The WORLD ENCYCLOPEDIA OF CONTEMPORARY THEATRE

AFRICA

The WORLD ENCYCLOPEDIA OF CONTEMPORARY THEATRE

AFRICA

EDITED BY
DON RUBIN, OUSMANE DIAKHATÉ
AND HANSEL NDUMBE EYOH

LONDON AND NEW YORK

First published in 1997
by Routledge
11 New Fetter Lane, London EC4P 4EE

Simultaneously published in the USA and Canada
by Routledge
29 West 35th Street, New York, NY 10001

as The World Encyclopedia of Contemporary Theatre, Volume 3, Africa

First published in paperback 2001 by Routledge

Routledge is an imprint of the Taylor & Francis Group

© 2001 The World Encyclopedia of Contemporary Theatre Corporation

Typeset in 9/10½ pt Sabon and Optima by MCS Ltd, Wiltshire
Printed in Great Britain by Biddles Ltd, Guildford and King's Lynn
Printed on acid-free paper

This encyclopedia is a project implemented with the support of UNESCO and at the request
of four non-governmental organizations. The opinions expressed in the various articals are
those of the authors themselves and do not necessarily reflect the point of view of the
sponsoring organizations.

British Library Cataloguing in Publication Data
A catalogue record for this book is available from the British Library.

Library of Congress Cataloging-in-Publication Data
A catalog record for this book is available from the Library of Congress.

ISBN 0–415–05931–3 (hbk)
ISBN 0–415–22746–1 (pbk)

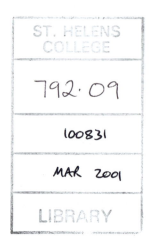

The World Encyclopedia of Contemporary Theatre would like to acknowledge with sincere thanks the financial contributions of the following:

REGIONAL SPONSORS

Department of Canadian Heritage
Ford Foundation
Japan Foundation
Ontario Ministry of Citizenship and
    Culture
Rockefeller Foundation
Routledge
Social Sciences and Humanities
    Research Council of Canada
UNESCO
York University

NATIONAL SPONSORS

Autonomous National University of
    México
Cameroon National UNESCO Commission
Canadian National UNESCO Commission
Cheikh Anta Diop University
Cultural Ministry of France
German Centre of the ITI
Higher Institute of Dramatic Arts,
    Damascus
Mexican National UNESCO
    Commission
Joseph S. Stauffer Foundation
University of Bordeaux
Herman Voaden
Woodlawn Arts Foundation

STATE SPONSORS

Apotex Foundation
Austrian Ministry of Education and the Arts
Samuel and Saidye Bronfman Family
    Foundation
Floyd S. Chalmers
Faculty of Fine Arts, York University
Finnish Ministry of Education
FIRT
Georgian Ministry of Culture
Greek Ministry of Culture
Calouste Gulbenkian Foundation
International Theatre Institute (Paris)

and National Centres in Bangladesh,
    Belgium, Bulgaria, Canada, Czech
    Republic, Finland, Hungary, India,
    Netherlands, Poland, Romania, Slovak
    Republic, United States, Switzerland
    and Venezuela
Israeli Ministry of Foreign Affairs,
    Division of Cultural and Scientific
    Relations
Japan Foundation Cultural Centre,
    Bangkok
Henry White Kinnear Foundation
Ministry of the Flemish Community
    (Cultural Affairs)
Moldovan Theatre Union
Organization of American States
Polish Ministry of Culture
Republic of Macedonia Ministry of Culture
K.M. Sarkissian and the Zoryan Institute
Conn Smythe Foundation
Turkish Embassy in Canada

LOCAL SPONSORS

Marion Andre
Arts Development and Promotions
Australia Council
Mariellen Black
Lyle B. Blair
Canadian Department of Foreign
    Affairs and International Trade
Canadian Theatre Review
Centre de Recherches et de Formation
    Théâtrales en Wallonie
Mr and Mrs Max Clarkson
Joy Cohnstaedt
H. Ian Macdonald
Freda's Originals
John H. Moore, FCA
Erminio G. Neglia
Farouk Ohan
Ontario Ministry of Skills Development
Peter Perina
E. Marshall Pollock
Rodolfo A. Ramos
Calvin G. Rand
Lynton Reed Printing
Don Rubin and Patricia Keeney
St Lawrence Centre for the Arts
Storewal International Inc.
Anton Wagner

Special thanks to:

Margrethe Aaby (Norway), Senda Akihiko (Japan), Eric Alexander (Netherlands), Ebrahim Alkhazi (India), Ina Andre (Canada), Toshi Aoyagi (Canada), Gaida Barisone (Latvia), Curtis Barlow (Canada), Alison Barr (United Kingdom), Isabelle Barth (France), Alexei Bartoshevitch (Russia), Shaul Baskind (Israel), Jean Benedetti (United Kingdom), Eric Bentley (United States), Don Berkowitz (Canada), Mariellen Black (Canada), Lyle B. Blair (Canada), Gaston Blais (Canada), Monica Brizzi (Italy), Robert Brustein (United States), John Bury (United Kingdom), Judith Cameron (Canada), Richard Cave (United Kingdom), Kelly Chadwick (Canada), Katarina Ćirić-Petrović (Serbia), Martin Cloutier (United States), Joy Cohnstaedt (Canada), Martha Coigney (United States), Communications Committee (International Theatre Institute), Leonard W. Conolly (Canada), Robert Crew (Canada), Renée L. Czukar (Canada), Michelle Darraugh (United Kingdom), Gautam Dasgupta (United States), Susan Frances Dobie (Canada), Francis Ebejer (Malta), Eldon Elder (United States), Krista Ellis (Canada), John Elsom (United Kingdom), Claes Englund (Sweden), Debebe Eshetu (Ethiopia), Martin Esslin (United Kingdom), Dickson Eyoh (Canada), Alan Filewod (Canada), Stephen Florian (Malta), Joyce Flynn (United States), Mira Friedlander (Canada), Julia Gabor (Hungary), Bibi Gessner (Switzerland), Madeleine Gobeil (UNESCO), Mayte Gómez (Canada), Sevelina Gyorova (Bulgaria), René Hainaux (Belgium), Bartold Halle (Norway), Peter Hay (United States), Ian Herbert (United Kingdom), Nick Herne (United Kingdom), César T. Herrera (Uruguay), Frank Hoff (Canada), Eleanor Hubbard (Canada), Huang Huilin (China), Djuner Ismail (Macedonia), Stephen Johnson (Canada), Sylvia Karsh (Canada), Naïm Kattan (Canada), Ferenc Kerenyi (Hungary), Myles Kesten (Canada), Valery Khasanov (Russia), William Kilbourn (Canada), Pierre Laville (France), George Lengyel (Hungary), Henri Lopes (UNESCO), Paul Lovejoy (Canada), Margaret Majewska (Poland), Lars af Malmborg (Sweden), Georges Manal (France), Suzanne Marko (Sweden), Bonnie Marranca (United States), Vivian Martínez Tabares (Cuba), Ruth R. Mayleas (United States), Giles R. Meikle (Canada), Atta Mensah (Canada), Paul-Louis Mignon (France), Ian Montagnes (Canada), Mavor Moore (Canada), Richard Mortimer (Canada), Judi Most (United States), Julia Moulden (Canada), Irmeli Niemi (Finland), Farouk Ohan (United Arab Emirates), Louis Patenaude (Canada), Oskar Pausch (Austria), André-Louis Perinetti (International Theatre Institute), Donald S. Rickerd (Canada), Roehampton Hotel (Canada), Mr & Mrs Irving Rubin (United States), Marti Russell (Canada), Raimonda Sadauskienė (Lithuania), Suzanne Sato (United States), Willmar Sauter (Sweden), Richard Schechner (United States), Petar Selem (Croatia), Małgorzata Semil (Poland), Mary Ann Shaw (Canada), Neville Shulman (United Kingdom), Mikhail Shvidkoi (Russia), David Silcox (Canada), Phillip Silver (Canada), Singer Travel (United States), Ron Singer (Canada), Mike Smith (Canada), Prince Subhadradis Diskul (Thailand), Anneli Suur-Kujala (Finland), Péter Szaffkó (Hungary), Teatro de la Esperanza (United States), Teatro del Sesenta (Puerto Rico), Jane Thompson (Canada), Carlos Tindemans (Belgium), Indrasen Vencatachellum (UNESCO), Janusz Warminski (Poland), Klaus Wever (Germany), Don B. Wilmeth (American Society for Theatre Research), Claudia Woolgar (United Kingdom), Piet Zeeman (Netherlands), Paul Zeleza (Canada).

DEDICATION

This series is dedicated to the memory of Roman Szydłowski of Poland (1918–83), a former President of the International Association of Theatre Critics. His vision for all international theatre organizations was truly worldwide and his tenacity in the service of that vision was genuinely legendary. It was Dr Szydłowski who first proposed the idea for a *World Encyclopedia of Contemporary Theatre*.

THE NATIONS
OF AFRICA

CONTENTS

• **AFRICA**

Contents • **The Nations and Their Theatres**

AFRICA

AN INTRODUCTION

OF NATIONS AND THEIR THEATRES

The encyclopedia has been with humankind since the ancient Greeks. Aristotle's works are certainly encyclopedic in nature; that is to say, they encircle particular aspects of knowledge, some extremely specialized, some more general. Pliny the Elder (AD 23–79) compiled a thirty-seven-volume encyclopedia of natural science. The largest encyclopedia seems to have been edited by the Emperor of China, Yung Lo, in the fifteenth century. Called the *Yung Lo Ta Tien*, it required 2,169 scholars to write it and ran to 917,480 pages in 11,100 volumes.

The *World Encyclopedia of Contemporary Theatre* (*WECT*) is a somewhat less exhaustive encyclopedia than Yung Lo's. When complete, we expect it to run to only 3,000 or so pages in a mere six volumes. However, Yung Lo sought to cover a much wider range of subjects than *WECT*. His goal was to examine nothing less than all of Chinese literature from the beginning of time.

WECT makes no such claims about its comprehensiveness. *WECT* is specifically an encyclopedia of nations and their theatres. The starting point is 1945, the end of World War II, a time of change politically, socially and culturally for much of the world. Sketching out a social and political context for each of the countries being studied, *WECT* seeks to explore in a comparative fashion each country's theatrical history since that time. The assumption from the beginning has been that theatre is an art form which grows from its society and which feeds back into it through reflection, analysis and challenge.

No other international theatre encyclopedia has attempted such a comparative, broad-based, cross-cultural study. The fact that virtually every one of our writers is from the country being written about adds still another level of authority and uniqueness to this work, which is attempting to present each nation's view of itself, a view not of politicians or propagandists but of each country's theatrical scholars and theatre artists.

It should also be made clear here that *WECT* is not intended as a guide to individuals, companies, festivals or forms. One will not find here analyses of Stanislavski, Brecht, Craig, Brook, Grotowski or Artaud. Nor will one find biographies of Soyinka, Fugard or Havel. *WECT* is also not the place to look for a history of the Comédie-Française or the Stratford Festival, Venezuela's Rajatabla or Japan's Tenjo Sajiki. Nor will readers find extensive documentation on the Carthage Festival or Edinburgh, on BITEF or Adelaide, on the Cervantes Festival or even Avignon.

The world of theatre is far too large and has become far too specialized for that. Information on the lives of everyone from playwrights to puppeteers, choreographers to composers, directors to designers can be readily found in a wide range of reference works available in every major language. There are book-length analyses and histories – some critical, some just documentation – of all the major companies and festivals that one could ever want to know about. There are also dictionaries available that focus on virtually every specialized theatrical subject from semiotics to cultural anthropology. Many fine theatre journals around the world maintain a valuable and continuing dialogue and documentation of current issues.

What has not existed before – and what *WECT* has attempted to create – has been a theatrical reference work looking at a wide range of *national* theatrical activity on a country-by-country basis from a specifically *national* standpoint. As we near the end of the twentieth century, as nations in many parts of the world finally shed their colonial pasts, and as new nations emerge in the aftermath of the collapse of the Soviet Union and Yugoslavia, such a gap in our cultural knowledge may seem curious. What, for example, does Romanian theatre look like to a Romanian in this postmodern world? Canadian theatre to a Canadian? What is of import to an Australian about his or her own theatre? To a Senegalese? A Brazilian? A Vietnamese? An Egyptian? And what of all the individual republics that once made up the Soviet Union, Yugoslavia and Czechoslovakia? What is the self-perception of theatre professionals in the new Germany, where two totally different systems were uncomfortably reunited as the 1990s began?

To allow the reader to draw conclusions and to allow comparability, each of *WECT*'s writers was given the challenge of bringing together just such a national impression in a very specifically structured essay which would include not lists of names and dates but rather a context – in some cases, contexts – for international comprehension. That is, each of *WECT*'s extensive national articles – ranging from 3,000 to 30,000 words per country (small books in some instances) – has been written so as to provide theatrical professionals and those concerned with research on the profession with not only the basic material they would need if they were going to work in or visit a particular country for the first time, but also the basic material necessary to identify international trends and movements in the decades since the end of World War II.

Those who already know their own or some other country's theatre very well, no doubt, will find the information contained on those countries useful but probably too basic. Even at 30,000 words, these articles cannot possibly replace the library that would be needed to completely cover the theatre of any one country. In any event, encyclopedias historically have been intended only as introductions. Indeed, it is difficult to imagine them being anything more than that on any given subject. The philosopher and encyclopedist Denis Diderot (1713–84) argued that encyclopedias should be seen as basic libraries in every field

but the reader's own. In this case, it is a theatre library for every country but the reader's own. To this end, we have asked writers to think of their ideal reader as a sophisticated professional from abroad.

In this light, we believe that *WECT* will be most important to readers for the breadth of its coverage; in this case, for the distance from home that each reader can travel through these articles. This is not in any way to suggest a lack of depth but rather to honestly recognize given limitations. *WECT* is therefore providing extended and extensive articles on every theatre culture in the world, more than 160 countries by the time the project is concluded. Looked at as a whole, they will be more than able to help theatre professionals in every part of the world put plays, companies, policies and productions into a national context, and in our complicated world this seems an important and unique contribution.

WECT material can be accessed in one of two ways: by either reading vertically (from beginning to end in any particular country) or horizontally (focusing on only a single subject such as Puppet (and Mask) Theatre or Dramaturgy across several countries). Having suggested earlier that this is not an encyclopedia of individuals, companies, festivals or forms, the fact is that one *can* identify individuals, companies, festivals and forms by referring to the index at the back of each volume or to the comprehensive multi-volume index planned for the final volume. By going to specific pages, the reader will then be able to follow the influence and development of particular figures or groups both within their own countries, within regions and ultimately in the world.

Whichever approach one is using, whether professionally focused or casual, it is probably useful at this point to understand the many section headings in each of the national articles and what each section is intended to include.

How To Use This Volume

Each national article in this volume is divided into thirteen sections: History, Structure of the National Theatre Community, Artistic Profile, Companies, Dramaturgy, Directing and Acting, Theatre for Young Audiences, Puppet and Mask Theatre, Design, Theatre Space and Architecture, Training, Criticism-Scholarship-Publishing, and Further Reading.

These sections are intended to provide the following information.

History: Each national article opens with basic geographical, historical and/or socio-political material. In the cases of countries whose histories may not be well known outside the immediate region, we have encouraged writers to provide a more extensive background than might be normally found. Included as well is a history of the country's major theatrical movements and events since 1945, treated on a decade-by-decade basis or treated thematically. In each case the intent has been to give the national writer flexibility in interpreting the material being discussed.

Structure of the National Theatre Community: This is essentially a demographic section intended to offer information on the types of theatres (commercial, state-supported, regional or municipal) and the numbers of theatres operating in a particular country, their geographical distribution and relative sizes (both in terms of employees and budgets). One will find in this section information on the various infrastructures that have developed (national associations, national and international linkages), unions, as well as information on the major festivals in the country and national awards.

Artistic Profile: A look at the major artistic trends and styles in music and/or dance theatre which have evolved within each country with particular emphasis on significant indigenous forms and their relation to cultural and religious practice. Where a significant spoken drama has emerged that too is discussed within this section.

Companies: An identification and discussion of the major professional troupes as well as an examination of those non-professional troupes (often connected with educational institutions) which have influenced national cultural practice in the performing arts.

Dramaturgy: Initially called 'Playwriting' this section heading was changed to its current title to allow WECT to recognize the many collectively created productions which have been done across the many continents as well as to acknowledge the significant role of the director in script development. In no way is this intended to demean the importance of the playwright whose work, we believe, still remains central to the process of theatrical creation and is at the centre of this particular section.

Theatre for Young Audiences: Within African cultural tradition, performances have almost always included young people and it is the exception rather than the norm in Africa to find companies working specifically for young audiences. Yet since 1945, a number of such companies have emerged and where they exist they are dealt with under this heading. By including this separate section, WECT is acknowledging the importance of this very special area of contemporary theatrical practice and its long-term effect on theatrical art worldwide since 1945.

Puppet and Mask Theatre: Sometimes linked with the **Theatre for Young Audiences** section but most often recognized on its own, puppet theatre is at once one of the oldest of the popular theatrical arts and, where it has been rediscovered by contemporary theatrical practitioners, one of the most avant-garde. Within this section we have asked writers to trace developments in the form from its theatrical mimetic roots (imitation of actors) to what has come to be known as Object Theatre, in which things take on a dramatic life of their own thanks, very often, to black light techniques that emerged during this period in eastern Europe. We have also asked our writers to look at experiments involving the interrelationship between live actors and puppets or live actors and objects. This is a fascinating and important area which theatre professionals ignore at their own imaginative risk. As for the inclusion of masked performances as well as discussion of the African *masquerade* tradition in many countries, its placement within this section seemed both appropriate and useful for the light it sheds on the development of puppetry and its links between the world of the living artist and other worlds which theatrical art clearly has the possibility to reach.

Design: This section examines the work of each theatre community's visual artists. In some cases this has been done thematically; in other cases, on a decade-by-decade basis since 1945. Again, we have asked our writers to avoid lists. Instead of just naming names, we have asked them to choose a small number of representative designers and discuss their individual work.

Theatre Space and Architecture: When we began, this section was simply titled 'Theatre Architecture'. The words 'Theatre Space' were added as the articles began to arrive. Many of our writers originally interpreted this section as being only about buildings created specifically as theatrical venues. Clearly this would have eliminated many of the experiments relating to theatrical space which began in the 1960s and are still with us today, experiments which seem to have begun in North America out of sheer desperation and which evolved in many parts of the world to the total breakdown of proscenium theatre with its visual accoutrements as an *a priori* requirement for theatrical events.

Training: This section discusses the most important theatre schools and other professional training programmes in each country, their types of curriculum and the traditions they follow.

Criticism, Scholarship and Publishing: The most important theatre research and documentation centres in each country, major performing arts museums and the types of critical approaches being taken by leading critics and theatre scholars are identified in this section. The discussions here range from journalistic reviewing to more analytical philological, anthropological, semiological, and/or other types of structural approaches. In some cases historical context is provided; in others, contemporary developments are emphasized. As well, writers have been asked to identify the most important theatre journals and magazines along with the major theatre publishing houses in their countries.

Further Reading: Most national articles conclude with a brief bibliography identifying the major works available within the national language as well as the most important works about the country's theatre that the authors are aware of in other languages. We have tried to follow the bibliographical form recommended by the University of Chicago Press but in some instances writers followed their own scholarly form leaving us with certain Chicago-style omissions. Though we attempted to fill these gaps it was not always possible. In general, however, enough information has been provided to allow the diligent reader to find the works mentioned.

To some, this structure may seem overly complicated and perhaps even contradictory in terms of allowing each writer or team of writers to identify and define their national theatres. But in every instance, the key was to maintain comparability country-to-country and ultimately region-to-region. It is our belief that as interesting and informative as each national article may be, the real value of *WECT* will ultimately lie in its ability to provide comparability of theatres world-wide, in its ability to allow directors, playwrights, dramaturges, designers, critics, scholars and even those in government to look across a wide range of theatre communities.

Certainly this structure was not arrived at quickly or casually and it continued to be refined almost until publication. When this project was first conceived by the Polish theatre critic Roman Szydłowski (1918–83) in the late 1970s, it was seen simply as an opportunity to provide accurate and up-to-date documentation for theatre critics who were being confronted more regularly than ever before with theatre from all over the world as part of their daily reviewing duties. Visiting groups were no longer rare and exotic events on a critic's schedule. They were appearing with amazing regularity and the best critics simply wanted to do their homework.

But where could a working critic go to find quickly information on Turkish *karagöz*, on Thai *Khon* or South Africa's Market Theatre? Critics just seemed expected to know everything and everyone. Even when some information did exist, the sources were too often out-of-date or existed only in a language not widely spoken.

Most scholars would probably point to the nine-volume *Enciclopedia dello spettacolo* as the standard reference in the field. Available, however, only in Italian, the vast majority of the documentation included there was gathered before World War II and was, to say the least, Eurocentric. Published after the war, this encyclopedia of world theatre history was certainly strong the further one went back in time. But despite the fact that non-European theatre generally and the twentieth century specifically were not especially well served, the *Enciclopedia dello spettacolo* did become a standard. Most libraries found it essential for their reference sections. By the 1970s, however, it was clearly out-of-date even in its approaches to some of its early material.

Through the years, less ambitious attempts were made. Along with specialized individual volumes, these were very useful but, because of their specificity or, in some cases, their purely academic approach, they were not always useful to theatre professionals. It was at this point in time that Roman Szydłowski proposed a new type of world theatre reference work to the International Association of Theatre Critics, one of many international theatre communications organizations that had sprung up in the wake of two world wars.

At this organization's Congress in Vienna in 1979, Szydłowski, its president, received wide support for the proposal but no clear directions on how to proceed. Within eighteen months, however, he had convinced the International

Theatre Institute's (ITI) Permanent Committee on Theatre Publications – a loose association of editors of theatre magazines and journals – to take up the challenge. The ITI, it was felt, being affiliated with the United Nations Educational, Scientific and Cultural Organization (UNESCO), at a higher level than the other international theatre associations, seemed to be the right agency to bring the idea to fruition on the world stage. At its 1981 Congress, this committee (subsequently to be called the Communications Committee) endorsed the idea and recommended it to the organization as a whole. It was the ITI's new secretary-general, Lars af Malmborg from Sweden, who decided that the project would be a concrete contribution to world theatre communication.

Malmborg, with the support of the ITI Executive Committee, brought the idea forward and in early 1982 called a meeting of interested international theatre organizations and individuals who might be able to help realize the project. It was from this meeting, held under the aegis of the Fine Arts Museum in Copenhagen, that specific plans began to be made. Four organizations – the ITI, the International Association of Theatre Critics (IATC), the International Federation for Theatre Research (FIRT) and the International Society of Libraries and Museums for the Performing Arts (SIBMAS) – agreed to combine efforts towards the realization of what was now being called the *World Encyclopedia of Contemporary Theatre*.

By 1983, with the support of the Faculty of Fine Arts at York University in Toronto and with the initial interest of a major Toronto publishing house, WECT was incorporated as an independent not-for-profit project under Canadian law. Initial grants came from York University, UNESCO and, the largest grant to that time, from the American-based Ford Foundation (thanks to a willingness to risk on a project that did not fit neatly into any previously established programme by its Theatre Officer, Ruth Mayleas). During 1984, representatives of the four sponsoring organizations met in Toronto (courtesy of Canadian philanthropist Floyd S. Chalmers) to set up parameters. Without this initial support and all the faith it implied in an unprecedented vision, WECT would never have got off the ground.

The year 1945 was established as a starting point though it was agreed that nothing ever really starts or ends neatly in the world of theatre. It was agreed that television and radio would not be dealt with but that music theatre and dance theatre would be included. It was agreed that a socio-cultural approach would be taken and that the relationship between theatres and the nations from which they grew would be explored. It was agreed that comparability would be emphasized and that writers should be chosen from within each country.

During 1984 an outstanding international team of editors was selected to coordinate the work and to advise in such specialty areas as theatre for young audiences (Wolfgang Wöhlert), music theatre (Horst Seeger), dance theatre (Selma Jeanne Cohen) and puppet theatre (Henryk Jurkowski) among others. Over the years the International Editorial Board would expand and contract as needs appeared or as particular individuals found themselves unable to continue the work. But throughout, the notion of self-identification for each national article was maintained and continued to be the primary reason why WECT searched for leading writers, critics, scholars and theatre professionals within each country.

The first full International Editorial Board meeting was held in Toronto in 1985 during the twenty-first World Congress of the ITI. There were five people present from North America, another five from Europe (including WECT's two associate editors, Péter Nagy of Budapest and Philippe Rouyer of Bordeaux) and another six from Latin America, Africa, the Arab countries and Asia/Oceania. It was one of our Asian editors who put the first question to the gathering. 'What exactly do we think *we* mean when we use the word theatre?' he asked. 'I'm really not sure there's a definition we can all agree on. And if we can't come to an agreement on this basic question, how can we possibly agree on anything else?'

The apparently simple question led to an enormously involved discussion about the various types of spoken drama that had evolved in Europe and North America. Objections were quickly raised that we were ignoring musical theatre forms and forms involving movement. Others objected that we were locked into text while our puppet theatre editor was concerned that we were leaving out everything from Wayang Kulang to Punch and Judy. Our African colleagues suggested that our preliminary definition seemed to be ignoring the social relationships in much African theatre, from wedding ceremonies to circumcision rituals. And what of traditional forms in Asia such as *Kathakali, Noh, Kabuki,* Chinese opera, or even the Vietnamese *Hat Boi*? What of folk forms in so many parts of the world? What of contemporary experiments?

What had appeared to be a rather innocent question in the beginning quickly turned into a life-or-death debate on the whole future – not to even discuss the international credibility – of the project. During the next few days, we turned to various standard texts on theatre in search of a suitable, internationally acceptable definition. It was a fascinating, though ultimately frustrating, exercise. To our amazement, we couldn't really find such a definition. Examinations of standard dictionaries – including the *Oxford English Dictionary* – were of even less help. Most simply defined 'theatre' as a building.

So we created our own international, intercultural working definition of the word. It is offered here not as a conclusion but rather as a starting point for a continuing consideration of what those of us working in the field mean when 'theatre' is spoken of in a contemporary global context.

> *Theatre*: A created event, usually based on text, executed by live performers and taking place before an audience in a specially defined setting. Theatre uses techniques of voice and/or movement to achieve cognition and/or emotional release through the senses. This event is generally rehearsed and is usually intended for repetition over a period of time.

By the time *WECT's* International Editorial Board next met, it had become clear from discussions with the various international organizations that *WECT* would have to respect various national differences in approaching this work and would have to take, as the American poet Robert Frost once said, 'the road less travelled by' in seeking its writers; that is, it would go to source for its information and interpretation in every instance. Indeed, *WECT* has through the years taken pride in this unique approach, slow and costly though it has been. But it has also been an approach which has led the project to develop close working relationships with theatre people *in* each of the more than 160 countries now involved in what has become the largest international cooperative venture in the history of world theatre, and certainly the largest international publishing venture in world theatre today.

In focusing the work this way, it was obvious that the *WECT* project was taking many risks. The approach was clearly going to make this a much longer project than anyone had ever dreamed of. By the time this work is concluded, it will have taken about fifteen years. The approach would also force us to find significant international funding at a time when economies were just beginning to go into recession in many parts of the world. As this third volume goes to press, funding has been assured for our *Asia/Oceania* volume from the Japan Foundation and we have opened discussions with a number of potential international partners on funding for the other two volumes in the series – *The Arab World* and the concluding volume, a *World Theatre Bibliography and Cumulative Index*. Discussions have already extended into the development of this series into a world theatre database in an interactive CD-ROM format.

But we believed when we started – and still believe – that our approach was one which would afford the best opportunity to ensure both the long-term goals and the highest standards of international scholarly excellence and accuracy. This approach was also one of the key reasons why UNESCO decided to support the project and why UNESCO ultimately named *WECT* as an official project of its World Decade for Cultural Development (1988–97). Such recognition is unusual for a scholarly work and we feel with some pride that it is an important model for future intercultural, interdisciplinary arts research.

A few words are needed here about world politics and its effect upon our work. For most people, political change is simply interesting newspaper fodder or the stuff to support opinions – pro or con – on particular subjects. The closer that politics gets to home, however, the more directly it impacts on one's reality and the more it affects how one goes about one's daily business. Political change has constantly impacted on *WECT's* reality and profoundly affected its already complicated work.

To give but one key example, when work began on our European volume, there were only two dozen or so countries to deal with, and those in eastern Europe were guaranteeing they would cover all our writing and translation fees for the region. That was 1985. By 1990, the two Germanys had become one (requiring a significant restructuring of our German material) while the USSR, Yugoslavia and Czechoslovakia went from three separate national entities to twenty-three separate countries (fifteen individual republics from the

Soviet Union, six from Yugoslavia and two from Czechoslovakia). Not only did the already completed major articles on the USSR, Yugoslavia and Czechoslovakia have to be completely revised and turned into what we decided to call 'historical overviews' but also new writers needed to be found and new articles had to be commissioned on each of the republics, republics that were, in many instances, in the midst of social, political or armed revolution. With such changes swirling around us, we read the newspapers each day with genuine trepidation. By the time of publication, the volume had expanded to some forty-seven articles. Suffice it to say here that trying to keep up with this ever-changing political landscape continues to be *WECT*'s greatest challenge, a challenge we are trying to meet through computerization and the establishment of *WECT* as an international theatre database.

It was precisely these political changes which Martha Coigney, president of the ITI, was referring to when she said, perhaps optimistically, at the opening of the ITI's 1993 World Congress in Munich that in the future it would no longer be wars between superpowers that people of peace would have to be concerned about, but rather confrontations between cultures. If this is so then we believe that *WECT* may well be able to make a real contribution in at least introducing those cultures to one another. *WECT*'s goal from the beginning has been nothing less than that.

In helping the project to achieve this end, many organizations, many theatre and government agencies, many foundations and individuals have played important roles. A list of the financial sponsors and those who have worked with us appears elsewhere but we would like to specifically acknowledge the ongoing help of UNESCO, the Ford and Rockefeller Foundations (Rockefeller came to *WECT*'s aid at precisely the moment that recession and the enormous political changes in Europe threatened to kill the project), the Faculty of Fine Arts and the Office of Research Administration at York University, the Canadian and Ontario governments, the German Centre of the International Theatre Institute and particularly Rolf Rohmer, who has long served as president of the project's International Executive Board. This project would not have survived without the help of the Canadian Centre of the ITI (especially Curtis Barlow in the early years of the project) and the various members of the

Canadian-based Board of Directors who worked to find funds to realize this work. The support of our two recent Board presidents has been particularly appreciated – Calvin G. Rand (founding president of Canada's Shaw Festival) and Professor Leonard W. Conolly, formerly of the University of Guelph and now president of Trent University in Ontario.

This project could also not have survived without the ongoing support of the Faculty of Fine Arts and the department of theatre at York University, its deans and its chairs (including Lionel Lawrence, Joyce Zemans, Joy Cohnstaedt, Seth Feldman, Ron Singer, Phillip Silver and Robert Fothergill) and especially the sponsors of the Walter A. Gordon Fellowship, York University's highest research award, which allowed me the time to bring the first volume to fruition.

This project would not have succeeded had *WECT* not had the active support and understanding of all the members of its International Editorial Board, particularly the wisdom and advice of Péter Nagy, whose diplomacy in the face of *WECT*'s own political struggles was never less than brilliant. Nor would it have succeeded without the stubborn belief in this project of its Managing Editor and Director of Research, Anton Wagner, whose work was long funded by the Canadian Social Science and Humanities Research Council, and the project's indefatigable administrators Donna Dawson and Catherine Matzig. Our editors at Routledge – Samantha Parkinson, Alison Barr, Michelle Darraugh, Robert Potts, Mark Barragry and Christine Firth – have been most understanding in working with us on what must have appeared to them a mad dream at times. Without their personal commitment and the corporate support behind them, *WECT* would still be in the planning stages.

If I have personally been seen through the many years of this project as its architect, I can only say that the building would never have stood without the strength, determination and belief of my wife and too rarely recognized co-visionary, Patricia Keeney. Against all her writerly instincts and sometimes against all logic, she bravely sat through meeting after meeting of every one of this project's boards, a duty she took on because she believed in the work. Without her faith and goodwill, *WECT* might well have foundered.

There are far too many people to thank here by name. It would be remiss to try, for too many would be left out. But to all of them, particularly to all our editors, writers, national editorial committees, ITI Centres and translators, to all the sponsoring and other organizations which supported this work, thank you for believing with us and in us. We trust that your patience and support will have proven to be worth all the time, the pain and the effort.

Don Rubin
August 1996

FOREWORD

AFRICAN THEATRE: FROM *ALI BABA* TO *WOZA ALBERT!*

It took a number of years for me to unearth a hidden reason why I appeared to prefer attending rehearsals of plays to watching the finished product. At the beginning of my rites of passage in a strange, taciturn land called England, one of my favourite pastimes was to sneak into the darkened halls of theatres where rehearsals were in progress. A casual stroll in the foyer admiring photographs and posters – and occasional costume and design displays – invariably resulted in a quick sidestep through the heavy doors and, when I was through, parting the heavy plush curtains and sliding into the nearest seat. A few moments' wait to ensure that I was undiscovered, and my eyes to get accustomed to the dark, then a stealthy advance into a more central seat closer to the stage but still at a discreet distance. Then hours of savouring the bubbling broth under preparation on the lighted stage, a broth of three principal ingredients: the actors and their uneven talents and sensitivities, the lone chef (sometimes with an assistant immersed in note-taking) and an unknown text. It did not seem to matter what play it was.

Naturally, I assumed that these escapades were simply characteristic of the putative *aficionado* of theatre, eager to watch and learn from directors and actors at work, and this was quite true of course. However, since this habit would not leave me even after decades – although now I have far less time and opportunity to indulge in it – I began to suspect that there was a consumer gratification involved, one that was related to, but also different from the responses of a paying audience to the formalized, structured product that is the finished performance.

It is difficult now to recall how I came to stumble on the hidden cause – at first merely suspecting, then becoming more and more confident that this was the only explanation. My formative diet of theatre was undoubtedly the guilty one: the Travelling Theatre of the coast of West Africa – also known as the Folk Opera or Concert Party. The rehearsals on which I am now fed, I concluded, were a kind of surrogate for the transitional nature of those other performances, a constant feast of improvisation – obviously more vibrant, more 'socialized' – than the rehearsals in the darkened halls of British theatres. Still, they both shared the characteristic of changing from day to day, of being totally *unpredictable*.

For the African troupe, the plush, acoustic curtains, spring-back seats, Circle, Stalls, Upper Balcony, the elevated stage with full technical and lighting complement – these are simply notions from outer space. There are exceptions of course – from Dakar to Cape Town – where the 'well-made' play finds its home in a well-made theatre. In the main, however, what prevailed in the 1940s and 1950s is still today's norm for the Travelling Theatre, and even its transfer on to television in many countries has not vitiated its unpredictable, iconoclastic stamp.

A long-suffering lorry trundles into town, plastered with posters. Half-dead with fatigue and lack of sleep, and long distances travelled on pot-holed roads, its inmates come suddenly alive at the approach of this new town where their next performance has been scheduled. Pieces of costume are fished out from baskets, cardboard boxes, tin boxes and cloth bundles

11

– the next moment, these travellers are transformed into a festive army and the lorry's spluttering engine noises are drowned in a rhythmic ensemble of drums, mouth organs, gourd rattles, penny whistles, iron bells, voices and the occasional trumpet and saxophone. This musical chariot roars through the streets, targeting markets, office blocks, the motor parks ... even hospitals. Sometimes leaflets are handed out – the travelling theatre is in town! Then to the venue to set up the semblance of a stage, organize security (against determined gate-crashers), select the ticket entry points and somehow manage to include an hour or two of rehearsals. A new scene, a new song, a new routine is added or substituted – the director-manager-producer-general factotum-cum-principal actor's mind has hardly stopped churning since the last performance!

The venue is of course an open-air arena – preferably with borders that are not too difficult to control, such as a market square, school playing-field, a semi-open family compound, any school or town hall, the premises of a friendly church and even sometimes, the porch of a public building where the street can be sealed off with official or simply 'obliging' assistance from the local police. Chairs and benches are hired or borrowed, with special armchairs at the front for specially invited guests, the local VIPs whose donations in specially printed envelopes go a long way to securing the economic tightrope on which many of these troupes exist. It has been a truly frenetic day. Nothing can be done about the non-paying guests who will perch on trees, on rooftops or gather at the windows of bordering houses but, at last, the paying guests and gate-crashers begin to gather. From the midst of the general mêlée the special guests arrive and take their places ... at last, the magic moment!

One end of an improvised curtain on a single wire is grabbed by a disembodied hand and run across the stage by its operator, who pretends he is invisible to the audience. Then on to the boards, a pulsating squad in a routine that owes no small part to the vaudeville tradition – the 'Opening Glee!' This song-and-dance sequence serves as a prologue, a welcome to the audience, a sung outline of the action of the play or simply a rousing number that has nothing at all to do with the night's main fare, an opportunity for social or moral commentaries ... no matter what – the purpose is to serve as an appetizer and induct the audience into a magic space, transformed into a biblical land, an abode of ghosts and supernatural beings, the world of Ali Baba and the Forty Thieves, the kingdom of Shaka the Zulu, the romantic palace of the love-lorn daughter of the 'king' of Sokoto, or the one-room shack of a coal-miner from Iva Valley, Enugu, in Eastern Nigeria where dozens of striking miners have just been shot dead by the colonial police:

Baba t'o bi wa, ko to jeun
Iya to bi wa, ko to jeun
Omo ti a bi o, ko to jeun
Ki la o fi kobo, ojumo se?
[To feed the father, whose offspring we are
To feed the mother, whose offspring we are
To feed the child, who is our own offspring
What miracle is expected on a penny a day?]

Indeed, a vast distance separates Ali Baba or Iva Valley, re-created on the squeaky boards of Lisabi Hall in Yaba, Lagos, by Hubert Ogunde, from *L'Exile d'Abouri* of Cheik N'dao at the modern Daniel Sorano Theatre in Dakar, Sénégal, a vast distance not simply in geography and time but in style and sensibility. Yet the concerns have hardly changed over the years – from mystical evocations from the supernatural world to anti-colonial denunciations of social introspection. This is not to suggest a seamless integration of various contending strands in African theatre – indeed, the word 'contending' could not be more apt. Theatrical writing that was the product of the William Ponty Normal School in French West Africa constantly rubbed shoulders with the Ghanaian *anansegro*, but only from the perspective of period, the chronological fact that both were taking place at the same time. One, however, submerged itself in the French canon, an imitation of dated French drama which William Ponty instructors had decreed for their colonial wards. The world of *anansegro* was strictly demarcated from that school, and nothing rubbed off in style, motifs or general theatrical sensibility on the stewards of French culture, and their theatre catechisms. The rebellion would come later, with the generation of dramatists such as Bernard Dadié, Cheik N'dao and Anta Ka.

By contrast, despite separation of styles, the East African Hassan's anti-colonial *Kinjekitile* is easily seen as simply continuing the tradition of Hubert Ogunde's *Bread and Bullets*, whose technique, on a higher level of improvisational development, is evident in the *Woza Albert!* of Mbongeni Ngema and Percy Mtwa of South Africa, *Woza* being in turn a blood relation of the seminal *Sizwe Bansi Is Dead*, a collaborative piece by Athol Fugard, John Kani and Winston Ntshona. The point we are trying to make here is that theatre, despite its many masks, is the unending rendition of the human experience, in totality, and its excitement lies indeed in its very unpredictability – perhaps this was the essence of theatre that remained the elusive constant, sought in alien settings outside that early childhood immersion – theatre, as a rehearsal of real life.

Could this perhaps be what leaves directors and dramaturges of the temper of Peter Brook so permanently unsatisfied and makes them turn towards Africa (and other places too) for some kind of revelation? Or Richard Schechner? And Eugenio Barba in the direction of the Far East, whose stylistic opulence he proceeds to import into his Theatre Laboratory in the distant setting of Norway? African playwrights are fortunate in this respect, having the tradition of 'the unfinished' within their environment, but that has not made them any less adventurous. A whole generation of playwrights and directors – Sony Labou Tansi (what a tragic loss), Femi Osofisan, the late Dan Kintu and Byron Kawadwa (traumatic losses both), Ben Abdallah, Abdul Anta Ka, Bode Sowande, Ola Rotimi, and so on – appear to be breaking this ancient-new ground, while the West Indian poet and playwright, Derek Walcott and the Brazilian Abdias do Nascimento have equally produced theatre with such resonant affinity to that African source that one would not be too far off to class them as playwrights and experimentalists of a neo-African tradition. However, all that belongs in the contumacious realms of classification, and has nothing to do with the 'consumer gratification' which after all, on whatever level that pleasure or stimulation operates, is the primary purpose of preparing a spectacle and inviting an audience to view it.

I really ought to concern myself with giving praise where praise is uncontroversial, and that is to the editor of this series, Don Rubin, and

his team at *WECT*. Don Rubin's vision and indefatigability have resulted in enriching the field of theatre documentation in an original and invaluable measure. I am glad to be able to share a mini-minuscule sense of collective fulfilment in the emergence of these volumes, as I was both an Executive Member, then President of the International Theatre Institute when the idea was born and the initial motions undertaken by the Institute. For many years since then, however, I have merely received distant news of the travails and progress of the ambitious project.

These are difficult times for the artistic world in many parts of the larger world. The steady decimation of the artist and journalist tribe in Algeria, the brutal state murder of Ken Saro-Wiwa of Nigeria in 1995, and the yet fresh memories of Dan Kintu, Byron Kawadwa and others, murdered under Idi Amin in 1977, cast long, opaque shadows on the horizons of unfettered creativity. (No less painful was the more recent loss in 1995 of that Congolese original, Sony Labou Tansi.) The art of the theatre is very exposed, its vulnerability being part of its very strength, its vehicle the human presence and its channel of effectiveness direct and unmediated, both intellectually and viscerally. Not surprisingly, tyrannies and totalitarian conditions home in on its practitioners as first-order threats and act against them with singular viciousness.

It is unlikely that this volume will assuage their primordial fears but then, it is not intended for their kind. Those for whom this extensive labour of love has been undertaken will, however, possess one more record of validation and rejuvenation for their vocation – be it as student, consumer or as practitioner. The world of theatre has something new to treasure, and to celebrate.

Wole Soyinka
Nobel Prize Laureate for Literature
Harvard University
Cambridge

AFRICAN THEATRE IN A GLOBAL CONTEXT

The American expatriate poet Gertrude Stein once said that the problem in dealing with Los Angeles as a geographical entity was that 'there's no there there'. For many brought up on the professionalized Euro-American spoken theatre or even on many formalized Asian sung and/or danced drama forms, the problem in dealing with Africa's dynamic performative traditions, most of which involve music and dance, is – to paraphrase Stein – the theatre there seems to be without theatre there. Which is to say that it is easy not to see the continent's sophisticated and often ancient theatrical traditions if one is looking only for theatre buildings, raised stages, complicated infrastructures, advanced technology, expensive sets and published scripts.

Sub-Saharan Africa – Black Africa, if you will – has a multitude of its own traditions and has evolved its own contemporary forms based on those traditions. In francophone Africa much of it is based on the griotic tradition rooted in each community's oral history. A number of francophone Africa's most theatrically advanced groups – particularly in Côte d'Ivoire – are, in fact, now re-examining the role of the *griot* through crossover forms that connect past to present, storytelling to collective creation.

In parts of anglophone Africa the Concert Party with its many well-known travelling companies brings together elements of burlesque comedy and communal improvisation, folk song and social satire. Particularly strong in east Africa are the still vital storytelling traditions and a powerful and extraordinarily advanced Theatre-for-Development movement,

a movement rooted in both urban and rural communities, a movement involving health, educational and social issues in the belief that it is possible to find communal solutions to communal problems.

Those who wish to connect to Euro-American theatrical styles – French cuisine when visiting, say, the ancient African cultural and educational centre of Timbuktu (in modern Mali) – there is no better connection to be found in sub-Saharan Africa than the plays of the Nobel Prize-winning Nigerian dramatist Wole Soyinka, whose unique voice brings the most dynamic of African performative traditions and mythology together with the socially rooted traditions of western spoken drama. His work has already taken its deserved place in contemporary theatrical discourse.

Purely spoken drama in Africa, however, is still very much of a minority art form, a late development that emerged as part of colonial impositions and missionary training within the indigenous communities, impositions that failed to respect or even recognize in many cases either ethnic differences (there are more than a thousand different ethnic groups in sub-Saharan Africa alone) or differing religious traditions. In many countries, the spoken drama was used to try and replace traditional forms but in only a few countries did it succeed. Nevertheless, important dramatists did emerge – Bernard Dadié and Bernard Zadi Zaourou in Côte d'Ivoire, Soyinka and Ola Rotimi in Nigeria, Sony Labou Tansi in Congo, Sénouvo Agbota Zinsou in Togo, and Athol Fugard in South Africa – to name just a few of the many original and profound talents.

Interestingly, since the mid-1960s, attempts have been made right across the continent by these and other dramatists to return traditional African performing arts to a more central place within the continent's theatrical experience, even in works that are essentially spoken. Many of these attempts – along with responses by governments in terms of funding support (or the ongoing lack thereof) and political censorship – are documented in this volume.

To look at these issues in a slightly different way, it would seem that an argument could be made that western classical art divided – probably by the end of the fourth century BC – into a populist art aimed primarily at entertainment and escape, and a more elitist and often state-controlled or state-supported art primarily aimed at discussion and/or at the moral education of the community. The Roman poet and satirist Horace certainly recognized this when he argued in his *Ars Poetica* for the value of bringing both approaches together, to reunite *delicare* with *docere*, delight with teaching, entertainment with learning. Too rarely, however, have the two come together in the west. Shakespeare was perhaps the most successful at achieving such union in English drama; Brecht the closest in the Euro-American tradition during the twentieth century.

But the dichotomy that took place in western art did not, for the most part, occur in traditional African art. Even today, elements of that earlier cultural wholeness can still be seen across the continent. Art within these traditional societies is not perceived of as *either* educational *or* escapist but rather both simultaneously. Even in crossover forms, it is this union that is most apparent, this sense of the totality of theatrical form. It is this, then, that non-Africans seem to have the most trouble with in trying to 'read' African theatre whose dances, songs, plays and even grammatical constructions are layered with recognizable significance to those properly attuned. It is also this that is at the root of the difficulties many Africans have in trying to read 'meaning' into disengaged western popular art.

Yet these differences must be articulated and recognized if one is to begin to grasp the nature of theatre in African culture. To do so, one must be open to larger definitions of the word than are normally found in western tradition, alternative definitions or perhaps just more accurate definitions. This is part of what our two African volume editors are suggesting when they make distinctions between tra-

ditional and modern theatre in their introduction to this volume. And this is what east African scholar Penina Mlama of the University of Dar es Salaam means when she speaks of the connections between artist and community in her survey of theatre in Tanzania. This is what Joseph Tomoonh-Garlodeyh Gbaba means when he speaks of the importance of traditional aesthetics in his examination of theatre in Liberia today.

Obviously, if one is *only* interested in spoken drama one will not be able to understand the essence of contemporary African theatre, the rich fusions that are being made now even by traditional artists or those who, trained in western dramatic form, are beginning to re-introduce indigenous traditions into their work. It is this that is at the root of *didiga* in Côte d'Ivoire, the modern *koteba* in Mali, much of Soyinka's work, and the work of many experimental Theatre-for-Development groups in east Africa. It is, in fact, among the most exciting of evolutions in the performing arts to be found anywhere in the world today. Living traditional forms in vital discourse with alternative dramatic visions.

It is also at the root of the new interdisciplinary science of theatre anthropology, an extraordinary late-twentieth-century investigation into the nature of the performative being created by groundbreaking theorists and practitioners in this growing field such as Victor Turner, Richard Schechner, Eugenio Barba, Jerzy Grotowski, Augusto Boal and, in his own way, Peter Brook. All are seeking to recognize and understand the role of the performative in daily life, to enlarge the notion of the theatrical to make all of us realize that theatre is not necessarily limited to a few hours in a closed, darkened building with a carefully prepared text being spoken to a group that has somehow been allowed entrance. It is an attempt to make us aware that theatre, the theatrical and the performative are quintessentially connected to universal human experiences: birth, death, rites of passage, marriage, namings and even funerals. The theatrical – as Africa well knows – is to be found in sporting events and in circuses, in storytelling and in public scenes, in dances and other mating events, in clothing and hairstyles. And, yes, the theatrical is even to be found in theatre buildings and scripts from Johannesburg's Market Theatre to Addis Ababa's National.

All of these are part of a continuum of the performative that we can and do participate in daily, a theatre that requires active rather than passive involvement, to be lived as well as watched. Not theatre *or* ritual but theatre *and* ritual. It is to an understanding of this – at once older and newer – sense of theatre that this volume is dedicated.

For the record, this is the first encyclopedia of the theatrical arts completely written by African scholars and theatre practitioners. Many did not believe when we began that the volume would ever come to pass. To be honest, at times neither did I. This last decade of the millennium is certainly not a time when scholarly support agencies have been willing to take financial risks in such groundbreaking areas nor is it a time when international cooperative initiatives in the theatre are being encouraged.

This makes these risks that were taken by so many that much more precious. No one risked more or was more committed to the realization of this volume than our francophone African editor, Ousmane Diakhaté of Cheikh Anta Diop University in Dakar, and no one was more determined that it be completed than our anglophone African editor, Hansel Ndumbe Eyoh of the University of Yaoundé (and later the University of Buea) in Cameroon. To them – and to the Rockefeller Foundation, which funded much of this volume – my sincerest thanks.

But there were more than a hundred others directly involved in this work – among them more than sixty writers of the national essays; a dozen or so translators in Canada and in Africa; our staff, Meredith Lordan, Catherine Matzig, Anton Wagner and Patricia Keeney at York University, who were untiring in the preparation of the final manuscript. The work could not have been completed without the belief, commitment and encouragement of the President of the Union of African Performing Artists – Ethiopia's Debebe Eshetu – and the many members of his board; without the patience and good advice of friends such as playwright Dickson Mwansa of Zambia and Indrasen Vencatachellum of Mauritius (and of UNESCO); without Professor Sylvia Bâ of Sénégal, my intellectual conscience in this work; without the Ghanaian-Canadian scholar Atta Mensah for his inspiring example and to his daring *ikanga*; without writer Henri Lopes of Congo (also of UNESCO), who expressed his belief and support for this work very early on; and without my friend and colleague Wole Soyinka, who has never stopped encouraging even when his own battles kept him at too great a distance. To all these people, I say simply, though we have not yet finished, my friends, I think we have made a useful start.

Don Rubin

OF INNER ROOTS AND
EXTERNAL ADJUNCTS

Theatre is one of the cultural elements that best exemplifies Africa. It is at the crossroads of the sacred and the profane, orality and the written word, of inner roots and external adjuncts. The product of an accretion of diverse forms, it is rooted in Africa's traditions while at the same time it continues to assimilate foreign theatrical traditions, especially those of Europe.

Long before cultural contact with Europe, Black Africa had its very own personal forms of dramatic expression. But in order to understand them one must banish all notions of theatre as it is thought of today – something dependent on text, on halls, on lights, sound and box-office returns. In this sense, African tradition has not handed down to us a specific theatrical system; rather it has handed down a series of functions, which themselves were modified under colonial influence and which gradually moved away from their roots though they were never eliminated completely.

The term 'theatre' itself has diverse, complex, contradictory and even antagonistic connotations in Africa. As well, the study of dramatic phenomena involves diverse approaches. Even in the west, the word 'theatre' denotes completely different realities, and what is meant by theatre in one country is not always the same as what is meant in others. It would be unwise, therefore, to expect to find in ancient Black Africa types of theatrical performances analogous to European forms. Rather than referring to the cultural traditions of Europe then, I shall look at the evolution of African culture from within its own unique dynamic and from within its own history.

It is the functioning of society itself which most directly dictates artistic expression in Africa, whose theatre is rooted in myths, rites and folk celebrations which externalize the beliefs, passions and concepts that preoccupy any given group. The fact is that early Africans never invented a generic term to designate these representations. They did not name their theatre; rather they lived it. In their scheme of things theatre was taken for granted. Theatrical art in Africa, therefore, is very ancient, its origins lost in prehistory. Yet it is part of every day in public places and at home. Everywhere theatricality is evident. The slightest pretext often gives rise to complex theatrical events where music, dance and verbal parody figure in equal parts. The African has always lived in close accord with theatre and the theatrical is an integral part of his or her identity.

In this sense early Africa offers an example of perfect harmony between theatre and society. If one considers the genres and styles of theatre in connection with the milieux in which they originated, if one tries to ascertain the specific elements that gave rise to African theatre and if one studies these indigenous forms as such, it can be concluded that theatre in ancient Black Africa can be clearly found in such elements as ritual gesture and communal celebration by large rural publics where these forms first emerged, artistic forms that synthesize spectacle and the spoken word, rhythm and dance, forms that integrate many modes of expression. It is to rituals, dances, masquerades, storytelling and folk celebrations with all their theatrical elements, then, that one must look for such an African definition.

The fact is that Africa is prodigiously rich in rituals of all kinds. Some are in a lighter vein and give rise to comic expression but the great majority have their origins in religious expression and magic. Intended as a discourse with supernatural forces – in order to channel them, control them, appease them or honour them – and to ensure the survival and equilibrium of the community, rituals were and still are shields defending the community against evil forces. Through gestures and actions believed to be endowed with supernatural powers, these rituals enable society to reaffirm, perpetuate and commemorate aspects of existence and beliefs deemed essential for the community's physical, moral and spiritual health. Such rituals are numerous and varied, going back to ancient times and elaborated differently by each of the continent's more than one thousand different ethnic groups. In this sense, each of these thousands of rituals constitutes the germ of a theatrical performance in its use of mask, dance and incantation.

While it is also true that ritual and theatre are not the same thing, it is evident that theatre, of all the arts, is the one most apt to use the same elements as those found in ritual. It is for this reason that so many African researchers and practitioners put ritual at the centre of both their reflection and their stage practice. Imbued with symbolic meaning and using a concrete language, rituals delineate spaces that are always seen as symbolic or mythic, places to come together, places for an exchange between the human and the divine or between human and human. Created by master-celebrants and shared with participant spectators, such ritual ceremonies designate specific roles – often supernatural – with actions and words rooted not in aesthetics but in their efficacy as part of the whole performance construct.

The root here is religion – in this case, animism – which permeates all activities and constitutes the basis for a whole network of customs. African thought is steeped in animism which places humanity at the centre of its concerns. God, in the African universe, needs people in order to be fully realized. It is people, by their sacrifices, their cultural manifestations and their incantations who give God meaning. In this way, each human being – in conjunction with his or her ancestors – participates in divine creativity. Such activities are performed in ritual ceremonies by recreating and representing (as Senegalese poet and philosopher

Léopold Sédar Senghor has pointed out) a mythic temporal dimension through artistic techniques utilizing masks, songs, poetry and dance; in short, through theatre. These are all the appropriate channels necessary to ensure communication with the divinities and to convey to them humanity's grievances and praises.

It is through such performative elements that the myths and legends on which African civilization is based are examined, scrutinized and reinterpreted. In such traditional ceremonies, for example, the mask is considered the material representation of a spiritual presence assuring the presence of the dead among the living. It can symbolize animals as well as humans. The mask therefore is an emblem, a sign that not only obliterates the personality of the wearer, but also identifies that person with a mythical ancestor or a supernatural being. It can also enable the wearer to take on the appearance of a being belonging to another species while retaining his own ancestral connections.

The mask in this sense tells a story as it seeks out a supernatural past or present that it both directs and invigorates, participating in either the cohesion of the group or aggressively in a hostile situation. It should be noted too that the mask is not simply something covering the face, but also includes those garments covering the wearer's body. Always displayed in motion (as dance) the dramatic function of masking is clear in all African communities. When connected to representations of gods, masking also almost always inspires dance and music, elements of social integration and the most characteristic elements of cultural life on the African continent.

From a standpoint of space, it is also clear that in ancient Africa, no ritual act had meaning separate from the place where it was performed or apart from the participants involved in it. Ritual space existed therefore only by virtue of the forces and the supernatural beings that manifested themselves in it. It was never neutral and was based on a particular socio-psychological conception of the world. Every ritual act made – and continues to make – reference to cosmic reality, and particularly to the space that represents in condensed form the infinite space of the cosmos. As a result everything that is done, said or performed in it is in its turn invested with a particular energy. Ritual space thus acquires the same enhanced value that is found in the platform stage in other parts of the world.

In most African religions, the ritual expresses a need to communicate with supernatural forces, especially with 'the dead who are not dead', whose spirits live on. This need for exchange between the supplicant and the gods is expressed through offerings, sacrifices, entreaties and prayers. The structure of ritual space (as marked off by the protagonist) always conveys the desire to bring together the celebrants and those who share the same preoccupations. A circle of participants is formed around the leader/shaman/sorcerer, which allows him to take on the collective force of the group, giving him greater efficacy in the performance of his magic. The circular space itself expresses the desire to bring the participants together and to create between them a fusion, a true physical and psychological interpenetration. It is an attempt at recreating a spatial form in which beliefs and collective conceptions can best be realized. Through this dramatic space an attempt is made to replicate the conditions of ritual communion where everything comes together. And, of course, in a space where spirits and humans reinforce one another in reciprocal fashion, in a space where sacred forces and supernatural beings manifest themselves, no arbitrary gesture can be tolerated. The power of the space itself then implies and explains the nature of the ceremony and determines the overall impact of the performance.

Such ritual ceremonies are conducted by celebrants who must establish contact between supernatural and quotidian reality. Through them, there is imitation of supernatural phenomena and an effort to make the celebrants one with such forces. These imitations involve movement, gesture, disguise and dialogue with the divinities. There are masters of ceremonies as well as actions that take place according to a 'script' which itself respects certain prescriptions.

The principal objective of this central action is, obviously, the efficacy of the ritual, but artistic arrangement and acting are not completely foreign to it. The dance, for example, despite its religious origin, is not merely physical movement of a sacred nature. Ritual dancers are also creators of beauty in so far as they also stylize their bodies and movements.

Secular comic theatre arising mostly from folk celebrations also existed and still exists in Africa, especially during harvest times and during family ceremonies. A collective entertainment, these performances' principal aims were to represent mores observed in daily life. The setting was generally simple and was largely dependent upon the whims of the masters of ceremonies and the events being celebrated. Featuring both men and women and intended for a large rural public, these performances varied from light amusement to the satirical and were characterized by virtuosity in areas such as mime, verbal artistry, acrobatics, song and dance. Still seen today on special occasions and performed by artists who are born into their caste and whose function is handed down from generation to generation, these local performances continue to be given before very large audiences.

Performed in the same types of spaces as the rituals, such comic performances are still primarily done for entertainment. As with ritual events, admission is not charged. Performed in public squares or in courtyards, the shows are done with the audience standing in a circle around the actors. A tree might serve as a stand for props and costumes as well as a backdrop.

In certain religious ceremonies the celebrants wear, painted on their body, the picture of a place, or sometimes just a stylized design representing a detail of a place. The dance often creates a moving décor through these costumes, or through lines made by the dancer's steps. The objects they wear or carry and especially the colours of the accessories (branches, feathers, animal skins), constitute a décor endowed with special powers to transform the nature of a site. In such events, the artists may themselves be the décor.

Acting techniques in all these ritual or ritually related areas must obviously be mastered. The actor must show an ability to use dramatic space not only through movements but also through pauses so that all the spectators are included. The actors must be constantly aware of the power of their gestures and voices. Indeed, whatever the type of space, the African actor will almost always re-create, by gesture or word, the traditional circular space.

In the secular comic theatre, the actor must also be a highly skilled acrobat, dancer and mime. Such performances, like those of the commedia dell'arte, depend a great deal on improvisation around a relatively limited series of stories drawn from the common heritage, which often mix serious and comic modes. Finally, it should be said that secular performances provide spectacles that are much more varied and lively than do the ritual ones where things tend to be much slower and more established by precedent. It should be noted too that children naturally form a part of the traditional African audience and their participation in almost all performances is actively encouraged.

Clearly, such a brief summary shows African theatrical art before contact with the outside world to be rich and complex. In the last half of the twentieth century, in fact, African secular theatre has returned to its own sources, and practitioners as well as researchers have once again found in these ancient forms the roots of a theatrical renewal and have again connected African theatre to those rituals, dances, masquerades, tales and folk celebrations which have for so long been the true centre of the continent's theatrical art.

This said, one cannot ignore the fact that the evolution of African theatrical art was interrupted by foreign invasion. First by Arabs and then by Europeans, these invasions affected all aspects of society, including the theatre. Certainly the Arab conquest, dating from the eleventh century and the subsequent introduction of Islam, did much to redirect – if not stifle – artistic expression. Christianity later changed the direction once again. Both these religions grafted themselves on to an existing system of thought that was quite rich and most original.

Early descriptions of African performances by foreigners – first by Arabs from the eleventh century (a period before colonization) then by Europeans during the colonial period – invariably missed the spiritual dimension spoken of here. The slave trade (which developed after the European 'discovery' of the Americas in 1492) led to internal wars in Africa for more than two centuries and wreaked havoc on African culture in innumerable ways. Relations between African states were perverted by the rush to satisfy the demand for slaves. Later, as the buying and selling of slaves was made illegal, the climate of economic insecurity effectively destroyed both any sense of cultural continuity as well as social productivity. Slowly, Africa began to withdraw into itself. By the nineteenth century, when European powers again turned their economic and religious attention toward Africa, they found not a series of culturally and economically robust states but rather states that had been already significantly weakened in material and moral terms.

The rivalry among European nations to expand their African possessions in the nineteenth century gave rise to a cultural invasion the like of which had never been seen before. To avoid war, however, an international conference was held in Berlin in 1884–5 in an attempt to resolve the conflicts created by Europe's lust for African territory. It was this conference which established the rules of occupation of the African territories and which divided the continent up among the European powers. By 1902 the conquest of Africa was almost complete, with the greatest beneficiaries being France, Great Britain, Portugal, Belgium, later Germany and, to a lesser extent, Spain and Italy. This is the origin of the qualifying adjectives 'francophone', 'anglophone' and 'lusophone' used throughout this volume.

Francophone Africa

The sub-Saharan countries referred to here as francophone Black Africa actually divide into four groups: the countries of the former French West Africa; the countries of the former French Equatorial Africa; the former French colonies of the Indian Ocean; and the former Belgian territories. A few remarks on each of these four groupings follow.

The countries of former French West Africa. Known in French as Afrique Occidentale Française (AOF) and created in 1885, these countries formed a kind of federal territory with its capital in Saint Louis and later in Dakar (both cities in Sénégal). Included in this grouping were Côte d'Ivoire, Dahomey (contemporary Bénin), French Guinea, Upper Volta (contemporary Burkina Faso), Mauritania, Niger, Sénégal and the French Sudan (now called Mali). Also included in French West Africa was the former German colony of Togo which later became a territory under French mandate. With the exception of the Arabo-Berbers (Moors) of Mauritania and the Touaregs of Niger-Sudan, all the peoples of this area are essentially black and belong to the Mandingo ethnic group (comprising Bambara, Malinké, Susu, Diola, Songhai, Mossi and Senufo); the Sudano-Guinean group (Fan, Ashanti, Baulé and Hausa) or smaller groups such as Wolof, Dogon and Peul (Fulani).

The countries of the former French Equatorial Africa. Known in French as Afrique Equatoriale Française (AEF), this grouping included four territories with Brazzaville as its capital: Congo-Brazzaville, Gabon, Ubangi Shari (now called the Central African Republic) and Chad. There is great ethnic diversity in this region, the principal group being Bantu.

The Indian Ocean colonies. Included here is the island of Madagascar; a single colony which comprised the Comoros Islands, Réunion Island, the French Coast of the Somalis and the island of Mauritius; and the Seychelles Islands.

The Belgian territories. These included the Congo, Zaïre, Rwanda and Burundi (the latter two originally German colonies mandated to Belgium in 1918 and dominated by two ethnic groups – Tutsi and Hutu).

By the eve of World War I, French and Belgian influence was clearly felt in Africa throughout the region and its cultural destiny became clearly linked to French colonial policies. In the domain of theatre, colonization created a double cultural life: a literary theatre written in French and performed in accordance with European models (what is referred to here as francophone Black African theatre) and a theatre drawn from those traditional forms spoken about earlier.

Francophone Black African theatre therefore is actually quite a recent phenomenon. Created between the two world wars, it emerged along with French expansion on the continent. Seeking to establish reproductions of their own culture, their own ways and even their own religion in Africa, French colonial policy was aimed at cultural assimilation, making Africans into proper French citizens, reshaping the culture of the African world along French lines. Such a policy included an emphasis on education and evangelization. These two cornerstones also introduced European theatre into Africa and were the principal forces in the birth of francophone Black African theatre.

Christian missionary education was certainly a key factor in its development. Making extensive use of dramatic representation in the teaching of the Bible, European-style playlets began to be seen in all regions where Christianity was implanted. On the occasions of Christmas and Easter, for example, the Ploërmels Brothers, who ran the Secondary School of Saint Louis (founded in 1841), organized a series of theatre performances as had their predecessors, the Sisters of St Joseph of Cluny and Abbé Boilat. Catholic school students throughout the colonies, especially in Gabon and Dahomey, were encouraged to put on their own French-language sketches on themes taken from the Bible. These productions, inspired by religious themes, were conceived exclusively on a European dramatic aesthetic and became the first examples of francophone African theatre. It was only with the development of secular schools in the 1930s that these evolved into more modern theatrical forms.

One major breakthrough came in 1913 when Georges Hardy, himself a playwright, became Director of Education of French West Africa. Under Hardy, the theatre would gain an important place in the schools. Writing in 1917, Hardy saw the theatre as a way for his students

> to avoid the fatigue, boredom, homesickness that could afflict these young people separated from their families for an entire year …. These ceremonies provided many surprises for the spectators: the surprise at seeing with what ease and with what sense of nuance our students interpreted the French texts, the surprise at realizing the eternal youth and universal appeal of [French] masterpieces.

This secular form of school theatre spread through the territories as more and more schools were established. But it was mainly at the William Ponty Normal School near Dakar that the most significant francophone Black African theatre work emerged. The first laboratory of francophone African dramatic art, the Ponty School's role in the birth of this theatre bears closer examination.

Named for Governor-General William Merlaud-Ponty (d. 1915) who left his mark on educational policy in French West Africa, the all-male Ponty School was the most famous of the training schools of the federation. Founded in Saint Louis in 1903 and transferred to the island of Gorée (off Dakar) in 1913, its major aim was to provide a basic European education for future African civil servants. Most of the black francophone colonial elite were trained there, especially elementary school teachers and those called African doctors (trained to give basic medical care). Students were admitted by competitive examination and were recruited from among the brightest in the territories.

School authorities at Ponty quickly realized the educational value of theatre and actively encouraged it. Teachers had students write plays for various occasions, plays in some instances based on research collected from their home communities. Not only did such exercises give the students a taste for theatrical research but it also led them into regional groupings to discuss the themes best suited for dramatization. In such an atmosphere, theatre at Ponty – and later across French West Africa – was nurtured.

At the end of the academic year 1932–3, a play composed by the student group from Dahomey (Bénin), *Bayol et Behanzin*, was produced along with a farce of Molière. This was arguably the first original French-African play written in the European style. (The other candidate for this honour is *Les Villes* (*The Cities*) by Bernard Dadié of Côte d'Ivoire, but the manuscript is now lost. This play dates back to about 1931 when Charles Béart became director of the primary school of Bingerville in Côte d'Ivoire.) Here too francophone Black African plays were produced, Dadié's among them.

The years 1936–7 marked the apogee of Ponty's theatre activities with student productions emerging from Côte d'Ivoire, Guinea and Dahomey. In 1939 the school was transferred to Sebikotane (near Dakar). Theatre continued to thrive. In 1948, on the occasion of the festivities for the Centennial of the Abolition of Slavery, students from the Normal School for Girls in Rufisque joined the 'Pontins' for the first time in a dramatic production.

After World War II, colonial cultural policy and educational policy both changed. As a result, theatre began to disappear from the curriculum. Nevertheless, the work done at the Ponty School clearly played a seminal role through the later activities of its graduates, several of whom founded troupes on their return to their respective countries. Especially noteworthy was the one created in 1938 by the Ivoirians François-Joseph Amon d'Aby and Coffi Gadeau, the Indigenous Theatre of Côte d'Ivoire, which became in 1953 the Cultural and Folklore Circle of Côte d'Ivoire. Another outstanding example was the theatre of the Guinean Fodéba Keita, a school teacher and Ponty graduate who founded the troupe that would become the forerunner of the Ballets Africains, a company that had great success on its world tours.

With this proliferation of dramatic activities, the colonial administration announced in 1953 that it would begin the construction of a series of Cultural Centres in each of the large cities of the federation. Conceived as meeting places for the urban African and European elite, such centres were actively supported by the government. A promotional information bulletin launched in 1954, *Trait d'union* (*Hyphen*) covered theatre extensively and included information on the publication of plays as well as reviews of productions and practical advice for aspiring artists.

In 1955, an ambitious dramatic competition was organized among the Cultural Centre groups, an event closely monitored by the colonial administration. All Cultural Centres were required to participate. After elimination rounds in each territory, a local final was held and then quarter-finals among neighbouring territories, the host town drawn by lot. Grand finals were then held in Dakar in the presence of the High Commissioner. The competition spawned considerable theatrical activity all across French West Africa. The Cultural and Folklore Circle of Côte d'Ivoire was the winner in 1955 and 1956; in 1957, the Cultural Circle of Banfora (Upper Volta) won. In addition, a contest for playwrights was also organized. This period of francophone Black African theatre, called (for obvious reasons) the 'period of Cultural Centres', lasted until 1958, the date of the breakup of the federation and the beginning of what would be called the Era of Independence (1958 to the present) when new forms emerged more adapted to the sociopolitical realities of Africa.

Under the influence of new authorities, many of whom were educated in the Ponty tradition, European-style theatre continued to be encouraged. Conditions seemed particularly favourable for the creation of national companies, the encouragement of amateur troupes and the construction of infrastructures for the theatre. Such efforts were made in most of the new states and most had governmental support. Even schools of drama to train Africans in those techniques were opened in Sénégal, Mali and Côte d'Ivoire. In these schools, there was a desire not only to conserve traditional values but also to benefit from the wise utilization of techniques that had been tried and tested throughout the world. In many countries, the theatre benefited greatly during this period and many African dramatic artists who had through the years moved to France began to return to their native countries.

As well, theatrical scholarship emerged. In 1958, the Senegalese critic Bakary Traoré published *Le Théâtre africain et ses fonctions sociales* (*The African Theatre and its Social Functions*), a first attempt at analysing the specificity of African theatre. Colloquia and international meetings were organized widely. Among these were a colloquium on Black African theatre organized by the University of Abidjan in Côte d'Ivoire in 1970, an Inter-African Theatre Seminar organized by the African Cultural Institute in 1978 at the National Institute of the Arts in Abidjan, and the Bamako Theatre Meeting in Mali in 1988. These meetings conducted extensive reviews of the situation of African theatre and gave both theorists and practitioners opportunities to become aware of problems and to find solutions.

During this period, dramatic writing also improved considerably. Playwrights from the Ponty and Cultural Centre periods were almost always amateurs. Most of them considered the theatre a recreational activity and with the possible exception of the plays of the Senegalese author Amadou Cissé Dia (*The Death of the Damel* and *The Last Days of Lat Dior*, both written in 1942), few important plays emerged. It was only after independence that dramatic writing flourished, plays of real aesthetic quality began to appear and publishing houses both in Africa and abroad began to take them seriously. Among these were Présence Africaine in Paris, Nouvelles Éditions Africaines in Dakar and Abidjan, and L'Harmattan in Paris. All contributed significantly to the distribution of dramatic works as did the Concours théâtral inter-africain (Inter-African Theatre Competition) created in 1968. One must note here as well the work of the French publisher Pierre-Jean Oswald and his African Theatre Collection.

Historical themes exalting the past – by far the most important trend – and satires of social and political mores dominated the dramatic literature of this period and produced writers whose reputation transcended national borders: Bernard Dadié of Côte d'Ivoire; Abdou Anta Kâ, Cheik Aliou N'dao and Thierno Bâ of Sénégal; Djibril Tamsir Niane and Condetto Nenekhaly Camara of Guinea; Seydou Badian of Mali; Guillaume Oyono-Mbia of Cameroon; and Maxime N'Debeka, Guy Menga and Sylvain Bemba of the Congo. It should also be noted that while the historical vein was predominant in West African countries, the playwrights of Central Africa had a preference for comic theatre.

Clearly this period qualifies as a great one in the history of Black African theatre yet it also showed the need for ongoing state support, especially in the development of infrastructure and equipment. With the exception of the Daniel Sorano National Theatre of Dakar, no other country in francophone Africa had a properly equipped theatre, and training in dramatic arts was barely supported. Few could make professional careers unless they were connected to national companies and therefore considered civil servants. For financial reasons, little thought was given to independent productions. Indeed, almost all the attempts to create private professional companies in the francophone community failed for lack of support. Nor was consideration given to the importance of amateur theatre, especially in those countries that had opted for professional state theatres.

Yet, despite the growth in dramatic activity, audiences were not significant. The problem was that French, rather than a local language, was used in the vast majority of productions. Even in the mid-1990s, more than 70 per cent of people who were called francophone Africans were still not proficient in the language.

But sophistication in theatrical forms and methods grew and universities began to develop curricula in the area of dramatic arts. Through the 1980s, many more professional troupes emerged and the level of amateur and university troupes grew. Even countries that were not particularly noted for the vitality of their theatre in the 1960s and 1970s were, in the 1990s, making a name for themselves both in Africa and internationally, among them Togo, Congo and Burkina Faso.

By the late 1980s and into the 1990s, plays had become much more militant and political than ever before, more innovative and more diversified in style. A class of professional theatre artists was emerging, many with a range of talents. The new francophone playwrights were often not only writers but also directors, actors, administrators and even theorists. Among them the late Congolese Sony Labou Tansi, the Togolese Sénouvo Agbota Zinsou, the Malian Gaoussou Diawara, the Ivoirian Bernard Zadi Zaourou, the Cameroonian Wéré-Wéré Liking (who was working mostly in Côte d'Ivoire) and the Burkinabe Jean Pierre Guingané, to name just a few.

Dramatic criticism in the 1990s, however, has no specialized publication anywhere in Africa. Sometimes in the general press, space is reserved for theatre while in the universities research is generally limited to dramatic structure, the principal interest being its connection to sources and the rehabilitation of African aesthetic forms including ritual, orality and dance.

The performing arts centre Mudra Afrique in Dakar was for some time the main reference for African dance. Created in 1977 by the Belgian choreographer Maurice Béjart on the initiative of Senegalese President Léopold Sédar Senghor (the centre operated early on with the support of UNESCO and the Calouste Gulbenkian Foundation), Mudra was an active and important Pan-African centre. Though it closed after only seven years of operation, its director, Germaine Acogny, continued to organize training programmes and in 1996 she founded a new Centre for Traditional and Contemporary Dance in Toubab Dialaw, a village located about 50 kilometres from Dakar.

Two other francophone artists of note are the Cameroonian Wéré-Wéré Liking and the Ivoirian Soulymane Koly, both of whom work mostly in Abidjan. Liking is the director of the Ki Yi Mbok Theatre, which attempts to treat Black African theatre experience in relation to ritual and puppets, while Koly, director of the Koteba troupe, uses music and dance as essential elements in his theatrical research.

Perhaps the most important area of artistic exploration in the 1980s and 1990s has been in the area of traditional folk tales. Many theatre specialists have been re-examining and experimenting with them as the basis of new dramatic techniques. An especially important example has been the work of the Didiga Company, created in 1980 out of a group engaged in research on oral tradition under the direction of professor and playwright Bernard Zadi Zaourou at the University of Abidjan. Two of his colleagues, Dieudonné Niangoran Porquet and Aboubakar Cyprien Touré, have also been adapting the oratorical art of the African *griot* and his musical accompaniments into a new dramatic form called the griotique. These are all areas worth watching closely. Still another has evolved in Togo, the transposition of the Concert Party tradition (also seen in other West African countries) into a dramatic form using formally structured music and dance.

Francophone Africa has long had connections with Europe, but it is only since the 1980s that African theatre artists have begun to develop exchanges among themselves. In spite of attempts at regional and sub-regional theatre meetings in Bénin, Burkina Faso, and Côte d'Ivoire, exchanges of productions are rare indeed. (The Festival of Theatre in Bénin,

organized by the French Cultural Centre of Cotonou, the Ministry of Culture of Bénin and the Kaïdara theatre, was first held in 1991. The International Theatre and Puppet Festival of Ouagadougou is organized every two years by the two principal associations of theatre artists in Burkina Faso. Côte d'Ivoire hosts a National Festival of School and University Theatre, begun in 1981–2, and an African Festival of Francophone Theatre first launched in 1994.) In 1993, the Agence de coopération culturelle et technique (ACCT; Agency for Cultural and Technical Cooperation) created in Abidjan the Market for Performing Arts in Africa (MASA). Outside of Africa, the foundation Afrique en créations, with headquarters in Paris, has greatly contributed to the development of the art through the promotion and production of African cultural products. This organization collects documentation on African performance generally and publishes a magazine called *Afrique en scène* (*Africa on Stage*) in collaboration with Radio France International and the ACCT.

Another international initiative is the Concours théâtral inter-africain, founded in 1966 during a colloquium of directors of broadcasting in francophone Africa and Madagascar. Now run by Radio France International, this contest, in spite of problems, has played a significant role in promoting francophone African theatre. More than 70 per cent of the plays presented in French before 1978 were, in fact, directly or indirectly linked to this contest. Involving all African and Indian Ocean francophone countries, the competition gave a large number of authors a forum to make their works known, to make contact with theatre troupes and to solicit productions in other countries.

The contest gives prizes to the best plays and contributes to their circulation, with the best plays being broadcast in all participating countries. Often the best play is also published. Produced in the author's own country, the production usually tours in neighbouring countries as well. Encouraging budding dramatists, the contest has introduced the works of writers including Guy Menga, Sony Labou Tansi, Sénouvo Agbota Zinsou, Guillaume Oyono-Mbia and Sylvain Bemba.

Another major international forum for francophone African theatre has been the Festival International des Francophonies (International Festival of the Francophone World) held annually in Limoges, France. Created in 1984, the festival has invited many African troupes to present productions there while a number of African dramatists have completed projects as writers-in-residence under festival auspices.

Still another French endeavour which has been helpful to African dramatists has been the Théâtre International de Langue Française (International Theatre in French) created in 1985 by the French director Gabriel Garran. Part of the Francophonie movement, its aim is to make known contemporary dramatic literature of French-speaking communities. As such it has staged several major African plays in France such as *Je soussigné cardiaque* (*I, the Undersigned Cardiac Case*) by Sony Labou Tansi (Paris, 1985), *Le Destin glorieux du Maréchal Nnikon Nniku, prince qu'on sort* (*The Glorious Destiny of Marshal Nnikon Nniku, Outgoing Prince*) by Tchicaya U Tam'si in collaboration with the Daniel Sorano National Theatre of Sénégal, and especially *Le Bal de N'Dinga* (*The Ball of N'Dinga*).

One should also note the contribution of the French director Jean Marie Serreau, who created Aimé Césaire's *La Tragédie du roi Christophe* (*The Tragedy of King Christophe*) at the First World Festival of Negro Arts in Dakar in 1966, later founded the Company of the Toucan in Paris, a troupe of black actors, which launched, among others, the Senegalese actor Douta Seck and premièred in France the plays of Bernard Dadié.

One helpful American initiative in this regard has been the work of Françoise Kourilsky's Ubu Repertory Theatre in New York and its associated publishing ventures. Ubu is also committed to the production of francophone plays in translation and has brought the work of many African writers to the attention of anglophone audiences and producers.

In 1983, UNESCO's International Theatre Institute organized an important meeting in Harare (Zimbabwe) under its then Secretary-General, the Swede Lars af Malmborg. This led to the creation of a Union of African Performing Artists headed by the distinguished Ethiopian actor Debebe Eshetu. In 1985 the ITI sponsored another gathering, this one under Secretary-General André-Louis Perinetti, and presided over by Nobel Prize-winning Nigerian playwright Wole Soyinka in which fifteen African countries reflected on the future of theatre in Africa, and in 1991 the Paris-based ITI opened its own regional office in Dakar to identify the needs of the performing arts in Africa and to support coordination and cultural exchanges. By 1994, the ITI had fourteen national centres in sub-Saharan Africa: Sénégal, Nigeria, Zaïre, Madagascar, Mali, Cameroon, Sierra Leone, Burkina Faso, Ghana, Uganda, Zimbabwe, Central African Republic, Kenya and Bénin.

Ousmane Diakhaté
Cheikh Anta Diop University, Dakar
Translated by Sylvia Bâ

Anglophone Africa

It is now generally accepted that there is a phenomenon called anglophone African theatre, just as it is accepted that there is something called European or American theatre. Ever since the Nigerian Wole Soyinka won the 1986 Nobel Prize, the question no longer occurs whether anglophone African theatre exists or not. Too many distinguished writers have emerged: the Kenyans Ngugi wa'Thiongo and Micere Mugo; the Nigerians Ola Rotimi, John Pepper Clark, Femi Osofisan and Zulu Sofola; the Ugandans Robert Serumaga and Rose Mbowa; the Tanzanians Penina Muhando and Ebrahim Husein; the Ghanaians Ama Ata Aidoo and Efua Sutherland; the Cameroonians Guillame Oyono-Mbia and Bole Butake; and the South Africans Athol Fugard, Zakes Mda and Gibson Kente, just to name a few whose

works have made a breakthrough internationally. Indeed, what we now talk about are the trends which are manifest in this theatre.

Beginning with its own traditional theatre – already discussed in some detail by my co-editor Ousmane Diakhaté – contemporary African playwriting first copied western forms, especially Shakespeare, Molière and Schiller, or adapted some of the classics of Greek theatre. This was followed by a period of experimentation and radicalization during which it assumed the language of Caliban. It later settled into what has come to be known as total theatre which is in essence a mixture of traditional African and western forms. Thematically, anglophone African theatre could be said to have gone from traditional celebration to colonial vilification and back to root sources and cultural affirmation, settling, at the end of the twentieth century, into socio-political and economic appraisal.

Critical assessments of many of the leading first-generation playwrights of anglophone Africa, especially Soyinka, J.P. Clark, Ene Enshaw, Sarif Easmon, Joe de Graft, Ngugi wa'Thiongo and Guillaume Oyono-Mbia, has been mixed. While their works have been much praised by earlier critics, especially in the west, the younger generation of African critics see in many of these writers' works, a kind of literary and artistic prostitution with the west, abandoning any attempt to communicate with their immediate audiences. The search for some universal frame of reference has often resulted in works which are sterile and emasculated. The derivations of J.P. Clark's *Song of a Goat* and *The Raft* are rather obvious. The former comes from traditions of the Greek dithyrambic ritual, while the latter derives from the myth of the journey into the unknown. Clark was, however, to turn his attention to local lore with his play *Ozidi*. Many of Wole Soyinka's early plays demonstrate this kind of derivation, with obvious Shakespearian echoes, although he is more imaginative in transforming his sources and instilling them with freshness and verve. Soyinka has been able to develop a more eclectic style, the result of a thorough process of experiential distillation. Playwrights like Sarif Easmon in *Dear Parent and Ogre* and Joe de Graft in *Through a Film Darkly* remain stuck in their drawing rooms, however, harnessed to the constraints of the proscenium arch through whose fourth wall we are compelled to peep into their characters' lives.

There were, though, some playwrights, such as the Cameroonian Guillaume Oyono-Mbia, who actually experimented with indigenous forms. A professor of English, he has regularly translated his own work into French. *Three Suitors, One Husband* is obviously influenced by Molièresque humour, but even in this play there is already a clear attempt at integrated drama.

While structural problems have continued to be the concern of many African playwrights, a more serious source of worry comes from the use of language and the exploitation of particular themes. Many of these playwrights have continued to use thematic content as an excuse for shabbiness of form, whereas in artistic creativity, one is inexorably linked to the other.

Moving from the ritual and historical presentations of Charles Béart's William Ponty days, to the Ghanaian Concert Parties and the Nigerian Yoruba Opera, dramatists and theatre practitioners have continued to seek to relate works to their environment by making them more relevant and functional. Drama, like other forms of art in Africa, has come to be seen not only from the point of view of entertainment, but equally as an avenue for self-criticism and self-actualization. Through drama, it is increasingly being realized, people can assert or inculcate positive social mores, so long as the drama-making process is community centred. While the structural framework of the plays has moved from tame derivativeness through eclecticism and sheer adventurism, the thematic range was also bound to reach out to new vistas. On the linguistic level, language has become more vivid, with strong local colouring, all responding to the new circumstances. The strident voices accusing the colonizers have turned their attention to attacking the *arriviste* Africans who now lord it over their own people. Franz Fanon captured this very well in the title of his book, *Black Skins, White Masks*.

The newer generation of anglophone African writers and other theatre practitioners is, on the other hand, even more daring in its treatment of themes and more direct in its statement of purpose. Language is simplified to make access easier; action is enhanced mostly to include dance, masquerade and ritual. This growing awareness of the impact of drama in a still largely illiterate society, has led to the creation since the 1980s of a Theatre-for-Development movement. This style of theatre is seen as the fastest means of communication with the public, but it is also being stifled in a number of countries with repressive political regimes, be these civilian or military. Playwrights like Ngugi wa'Thiongo and Wole Soyinka have been incarcerated while others like Ken Saro-Wiwa have been executed in countries as far apart as Nigeria and Kenya. The work of theatre practitioners throughout the continent, in fact, continues to be looked upon with suspicion, especially with the growing awareness that theatre is subversive because of its congregational effect. Obviously when the theatre-making process becomes so demystified as to return it to its roots, it can awaken social and political consciousness and mobilize a revolutionary potential.

For many dramatists and theatre practitioners in anglophone Africa then theatre has come to be seen as a means of social and political evangelization, spreading dissent to the masses. It has become a means of consciousness-raising, of developing critical awareness, with local populations helping to write the script, do the directing, and even acting in the performances for which they also remain the final beneficiaries. The process itself is analytical, critical and complementary, generating solutions within the community and examining the various constraints that limit the scope of the action of the community. This movement – which started in Botswana and Lesotho – has spread throughout English-speaking Africa and has made a large impact in southern and eastern Africa (Tanzania, Uganda, Kenya, Malawi and South Africa) as well as in western Africa (Nigeria, Sierra Leone and Ghana).

The term 'popular', however, needs to be defined. In the broadest sense of the word, it implies that which has the widest possible audience appeal, something that cuts across the greatest number of social barriers. It can also be used to mean that which is rooted in the masses against that which limits itself to an elitist class.

Yet for all this, as previously indicated, it is anglophone Africa's playwrights who have brought world attention to the continent's theatre. The foremost of these is without doubt the Nigerian Wole Soyinka, the 1986 Nobel Prize-winner for literature. Soyinka has also written a substantial number of prose and poetic works as well as numerous theoretical essays. Educated at the University of Ibadan in Nigeria and the University of Leeds in Britain, he has become the conscience of his country during its many totalitarian regimes. Although it has been said that his plays have the imprint of African sensibility and symbolism and express a deep awareness of the African culture, critics also claim that they are barely understood in Africa. Paradoxically, non-Africans are among his most ardent admirers. He also remains the most studied African playwright and has been the subject of numerous books and articles, as well as of dissertations and theses around the world.

The Nigerian dramatic scene is certainly the most vibrant in anglophone Africa. The universities, about thirty in the 1990s, are hubs of these activities. Most now have repertory troupes with resident playwrights and directors. Many boast drama departments as teaching units. Lagos and Ibadan are clearly the seats from which Nigerian theatre radiates with

the performing facilities in Lagos and the pioneering work done at the Mbari Club of Ibadan largely responsible.

Yet there are other centres in anglophone Africa: Ghana, where the plays of Ama Ata Aidoo and Efua Sutherland show influences of the Ananse storytelling tradition while the University of Legon at Accra has been a focal point of work which is today led by people like Kofi Anyihodoo.

In Sierra Leone, a robust 'Creole' theatre tradition has developed in the work of Raymond Sarif Easmon, Yulisa Ahmadu Maddy, Thomas Decker (who translated Shakespeare's *Julius Caesar* into Krio) and wrote two Krio plays, *Nar Mami Born Am* and *E day E nor do*, and Raymond de Souza Johnson.

Cameroon, Africa's only officially English/French bilingual country, belongs to both the Francophonie and the Commonwealth. The first playwright from English-speaking Cameroon was Sankie Maimo, who started writing in Nigeria in 1959 and followed mostly the manner of modernity and tradition of the first generation of Nigerian playwrights. He was joined by anglophone Cameroon's most prolific playwright, Victor Elame Musinga, who started making incursions into social criticism. In the late 1970s a new breed of anglophone Cameroonian dramatists, championed by Bole Butake, emerged. The work of many of these playwrights could be associated with the kind of revolutionary attempts of Femi Osofisan in Nigeria. Of Cameroonian playwrights, though, the most important in terms of outreach remains Musinga with more than twenty plays to his credit.

The University of Makerere in Kampala, Uganda, was largely responsible for training the first crop of theatre artists in East Africa – Uganda, Kenya and Tanzania. The countries of this region, as well as many of those in southern Africa, went through a colonial situation which saw the importation of cultural values mostly from Britain. It was not until the advent of independence in the early 1960s and the awakening of African nationalism that attempts at validating indigenous culture began to manifest themselves. The Kenyan National Theatre in Nairobi, for example, was closed to plays by nationals until the mid-1960s.

In most of East Africa, repressive regimes gave rise to two types of theatre. The first was an elusive theatre which communicated through signs and symbols. This was seen in the work of John Ruganda, who in *The Burden*

(1971) attacked dictator Idi Amin's penchant for having many wives and mistresses. The period of the rule of Milton Obote during 1962–70 and then again from 1979 was characterized by intense repression, but playwrights like Wycliffe Kiyingi, in his radio series, *Wokulira*, kept the liberation struggle burning. Because of the attempt to evade reprisals, many of the plays during this period were quite obscure. Robert Serumaga, for instance, began writing drama in the absurdist vein. Rose Mbowa's 1987 production of her play, *Mother Uganda and Her Children*, was written after Bertolt Brecht's *Mother Courage*. Besides presenting the ethnic and cultural diversity of Uganda using its dances, rituals, folklore and customs, *Mother Uganda* became a review of the history of the country, marking decisive stages of the life of an average Ugandan, turning out to be a political allegory with the key issue being ethnic diversity and national unity.

Kenya suffered a similar malaise in the early 1960s when its theatrical scene was dominated by western imports from London. It was not until independence that people like Ngugi wa'Thiongo and Micere Mugo wrote and produced *The Trial of Dedan Kimathi* and *The Black Hermit*. *The Trial of Dedan Kimathi* dealt with the Mau Mau uprising that heralded the advent of independence, while wa'Thiongo's *The Black Hermit* examined the problems confronting a young man just returned home from studies in England between westernization and traditional Africa.

The Kenyan National Theatre based in Nairobi was Kenyan only in name, because it became an exclusive preserve of performances of non-Kenyan plays. Much of the early theatre by Kenyans was a revaluation of the consequences of independence. Ngugi wa'Thiongo's *Ngahika Ndeenda* (*I Will Marry When I Want*) was performed by the Kamiriithu Community Educational and Cultural Centre, a group of adult education pupils, much to the consternation of the authorities, and this led to the razing of an open-air theatre which had been constructed by the villagers, the banning of the play and Ngugi wa'Thiongo's consequent incarceration, and his eventual self-exile in England. While a lot of important work still continues to be done as part of the Kenya's Schools and Colleges Annual Theatre Festival, not much impressive work has lately emerged.

Zambia was also a seat of European theatre from the white settler community. National work was done by the University of Zambia Drama Society and the Zambia Dance Company which produced mainly West African plays, including Wole Soyinka's *The Road* in the 1970s. Later, work was taken out into the countryside and began to embrace Theatre-for-Development. Beginning with a workshop in 1979 which brought together seventy-seven participants made up of community development, adult education and theatre artists, Theatre-for-Development resource persons came from Botswana, Tanzania, Canada, Swaziland, the USA and from the liberation movements then operating within the region.

For a long time, Malawi remained behind a virtual 'iron-curtain' because of the benign dictatorship of Hastings Banda. Theatre was to develop within the country but rather than direct presentation, most of it became highly symbolic and resorted to innuendo to escape censorship.

As elsewhere in Africa, traditional festivals, rituals and ceremonies abound which are all of a highly theatrical nature. The most notable in Malawi is the Nyau which has been described as the performance of masked mimes and the ceremonies surrounding them.

The popular theatre also came to occupy centre stage in Malawi, under the leadership of Chris Kamlongera. Until recently, however, much of the theatre work in Malawi has come under the scrutiny of the Censorship Board which has a comprehensive mandate to expunge plays of indecency and obscenity, and any material likely to be repulsive or defamatory. This, of course, was very inhibiting to the playwrights and limited the scope of their work.

South Africa's 'white' theatre mostly followed traditions from the western world, while its 'black' theatre included works of protest, resistance and committed expression actively opposing the political-cultural status quo. A robust musical drama was developed during the apartheid period, first as confirmation of the traditional basis of African culture, and later as a force to be reckoned with in the search for freedom. Musicals like *Umbathala*, an adaptation of *Macbeth*, *Ipi Tombi*, *Sarafina* and *Asinamali* (*We Have No Money*) were mounted and toured extensively in Europe and America, as either symbols of the cultural richness or the freedom struggles of the Blacks. In these performances

Song, music, dance, movement, are forged into a means of expression, a language of its own right, with which the group ... communicates with each other, enacting their hopes and desires, their fears of rejection, their ideals of individual happiness and social participation and integration.

(Breitinger 1992:137).

However, besides musicals, an exciting theatre developed which was championed by those who strove to awaken the world to the plight of Black South Africans. Much of this theatre happened in the townships in a rather impromptu manner and through improvisations. Several theatre personalities emerged in the 1970s and 1980s, both black and white, all of whom fought hard against the apartheid system. Powerful playwrights such as Athol Fugard and actors Winston Ntshona and John Kani came to attack the inequities of the apartheid system in plays such as *The Island* and *Sizwe Bansi Is Dead*, while others like Percy Mtwa and Mbogemi Ngema performed *Woza Albert!* (1981), an enactment of Jesus' second coming in South Africa. Mtwa and Ngema both came out of the musical experiences of Gibson Kente, but broke away from what they considered a stagnant form of performance to embrace a more dynamic format, which developed through workshops and addressed itself directly to the blacks in the townships. Mtwa and Ngema later split and produced other plays including *Bopha* by Mtwa and Ngema and founded the Committed Artists, a group of unemployed youth who dramatized their experiences in apartheid South Africa.

Most of the plays written by Black South Africans during this period articulate the dignity of the oppressed, the injustices of the oppressor and the urgency of political change. With growing materialism, much of the theatre work became commercialized and compromised some of the ideologies initially expressed in earlier works. Works such as *Asinamali* (1984), *Sarafina* (1987) and *Township Fever* (1990) came to be severely criticized for the points of view which they expressed, which differed from those held by the suffering masses, which these works claimed they portrayed. Subsequently, South Africa's theatre moved from a theatre of confrontation and resistance to one of reconciliation as the apartheid system crumbled and gave way to a more nationally accepted system that promoted racial equality and that helped to heal the wounds of the past.

There is as well in most of Africa an interest in theatre for young audiences though in many countries it is perceived to be theatre *by* young people, often taking place within the context of theatre-in-education courses.

Clearly, contemporary anglophone African theatre did not emerge smoothly from the past but rather from a fragmented history of both traditional African and western influences. There are still the rituals and festivals in the countryside which today largely inform the structure and techniques of African theatre. One sees these clearly in the use of storytelling, folk narrative, the use of *griot*, the rituals, as well as the enhanced use of proverbs and the promotion of concepts such as negritude. Historical themes are dealt with alongside the problems of becoming which face today's decolonized African, caught between the black skins and the white masks of yesteryear. We have seen transpositions and adaptations of plays from ancient Greece and more recent western drama; plays which deal with the problems of colonization and the struggle for independence; plays of protest and those with a political bias; and we have seen the movement towards Theatre-for-Development, where a genuine attempt has been made finding theatre's traditional social function.

The history of Africa has not been the same from one anglophone country to the other, although the major periods have been similar – pre-colonial, colonial and post-colonial. Experiences have differed depending on the specific colonial power, the location of the country and the natural resources which it possessed. Though African countries gained independence much earlier, it was not until the early 1980s, for example, that Rhodesia became Zimbabwe and it was not until the 1990s that majority black rule was installed in South Africa. Dramatists in every country took part in this liberation struggle, both from the colonial powers and from the *arriviste* African leadership which followed. Soyinka's Nobel Prize gave international confirmation of the emergence and achievements of all African writers and reinforced the notion that the dramatist in Africa is a combatant whose activities go far beyond the stage.

Hansel Ndumbe Eyoh
University of Buea
Buea

THE GREAT ODE OF HISTORY

MUSIC AND DANCE IN AFRICA

Africa is the second largest land mass in the world and boasts the world's longest river (Nile), the world's largest inland lake (Victoria), the world's greatest falls (Musi O Tunya (Victoria) – the River That Thunders) and the world's largest desert (Sahara), all surmounted by great peaks like Kilimanjaro, Kenya, the Ethiopian Highlands and Cameroon Highlands. It is this Africa that awaits a giant – a master music and dance director with the composite vision of Soyinka, Ngugi, Oyono-Mbia, Opoku, Tewfik al Hakim and Fugard, that awaits more Blacks, more Arabs and more Caucasians who will together conduct a chorus (formed by all the spirits of the different climes of Africa) called The Great Ode of History. This Ode will be in a thousand keys with another thousand kinaesthetic parts, and it will give a full picture of the broad typography and variety of Africa's musical and dance heritage, a heritage bequeathed to us by millennia, by the human dwellers of tropical rainforests, by those who lived and still live in vast stretches of woodland, grassland, scrubland, desert oases and the swamps of river basins, by climes reflected vertically here and there along the slopes of highlands and snow-capped mountain tops in tropical climes. This Ode will proclaim African music and dance in its full historical glory rising from the painted caves and open-air art galleries of the continent's prehistory.

In this article, however, I can hope to reach only the lower shadows cast by this world Ode in music and choreography.

Why such dominance of music and dance in African cultures? The answer is perhaps best illustrated by a Kikuyu (Gikuyu) legend. As it is told, after careful consideration of how a set of new laws could be propagated effectively, a Council of Elders resolved to put them into songs and to get dancers to tour the land with them (see Neher and Condon 1975). In such times – not so long past – the performing arts still carried such strength as communication vehicles. Even Jomo Kenyatta, a trained anthropologist who later became president of Kenya, provided such evidence in his book, *Facing Mount Kenya: The Tribal Life of the Gikuyu* (1961), a work filled with many references to musical instruments, occasions for music-making and dancing, all stressing the significance of these arts in popular culture.

Citations from Africa's most distant past, though fewer, speak of older dance and musical arts with insistent conviction. The prehistoric cave painters and artists of open-air galleries documented such scenes of music and dance (see Gillon 1984). Arab travellers crossing the Sahara to West Africa, old sailors, Christian priests and nineteenth-century explorers left further records of music and dance for those concerned with the search for an African heritage in these arts, a heritage taking us back before the interventions of Islam (from the seventh century onwards) and before Christianity (from the fourth century in Ethiopia), a religion which flared with renewed spirit across the continent in the nineteenth century. (See, for example, Abdullah Abu-Ubayd al Bekri,

The 1995 Ra-Jean Marie's Company production of the *hira gasy* (*Malagasy Song*), Madagascar.

Al-Masalik wa l'Manalik, cited by Davidson 1964: 71; Ibn Battuta, Muhammad ibn Abdullah, quoted by Gibbs 1929: 324–5; Father Dos Santos [1586], quoted by Theal 1901; H.M. Stanley 1974).

The vicissitudes of these artistic forms – and indeed almost all the arts of Africa – may be inferred by trying to view their development from today's existing hybrids: the *highlife* (Ghana), *marabi* (South Africa), *soukous* (Zaïre and Congo), *taarab* (East African pop music) and so on until one finds the original cultural confluences which the earliest musicians and dancers confronted, mixing new ideas with proven local ones and creating innovative artistic responses. Combining this with scholarly analyses of heritage African music and dance that are least susceptible to change – performing arts from old shrines and highly revered rituals of life-cycle junctions, including burial and other traumatic commemorative events – may prove much that is important about both Africa and art.

Even with the promise of scientific scrutiny, the most rigorous examinations could assure only high probability, not assurances in these areas. As well, some artistic heritages across this vast continent will not have withstood the bombardments from external cultures as well as others. Yet the music and dance being recorded and videotaped may well be eloquent evidence for the authenticity of Africa's performing arts history.

Here is but one example – a time count for a *kadodi* (also called a *mwaga* or an *ingoma*) dance by Masaba youths done before their circumcision rites which will see them accepted into the community as adults. The master drummer's part spells out the extraordinarily complicated count patterns and is the most recurrent phrase: six clearly audible beats in the first bar of the phrase that are maintained throughout; a second bar with stress patterns highlighting alternate impulses producing three audible counts; two succeeding bars with stress patterns spaced out in counts of two; and two final bars which repeat this phrase pattern. The whole phrase thus depicts a count pattern of six, three, two plus two. Or, if the listening ear prefers, a pattern of six followed by patterns of three and four.

Music comes to everyone as combinations of such elements. In African music, the twin elements of time and time division often stand out as the most dominant. In this illustration, some discerning ear may indeed be able to clearly identify the phrase along the line of this analysis and see it as one whole time unit with components that produce three distinct rhythms. Frequently in African music, two or more lines of distinct time run concurrently and yield between them an additional time line, producing in the ear three or more sequences out of two, four out of three and so forth.

Such time sequences may not be clear to every listener but if dancers are involved they will be further delineated in movement patterns. Partly such recognition is the work of ethno-musicology, which has broken through the obscurities of African music to identify such phenomena, to alert listeners to be aware of such dynamics as time multiplication as they experience African music. These may be noted between singing on the one hand, and accompanying claps on the other, or between a chorus and a decorative vocal part sung above it. To truly understand such patterns, one must examine far more closely royal drum orchestra music, something we are unable to do in this limited space. Suffice it to say that such royal music has nurtured and preserved treasures of rhythmic creativity and management. The royal *bakisimba* orchestra of Buganda; *dundun* orchestras of Yoruba royal houses of Nigeria; *fontomfrom* orchestras of Akan royal houses in Ghana; and *ntore* orchestras of Rwanda furnish good examples.

At the centre of music and dance are, of course, the drum and drum orchestras. But there are other instruments as well. In a short survey one can hardly speak of the variety of sizes, tone qualities, and pitch and dynamic ranges of all the musical instruments but a brief viewing of the great stock and spread of this heritage may bring wider perspectives to this view of the variety in musical sound in Africa. A division of these musical instruments into four main classes is a widely accepted method of approach since all the major world cultures account for their examples within these classes.

In class one are many self-sounding musical instruments (usually called *idiophones*) incorporating rattles and bells of many kinds. Of widespread interest in this class are scooped out wooden cases great and small, fondly referred to as slit drums. They are also idiophones by reason of producing sound from the vibration of their entire body surfaces. They are struck with fists or heavy sticks to communicate their presence to great distances. They are used as signals, message bearers or as articulate deep-voiced participants in important ensembles and orchestras. Also noteworthy in this class are the great variety of hand pianos ranging in size from the palm of the hand (with high-pitch notes) to giant versions (exploited for their booming sounds). Of the hundreds of names for this instrument, the *mbira* of the Shona of Zimbabwe should be specially noted because of the wide variety of this instrument and the centrality of its place in traditional social institutions there.

Perhaps the most interesting thing to remember about the *mbira* is its wide African provenance. The earliest known reference to it comes from the writings of Dos Santos, a Roman Catholic priest, who wrote in 1586 of southern (central) African models (see Theal 1901). Even then, he spoke of these as old, traditional, popular instruments.

Vying for pride of place with the hand-piano in the idiophone class is the xylophone, an instrument also bearing many names on the African continent. A few of these have loomed prominently in literature. Seeking refuge from the temptation of giving too much space to this instrument, only four are listed here: *timbila* of Mozambique, *entaala* of Buganda (Uganda), *silimba* of the Lozi of Zambia, and *gyil* of the Dagaba (Ghana).

Hugh Tracey (see e.g. 1969), a well-known champion of the idea of preserving traditional African music, an extensive collector and publisher of recordings and an extensive writer on the subject of African music, described the sound produced by this instrument as 'wood music', thus highlighting the primary source of the sound but not ruling out the wide variety of sound quality coming from the African xylophone, which ranges from resonant and booming in the Ghanaian and Mozambican examples to the rich and brilliant far-carrying qualities of *mbaire* varieties from the Kisoga (Uganda).

In the second class of musical instruments – the *membranophones* – are drums in a wide range of sizes and producing sounds of unexpected variety. These include the rarely heard boom of the *maoma*, the largest drum found in the full royal ensemble of the King of the Barotse of Zambia to the wailing double bass qualities of the friction drum, the *namalwa* of the Ila people of Zambia.

In the third class we have the strings – *chordophones*, which are either plucked or bowed. The *gonje*, the Dagbamba form of the West African violin, is the backbone of one of the big royal ensembles of the Ya Na's palace. Playing largely in unison, its sound fills the atmosphere at festivals and on special occasions to delight important visitors. But the main characteristic of this instrument is its virtuosity in praise music. Musicians of East Africa may well outdo those of West Africa in their excellence and variety in stringed instruments. Often cited in literature are the *entongoli* (plucked lyre) found among the Busoga and Buganda, the bowed one-string *indingidi* of the Bakiga and the plucked *opuk* of the Acholi of Uganda. But one may cite a veritable area of bowed one-string violins from the northern and the upper eastern regions of Ghana, northern Nigeria, Burkina Faso, Niger, Mali and even further north, where these West African regions share the velvety sonorities and ecstasies of bowed string virtuosity.

Variety of sonority and virtuosity also characterize African instruments in the fourth class – *aerophones* or wind instruments. Most typical are flutes, trumpets, horns and clarinets. The occasional oboe (in the form of the *alghaita* of northern Africa) is also noteworthy.

The varieties of pitch levels, and weights of sound, shimmer (even rasps of sound) and metal sounds are astounding. Many of these can be heard in ensembles which produce varying traditions of pitch combination and orchestral blends. Beyond the rich music is its connection with local lore and ritual. Players rarely talk of such things to strangers.

The arts co-mingle in Africa and nowhere is this clearer than during festivals where all the disciplines – including costume – come together in full regalia. At the annual Arts Festival in Zambia, for example, the item to receive the highest ovation without fail every year is the appearance of the *chimbuza*, a type of spirit medium from the Tumbuka areas of the Eastern Province. He is truly resplendent in his crossed-shoulder bands, broad sleeves and head gear surmounted by stiff upraised tassels set in immaculate beadwork with close-knit borders featuring chevrons in patterns of blue, white, red, pink, light brown and many shades between. Also striking are his shoulder pad rosettes in red, white and blue flowing down the upper arm. From the pelvis to the upper leg is a skirt tightly girded at the waist. On the calves of both legs are rafted pod rattles. All this is highlighted by smooth bare skin and the presence of a dancer whose craft never clouds his resplendent dignity.

Most of the movement of the *chimbuza* is in the flexing and flipping of his arms. In his right hand is a horse-tail switch which helps articulate the arcs and angles described by the arm movements. In timely counterpoint to all this are bends of the neck and occasional twitching of the head, all in flowing coordination. This is a dance of stately grace imbued with energy generated from the legs and the feet. The actual force would elude the onlooker if the pod rattles worn on both calves were silenced. Their

Renowned solo *chimbuza* dancer Mkandawiri with a *vimbuza* orchestra and chorus.
Photo: Zambia Information Services.

dry insistent sounds, however, activated by the rapid stamping in clear rhythmic patterns, penetrate the welter of orchestral sound from the accompanying drums and singing voices. In traditional contexts, the *chimbuza* is a conduit between himself and the spirit world, mediating and receiving communications, sometimes emerging to join in the singing and adding to it with well-timed exhortative shouts while being propelled in barely visible steps controlled only by his toes.

Visual art and music are blended here with dance, and one is able to interpret hand movements and facial expressions, another semantic element added as a fourth dimension of this artistic feast.

One can also look at performances of the Barotse of the Western Province of Zambia, specifically the *kayowe* dance. This again is vigorously accompanied by drums and a chorus. In a highly mimetic dance routine, two dancers – male and female – depict a hilarious courting scene resplendently costumed in the visage of cock and hen. After a few tell-tale antics, the cock gathers courage to make his intentions clear to the hen who initially indicates shyness but quickly withdraws her resistance. Familiar human experience is clear. What draws real laughter and pleasure are the skills of the dancers in this well-paced (slow to fast) winged *pas de deux* veering toward the peripheries of reality.

Clearly dance is an old human art in Africa. Henry M. Stanley furnishes still another vivid picture. The place is described as 'Usiri' in northeastern Zaïre. As he tells it, the dancers are arranged in thirty-three rows with thirty-three men in each forming a perfect square. With spears in each hand, the dancers cause reflections of polished metal to flash before one's eyes while they loudly sing and slowly move in unison with stamping feet that shake the earth a hundred metres away. The dancing phalanx moves in steps of not more than 15 centimetres (6 inches) long. Stanley does not tell us the shape of the moving steps nor the significance of the figure of 1,089 dancers. But other surviving examples across the continent depict similar movement and dynamics within combat which the dance apparently re-enacts. Hugh Tracey has described and illustrated other martial performances from southern Africa such as the *ngoma* performed by the Ngoni in the Cewa and Tumbuka areas of Malawi and Mozambique. Special features here include the knobkerrie banged occasionally on the shield and the luxuriant sisal which decorates the lower legs, which are occasionally flung up above shoulder level and then swung back to the ground with a heavy stamp.

Comparable to these are the large dance suites of east and central Africa performed under various names in homage to kings and notable visitors. The Banyarwanda of Rwanda, Burundi and Uganda call their dance *ntore* (the dancers too are known as *ntore*). With minor variations, this dance may also be seen among the Bakiga and Banyankore of Uganda. The accompanying drums are usually six or seven in number. Drummers and dancers are drawn from the ranks of the aristocracy where they go through a system of rigorous training from boyhood.

The usual beginning is in slow single beats which progressively double up, and through decorative acoustic accents by the drum. Single strokes in whole note values will start the dancer on those beats, with time to gently rock the body forward and backward. Eventually the beats change into half-notes, then quarter notes and soon progress into eighth notes, by which time faster drums introduce more decorative accents to form the characteristic rhythms. The accompanying singing intensifies, changes to a higher key (often a major third higher), leaps increase in height and stamping

grows heavier. At this thunderous point of animation the drumming abates and another round of dance ensues.

In a different pattern but also in large extended forms are the *bwola* dances of the Acholi of northern Uganda. Here we have a nuclear set of three drums which lead from the centre a large moving circle formed by hundreds of dancers, each carrying his own personal drum with which he plays responses to the nuclear ensemble while a thunder of voices provides a strong, powerful vocal chorus. At signals from the centre, the dancers change direction.

Another sparkling array of dancers may be found among the Lobis of West Africa, whose people spread across the borders now shared by Burkina Faso, Côte d'Ivoire and northwest Ghana. During the dry season rituals were required to bring forth rain. In costumes studded with cowrie shells and surmounted by feathers over arc-shaped caps with glass spikes to reflect sunlight (and thus symbolize the sun and its power and energy) the worshippers dance praises to the spirits of the grasslands and woodlands which preserve all growing things. Resplendence is the keynote here and it is enlivened with flutes, finger bells, forged iron bells and drums.

By far the most frequent are dances by individuals and small groups. The numerous *chimbuza* votaries of Tumbuka in southern Africa have already been referred to. Significant also are the many court dancers in many parts of Africa. Perhaps the most travelled are the *bakisimba* dancers of Buganda in Uganda. In small groups of men and women, winsome patterns of shuffle steps, stylized hops and leaps carry the body in various linear formations varying the speeds of travel and dynamics of limb movements. Originally formed hundreds of years ago to entertain and edify the kings of Buganda, the charm and grace of this dance popularized it among the ordinary folk and *bakisimba* bands sprang up all over Buganda; but outside royal contexts the dance developed faster versions known as *nankasa* which often portrayed and commemorated scenes from Kiganda life. The most popular of these enactments was the wedding dance called the *embaga*.

As for the technical repertoire, most of the examples thus far given depict the most obvious technical element – namely, space management. But large dance groups also draw attention to the element of flow, often

A dance of the Samo 'rain-people' in Burkina Faso.

simultaneously relating the centre of the defined space to its outer rims. In the spiral line movement of the Acholi *bwola* dance, and dances of similar character, this feature of varying focus is set in strong relief. Smaller dances, in contrast, such as the Lozi romance of the cock and the hen, capture the spectator's imagination and lead it into this enactment which is virtually in one spot. Here the mind of the spectator quickly adjusts its scale of perception to the different magnitude and the slightest twitch of the cock's 'shoulders' is amply accommodated within the scale.

All these dancers sensitize the audience to spatial elements and body surface arts that might otherwise go unnoticed. But above all, the dance is an exhibition of the human body in motion. Even when the art of movement is drawing attention to the skillful manipulation of the body as a whole, the individual body parts are manipulated to throw focus, portray weight or lightness, to speed or set up counterpoints depicting various elements in concurrent motion. The *adowa*, one of the most popular dances of the Ashanti of Ghana, for instance, is danced before kings, at grand funeral celebrations, at big national events and enjoyed by audiences for its great variety of movement – a

graceful wave travelling laterally from the neck through the pelvis, the rhythmic exhibition of contrasting levels through heel raising and gentle leaps with the feet barely leaving the ground, almost wafting the body along, hands circling with palm and the back of the hand taking turns depicting a suppleness that can only confess purity and goodwill. All this is quietly confirmed in the smaller circles described by the forefingers in concurrent gentle motion counter-clockwise. In this dance, the body works itself into a perfect flexibility and the dancer's pride is clear in his or her neatly coiffed hair (*densinkran*), smartly made costume (usually based on models of traditional Ashanti dress), and ankle beads of precious stones. *Adowa* is danced by both males and females, with the latter predominating. Each individual in the ensemble has an opportunity to star.

Since the 1980s, African dance has been exhibited around the world by faithful stewards who have successfully enlarged rural genres and trimmed mammoth-size festival dance traditions to fit the varying sizes of world stages while attempting to maintain the integrity of the original African experience, making it intelligible to international audiences.

Even away from traditional culture, dance and music have still been dominant forms. In South Africa, *King Kong* was a musical staged in 1959 filled with urban songs and jazz-oriented orchestration. King Kong, the boxer and hero of the story, is a twentieth-century urban hero in Harry Bloom's terse script and Pat Williams's spare lyrics backed by Todd Matsikiza's musical conception. In many senses, this jazz opera stands at the centre of an active cultural confluence. Interestingly, it was the westernization of some of the music which was challenged amid the enthusiastic press that welcomed the work both at home and abroad. Some resented the heavy orchestration and thematic development.

Gibson Kente's *Sikalo*, another musical, played to capacity houses during the mid-1960s and used more traditional African song idioms as well as township songs and traditional thematic elements in his story.

Oba-Koso by Nigeria's Duro Ladipo was well received at the Commonwealth Arts Festival in Britain in 1965, after an extended run in Lagos. This is a folk opera based on the legend-filled biography of Shango, a king of Oyo during the thirteenth or fourteenth century. The music here was based on Yoruba traditional idioms.

Djoliba, another important work using dance and music, is a ballet based on a Guinean legend. The awe-inspiring atmosphere of the forest is created in dance as are the gruelling battles between the devil serpent's monsters and the hero. The triumphal rescue of a virgin is vividly depicted in splendid dances and brilliant music by a range of instruments and voices. There is also a constant reference to contemporary Guinean life and its new social and political values.

One could mention also *Sombo Malimba*, a dance-drama choreographed for the Zambia Dance Troupe and presented at Expo '70 in Osaka, after a short run in Zambia. It subsequently received ovations during a tour of the United States. Its dance items were all taken from traditional sources – the tale of the unsmiling daughter of a king – as was the music.

In Ugandan Robert Serumaga's *Renga Moi* (1972) actors came to life through song, dance and action, working out conflicts and resolutions with hardly any speech. The dynamic use once again of traditional music, dance and semantic movement lifted this work far above ordinary pantomime and pageantry. The sources of *Renga Moi*'s artistic vocabulary can be found right across the spectrum of Ugandan life.

Even more modest forms like riddles, proverbs, narrative arts and praise poetry are frequently integrated with music and dance in works by African authors, composers and choreographers. Given more space one could speak as well of many other old and new groups which show that these trends have continued. Among them, Pangols – Spirit of West Africa (Sénégal), Abibigromma (Ghana), the Ghana Dance Ensemble, the Black Pearls (Uganda), the Ballet Guinea (directed by Fodéba Keita), the N'dere Dance Troupe (Uganda), and the Pan-African Orchestra and its traditional African instruments (Ghana).

Within Africa's universities too the recognition of the importance of music and dance is clear. One must note this trend from 1962 at such institutions as the University of Nigeria at Nsukka, the University of Ghana at Legon (Accra), the University of Ife, Ile-Ife (now renamed Obafemi Awolowo University), Makerere University in Kampala, Cape Coast University in Ghana, the University of Ilorin in Nigeria, and the University of Port Harcourt in Nigeria among others.

Legon, Makerere and Ilorin each began their performing arts departments with joint studies in music, dance and drama. Makerere and Ilorin, in fact, required every student in her/his first or second year to study all three disciplines with specialization only in their final year(s). At Legon, dance was a key part of the music and drama programmes as well. It can be said that in most cases, African universities have mandated their students to take courses across all three disciplines.

I myself made a proposal to the University of Cape Coast in 1975 urging the continuation of such joint studies there. The proposal said, in part,

> Artistic life in Africa over the past fifty years stresses the need for reuniting the kinaesthetic and dramatic arts with music in the service of society. Evidence from the long established arts of Africa and later developments (e.g. new choral as well as traditional court music, instrumental ensembles and new African theatre forms) confirms the viability of music and the other performing arts as self-sufficient arts worthy of preservation and continued separate development as music, drama or dance. Nevertheless, performances which have communicated best with wider audiences in Africa have been those that have combined the three genres of music, drama and dance, and looked in the direction of new forms of integrated arts.

The universities have not limited their work in the performing arts to African music. Many over-emphasize western music which bears its own reflections of African music. From the 1850s onwards, the educated African had been won over to western music – thanks to the missionary schools. Church hymns were translated into African languages and sung to hymnbook tunes. A lot of these tunes became popular. After the organ was introduced, some schools and teacher training colleges acquired portable ones and taught gifted students. Before long, being an organist and playing western music on it became a position of pride. The few who had such access to the organ responded far beyond expectations.

By the mid-1930s, private music schools had sprung up from Bathurst (now Banjul) to Mombasa and from Cape Town to Cairo, successfully preparing students for Grade and Diploma examinations in music theory and instrumental playing (set and graded, of course, by overseas colleges and academies of music). Many organists even appeared on church occasions in academic gowns.

At the same time, other gifted young people

taught themselves the foreign pop music of their times, especially the music from England and the United States. By the mid-1940s ragtime, boogie-woogie and swing were at home in many African countries, being played by well-known bands. Among them were Ghana's Damas (Male) Choir, E.T. Mensah and His Tempos Band, King Bruce and His Ramblers Dance Band, Pan African Orchestra, Rag-a-jazz-bo and the Sugar Babies. Other well-known groups included the Mayfair Orchestra (Nigeria), Nyonza Singers (Uganda), and two South African groups, Jazz Maniacs and Rhythm Kings.

Between these bands and the many composers and teachers connected with them came hybrid forms of music – African pop – which people were not only singing and dancing to but also singing or listening to in churches and schools. Soon came the new anthems, new patriotic songs of nationalism, new sonatas and even symphonies of African mould. Dance did not follow western patterns but struck new ones, exploring new methods of extension and exploitation of space along with unprecedented conceptions of tempo and gymnastics.

All of these elements are products of and contribute to the dynamism and creative energy that is the theatre in Africa as we approach the year 2000.

Atta Annan Mensah
York University
Toronto

Further Reading

Davidson, Basil. *The African Past*. London: Longman, 1964.

Gibbs, H.A.R. *Ibn Battuta: Travels in Asia and Africa*. London, 1929.

Gillon, Werner. 'The Rock Arts of Africa'. In *A Short History of African Art*, 36–54. Harmondsworth: Penguin, 1984.

Kenyatta, Jomo. *Facing Mount Kenya: The Tribal Life of the Gikuyu*. London: Secker & Warburg, 1961 (first published 1938).

Neher, William, and John Condon. 'The Mass Media and Nation-Building in Kenya and Tanzania'. In *The Search for National Integration in Africa*, eds. David R. Smock and Kwama Bentsi-Enchill, 223–4. New York: The Free Press, 1975.

Stanley, H.M. *Coomassie and Magdala*. London: Samson, Low, Marston, 1974.

Theal, G.M. *Records of Southeastern Africa*, vol. 7. Cape Town, 1901.

Tracey, Hugh. *Codification of African Music and Textbook Project*. Roodeport, South Africa: International Library of African Music, 1969. 54 pp.

AFRICAN PUPPETS AND MASKS

LINKS IN A HISTORICAL CHAIN

African puppetry has long been connected to various artefacts used in ritual such as statuettes, dolls and masks and is significantly different from the European concept of the puppet as a mainly miniaturized inanimate figure displayed or manipulated as part of a narrative or dramatic performance.

Though Black African culture has not generally been influenced by the European form of this art, one can assume that the examples brought by European merchants and colonizers in the seventeenth, eighteenth and nineteenth centuries accelerated in some areas a slow transformation of ritual-related indigenous mask art into an art in which the foreign style of puppet entertainment could also flourish.

Without doubt, it was a foreign style, to begin, the animation of African and European figures differs significantly. Not only might ritualistic objects in African culture be articulated and/or made to move but also statuettes on pedestals could have articulated limbs and be manipulated. One might even see in this a link in a historical chain leading toward the global secularization of the puppet, a link found only in Africa.

The fact that both African masks and articulated statues have similar construction features and functions makes classification even more difficult. African masks, for example, often have movable parts but this in itself does not make them puppet masks. Full body masks also exist which remind one of lifesize or enlarged puppets closely connected to their manipulators. Various helmet-type masks also linked both mask and puppet elements. Usually embellished by small, finely elaborated, sometimes surrealistic figures at the top, such masks usually held symbolic meaning. But were they puppets? Is it appropriate even to call them puppets? Their size certainly does not help in answering the question. Some were only a few inches high while others were almost lifesize.

Though the origin of African masks and puppets is not known for certain, it seems clear that most were rooted in death cults, the assumption being that they were themselves created by magicians, sorcerers, or, in some cases, witches. Some are spoken of in myth as is the case of the Ibibios legend of Akpan Etuk Uyo who, like the Greek, Orpheus, went to the Kingdom of the Dead where he saw a puppet play and, like Prometheus, brought this secret information back to the people on earth. Again like Prometheus, he pays for his transgression, in this case with his life. From such stories one can see that partly due to their inanimate nature, puppets were generally seen as intermediary objects, somewhere between human beings and gods. In certain rituals, returning initiates were considered still to be in an intermediate state and therefore they painted their bodies with skeletons and, significantly, moved as puppets.

In general, African puppets and masks are made of wood, bamboo, straw and/or cloth, often ornamented with bright paint, bits of string, tin and even hair. Manipulation is done in several ways ranging from a form which in Europe is called the *marionnette à planchette* (toe-puppet) to the rod-puppet and string-puppet to the simple marotte (moving head). Many have complicated and specialized construction such as the instrument-puppets used in Bembe musical events. Other figures grew from the mask tradition: headdress-puppets, shoulder-puppets, face-puppets, and body- and shield-puppets. Normally manipulators were not revealed although their covers rarely hid them completely. In most cases manipulators manifested their presence only to show some magical function of the puppet.

It should be noted here as well that the African use of puppets and masks in rituals was quite similar to the magical and religious use of puppets on other continents. Wherever they appeared, they were meant to bring supernatural powers to a ceremony and to the village as representations of departed ancestors, demons and gods (sometimes in the shape of mythical animals). Some have suggested that the masks and puppet figures were the incarnation of the supernatural beings themselves while others argue that the participants were always conscious of the fact that the artefacts were simply representations and were always aware of the double function of the presentation (the carrier of the object and the object itself; that is, the god in the form of the mask and the puppet). The belief in the magical power and the use of the figure as mediative object allowed both serious as well as comic actions. In other words, people allowed themselves 'to play' with their gods.

Those who actually wore the masks could cover their faces or bodies or they could just hold them in their hands in front of them. They could also attach them to an elbow or a knee. Meaning itself depended on the theme of the ritual and very often had its own semantic code. Involving dancers either in or out of masks, singers, musicians, drummers and puppeteers, such performances were part of a repertory in which dancing masks and performing puppets were often similarly used.

All sacred objects had to be created by those initiated into the mysteries of that art, often a special association which was able to recognize and respond to ritualistic taboos and ritualistic principles concerning the choice of raw materials and proper times for their collection. It was most often the village blacksmith – himself often a sorcerer – who executed these tasks.

Rich in artistry and style and changing from region to region, these mask and puppet manufacturers showed invention and a genuine sense of fantasy as they explored even grotesque and horrifying images. Creating representations of humans, animals and other recognizable objects, the artists tended to show only certain characteristics, meaning that only rarely was the representation mimetic. Rather, reality was distorted, reduced to essential features (in some cases this was the quasi-geometrical vision now so clearly recognized as an inspiration for the cubists). A puppet creator might make and manipulate only that element which was essential to the ritualistic performance such as a hand or a phallus. On occasion the effect was absolutely surrealistic such as when a disembodied hand was raised toward a disembodied head.

Puppets also served fertility rituals as imitators of sexual intercourse and took part in initiations. Their presence, in fact, was essential in various acts of divination and even as part of funeral rituals (the most famous of these was the Niombo of the Bwende peoples in Zaïre, a funeral ritual that points to possible links with ancient Egypt).

When European travellers to Africa introduced puppets for pure entertainment in the nineteenth century, audiences understandably had trouble making sense of them. Nevertheless, such performances continued almost unchanged through the 1950s. Throughout this period, however, African puppet traditions slowly changed from pure ritual to what can be seen as theatrical entertainment. This was accompanied by the loss of certain traditional puppet figures, especially those used to represent sexual acts. Though many puppets were slowly secularized, performances still took place only on occasions such as feast days, initiations, circumcisions, marriages, harvest celebrations or visits by important guests.

Normally done outdoors on improvised stages, the performances – like the actual shapes of the stages – varied widely. For smaller puppets, the stage would consist of pieces of cloth (sometimes simply skirts sewn together) hung between two poles or trees; more professional groups might use a square canvas with a hole in the centre for the puppets to appear through. Sometimes a triangular canvas would be placed above hollow spaces such as a canoe. Even coverings on a performer's body could be used as a puppet stage.

Secular shows might consist of a series of short sketches depicting village life or local animal life. The puppets themselves rarely spoke, with narrators widely used. Only in exceptional cases did puppets actually deliver lines and when they did voices were usually distorted by use of a special flute. Both puppets and live performers would normally address their words directly to the audiences and the audience was expected to respond.

Though shows might be elaborate, in general they were not and short sketches from familial life would dominate. Quite popular were stories of unfaithful wives which usually ended with the wife being returned to her mother (if her lover could not compensate her husband). In cases where the husband was murdered by the lover, the husband's ghost would haunt them from the other world. Still other pieces dealt with criminals ending with the criminal's hand being cut off. In this way African puppet theatre maintained a didactic tradition and confirmed local mores and values.

Satirical pieces featured many local characters and types such as the dishonest merchant, the colonial administrator, the European missionary and the court official, all aiming at the correction of corruption, thievery, stupidity, imitation of Europeans, violation of taboos and even health issues.

Many such performances show ongoing links with ritual puppetry and are still done by 'non-professional' puppeteers. As for European models, in francophone Africa it was Guignol; in anglophone Africa a variety of European styles were seen and several permanent groups emerged, especially in modern Zimbabwe and South Africa.

South African puppetry, in particular, was recognized by state authorities as an important instrument in the realization of colonial social goals. South Africa's National Popular Theatre Programme, for example, aimed at promoting self-reliance among the largely non-literate rural population of Botswana in the late 1970s.

However, the traditional sacred role of the puppet remained for many Africans and no unconsecrated person could play with a puppet without punishment. Indeed, those wishing to work with puppets in the more European style were often required to undergo ritual exorcism before being allowed to begin training. Though such taboos are now all but gone occasional examples still emerge.

Many groups now use puppets as a part of theatre for social action, as part of children's education, as part of youth rehabilitation, or even as part of social campaigns. Official support for such work has helped to create national puppet theatres in Togo, Mali, Zaïre, Burundi and Côte d'Ivoire. Most of these companies work from specific national traditions but some have a clear European style (for example, Themaz Puppet Theatre of Zaïre).

During the 1980s and 1990s, a number of joint African-European companies emerged in such countries as Côte d'Ivoire and South Africa. The former achieved success with a show about the legendary hero Sunjata in *Sunjata, L'Epopée Mandigue* (*Sunjata, The Mandingo Epic*) and the latter in several multi-national and multiracial companies which were engaged in the struggle against apartheid.

Henryk Jurkowski
Warsaw

AFRICAN THEATRE AND THE QUESTION OF HISTORY

The discussion of the history of African theatre has always presented a number of invisible pitfalls. Because of the strong discernible links between contemporary African theatre and the indigenous resources of dance, storytelling, masquerade and mime, there is a tendency to postulate a seamless relationship between theatre practice and such indigenous resources and to pursue their histories as essentially the same and moving in the same direction. There are of course many advantages in tracing the state of theatre and of indigenous forms as having the same inextricable roots and being affected by the same historical processes, but there is a sense in which this standpoint prevents theatre in Africa from being seen as a specifically constituted transformative domain continually responding to a variety of both internal and external influences in order to produce a theatrically mediated understanding of reality.

The analysis of the history of African theatre practice is constrained by a certain 'tyranny of teleology'. As a paradigm of pre-colonial, colonial and post-colonial politico-historical realities is deployed, not only is the loss of the vitality of indigenous culture lamented, but also the role of contemporary theatre is read in terms of the re-production of the lost indigenous ethos. This has been termed 'golden ageism' by David Kerr in his *African Popular Theatre* (1995). He sees this tendency as paralleling economic development theory generally, in which all social and cultural forms are analysed within a teleological framework that has modernization and westernization as the

key motors of change. He himself sidesteps this form of analysis by tracing the various ways in which African pre-colonial indigenous genres, as they fed modern theatre forms, were often subtle mediations of indigenous economic and social systems and of class formation and historical change.

The central problems in analysing the history of African theatre seem to involve, first, how to describe change without necessarily being teleological, and second, how to define the ambit of theatre practice so as to discern its lineaments as a form simultaneously working on history as well as being worked by it. The key thing is to perceive theatre in Africa as a form of process in dialectical relationship to a wide variety of forces both material as well as politico-historical. Thus it is not enough merely to trace the ways in which indigenous resources are transferred into African theatre practice; this needs to be matched with a precise analysis of African theatre's specific differences from indigenous resources and the historical significance of these differences.

Cultural contact with the west through colonialism unleashed a variety of contradictory effects on African culture. Among the more positive effects was that with the inception of colonialism, indigenous cultures subtly redefined their conceptual ambits so as to take account of the new cultural threat. There were various forms of such redefinitions. Among the Yoruba of Nigeria, for instance, one way in which the new cultural threat was negotiated was by figuring the Christian God as synonymous with the Yoruba high god, Olodumare. This allowed the *babalawo*, the priests of the Ifa divination cult, to proceed with their interpretations of personal problems brought to them for resolution by both Christians and non-Christians alike in the light of the subtly redefined ambit of *orisha* worship (see Barber 1990; Yai 1993). Thus, indigenous traditions participated in the history of their own formation and selectively syncreticized with dimensions of the invading culture in order to define a new mode of worldliness. The process of redefinition, however, never really stopped with the end of colonialism.

Something of the complexity of the processes of transformation can be seen in the area of popular theatre, especially in the West African Concert Party and Yoruba Travelling Theatre traditions. Travelling Theatre and Concert Parties are famous for their fluidity and their dependence on memory and improvisation for sustaining the spirit of their productions. As this theatre related to a burgeoning urban sphere composed of an 'intermediate' class – neither agrarian nor elite but mainly comprising partially literate motor mechanics, drivers, tailors, petty traders, bricklayers and primary school teachers – the theatre itself began to be constituted as an amalgam of both oral and literary influences. Karin Barber describes this phenomenon in relation to Yoruba Travelling Theatre, but it can be taken to represent the tendency in popular theatre more generally:

> All addressed larger, more anonymous and often dispersed publics than older genres such as masquerade, festival drama, and oral poetry. Circulating between live performance, electronic media and print, themes and motifs gained wide dissemination in multiple forms. The popular theatre is a central site in these fields of mutating discourse, feeding on histories, novels, newspapers, street talk, oral anecdotes, sermons and tales for its sources, and supplying magazines, television, records, radio, films and video materials to recirculate.
>
> (Barber 1995: 8)

Clearly, the relationship that these popular theatres have with indigenous resources cannot be discussed in isolation from the ways in which they relate to other media, or from their mode of aspiration or the modern-day context of production of their meanings.

The transfer of indigenous genres into the space of popular theatre obeys another process that can be termed the process of the commodification of indigenous culture (or, of culture more generally). The process of commodification is tied inextricably to that of nation-state formation as well as to commercial impulses. At independence it was important for African countries to project a sense of unity that would cut across narrower tribal affiliations. It was crucial to dissociate certain indigenous symbols and genres from their specific local contexts and to project them as things that members of an emergent nation could seize upon both for self-apprehension and for the definition of a place in the world. And so in Ghana, for instance, the practice of speaking through an *okyeame* (a staff-bearing linguist or interpreter of the king's word), which is an important feature of Akan courts, was transferred to a higher national arena. To this day, Ghana has a State Linguist who is always present at important state functions such as the swearing-in of the head of state or the opening of Parliament. The State Linguist is paid by the state and is entitled to a state pension.

The complex links between the commercial and nationalistic impulses behind commodification of the indigenous sphere can be seen in the creation of what could be termed 'recreational identities'. Recreational identities may be defined as those identities created around sporting events and other forms of entertainment that depend heavily on spectators or the public. It is interesting to note in this respect how the current anthem for the South African rugby team was derived from *Shosholoza*, a song initially sung by migrant Zimbabwean workers in a traditional imitation of the sound made by a moving train. For a long time it was a song associated with anti-apartheid sentiments. The song was given a multiracial and national dimension during the 1995 Rugby World Cup held in South Africa, when an excited mix of Blacks, whites and Coloured South Africans sang *Shosholoza* for all they were worth in support of their national team. The *Shosholoza* tune does not strictly qualify as an indigenous genre, yet its journey into the form of a nationally rehearsed sports song offers a useful insight into the potentially commodified trajectories of any indigenous song or genre. The point, then, is that the transfer of indigenous elements into contemporary African theatre needs to be analysed within a framework that pays attention to the complex processes of commodification both positive and negative.

Perhaps the area of least research and theorization is on the theatre's encapsulation of a variety of sources and the implication this has for discussing the theatre's effects. The issue itself needs to be formulated historically, for the impact of theatre in Africa must not be read homogeneously across time. As a general rule, and partly as a way of differentiating the nature of African theatre from western forms, the sense of a smooth and participant relationship has frequently been suggested as appropriate for discussing theatre–actor–audience relations. But what precisely is the nature of the audience's relationship to African theatre, considering that it is frequently mediating a variety of forces from both indigenous and modern culture as well as from orality and literacy? A useful way of discussing this would be to consider African theatre as a form of 'intermedium'. The term itself, with a theoretical history in the writings of Dick Higgins (1984) and others, may be defined in terms of the ways in which certain forms of theatre bring together disparate genres and materials without necessarily subjecting them to a hierarchical system of signification, thus forcing the audience to participate in a process of deriving meaning from the performance. There is a playing through and across a variety of cultural texts and resources which ensures that the relationship between audience and the theatre is an active and negotiated one. (See Nick Kaye (1996) for a particularly nuanced discussion of the history of the term and some of its contemporary applications in western theatre.)

Many African plays seem to propose organic forms of closure which in turn suggest a commonly shared horizon of expectations with audiences. This seems to be especially the case in popular theatre where there is often a discernible movement towards a moral conclusion. But considering what has already been noted about the various genres that come into play, it is evident that even popular theatre imposes a form of negotiation for the audience if only because there is a problem of recognition inherent in the bringing together of a variety of disparate materials. The lineaments of African theatre as an intermedium become even better clarified in the work of playwrights who seek a variety of alienating effects as a way of achieving a form of contemporary political and social critique.

Notorious examples of how plays refuse easy closure are provided in the work of Wole Soyinka. It must be said in passing that there is a tremendous amount of work yet to be done

on Soyinka's contribution to African and world theatre. Both *A Dance of the Forests* and *The Road* have been noted as 'difficult' plays that do not seem to make meaning in and of themselves. These two plays actually fully illustrate the notion of theatre as an intermedium. The form of these plays rehearses the mode of their unresolved contradictions not only in conceptual terms, but also in terms of the variety of cultural materials brought into play. Even though Soyinka's is obviously a special case, it provides us with the sense in which African theatre creates an intermediary space by which audiences are drawn into an active process of meaning and making. This occurs even in instances where the plays seem to be merely celebrating indigenous culture. Thus the plays of Ghanaian Mohammed Ben-Abdallah have a deliberate alienating effect with a recourse to strong bawdy language while at the same time attempting to celebrate something of the wealth of indigenous Hausa culture within the postcolonial world of corruption and disenchantment. The point is that African playwrights are producing theatre as an intermedium precisely as a conduit for meditations on historical processes.

The notion of African theatre as an intermedium could also be useful for analysing the fast-expanding television and video industry in Africa. The possibilities made available by video in particular are evident in the wide popularity of amateur video film productions which seek to integrate the indigenous ideas with technologically sophisticated ways of expressing them. And so it is now possible to see ghosts and spirits on screen along with talking animals and trees where before these had to be suggested by a variety of means with a lot depending on the audience's own imagination. Another dimension has also been opened up in popular African television soap operas which often serve as important opinion-forming programmes. The Nigerian activist Ken Saro-Wiwa, executed by his government in 1995, reached thousands of homes weekly in the mid-1980s through his *Basi and Company*, a television series that dealt with the get-rich-quick mentality of urban youth and which drew heavily on indigenous notions of justice.

It would, however, be facile to stop merely at discussing the form of African theatre without attempting to reintegrate the insights gained back into the wider context of African socio-political realities. To echo Guy Debord (1983:4), the theatre spectacle is not 'a collection of images, but a social relation among people, mediated through images'. The ways in which contemporary African theatre mediates social relations is an array of great complexity. What needs to be discussed to shed light on this is the framework of institutional support and patronage of the arts in Africa, the international networks of reviews and critical commentaries, and the very modalities by which the meanings of the various theatres are disseminated in the public domain through tours, shows, advertisements and broadcasts. All these form an ensemble of social effects of great, if mediated, power. Once again the questions need to be posed historically. When Hubert Ogunde's plays were banned by the colonial government in Nigeria, it was precisely because of the perception that they would arouse anti-colonial sentiments (see Clark 1979). The same tactics of containment were applied by the Kenyan government to Ngugi wa'Thiongo in the late 1970s when he sought to develop a peasant and popular basis for all stages of the production of *Ngahika Ndeenda (I Will Marry When I Want)*. He was arrested and detained for attempting to celebrate the fact that ordinary people were the makers of their own history.

It must be noted, however, that even as such initiatives are banned or frustrated by governments, the space voided by them is quickly occupied by forms of institutionally inspired theatres. The form of Theatre-for-Development, and more recently in Zimbabwe, the phenomenon of theatre road-shows for the advertisement of manufactured products, are clearly attempts at redefining people's attitudes to developmental policies and to industry by means of theatre. The place of contemporary theatre in Africa cannot be fully comprehended without account being taken of the subtle and not so subtle ways by which institutional forces attempt to impact on the lives of ordinary people through theatre. We need to develop a rigorous critical idiom by which to analyse all these dimensions of African theatre if we are going to make any sense of its relationship to history.

Ato Quayson
Pembroke College
University of Cambridge

Further Reading

Barber, Karin. 'Discursive Strategies in the Texts of Ifa and the "Holy Book of Odu" of the African Church of Orunmila'. In *Self-Assertion and Brokerage: Early Cultural Nationalism in West Africa*, eds. P.F. de Moraes Farias and Karin Barber. Birmingham: CWAS, 1990.

———. 'Literacy, Improvisation and the Public in Yoruba Popular Theatre'. In *The Pressures of the Text: Orality, Texts, and the Telling of Tales*, ed. Stewart Brown. Birmingham: CWAS, 1995.

Clark, Ebun. *Hubert Ogunde: The Making of Nigerian Theatre*. Oxford: Oxford University Press, 1979.

Debord, Guy. *Society of the Spectacle, 1967*. Detroit, IL: Black and Red, 1983.

Higgins, Dick. *Horizons: The Poetics and Theory of the Intermedia*. Carbondale: Southern Illinois University Press, 1984.

Kaye, Nick. 'Site/intermedia'. *Performance Research*, no. 1 spring (1996): 63–9.

Kerr, David. *African Popular Theatre: From Pre-colonial Times to the Present Day*. London: James Currey; Portsmouth, NH: Heinemann, 1995.

Yai, Olabiyi. 'In Praise of Metonymy: The Concepts of "Tradition" and "Creativity" in the Transmission of Yoruba Artistry over Time and Space'. *Research in African Literatures* 24, no. 4 (1993): 29–37.

THEATRE IN AFRICA

THE ART AND HEART OF LIVING

Before his untimely death in 1995 from AIDS, the distinguished Congolese playwright Sony Labou Tansi, artistic director of the Rocado Zulu Theatre in Brazzaville (founded in 1979), agreed to write the major National Article on Congo for the *World Encyclopedia of Contemporary Theatre*. That article, primarily a personal overview of some key elements in Congolese theatre – both traditional and modern – was prefaced by an even more personal testimony which he asked *WECT* to publish as well, a statement of 'love' written in profound anger and discontent. It is offered to readers here as one of Sony Labou Tansi's last public statements on the humanizing role of art as well as an insight into the depth of anger still felt toward the outside world by so many Black African artists.

Don Rubin

Over and over again we have heard tales of certain 'primitives' who allegedly indulge in incessant tribal warfare, killing and hunting one another without rhyme or reason, coupling like animals. They are generally conceived of as gatherers and hunters totally bereft of any creative or artistic ardour. Nor do we detect in them any of that crying hunger for what we know of as beauty in their makeup, something we assume to be innate in the human being. Much ink has been spilled and many pronouncements have been made that relegate such presumably subhuman creatures beyond the pale of the human family.

All such rhetoric has been based on the apparently obvious assumption that *they* have not produced a civilization that is quite like other parts of the world, a civilization identifiable with the outward eye or a civilization that is clearly connected to some Christian notion of the human spirit. All the creativity of these unfortunate people has been reduced to the commonplace, their art invalidated and their thinking limited to the elemental.

When their continent was 'discovered' by Europeans (as if it had to become known to Europeans to exist officially), the official Bulls of Alexander VI confirmed what Pope Nicholas V had suggested: Blacks were probably not truly human. Over the next few centuries millions of Africans were sold into slavery (at least 2 million Africans of the 'highest quality' sold to Brazil alone), 'quality' being decided by the intellectual authorities of the day and generally being defined as those who were likeliest to survive the most bestial of conditions. The moral approval of such activity by the colonial powers of the time was to be seen in the purchaser's arrogance as well as in the suffering of their charges. A whole new world was built on the sweat, blood and stench of dead black bodies.

Modernizations improved the commercial aspects of slavery and deepened the prejudices. Regarded in the beginning by many in the world as a people without a soul and without a culture, the descendants of these slaves continued to face such attitudes through most of the twentieth century. In actual fact, slavery merely travelled elsewhere and returned home under new names, names designed to spare later popes the pain of revealing the true colour of those with a Black Soul.

45

The scenario, in fact, remains unchanged in both its mathematical certitude and the depth of its thinking. Modern slavery belonged to a time when black hands simply had to be brought to more profitable lands. Colonization, on the other hand, created a magic formula whereby black slaves were forced to work on their own lands, now owned by others. In the colonial formula their lands were controlled by European royalty, people like Léopold II of Belgium (until he bequeathed his immense property – in this case the État Indépendant du Congo (Independent State of the Congo) – to the Belgian people through various real estate companies).

Eventually they realized that it did not pay to have their colonies run by corrupt European officials so the notion of Black African independence was hastily cobbled together. In less than twenty-nine months the rules changed. Once more, though, Black Africans were allowed to bear the stigma of a new dimension in the evolving theory of slavery: the replacement of corrupt Mother Country officialdom with corrupt native officialdom: the roots of both neo-colonialism and neo-slavery.

The advantages of this new state of things were clear for the new political popes: no longer did they need to discuss the terrible issue of the colour of the Black Soul. They were spared as well further debate on the fundamental reasons why God was impelled to create such peoples: 'so black, so thick-lipped, so wide-nosed, so crinkly-haired, so incapable of creativity or thought'. Above all, these people were clearly unable to erect things in stone or clay.

All this to lead up to the subject of theatre in Africa? Yes. Otherwise all that I write here would be locked into a cupboard of prejudice. My choice is to hate or to speak out. It is always better, I think, to speak out. It is possible to contradict an opinion but it is much more difficult to contradict unspoken hatred.

And hatred still exists. History is still closed against Black Africa in spite of openings carved out by a few great people like Picasso, the cubists, Lincoln, Schoelcher and a few other geniuses of hope. We children of idol worship do have much to say. We are pleased and proud that when we speak it is not hatred being voiced but rather the desire to challenge blind prejudice and the arrogance of those who have appointed themselves the high priests of history.

I wish here to simply challenge the notion – still very much alive in the world – that denies the existence of theatrical expression among the so-called primitive peoples of Black Africa. The origin of theatre in the rites of religion is well documented world-wide and it is no less so for Africa. But in Africa it is connected to *our* religions, not to those of the European colonizers who assassinated our art when they assassinated our religion (the art and heart of living for us).

Yet it is still alive in our lives and in our traditional beliefs. It can be found in my own country in such forms as the *wala* (theatre of war), *kingizilia* (theatre of healing), *lemba* (theatre of wisdom), *nkoloba* (theatre of talking wood/puppets/masks) and in the *miloko* (theatre of confrontation with the dead).

All of these fit my own definition of theatre: a coming together of human beings who have agreed on a place, a time, a story and who take roles and wear costumes in order to act out for one another tales from and of existence. All these forms create theatrical magic, that magic which, under the pretext of recounting a fable, re-creates the illusion of a moment of life. In all these forms, theatre is used to make direct statements about people connecting with people to construct a better world, a world of brotherhood, a world where the expression *bâcler son destin* (botching one's destiny) will no longer apply.

Sony Labou Tansi

THE NATIONS AND THEIR THEATRES

ALGERIA

(Arab World Volume)

ANGOLA

(Overview)

Located on the west coast of Africa between Congo and Zaïre to the north, and Namibia and Zaïre to the south and east, Angola is a relatively large country of 1.25 million square kilometres (481,400 square miles), larger in land area than France, Portugal and the United Kingdom combined. Historically composed of Bantu peoples who moved into the region in the fourteenth and fifteenth centuries from central Africa, the land was named for Ngola, the ruler of the ancient Kimbundu kingdom.

The Kimbundu still remain one of the country's largest ethnic groupings, the others being Ovimbundu and Bakongo. Though the official language is Portuguese, various Bantu dialects are widely spoken across most of the country. Angola's 1994 population was 9.8 million; the national literacy rate was 42 per cent.

The Portuguese explorer Diego Cão reached this part of Africa in 1482 while searching for a sea route from Europe to India. The Portuguese founded the capital city of Luanda in 1575 but it was not until 1918 that Portugal gained complete control of the region. Major revolts against Portuguese control from 1961 led to a long war in the northern part of the country. The military took control of Angola in 1974 and in 1975 it proclaimed independence. Civil war, however, continued to spread.

During the long period of colonization, Angola's rich traditions of music, ornamentation and oral history were put aside in favour of the cultivation of the Christian faith and the well-being of the Portuguese Empire. This led not only to enormous human suffering and economic waste but also to cultural loss as well. Traditional religious ceremonies, for example, which constituted much of the spiritual life of the native people, were deemed to be sacrilegious and were banned. The same occurred to myths, legends, hymns, chants and other cultural traditions. As ethnologist José Redinha has put it, Angola experienced 'the presence of an inhibiting transculturation phenomenon' and as a result its native cultural identity was profoundly violated. As another example, during missionary-sponsored dramatic performances, only whites were allowed to play members of Jesus' family while in other biblical scenes, the portrayal of evil characters had to be done by black or masked actors.

During the late nineteenth century, all public theatrical events had to be registered in the pages of the *Boletim Oficial do Governo Geral da provincia de Angola* (*Official Bulletin of the Governor-General of the Province of Angola*), a news organ with multiple functions. The bulletin is useful as a source of theatrical information: one learns that many of these performances were attended by official visitors to the country, a relatively large number from France.

By the early part of the twentieth century, various amateur theatre troupes were in existence in the city of Luanda. Many of the old theatres, in fact, still exist, buildings where, according to historian José de Almeida Santos, 'the local amateurs triumphed in melodramas of love and heroism as well as in picaresque farces'. Among these troupes were Teatro de Previdência, Sociedade União, Sociedade Prazer Dramática dos Jovens (a youth theatre) and several French military theatre groups.

In the years after World War II, two native Angolans – Domingos Van-Dunem and Norberto de Castro – helped to create the Club de Teatro de Angola, but their attempts to generate wide interest in theatre ultimately failed, partly because colonial policies continued to restrict their actions. In the 1950s, the Companhia Teatral de Angola was founded in Luanda and it set the post-war standard for non-subsidized amateur groups.

Beyond this, the country hosted a number of touring groups from Europe which generally failed at the box office since these foreign performances had no particular meaning to local audiences. It was not until 1971 when the Teatro Experimental de Cascais, an experimental theatre group from outside Lisbon, visited the country that alternative visions were offered and the works of writers such as Lope de Vega, Racine, Yves Jamiaque and Gervasio Lobata were seen for the first time.

Yet Angolan writers did exist from 1945 on and certain of their plays were at least published earlier. Among them was Henrique Galvão, who in 1935 wrote *Como se faz um homen* (*How a Man Is Made*). In 1936 he adapted a poem of Silva Tavares for the stage, *O Velo d'oiro* (*The Golden Fleece*) and in 1939 he wrote *Colonos* (*The Colonists*). In 1940 the National African League journal *Angola* published a play by Padre Benevuto Santos about Dom Nuno Alvares Pereira called *O Condestável* (*The Supreme Commander*). Also in 1940 Alfredo Cortez wrote *Moema*, a play set in the city of Benguela.

It was the National African League which spurred most of the interest in Angolan theatre through the 1940s and especially after World War II in an effort to defend African interests. The League sponsored musical performances and recitals and even Samba groups following the South American music and dance style then in vogue. Most of the group's work tried to reflect both the local environment and the local lifestyle while emphasizing social and political issues.

Among the well-known artists working in such performances were Liceu (Carlos de Aniceto Vieira Dias), the Araujo Brothers (Oscar, Mario and Cesar), Xico Machado (Francisco Arnaldo de Assis Machado), Lacerda (Antonio Ferreira), Horacio Horta, Helena Portugal, Gertrudes Craveiro and Mirumba (Guilherme Cordeiro) to name just a few.

In 1948 the music theatre group Conjunto Ngola Ritmos (Angola Rhythms) appears and in 1950 the Grupo Experimental de Teatro, the latter influenced by the Brazilian group Teatro Experimental do Negro (Negro Experimental Theatre) and the naturalistic style of its leader Abdias do Nascimento.

There were several attempts to develop ongoing indigenous theatre activities in the 1950s and 1960s ranging from the presentation of an Angolan street carnival to the work of the group Ngongo. Most were stopped by police officials as threats to public security. Ngongo is particularly significant because of its attempts to stage tales, legends, sketches and audience participation pieces following more traditional oral folk forms. During the battle for independence these forms would emerge once more in performances staged by newer groups such as Tchingange which offered a large number of improvised performances in factories, shops, schools, hospitals and even important sugar

The Companhia de Dança Contemporânea's production of *Tira a Máscara! Qual Máscara?*
Photo: Rui Tavares.

The Companhia de Dança Contemporânea's production of
A Propósito de Luedi.
Photo: Rui Tavares.

refineries in the interior. Its anti-colonial, anti-government positions were clear in such plays as *Poder Popular (People Power*, 1975) and its work was typical of the didactic, political approach to theatre at this time in Angola.

As some of these groups were closed down, others emerged and in 1976 a National School of Theatre was formed. The most important of the groups at this time were Xilenga-Teatro (founded 1977) which staged oral narratives from the Tsckokwe culture, and Elinga-Teatro, founded in 1990 and still operating in 1996. Two other groups deserving of note here are the Grupo Experimental de Teatro (connected to the Ministry of Culture) and Kapa-Kapa, a collectively based group under the direction of Nôa Wete, a director and playwright. For the most part, all these were and still are amateur groups or, at most, semi-professional. None is subsidized.

Among the country's playwrights, the following are of particular note for trying to maintain an active theatrical tradition: Antonino Pereira do Santos Van-Dunem, author of *O Patrão não tem corage (The Boss Lacks Courage,* 1945); Domingos Van-Dunem, author of *Kioxinda* (1967), *Auto de Natal* (*Christmas Play,* 1972), a play written in the Quimbundo language as part of the movement of rediscovery of indigenous values, and *O Panfleto* (*The Pamphlet,* 1989); Orlando de Albuquerque, author of the political plays *Ovibanda* (1975) and *O Filho de Nzambi* (*Nzambi's Son,* 1975); and Manuel dos Santos Lima, author of *A Pele do Diablo* (*Devil's Skin,* 1977).

Other Angolan playwrights include Armando Correia de Azevedo, author of *A Taberna* (*The Tavern*) and *Muji*; Artur Pestana (Pepetela),

author of *A Corda* (*The Rope,* 1978) and *A Revolta da casa dos Ídolos* (*Revolt in the House of Idols,* 1980); Henrique Guerra, author of an adaptation of Brecht, *O Círculo de giz de Bombó* (*Bombo's Chalk Circle,* 1979); Jorge Macedo, author of *Sequeira Luis Lopes ou o Mulato dos prodigios* (*Sequeira Luis Lopes or the Prodigious Mulatto, 1991*) and *Tutumbagem*; João Maimona, author of *Diário com a Peripécia* (*Diary with Peripetia,* 1987); José Mena Abrantes, author of *Ana Zé e os escravos* (*Ana Zé and the Slaves,* 1986); and several Angolans of European origin including Angerino de Sousa, José de Almeida Santos, Ribeiro de Almeida and Lilia Fonseca.

Domingos Van-Dunem
Translated by Maria-Clara Versiani Galery

Further Reading

Almeida Santos, José. *Paginas Esquecidas de Luanda de Ha Cem Anos* [A century of writing from Luanda]. 4 vols. Luanda: Da Camara, 1970.

Altuna, Padre Raul Ruiz Asùa. *Cultura Tradicional Banto* [Banto traditional culture]. Luanda: Secretariado Diocesano de Luanda, 1985.

Bastin, Marie-Louise. 'Ritual Masks of the Chokwe'. *African Arts* 17, no. 4 (August 1985): 40–4.

Redinha, José. *Etnias de Culturas de Angola* [Ethnic cultures in Angola]. Luanda: Instituto de Investigação, 1974.

Van-Dunem, Domingos. 'Para a história da falta de Teatro em Angola' [Toward a history of Angola's lack of theatre]. *Revista Noticia* (January 1968).

BELGIAN CONGO

(see **ZAÏRE**)

BÉNIN

In the early seventeenth century, three major kingdoms flourished in the territory that is presently known as Bénin: the kingdoms of Ardra, Jakin and Dahomey. By the eighteenth century, the powerful Dahomey nation – interested in selling slaves to European traders – began to assert power over the whole area including its Ardra and Jakin neighbours. In 1738, however, the Yoruba overthrew them and for the next hundred years tributes were paid to the Yorubas by the Dahomians.

King Gezo restored autonomy to Dahomey in the late nineteenth century by bringing together a powerful army that included a band of female warriors. As well, Gezo signed the first trade agreements with France (1851), agreements that were not, however, accepted by subsequent Dahomian rulers. As a result, in 1894 France forcibly deposed King Béhanzin and made Dahomey part of its colonial holdings in West Africa.

Ruled by France under the name of Dahomey and Dependencies, it was not until the years after World War II that the territory began to be given gradual control over its own affairs. In 1952 it was allowed to elect its own legislature and in 1960 it became a fully independent nation. It subsequently joined with Côte d'Ivoire, Upper Volta (now Burkina Faso), Niger and Togo to create a French African economic union, the Conseil de l'Entente.

A series of *coups d'état* followed in the 1960s and in 1970 a Government of National Unity was formed. In 1972, however, still another coup saw the military again take control. In 1975, the country's name was officially changed from Dahomey to Bénin, the same year that the government formally took over maintenance of the country's elementary schools.

With only a 121 kilometre (78 miles) coast along the Gulf of Guinea, Bénin occupies a long, narrow strip of land in West Africa. Bounded by the enormous republic of Nigeria to the east, Niger and Burkina Faso to the north and Togo to the west, Bénin covers an area of some 112,600 square kilometres (43,500 square miles) and had a 1990 population of 4.7 million.

The country has forty-two ethnic groupings, the most important being Fon, Adja, Yoruba, Dendi and Bariba. French remains the official language but at least ten different tribal languages are quite common. With only 30 per cent of the country divided fairly closely between the Muslim and Christian religions, 70 per cent of the country follows traditional animist beliefs. Well over 80 per cent of the country's exports flow to Europe, including crude oil, cotton, palm products and cocoa. Bénin had an external debt of some $1 billion in 1989 but an annual per capita income of only $360.

Bénin's capital is officially Porto-Novo and the country's administrative functions are centred there but its largest city, Cotonou, is the *de facto* capital as well as the economic centre. Most of the country's schools of higher education,

including its one university, the National University of Bénin, are located in these two cities – less than 30 kilometres apart – which together have a population of some 700,000.

French colonization profoundly and clearly affected both the history and social evolution of the country, uprooting the deeply ingrained traditional cultural life while substituting another. The result was a series of cultural mutations involving forms that must be considered theatrical and dramatic. Within such a traditional society, public events follow clearly recognized structures that are inherently dramatic and which are common in societies requiring initiation for full entry into them. Among these are the Egun, Zangbeto and Gèlèdè societies in the southern part of Bénin and those groups that were influenced by them such as the Aguélé. Masked dancing is another element common to all of them. In the north, the Bio N'kuro both sing and dance on public occasions while dancing marionettes are found in Dagbé (in the province of Ouémé). Public storytelling is yet another established form that can be found throughout the country.

A 1980 production by the company of students of the National University of Bénin.
Photo: Ehuzu.

Though some of these performances clearly reflect a desire to celebrate a divinity, many are not directly connected to religion. Some are propaganda pieces for particular cultural groupings; others are a way of representing myths to their communities; still others are an attempt to dramatize specific spirits with a view to exorcizing them. Rooted in a desire to objectify such phenomena, these dramatic events also allow initiates to become participants (actors) in the performances whether it is for the cult of the dead (as in Egun or Kouvito) or as guardians of public safety as in Zangbeto.

Functioning as entertainment, education and social integration, such traditional performances follow precise dramatic criteria while still being flexible enough to allow for innovation. The *adjogbo* dance provides some of the most remarkable examples of this. Even within traditional griotic storytelling, the storyteller is able to integrate into a harmonious whole such diverse elements as proverbs, songs and dances.

Such events were open to anyone within the society and the idea of charging a fee to watch and participate in them was simply not part of the culture. As a result, audiences were always large and enthusiastic, and cut across the entire community – initiates and non-initiates, children and adults, women and men, poor and wealthy, actors and spectators. Truly popular, the appeal and significance of such events can clearly be found within this extraordinary social communion.

To a very great extent, it was these cultural structures that were most affected by French colonization and the establishment of a centralized administrative structure in the colony. Other major changes included the generalized use of coinage, the rapid development of urban centres (which accentuated the disequilibrium between city and country) and the gradual development of clear social classes. All these were both signs and catalysts of the rapid changes taking place in the land.

Eventually French missionaries began to use European-style spoken theatre for evangelical purposes and it was not so long after that that European plays began to be seen on public stages in cities in the south of the country. Most of the performances were held outdoors, usually in church courtyards, but eventually these performances made their way into church-run schools as well.

In such churchyard performances, actors were drawn not only from the missionaries themselves but also from the newly converted. In school performances it was the children who took the roles of saints and personages from the Bible. Moralistic sketches on Christian themes began to be seen more often. Christian holy days such as Christmas, Epiphany, Easter and Whitsuntide always boasted such performances, first in local languages and eventually in French. To this day in Porto-Novo, plays by one of the priests most active in this endeavour – Father Aupiais's *The Three Wise Man* and *Herod* – are still shown at Christmastime.

It was not so long after this that other aspects of European theatre began to be introduced: the Italian-style stage, the use of settings, curtains and, of course, paid admissions. This could be seen not only in the church schools but also in the public schools. The colonial administration realized quite quickly the uses to which European theatre could be put.

The school with the highest social and educational status in what was called French West Africa at the time was just outside of Dakar in modern Sénégal – the William Ponty Normal School. It was here where the first 'well-educated' Dahomians received their initiation to European-style education, including schooling in spoken drama. At the end of each school year a Festival of Native Arts was also organized, in which students were encouraged to put on plays showing the traditions and customs of their native lands.

One such play – perhaps the first European-style play on a Dahomian theme – was *La Dernière Entrevue de Béhanzin et de Bayol* (*The Last Meeting of Béhanzin and Bayol*). A historical drama, the play shows the enormous influence of colonial ideology on the students and was quite typical of the Ponty School style. That same year, Dahomey students produced a choral drama, *Ma bi si ayé*.

Over the next few years more new plays began to come from the Dahomian students at Ponty – *Le Mariage de Sika* (*Sika's Wedding*) in 1934; *L'Élection d'un roi au Dahomey* (*The Election of a King in Dahomey*) in 1935; and *Retour aux fétiches délaissés* (*Return to the Abandoned Sorcery*) in 1936, a play about the misfortunes of a family caused by the anger of its ancestors.

At the Colonial Exhibition in Paris in 1937, a number of productions from the Ponty School were included and widely praised. The plays had equal appeal back in Dahomey and the Dahomian Ponty students became even more confirmed in their commitment to European styles. For students at home who could see these productions only when the elite returned from the Ponty School, these plays seemed to be models of a new type of theatre and the work was both influential and popular.

To the colonial powers interested in controlling the activities and the education of the new elite, such performances also guaranteed the stability of the colonial system as these students grew, took power themselves and sought new entertainment reflective of their new lifestyles.

By 1952, the colonial administration also helped to create a series of *Cercles culturels* (Cultural Circles) in Dahomey as in other French colonies. From this point on the different groups began to compete with one another for best productions and best plays in local and eventually interregional festivals. In 1957, for example, a group calling itself Les Scouts du Dahomey staged three different productions: *Kotodja*, a warrior's dance; *Houékodé*, a historical drama in three acts; and *L'Étudiant* (*The Student*), a satire on conflict between tradition and modernism. Troupes for these

competitions were selected on a colony-to-colony basis.

In the schools, the European classical repertoire was also produced more frequently, especially Corneille, Racine and Molière. As the years passed, a polarization became apparent between the minority of the population that was literate and preferred the new literary plays, and the majority, which was illiterate and preferred traditional styles of performance. For the most part, the minority lived in the cities; the majority in rural areas. It was only in the cities that both styles could be seen.

Through the 1960s one could actually see the forms beginning to blend. During that decade, the idea of paying for public entertainment was also gradually accepted and groups were formed that introduced, with varying degrees of success, performances in spaces that were now being designed to handle the new literary theatre. Some of the new groups even began to blend the two styles in such a way as to show aspects of local culture, and the beauty of its folk wisdom, its songs and dances. On occasion, these were intertwined with short sketches or simple pieces about everyday life or local history.

The 1994 production by the Théâtre du Cri of Pierre Corneille's *Cinna*.
Photo: Ahounou.

Clearly such an interest grew out of an evolving African nationalism during the 1950s and its urge to affirm African rather than European cultural values. New folk theatres came into being, attempting to turn the eyes of sophisticated and educated young Africans away from the glamour of western ways and back toward an awareness of their own rich heritage. Among the earliest of these was Troupe théâtrale et folklorique d'Ekpè founded in 1953 by Télésphore Sagbohan (b. 1936).

From the same influences and interests grew the Ensemble National du Dahomey (National Company of Dahomey), founded in 1962, under the direction of Flavien Campbell (b. 1925). The troupe represented Dahomey abroad that same year when it was invited to the Theatre of Nations Festival in Paris. In 1964 the troupe appeared in West Berlin, in 1966 it played at the First Festival of Black Arts in Dakar, and in 1969 at a festival in Côte d'Ivoire.

The Ensemble folklorique des ballets Daho-Negro (Daho-Negro Folk Ballet Ensemble) first appeared during the Cotonou Fair in 1965. Founded by the Senegalese Edouard Gaye, the group later toured Greece and the Netherlands with its blend of theatre and dance. By 1970, using the name Ballets Africains, it staged a major historical play called *Les Nègres d'Agadja et Houffon* (*The Blacks of Agadja and Houffon*). Soon, however, the group disbanded though certain elements of it were later reunited in Les Ballets Egblémakou, still thriving in the 1990s though mostly performing for tourists in search of the exotic, or on official state occasions.

In addition to these relatively important groups, there also existed during the 1960s a number of others, less widely known and with shorter artistic lives. Among these were the Union folklorique et théâtrale des jeunes de Jéricho (Young Jericho Folk and Theatre Union), the Jeunesse théâtrale et folklorique dahoméenne (Dahomian Youth Folk Theatre) and the Ensemble folklorique dahoméen (Dahomian Folk Ensemble).

Even these folk-based troupes were staging literary plays as well, often in French. The Ekpè group, for example, slowly moved away from an exclusively sung and danced repertoire to scripted productions – Fofana Moctar's *L'Appel du fètiche* (*The Call of the Sorcerers*) in 1963, Dandoli Mahamane's *L'Aventure d'une chèvre* (*The Adventure of a Goat*) in 1964, Abdou Anta Ka's *La Fille des dieux* (*Daughter of the Gods*) also in 1964, and

Maurice Mêlé's *Dahomé* in 1967.

It was, however, a group founded in 1965 in Porto-Novo that evolved spoken drama in the country to its highest point. Calling itself Les Cerveaux Noirs (Black Brains) and composed of a group of young and literate Dahomians, the group's major successes at this time included two plays by Jean Pliya (b. 1931) – *Kondo, le Requin* (*Kondo the Shark*), which was played thirty-six times between 1966 and 1968, and *La Secrétaire particulière* (*The Private Secretary*) in 1970. Another success was with Guy Menga's (b. 1935) *La Marmite de Koka Mbala* (*Koka Mbala's Pot*) in 1969.

Another 1960s group of note was Les Muses (The Muses), founded in 1967 in Cotonou at a local secondary school by director Boniface Makponsè (b. 1951). Among the company's major dramatic successes were *Agadja et le royaume d'Oyo* (*Agadja and the Kingdom of Oyo*, 1970), an adaptation of an anonymous historical work; *Le Royaume de Savi et princesse Naguézé* (*The Kingdom of Savi and Princess Naguézé*), *Le Sacrifice du sang* (*Blood Sacrifice*) and *Madi Awa*. Several other troupes were founded at secondary schools at this time but most of them, including Les Coeurs d'Ebène (Ebony Hearts) founded in 1970 at Lycée Houffon, had less success.

Through the early 1970s, theatre in the country was led by Les Cerveaux Noirs and by the many secondary school and university groups that had now come into existence. By the mid-1970s, however, energies had peaked. Earlier successful plays continued to be repeated but few new plays of note emerged. This was further complicated by an increasingly difficult political situation, which meant that plays had to be chosen with very careful consideration of their subject matter.

At the first national festival of the arts held in 1976 – a festival known by its acronym, FESNAC – a new play by Makponsè called *A lute continua* (*The Continuing Struggle*) won first prize. Staged by Les Muses, the success of this new play attracted wide attention, but at the second FESNAC the company retreated to the much safer *Agadja*, which had won third prize at the Cotonou Fair in 1970.

Most of the major groups continued to back away from written texts over the next decade and few new plays were even published. Among the few plays of note to make it into print at this time were Séverin Akando's (b. 1952) *Révolution africaine* (*African Revolution*, 1975), André Pognon's (1905–92) *Le*

Trône vacant (*The Vacant Throne*) (1975), Henri Hessou's (b. 1956) *L'Aventurier sans scrupules* (*The Unscrupulous Adventurer*, 1982), and Justin Hounkpodoté's *Enquête sur le terrain* (*Investigation in the Field*) in 1983.

Political and social changes during the 1970s were reflected in a group of plays that is still read in schools though they are rarely produced. These include works by Lucien Gangbadjo – particularly *Triomphe éclatant* (*Resounding Triumph*); Séverin Akando – particularly *Le Mariage n'aura pas lieu* (*The Wedding Will Not Happen*); and several plays by Pascal Gnanho – *Les Dieux ont trahi* (*The Gods Have Betrayed*), *L'Agression* (*The Attack*), *Le Paradis est plutôt un enfer* (*Heaven Is Pretty Hellish*) and *Le Tribunal de la dernière instance* (*Court of Last Appeal*).

Three plays by Sani Sourakatou highlighted a renewal of French-language, socially rooted playwriting during the 1980s. Sourakatou's most produced works are *Attention professeur* (*Watch Out, Professor*, 1988), *Décision finale* (*Final Decision*, 1989) and *Binta Foulana* (1991). Other plays of note from this period include Camille Amouro's (b. 1963) *Ghôli* (1988); and Akambi Akala's (b. 1954) 1990 success, *Le Délégué de Kovêdji* (*The Delegate from Kovedji*). Most of these works were presented by student companies.

One of the significant features of the 1990s has been the production by various groups of plays from other African countries, for instance, plays by the Chadian dramatist Naindouba Maoundoé – *L'Étudiant de Soweto* (*The Student from Soweto*); by the Cameroonian Patrice Ndèdi Penda – *Le Caméléon* (*The Chameleon*); by the Senegalese Mbaye Gana Kébé – *Notre futur enfant* (*Our Unborn Child*); by the Nigerian Wole Soyinka – *The Lion and the Jewel*; by the Ivoirian Bernard Dadié – *Béatrice du Congo* (*Beatrice of the Congo*); and by the Congolese Sony Labou Tansi – *Je soussigné cardiaque* (*I, the Undersigned Cardiac Case*) and *La Parenthèse de sang* (*Parentheses of Blood*).

Between these major areas of traditional performance and scripted performance lies collective creation, first seen in Bénin in about 1970 when the Troupe théâtrale de l'IRAD staged *École et tradition* (*School and Tradition*) under the direction of Lazare Houétin (b. 1944). Following Houétin's return to the country after a period of theatre study in France, he convinced Les Cerveaux Noirs to turn toward this new genre. The result was the

politically controversial but immensely successful *Yovo hélu wé, Akowé hélu wé* (*Beware White Man! Beware African Intellectual*). State authorities were not pleased with the show, but were unable to prevent its performance. A second collective was an equal success – *Kooyi Gnan, to we non blo to do* (*All the Same, the People Should Have the Say in Politics*).

After 1974, though, Les Cerveaux Noirs seemed to lose direction even in its collective work although the group survived through 1985. In that year it staged one of its last collectives, *Le Bal des ténèbres* (*The Ball of the Shadows*), another socio-political satire. Again the authorities caused problems for the group, and Les Cerveaux Noirs eventually had to close down. Yet the group had proven the effectiveness of the collective form.

Other troupes also worked effectively in this style including the Ensemble artistique et culturel des étudiants (EACE; Artistic and Cultural Student Ensemble), whose 1988 production *Il était une fois* (*Once Upon a Time*) was banned by the state censor and could not be performed until 1990 when a new openness began to pervade the country. In 1988 the company Les Muses, now working on a professional basis, staged a collective entitled *La Trompette du crépuscule* (*Trumpet of the Dusk*), which severely criticized totalitarianism. Still another group working collectively, Zama-Hara, has continued to produce social satires since its founding in 1975.

Given the wide range of producing styles being seen in Bénin, it was not surprising to find a company being created in 1984 dedicated to finding 'a mode of dramatic expression proper to Africa'. Calling itself the Troupe d'initiation et de recherche en art dramatique (TIRAD; Troupe for the Initiation and Research into Dramatic Art) and founded by Tara Daniel Tindjilé (b. 1953), its most original production has been *Les Traqués* (*The Hunted*) in 1985. A poetic drama built around the theme of Africa's destiny, it blended song, dance, story, poetry and history. The company's later productions have tended toward more traditional styles usually based on plays by African or French authors.

Collective creation left other marks on Bénin theatre as well. Most groups now use local languages in performances rather than French; the dominance of the playwright has been replaced by the dominance of the group; and literary theatre itself left the control of a dominant upper class and became a more democratic, demystified, popular art.

The 1988 Les Muses's production of *Trumpet of the Dusk*.

With the stranglehold of French therefore broken on the stage by the 1980s, even the storytelling tradition began to be explored once again. Perhaps the country's most famous company working in this style has been Tow-akonou, founded and directed by the storyteller Déhumon Adjagnon (1930–85). Performing almost exclusively in the Goun and Yoruba languages, its goal was simply to amuse through the telling of moralistic stories based on everyday experiences and accessible to everyone. After the death of its founder, however, the group diminished in both the frequency of its performances and in its theatrical vigour. Others working in a similar style included Odidere Ayekooto, Duniyan, Tani Mola, Les Griots du Bénin and Qui dit mieux? (Who Can Top This?), the latter group composed exclusively of women.

Several groups have also worked since 1985 in the field of Theatre for Social Action to bring awareness of health and education issues to the country. Encouraged in their work by United Nations agencies such as UNESCO and UNICEF, productions have been done on a range of subjects including dental health, sexual education for young people and AIDS. In 1990, the women's group Qui dit mieux? produced a show called *Femme et SIDA* (*Women and AIDS*).

Also in 1990, the country's first national theatrical organization was created: l'Association nationale des artistes et troupes de théâtre et de ballet (ANNATTHEB; National Association of Artists, Theatre and Dance Companies). In 1991, an international theatre festival was held for the first time in Cotonou, attracting troupes from across francophone Africa.

Structure of the National Theatre Community

There are ten theatre troupes in the 1990s that produce on a regular or nearly regular basis. All operate under the 1901 law for associations, which means that each is run by a democratically elected board of directors, which has responsibility for the overall administrative and technical functioning of the group.

For the most part, theatre people cannot survive in Bénin on their theatrical work alone meaning that most would be classified as amateurs. This said, many have had professional training at specialized schools in either Africa or Europe.

State support to these companies is virtually unknown although Zama-Hara, Les Messagers and EACE have occasionally received support from international humanitarian organizations for their work in educating the public on social issues.

Artistic Profile

For a discussion of the artistic styles operative in Bénin see the opening historical section.

Companies

Bénin's most important theatre groups include Les Muses du Bénin, Zama-Hara, EACE, Towakonou, Troupe théâtrale et folklorique d'Ekpè, Qui dit mieux?, CACUZ, CENAC, SAPAC, Douniyan and Les Messagers. All work for the most part in and around Cotonou and Porto-Novo. There is no national theatre company.

Dramaturgy

About half a dozen playwrights in Bénin have produced regularly. Among them are Jean Pliya, Séverin Akando, Henri Hessou, Maurice Mêlé, André Pognon and Justin Hounkpodoté. Their plays are discussed in the opening historical section.

Directing and Acting

Directing as a theatrical art is a completely post-World War II phenomenon in Bénin and

The 1992 EACE production of *Le Procès*.
Photo: EACE.

evolved with the emergence of particular theatre companies. Two directors who came to the fore in the 1980s were Tara Daniel Tindjilé and his troupe TIRAD, and Akambi Akala with Zama-Hara. Tindjilé took his inspiration mainly from African tales, myths and poems while Akala integrated song and dance into his theatrical language.

Other directors of note include Boniface Makponsè with Les Muses, Hyppolyte da Silva (b. 1942) with Les Messagers, Antoine Dadélé (b. 1954) with CENAC, and Lazare Houétin with IRAD. It should be noted as well that Houétin, Tindjilé and Akala are accomplished actors as well and are often seen in their own productions.

Bénin's best known professional actor is Tola Koukoui (b. 1943), who lives and works primarily in France.

Theatre for Young Audiences
Puppet and Mask Theatre

Bénin does not possess a troupe that specializes in theatre for children since children naturally form a part of the traditional African audience. Theatre for children is therefore generally considered as theatre by children and is seen in the schools as a cultural activity used to celebrate important occasions such as Christmas or Commencement.

From the 1970s onward, school performances have also gone out into the community. Troupes involved in theatre for social action such as CAEB have used children in their shows, which often incorporate traditional folk dances and songs.

As for puppets, these are especially familiar in the southern part of the country and can be seen in their purest form in villages such as Dagbé in the Ouémé. It is in this area that puppet masters work with specific figures, usually only one or two, and almost always a man and a woman.

The shows are not mounted in miniature theatres as they have traditionally been in

Design for the 1992 EACE production of *Le Procès*.
Photo: Ahounou.

Europe but rather in open spaces. The only exception to this has been shows seen on national television, which offers puppet shows within their own proscenium stages.

Masks are used in many festivals. They are seen primarily in performances held as part of ceremonies by societies requiring rites of initiation.

Design
Theatre Space and Architecture

Traditional African performance takes place in public squares. At such outdoor events, always open to the public free of charge, one may see anything from indigenous dances to short scripted pieces.

Spoken plays are more formally staged. Only the Centre culturel français in Cotonou (800 seats) and, more recently, the Palais Royal in Porto-Novo, the Museum in Ouidah and the Centre culturel français in Parakou (1,000 seats) offer acceptable facilities.

The two cultural centres are the only spaces that offer their own sound and lighting equipment. Those wishing to use such facilities must rent them or make do with cinemas, community centres or sports halls. One such, the Sports Hall in Cotonou seating 2,500, has, in fact, been renamed the Hall des Arts.

Training
Criticism, Scholarship and Publishing

There is no theatrical training school in Bénin. As a result, the small number of people wishing to receive professional training and the even smaller number of people who can afford it must go abroad. Paris is the goal in most cases. From time to time workshops are offered by some of the troupes or by visiting professionals under the auspices of the Centre culturel français.

Few plays from Bénin have been published either at home or abroad. Internationally only two plays have reached print, both by Jean Pliya – *Kondo, le Requin* and *La Secrétaire particulière*. Both were issued by the Cameroonian publisher, Éditions CLE in Yaoundé.

At home, plays by five different writers have been published: Séverin Akando (*Révolution africaine*, Édition Typo-Press, 1975); Henri Hessou (*L'Aventurier sans scrupules*, Édition la Récade du Bénin); Maurice Mêlé (*Danhômê*, Imprimerie Rapidex, 1965); André Pognon (*Le Trône vacant*, Édition ABM, 1975), and Justin Hounkpodoté (*Enquête sur le terrain*, Cotonou, 1983). In each case, publication was subsidized by the writers themselves. It should also be noted that most of the aforementioned publishing houses are little more than printing presses that can be hired by anyone with the funds to do so.

There is no theatre or performing arts magazine and most of the writing on theatre is of a journalistic variety. In-depth criticism is limited to the work of academics and students at the National University of Bénin.

Guy Ossito Midiohouan, Akambi Akala
Translated by Helen Heubi

Further Reading

Huannou, Adrien. *La Littérature béninoise de langue française* [Béninese literature in the French language] Paris: Karthala ACCT, 1984.

Koudjo, Bienvenu. 'La Pratique théâtrale au Bénin' [Theatre practice in Bénin]. *Notre Librairie* 69 (May–July 1983): 72–7.

——. 'Théâtre, rites et folklore au Dahomey' [Theatre, rites and folklore in Dahomey] Doctoral dissertation, Université de Paris III, 1976.

Midiohouan, Guy Ossito. 'La Pratique théâtrale en République Populaire du Bénin depuis 1945' [Theatre practice in the People's Republic of Bénin since 1945] In *Semper aliquid novi: littérature comparée et littérature d'Afrique* [Always something new: Literary comparisons and African literature], eds Janos Riesz and Alain Ricard, 357–68. Tübingen: Gunther Narr Verlag, 1990.

Nevadomsky, Joseph. 'Kingship Succession Rituals in Benin'. *African Arts* 17, no. 1 (November 1983): 47–54.

Savarolles, François. 'La Troupe théâtrale et folklorique du Bénin: les filles des amazones' [The theatre and folklore troupe of Bénin: Daughters of the Amazons]. *Afrique* 63 (January 1967): 22–5.

BURKINA FASO

Formerly the French colony of Haute-Volta (Upper Volta), Burkina Faso is a landlocked country in West Africa. It is bounded by Mali to the north and west, Niger and Bénin to the east, and Togo, Ghana and Côte d'Ivoire to the south. It has an overall land area of 274,100 square kilometres (105,800 square miles) and its 1994 population was estimated at 10.1 million. The capital and largest city is Ougadougou.

A multi-ethnic, multi-religious society comprising some sixty ethnic groups each with its own language, customs and traditions, Burkina Faso's largest group is the Mossi whose ancestors came to modern Burkina Faso in the eleventh century from what is now the northern part of Ghana. The Mossi Kingdom was one of four medieval kingdoms established in the region between the eleventh and sixteenth centuries. Among other important ethnic groupings are Gurunsi, Senufo, Lobi, Bobo, Mande and Fulani (Peul).

The first recorded Europeans to visit the area came in the late nineteenth century. By 1896, the French were sending in an army to claim Ougadougou as a protectorate and in 1919 the French created the colony of Haute-Volta with much the same boundaries as the country has today. Part of French West Africa, in 1932 the colony was subsumed by its neighbours but in 1947 it regained its separate status. From 1947 to 1960 – despite the continuing movement of some 20 per cent of the male population each year to neighbouring countries for seasonal work – an independence movement grew which resulted in formal independence from France in 1960.

A military coup took place in 1966 which resulted in the suspension of the first constitution. A new constitution was introduced, in 1970 but in 1974 it too was suspended and the military again resumed power. In 1977 a third constitution was brought in. In 1984, the country changed its name to Burkina Faso and its citizens thereafter became known as Burkinabes. There are three major religious groupings – animism, the traditional religion which is still practised by nearly two-thirds of the population, Islam and Christianity. In 1993, the literacy rate stood at just over 18 per cent.

The history of the country's theatre can be briefly analysed under three separate headings: traditional performances, theatre under the colonial system, and theatre since independence.

All important occasions – births, namings, passages into adulthood, marriages, deaths, enthronements and funerals, for example – are marked by traditional rites designed to ensure the integration or confirmation of the individual as belonging to one or another social grouping which is responsible for that person's existence from cradle to grave. These rites – often community productions involving significant performative activities – can be esoteric depending on the nature of the ceremony and the particular ethnic group involved.

For example, with the Dagari (Dagaba), burial and funeral are twinned in one ceremony which lasts for several days, during which time the friends and relatives of the deceased perform before the richly dressed body, which presides in an armchair over a re-enactment of the important moments of his or her life. It is a moral duty for every member of the family to take an active part in this performance whose actors are chosen only at the time. All of this is attended by a large audience of community members. It

Kedougou 'red dancers', Mossi.
Photo: Michel Huet.

should also be noted that such ceremonies are done only in the language of the community, some of whose linguistic codes are secret.

The lives of Burkinabes are also lived according to various social, often performative, rituals. These vary from everyday greetings (which recognize different people by their age, sex and social status) to more complex social 'games' that are closer to Augusto Boal's invisible theatre than they are to Aristotle's concept of mimesis. For example, two members of a community might greet one another with what would be seen by outsiders as extended verbal and sometimes even physical abuse. Such encounters can be so violent that bystanders cannot be sure whether they are serious or not until both protagonists burst out laughing and shake hands in friendship.

Such traditions, whatever their nature, are intended to strengthen the social order. None – since they date from pre-colonial times – has any significant capacity for social or political protest. Most, in fact, are often of a religious nature. Such performative events, unfortunately, are now being seen less and less. Indeed, many historically important cultural

modes of expression are now undergoing a process of marginalization. Though relegated to folklore, they nevertheless provide a rich mine for modern theatre practitioners who are using this material to create newer forms that can reach even wider audiences. It should be said as well that the artists versed in traditional forms – whether musicians, dancers, storytellers or public actors – remain the best trained and the most cultivated in their fields and are, as a result, best known to the public.

During the colonial period, European-style theatre in French West Africa was born first at the École Primaire Supérieure in Bingerville (Côte d'Ivoire) and then flowered from the 1930s at the École Normale Supérieure William Ponty (William Ponty Normal School) in Dakar.

Though numerous Burkinabe students participated in the Ponty theatre classes and performances, none achieved the prominence while there of the Guinean Fodéba Keita, or the Ivoirian Coffi Gadeau. It was only after returning home and re-establishing contact with their own people that Burkinabe graduates revealed their skills in the new spoken dramatic arts.

During the 1950s there were clear signs of this growing theatrical activity in the country's major cities. One was the increase in cultural and educational associations such as the Cercle amical (Friendship Circle) in Banfora and the Foyer amical (Friendship Hostel) in Ouagadougou. Many of these groups staged European plays while others adapted ethnic dances to the stage. Among the most dynamic of these groups was the Ougadougou troupe led by Jean Ouédrago. Similar developments were occurring in Bobo-Dioulasso through religious associations such as the Jeunesses catholiques (Catholic Youth). Yet the country as a whole lacked the resources and the cultural infrastructures that were beginning to be seen in the rest of West Africa.

The appointment of Bernard Cornut-Gentil in 1951 as High Commissioner of the French West African federation had repercussions on each nation's theatrical life. On the High Commissioner's recommendation, Journées d'études (Study Days) were held in the federation capital of Dakar in 1953. It was decided at these meetings to create cultural centres in all the principal cities and towns of the territories, to hold a competitive drama festival for the whole of French West Africa and to publish a bulletin linking each of the cultural centres. This latter

A masked dancer at the annual Bobo purification rites.
Photo: Michel Huet

would be called *Traits d'union* (*Hyphen*) to indicate the ongoing relationship between them. A Burkinabe – Lompolo Koné – was named its first editor.

In 1955, the first festival was held in Dakar with the troupe from the cultural centre at Banfora one of the finalists with its production of *La Légende de Teli Soumaoulé* (*The Legend of Teli Soumaoulé*), a collective creation based on a scenario by Lompolo Koné. Other centres in Burkina Faso were beginning to offer equally interesting performances. Among them were the cultural centres at Bobo-Dioulasso, Ougadougou, Ouahigouya, Koudougou, Gaoula, Fada, Dori and Kaya.

In 1957 the Banfora troupe again reached the finals, this time with its production of *Au Pays des paysans noirs* (*In the Land of Black Peasants*), an adaptation of the novel *Les Paysans noirs* by Robert Delavignette. This competition, the last to be organized in French West Africa as such, was, like the others, an effective governmental tool for the support of theatrical creation and a useful yardstick for its development. Between 1953 and 1959, for example – the years just prior to independence – the number of cultural groups (*amicales* as they

were called in the larger cities) grew from half a dozen to more than fifty. Theatre was the main focus attracting the most participants and gaining the greatest prestige. Western-style theatre was slowly becoming part of community life.

Because of theatre's growing popularity, the church – long a vigorous opponent of traditional performance, which it considered pagan – itself began to use theatre as a means of Christian propagation. In most of the larger churches – with the help of youth movements like the Jeunesse étudiant chrétienne (Christian Student Youth) and the Jeunesse agricole chrétienne (Young Christian Farmers) – liturgical theatre troupes were formed whose challenge it was to represent the lives of Jesus and the saints for the edification of Christian audiences.

For a long time these shows were performed exclusively in French, it being out of the question for the church to deviate from the basic principles of colonial culture which required the language of the mother country to be propagated in every way possible. Nevertheless, according to critic Bakary Traoré in his valuable study 'Le Théâtre négro africain et ses fonctions sociales' ('Black African Theatre and its Social Functions') which appeared in *Présence*

Africaine in 1958, the church in Burkina Faso was one of the first in Africa to use local languages in its worship services. As he put it,

the only representatives of the governing powers who attempted to translate anything into a local language were the white fathers in Ougadougou in Upper Volta and the anglo-American protestants in Nigeria.

Similar experiments in theatre in the vernacular (particularly in the Mossi language) were being made at this time in the diocese of Koupèla.

Acting styles in this religious theatre, however, were clearly European. The actors, chosen from the ranks of the most committed believers, were trained to imitate as closely as possible the reactions of the characters they portrayed. In each case, local priests were in charge of the performances which took place within the various Roman Catholic missions.

It is of interest to note that all seminarians began to receive systematic training in playwriting and play directing at this time so that they could write plays or direct actors when they had their own parishes. This said, the fact is that only a small percentage of the young seminarians actually became fully fledged priests. For example, of five young theatre instructors at the University of Ougadougou when that department began, four received their early training at a seminary.

Since the William Ponty Normal School focused its energies on teachers, it can also be said that the art never left its *alma mater*. Many of the Pontins became directors of cultural centres while others became involved in school theatre as teachers. It was this activity within the school theatres which led to the creation of two annual national festivals: the Festival national des arts du secondaire et du supérieur (National Arts Festival of Primary and Secondary Schools) and the Prix du meilleur spectacle à l'école primaire (Primary School Best Performance Prize).

Following independence in 1960, theatre also became part of the cultural policies of the young state. Cultural centres were quickly transformed into Maisons des jeunes et de la culture (Youth and Culture Houses) and the national theatrical competitions ceased. Many of the leaders of the former cultural centres, in fact, were promoted to important political positions.

The first major theatrical performance of the post-colonial era took place in October 1961 at Ougadougou as part of the celebrations of the first anniversary of independence. Combining theatrical forces for the occasion were artists from the Youth and Culture House of Ougadougou and the Troupe Yennega of Félix Boyarm. Through the rest of the 1960s, however, the state all but withdrew from cultural activities encouraging in its place private institutions and private support.

Replacing many of the cultural animation activities of the state were efforts by the independent Association voltaïque pour la culture africaine (Volta Association for African Culture) founded in 1963 and the Cercle d'activités littéraires et artistiques de Haute-Volta (Literary and Artistic Activities Circle of Upper Volta) founded in 1966. The former concentrated on the organization of lectures and debates while the latter organized (until 1973) an annual multidisciplinary festival involving all the artistic and cultural sectors of the country. The finals of this festival were held in the capital in the presence of top state officials.

Theatre was strongly represented at these festivals and frequent winners included the Troupe Yennega, Sotogui Kouyaté's Troupe de la Volta and Karim Laty Traoré's Cercle de l'amité. Among the playwrights whose work was first seen during these events were Yaya Konaté, Karim Konaté, Harouna Ouédraogo and Sibiri Traoré Omar.

In 1971, the state decided to once again become involved in cultural activities and created a cultural administration which operated through various ministries. One of its first ventures was the organization of a new festival strictly for the Youth and Culture Houses. From 1971 to 1983, this festival – Semaines de la jeunesse (Youth Weeks) – worked relatively well giving opportunities to both rural and urban groups to have regular and intensive seasons. Though these festivals were only modestly funded and the troupes often quite unstable, the Semaines de la jeunesse had several positive effects: they brought theatre into remote areas of the country and helped people become aware of their own cultural identities. As well, most of the plays that were seen were by Burkinabe writers, often in local languages and most dealing with local themes. On the negative side, the private troupes were all left on the sidelines.

This latter problem was solved in 1983 when the Youth Weeks were replaced by Semaines nationales de la culture (National Culture Weeks) allowing the private troupes to participate again. Encouragement of cultural activity generally grew with literary competitions (Grand prix des arts et lettres/Grand Prize for Arts and Letters) and more theatre festivals. Again, new playwrights emerged – Sowié Moussa Théophile, Jean-Pierre Guingané, Zongo Martin, Jacques Prosper Bazié, Tinga Issa Nikiée and Ousmane Ouédraogo among others.

New troupes emerged even in places where none had existed before: in political groups, in government agencies, military garrisons and in private associations of all kinds. The Semaines nationales de la culture provided an opportunity for all these troupes to take the stage, first locally and then nationally. Theatre became not only an art but also a vehicle of expression, often political.

The festival also led to the creation of new groups such as the Théâtre Conago Désiré in Ougadougou, Théâtre Nani Palé in Gaoua, Théâtre Populaire in Koudougou and Théâtre de l'Amitié in Bobo-Dioulasso. By 1990, ten prize-winning plays had been published.

Structure of the National Theatre Community
Artistic Profile

Companies

Theatre in Burkina Faso is still essentially connected to the amateur tradition although a growing number of semi-professional companies is to be noted. Even in the most stable theatre groups, however, company members have to find their salaries in other sectors.

This said, theatrical performances can be found all over the country and all celebratory occasions worthy of the name seem to include a stage show. Sometimes it is by a private troupe hired for the occasion which is able to stage something from its regular repertoire. More often it is a pick-up company which is hired for the occasion and which will disappear when the event is over.

Religious occasions, for example, call for theatre groups connected with religious institutions, both Christian and Muslim, to perform. State occasions see performances by military theatre groups. There are as well handicapped groups such as the Mal Voyants de Nongtaba (The Blind of Nongtaba) which, as their name indicates, is made up of blind artists.

Because of this approach to theatrical work, it is impossible to offer an accurate count of the number of companies working at any given time in Burkina Faso. Nor is it possible to conduct any formal research on this level. Even style is difficult to pinpoint since so many of these groups veer between European spoken theatre and traditional storytelling. Only the groups performing in schools remain consistent in style. During the school year they present plays in French for other students; during holiday periods they often establish their own community companies and do plays on social issues such as immigration, the exodus from rural areas, drought and education. Most of these performances are jumping off points for debates in which the whole village participates. These school groups are an important step in initiating the public into theatrical art. They not only train future public officials – administrators and politicians – but also serve as role models for the villages and the Youth and Culture Houses.

Of the semi-professional groups – that is, those companies with some stability – the oldest is the Théâtre de la Fraternité (Brotherhood Theatre), established in 1974–5 as the Troupe théâtrale du Lycée municipal de Ougadougou (Theatre Troupe of the Ougadougou Municipal School) by Jean-Pierre Guingané. The company changed its name when it separated itself from the school in 1979. This is one of the troupes that has led the country's theatre community by example with its emphasis on socially relevant theatre. It has produced both European-style spoken drama and pieces involving Theatre-for-Development techniques.

Many of the Théâtre de la Fraternité's shows include songs, instrumental music and ethnic dances, and use various types of presentational techniques from proscenium to theatre-in-the-round. The company produces in several languages and though its administrative structures are more or less permanent its personnel change regularly. Guingané, a historian and a playwright, has remained with the company through the years as its most consistent director.

Two other semi-professional troupes of note are connected to state-supported institutions – the Ensemble artistique de la radio et de la télévision (Artistic Group of the State Radio and Television) and the Troupe de la compagnie du génie militaire (Military Troupe).

The Artistic Group of the State Radio and Television functions as the *de facto* national company. Its director is appointed by the Cabinet. Its regular employees receive a monthly salary while others are hired and paid per appearance. The company was founded by Karim Konaté and Sou Jacob.

The Military Troupe is considered the cultural sector of the military even though not all the actors are in the army themselves. Material and financial needs of the troupe are provided through the auspices of the Ministry of Defence.

Other semi-professional groups include Troupe Yennega, the first private troupe in the country – it operated from 1958 to 1968 – and tended to produce French-language classics; Atelier théâtral burkinabé, founded in 1978 by Prosper Kampaoré, which has been influenced by Augusto Boal's Forum Theatre concepts and which works in a socio-political way; Mutuelle Nouvelle Génération (New Mutual Generation) which tends to stage pieces involving mime and dance; and Compagnie Louis de Gonzaque Yaméogo (operating 1966–70) which was composed mostly of intellectuals and students and became the first experimental group in the country.

Other groups of note included La Troupe de la Volta (1966–71), founded by Sotogui Kouyaté (later a professional actor in Paris), one of the best of the Cultural Centre groups focusing on the techniques of the *griot*, the traditional storyteller and ethnic dance; le Cercle de l'amitié (1968–75), founded by Karim Laty Traoré and Sidibé Mamadou, an offshoot of the Troupe de la Volta which worked in similar ways; and le Théâtre de la solidarité africaine (1969–75), founded by political and labour organizer Philippe Ouédraogo whose work reflected these leanings.

Other troupes not yet spoken about that emerged subsequently – the second generation troupes – include the French repertoire troupe l'Atelier théâtral de Ougadougou (founded in 1967); La Troupe Soweto, the only troupe run by a woman, Joëlle Ouattara, formed expressly to work against apartheid in South Africa; Troupe Koulé Dafro, founded in 1979 in Bobo-Dioulasso; the satirical Troupe Ouezzin

Coulibaly, founded in 1980 by Dieudonné Coulibaly in Bobo-Dioulasso; and Troupe de la promotion, founded in 1986.

All theatre companies in the country are set up as non-profit cultural associations (or are attached to such associations). As such all are subject to a law (August 1959), which obliges them to be non-political. The same law requires that they have a board of directors elected by the members. Most survive by selling memberships, soliciting donations and through box-office income.

In total, there are fifteen semi-professional troupes, all in Ougadougou or Bobo-Dioulasso. Each group produces an average of two shows per year.

Dramaturgy
Directing and Acting

About two dozen writers have had plays staged by one or more theatres in the country. Among those whose works have been published are Sawadogo Barthélémy (*Révolution*, in French and Mossi), Jacques Prosper Bazié (*Amoro*), Wenceslas Compaoré (*Tiibe ou la fille de Tiibo/Tiibe or the Daughter of Tiibo*), Pierre Dabiré (*Sansoa*, 1969), Jean-Pierre Guingané (*Le Fou/The Madman*, 1986), Nikèma Tinga Issa (*Daniel ou le salaire de l'ambition/Daniel or the Fruits of Ambition*) and Prosper Kompaoré (*Les Voix du silence/Voices of Silence*).

Other important playwrights include Karim Konaté (*Yannega*), Yaya Konaté (*Oedipe noir/Black Oedipus* and *La Bataille de Noumoudara/The Battle of Noumoudara*), Sotogui Kouyaté (*La Complainte du caïman/The Lament of the Cayman*), Zongo Martin (*La Nassa de Tinga*), Sawadogo Moussa (*L'Oracle/The Oracle* and *La Fille de la Volta/Daughter of the Volta*), Tinga Issa Nikiée, Sibiri Traoré Omar (*Allah Manson/The God Manson*), Harouna Ouédraogo (*L'Heure de la vérité/Hour of Truth*), Mikinam Ouédraogo (*Les Trois libertés/The Three Liberties*), Yamba Elie Ouédraogo (*Coopération ou conspiration/Cooperation or Conspiracy*), Ouédraogo Ousmane (*Et le peuple lave son linge (And the People Do Their Laundry*) and Sowié Moussa Théophile (*Tiomboulan*).

Theatre for Young Audiences
Puppet and Mask Theatre

In traditional theatre, children and young people are always included as part of the audience. As such there are no specific 'theatre for young audience' groups operating in the country.

One of the most popular shows which Muslim children perform in themselves is called *dodo*, a performance involving music, dance, songs and the many young actors in makeup and masks dressed as animals. Performed during Muslim holy days, the popular success of the *dodo* has led to the creation of an annual *dodo* carnival at the end of Ramadan, in which some twenty youth groups take part.

Design
Theatre Space and Architecture

Traditional performances take place outdoors in any public space large enough to hold the audience which usually stands in a large circle around the performers.

Western-style theatres do not really exist except within the numerous Youth and Culture Houses across the country and within the foreign Cultural Centres. Most of these are modest – a small proscenium auditorium and limited seating. Few have technical facilities of any real note.

Training
Criticism, Scholarship and Publishing

About a dozen Burkinabe plays have been published within the country and a smaller number outside, mostly in Abidjan.

Drama criticism is little developed except at university level where it has no effective way of expressing itself to a wider public or even among academics. The university has no performance journal that appears regularly.

What theatre reviewing there is lies in the hands of journalists who write for the two government newspapers: the daily *Sidwaya* or for the weekly *Carrefour africain* (*African Crossroads*). Radio covers many events but is not sufficiently decentralized, while television is available almost exclusively to those who live in the capital.

Jean-Pierre Guingané
Translated by Helen Heubi

Further Reading

Benon, B. 'Deux expériences théâtrales: Jean-Pierre Guingané et le Théâtre de la Fraternité, Prosper Kampaoré et l'Atelier Burkinabé' [Two theatre experiments: Jean-Pierre Guingané and the Théâtre de la Fraternité, Prosper Kampaoré and the Atelier Burkinabé]. *Notre Librairie: La Littérature du Burkina Faso* 101 (April–June 1990).

Bovin, Mette. 'Provocation Anthropology: Bartering Performance in Africa'. *The Drama Review* 32, no. 1 (spring 1988): 21–41.

Boyarn, F. 'Le Théâtre en Haute-Volta' [Theatre in Upper Volta]. *Premières Mondiales* 30 (1962).

Cornevin, Robert. 'Théâtre et histoire: légendes et coutumes de la Haute-Volta' [Theatre and history: Legends and customs of Upper Volta]. *France-Eurafrique* 231 (1971): 28–30.

Deffontaines, Thérèse-Marie. 'Théâtre-Forum au Burkina Faso et au Mali' [Forum theatre in Burkina Faso and Mali]. *Notre Librairie* 102 (July–August 1990).

Guingané, Daogo Jean. 'Le Théâtre en Haute-Volta, production, diffusion, structure et public' [Theatre in Upper Volta, production, development, structure and publication]. PhD dissertation, Université de Bordeaux III, 1977.

Guingané, Jean-Pierre. 'Théâtre et développement au Burkina Faso' [Theatre and development in Burkina Faso]. *Revue d'Histoire du Théâtre* 160 (1988): 361–73.

Irwin, Paul. *Liptako Speaks: History from Oral Tradition in Africa*. Princeton, NJ: Princeton University Press, 1981.

Ki, Jean-Claude. 'Le Théâtre dans le développement socio-culturel en Haute-Volta' [The theatre in socio-cultural development in Upper Volta]. PhD dissertation, Université de Paris III, 1974.

Pageard, Robert. 'Théâtre africaine à Ouagadougou' [African theatre in Ouagadougou]. *Présence Africaine* 39 (1961): 250–3.

Pieces Théâtrales du Burkina [Plays of Burkina]. Ouagadougou: Ministère de l'Information et de la Culture, 1983. 157 pp.

Traoré, Bakary. 'Le Théâtre négro-africain et ses fonctions sociales' [Black African theatre and its social functions]. *Présence Africain* (1958).

Voltz, Michel. 'Voltaic Masks'. *The Drama Review* 26, no. 4 (winter 1982): 38–45.

Zimmer, Wolfgang. Repertoire du théâtre burkinabé [Burkino Faso theatre repertoire]. Paris: L'Harmattan, 1992. 138 pp.

BURUNDI

Located on the shores of Lake Tanganyika in central Africa, Burundi is bordered by Tanzania on the east and Zaïre on the west and shares both a border and close historical ties with Rwanda on the north. In 1992, it had an estimated population of approximately 5.5 million living in a land area of some 27,800 square kilometres (10,800 square miles).

Inhabited by the Barundi people, a grouping made up of three major ethnic groups – the majority Hutu (or Bahutu, a Bantu people), Tutsi (also called the Batutsi or Watusi, a Hamitic people) and Twa (or Batwa, also known as Pygmies) – all of whom share the same language, Kirundi. French and Kirundi are the languages of national administration. About 80 per cent of the population are Christian with the remaining 20 per cent either Muslim or followers of traditional African religions.

One of the last regions of Africa to become a European colony, Burundi became part of the German East Africa colony in 1896 along with Ruanda and Tanganyika. In 1916, the League of Nations placed Burundi and Ruanda under Belgian rule calling it Ruanda-Urundi. Following World War II, it became a United Nations trust territory under Belgian control. In 1962, Ruanda-Urundi became two independent nations – Rwanda and Burundi.

There are fifteen provinces in Burundi with the capital in Bujumbura. The second most important city is the historical capital, Gitega.

Until 1966, Burundi was a monarchy and thereafter a republic. In 1966, an army coup led to the abolition of the monarchy and that same year Michel Micombero, a former army officer, proclaimed himself president of the country. In 1976, he was deposed by another army coup and Jean-Baptiste Bagaza was appointed president. Major Pierre Buyoya overthrew Bagaza in 1987. During his time in office, Buyoya started a democratization process allowing many political parties. In 1993, multi-party elections brought a civilian government into power. In the years since 1993, civil war between Hutus and Tutsis has caused immense damage – economic and cultural – within the country. By 1996 more than 100,000 had died.

Burundians have a long cultural history with traditions in storytelling, music and dance. Though western-style theatre was seen from the beginning of the colonial period, it did not engender any deep enthusiasm in Burundi until after about 1945. Even then, ongoing ethnic tensions made daily life in Burundi dramatic enough. The only difference between an ordinary citizen and an actor on stage was that for the ordinary citizen the action was not imaginary and the daily dramas were not being observed but rather lived by social groupings in constant perturbation. As well, since most Burundians were illiterate, they preferred their own oral literature to a written one from the west.

As for organized theatrical activities, these emerged most significantly after independence when schooling became a right as opposed to a privilege for most people. Western-style theatre was included in school activities and performances were given of various European classics. By 1967, however, a Burundian had actually written a play in the new style – *Abuzukuru ba Kimotabugabo* (*Grandchildren of the Whole Man*) by Emmanuel Nziko-banyanka. Nzikobanyanka followed the success of this play with two others – *Nagasaga* (*Farewell*) and *Karaba Undabe* (*Wash Yourself, Then Look At Me*).

Other young playwrights followed his lead and several had their plays produced. Among them were Séverin Mfatiye, author of *Semasunzu Yasize Araze* (*Semasunzu's Will*), Fidè Ngenze-buhoro, author of *Mwambiro* (*Yeast*) and *Urwinjizo* (*Rite of Passage*) and Candide Niyon-zima, author of *Ubuntu mu Bantu* (*Dignity of the Human Race*). All were written in Kirundi.

French-language theatre did not emerge until after 1975 when plays by Louis Kamatari and Ambroise Niyonsaba won awards in the Concours théâtral inter-africain (Inter-African Play Competition): Kamatari for *Soweto ou le cri de l'espoir* (*Soweto or The Cry of Hope*) and Niyonsaba for *La Métamorphose* (*The Metamorphosis*).

In 1996, the National Department of Culture – which keeps a catalogue of all publications – had listed 141 Burundian plays written in Kirundi and 127 in French. Of these, 34 (18 in Kirundi and 16 in French) were written by Marie-Louise Sibazuri. There were also four plays written in Swahili and 2 in English.

Structure of the National Theatre Community

Burundi's theatre is essentially amateur although a number of semi-professional theatre artists and groups do exist. The largest number of groups are within the secondary school system, usually connected to language training classes, where both classical European and modern Burundi plays are regularly staged by students.

The next largest grouping would be what can be called 'guild' companies since the actors who compose the groups are all in the same line of work when not on stage. For example, they may all come from the field of transporta-tion, postal services or television. These guild companies generally stage only one production a year with the flexible rehearsal time that implies. Most of the groups receive some sub-sidy from their guilds.

Before the war that began in 1993, there were four semi-professional troupes: the so-called 'Laugh' troupe, the Pili-Pili, the Luxa and the Ada, each presenting two shows annually.

There were also two professional troupes – the Mutabaruka and the Geza Aho – which took turns producing plays every three months or so even during the war, and received direct funding support when they were commissioned to do a play on a particular subject. The radio theatre troupe, Ni Nde, also produced weekly radio dramas and was supported by the national radio and television authority.

Burundi has no specific theatre festivals for western-style plays although in 1983 and 1990 there were two national competitions. Produc-tions tend to be shown on the last weekend of each month. Ticket prices range from double to five times the cost of film tickets and, at minimum, about six times the cost of a loaf of bread.

Touring is rare and there are no unions or theatrical organizations in operation. In 1996 plans were being drawn up, however, for the creation of a theatre society to be called SAADRA.

Traditional performative events, on the other hand, include celebrations for births, wed-dings, deaths, entrance into adulthood and the like. These occur throughout the year and involve a wide variety of performance styles.

Artistic Profile

Companies
Dramaturgy
Directing and Acting

A range of theatre styles can be seen in Burundi including traditional community events involving dance and music, western-style performances of classic plays within the university community, popular theatre events in Kirundi for the wider community (including children), café theatre in the Centre culturel français and marionette and radio/television theatre.

The Geza Aho production of *Barukwege Mwene Niyomuo*.

In 1996, there were only two active companies because of the war: the Ni Nde group which, because it works on radio and television, has a wide national audience and is composed of professional artists; and the Geza Aho which does popular theatre in public halls and has had success in dramatizing traditional tales with dance, drums and song and has also videotaped a number of its performances. Other performing groups suspended their activities because of the unstable political climate.

Most western-style plays follow, consciously or unconsciously, the traditions of indigenous dramatic art – speed for debates and arguments, slowness for complaints etc. In many scripts, dialogue, song, dance, storytelling and even lullabies are interwoven depending on the audience and the circumstances. If the intended audience is young, dialogue will be kept light with a simple, short repartee; for a more mature audience, a text is often enriched with adages and precepts with messages buried so that only initiates understand them.

Some work is being done in theatre for social action and Boal's notion of Theatre of the Oppressed has been attempted. In such performances the audience is encouraged to become involved.

The country's most experienced director is Tharcisse Kalisa-Rugano, former director of the Mutabaruka company.

Theatre for Young Audiences
Puppet and Mask Theatre

On the whole, Burundian theatre does not distinguish between the ages of the audience. Children in traditional theatre attend the same events as adults and this has been carried over into western-style theatre, especially theatre for social action. One of the few events actually to use children as performers was a UNICEF-sponsored performance about AIDS.

There is only one puppet theatre in Burundi, located in the capital. Boasting a very successful repertoire of short plays, the Puppet Theatre, as it is called, is not particularly well known by the general public but it has a steady following among both young and old.

Performances are given whenever a group of ten or more makes a request.

The mask tradition is almost entirely non-existent in the country and masks are worn only when animals are represented on the stage.

Design
Theatre Space and Architecture

Though there are over a hundred spaces in Burundi that are used with some regularity for theatre events, technical support and design are rarely a significant part of the work. Most theatres have rudimentary equipment and in some there is only a raised platform and some curtains. The largest auditorium has 750 seats and the smallest 200.

The best auditoriums are in Bujumbura, the capital, and in Gitega. These include the auditorium of the Islamic Cultural Centre, the French Cultural Centre, the campus of Kiriri University and the commercial Odeon Palace.

Training
Criticism, Scholarship and Publishing

Without a school of theatre in the country, artists are left to their own imaginations and skills on stage. As a result, improvisation is a talent that is highly regarded.

There is also no centre for theatrical research or any company which publishes theatre texts. Criticism is practised informally among playwrights themselves. To date, no books have been written specifically on theatre in Burundi.

Marie-Louise Sibazuri
Translated by Helen Heubi

CAMEROON

An independent nation since 1960, the Republic of Cameroon covers an area of some 475,500 square kilometres (183,600 square miles) in the western part of central Africa. With its southern borders dipping below the equator and its northern tip touching Lake Chad and the Sahara, the country – geographically and culturally – has been appropriately called 'Africa in miniature'. Its population of some 12 million people includes more than 250 different ethnic groups – Bantu in the south, Peul (Fulani) and Fulbe in the north, Tikar in the west and Pygmies and Maka in the east.

It was the Carthaginian navigator Hanno who in the sixth century became the earliest European to explore the Atlantic coast of the territory and who named the 4,070 metre high Mount Fako the 'Chariot of the Gods'. In 1471, the Portuguese explorer Fernão do Po began an exploration of the Wouri River near what is today's port city of Douala. Believing the enormous numbers of crayfish he found there were prawns, he named the river Rio dos Camarões (river of prawns). When the Spanish later arrived, they changed it to the Spanish *camarones*, a name that eventually became Kamerun, the Cameroons, Cameroun and Cameroon, depending on which European nation was occupying it. For the most part, the country's southern area came under European and thus Christian influence while the northern area was exposed more to Arabic and hence Islamic authority.

Germany annexed the country in 1884 as part of a European colonial division of Africa and established vast plantations and cash crops such as bananas, palm kernels and peanuts. When Germany was defeated at the end of World War I, it lost its African colonies and under the Treaty of Versailles in 1919 Britain and France divided up Cameroon. In 1960, after a decade of civil unrest, the eastern part of the country gained its independence as the Republic of Cameroon. The following year, the British Cameroons held its own referendum which resulted in Northern Cameroon becoming part of Nigeria on 1 June, 1961 and Southern Cameroon joining what was to be called the Federal Republic of Cameroon. In 1972 the name was changed to the United Republic of Cameroon and in 1984 simply to the Republic of Cameroon.

Bordered by Nigeria to the west, Gabon, Equatorial Guinea and Congo to the south, and Chad and the Central African Republic to the east, the country's political and cultural autonomy is a complex one to maintain. Also, the existence of two different official colonial languages – French and English – provides its own problems with both linguistic groups vying for hegemony. Yet the country has managed to retain a genuine stability despite these pressures.

Even during the years prior to independence, the liberation war against the French was fought as much on linguistic and literary terrains as on the ground itself. It was not until the liberation forces, led by the Union des Populations du Cameroun (Cameroon People's Union), were subjugated and their leaders replaced by a group more acceptable to the French that independence was achieved. Unfortunately, from independence through 1982, the country wound up being governed as a dictatorship by Ahmadou Ahidjo (1928–92) which left Cameroonians prisoners in virtually every sense of the word.

Censorship in all cultural matters was extensive and draconian laws were passed to enforce them. As a result, many artists went into exile at this time, among them novelists such as Mongo Beti (b. 1930), Ferdinand Oyono (b. 1930) and Francis Bebey (b. 1926). Those playwrights who remained in the country evolved of necessity a symbolic and indirect style.

The plays of this period castigated not only colonialism but also its new Cameroonian equivalents. Many writers affected a naive and often comedic style of speech in their work. Developing a shared understanding of what was being said, their audiences were able to follow the thematic thrust of these works through even the most apparently innocent statements. Not surprisingly, the symbolic theme of marriage came to predominate.

On the other hand, plays of pure indictment and more direct statement – for instance, *Africapolis* (1978) by René Philombe (b. 1930) and *Politicos* (1974) by Jean Evina Mba – rarely made it to the stage. Dissent in the theatre had to be guarded during these years with political control exercised in various ways. Public performances were subjected to administrative authorizations and few public performance areas were made available. Though many plays were produced on radio, this medium too was ultimately controlled by the state.

When Paul Biya (b. 1933) took over as president from Ahidjo in 1982, writers hailed the change and looked forward to a new period of democracy. Ahidjo, however, would not give up control of the party and a dual leadership emerged. Nevertheless, Biya somewhat liberalized the press and allowed more public expression. Several dramatists emerged particularly in and around the University of Yaoundé.

The plays from this period – though their plots were often slight, sometimes even frivolous – retain their social commitment and interest. 'Under' written in an attempt to circumvent censorship, the plays allowed for much improvisation both in rehearsal and performance. Scripts which would appear to play in less than an hour would often run three hours or more in production with dance, music, mime and much new dialogue added.

In 1963, L'Ensemble national des danses traditionelles du Cameroun (Cameroon National Traditional Dance Ensemble) was founded, bringing together dances from various parts of the country. Though Cameroonian in one sense, these pieces, once taken out of their specific cultural contexts, were also somewhat incoherent as an image of one large and complicated multicultural country. A variety show rather than a cultural whole, performances by the group nevertheless represented the new Cameroon around the world and received positive reviews for their colour, vigour and variety in such centres as Moscow, New York, Dakar, Algiers and Osaka. In 1977 the company was reorganized and expanded, now with separate ensembles for dance, music and drama.

Such performance activities have long played an important role in Cameroonian life. Part of the rituals connected with birth, death and other rites of passage, the oral nature of these events has made scholarship and comparisons with Graeco-Roman theatre and drama quite difficult. Additionally, the intervention of colonization and the imposition of European forms on indigenous theatre traditions has meant that their own evolution was severely disrupted and their growth stifled. By imposing a western way of doing things as part of Europe's 'civilizing mission' local traditions and cultural activities became for many years relegated to the realm of anthropological rather than artistic study.

Certainly celebration and ceremony needed to be more deeply understood as did traditional forms of art which have long been open to the community, quite often in a participatory way. The notion of charging to 'see' performances is still considered odd by many and has no place at all when connected to celebratory events such as namings, initiations, betrothals, marriages or burials. Such events – sometimes simple, sometimes complex – are also connected to the celebration of the coming of different seasons, planting and harvesting, and can involve great pomp and circumstance.

Most activities carried out during these occasions are quintessentially histrionic, usually beginning with the traditional 'breaking of kola nuts' and the 'pouring of libations'. Very much part of such events as well is the notion of roleplaying, a clear attempt by the participants to understand not only the environment but also the psychic responses to it by each individual.

Theatre in this sense is often seen as part of the whole rather than as something separate from it, and performance in its various forms is seen as inclusive rather than something separated into genres such as music, dance or speech. Much African theatre is already 'total theatre' and western developments in this direction can be seen as simply catching up with

The *Ngondo*, a Douala traditional festival.
Photo: Ndedi.

existing African performance concepts. Much Cameroonian theatre is therefore syncretic in nature, growing from folk-based narrative performance but over the past century being clearly influenced by the European medieval didactic tradition as well as by plays of classical writers such as Molière and Shakespeare. It is from all these influences that the modern Cameroonian theatre has developed.

The first Cameroonian plays to be written in a European style had actually begun to appear in the late part of the nineteenth century and the early twentieth when the country was under German colonization. Among the earliest of these dramatists was Njoh Dibongue (b. 1869 or 1870) who was sent to Germany to study law and literature. On his return home, he wrote an etiological drama called *Abenteuer Eines See Offiziers*, about the marriage of a marine officer. Written in German, the play on a deeper level is a debate between Mother Earth and Neptune.

Other writers of the period tried their hand at the form as well. Among them were Tongoo Diboundou and Kingue Kwedi, both evangelists. Diboundou, writing in his own language

of Doula, wrote about the ten virgins while Kwedi wrote in French in 1912 a play called *Une Famille à l'attente de nöel* (*A Family Awaiting Christmas*). Yet another religious drama, *L'Annonce de l'enfant Jesu* (*Waiting for Baby Jesus*) by an unknown author was also performed in Douala that same year. Even the expatriate Ridel wrote two plays in German at the time, *Tolongi* and *Der Lieb Sie*, both of which were regularly performed in Douala and Yaoundé between about 1910 and 1916.

With the political changeover after World War I from German to British/French control, both the educational system of the country and the cultural systems began to change. Nevertheless importance was still placed on plays in the colonial languages and works in these languages had the best chance for production. Among them, *Un Jeune homme à la recherche d'une conjointe* (*A Young Man in Search of a Wife*, 1919) had the most success. In 1928, three such plays were performed before the French Resident Governor at the Catholic Church in Mvolye (Yaoundé) – *Yesu Mongo* (*Little Jesus*), *Le Diable dans la bouteille*

(*Devil in the Bottle*) and *Guignol joue sa femme* (*The Clown Taunts His Wife*). Except for these examples, by the 1940s it was still the traditional African events rather than the more literary European-style spoken theatre that dominated. It was the same in the English-speaking part of Cameroon.

In 1942, a group of students at the Normal School in Kake, Kumba, produced with their British principal Charles Low a script called *White Flows the Latex, Ho!*, a musical comedy about life on the plantations and in the military. In the French-speaking part of Cameroon, administered by France as a mandated and later a trust territory under the United Nations, Jean Baptiste Obama (b. 1926) produced *Mbarga Osöno*, an adaptation of Molière's *Scapin* (1943). Lamenting the occupation of France itself during the war, writers wrote of the country's misfortunes in plays such as *Hitler or the Fall of the Hydra* (1944), a play by Louis-Marie Pouka Mbengue (1910–90).

After the war, the first professional theatre troupe in the country was established – L'Association des jeunes artistes camerounais (AJAC: Association of Young Cameroon Artists). Founded in 1955 by Stanislas Owona (b. 1928), a playwright, actor and director, the group staged several of Owona's plays, among them *Le Mariage d'Ebubudu* (*The Marriage of Ebubudu*) and *Le Chômeur* (*The Vagrant*). Two other Cameroonian plays of note also written at this time were *Trois prétendants ... un mari* (*Three Suitors ... One Husband*) by Guillaume Oyono-Mbia (b. 1939), then a student, and *I Am Vindicated* by Sankie Maimo (b. 1936), then a teacher. Both were staged in 1959, the first at the Collège Evangélique de Libamba and the latter at the Mayflower College in Ikpenne, Nigeria.

With the creation of the Ensemble National, on the other hand, according to Alain Gheerbrant, a spokesman for the new company, the goals began to change in an effort to recognize in African performance all the elements that have constituted the basis of the performing arts from time immemorial. One can find the finest expressions of mime, great tragedy worthy of the Greeks ... I am thinking of the Fali funeral rituals. One can find romantic drama, court dances; in sum, all that through the centuries has contributed to the creation of dramatic art. The sole difference is that there is less dialogue than in western theatre ... here the body participates as much as the spirit.

Also, the arts were to help promote national unity. Cameroon, in fact, was not the only African country to use the arts in this way. Similar attempts were made in Guinea with Les Ballets Africains, in Zaïre and in South Africa. With the Ensemble National, the dances covered a wide range of regions and styles and though they retained their overall exuberance they lost much in their transition to public stages. Lacking a genuine social significance or function, these works were selected not for meaning but rather for their ability to be choreographically rich and spectacular. Looked at more were elements such as space, time, energy, body posture, arm gestures and geometric formation. Context, in this sense, had all but disappeared.

Looking back over the country's development since independence it can be fairly said that the arts have reflected both its liberal and strongly centralized tendencies. From the protest literature of the dictatorship years, the number of viewpoints has spread both culturally and politically. In the mid-1990s for example, some 120 different political parties were in operation, each with its own point of view – and each with its own cultural supporters – all determined to be heard on the key issues affecting Cameroon's future.

Structure of the National Theatre Community

There are at any given moment more than a dozen theatre groups operating in Cameroon, most of them in and around the capital of Yaoundé. Only the Ensemble National receives financial support from the government, generally through *ad-hoc*, extra-budgetary items. Other troupes find production support where they can, mostly from universities and/or from foreign cultural services (French Cooperation, Gothe Institute, British Council and American Cultural Centre). International organizations such as UNICEF (United Nations Children's Fund) and GTZ (German International Development Agency) also sponsor theatre activities.

A National Cultural Forum was held in 1990 aimed at creating a state cultural policy

Gilbert Doho's 1989 production of his drama *Wedding of Ashes* at the Hilton Hotel.
Photo: Tagas Vince.

and a basis for government support. While this resulted in the creation of a Ministry of Culture in 1992, the notion of national funding for the arts is still far from being implemented.

In 1968, the country's first theatre union was created – Union des Associations d'Art Dramatique du Cameroun (UNADRAC: Union of Cameroon Drama Associations) – and there is as well an authors' rights association. The latter was formed in 1980 and reorganized in 1990 under the name SOCINADA (Société Civile Nationale des Droits d'Auteur). Officially supporting all creative authors, it tends to focus on musical composers.

There is no system of national theatre awards and other than the Ensemble National, most theatre artists would be classed as semi-professionals or amateurs since they are required to take on non-theatrical work to survive on a daily basis.

Many theatre artists find additional work on CRTV (Cameroon Radio and Television station) which was inaugurated in 1985. Under its first director-general, Etoga Ely (b. 1933), a relatively large number of national plays was produced and this has continued under the director-generalship of Gervais Mendo Ze (b. 1945). Most were filmed directly from the stage rather than being adapted specifically for television. Economic crises in the 1990s have led, however, to a reduction in the number of plays seen on television and to an increase in the number of foreign situation comedies being shown.

Among the leading directors of television drama in the country have been Daouda Moutchangou (b. 1948), Richard Lobe (b. 1949), Thomas Gwangwa'a (b. 1963), Vanessa Sona (b. 1963), Vincent Ndoumbe (b. 1960), Blandine Ambassa (b. 1960) and Robert Ekukolle (b. 1964). Gwangwa'a and Ndoumbe also have been part of two major arts programmes, *Focus on Art* and *Accord Majuscule*, both important in the promotion of national theatre activities.

A Cameroon Centre of the International Theatre Institute was founded in 1988 with Ambroise Mbia (b. 1943) and Bole Butake (b. 1947) as its first president and secretary-general, respectively. This centre initiated the 1988 Colloquium on Cameroon drama and also the Yaoundé Theatre Days, which have since become an annual event.

Artistic Profile

Traditional performative events within each community are generally participatory and involve music, dance and much symbolic enactment. When replicated on stages of theatres such as the Ensemble National, they tend to make up in energy and spectacle what they lose in fidelity and significance.

One example of this is the *maindo*, an expiation ritual that originated among the Pygmies of southeast Cameroon. A celebration of the invincibility of a woodland spirit, the *maindo* reflects humanity's relationship with various supernatural forces that hover above it. It is an attempt to connect both physically and emotionally with them, an encounter ultimately between humanity and the divine.

The performance is usually done in a village square. Musicians and magicians are dressed in full ritual costume. After an opening musical segment, the lead magician goes to the forest and returns with a wounded masked creature. When it attempts to escape, it is pursued in music and dance by the magicians who succeed in overpowering it. As the music builds, the creature – which first appears as a bundle on the ground – begins to gyrate, slowly growing to 4–5 metres. When the music has hit its height, the creature disappears back into the forest.

When transferred to a closed, indoor, proscenium stage, such a performance is bound to lose much of its magic and mysteriousness. Within the village, only specially chosen people may perform it. Since the company's creation, the *maindo* has been seen regularly as part of the Ensemble National's repertoire.

The same is true of the folk narrative, several styles of which exist within the country. Connected to the *griot* tradition, these are chanted or sung performances which transmit the history of the community, teaching community traditions and mores, articulating the values of the group, utilizing and establishing symbols and ideals. In such an environment, the performer's role is essential to the very fabric of the community and has been developed into an extraordinarily high art.

Another artistic form of note is the *mvet*, found mainly in the South and Central Provinces of Cameroon as well as in the northern parts of Gabon, Congo and Equatorial Guinea. The *mvet* is built around a performer with exceptional verbal and rhythmic memory who has complete familiarity with large and varied stock of standard or formulaic phrases and themes. The form includes not only the use of voice but also movement, music, mime and dance. The *mvet* virtuoso (*mbomo mvet*) must be able to impersonate various characters and be a master of witty repartee to hold an audience during narratives that sometimes go on for an entire night.

In a *mvet* performance, usually outdoors, the members of a family or a village gather in a semicircle around the performer (and his orchestra where there is one) and the performance slowly begins. Time and space are being utilized in a fluid way. Often functional, these pieces tend to be somewhat didactic as they seek to release community feelings. They often comment on social changes as well. The form's basic elements include impersonation as well as the use of colour, texture and movement and deal with states of existence and emotional qualities. The conclusion tends to underscore the meaning and relevance of the whole. As in most of these forms, the audience, which is usually familiar with the story, is encouraged to comment on and interact with the performer whose skill is judged by his narrative imagination.

Another style with a special Cameroonian bent in the theatre is that of stand-up comedy using a particularly crude type of language, most often in French. Although critical opinion tends to be harsh on these 'humourists' because of what is said to be their vulgarizing influence on the quality of language, they have succeeded where many others have failed in actually bringing people into the theatre. Among the best known during the 1980s and 1990s have been Dave K. Moktoi (b. 1955), Essindi Minja (b. 1958), Tchop-Tchop (b. 1965), Njike René (stage name Masa Atré, b. 1958), Daniel Ndo (b. 1948), Jimmy Biyong (b. 1955), Kouokam Narcisse (b. 1955) and Dieudonné Afana (stage name Jean Miché Kankan, b. 1952).

Since the late 1980s, several attempts at creating a more western-style dance-drama have been made. Two such attempts were *Djeki la Njambè* (1988), based on the folk narrative of the same name from the Littoral area, and *The Courageous Cry* (1994), written and directed by the Nigerian Edet Ekpenyong and sponsored by the British Council. The *Djeki* performance featured the septuagenarian

Titi Koulle and was coordinated by University of Douala professor Grace Tonde Ekoto.

Companies

From its official founding in 1977, the Ensemble National has been the country's largest and most active production company with separate groups working in dance, spoken drama (almost exclusively in the French language) and music. The dance company in the beginning had some 140 members and produced regular seasons. By the mid-1990s, however, the troupe had been reduced for economic reasons to about 30 members, all paid on a per performance basis. Its first director was Philippe Dauchez of France.

The Ensemble dance troupe usually works with the Ensemble musicians and one can see in any performance not only dancers but also a wide variety of instruments as well as singers who chant and recite. Its orchestra includes varying sizes and styles of drums, string instruments, bow-lutes, rattles, clappers, whistles, xylophones, horns and trumpets.

Costumes for Ensemble performances include fine headgear, masks, and voluminous dresses including material from tree bark, animal skins, cotton, raffia, leaves, feathers and cowries. Masks are often carved and patterned after human or animal figures – comic or tragic, male or female – but are never presented naturalistically. In their village settings, some of the masks are said to have spiritual attributes although this is obviously not the case when they are replicated for the performances. This said, many of the dancers make certain they are expiated before donning them.

Prior to the creation of this company public performances on this model could be seen, mainly in the French-speaking part of the country, in the French Cultural Centres in Yaoundé and Douala, at the American Cultural Centre in Yaoundé and in various college and church halls around the country.

Perhaps the best-known director of the Ensemble National has been Ambroise Mbia. Beginning his career in agriculture he later became interested in acting and migrated to Paris for a time. In 1977 he was secretary-general of the Festival of Art and Culture held in Lagos. Later returning to Cameroon, he was appointed head of the Cameroon Cultural Centre, in 1986 Deputy Director of Culture and in 1995 Deputy Director of National Heritage. Creator of the Yaoundé Theatre Days in 1989, his stage productions of mostly African plays have tended to be on the spectacular side. Director of the Ensemble National from 1978 to 1984, his major production there was a 1982 production of Ivoirian Bernard Dadié's play, *Beatrice du Congo* (*Beatrice of the Congo*), still the most expensive production ever mounted in Cameroon.

Another director of the Ensemble National, Francis Njoumouni (b. 1948), was also trained in France. His most important productions with the company included Soyinka's *The Lion and the Jewel* (1987) and Jean Evina Mba's *Politicos* in 1988. Following the latter production, he was dismissed as the Ensemble National's director and, though he has since become head of Cultural Animation, has generally kept away from directing.

Geneviève Bounya Epée née Kuoh (b. 1955) was named director of the Ensemble National in 1989 but the limited nature of the company's repertoire as well as the theatre's depressed financial situation during this time made it difficult for her to make any significant impression.

French-born Jacqueline Leloup (b. 1945) was instrumental in the development of theatre within the University of Yaoundé and her early work had support from both the university and the French Mission for Cooperation and Cultural Action. In 1975, Leloup created a Club d'Art Dramatique (Dramatic Arts Club) which soon became the Théâtre Universitaire (University Theatre). Shortly thereafter, an English section was created by playwright and theatrical animateur Hansel Ndumbe Eyoh (b. 1949) who had recently returned to Cameroon after completing a doctorate at the University of Leeds. First calling the troupe the Barombi Players, then the Yaoundé University Experimental Theatre and finally in 1982 the Yaoundé University Theatre, Eyoh and Leloup both received support from the university for their work. In addition Leloup was able to count on continuing additional support from the French government.

Her shows from 1975 to 1985 tended to be fully produced while Eyoh's, which focused more on local concerns, were much more modest in style. Doing one major show per year, Leloup's only attempts at staging national work were her controversial adaptation of Sophocles' *Oedipus Rex* under the title *Guiedo* (1983) and *Meyong Meyome au royaume des morts* (*Meyong Meyome in the Land of the*

Jacqueline Leloup's 1984 Yaoundé University Theatre production of *Guiedo* with Teufack Auber in the title role.
Photo: T. Tchatse.

Dead, 1985). Eyoh's smaller productions, on the other hand, included Soyinka's *The Lion and the Jewel* (1982), Fugard's *Sizwe Bansi Is Dead* (1983) and Bole Butake's *The Rape of Michelle* (1985). Leloup later left Cameroon for the Republic of Congo, eventually returning to France. Eyoh remained at the university until 1986 when he was appointed Director of Cultural Affairs in the Ministry of Information and Culture.

Replacing Leloup and Eyoh at the university were Gilbert Doho (b. 1954) and Bole Butake, Doho running the French-language Théâtre Universitaire and Butake running the English-language University Theatre. Butake maintained Eyoh's small production tradition while Doho, who did his graduate work in theatre at the University of Lyon, turned his group away from the international repertoire and into a much more socially committed company with himself as both playwright and director. By the 1990s, however, both troupes found it difficult to fund their performances, even within the university, due to the growing argument for 'anglophone rights'. The university's support of this position was seen as anti-government.

Among earlier troupes of note in Yaoundé which regularly staged new plays, mostly at the French Cultural Centre, were the Associations des jeunes artistes Camerounais (Association of Young Cameroonian Artists), a troupe founded by playwright-director Stanislas Owona (b. 1928); Le Négro Star (Negro Star) founded by Adolphe Mballa (b. 1947); L'Avant-Garde Africaine (African Avant-Garde) founded by Dikongue Pipa (b. 1945); Les Compagnons de la Comédie (Comedy Companions) founded by Marcel Mvondo (b. 1938); and the most ambitious of the groups, Les Tréteaux d'Ebène (Ebony Stage) begun by Charles Nyatte (b. 1946).

Other groups were Les Étudiants Associés (Associated Students) begun by playwright Raymond Ekossono (b. 1954); Les Étudiants du Rénouveau (New Deal Students) founded by Rabiatou Njoya (b. 1945); Le Théâtre Saisonnier (Seasonal Theatre) founded by Lucien Mamba (b. 1941); and the Flame Players, founded in 1988 by Godfrey Tangwa (b. 1947).

Several actors in the Ensemble National also have created their own occasional groups. The best known has been Keki Manyo's (b. 1954) Les Perles Noires (Black Pearls) which has tended to stage mostly foreign plays from school syllabuses.

Yaoundé has always dominated the country's theatrical life to the point that it is sometimes forgotten that other cities and towns also have their own theatres. Douala and Buea follow Yaoundé and there is also some theatrical activity to be found in Bamenda, Bafoussam and Garoua. The best known troupe in the provinces is the Musinga Drama Group founded in Buea in 1974 by Victor Eleame Musinga (b. 1944).

Dramaturgy
Directing and Acting

Cameroonian dramatic literature draws extensively from myths and legends as well as from the popular folklore. The myths help audiences maintain connections with their ancestry and provide a continuous transmission of knowledge and wisdom, while legends help reinforce notions of patriotism and loyalty. These are clearly reflected in contemporary plays, especially in those which tend toward social relevance in subject matter.

Unlike Ghanaian dramatic literature, which often emerged from the Concert Party tradition,

Daniel Nguelle as the Sorcerer in Jacqueline Leloup's 1984 Yaoundé University Theatre production of *Guiedo* at the French Cultural Centre.
Photo: T. Tchatse.

or Nigerian drama, which emerged in part from Yoruba Opera, Cameroonian drama did not grow directly from the traditional dance or narrative performance but it has continued to be informed by them. The growing attempt in the years after World War II – a response to colonialism – has been to return to root sources. The emergence of the Negritude movement in the 1940s (the recognition and identification of African equivalents of European ideas and traditions), led by the Senegalese poet and statesman Léopold Sédar Senghor and the West Indian Aimé Césaire, as well as the reawakening of the 'African Personality' in the late 1950s, provided a new orientation to Africans in valorizing their own culture. Both these movements and their many interpretations – along with the theatrical examples of Wole Soyinka's plays – have provided impetus for contemporary Cameroonian drama both in opposition and affirmation.

Perhaps the first modern Cameroonian dramatist of note is Guillaume Oyono-Mbia (b. 1939) whose 1959 Molière-styled comedy,

Trois prétendants ... un mari, is still one of the staples of national dramatic literature. The play is not only read in schools but also produced. It has been translated into English, Swedish, Spanish and Russian. Other plays by Oyono-Mbia include *Jusqu'à nouvel avis* (*Until Further Notice*, 1970), *Notre fille ne se mariera pas* (*Our Daughter Won't Marry*, 1973, later made into a film by the Cameroonian Daniel Kamwa), *Le Train spécial de son Excellence* (*His Excellency's Special Train*, 1976) and *Le Boubier* (1989). During the 1990s, Oyono-Mbia turned away from the stage, saying that his plays had been exploited by publishers and producers who all made money from them while he himself earned nothing. His later work has tended to be in the short story genre. Published in both Britain (Methuen, 1968) and in France (ORTF/DAEC, 1973), his plays have been produced by the Concours théâtral interafricain (Inter-African Theatre Competition) and by the BBC.

Many other Cameroonian dramatists, inspired by Oyono-Mbia's success, have also tried their hands at writing for the Radio France Concours. Between 1966 and 1982, in fact, Cameroonian writers submitted 845 scripts to Radio France and won an unusually large number of prizes. Among the winners were Jean Baptiste Obama (b. 1926) with *Assimilados* (*Assimilated*), Antoine Epassy (b. 1952) with *Les Asticots* (*The Guys*) and Protais Aasseng (b. 1954) with *Trop c'est trop* (*Much Too Much*).

Among established English-speaking dramatists is Sankie Maimo whose first major success was with *I Am Vindicated* in 1959. Among his important later plays are *Sov-Mbang the Soothsayer* (1968), *The Mask* (1970), *Succession in Sarkov* (1981), *Sasse Symphony* (1989) and *Retributive Justice* (1992). Like Oyono-Mbia, Maimo too has proven an effective writer in the short story genre.

Among the writers who emerged since the liberalization of the 1970s have been Victor Eleame Musinga, Alexandre Kum'a Ndumbe (b. 1945), Joseph Kegni (b. 1947), Bidoung Mkpatt (b. 1952) and Bole Butake. Musinga has more than ten plays to his credit including *The Tragedy of Mr No Balance* (1976) while Ndumbe's output includes *Ach Kamerun unsere Deutsche Kolonie* (*Oh Cameroon, Once a German Colony*, 1970) and *Cannibalisme* (*Cannibalism*, 1973). Butake's most recent plays include *And Palm Wine Will Flow* (1990) and *Shoes and Four Men in Arms* (1994).

Other writers of note who emerged during the 1980s and 1990s have been Hansel Ndumbe Eyoh, Bate Besong (b. 1958), Victor Epie Ngome (b. 1952), Babila Mutia (b. 1958), Benedicta Mufuh (b. 1954), Désiré Naha, Pierre Makon (b. 1954), Joseph Kengni (b. 1947), and one of the country's few women writers, Mbarga Kouma Charlotte (b. 1941). Gilbert Doho (b. 1954) came to note with the 1989 play *Noces de cendres* (*Wedding of Ashes*) and *Le Crane* (*The Skull*, 1995) while

Emmanuel Tabi as the Chief in Bole Butake's 1991 University of Buea production of *And Palm Wine Will Flow*.

Eyoh's latest play was *The Reserved Forest* (1995).

Perhaps the country's best known director and actor is Wéré-Wéré Liking (b. 1947) who has worked extensively in theatre involving music and dance. In 1984 she moved to Abidjan in Côte d'Ivoire, where she continues working with her troupe, Ki Yi Mbok. She made her first appearance in Cameroon in 1978 with a production called *Ngonga*.

Theatre for Young Audiences
Puppet and Mask Theatre

The major children's theatre in the country is Théâtre du Chocolat (Chocolate Theatre) founded by Roger-Joseph Etoundi (b. 1955) who works under the professional name Etoundi Zeyang. Etoundi first began staging shows for children in 1981 when he created the

first episode in what has become a continuing series for the company called *Les Aventures de Bobo et Mangetout*. These are two slapstick characters – Bobo, very thin and witty; Mangetout (Eat-all), very fat and stupid, representative of the nouveau riche – who have become

Hansel Eyoh's 1990 Yaoundé Children's Theatre Collective production of his play *Munyenge* at the Goethe Institute, Yaoundé.
Photo: Hansel Eyoh.

immensely popular. More than thirty shows have been created to date using the Bobo and Mangetout characters.

Another group working in this field, Bounya Epée's (b. 1955) Black Expression, felt it necessary for children's theatre to include social problems rather than avoiding them. Working mostly in Yaoundé, the group during its short existence in the 1980s staged a number of effective productions including the widely praised *Baïnou, le Paresseux* (*Baïnou the Lazy*).

In 1989, Hansel Ndumbe Eyoh founded the Yaoundé Children's Theatre Collective. The next year, the group performed in Lingen, Germany, at the First World Festival of Children's Theatre

staging his play *Munyenge*. In 1991, the group did a second production, *The Magic Fruit*, but disbanded shortly thereafter.

Though puppetry in the European sense does not really exist in Cameroon, there is a mask tradition in the country as well as a masquerade tradition featuring children wearing masks especially around Christmas and Easter. Similar to the North American Halloween tradition, children go from house to house hoping for treats or money.

The only European-style puppet group to have been seen in the country to date was in 1988 when a German company played at the Goethe Institute in Yaoundé.

Design

There are few trained designers in Cameroon. This said, three designers from the Ensemble National were trained in China – Emmanuel Ambah (b. 1955), Kouam Tawadje (b. 1954) and Ndebi Ndebi (b. 1955). None of the three,

however, has worked regularly enough either at the Ensemble National or anywhere else to make a living. As a result, all three have moved on to other work in graphic arts and television.

Theatre Space and Architecture

Cameroon's only purpose-built theatre is the Palais des Congrès in Yaoundé (the Yaoundé Conference Centre), built by the Chinese and commissioned by Ahmadou Ahidjo as his last public act as president in 1982. Towering over the city near Mount Febe Hill, the Centre has a 1,500 seat multipurpose performance hall with an ultra-modern stage boasting the country's best sound and lighting equipment. Unfortunately, costs of hiring the hall are beyond the possibilities of most of the country's theatre groups.

More accessible in terms of costs and location are facilities at the French Cultural Centre whose proscenium theatre seats about 400. The Cameroon Cultural Centre, on the other hand, is home to the Ensemble National. Refurbished in the early 1980s, it was by the mid-1990s, however, in need of yet another restoration.

The University of Yaoundé (formerly the Federal University of Cameroon and since 1993 known as University of Yaoundé I) has several amphitheatres which are regularly used for theatrical events. The most popular one is Amphi 700, built in 1973 as a lecture hall but remodelled in 1980 as a theatre.

Other spaces used for theatrical performances include stages of various sorts at the Goëthe Institute (150 seats), the Hilton Hotel (up to 700 seats), Catholic University, the École Normale Supérieure, the National School of Posts, and the National School of Administration and Magistracy.

In the provinces, cinemas, churches and college halls tend to be used. Most of these facilities have poor acoustics and little technical equipment.

Hansel Eyoh's 1992 Yaoundé University Theatre production of his drama *The Inheritance* at the Hilton Hotel.
Photo: Hansel Eyoh.

Training

Professional training is one of the country's weak points. Though Cameroon has innumerable talented people in all fields – acting, directing, playwriting, set and costume design and even lighting and sound – few have been formally trained. Often playwrights simply bring together people they know and stage plays themselves as best they can. As a result of this situation, it is not surprising to find writers also playing leading roles and serving as their own promotion managers.

On the academic side, within the University of Yaoundé an optional programme in theatre arts has existed since 1980 under the Faculty of Letters and Social Sciences while in 1989 a Master's degree in Performing Arts was introduced. Many of the Master's degree graduates have subsequently gone into education where they have begun to include dramatic literature and theatre performances in secondary school curricula. In the early 1990s, degree courses in the performing arts were introduced at both the University of Yaoundé I and at the new University of Buea.

Professional workshops have been offered on an occasional basis at the Ensemble National since 1976, with guests usually brought in from abroad.

Criticism, Scholarship and Publishing

Scholarship in theatre has been a fairly recent phenomenon in the country. A colloquium on Cameroon theatre was held in 1988 and the proceedings were published under the title *Théâtre Camerounais: Cameroonian Theatre* and this remains a useful source of information. In 1994 a conference on Cameroon literature was held at the University of Buea at which several papers on Cameroon drama were presented. During 1995 a colloquium specifically on Cameroon drama was held at the French Cultural Centre in Yaoundé.

Other than the published results of the above conference proceedings, most information is available in doctoral dissertations written by Cameroonians studying in Britain, the United States, France and Nigeria.

Useful information can be found in Banham and Wake's *African Theatre Today* (1976), Dorothy Blair's *African Literature in French* (1976), Anthony Brench's *Writing in French from Sénégal to Cameroon* (1967), Oyin Ogunba and Abiola Irele's *Theatre in Africa* (1978), Michael Etherton's *The Development of African Drama* (1982) and in Richard Bjornson's *The African Quest for Freedom and Identity* (1991). A bibliography of Cameroon theatre was published in 1986 by Wolfgang Zimmer.

Valuable information on both Cameroonian and African theatre generally can be found in issues of *African Theatre Review*, a respected but short-lived journal whose three issues were published between 1985 and 1987 under the editorship of Siga Asanga of the Department of African Literature at the University of Yaoundé. Several articles on Cameroon theatre have also appeared in journals and newspapers such as *Abbia, Cameroun littéraire, New Horizons, Ngam, Cameroon Tribune* and *Cameroon Post*.

Though very few Cameroon plays have been published, more than 2,000 have been written. Most exist only in typescript format and disappear far too quickly.

Hansel Ndumbe Eyoh, Bole Butake,
Gilbert Doho, Asheri Kilo,
Oyi-Ndzie Polycarpe

Further Reading

Asanga, Siga, ed. *African Theatre Review.* Department of African Literature, University of Yaoundé, Vols. 1, 2, 3, 1985–7.

Banham, Martin with Clive Wake. *African Theatre Today.* London: Pitman, 1976.

Bjornson, Richard. *The African Quest for Freedom and Identity.* Bloomington, IN: Indiana University Press, 1991.

Blair, Dorothy. *African Literature in French.* London: Cambridge University Press, 1976.

Brench, Anthony Cecil. *Writing in French from Sénégal to Cameroon.* London: Oxford University Press, 1967. 153 pp.

Butake, Bole and Gilbert Doho. *Le Théâtre camerounais/Cameroonian Theatre: Proceedings of the Conference on Cameroon Theatre.* Yaoundé: BET, 1987.

Cornévin, Robert. *Le Théâtre en Afrique noire et à Madagascar* [The theatre in Black Africa and Madagascar]. Paris: Le livre africain, 1970. 334 pp.

Doho, Gilbert. 'L'Espace dans le théâtre africain' [The African theatre space]. PhD dissertation, Université de Lyon II, 1983.

———. 'La Vie théâtral au Cameroun de 1940 à nos jours' [Theatre life in Cameroon since 1940]. PhD dissertation, Université de Paris III, 1992.

Etherton, Michael. *The Development of African Drama*. London: Hutchison, 1982.

Eyoh, Hansel, Ndumbe. *Beyond the Theatre: Interviews with Selected Popular Theatre Practitioners*. Bonn: DSF, 1992.

———. 'Changing the Set: 30 Years of Cameroonian Drama'. In *Small Is Beautiful: Proceedings of the International Federation of Theatre Research 1990 Conference*, eds Claude Schumacher and Derek Fogg. Glasgow: Theatre Studies Publication, 1991.

———. 'The Development of Drama in Cameroon: 1959–1979'. PhD dissertation, University of Leeds, 1979.

———. *Hammocks to Bridges: An Experience in Theatre Development*. Yaoundé: BET, 1986.

Hourantier, Marie-José. *Du rituel au théâtre* [From ritual to theatre]. Paris: L'Harmattan, 1984.

———, Wéré-Wéré Liking and Jacques Scherer. *Du rituel à la scène chez les Bassa du Cameroun* [From ritual to the stages of the Bassa of Cameroon]. Paris: A.G. Nizet, 1979.

Kasteloot, Lylian. *Les Écrivains noir de la langue française* [Black writers in French]. Brussels, 1965.

Kilo, Asheri. 'The Development of Cameroon Anglophone Theatre'. PhD dissertation, University of Leeds, 1991.

Magnier, Bernard. *Théâtre d'Afrique noire* [Theatre in Black Africa]. Paris: Présence Africaine, 1984.

Melone, Thomas, ed. *Mélanges africains* [The African mix]. Paris, 1973.

Notre Librairie 99, Paris: CLEF, 1989.

Nouvel du Sud. Special issue (June–July 1987). Paris: Silex, 1987.

Ogunba, Oyin and Abiola Irele, eds. *Theatre in Africa*. Ibadan, Nigeria: Ibadan University Press, 1978.

Ongoum, Louis Marie and Celestin Tcheho. *Littérature orale de l'Afrique contemporaine: approches théoriques et pratiques* [African oral literature: theory and practice]. Actes du colloque international. Yaoundé: CEPER, 1989.

Présence Africaine. *Actes du Colloques d'Abidjan sur le théâtre négro-african* [Proceedings from the Abidjan Colloquium on Black African Theatre]. Paris: Présence Africaine, 1967.

Revue Écriture 4 and 5, Département de Français, University of Yaoundé 1.

Scherer, Jacques. *Le Théâtre en Afrique noire francophone* [Francophone Black African theatre]. Paris: Presses Universitaires de France, 1992.

Zimmer, Wolfgang. *Bibliographie du théâtre camerounais* [Bibliography of Cameroonian theatre]. Sarrebruck: University of the Sarre, 1983. 79 pp.

———, *Répertoire du théâtre camerounais* [Repertory of Cameroonian theatre]. Paris: L'Harmattan, 1986.

CHAD

(Overview)

Located in north central Africa, landlocked Chad extends from the Sahara Desert in the north – and its border with Libya – to tropical Africa in the south where it shares borders with Cameroon and the Central African Republic and to Niger and Nigeria in the west and Sudan in the east. Chad has an overall land area of 1,271,000 square kilometres (490,700 square miles), about twice the size of France.

With more than two hundred ethnic groups, Chad had an estimated (1994) population of just under 5.5 million. Of these, the majority are Muslims in the north and central parts of the country and non-Muslims in the rest. Over one hundred different dialects and/or languages are spoken in the country with French and Arabic as the official languages country-wide and Sara and Sango as additional official languages in the south. Chad is politically divided into fourteen prefectures. Most of the population are farmers who live near Lake Chad and in the Logone and Shari river valleys in the south. Civil war, drought and food shortages have caused major problems in the country in the years since World War II.

Over many centuries, major African empires flourished in this region around Lake Chad including the Baguirmi, the Kanem, the Bornu and the Wadai. Arab conquerors introduced Islam in the eleventh century. French explorers reached the area in the 1890s as the power of local African empires was declining. By 1913, the French controlled the entire area.

In 1940, following the German occupation of France, Chad became the first French African territory to support the Free French, an action which prevented the German takeover of other French African colonies. A major Allied supply base, Chad, after the war, took control of its own government by agreement with France and fifteen years later – in 1960 – became an independent republic.

The first president of Chad was François Tombalbaye who in 1962 banned all political parties but his own. This led to protests which were exacerbated when conflicts broke out between Muslims in the north and those mostly non-Muslims living in the south. Military aid from France continued between 1969 and 1975 and then again in 1978.

In 1975, Tomalbaye was killed during a military coup and Félix Malloum became the new president with Hissène Habré, former head of the northern army, the new prime minister. A provisional government representing the major ethnic and religious groups was established in 1979, ending the country's thirteen-year civil war. Despite various reforms in the years since, more than 75 per cent of the country was still illiterate in 1995.

It can be said with some accuracy that virtually all important celebratory events in Chad from births to weddings and funerals still include theatrical elements – dance, music and significant amounts of storytelling. Many modern ventures into western styles of theatre have included some of these elements as well.

It was the arrival of the French colonists in the late nineteenth century which introduced a European style of theatre in the country mostly in schools and through missionaries. Various *ad-hoc* efforts led to the formation of two amateur groups in 1939, one through the scouting movement called Coeurs Vaillantes

(Valiant Hearts) and another through the Christian youth movement called the Ames Vaillantes (Valiant Souls). Performances by these groups were meant chiefly to arouse the interest of indigenous populations in biblical scriptures in much the same spirit as the Mystery plays of medieval Europe.

The country's first independent theatre company – La Comédie du Chari – was founded in 1967 through the Centre Culturel Français (French Cultural Centre) in the capital, N'Djaména (then called Fort Lamy). Two years later, a national theatre company, the Théâtre National du Chad, and a national dance troupe, the Ballet National du Chad, were established.

The creation of these groups was made possible by a series of changes in the structure of the government during the decade as culture become an independent office within the National Ministry of Education. The newly formed Direction de la Culture became responsible for coordinating and animating all cultural affairs as well as for surveying cultural activities both in and outside of schools. This included community cultural activities, folk culture and animation within the various Regional Cultural Centres.

Despite the new interest, however, the Théâtre National du Chad has essentially remained an amateur group though it has had a paid, professional director. Most of its actors are students who stay with the group for only a season or two until they finish their studies and then move on. Though the company receives modest state support, it is clearly not enough to change its status significantly.

One of the few groups to work regularly enough to claim at least semi-professional status has long been Le Théâtre Vivant Baba Moustapha. This company is also the only one from Chad to ever play outside the borders: in 1986 it played in Cameroon; in 1988 in the Central African Republic; and in 1989 it played in Bénin, Togo and Burkina Faso. Several actors from the group have also studied in France.

With the Moustapha company providing inspiration, theatre activity has grown and in 1995 some forty-three groups were operating, at least one in virtually every city of any size. Playwrights have also emerged from several of these groups. Among them are Samuel Bebnone Palou, Baba Moustapha, Maoudé Naindouba, Dangde Laobele Damaye and Kari Djimet (the pen-name of Garang Ko-Tourou).

Bebnone Palou is the author of Chad's major historical epic, *Mbang Gaourang*, which examines the rulership of the King of Baguirmi, who signed the agreement making Chad a French Protectorate.

Baba Moustapha and Maoudé Naindouba both tend to write more political plays. Moustapha's *Makari aux épines* (*Makari of the Thorns*) is a caustic criticism of the corrupt dictatorial regimes that the old colonial system instigated and encouraged while Naindouba's play, *L'Étudiant de Soweto* (*Soweto Student*), deals with apartheid in South Africa. The latter play won the Ninth Concours théâtral inter-africain (Inter-African Theatre Competition) in 1978.

Laobele Damaye's *Les Arrivistes* (1974) is a satire on contemporary corruption and nepotism, two plagues that have afflicted many African nations late in the twentieth century. The play was widely produced in 1975–6.

Moustapha and Kari Djimet have both written social satires as well, Moustapha in *Achua ou le Drâme d'une fille-mère* (*Achua or The Drama of an Unwed Mother*) and Djimet in *Le Crime de la dot* (*Crime of the Dowry*).

As for spaces, traditional performances are always held outdoors and are part of regular holiday periods while performances of spoken dramas are generally held in cultural centres or conference halls. In N'Djaména, the most popular venues are the facilities of the Centre Culturel Français with 410 seats; the 300-seat Maison des Jeunes et de la Culture; and the conference hall of the Ministry of Foreign Affairs which holds 1,200. In 1993, a Maison du Peuple was inaugurated, a space devoted almost exclusively to theatrical activities.

There are no training schools for theatre within the country, meaning that anyone interested in pursuing advanced skills must go abroad and those so interested usually go to France. Likewise, there are no publications in the country dealing with theatre or dramatic activities nor have scholars at the Université du Chad shown much interest in the subject. The few plays to have appeared in print have also been published abroad, again mostly in France and usually with the support of UNESCO and/or the Concours théâtral inter-africain.

Garang Ko-Tourou
Translated by Helen Heubi

Further Reading

Bebnone Palou, Samuel. *Mbang Gaourang*. Paris: UNESCO.

Djimet, Kari. *Le Crime de la dot* [Crime of the dowry]. Paris: UNESCO.

Moustapha, Baba. *Achua ou le Drâme d'une fille-mère* [Achua or the drama of an unwed mother]. Paris: UNESCO.

———. *Le Commandant Chaka* [Commander Chaka]. (Monde noir poche, no. 19). Paris: Hatier/CEDA, 1983.

———. *Makari aux épines* [Makari of the thorns]. Paris: NEA/CLE, 1979.

Naindouba, Maoudé. *L'Étudiant de Soweto* [Soweto student]. Paris.

CONGO

(Overview)

The country that is now known as the Congo lies across the Equator on the western side of central Africa. Once part of the powerful Kongo nation which lived along the most important river in central Africa, the 2,900 mile Congo River, the country shares borders to the south and east with Angola and Zaïre and to the north and west with the Central African Republic, Cameroon and Gabon.

The earliest settlers in the region were Pygmies, who lived throughout modern Congo and Zaïre from about the year AD 1000 when they were pushed into the region as the Bantu people of Cameroon moved southward. Today they are found only in the northeast of the country. The Congo covers an area of some 349,000 square kilometres (134,800 square miles) and has a population of just under 2.5 million people (1994).

The largest of the fifteen mostly Bantu ethnic groups in the region is the Bakongo who live chiefly in the Brazzaville area. Within this group are found the twelve original clans of the Kingdom of Kongo presided over by the *Meni-Kongo*, a ruler elected by universal suffrage from the twelfth century onward. Other ethnic groups include Batéké, Vili, M'Bochi and Sangha. Several Bantu languages are spoken in the Congo but French remains the official administrative language.

The first European to have set foot in this area was the Portuguese navigator Diego Cão, who encountered the mouth of the Congo River as he sailed down the west coast of Africa in 1482. Over the next 350 years the area became a lucrative centre for the slave trade until the Treaty of Vienna in 1815 outlawed the practice. French and Scandinavian missionaries began to arrive in the region in the early 1700s but did not travel very far inland until the late 1800s. In 1874, the English explorer, Henry Stanley, began a three-year exploration of the length of the Congo River with a group that included three white men and three hundred Africans, more than half of whom died during the voyage.

In 1880, Pierre Savorgnan de Brazza (1852–1905) established a trading post that would become modern Brazzaville and his treaties with the Batéké leaders helped establish a strong French presence in the area. In 1903 France gave the name Middle Congo to the region and in 1910 the Middle Congo – along with Chad, Gabon and Ubangi-Chari – became part of the territory known as French Equatorial Africa. In 1958, French Equatorial Africa was dissolved and after a period as a self-governing member of the French Community, the Congo in 1960 became independent.

The country is now almost evenly divided between those who practise Christianity and those who follow traditional animist beliefs with a small percentage of Muslims in the northeast part of the country. About 70 per cent of the population lives in or between the port city of Pointe-Noire on the Atlantic coast and the capital city of Brazzaville, some 250 miles or so to the east.

As for Congolese theatrical activities, most relate to traditional cultural rituals and forms and most include a range of activities including storytelling, music and movement. Four of the forms – *kingizila*, *lemba*, *nkoloba* and *miloko* – are based on a repertoire of texts that are most often sung. The key artists (*bisi kwimba*) are a hereditary lineage of troubadours who maintain the forms and skills and pass them down from generation to generation.

Over the centuries, *bisi kwimba* have survived various attempts by zealous missionaries determined to wipe out 'heathen' forms and styles. Among the most famous *bisi kwimba* have been Moni-Mambou, Ngabiyelo and Bangu, artists who, in many cases, had to disguise their art under other names or masquerade under false totems. The most famous traditional performance piece is called *The Grand Tax*.

The *kingizila* itself is closely connected to health and healing. Two forms of *kingizila* exist – one involving the people as a whole and another restricted only to royalty and known as the *mfumu*. In both forms, an ill person is at the centre and the purpose of the art is to make them well. If the central figure is a commoner, the event is public; if a royal personage, the event is private. The event, the performance, the curative 'script' is repeated fourteen times over forty-two days (i.e. once every three days). At the end of this period, the patient is either cured or declared possessed (*yeza*). Clearly this is not theatre in a European sense but it is nevertheless enacted ritual, rehearsed and repeated with a specific social goal in mind.

Other performative forms are equally diverse. The *lemba*, for example, is a kind of theatre for the very wealthy and could take years to prepare. Among the elements needing to be clearly set is the defined trail (*lumbu* or fence) leading to the performance area; the costumes, which had to be satisfactory to the actor or the performance could be postponed; and the teaching of each participant an important truth or secret (*mpungu a lemba*). The director of the event as a whole is known as the *nganga a lemba* or *lemba* doctor. Looked at in this light, the *lemba* can be seen as a theatre of wisdom.

Another type of performance involves *nkolabas* or wooden statues. Akin to puppet theatre, it involves three couples, a musician and a narrator (in many cases two statuettes play the roles). The *nkolaba* story could be set anytime – past, present or future. Involving music and drawing from a well-known repertoire of songs – dramatic, comic or tragic – the performance is put together by a master director called *nganga a nkoloba*.

Still another theatrical form found in the Congo is *miloko*, a theatre of confrontation with the dead. The assumption here is that both the living and the dead have responsibilities to their society. When the dead, as on occasion happens, neglect their duties, the living are encouraged to express their complaints. First, invocations are offered. If these do not suffice, a fable is constructed in which the living and the dead are presented in confrontation. Each are represented by specific performers. Those who play the dead must enter into communication with those whom they represent and present their cases. Such performances take place at night, usually in a village of the dead (a cemetery) where the dead may be contacted. The event takes place under a giant tree which represents all of nature and which acts as a witness.

One final form of traditional performance is the *wala* or theatre of war. There are two forms of *wala* – one originating as dance for the warriors themselves, and another done in a designated place by spiritual shamans who recall in story form the battle sagas of the nation. It is the floor itself – *wala-wala* – which gives the form its name (*wala-wala* itself means literally 'drawing the role').

For the Congolese, war was the art of killing an enemy according to laws known to men and gods, an experience in which warriors fight to prove who is the better man. The battle continues until one of the fighters acknowledges publicly that the other was better or until one dies. This is reflected in both the dances of the warrior and the ritual enactments of the shaman. In both forms, the participant-performers draw lots for roles, for costumes and for positions in the performance area as well as for the seated postures known to be the most difficult to master. An audience is allowed to watch on the basis of age, social position and their ability to contribute to the action in some way. The *wala* is performed only in moonlight.

The fact is that colonial administrations and missionaries could not accept these performance displays or their purpose which was – no more nor less – to harmonize forces within the community. Eventually such events were degraded. This was the cause of the destruction of many traditional African cultures, perhaps a fundamental one in the process of colonization.

The introduction of colonial schools and religious systems included the introduction of colonial theatrical forms as well. French classics especially were included in schools and the writing of colonial-style plays – eventually with serious messages for African audiences – followed.

In the years just before and after independence, especially in Brazzaville, a western-style theatre came to life along with an Association of Congolese Theatre directed by Maurice Battambica. Battambica staged a number of his own plays through this association, among them *Le Maître d'école a tué sa femme (The Schoolmaster Has Killed His Wife)*. Another writer of note emerging from this association was Guy Menga, who denounced the clash of traditions in his play *La Marmite de Koka-Mbala (Koka Mbala's Cooking Pot*, 1969) as well as starting, with Patrice Lhoni, the Théâtre Congolais in Brazzaville. Other groups emerging at this same time included Théâtre Municipale and Kamango Players, the former in Brazzaville, the latter in Pointe-Noire.

A theatre school was opened in the 1970s, CFRAD (Centre for Training, Research and Dramatic Art). Part of its goal was a revival of interest in traditional theatrical forms. One play to grow from this work was Ferdinand Mouangassa's *Nganga Mayala*, about a king who dies and the woman who replaces him. Despite its attempts, however, the CFRAD experiments failed to develop an active Congolese theatre and by the 1970s the traditional French repertoire returned more strongly than before and eventually CFRAD disappeared.

Through the next decades, still other Congolese playwrights of note were to be seen: Sylvain Bemba (b. 1934), Sony Labou Tansi (1947–95), Caya Makhélé, Maxine Ndebeka (b. 1944), Gilbert Kiyindou and Tchicaya U'Tamsi (Gérard Félix Tchicaya, 1931–88). Bemba, a novelist and radio dramatist, wrote his first play, *L'Enfer c'est Orfeo (Hell Is Orfeo*, 1966), under the pseudonym Martial Malinda. A satire on social injustice, the play utilizes an African vernacular. Other Bemba plays include *L'Homme qui tua le crocodile (The Man Who Killed the Crocodile*, 1973), *Une eau dormante (Still Water*, 1975), *Tarentelle noire et diable blanc (Black Tarantula and White Devil*, 1976), and *Un foutu de monde pour un blanchisseur trop honnête (A Rotten World For an Honest Laundryman)*.

N'Debeka, born in Brazzaville, is the author of three plays, *Le Président* (1970), *Les Lendemains qui chantent (Happy Days Will Come)*, and *Equatorium* (1983), published in English by Ubu Books in New York.

Tchicaya, a poet, is the author of the drama *Le Zulu* (1972); *The Glorious Destiny of Marshal Nnikon Nniku* (1979), a comedy-drama about the rise and fall of a megalomaniac; *Le Bal N'Dinga,* a poetic dance-drama; and three novels.

The work of these writers was regularly seen despite the fact that performance spaces were all but non-existent in the country and public subsidy virtually an unknown concept.

It was during the 1980s that several new groups sprang up – Théâtre du Marigot in the commercial centre of Pointe-Noire; la Troupe de l'Amitié (Friendship Troupe), le Zola Théâtre, le Théâtre de la Grande École (Grand School Theatre), le Théâtre de l'Éclair (Lightning Theatre, originally Les Frères Tchang), La Troupe Artistique Ngunga and a state-run Théâtre National, all in Brazzaville.

Each carved out a particular area of theatrical expertise: Les Frères Tchang in mime; Grand École in popular boulevard comedies; Amitié doing more classical work; and Ngunga doing collective works involving music, movement, script and masks under the direction of Matoondo Kubu Touré. Some of Ngunga's work was particularly daring. The play *Nkassa*, for example, is about the promised land and took two nights to perform. This production, staged in the late 1980s, won the Ministry of Culture's First Prize for Theatre, an award established during the decade along with the Ministry's Cultural Weeks.

After writer Emmanuel Dongala became the director of Les Frères Tchang and the company changed its name to Théâtre de l'Éclair, it produced its major critical and popular success *Le Premier Matin du monde (The First Morning of the World)*. Like most Congolese groups, the company was hampered by a lack of women willing to work in the theatre. Performing on stage in the Congo is still considered a morally dubious career for a woman and the few who do are often snatched up by television and film.

During the 1980s the Department of English at Brazzaville's Marien Ngouabi University (founded 1972) established an active extracurricular theatre programme under Irish-born Malachy Quinn. The group staged plays by a wide range of writers from John Millington Synge to Wole Soyinka (*The Lion and the Jewel*), and also staged English-language productions of plays by Congolese writers such as Guy Menga (*Koko-mbla*) and Rémy Medou-Mvomo (an adaptation of his novel, *Afrika'ba*).

Perhaps the most dynamic theatre group of the modern period was Rocado Zulu Theatre based in Brazzaville. Founded in 1979 by playwright-director Sony Labou Tansi and operating regularly even beyond Labou Tansi's death in 1995, the company premièred most of his plays including *Conscience de tracteur* (translated as *The Second Ark*, 1979), *Qui a mangé Madame D'Avoine Bergotha?* (*Who Has Eaten Madame D'Avoine Bergotha?*, 1984), *Le Cercueil de luxe* (*The Luxury Coffin*), *La Rue des mouches* (*Street of Flies*, 1985), *Antoine m'a vendu son destin* (*Antoine Sold Me His Destiny*, 1986), *Moi, veuve de l'empire* (*I, Widow of the Empire*, 1987), *La Peau cassée* (*Broken Skin*), a co-production with the French company Fartov et Belcher from Bordeaux, and *La Légende de l'invention de la mort* (*The Legend of the Invention of Death*). Among Labou Tansi's most powerful dramas are *Le Parenthèse de sang* (*Parentheses of Blood*), produced at the Kiron Space in Paris in 1984, and *Je soussigné cardiaque* (*I, The Undersigned Cardiac Case*). Both plays were written in 1981.

A graduate of the prestigious École Normale Supérieure of Central Africa, Labou Tansi is also the author of four novels, poetry and many short stories. His plays focus on post-colonial Africa and often revel in absurdist illogicality.

In 1982, the Rocado Zulu won the Radio France Internationale's Grand Prix du Théâtre vivant (Grand Prize for Live Theatre) and was also the first company to win the Congo's Prix National du Théâtre (National Prize for Theatre) of the Ministry of Culture. The company played at the Festival de la Francophonie in France on several occasions as well as in Belgium.

Other works produced by the group include *Baiser d'avril* (*April Kiss*) by Nicolas Bissi, *La Tragédie du Roi Christophe* (*The Tragedy of King Christophe*) by Aimé Césaire, *Ils sont encore là* (*They're Still Around*, an adaptation of *Tribaliques* by Henri Lopes) and Sylvain Bemba's *Eroshima*. The group performed most often at the Centre Culturel Français.

Staff, based on a draft by
Sony Labou Tansi
Translated by Helen Heubi

Further Reading

Biahouila, Lucien. 'Théâtre et communication: problèmes de langues au Congo' [Theatre and communication: The problems of language in the Congo]. PhD dissertation, University of Paris III, 1983. 263 pp.

Chemain, Roger, and Arlette Chemain-Dégrange. 'Un théâtre militant' [A militant theatre]. In *Panorama critique de la littérature congolaise contemporaine* [A critical overview of contemporary Congolese literature], pp. 105–35. Paris: Présence Africaine, 1979.

Jadot, Joseph M. 'Le Théâtre des marionnettes au Congo Belge' [Marionette theatre in the Belgian Congo]. *Bulletin des Seances* 21, no. 3 (1950): 559–69.

'Le Théâtre au Congo' [Theatre in the Congo]. *Het Toneel* 6 (1956).

'Le Théâtre congolais' [Congolese theatre]. *Afrique Chrétienne* 7, no. 46 (1967): 17–19.

Menga, Guy. 'Quel avenir pour le théâtre en langue française au Congo?' [Which route for French-language theatre in the Congo?]. *Culture Française* 3–4, no. 1 (1982–3): 45–8.

Tati-Loutard, J.B. 'Itinéraire' [Itinerary]. *Notre Librairie: La Littérature congolaise* 92–3 (March–May 1988).

CÔTE D'IVOIRE

Known in English until 1986 as the Ivory Coast but now officially called by its French name, the Côte d'Ivoire is a square-shaped country of some 319,800 square kilometres (123,500 square miles) lying north of the Equator in western Africa. Bounded on the north by Mali and Burkina Faso, on the south by the Gulf of Guinea, on the east by Ghana and on the west by Liberia and Guinea, Côte d'Ivoire is the world's third largest producer of coffee and the largest producer of cocoa. Composed of more than sixty ethnic groups, the four major linguistic and cultural entities are Akan, Mandé, Voltaic and Kru. In 1995, the country had a population of just over 13.5 million people.

Archaeological evidence indicates the presence of societies in this region of western Africa dating far back into human history. During the medieval period, the northern part of modern Côte d'Ivoire was part of the trans-Saharan trade networks and it was through these networks that Islam was introduced to the country. Followers of Islam in 1995 still made up approximately 25 per cent of the population with Roman Catholics making up another 20 per cent. However, animistic beliefs still predominate in most of the country.

With the fall of the ancient Mali kingdom to the north in the sixteenth century, the population in the area increased significantly. In the late seventeenth century the Bouna kingdom was created by Bounkani, an immigrant from the ancient Kingdom of Ghana, not to be confused with the modern political entity of the same name. The Bouna kingdom became an important early centre of Islamic learning. Ashanti wars in the late seventeenth century again increased the population.

European explorers and traders – mostly French and Portuguese – began sailing into the area in the late fifteenth century seeking slaves and ivory. It was these early French traders who began calling this part of western Africa 'Côte d'Ivoire'. By the eighteenth century trading posts had been established and trade flourished expanding into palm oil and gold. During the 1830s, coffee plants began to be imported for the first time.

In 1893, the French took control of the area creating a protectorate ruled through a French governor. Borders were set in 1898 but there was significant resistance to head taxes and forced labour on the increasing number of colonial plantations. Ivoirians were conscripted to fight on the French side during World War I and it was not until the end of the war that Côte d'Ivoire was considered 'pacified'. The country's present borders were established just after World War II.

At the same time, Ivoirians began to make demands for an increased voice in government. Deputies were eventually allowed to be elected to the French National Assembly and one of them, a physician, Félix Houphouët-Boigny (b. 1905), became a leader in the country's independence movement. On 26 March 1959 the country became a republic and on 7 August 1960 the independence of Côte d'Ivoire was formally recognized. Houphouët-Boigny was elected the first president of the new republic and he remained in power as head of a single party regime for the next thirty years. In 1990, a multi-party government came into being.

To comprehend some of the complexities of modern Ivoirian culture, one must understand that each of the four major ethnic groupings spread not only across the country but in some

A traditional masked dance from western Côte d'Ivoire.
Photo: Barthélémy Kotchy.

cases beyond the modern borders to share roots and traditions with related ethnic groupings in several other countries.

The Akan, for example, came from ancient Ghana and form a mosaic in which some tribes have a state of their own while others do not. This grouping is essentially matrilinear in contrast to the Mandé which is patrilinear. The Voltaic grouping also exists all across western Africa and can be found not only in Côte d'Ivoire but also in Mali and Burkina Faso. For many Voltaic, existence is controlled by the Poro, a secret society with a belief in a mystical universe. The Kru, who migrated to the area from modern Liberia in the sixteenth century, are composed of two large groupings of twenty-one different ethnic groups.

Abidjan is the economic and cultural capital of the country while the city of Yamoussoukro is the country's political capital. Bouaké is the second largest city in the country. The country's official language is French; the five African languages which predominate are Yacouba, Senoufo, Baoulé, Agni and Dioula, the common market language. During the

1970s and 1980s, the country attracted many nationals from other African and Arab states seeking employment opportunities. In the mid-1990s, a large number of French and Lebanese nationals were also living in Côte d'Ivoire.

As is traditional in many African societies, people are born into certain trades including the arts. Musicians and dancers tend to come from long lines of musicians and dancers as do those storytellers and praise singers who record and maintain the stories of individual families and tribes, the *griots*. Others in these categories include carvers of masks and acrobats such as the popular stilt walkers.

During the nineteenth century, a significant split emerged between those wanting to follow the older ethnic traditions and those – especially among the social elite – who wished to follow a more European, essentially French, cultural model. One of the centres of the French educational and cultural model was based in Dakar, Sénégal, the William Ponty Normal School. Among those who went to the Ponty School were three Ivoirians who returned to create the Cercle culturel et folklorique de

Côte d'Ivoire (Côte d'Ivoire Culture and Folk Circle), known locally as the CCFCI.

These three graduates of the Ponty School – Coffi Gadeau (b. 1915), François-Joseph Amon d'Aby (b. 1913) and Bernard B. Dadié (b. 1916) – helped make this company a centre of indigenous spoken drama with each writing several plays. Critics, in fact, began speaking of a Théâtre Ponty style, a style at once rooted in local culture while still managing to maintain traditional European ideals of moral elevation and entertainment. In 1977, Dadié became Minister of Cultural Affairs.

Writing of the group in 1988 in a book entitled *Le Théâtre en Côte d'Ivoire des origines à 1960 (Theatre in the Côte d'Ivoire from Its Origins to 1960)* Amon d'Aby explained that

> while seeking to entertain, the Ponty Theatre style was inspired by history, folklore, religion and social problems. *Bayol and Béhanzin, Péroz and Samory, Sokamée, Le Mariage de Sika (Sika's Wedding)* and *Assémien Déhilé* were the first major works of this theatre, and had a powerful influence

upon the evolution of dramatic art throughout the territories of French West Africa.

During the period just prior to independence, an École national d'art dramatique (National School of Dramatic Art) was founded (1959) and two French theatre teachers were named as its director and assistant director. The theatre school became a popular location for seeing spoken drama including classical plays such as Molière's *The Misanthrope* and Beaumarchais's *The Barber of Seville*.

Between 1961 and 1964, students of the school played in various spaces in Abidjan, including at the City Hall, to a mixed elite of French and Ivoirians, again doing Molière along with more modern pieces such as *Papa bon Dieu (Daddy God)* by Louis Sapin and *Un nommé Judas (A Man Called Judas)* by Claude-André Juget.

At the end of 1964, the École nationale d'art dramatique became the École nationale de théâtre (National Theatre School) and was integrated into the new Institut national des arts (INA; National Institute of the Arts) and

The 1977 National Theatre School production of Bernard Zadi Zaourou's *The Sofas*, directed by Blaise Bah and Ebouclé Kodjo.
Photo: Alexandre Dagry.

placed under the direction of the Secretary of State in charge of Cultural Affairs. Also connected to the new institute was the École nationale des beaux-arts (National School of Fine Arts) and the École normale de musique et de danse (Teachers' School for Music and Dance).

This multidimensional institute was the idea of Albert Botbol, a French expert from UNESCO. As part of its mandate, the National Theatre School not only would train actors, directors and technicians but also would be required to mount a certain number of productions each season. According to Botbol, 'the INA must work as an instrument of cultural promotion to ensure the harmonious balance sociologically required by the economic progress of the Côte d'Ivoire' (Fraternité-Matin, 10 November 1966).

Clearly, the fundamental objective of INA was the promotion and creation of an Ivoirian dramatic art, an art rooted both in the national culture and in the western dramatic tradition. To this end, workshops began to be organized by French theatre specialists such as Henri Cordreaux in 1966 and Georges Toussaint in 1967. The latter workshop resulted in the production of Dadié's most important play, Monsieur Thôgô-gnini. This play, first staged at the Centre culturel de Treichville before a large audience of officials, political and cultural leaders and administrators, marks the real beginning of the modern Ivoirian theatre. The play continued to be performed for the next three years in Abidjan as well as in other cities across the country. A satirical comedy, the play, concerned with the abuse of power, has a clear political message which has continued to remain in the national collective memory.

In 1970, Jean Favarel, formerly a member of the Grenier de Toulouse, became Director of INA, though Ivoirians were in charge of the component schools and groups. While audiences slowly diversified during the decade, they still included a majority of university students and university graduates, and people in influential positions. During the 1970–1 season, Favarel himself staged productions of Gogol's The Government Inspector and Toussio by the Ivoirian dramatist Gaston Demangoh (b. 1940).

During the 1971–2 season, a full programme of theatrical productions was offered, the first such season in Côte d'Ivoire history. The plays included an adaptation of Pierre Basson's French novel La Tête (The Head); a Moroccan play by Jean Huberty Sibnay called La Tribu (The Tribe); Eugène Ionesco's The Lesson; Nigerian dramatist Wole Soyinka's The Swamp Dwellers; and Les Sofas (The Sofas) by the Ivoirian dramatist Bernard Zadi Zaourou (also known as Bottey Zadi Zaourou, b. 1938). Zadi Zaourou would later create a Chair in African Literature at the University of Abidjan.

From this point on, several streams of theatrical research emerged both among professionals and amateurs, streams which led to rich experiments in new artistic forms and other streams which led to a rediscovery of the black African cultural heritage. The goal was nothing less than the creation of a new artistic language rooted in the dramatic traditions of Africa.

With the emergence of a large number of amateur troupes in the 1980s and 1990s came a fresh willingness to tackle difficult and controversial subjects with many of these groups taking on social issues in their productions. Among the controversial subjects they have dealt with have been the misuse of public funds, corruption, mismanagement, tribalism, nepotism, intergenerational conflict, juvenile delinquency and the movement from a rural to an urban environment. These companies have appealed to large audiences and have been regularly more commercially successful than professional productions and those in more experimental areas.

In 1989, a National Federation of Amateur Theatre was formed, growing from the success of the first national festival of amateur theatre which was held in 1985. This movement expanded through the mid-1990s and received new support when the university professor Henriette Dagri Diabaté was named the country's new Minister of Culture.

Structure of the National Theatre Community

For the most part, the state has paid little attention to the arts in Côte d'Ivoire. One of the few exceptions came during the tenure of Bernard Zadi Zaourou as Minister of Culture when loans were made available to groups to mount productions, but this was very much the exception rather than the rule. In general, both in the professional and the amateur spheres, the existence of the Ivoirian artist has remained precarious.

Most theatre groups are required to pay rental for performance spaces. The result is that tickets for theatrical performances are usually double or triple that of films, about twenty times the price of a loaf of bread.

Though there are no theatrical unions *per se* there are two unsubsidized support organizations. These are Fédération des théâtres populaires (Popular Theatre Federation) run by Dieudonné Niangoran Porquet (b. 1948) and Fédération nationale de théâtre (National Theatre Federation) headed by Pierre Ignace Tressia. Both organizations have managed to avoid any kind of systematic interference from the state censorship apparatus.

As for performance events, Côte d'Ivoire has been the standing host for two festivals of African francophone theatre. The biggest of these, Festival africain du théâtre francophone (African Festival of Francophone Theatre), is funded by the Ministry of Culture and the Agence de coopération culturelle et technique (ACCT; Agency for Cultural and Technical Cooperation), and is judged by an international jury which in 1994 included experts from Sénégal, Cameroon, Burkina Faso, Bénin and Côte d'Ivoire. Awards were given to companies from Niger, Bénin, Guinea, Burkina Faso, Togo and Côte d'Ivoire. The Grand Prize of Friendship and African Cultural Cooperation went to the Théâtre national of Guinea.

The festival has also set for itself the arduous task of formulating new strategies for the economic, social and cultural development of all African states. The festival is seen as a fertile field for cultural exchange, especially among the francophone countries, and a unique opportunity for communication among African theatre artists.

The other festival is supported by the Ministries of Culture and National Education – the annual Festival du théâtre scolaire et universitaire (FESNATSU; Festival of High School and University Theatre). Begun in 1982 as an initiative of Bernard Dadié and expanded in 1986 to include primary schools as well, the festival also receives support from municipalities and is designed to develop an early appreciation of theatre in young people. It is seen as a contribution to general education and as an opportunity to provide some experience for developing artists. Known by its acronym, FESNATSU awards prizes for best group, director, actor and actress and for the best original play. In 1995 the director of the festival was Kouassi Dènos Koffi. Through the years national participation has steadily increased in FESNATSU with more than 50 per cent of the country's 250 or so schools sending performances.

Apart from these, Côte d'Ivoire has been the host since 1993 of the Marché des arts du spectacle africain (MASA; African Performing Arts Fair). Held annually in Abidjan and financed by ACCT, the Ministry of Culture and a grant from the European Union, it seeks to provide touring opportunities for productions and to encourage encounters between artists and potential marketers of the performing arts from around the world.

MASA is also intended as an opportunity for African artists to meet one another and discuss their work. To this end workshops are held for musicians, dancers and actors to exchange experiences and to discuss problems and perspectives. A full report is published after each festival by ACCT.

Artistic Profile

Companies

The professional theatre community in Côte d'Ivoire has tended to think of itself as the cradle of theatre experimentation in Africa. As a result, examination of new forms – especially as they relate to indigenous African models – has been widely encouraged.

In the mid-1980s, these generally experimental interests had coalesced under the general rubric of Research Theatres and had moved in three basic directions. The first of these consisted of the creation of new theatrical institutions based on the study of Black African civilization. In this work, the aesthetics of western theatre were refuted in favour of a black sensibility and style which was seen to be still very much alive in traditional culture.

This trend was reflected in the play *La Griotique* written jointly by Dieudonné Niangoran

Porquet and Aboubakar Cyprien Touré (b. 1949). Rooted in a reaffirmation of the role of the *griot*, the master troubadour of African oral tradition, the first shows in this new griotic genre were based on the poetry of young African writers and enacted on a stage using the specific language of the *griot*, a plural voice where parable and gesture are imbued with rhythm and accompanied by music, an essential ingredient in this tradition. The *griot*'s art includes spoken word, chant and song. Depending on the occasion, the *griot* can be a historian, a teacher, a mediator or even a healer, all these roles being rooted in language. Known as People of the Word and a caste apart from others, it is this unique griotic tradition that Porquet is working with.

A second stylistic approach emerged in the work of Zadi Zaourou, who turned to the *didiga*, rehabilitating and restoring this ancient artistic tradition and adapting it for the contemporary theatre. *Didiga* is based on the traditional notion of what can be described as 'the unthinkable'. It deals with subjects that are beyond quotidian logic, attempting to shock the viewer with stories inspired by everyday life. In these works, the familiar is challenged by the irrational. This tension between the strange and the familiar is intended to awaken the spectator to a new awareness. Underlined and sustained musically by the bow (*dodo*) and the flute (*pédou*), the form also adds in the use of colours: red for change, black for tradition, and white for death.

Among the most interesting and important works in this style have been Zadi Zaourou's *La Termitiére* (*The Termite Nest*), *Les Rebelles du bois sacré* (*Rebels of the Sacred Grove*), and *L'Oeuf de pierre* (*The Stone Egg*). Perhaps the most successful work in this form was his *Le Secret des dieux* (*Secret of the Gods*, 1984).

A third trend in this evolving theatrical research has been the development of a black dramatic sensibility using African languages. Seeking both thematic and aesthetic originality, the aim is to create a pure and authentic stage language, form and technique which reflect indigenous experience without reference to non-African traditions.

Utilizing music and dance, and often rooted in collective creation, this last trend could be seen clearly in Ahmadou Kourouma's (b. 1927)

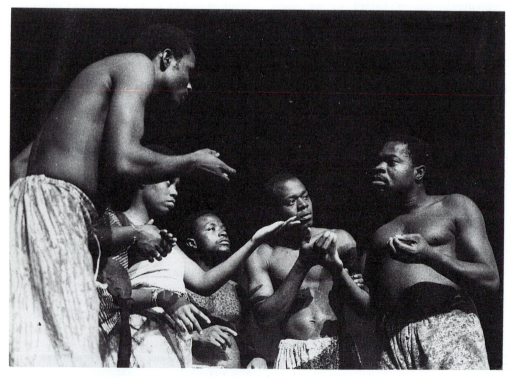

The 1973 National Institute of the Arts production of *I Am Myself*.
Photo: Barthélémy Kotchy.

Tougnantigui ou le diseur de vérité (*Tougnanti-gui or the Speaker of Truth*). Created with actors from INA in 1972 under the direction of Moro Bitty, it was quickly recognized as a new and important direction in Ivoirian theatre. In a similar style was *C'est quoi-même?* (*What Is Happening?*), another INA creation staged in 1973.

This style became dominant and was perfected after 1975 in the work of Soulymane Koly, a Guinean of French nationality who created the Ensemble Koteba as a vehicle for African musical theatre and modelling his work on the traditional Malian *kotéba bambara* form, a style also used in the work of the group Théâtre rituel (Ritual Theatre).

The traditional *kotéba* has two essential parts – the first danced, the second chanted. Each part could last several hours. The danced part includes drumming, singing, clapping (usually by young girls) and the ringing of bells. The second part – also accompanied by dance and music – usually features sketches involving a range of traditional characters from everyday life and defined by established physical and psychological traits. These include the unfaithful wife, the victim of elephantiasis who limps along with enlarged testicles, the leper with twisted hands, the blind man, the boastful hunter, the smooth talker, etc. During colonial times, other characters were added – the white commander, the interpreter, the native police-man and so forth. Focusing on everyday problems and especially marital relations, the *kotéba*'s immediacy and sense of fun makes it both popular and participatory.

Koly's work in spectacular musical pieces such as *Didi par ci, Didi par là* (*Didi Here, Didi There*), *Fanico*, *Adama Champion* and *Atoukassé* depicts many of the social problems of the new urban life in Black Africa, especially in Abidjan where his group is based. The company's work is didactic as well as playful, emotionally moving and offering a clear moral. This work also consistently uses the street French of Abidjan.

Koly's 1992 production in this style, *Waramba-Opéra Mandingue*, was a grand, popular saga in which tragedy, lyricism, humour and derision were blended into a combination of monumental forest polyphonies and the haunting lyricism of the Mandingan homeland. Inspired by heroic frescoes and Mandingan melodies and hymns from legendary times, the piece attracted a wide and appreciative public.

The work of the Ki Yi Mbok Theatre, created in 1980 by Cameroonian-born Wéré-Wéré Liking, is also derived from Black African rituals, mostly found in Côte d'Ivoire, Cameroon and Mali. Connected to initiation, death and healing, they are re-created in this group's work using an innovative stage language, images, symbols, masks, colours, sounds, rhythms and even odours. This work tends to be expressed through dance, gesture, posture, voice, props and lighting. The group aspires to reinvent ritual for the illumination, education and initiation of both spectator and actor. The group often includes marionettes in its work.

Among Ki Yi Mbok's important creations in this style have been *Les Mains veulent dire* (*The Hands Tell the Meaning*), *La Puissance de UM* (*The Power of UM*), *La Rougeole-arc-en-ciel une nouvelle terre* (*Measles Rainbow, a New Land*), and *Orphée-l'Afrique* (*Orpheus-Africa*).

An offshoot of the Ki Yi Mbok style is the Bindkadi-So, created by the French-born Marie-José Hourantier. It too seeks to renew art through ritual. Other directors working in this way are Saïdoo Bocoum, Martin Guedeba, Antoine Soudé, Mory Traoré and Ignace Alomo.

The Atelier Théâtre Attoungblan, founded in 1984 by Alexis Don Zigre, is more text-based than the other Research Theatre groups and has developed its own avenue of work which seeks to combine new forms with the aesthetics of socially rooted theatre. Based in the art of the traditional African storyteller, the group uses corporal expression in the extreme and traditional African symbolism to create a series of profoundly expressive images. The group's best work has been in *A qui la faute?* (*Whose Fault?*), *L'Enfer c'est nous* (*Hell Is Us*) and *Carrefour* (*Crossroads*).

The Sekedoua Company of Ignace Alomo has also been inspired by the griotic tradition and has mounted several one-person productions involving the use of storytelling.

Y Mako Teatri, on the other hand, tends to come close to happenings and performance art in its work evolved from the Augusto Boal-inspired Invisible Theatre. In these productions – usually taking place in a public area – the audience is composed of those who just happen to be there and they generally do not know that they are part of a theatrical performance. The group attempts to draw attention to social problems by staging unannounced events in different neighbourhoods. Y Mako was founded by Clause Gnakouri and Luis Marquès.

Wéré-Wéré Liking, artistic director, Ki Yi Mbok Theatre.
Photo: Courtesy du Maurier Ltd. World Stage Festival, Toronto.

Wéré-Wéré Liking's 1994 Ki Yi Mbok Theatre touring production of *Singue Mura*.
Photo: Courtesy of du Maurier Ltd. World Stage Festival, Toronto.

Groups working in the field of theatre for social action include Union théâtrale de Côte d'Ivoire of Daniel Adje and Le Soleil de Cocody of T. Vincent Diallo.

About the only Ivoirian theatre group working with a subsidy is the Compagnie nationale d'art dramatique (CNAD; National Drama Company) founded in 1993 with a grant from the Ministry of Culture. The company hires local professional actors and is rooted in more traditional text-based theatre.

Some amateur troupes of note have been Amadou Diallo's Djibioua de Divo, Moussa Kourouma's (b. 1942) Les Compagnons d'Akati, and Fargas Assande's N'Zassa Théâtre.

Dramaturgy
Directing and Acting

The first generation of Ivoirian playwrights was clearly modelled on the French school of drama. It saw the production of plot-based scripts generally rooted in well-known stories, legends and historical subjects. Expressed in a recognizable dramatic language and a traditional European style, the earliest plays were staged at the École primaire supérieure (Advanced Primary School) at Bingerville, near Abidjan, and then evolved further at the William Ponty Normal School in Dakar.

Characterized by simplicity of language and plot, its chief aim was to reflect reality in a clear and entertaining way. Created within a colonial context, political content was rare in such plays and, in the early work of Amon d'Aby and Bernard Dadié, an ethnographic approach dominated. In short, the Ivoirian oral tradition was reshaped to fit the norms of French spoken drama.

A typical example is Dadié's *Assémien Déhilé*. Now considered the classic example of the so-called Ponty style, it is one of the first plays to make its author famous. Amon d'Aby later wrote in his study, *Theatre in the Côte d'Ivoire from Its Origins to 1960*, that in this play Dadié confirmed the orientation of the early authors: 'everyday life, folklore, history, rituals. These were the cultural elements mined in this body of work which proved a revelation for Ivoirians'.

Essentially dramatizing spoken stories, Dadié was clearly shaping mythical material into a European dramatic form. The play is built around three tableaux linked by the dramatist's storytelling abilities. Yet the essence of African language can still be found – the silences, the proverbs, the rich metaphors – and the resulting script is both entertaining and accessible to a wide audience.

This trend lasted until about 1966 when Dadié, having seen a play by Aimé Césaire in Berlin, began to change his approach to playwriting. This evolution from the Ponty style to the Césaire style placed Dadié in a transitional zone between two generations of playwrights with different ideals and approaches. Dadié's new mode corresponded to his own experience as a Black African living through different periods of Ivoirian history – the colonial period and the period of decolonialization.

The grandeur of Dadié's themes after this point clearly reflects the social and personal tensions arising in him from the upheavals of an Africa suffering deeply as it sought to define its own path. His first major work in this new style, *Monsieur Thôgô-gnini*, is again a model for its time. Though classical in structure, the play contains a clear counterpoint in terms of storyline. It is the interweaving of threads which gives the play much of its joy. In it, tragi-heroic forms are telescoped upon more elliptical forms as well as upon the epic. Also building on the storyteller's art, the ending of the play, in which power moves to the people themselves, presents a clear vision for Africa following independence.

All of Dadié's subsequent work, essentially tragic, expresses his humanitarian idealism against a specific socio-political background. For him, liberty and justice are fundamental values which represent a more humane society. *Les Voix dans le vent* (*Voices in the Wind*) is an allegorical play explicitly dealing with this reality. In it, he parodies the experience of a despotic African leader trying to lead a people toward independence. Utilizing a cinematic style with numerous flashbacks, several essentially autonomous sequences parody the leader's irrational behaviour with humour and irony.

Several of his later plays such as *Béatrice du Congo* (*Beatrice of the Congo*) and *Iles de tempête* (*Islands of the Tempest*) deal with a similar theme as *Les Voix dans le vent* depicting in a humorous manner various tragic consequences of the life of an autocratic leader. The action in these later plays, however, while more varied, is often at the expense of the lyricism found in his earlier work.

Yet the ideological content of Dadié's later

work never detracts from his essential artistry. Symbolism and realism, satire and ballad all coexist in a most original way. His politicians are effigies which is, in fact, his real experience with most of them. His plays often form a triptych, each view representing a different aspect of the same theme: a thirst for power leading to a shameless exploitation of people which leads to a people's revolt and the ultimate fall of the protagonist.

The post-independence generation which followed Dadié tended to write more explosive plays. Breaking away from the traditional European style, these later plays, nevertheless, kept their increasingly political orientation. Here the dramatist becomes a spokesperson for a tormented conscience, for people persecuted by their own, for justice. The use of history as a way to distance the audience from daily realities constituted a new approach to Ivoirian dramaturgical aesthetics. Even so, the tone tended to become more virulent and the humour and irony more incisive as contradictions became clearer.

In *Le Respect des morts* (*Respect for the Dead*), Amadou Koné (b. 1953) depicts through dialectical argument a conflict between traditional and dynamic values within African society. This antimony is expressed in verbal pyrotechnics showing an Africa clinging to its past. To preserve or to innovate? That is Koné's key question. Despite this, the language he uses is accessible to a wide audience.

The plays of Charles Zégoua Nokan (also known as Zégoua Gbessi Nokan, b. 1936), both in theme and dramatic action, are even more revolutionary. His first play, *Les Malheurs de Tchakô* (*The Misfortunes of Tchakô*), is a veritable labyrinth of relationships. Through psychological and ideological interferences he creates a complex dramatic situation which reflects the experience in many post-independence African countries. The misfortunes of the solitary, individualistic hero condemn him to immobility partly because of his relations with the authorities while his situation expresses a social reality where political intrigues reach a peak of dramatic intensity. A contradictory figure torn between the people and power, the protagonist becomes in the end an enigmatic marionette.

Nokan's subsequent works are simpler yet even more explosive. In *Abrah Pokou ou une grande africaine* (*Abrah Pokou or A Great African Woman*), Nokan deals with the relationship between love and politics. He uses a technique of discontinuity where the dramatic action appears to slow down. It is the resurgence of class conflict as well as the rapidity of the denouement which reinforces the meaning of the play. Utilizing a Baulé legend and tempering it with a Marxist viewpoint, Nokan elucidates the problem of a people rooted in a retrograde feudal system based on slavery who attempt to transform it into a socialist democracy. The use of legend gives a further epic density to the play while Brechtian distancing techniques add several additional layers to it.

All of Nokan's theatrical work is built on a revolutionary optimism connected to the dynamics of history. His plays denounce all forms of oppression and injustice. Devoid of psychological motivation and traditional dramatic action, these works are based on the ideological evolution of a collective hero. These are difficult and revolutionary plays which have as a result not been seen much on Ivoirian stages.

After his own early plays, Zadi Zaourou departed as well from conventional dramatic styles to develop his own form of theatre, a form already spoken of in the **Artistic Profile** section, called the *didiga*. This is a form of total theatre bringing together dramatic language and symbolism and tied together with a rhythmic narration and music. Though poetic, the form nevertheless is generally used for a violent denunciation of shameful political practices. His plays in this style – especially *L'Oeil* (*The Eye*) and *La Tignasse* (*The Mane*) – show his complete break with the architecture of Aristotelian theatre.

The narrative form of *didiga* places the dramatic hero in the midst of psychic and metaphysical phenomena which vie for his attention. Used as well is the notion of African irrationality to accentuate the overall symbolic tone of the art. The protagonist, in this context, is an instrument of justice whose mission is to defend ordinary people against external forces.

In Zadi Zaraou's *La Termitière*, key roles are played by music, verbal symbolism and gestures, which all combine to tell the story of a society in crisis. The gestures become ritualized while silence in the midst of speech brings a telling esoteric tonality to the work. This symbolism, however, is often a difficult barrier for spectators to cross.

Dieudonné Niangoran Porquet's work, on the other hand, is rooted in the aesthetics of the *griot*, their narrations, gesture and music. Also breaking from European dramatic form, this work stresses dance and song as a support for the words. As critic Aboubakar C. Touré says, 'Even if the dance opens the show, the dancer knows that the theme developed... must be in relation to the text, and that this theme must also be reflected in the singing, the instrumental accompaniment and the text' (quoted in Barthélémy Kotchy's study, 'New trends in the theater of the Ivory Coast (1972–83)', p. 242).

From a textual point of view, the *griotique* uses a new form called by Niangoran Porquet *griotization*. This combines poetry and music which becomes more intense as the action develops. A solo performance which alternates with an ample epic style, these two elements cross-pollinate creating a skilfully set up explosion of musical sequences that integrate, as Niangoran Porquet says, African literature and history.

Although performances in this style are numerous, actual written texts are rare except for their occasional appearance in collections of poetry. Even then, these poems make difficult reading because of their multiple images and allusions. Even individual lines are punctuated by music using specific instruments such as a *tom-tom, kora* or *balafon*. Several of Niangoran Porquet's works in this style have been published as *Mariam et griopoèmes* (1978).

Such a griotic architecture is innovative in its attempt to transcend the traditional combinations of words and music used by the *griots* themselves. Yet the breadth as well as the lyrical discourse makes this genre static and often devoid of conflict. What remains of interest is the development of a pure dramatic lyricism with its many opportunities for improvisation.

For younger dramatists, text has become an invitation more to search for their own forms and meanings than anything else. In working with younger dramatists, Ivoirian directors have developed a new sense of the marvellous and the imaginary on the stage, elements which have allowed a fuller emotional and lyrical expression for a whole new generation of theatregoers.

Theatre for Young Audiences
Puppet and Mask Theatre

There are no companies in Côte d'Ivoire specifically working in the fields of youth theatre or marionette theatre. Virtually all primary and secondary schools in the country offer theatrical productions as a way for students to learn about both themselves and the art form. Only the Ki Yi Mbok Theatre can be said to utilize marionettes regularly in its productions.

Design
Theatre Space and Architecture

Costumers and set designers are virtually unknown in Côte d'Ivoire although the Ministry of Culture occasionally organizes workshops covering basic training in these areas. Nevertheless, this can hardly be considered training for specialists. In general, the director of each production takes responsibility for these visual elements.

As for theatre space, Côte d'Ivoire has inherited a European tradition in the design of theatres, which is not necessarily effective for African dramatic art which relies much more on the interaction between actor and audience and works best in a theatre-in-the-round and in an open-air situation. In these cases, audiences simply surround the performers in a circle of whatever width is required. This can be seen clearly in the open-air performances of artists such as Nomel Okro (b. 1902) of the village of Ousrou (Dabou). But it is also a custom on the wane as municipalities build community centres with 'proper' performance spaces.

In Abidjan there are six cultural centres of this newer type and all have spaces that can be used for theatrical performances. The most important of these European-style theatres is the Centre culturel français inaugurated in 1969 and seating just over 500. Others of note include the Centre culturel de Treichville and the Centre culturel d'Abobo.

There is a theatre at the Cocody Cité reservoir – the Théâtre de la cité – but it is no longer being used for theatrical purposes.

In the interior, the city of Yamoussoukro has an amphitheatre seating nearly 1,000 at the Lycée scientifique while in the city of Bouaké there is a 500-seat theatre at the Centre culturel Jacques Aka, a gift from France.

Other urban centres in the country make do with cultural and community centres from the colonial period, most of which are rapidly deteriorating.

A 200-seat open-air theatre in Abidjan has also been used in recent years for the *didiga* theatre of Zadi Zaourou while the Ki Yi Mbok Theatre now has its own 300-seat space.

Among multipurpose facilities offering space to theatrical troupes are the Cinéma Ivoire (400 seats) and the Palais des congrés, both in Abidjan, and various other cinemas in urban neighbourhoods. All usually rent for exorbitant rates.

Training

The major training institution in the Côte d'Ivoire from 1959 to 1980 was the École nationale d'art dramatique (ENAD). Often underfunded during its existence, it closed for lack of money in 1980 but reopened in 1992 when it gained a new lease on life with the creation of the Institut supérieur des arts de l'action culturelle that year. The school has expanded into the field of dance training and is now known officially as the École nationale de théâtre et de danse (ENTD). In 1995 the school was under the direction of Jeanne Menzan Kouassi.

ENTD takes students who have graduated from high school whether they are young and talented or mid-career professionals seeking to obtain additional skills. It offers courses in voice and speech, interpretation, stage management,

The 1995 ENTD production of Albert Camus's *Caligula*, directed by Ebouclé Kodjo and Menzan Kouassi.
Photo: Alexandre Dagry.

directing, movement, singing and dance. ENTD, together with the Institut national supérieur, provides a broadly based applied training in theatre and the performing arts generally.

In 1994, the University of Abidjan at Cocody created a training programme in performing arts research within the Faculty of Arts. This programme offers university-level instruction in theatre and cinema, instruction formerly given through the Département de Lettres Modernes. The programme offers studies in criticism, semiotics, aesthetics and theory, the psychology of art, film and theatre administration. The programme leads to advanced work including teaching certificates, Master's degrees and doctoral study.

Criticism, Scholarship and Publishing

There is no autonomous research centre for theatre scholarship nor is there a dedicated theatre journal in Côte d'Ivoire. Individual production reviews tend to be written by journalists in local newspapers while academics generally publish articles in journals from the University of Abidjan.

The two most important of these journals for arts criticism are the *Annales de l'Université d'Abidjan* and the *Revue de littérature et d'esthétique négro-africaines*. Both are issued by the university's Publications Service. Ivoirian theatre academics also publish regularly in the journal *Présence Africaine*.

In most published essays on theatre, text is approached as literature with some critics adding in sociological, national or semiotic elements to their work. Ideological approaches are also found regularly. Leading academic critics of theatre include Barthélémy Kotchy

(b. 1934), Valy Sidibé (b. 1953) and Abou-bakar C. Touré. The most important of the journalistic critics is Koffi Raphaël Atta.

Among the major studies of Ivoirian theatre are Kotchy's *La Critique social dans l'oeuvre théâtrale de Bernard Dadié* (*Social Criticism in the Theatrical Work of Bernard Dadié*, 1984); Nicole Vinci Leoni's *Comprendre l'oeuvre de Bernard Dadié* (*Understanding the Work of Bernard Dadié*, 1986); and Marie-José Hourantier's *Du rituel au théâtre* (*From Ritual to Theatre*, 1984).

A large number of monographs and studies on Ivoirian performing arts exist, only some of which have been published.

Barthélémy Kotchy, Valy Sidibé
Aboubakar C. Touré
Translated by Helen Heubi

Further Reading

Abibi, Azapane. *La Communication dans le théâtre de Bernard Dadié* [Communication in the theatre of Bernard Dadié]. PhD dissertation, Université de Bordeaux III, 1978.

Aiko, Koudou. 'Univers dramatique et pouvoir politique: le théâtre ivoirien 1960–1975' [Dramatic universe and political power: Ivoirian theatre 1960–1975]. PhD dissertation, Université de Paris X, Nanterre, 1979.

Amon d'Aby, François-Joseph. *Le Théâtre en Côte d'Ivoire des origines à 1960* [Theatre in Côte d'Ivoire from its origins to 1960]. Abidjan: CEDA, 1988.

Amon d'Aby, François-Joseph, Bernard Dadié and Germain Coffi Gadeau. *Le Théâtre populaire en République de Côte-d'Ivoire* [Popular theatre in the Republic of Côte d'Ivoire]. Abidjan: Cercle Culturel et Folklorique de Côte d'Ivoire, 1966. 230 pp.

Aniegbuna, Ikeh E.F. *La Satire et la mutation sociale dans les théâtres de Bernard Dadié et Wole Soyinka* [Satire and social change in the theatre of Bernard Dadié and Wole Soyinka]. PhD dissertation, Université de Paris III, (1980).

Bana-Kouassi, Jeanne. *Le Théâtre ivoirien: l'image et la place de la femme dans ce théâtre* [Ivoirian theatre: the image and the place of women in that theatre]. Paris: Université de Paris III, 1985. 105 pp.

Bile, Isaac. 'Rituels et théâtre en Côte d'Ivoire' [Ritual and theatre in Côte d'Ivoire]. *Mask und Kothurn* 29 (1983): 261–71.

Coulibably, Mawa. 'Lecture de *Les Sofas, L'Oeil, Fer de lance*' [An interpretation of *Les Sofas,*

L'Oiel and *Fer de lance*]. PhD dissertation, Université de Paris X, Nanterre, 1983.

———. 'Place et rôle de la musique dans le théâtre négro-africain moderne' [The role of music in modern Black African theatre]. *Annales de l'Université d'Abidjan*, Series D (Lettres) 4 (1971).

———. 'Les Sources du théâtre négro-africain' [Sources of Black African theatre]. *Revue de littérature et d'esthétique négro-africaines* 2 (1979).

Dagry, Lucie. *Images et mythes de la femme dans le théâtre de Dadié* [Images and myths of woman in the theatre of Dadié]. Paris: Université de Paris III, 1984. 87 pp.

Etienne, J. 'Activités théâtrales en Côte-d'Ivoire' [Theatre activities in Côte d'Ivoire]. *Premières Mondiales* 30 (1962).

'40 Ans de théâtre ivoirien' [40 years of Ivoirian theatre]. *Eburnea* 66 (1972): 17–32.

Hamilton, Issac Bile. 'Rituels et théâtre en Côte d'Ivoire' [Ritual and theatre in Côte d'Ivoire]. *Maske und Kothurn* 29 (1983): 282–91.

Holas, Bohumil. *Craft and Culture in the Ivory Coast*. New York: International Publications Service, 1968.

Honsch, Marlène. 'Le Pouvoir et l'argent dans l'oeuvre romanesque et théâtrale de Bernard Dadié' [Power and money in the novels and plays of Bernard Dadié]. PhD dissertation, Université de Paris III, 1981.

Hourantier, Marie-José. *Du rituel au théâtre: contribution à une esthétique théâtrale négro-africaine* [From ritual to theatre: contribution to a Black African theatre aesthetic]. Paris: L'Harmattan, 1984.

Kodjo, Léonard. 'Les Personnages du théâtre de Ponty' [Characters in the Ponty theatre]. *Revue de littérature et d'esthétique négro-africaines* 3 (1981).

Kotchy, Barthélémy. *La Critique sociale dans l'oeuvre théâtrale de Bernard Dadié* [Social criticism in the theatrical work of Bernard Dadié]. Paris: L'Harmattan, 1984.

———. *Elements culturels et formes de représentation dramatique en Afrique noire: le cas de la Côte d'Ivoire culturale* [Cultural elements and forms of dramatic representation in Black Africa: the case of Côte d'Ivoire]. PhD dissertation, Université de Paris VIII, 1983.

———. 'New Trends in the Theater of the Ivory Coast (1972–83)'. Translated by Clive Wake. *Theatre Research International* 9, no. 3 (fall 1984): 232–53.

———. 'Le Théâtre aujourd'hui en Côte d'Ivoire: une interview avec Soulymane Koly, directeur du Groupe Theatral "Koteba", Abidjan' [Theatre today in Côte d'Ivoire: an interview with Soulymane Koly, director of the Koteba Theatre Group, Abidjan]. *Komparatistische Hefte* 3 (1981): 68–78.

Liking, Wéré-Wéré and Marie-José Hourantier. 'Les Vestiges d'un kotéba' [The remains of the kotéba]. *Revue de littérature et d'esthetique négro-africaines* 8. Université d'Abidjan (1981).

Logobo, Kpale. 'Influence de la tradition orale, sur les arts dramatiques en Côte d'Ivoire: la cas du didiga' [The influence of the oral tradition on theatre arts in Côte d'Ivoire: the case of *didiga*]. PhD dissertation, Université d'Abidjan, 1986.

Ojo, S. Ade. 'L'Écrivain africain et ses publics: le cas de Bernard Dadié' [The African writer and his audience: The case of Bernard Dadié]. *Peuples noirs, peuples africains* 32 (March–April 1983): 63–99.

Porquet, Niangoran. *Mariam et griopoèmes*. Paris: Oswald, 1978.

Sidibé, Valy. 'La Critique du pouvoir politique dans le théâtre de Bernard Dadié 1966–1980' [The critique of political power in the theatre of Bernard Dadié 1966–1980]. PhD dissertation, Université de Paris III, 1984.

——. 'L'Image de la femme dans le théâtre de Bernard Dadié' [The image of woman in the theatre of Bernard Dadié]. *Revue de littérature et d'esthetique négro-africaines*, 9 (1988).

Touré, Aboubakar C. 'Le Théâtre négro-africain: paradoxe ou vérité esthetique. Le cas ivoirien 1932–1972' [The Black African theatre: paradox or aesthetic truth. The Ivoirian case 1932–1972]. PhD dissertation, Université de Paris VIII, 1979.

——. 'Controverses sur l'existence de l'art du théâtre en Afrique-noire' [Arguments on the existence of the art of theatre in Black Africa]. *Revue de littérature et d'esthetique négro-africaines* 8. (1987).

Vinci Leoni, Nicole. *Comprendre l'oeuvre de Bernard Dadié* [Understanding the work of Bernard Dadié]. Paris: Saint-Paul, 1986.

DAHOMEY

(see **BÉNIN**)

DEMOCRATIC REPUBLIC OF CONGO

(see **ZAÏRE**)

EGYPT

(Arab World Volume)

ETHIOPIA

Unlike most of Africa, Ethiopia has a history of self-rule dating back to nearly 1000 BC. Covering an area of 1.22 million square kilometres (472,000 square miles), it is located on the eastern horn of Africa and, since the independence of Eritrea, a small nation created on Ethiopia's northern border along the Red Sea in 1993, is officially landlocked. Bordered to the east by Djibouti and Somalia, to the south by Kenya, to the west by Sudan, Ethiopia had an estimated population in 1994 of 54.9 million, making it one of the most populous nations in Africa.

Most Ethiopians in the 1990s are either Orthodox (Coptic) Christians or Muslims, with less than 17 per cent of the population being Roman Catholics, Pentecostals, Jews or animists. The major ethnic groups are Amhara, Tigre, Gurage, Adere (Semitic peoples – the descendants, according to some scholars, of immigrants and traders from the Arabian Peninsula some two thousand years ago),

Oromo (the country's majority), Sidama, Afar, Saho, Somali, Konso (Cushitic peoples) and the Sudanic peoples of western Ethiopia, who speak Nilo-Saharan languages and include the Koman, Kunama, Berta and Annuak peoples.

There are four factors central to an understanding of Ethiopian theatre as it appears in the twentieth century: the question of language, or, more specifically, literary and cultural language; the role of religion in cultural production through the centuries (and the relationship of religion and language); foreign influence or invasion (often religion-motivated) in a country proud of its record of independence; and the contribution of these factors to the politicization of Ethiopian theatre today.

Sabean and Greek were the official languages of the nascent Ethiopia just before the birth of Christ. Ge'ez, a local Semitic language, was spoken by the masses when the Axumite Empire (which had strong trade links with Byzantium and southern Arabia) ruled northern

Ethiopia in the first ten centuries AD. There is still a form of the Greek word *teatron* in Ge'ez. The Axumite King Ezana was converted to Christianity around AD 300 with the Orthodox patriarch in Alexandria retaining the power to ordain Ethiopian bishops for the next sixteen hundred years. The Old and New Testaments were translated into Ge'ez during his reign.

The Zagwe dynasty emerged from the disintegrating Axumite empire – a generic king from this dynasty providing the twelfth-century European myth of Prester John. The *Kebre Negest* (*The Glory of the Kings*), written in the early fourteenth century, is the first record of the claim made by Ethiopian monarchs up to and including Haile Selassie I (1930–74) of their descent from King Solomon and Makeda, Queen of Ethiopia. The son of this union, Menelik I, was the progenitor of the Solomonic dynasty. When he came of age, he travelled to Jerusalem to see his father and returned having stolen the Ark of the Covenant. This narrative enables the Ethiopian church to claim Ethiopians to be a chosen people. The legitimization was (and still is) a particularly useful strategy for unity in the face of the growth of Islam in the surrounding territories.

The greatest incursion of Islam in Ethiopian history was spearheaded by Ahmad ibn Ibrahim al-Ghazi (1506–43) – or, to Ethiopians, Ahmad Gragn (Ahmad, 'the left-handed') – who led a *jihad* against the Solomonic empire in 1527. The Christians were devastated and churches were destroyed. Six years later they sent to Europe for help, and the call was answered by the Portuguese. The major results of this conflict were an immense weakening of the Ethiopian church, and thus of Ethiopia, and the presence of Portuguese missionaries who promptly tried to convert Ethiopia to Catholicism. Although two successive kings were persuaded, the people rebelled and the Jesuits were expelled. These two violent encounters went far in the shaping of Ethiopia's attitude to the outside world.

The encounters also alerted the church to a need for defensive tactics. One of the strategies adopted was control of the written word and any other kind of cultural production which might threaten the supremacy of the Orthodox church. Although Amharic began to supplant Ge'ez as the vernacular (and Ge'ez supplanted Greek and Sabean) by the tenth century, it does not seem to have been written until the fourteenth. Ge'ez became the language of the

priests, the erudite and the nobility, and thus a locus of control. The Portuguese, for their part, encouraged liturgical writing in Amharic, but once they had left, this development became anathema to the ruling classes. Literary writing in Amharic did not resurface until the reign of Tewodros II (1855-68), who attempted to break the church's monopoly by making Amharic the language of state as well as of the people. Ge'ez now occupies an equivalent position to Latin in Italy, and Amharic has been the official language of Ethiopia for the last century, with English as the second language of the state, and the language of university education. Ethiopian literature (here ignoring, of course, an immensely rich oral tradition in all vernaculars) was, however, devotional and almost invariably in Ge'ez until the beginning of the twentieth century. This reflects the degree of control exercised by the church over cultural production, and goes some way to explaining the complete lack of theatre as an institution in Ethiopia until the beginning of the twentieth century. It is important to note in the discussion that follows that although there have been productions of plays in Tigrigna (the Semitic language of Tigre) in Asmara and Mekelle, very few, if any, plays are written in Ethiopian languages other than Amharic.

Religious education had two main areas of cultural production: *kine* – poetry which relies heavily on the capacity of Ge'ez for double- or even triple-entendre – and *zema*, or religious music. (*Kine* in Amharic is a very recent phenomenon – the poet-playwright Yoftahé Negussé (d. 1949) among others, thus attempted to elevate Amharic to the literary status that Ge'ez enjoys.) Both disciplines obey a complex system of rules in which practitioners are trained from childhood. Traditional reverence for *kine* in particular translates into a disproportionate concentration on verbal artistry in contemporary plays, a large number of which are in verse. *Kine* and *zema* were occasionally combined when an inspired poet produced an exceptionally good piece of work which was then put to music. *Shibsheba*, or religious dance, was always part of such occasions which tended to take place at the graduation of a poet or at religious or court ceremonies. Accomplished scholars (who were always church scholars) often recited pieces created for the occasion.

Orthodox church services, often three or four hours long, might be seen as theatrical events. Outdoor spectacles are also part of the church year, the most spectacular being *Meskel*, or the Feast of the Cross, and *Timkat*, or the Baptism of Christ. In the latter, processions of priests and deacons dressed in extravagant embroidered robes and carrying decorative staffs and colourful gilded umbrellas sing and dance to the rhythm of drums and ululations of women as they accompany a copy of the Ark of the Covenant (which resides in the Holy of Holies of every Ethiopian church) on a journey away from and back to its resting place. Considering such events outside their religious context would be seen by Orthodox Ethiopians as inappropriate, but a highly developed sense of occasion is evident at these times. Other ceremonies such as weddings and funerals have been considered by modern scholars to be a form of traditional folk theatre since celebratory dances and professional mourners often follow a narrative thread, but again, distinctions must finally be made according to the intended purpose of the ceremonies. Ethiopians in the south and west of the country who are not so steeped in Semitic Christian traditions follow religious rituals that are much closer to those of other African nations.

The Italians established strong beachheads in southeastern Eritrea during the late 1800s but despite their modern equipment were defeated by Menelik II (1843–1913) at the battle of Adwa in 1896. During his rule, the country began to be modernized and the capital Addis Ababa ('new flower') was established. In 1917 Empress Zawditu (1876–1930) was crowned, and pledged to rule through her regent, the heir-apparent Ras Tafari, later Emperor Haile Selassie I, and the last monarch to claim the Solomonic lineage. He opened the country to international trade and in 1923 led Ethiopia into the League of Nations. Twelve years later, Italy under Mussolini invaded the country and Haile Selassie went to the League for help.

The Emperor returned to Ethiopia in 1940, aided by the British, and reigned until 1974 when he was overthrown by a military coup led by Colonel Mengistu Haile-Mariam. Shortly after, land, financial institutions and major companies were nationalized and Ethiopia was declared a socialist state. Land reform and health and literacy programmes were established. In 1979, all political groups were effectively abolished and replaced by the Workers' Party of Ethiopia. Following national elections, the provisional Military Administrative Council was abolished in 1987. After a succession of defeats in the civil war that had been raging for nearly thirty years, Mengistu fled Ethiopia for Zimbabwe on 21 May 1991, and the Ethiopian People's Revolutionary Democratic Front (EPRDF, formerly the TPLF, or Tigre People's Liberation Front) under Meles Zenawi marched into Addis Ababa and took power. Except for Eritrea, which gained independence at this point, he controlled most of the country by 3 June 1991, and continued to rule through 1997, attempting to establish Ethiopia as a democracy. This is a difficult task in a country accustomed to centuries of monarchic rule succeeded by a military dictatorship but it has produced a very different politico-economic climate in which Ethiopian theatre is flourishing.

The development of Ethiopian theatre can be classified into six quite distinct stages. Credit for writing the first Ethiopian play goes to Tekle-Hawaryat Tekle-Mariam (see **Artistic Profile**), author of *Yawrewoch Komediya* (*Comedy of the Animals*), a satirical adaptation of the fables of La Fontaine. It was performed by students for members of the court at a hotel in Addis Ababa between 1912 and 1916, and was so effective that all dramatic activity was promptly banned until the coronation of Emperor Haile Selassie I in 1930. This illustrates the highly politicized nature of Ethiopian theatre from its very inception.

Between 1930 and 1935 theatre was a stronger presence in the schools than among the public. The Minister of Education, Sahle Sadalu, saw theatre as an important educational tool (it has since been seen as a useful tool of indoctrination, particularly by Mengistu's Marxist government) and built Ethiopia's first stage at the Lycée Menelik II in 1934. Schools in the capital were centres for theatrical experimentation – for example St George School, where poet-musician Yoftahé Negussé (1916–50) was a teacher. He was trained in both *kine* and *zema*, and his work is a cornerstone in the foundations of Ethiopian theatre. Haile Selassie I would later commission Yoftahé Negussé and Melaku Begusaw to create a series of plays celebrating Ethiopian history, the Emperor and the church.

There was no theatrical activity in the five years after the Italian invasion of 1935, but theatre was established in earnest when the Emperor was restored to power in 1941. There is no information surviving about Italian-sponsored productions.

The Hager Fikir (Patriots) Association which had been formed before the war reappeared after the Italian occupation as a discussion group which began to perform plays it had developed by improvisation, and finally became a theatre company. It was composed of those who had returned from exile in Europe. The room used for performance is now the second space at the Hager Fikir Theatre. The Municipality Theatre Company consisted of those who had stayed in Ethiopia and faced the Italians, and there were strong political frictions between the two groups. The latter group performed, for example, Yoftahé Negussé's *Afajeshion* (*You Got Me Caught*). Written while the Emperor was in exile, it questioned the way in which he had handled the war and quickly became the first genuinely popular play written in Amharic. Early directors include Afework Adafre (b. 1904) and Tesfaye Tessema (b. 1907). There were also a few private companies at the time – among them the Andenet (Unity) Theatre Company directed by Mathewos Bekele, and a company led by the actor Melaku Ashagre.

Emperor Haile Selassie commissioned the 1,400-seat Haile Selassie Theatre (later the National Theatre) in 1955 for the Imperial Silver Jubilee. In 1956, the Municipality Company was given the building. According to some theatre historians, this was a strategic move on the Emperor's part, since it quietened the resistance fighters. In its early years, the theatre was run by Austrians Franz Zulveker and Richard Hager, and the company staged lavish productions of historical and religious dramas, often with costumes imported from Europe. The opening production at the National, *David and Orion* by Prime Minister Mekonnen Endalkachew, was typical. Probably the most famous production of this era was the tragedy *Tewodros* (1959) by Girmachew Tekle-Hawaryat, son of the first Ethiopian playwright and a member of the Emperor's cabinet. These plays were staged by directors who were not working in a language they knew, and tended towards the spectacular and declamatory.

From the beginning, there was a radical split in perception with regard to theatre practitioners in Ethiopia. While early playwrights were often members of the nobility or of the cabinet, and always highly educated in both the traditional and the modern manner, the companies of actors were varied, often including *azmari*, or minstrels. These minstrels sing at feasts, and live by their wits, often composing songs on the spot from tidbits of gossip. They

are both held in contempt (particularly female *azmaris*, who are a byword for looseness) and feared for their perception and command of language. The acting profession is still regarded with a certain amount of suspicion.

In 1960 an Ethiopian who had recently returned from Europe, Tsegay Gebre-Medhin (b. 1937), was chosen to run the Municipality Company at the National Theatre. The third period in the history of Ethiopian theatre began when the National started to focus on plays that were more socially relevant and sophisticated. With the company's leading actor, Tesfaye Gessesse (b. 1937), who also returned from training abroad in 1960, Tsegay established a school which produced a number of outstanding actors, including Wegayehu Negatu (1944–89), Debebe Eshetu (b. 1944) and Alem-Tsehay Wedajo, the most prominent woman in Ethiopian theatre to date.

Ethiopian theatre moved suddenly into a different phase with the Marxist revolution of 1974. Plays became even more political – this was the heyday of agitprop and protest plays by authors such as Melaku Ashagre, Tekle Desta, and Tsegay Gebre-Medhin. With regard to the profusion, relevance, quality and particularly collaboration of artists from different genres in the major works produced, this was a golden age for Ethiopian theatre. A sharp increase in theatre attendance testifies to this fact.

In 1979 a theatre arts department was established at the University of Addis Ababa and a different generation of actors, directors and writers began to emerge. In 1983 the government established a body which would centralize the selection of plays to be produced at the major theatres. Although, to some extent, this body functioned to control corruption in the playhouses, it also acted as a censoring organization. As Mengistu Haile-Mariam's government became more and more hardline, imprisonments and banned plays became the norm and the theatres fell back on translations and history plays, relying on the audience's well-developed capacity to understand oblique political allegory.

What could be called the sixth period is from 1991 to the present. The political future of Ethiopia is very uncertain, and the government in the 1990s has begun to break the monopoly of Amharic. While this allows more freedom of expression to individual groups, it has also created an atmosphere of inter-ethnic suspicion and misunderstanding. The euphoria of being rid of a ruthless dictator and the excitement of the democratic experiment cannot hide the fact that Ethiopia is now poorer than it has ever been and has more social problems than ever before. Both sides provide simple subject-matter, and Ethiopian theatre is expanding into a strong industry.

Structure of the National Theatre Community

There are five government-owned theatres in Ethiopia, all of which are located in the capital, Addis Ababa. The National Theatre is the largest of these, seating 1,400 people, and is under the aegis of the Federal Ministry of Information and Culture. The other four theatres are the Ras (literally 'Head', but also one of the highest possible ranks in the Ethiopian monarchical system) Theatre, Hager Fikir (Patriots) Theatre, the Municipality Theatre and the Youth Theatre. The latter four are administered by the Addis Ababa Administrative Region Ministry of Information and Culture.

All five government-owned theatres are run similarly. Each is divided into five departments: planning, programming and public relations; administration and finance; general services; film; and performing arts. Theatre is classified under the latter section, which also includes traditional and modern music and dance. The buildings are also used as cinemas.

With few exceptions, the job of direction is given to in-house staff and there is a particular company attached to each theatre. The actors are permanent employees of the government and the playwright is usually an outsider.

The theatres are run on budgets provided by the government with 47 per cent in tax paid on each ticket. The money left is divided among the playwright (30 per cent), director (10 per cent) and actors (10 per cent). On average, tickets at these theatres cost the equivalent of one packet of cigarettes. In the National Theatre, for example, an average audience would be about a thousand people and the play would run once a week for about seven months. Profit-sharing is slightly different for a private company such as the Candle Theatre Company (founded 1995): after paying the same taxes, the playwright would receive 35 per cent of what remained, the actors 25 per cent, the director 15 per cent and 25 per cent would go toward the running of the theatre. This is the only private company in Ethiopia which runs its own venue, however; other companies must rent space for each production. It is noteworthy that the playwright, in each case, receives the biggest percentage.

Under the regime of Mengistu Haile-Mariam, all plays for prospective production at the government-owned theatres had to be submitted to a script-evaluation committee established within the Ministry of Culture in 1983. In the 1990s these theatres have the right to carry out their own script selection. However, directors are painfully aware of the repercussions of producing 'unsuitable plays', and in effect act as their own rigorous censors, painstakingly comparing all submitted scripts to the new constitution. This often leads to the 'safety' of staging translations, often Shakespeare; the 1995–6 season saw, for example, a production of *Hamlet* (in a translation from Haile Selassie I's time) at the Municipality Theatre. 'Safety' is subjective, however: John Ryle, reviewer for the *Guardian* (15 December 1995), points out the audience's enthusiastic capacity for reading relevant political allegories into the play.

The large theatres produce shows all year round. Although prior to the revolution of 1974 theatre was an evening event, curfews and major limitations on transport meant that the Sunday matinée became the major theatrical event of the week. The Sunday shows generally last from two-and-a-half to three hours, although they may often be longer. Recently theatres have begun to add late afternoon shows during the week, Saturday matinées, and Sunday morning children's shows (although the latter have now been dropped). While the weekend shows are full-length plays, weekday offerings are generally variety shows which may include comedy sketches and traditional and modern dance and song. These additions to the repertoire mean that the state theatres have become busy theatrical centres rather than six-day cinemas. One mid-1990s week at the Ras Theatre, for example, saw a variety show on Wednesday evening, a double bill of two short plays on Friday night, a matinée called *Saturday Comedy*, and the usual major play on Sunday. While plays are seen year-round – there is no specific theatre season as such – the period between June and September (the rainy season) is considered a peak time. This is because the stadium closes and soccer is no longer an alternative, and also because teachers posted to the provinces return to the city at this time.

The Addis Ababa University Theatre Arts Department Playhouse and the University Cultural Centre are two major theatre centres in the capital. The University Theatre is located at the Graduate Faculty Campus (formerly the German School), and does not have its own permanent staff. Shows produced here are usually student projects, and thus usually run during the academic year. It has become a vigorous centre of innovation, and is well respected among theatregoers.

The University Cultural Centre is one of the oldest theatre centres in the country. It has its own artistic director, a small administrative staff, and an amateur company which consists mainly of singers, dancers, and musicians. It does, however, sponsor and produce its own shows, as well as providing theatre space and facilities for outside groups. In 1996, the Centre produced *Albino*, a collective creation. Directed by Dagmawi Fisseha (b. 1958), *Albino* addressed contemporary social issues such as unemployment.

During the early 1990s, there was a proliferation of private theatre companies in the urban centres of Ethiopia, not least in the capital. Two major factors have contributed to this growth. The first is the overthrow of the Derg (Mengistu Haile-Mariam's militaristic Marxist regime) and the incumbent government's promise of a commitment to democracy. The resulting liberalization of the economy has allowed individuals to conduct theatrical examinations of social and political issues. There are others who have seen the possibility of profit in a still small industry.

Second, the government in the mid-1990s carried out wholesale dismissals of senior managers in the state-run theatres and they have proceeded to practise their art independently. None of the new private companies is subsidized. There are also companies being established outside Addis Ababa, in Dessie, Nazareth, Awassa, and Bahr Dar.

Rehearsal times at a theatre like the National may be nine months, or at a private theatre like the Candle Theatre, not less than six months. At the latter, this is mainly because the actors are not full-time professionals, and rehearsals are iimited to weekends. Private companies do go on tour: Mengistu's government ensured the establishment of community halls in almost all major provincial towns. The length of time a company spends in a town depends on the size of the audience, although it is not usually more than four days, and a market researcher is sent two or three days in advance of each booking to acquire the space and assess the potential size of the audience. Touring has its own dangers. After the passing of language laws in the early 1990s, thugs – allegedly dissatisfied members of provincial audiences – lynched the actors in Tsegay Gebre-Medhin's play *Ha-Hu Weyem Pe-Pu* (*ABC or XYZ*).

Ethiopia has no theatre festivals. There is a yearly award for the writing of children's plays; the first prize is 1,000 birr, the second about 300. Other prizes are awarded on state occasions rather than on a regular basis. There is a Union of Ethiopian Theatre Professionals but it is not especially active. However, it did achieve the 10 per cent share of profit for actors at the government-owned theatres. This is additional to the government salaries that the actors receive which range from 500 birr a month for an actor with a BA degree to 300 birr a month for one without. Established actors receive about 75 birr per performance, equivalent to about ten packets of cigarettes.

Recent developments include the growth of a diasporic theatre community and the production of Ethiopian plays abroad. An example of the latter is the production of Tsegay Gebre-Medhin's historical drama *Tewodros* at the Arts Theatre in London in 1987. There are also companies and playwrights among the large Ethiopian diaspora in the United States, often established by theatre professionals who have fled Ethiopia – for example, Haymanot Alemu and Tesfaye Lemma produced a version of Tsegay's *Mother Courage* (only the title is bor-

1993–4 production of *Love in America* at the Ethiopian National Theatre in Addis Ababa.

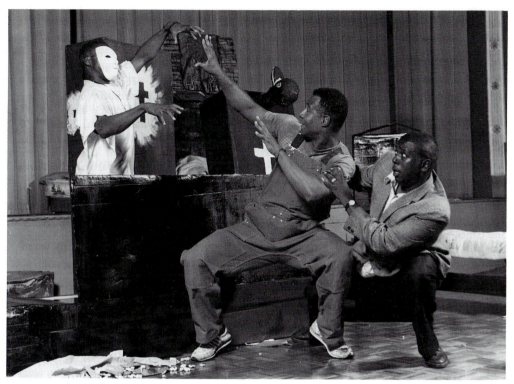

Ethiopia's diaspora theatre community is an active one, especially in the US and the UK. Above is a scene from the Ethiopian play *The Coffin Dealer and the Grave Digger* at the Park Theatre in Oakland, California.

rowed from Brecht) in the United States. Another important trend is the importing into Ethiopia of plays written by exiles in the United States; *Love in America* by Fikre Tolossa is a recent example. Ayalneh Mulat's (b. 1949) *Deha Adeg* (*Child of Poverty*) was translated, adapted, and directed by Aida Edemariam at Oxford in 1994, and then at the 1995 Edinburgh Festival Fringe. In April 1996 the London *Stage* reviewed a play produced by Ethiopian Jews in Israel.

Artistic Profile

There cannot be said to be clear genre specialization by either the state-run or the private companies; the general trend is towards diversification and the attracting of large audiences. The Sunday matinées at the government theatres are always full length, but they can be tragedies, comedies, melodramas, historical plays, original works, or translations. They do not usually contain music and dance, although these were major elements in the protest and agitprop plays of the 1970s (the transition period between the now-disliked imperial regime and the Marxist regime that had just come to power) produced at the Hager Fikir and other theatres.

Although music and dance are fundamental to traditional Ethiopian performances, *Ye Listro Opera* (*The Shoe-Shine Boy's Opera*, 1990) – or, as it was called after government pressure *Ye Godana Opera* (*Street Opera*) – was the first major play in over a decade to incorporate music and dance as essential components of its structure. Directed by Abate Mekuria and produced at the Municipality Theatre, its reception was mixed. Although part of the reason might have been the slang-studded dialogue and fairly loose plot-line, this is a standard reaction among an urban audience weaned on naturalistic drama. It is interesting

Ababa University, an audience member made the radical suggestion that the lady in question, who does not receive a single line of script, should make the choice.

Another of Fisseha Belay's plays rooted entirely in Ethiopian custom is *Alkashena Zefagn* (*The Mourner and the Minstrel*). This play was produced in 1988 at the Addis Ababa University Theatre and in 1994 at Hager Fikir. The play explores the paradoxical world-views of two traditional artists – the minstrel who sings at celebrations, and the professional mourner who sings at funerals.

Weteté was workshopped at the Addis Ababa University Theatre in 1987 and is probably Fisseha Belay's most important achievement to date, as he not only uses traditional materials but also attempts to re-create a truly indigenous theatre both in form and content. *Weteté* is a creation of the now obviated (thanks to the World Health Organization) traditional smallpox vaccination ceremony. According to traditional Amhara belief, *weteté* and *maré* ('my milk' and 'my honey') are the terms of endearment given to the feminine spirit associated with smallpox.

The traditional healer carries the *weteté* from one village to another to vaccinate anyone who has not been vaccinated before. The transportation of the *weteté* is accompanied by villagers who sing praise songs and dance to appease the spirit whom they describe as a beautiful young woman riding a winged horse. They ask her to be lenient on those whom she is going to inhabit (vaccinate), and hold a feast in her honour. After the vaccination, the praise songs are supplemented by storytelling and improvisations which it is hoped will alleviate the pain of the after-effects of immunization. In Fisseha's play these events are framed by the narration of a character who has lost his sight through smallpox.

Fisseha Belay is not the only playwright to draw on tradition – almost all Ethiopian writers use their heritage in some way, either as a dramatic device or as an object of investigation. The late Mengistu Lemma's *Tsere-Colonialist* (*Anti-Colonialist*, 1978) has as its central theme traditional Ethiopian astrology: it tells of a traditional church scholar who survives and triumphs through the Italian occupation by using knowledge outlawed by the Ethiopian Orthodox Church. In *Zikegnaw Joro* by Tsegay Gebre-Medhin (*The Lower Ear*, Congress Hall, 1989) the traditional thief-catcher ('Leba Shay') is foregrounded. These thief-catchers were given special potions, then, held by a leash, asked to smell out the culprit. In the play, this character went into the audience and confronted senior government and party officials.

Tsegay Gebre-Medhin is probably the best known Ethiopian playwright both within and outside the country. He has written plays in English, most notably *Oda Oak Oracle* – printed in London in 1965 and described by Albert Gérard in 1971 as 'one of the finest plays to have been written in Africa' – and *Tewodros*, first performed before the Emperor on 5 May 1963 to inaugurate the Creative Arts Centre at Addis Ababa University and produced fourteen years later at the Arts Theatre in London. He is renowned within Ethiopia for the elevation, subtlety, and complexity of his language (a mixture of Ge'ez, Oromo and Amharic), his larger-than-life characters, and his translations from Shakespeare: *Othello*, *Macbeth* and *Hamlet*.

Tsegay's original plays are chronicles of Ethiopian social and political history. His most recent play, for instance, *Ha-Hu Weyem Pe-Pu* (1992), investigates current political developments in Ethiopia, especially the issue of ethnicity. The two central characters in this play are the sons of the two main characters in *Ha-Hu Besidist Wer* (*ABC in Six Months*) a play written twenty years previously at the outbreak of the 1974 revolution. Both plays revolve around a character who remains off-stage, Sergeant Tassé, his house, and his son's dysfunctional family. Both plays treat current national issues in an episodic – even a fragmented – manner, and the overall story has less significance than the individual scenes. Both plays use a chorus that is entirely integrated within the world of the play. In the earlier play, for example, there are two types of chorus characters – *lalibelas* (who beg in song not because they need to beg but because they have been cursed with leprosy if they do not live in this way) and mourners.

Early plays at the Hager Fikir Theatre were not formally scripted – the director would provide an idea around which the actors would develop dialogue, sometimes in verse. Even in plays that were scripted, much space was still left for improvisation by the actor. A stage direction in one of the plays produced at this theatre reads 'After the table is set for both adults and children, they pray. One of the children begins to eat before the prayer ends. All eat, and feed each other affectionately, and the meal is followed by a children's song. As they are leaving, they say'. Expanding parts of a play that had caused amusement was a convention at the Hager Fikir. After a few shows, the original play could disappear behind the new construct of improvisation and audience reaction.

In the 1900s, a handful of plays have been produced that have been the result of collective creation – lengthy pre-production, improvisation and research. Among these is *Lattë* (*The Bachelor*, 1987), created by the Ras Theatre Company; *Ye Cupid Kest* (*Cupid's Arrow*, 1988–9), scripted and directed by Tamirat Gebeyehu (b. 1965) at the Theatre Arts Department; and *The Shoe-Shine Boy's Opera*, scripted and directed by Abate Mekuria. All these plays deal with contemporary social issues: *Lattë* addresses marriage in modern Ethiopia; *Ye Cupid Kest*, the social and academic reasons behind fatal romances at Addis Ababa University; and *The Shoe-Shine Boy's Opera*, the plight of Ethiopia's lower classes.

Directing and Acting

Until Austrian directors worked at the National Theatre in the 1960s, the role of the director was not clearly distinguishable from that of the playwright. Even in the 1990s, outside the government theatres, plays are usually written and directed by the same person. Early Hager Fikir plays were created through improvisation. The artistic director, who was also the director of many of the shows, would assign characters to the actors based on their physical characteristics and acting styles, and give them a skeletal plot. Then the assistant directors would work with the actors to develop the play which was usually a succession of loosely related scenes and verse dialogue. Directing was thus conceived as the provision of a framework rather than the interpretation of a text.

The Austrians' effect on the National Theatre not only was to make the role of the director much more distinct, but also, since they compensated for their lack of understanding of the plays with lavish sets and costumes, reduced the role to not much more than stage-designer. Little has changed since then, and the part the director plays is still not very clear to most audience members.

Abate Mekuria is one of the few directors who has made a real impact on Ethiopian theatre. Most of the plays he has directed were written by Tsegay Gebre-Medhin, and are full of long speeches written in a highly allusive, extremely educated register. Abate's talent is to transform these otherwise heavy and even boring speeches into absorbing dramatic scenes. He has good control of crowds, and his larger-than-life direction suits both Tsegay's plays and the vast government stages.

Melaku Ashagre, a notable director and playwright, spent his entire working life at the Hager Fikir Theatre and epitomizes the artistic style of the company. His *métier* was the farcical, and he has left behind him a style that caters to the tastes of the conservative Ethiopian audience. Both his plays and his direction were full of stock characters and interpretations.

Tekle Desta is another important director and represents those who come to the job after years of apprenticeship in acting. Getachew Abdi also began as an actor, and has a flair for the visual. Sahlu Assefa who, like most of his contemporaries, lost his job in the government theatre when the regime changed, was one of the rising directors of the late 1980s. Two of Sahlu Assefa's most memorable works are *Blacha Abba Nefiso*, by Berhanu Zerihun (the story of a warrior at the battle of the Adwa who chooses to commit suicide rather than surrender to the Italians) and *The Merchant of Venice*, starring Debebe Eshetu. Sahlu Assefa is known for his extensive research and 'authentic' productions.

Manyegezawal Endeshaw represents a new crop of directors coming from the University Theatre Arts Department. His predilection for the fantastic is a welcome departure from the dominant naturalistic style. Nebiyou Tekalign, a graduate of the Theatre Arts Department, is probably one of the most promising directors in Ethiopian theatre in the 1990s. He is more interested in experimentation with styles, and is the director of the handful of plays in languages other than Amharic.

Acting style in the government theatres is dictated by their size. Projection is a perennial problem, and this, combined with the wordy poeticism of many playwrights, results in a declamatory, static style of acting. The National Theatre was initially built as an Opera House and is so large that actors must often come forward to the edge of the stage to deliver their lines.

The previous generation of outstanding actors includes Wegayehu Negatu and Debebe Eshetu who both dominated the stage (and Debebe Eshetu in films as well) from the 1960s until 1989, when Wegayehu died. For many Ethiopian theatregoers they epitomize classic Ethiopian acting. Their contemporaries include Awlachew Dejene and Telela Kebede (in *Ha-Hu Besidist Wer*). Most Ethiopians know the latter as a gifted singer. She is an illustration of the nature of Ethiopian theatre in the golden era: Tsegay incorporated her voice, and even entire musical numbers by her, into his plays. Asegedech Habte, who played Mother Courage in Tsegay's play of the same name, is one of the first Ethiopian actresses. Asnaketch Worku appeared in many of Tsegay's plays at the National, and is also better known as a singer and musician.

Prominent actors of a slightly younger generation include Fekadu Tekle-Mariam, famous for his portrayal of Tsegay's Tewodros, and Abebe Balcha, a full-time lawyer known for his Othello. Jemanesh Solomon is often in Fissahe Belay's plays, her major début being in *Yalacha Gabecha* (*Marriage of Unequals*) by Mengistu Lemma, directed by Abate Mekuria at the Municipality Theatre. She was a rising star who graduated from the university in 1988 and worked as an actress until 1994, when she left for the United States. She was also artistic director at the Municipality Theatre, succeeding Abate Mekuria in 1990. Elsabet Melaku made her début in the same play, was the lead in Tamirat's *Ye Cupid Kest*, and appeared in an Amharic translation of Harold Pinter's *The Lovers*. Alem-Tsehay Wedajo was in most of Tsegay's plays, and is known for her Ophelia. She was the head of programming and production at the National Theatre and was the director of the Ethiopian Theatre Professionals Association. She later left for the United States. Current male actors of note include Getenet Eneyew and Teferi Alemu (also artistic director of the Hager Fikir Theatre).

Theatre for Young Audiences
Puppet and Mask Theatre

Between the accession of Emperor Haile Selassie and the Italian invasion, theatre was almost a stronger presence in the schools than it was among the public, and it is still strong in the former. At the Sandford Community School, at least three major plays are produced each year, not counting those provided by every individual class before the Christmas holidays or the end of the school years.

Youth participation in theatre increased greatly in the mid-1970s, under Colonel Mengistu's regime, because performing troupes called *kinet* were set up in all the *kebelles* (the smallest administrative divisions of the country). The plays that were produced by these groups were not markedly different in their thematic preoccupations from those produced by more professional or independent companies, and were usually agitprop productions performed under the watchful eyes of government censors or propagandists. Youth theatre differed in that it tended to be included in variety shows – a form that had been popularized on a larger scale in the 1940s on the stage of the Hager Fikir Theatre. This larger form was still occasionally used in the early 1980s where many different schools performed one after another, the evening ending with Marxist/Socialist proclamations.

The content and artistic value of plays produced under such circumstances was therefore limited. But the main importance of the work produced by the *kinet* troupes was the opportunity to experiment at an early age with traditional dance and song. Of secondary importance was the production of a pool of future professional artists. Apart from the *kinet*, youth audiences were catered for by occasional sketches on the educational radio station *Legedadi* and weekly shows on national television and radio. Also in the mid-1980s the three major theatres in Addis Ababa began to produce children's shows every Sunday morning.

In 1990 a grant was secured from the Japanese government, and the first children's playhouse was opened at what had previously been the YMCA (Young Men's Christian Association) of Addis Ababa. German artists also provided workshops specifically related to children's theatre.

Among the playwrights now writing for this audience are Haile-Mariam Seifu, Alemayehu

Gebre (who won the prize for children's writing in 1989) and Ayalneh Mulat. Popular plays produced recently include *Doyo* and *Teraraw Genfo* (*Porridge of the Mountain*).

The recent plays make extensive use of puppetry, masks, makeup, physical action, and traditional songs and games. Like Ethiopian folk tales, the plays are dominated by animal characters and fantastic plots, neither of these being significant elements in mainstream Ethiopian theatre. While potentially contributing towards the emergence of a more truly Ethiopian theatre in form and content, the new trends in children's theatre may also begin to free adult plays and audiences from the imprisonment of naturalism. The nascence of children's theatre has given theatre practitioners new venues and a new audience.

Sunday morning shows more or less ceased in 1994, leaving the field entirely to the newly established children's playhouse which suddenly undercut the vigour of an emerging genre. In 1996, however, Ayalneh Mulat and the Kendil Theatre Company had five children's plays on stage on Saturday mornings: *Enatena Lej* (*Mother and Child*), *Balena Mist* (*Husband and Wife*), *Wekaw*, *Condom*, and *Yaleedme Gabecha* (*Early Marriage*), this last requested by the Committee for Preventing Harmful Customs. Actors in training perform to audiences of not less than a hundred children every Sunday morning. The plays focus on social issues in as entertaining a way as possible, although Mulat, who has written four of the plays, insists on having serious or unhappy endings so that the plays will be remembered.

Puppets are not native to Ethiopian theatre, although they have been used sporadically on educational television. Touring European puppet shows have been hosted at the Italian and other cultural institutes. In the 1990s their use has been the result of collaboration with visiting European artists, and most of the productions in the Children's Theatre (the former YMCA) have involved puppetry.

The most important work in this form of theatre to date is the 1996 Addis Ababa University theatre arts department production of the story of King Solomon and the Queen of Sheba, co-sponsored by the Alliance-Française and Addis Ababa University Theatre. The production made use of choral songs, an increasingly important element in Ethiopian theatre.

Design

Most directors also take on the role of designer, although all the government theatres do have in-house designers who are usually graduates of the Addis Ababa School of Fine Art. Demissé Shiferraw is one of the very few well-known designers. Tadesse Mesfin, another designer of note, left the country for political reasons. Mesfin Habte-Mariam works at the Municipality Theatre and is partly responsible for its move towards a more symbolic and economical stage design.

During the 'golden era' of Ethiopian theatre – between 1974 and 1978 – there was close collaboration between established artists in different fields. For example, the set of Tsegay Gebre-Medhin's *Ha-Hu Besidist Wer* was designed by the late Ethiopian abstract artist Gebre-Kristos Desta who was then an instructor at the School of Fine Art. (The same set was used for *Ha-Hu Weyem Pe-Pu* twenty years later.) The music for *Ha-Hu Besidist Wer* was composed by an Armenian, Captain Nalbandian, Mulatu Astatke (a giant of Ethiopian classical music), and Mer'awi Setot.

In 1996, a production at one of the large government theatres had a budget of 30,000–40,000 birr, two-thirds of which was spent on the set. The stages are huge and the pressure is to fill them. In contrast, the original Hager Fikir Theatre (now the second space) had fewer than 300 seats and a stage that was often just big enough to hold the cast and therefore used no set at all. A simultaneous pressure is the demand for naturalism. If, for example, a house is called for by the script, then a set not much different from (and possibly more expensive than) a real house is built. In a country where much of the population is lucky to have some sheets of corrugated steel as shelter, this type of expenditure is seen as inappropriate. In the Municipality Theatre the stage is smaller and sets are more minimalist or representational.

Painted scenery and backdrops are sometimes used but there is often no set at all. The average Ethiopian audience is far more interested in the plot and verbal artistry of a play; sets, costumes and lighting are a bonus which the theatre company is not expected to provide if it does not have the resources. Thus private, under-funded companies do not feel forced to have sets or lighting. Costumes are important, but more as aids to characterization than naturalistic recreation.

In 1984, to commemorate the establishment of the Workers' Party of Ethiopia and the tenth anniversary of Mengistu's government, millions were spent on spectacular monuments and light displays all around the capital. These displays were mainly the work of Korean directors. This sudden emphasis on mass choreography and large symbols found its way into plays of the period, for example Getachew Abdi's *1928* (the Ethiopian date for the massacre by the Italian governor, Rodolpho Graziani, of over 10,000 Ethiopians in 1937) produced in 1989–90 at the National Theatre.

Theatre Space and Architecture

Plays take place both inside and out of doors, although, except for deliberately experimental performances at the university, outdoor performances are invariably a result of a lack of space. Touring theatre companies use makeshift stages in school halls, community halls, storage facilities or tents. There were more outdoor performances when the *kinet* groups emerged in the late 1970s, and performing troupes from the army often staged shows on hillsides. Outdoor performances use little or no scenery or lighting, and there is a strong tendency to retain the audience–performer delineation that would be caused by a proscenium or thrust stage.

Conscious attempts have been made at the Theatre Arts Department to explore different uses of theatre space. Most of these attempts have been motivated by expatriates and instructors at the Department. For example, *Oedipus the King* was directed in the early 1980s by Robert MacLaren on the steps of the Graduate Faculty, Jane Plastow used every imaginable space in the theatre for *The Caucasian Chalk Circle*; Clifford Coker directed Kenyan Ngugi wa'Thiongo's *Black Hermit* in-the-round in 1987, and in 1988 Mark Russell staged *Defiance* by turning the theatre into a total acting area.

Experiments with space by Ethiopians include *Hod Yefjew* (*Powerless Resentment*, 1987), written and directed by Fisseha Belay, where the audience was placed on the stage with the actors in the auditorium, and *Oedipus the King*, directed by Abate Mekuria in 1994, and staged around a fountain commonly known as the 'kissing pool' in the university grounds.

None of the theatres currently in use – not even the University Cultural Centre – was initially built as a theatre (except possibly the Municipality Theatre which nevertheless feels more like a conference hall). The National Theatre was a cinema that the Italians left unfinished when they departed. The Hager Fikir Theatre was built for a photo exhibition of the Emperor's visit to the United States, while the second space (which is a very good, intimate theatre space, although rarely used now as such) and today's bar were a pool club for Italian officers. The Ras Theatre was a cinema until it was converted into a theatre at the end of the 1970s, and the university Cultural Centre was a banquet hall when the main campus of the University was still an imperial palace.

Except for the University Cultural Centre and the space attached to the Theatre Arts Department, all the theatres have fixed seats, proscenium or thrust stages, and accommodate audiences of between 1,000 and 1,400 people. The Kendil Theatre has an end-stage.

Other performance spaces include Congress Hall, which seats up to 2,000 people but is rarely used as a theatre, and scores of 'Hulegeb Adarash', multipurpose halls which were built in all major towns and cities during the 1980s, and which do not have specific companies attached to them.

Training

In 1945 an advertisement appeared on national radio asking for people who wanted to be trained to act or work in the theatre. The advertisement was placed by the Municipality Theatre Company. Hager Fikir Theatre had an apprenticeship programme where children were taken from the priest's schools from as early as 9 years old. At first they sang, then were gradually trained as actors and playwrights.

In the mid-1970s Tsegay Gebre-Medhin established a theatre school at the National Theatre. This short-lived theatre school produced prominent graduates such as Alemtsehay Wodaje. Between 1945 and 1975 theatre training proceeded in a fairly *ad-hoc* fashion, where people either learned on the job, or went abroad. Among the latter group were Tesfaye Gessesse (playwright, director, actor, and now chair of the Theatre Arts Department of the university) who took an MA at Northwestern University (Illinois, United States) and Tsegay Gebre-Medhin, who was trained in England at the Theatre Royal in Windsor and the Royal Court Theatre in London. Most theatre practitioners at this point, however, were self-trained or came from other disciplines: Mengistu Lemma, a well-known writer of comedies, for example, began a degree at the London School of Economics. He did not, however, finish it. In the late 1970s, when Mengistu Haile-Mariam's Marxist government was well established, many theatre workers such as Behailu Mengesha, Getachew Abdi, and Sebhat Tessema were trained either in the former Soviet Union or in eastern European countries.

In 1990, the Ministry of Culture in Addis Ababa offered a series of free summer workshops aimed at teaching young people all aspects of theatre work with an emphasis on writing and acting. Because of the lack of resources that all theatres in Ethiopia must deal with, technical aspects of productions are usually limited, and little training takes place in this area. That first summer, one hundred students were accepted, and thirty graduated; in 1995, between two thousand and three thousand students applied. Again, one hundred were accepted, and forty graduated. The government has now withdrawn its subsidy, and the future of the programme remains to be seen; the demand for it, however, is undeniable. Graduates of this programme tend to start their own companies, or to find jobs in the state-run theatres.

In 1979, a Theatre Arts Department was opened at Addis Ababa University, and it is now the main centre in Ethiopia for theatre training and research. Courses taught include performance, playwriting, directing, theatre history (both Ethiopian and European), stagecraft (properties, design, makeup, lighting – although these are restricted by the availability of resources), stage-management, media (film, television, radio), creative writing (nondramatic), theatre in society, and traditional drama. Class sizes vary between fifteen and thirty students, and are in fact getting smaller rather than larger.

The department faces two main problems. First, acting is not regarded as a profession that needs training. It is also not as prestigious as careers in engineering or medicine. Connected to this is a lack of support from the university itself. For example, in the early 1980s the Theatre Arts Department conducted a two-year series of skill-upgrading workshops for theatre professionals already active in the industry. The university, however, refused to grant the graduates diplomas since general entrance requirements had not been met. The programme has been suspended. Second, there was friction between the university and nonuniversity theatre communities, the latter being dominated by the older generation, most of whom had no formal training or who had been educated in eastern Europe. The establishment of the Theatre Arts Department was, however, a major turn for the better for both the practice and the theory of Ethiopian theatre. Less than twenty years after the department's inception, the Ras, the National, and the Municipality Theatres were being directed by university graduates, which led to a better working relationship between the two communities.

In 1995, a private theatre training centre was established at the Kendil Theatre Company. It has two streams – a full-time, two-month course, and a nine-month, part-time course on weekends. In 1966, the latter was attended by 145 students. Young actors are taught Ethiopian drama, literature, music and folk dance, with general lectures given in the mornings by former university professors. Workshops and practical experience are included.

Criticism, Scholarship and Publishing

The only theatre research centre in the country is the Addis Ababa University Theatre Arts Department.

There is an annual conference held in June by the Institute of Language Studies at Addis Ababa University, and this is the main forum for theatre research. Occasionally, papers have been presented at the International Conference of Ethiopian Studies. In 1994–5 the first conference on Ethiopian theatre was held in Addis Ababa.

In 1984 Hager Fikir Theatre celebrated its golden jubilee. There were special performances of early plays, and their production processes – the way in which the plays had been developed and rehearsed – were re-created. There was also an academic conference organized to mark the occasion.

There are no theatre journals or equivalent publications, and after 1974 plays themselves were hardly ever published. However, there is a great deal of unpublished material at the Theatre Arts Department – for example, the exhaustive *A Preliminary Investigation of Dramatic Elements Within Traditional Ceremonies Among the Annuak, Majenger, Nuer and Shako Nationalists of Illubabor Administrative Region, South Western Ethiopia* by Abone Ashagre and Peter Harrop.

Since Ethiopian playwrights and other theatre professionals work in an indigenous language, they have been denied the attention given to their African counterparts by international researchers – in fact, Ethiopia is treated as a distinct area in almost all work on African theatre. Albert Gérard's *Four African Literatures: Xhosa, Sotho, Zulu, Amharic* (1971) is a solid, if somewhat over-critical, guide to the literary beginnings of Ethiopian theatre. Probably Jane Plastow's *Ethiopia: The Creation of a Theatre Culture* (1989) is the only major work done on Ethiopian theatre in recent years. A handbook on acting in Amharic called *Mestawet* (*Mirror*) was printed in Germany in 1995 and is the second educational book on theatre in recent years. The first was Debebe Eshetu's important translation of Stanislavski's work in about 1983.

Strained relations between the west and the Ethiopian government before 1991 are one reason for this lack of scholarship. Before 1974, plays by major Ethiopian playwrights such as Tsegay Gebre-Medhin had been translated and printed in Europe. Paradoxically, Ethiopian theatre took massive strides after 1974. Another reason is the shortage of theatre scholars within the country itself.

Major government-owned newspapers carry reviews of new productions in their weekly 'Culture' section. These reviews are extensive, but since they are usually written by individuals with very little knowledge of the theatre, they often fail to provide an informed opinion. Those written by knowledgeable reviewers tend to be suspect; bias is difficult to avoid in such a relatively small community.

Tamirat Gebeyehu, Aida Edemariam
(with draft material by Debebe Eshetu)

Further Reading

Aklilu, Amsalu. 'Acher Ye Ethiopia Sine-Tsehuf Tarik' [A short history of Ethiopian culture]. Unpublished. Addis Ababa University, 1976.

Ashagre, Aboneh, and Peter Harrop. *A Preliminary Investigation of Dramatic Elements Within Traditional Ceremonies Among the Annuak, Majenger, Nuer and Shako Nationalities of Illubabor Administrative Region, South Western Ethiopia*. Report prepared for the Research and Publication Office of Addis Ababa University. Theatre Arts Department, Addis Ababa University, 1984.

Gebeyehu, Tamirat. 'Ye Leb Woled Serawochen Be Tenetenet Sele Makenaber' [Adapting creative works for the stage]. Unpublished. Theatre Arts Department, Addis Ababa University, 1989.

Gérard, Albert. *Contexts of African Literature.* Amsterdam and Atlanta, GA: Rodopi, 1990.

——. *Four African Literatures: Xhosa, Sotho, Zulu, Amharic.* Berkeley and Los Angeles: University of California Press, 1971.

Gessesse, Tesfaye. *Acher Ye Ethiopia Theatre Tenat: Kemegemeriyaw Eske Kebede Mikael* [A short study of Ethiopian theatre: from the beginning to Kebede Michael]. Proceedings of the Third International Conference of Ethiopian Studies. Addis Ababa: Institute of Ethiopian Studies, Haile Selassie University (Addis Ababa University), 1996.

Leiris, Michel. *La Possessione e i suoi aspetti teatrali tra gli Etiopi di Gondar* [Possession and its theatrical aspects among the Ethiopians of Gondar]. Milan: Ubulibri, 1988. 86pp.

Levine, Donald. *Wax and Gold: Tradition and*

Innovation in Ethiopian Culture. Chicago and London: University of Chicago Press, 1965.

Mantel-Nieóko, Joanna. 'Ethiopian literature in Amharic'. In *Literatures in African Languages: Theoretical Issues and Sample Surveys*, eds. B.W. Andrzejewski, S. Pilaszewicz and W. Tyloch. Cambridge and New York: Cambridge University Press, 1985. 672 pp.

Marcus, Harold. *A History of Ethiopia*. Berkeley, Los Angeles and London: University of California Press, 1994.

Messing, Simon D. 'A Modern Ethiopia Play: Self-finding in Culture Change'. *Anthropological Quarterly* 33 (1960): 149–57.

Plastow, Jane. *Ethiopia: The Creation of a Theatre Culture*. Manchester: University of Manchester Press, 1989.

Ullendorf, Edward. *The Ethiopians: An Introduction to Country and People*. Oxford: Oxford University Press, 1960.

Zewde, Bahru. *A History of Modern Ethiopia: 1855–1974*. Addis Ababa: Addis Ababa University Press, 1992.

GHANA

Situated on the west coast of Africa and occupying approximately 238,600 square kilometres (92,100 square miles), Ghana is bordered on the west by Côte d'Ivoire, on the east by Togo (formerly French Togo) and to the north by Burkina Faso (formerly Upper Volta). Previously known as the British colony of the Gold Coast, Ghana became independent in 1957 and was joined that same year by British Togoland. The creation of the new nation made it the first Black African political entity to become independent since the founding of Liberia in 1847. With Kwame Nkrumah (1909–72) as its first prime minister, the country was declared a republic in 1960.

Within modern Ghana's boundaries – artificial structures essentially established by the colonial powers at conferences in Berlin in 1884 and 1885 – live some 19.1 million people, 54 per cent of whom were under 18 in 1995. In the population are to be found speakers of some forty-four African languages, the most important of which are Akan, Dagbani, Ewe, Ga, Hausa, Moshi and Nzima. The present distribution of the speakers of different languages reflects population movements over a long period, with influxes from west, north and east being remembered in myths and legends. Nevertheless, English is the main official language, while Akan is spoken by a significant proportion of the population. Theatre flourishes in other languages as well, particularly in Fanti (part of the Akan group).

The capital of the country, Accra, is situated on the coast and, like capitals in all countries in similar stages of evolution, absorbs a disproportionate amount of government expenditure. Migration to the cities and larger towns is a feature of internal population movements with cities such as Accra and Kumasi acting as magnets for young people seeking economic opportunities.

The country is rich in minerals, particularly gold, but also manganese, diamonds, and bauxite. It was, however, the gold that impressed the Portuguese who first arrived in the 1450s and who, at the beginning of the 1480s, established a fort at Edina, later called Elmina.

Interest in gold gave way to traffic in human beings. For centuries the slave trade fostered wars and raiding, created instability and robbed the territory of able-bodied people. Although officially stopped in 1807, the buying and selling of human beings continued and the scars can still be traced in the language and mores of Ghanaians. Although treated in dramatic texts and in dance drama sequences, the implications of the slave trade, which involved Africans as both victims and exploiters, represent a potentially divisive experience: a part of the past that a nation building a sense of unity can dwell on only at great risk.

In the period following the formal abolition of the slave trade the Ashantis invaded coastal areas. After various skirmishes leading to the decisive battle of Katamansu in 1826, the British assumed responsibility for the region. The establishment of this colonial presence was marked by the signing of the Treaty of Friendship, known as 'The Bond of 1844', between Britain and the Fanti chiefs, who inhabited what are now parts of the Central Region near Cape Coast.

A series of wars with the Ashantis followed, and a decisive point was reached in 1874 when a British punitive expeditionary force under Sir Garnett Wolsey entered Kumasi. From there agents moved north signing Treaties of Friendship with chiefs in what became known as the Northern Territories. Despite this advance, tension continued in the centre of the country. In 1896, Otumfo Agyeman Prempeh I was taken prisoner and sent into exile in the Seychelles, but resistance continued. In 1901 the Ashanti Kingdom was annexed as a British colony and the Northern Territories formally became a British protectorate. In 1919, as part of a redistribution of what had been German colonies, part of Togoland also fell under British rule.

Politicians have tried to impose a sense of identity on the country, sometimes using the performing arts. But because of the country's diversity and history, the term 'Ghanaian' can be used only with trepidation. In the paragraphs that follow the word is used with full cognizance of the dangers inherent in generalizations.

It may be useful to examine in greater detail the growth of the articulate tradition that defined itself in terms of opposition to the European presence, an opposition centred in Cape Coast. Situated just a few miles from Elmina, Cape Coast was a mercantile, missionary and educational centre. It was there that English-style education was first available, initially for the mixed-race children fathered by Europeans, and it was there in 1897 that the Aborigines' Rights Protection Society was formed. That society, tiny in terms of members but significant within the evolution of the country, led the opposition against British influence and power through the law courts.

Its membership included many who had been educated in London, among them John Mensah Sarbah (1864–1910), a lawyer and author of major books on law; Joseph Caseley-Hayford (1866–1930), and Kobina Sekyi (1892–1956), both writers. Through their works, particularly in Hayford's *Ethiopia Unbound*, and Sekyi's play *The Blinkards* (1915), comes a powerful sense of racial and cultural confidence. Caseley-Hayford was a prime mover in the organization which brought together the new coastal elite in a regional grouping: the West African National Congress, founded in 1917. Other important spokespeople who used a dramatic form to engage in debate with the British included J.B. Danquah (1895–1965) and F.K. Fiawoo (1891–1961), one an Akyem, the other a Ewe. In *The Third Woman* (1943) and *The Fifth Landing Stage* (originally written in Ewe and entitled *Toko Atolia*, 1943), they confronted European assumptions.

During the first decades of the century, the Gold Coast continued to be drawn into contact with other countries through increasing involvement in the world economy and as a result of the activities of colonial officers, missionaries and teachers. Imported elements began to be fused with a fundamentally agrarian and pastoral society, and in coastal and riverine areas, with communities of fisherfolk.

In terms of theatre, this meant that the festivals, rites, rituals and entertainments of the region (including music, dances and storytelling) which all existed within a specifically West African framework were brought into contact with imported traditions such as school plays, Empire Day celebrations, church cantatas, club entertainments and cinema. The interaction was particularly significant in Tarkwa, where gold mines were situated; in the twin towns of Sekondi-Takoradi from which cocoa and timber were exported; and in educational, administrative and missionary centres, such as Cape Coast, Kumasi and Accra. The most remarkable syncretic convention to emerge was that of the Ghanaian 'Concert Party', a form of performance whose beginnings can be traced to the city of Sekondi in about 1918 and whose artistic structure will be discussed later.

World War II and its aftermath prepared the way for political and theatrical developments, including a rising tide of anti-imperial sentiment. A nationalist political party, the United

A typical Concert Party stage in a compound house.
Photo: Bokoor African Popular Music Archives.

Gold Coast Convention, was established in 1947 by a group of distinguished local men including lawyer and playwright J.B. Danquah. Its aim was to secure self-government for the people of the Gold Coast 'in the shortest possible time'. Following shootings at Christiansbourg and the rioting that followed, six leaders of the party, including Danquah and Kwame Nkrumah, were arrested by the British.

The events which followed showed that the British were prepared to make certain concessions, reflected by the appointment of a Committee on Constitutional Reform, and that Nkrumah was determined to set the pace for the process of decolonization. American-educated, with a Marxist-influenced approach to national problems and a commitment to Pan-Africanist ideals, Nkrumah embodied a new approach to politics in the country. On 6 March 1957, under the name of an ancient West African kingdom, the country became independent: the Gold Coast was now to be known as Ghana.

Guided by a belief in socialism and Pan-Africanism, the new government began to implement a controversial Five Year Development Plan in which a number of major projects, controlled by the state and including the building of the Akosombo Dam, the development of Tema Harbour and the construction of the Tema–Accra motorway, were set in motion.

These changes were also linked to significant developments in theatre, many of them guided by the Ghana Institute for Arts and Culture (GIAC). Among these were the creation of a company called the Experimental Theatre Group and the establishment of a Workers' Brigade Drama Group to put on political Concert Party-style productions. The early years of independence also saw the construction, thanks to the new Arts Council and US funding bodies, of the Accra Drama Studio.

During this same period, Saka Acquaye (b. 1928) composed and directed a series of 'folk-operas' which combined music, dance and drama. Several – *Obadzeng*, *Bo Mong* and *The Lost Fisherman* – were dispatched on cultural visits, sometimes as far away as the Soviet Union. The theatre thus became directly involved in Nkrumah's desire to be 'non-aligned' in the dangerous east–west political game of the time.

The period also saw the flourishing of the enterprising playwright Efua Sutherland (1924–96). More than anyone else, she articulated a vision of what the local theatre might become, and in many ways embodied the Ghana National Theatre Movement at this time. However, as the years passed and the euphoria which had accompanied independence faded, Nkrumah's government lost favour. There was also opposition to his push to make the country a one-party state as well as discontent with blatant corruption in high places, anger at the passing of the Preventive Detention Bill, uncertainty about the implications of his ideas about 'African personality', rage at the death, in detention during 1965, of Danquah, concern at the proliferation of state-owned industries, and disappointment at their failure to make a profit.

There was also indignation in many places at the extent to which Nkrumah had encouraged a personality cult around him. As essential commodities became more difficult to obtain, challenges to Nkrumah's position mounted and theatre censorship began to be felt. The honeymoon between him and the arts ended. As early as 1959, censorship could be clearly felt: the headmaster of Achimota School that year was forced to step down after playing the Mayor in a staff production of *The Government Inspector*. The production was read as an attack on the government. Matters became worse when Ibsen's *An Enemy of the People* was also rejected as being politically unsuitable to mark a conference of visiting heads of state.

In 1966, Nkrumah, out of the country on a visit to China, was overthrown by a coup. A National Liberation Council was set up which held power until 1969, when elections took place and Kofi Busia and the Progress Party came to power. This Second Republic represented a brief period of liberal, though, many felt, indecisive, rule. In 1972 members of the armed forces, led by Kutu Acheampong, moved once again. The next seven years saw a period of widespread corruption and uncontrolled abuse of rule by the National Redemption Council, and experiments with a Supreme Military Council and a cynically conceived Union Government before Lt General Akuffo launched a palace coup. This did not satisfy younger elements within the forces and in 1979 Flight-Lieutenant Jerry Rawlings (b. 1947) emerged as the leader of another coup that placed the Armed Forces Revolutionary Council in control.

Rawlings and the Council returned the country to civilian rule, under Hilla Limann and the People's National Party in 1979, but observed events closely. In 1981, in what was seen as his 'second coming', Rawlings overthrew Limann and ruled through the Provisional National Defence Council until 1992 when he was elected president. Under pressure, Ghana made structural adjustments advocated by international financing bodies such as the World Bank. To the surprise of many Ghanaians, the country has been held up as a model of what can be achieved if the 'medicine' prescribed in Washington is taken.

Summarized in this way recent Ghanaian history is somewhat confusing. It is perhaps more helpful to see the country during its modern history swinging between the rhetoric of east and west, of ideologically oriented 'African Socialism' united with an African personality on the one hand and liberal humanism going hand-in-hand with capitalism and a commitment to individual freedom on the other. The movement between poles is complicated by the changing world in which the various groups and individuals have had to operate.

There have been momentous changes since World War II and, as a result, the passing of the old colonial order has been followed by the passing of the tight hegemonic system in which the world was divided between east, west and the non-aligned. To the economic forces represented by multinational companies, and the futures markets on which the prices of primary products are fixed, must be added the post-war policies of the new colonialists including the World Bank and the International Monetary Fund.

These, crudely sketched, are some of the political and economic forces that have shaped recent Ghanaian history, and that have, inevitably, affected its theatre. The heady days of the 1950s and early 1960s, when Ghanaians were exhilarated by nationalism and by the sense of being at the forefront of an Anti-Colonial and Pan-Africanist movement whose time had come have long since passed. So too have the brief periods of euphoria and revolutionary fervour that accompanied coups. There have been times when artists – or, at least, some artists – and government have worked closely together. This was particularly true in the early years of Nkrumah which saw the rise of nationalism, and the arrival of independence under a leader who was committed to state involvement in all aspects of the economy and society.

Under Rawlings, in khaki and mufti, the state has been supportive of certain aspects of theatre life, and individual activists have even

been able to rise to positions of power within the structures he has encouraged. Playwright and teacher Asiedu Yirenkyi (b. 1946), for example, became Minister of Culture at one point and was able to establish a tiered system of arts festivals. A little later, Mohammed Ben-Abdallah (b. 1944), who held a variety of government posts, pushed the formation of a National Commission on Culture that recruited some of those who had taken courses in drama at the University of Ghana, and produced a framework for nation-wide support for the arts. He also negotiated various plans which led to the construction of a National Theatre in Accra and the reconstruction of the Drama Studio at Legon near Accra, as part of a Chinese construction programme. Government support can still be seen through its input into the University of Ghana's School of Performing Arts and into the National Theatre.

On the other hand, much has been left to the initiative of amateur enthusiasts to do what they can: creating spaces, developing talents and carrying out experiments. The atmosphere in which they have had to work has often been poisoned by fear of repercussions, what opposition politician Adu Boahene has called 'a culture of silence', and for several years, under both Nkrumah and Rawlings, many were wary of expressing controversial opinions.

Nevertheless, the state has also provided support for amateur companies including the Drama Studio Players, Ghana Theatre Club and Ghana Playhouse. Their repertoires were generally text-based and reflected the extent to which the country was responding to European-style drama. Plays by local dramatists and by important international writers began to be seen. During the early 1960s, for example, Drama Studio Players put on a series of productions that included plays by Efua Sutherland such as *Odasani*, *Foriwa* and *Edufa* while the Theatre Club did García Lorca's *Yerma*, Strindberg's *Miss Julie* and *The Stronger*, F.K. Fiawoo's *The Fifth Landing Stage*, Lorraine Hansberry's *A Raisin in the Sun* and the Haitian writer Felix Morrisseau-Leroy's *Antigone in Haïti*.

Theatres also looked to other West African playwrights such as Sarif Easmon, James Ene Henshaw and Wole Soyinka. During the early 1970s they concentrated on Ghanaian work such as Danquah's *The Third Woman* and Sekyi's *The Blinkards* but their choices shifted as ideological winds changed. The search for texts that offered opportunities for spectacle,

The Legon 7 production of *The Interlopers*, based on Wole Soyinka's *The Interpreters*. Photo: Don Gentner.

music and dance accounted for their decision to put on *Hassan* by James Elroy Flecker; a taste for melodrama prompted selections such as *The Yorkshire Tragedy*.

The desire to establish a company that would travel extensively and combine music, dance and dialogue burned in the heart of Efua Sutherland, and in 1968 she was able to establish the Kusum Agoromba group. Professional and mobile, the twenty-person company operated from the Drama Studio and offered 'quality plays in Akan'. Their programme included Sutherland's own works, such as *Foriwa* and *Odasani* (an adaptation of *Everyman*) as well as *Blood Is Mysterious, The Rumour Monger's Fate, God's Time Is Best, Love For Your Neighbour* and *Ananse and the Dwarf Brigade*. This last was an example of the continued search for a theatrical tradition within an indigenous storytelling tradition. Productions offered to schools, colleges, churches, community centres and other institutions were varied and impressive. A remarkable record of miles travelled and productions mounted was established by this pioneering company, and although the funds that supported it ultimately ran dry, members of the group continued to work in the theatre.

In 1983 the University of Ghana established its own professional company, Abibigromma, officially a research wing of the School of Performing Arts. Some of its members were recruited from among those who had earlier graduated from the School, and the company was overseen and sometimes directed by members of the School's staff. Early productions included *Death and the King's Horseman* (Soyinka), *Omero Tulige* (Tamakloe), *Sleeping Beauty* (choreographed by Adinku), and *Sizwe Bansi Is Dead* (Fugard, Kani and Ntshona). Members of the company also participated in Ben-Abdallah's *The Land of a Million Magicians*.

When the new National Theatre was opened in 1993, many members of Abibigromma were offered employment there. Some moved but many did not and as a result two separate companies existed for a time – the only two professional theatre companies in the country – and both calling themselves Abibigromma. Their repertories have been very different though echoing the rhetoric that went back to Kunsum Agoromba and beyond.

Both, however, have aspired to employ all the arts in 'total theatre' productions. In 1994, Abibigromma (Legon) did *Ananse in the Land*

Femi Osofisan's 1994 Abibigromma (Legon) production of his *Nkrumah Ni...Africa Ni...*.
Photo: Eckhard Breitinger.

of Idiots (Yaw Asare), *Who Raped the Ramatu Sisters?* (choreographed by Cecilia Yelpoe with Yaw Asare) and, under the direction of Femi Osofisan who was also the playwright, *Nkrumah Ni... Africa Ni...*.

During the same year, Abibigromma (National Theatre) put on a season that included two works by Caribbean authors – *Old Story Time* by Trevor Rhone, and *The Playboy of the West Indies*, an adaptation by Mustapha Matura. Both were directed by visitors, one (Anton Phillips) from the United Kingdom, the other (Steven Gerald) from the United States.

The economic base that existed at independence was eroded from the mid-1960s by over-ambitious policies, corruption and economic disasters. The articulate middle class that once formed the vanguard of the national theatre movement saw a marked drop in its standard of living during the decades and the limitation of its ability to create opportunities to take part in or attend theatrical activities. The challenges of television, and more recently video, while providing employment for performers, dealt further blows to the theatrical tradition. They have eaten deep into the audiences on which the troupes depend.

There are nevertheless a number of newer groups that have emerged, some interested in using drama for various kinds of community development, and there is a continuing interest by foreign cultural agencies in supporting local theatre. The British Council has been such a supporter for many years, while Germany and the United Stated are among the countries which have more recently become involved in providing such assistance.

Structure of the National Theatre Community

In speaking of the structure of the national theatre community, it is easiest to start by identifying specialized *places* for performance and to draw attention to some of the groups that act in them. The National Theatre is one such. Constructed with a loan from China, it occupies a site in Olympic Park near the centre of Accra and is the base for Abibigromma (the National Theatre company), the National Orchestra and National Dance Ensemble. The building, which is run by the National Theatre Corporation and which opened in 1993, took some thirty months to build and affords the companies various rehearsal, office and workshop facilities. There are dressing rooms, makeup rooms, green rooms, and a number of performance and exhibition areas.

The National Theatre opened with a production that brought together the National Dance Ensemble, National Symphony Orchestra and the National Theatre's own drama company. The first play produced there was *The Leopard's Choice*.

As might be expected with such a large building, and one which requires air conditioning, rental charges are high, and few groups – even though they are not required to pay full rates – can afford to work there. Performances in the National Theatre are, therefore, few and far between – though Saturday afternoon variety shows have proved popular and are presented regularly.

Elsewhere, theatre in Ghana exists in a variety of forms and locales. An indication of the diversity can best be suggested by noting here the experience of students from the School of Performing Arts at Legon who, during the first eight months of 1994, performed in the following places: in front of a three-storey teaching block at the West African Secondary School, Adenta; in the largest open space, one often used for children's games at Christian Village, situated a few miles from the Legon campus; in a closed-off street of town-planned and overcrowded Ashaiman, near Tema; in a space between cowsheds and the home of

God, Lucifer and Gabriel in the Legon Road Theatre production of *The Fall*.
Photo: James Gibbs.

herders from the north who had taken their beasts south to sell them, on the edge of Ashaiman; on the lush lawn of an open-air restaurant near high-rise flats in one of the middle-class residential districts of Tema; in the Achimota lorry park just off the busy Nsawam Road; under a tree opposite a chief's simple dwelling in Tamale; on open, sandy ground in Bolgatanga where a few trees provided the set for a play about protecting plants; in the Drama Studio on the university campus (many times); in the main auditorium of the National Theatre; in the Courtyard Theatre at the same venue; on a stage erected within Cape Coast Castle – originally a fortress for invaders and a prison for captives awaiting sale; in the Arts Centre, Accra; and in the garden of a lecturer's home in the township of Madina near Legon. Many of the more obviously improvised of these venues were chosen because of the overriding desire to take a production to a particular audience, or to create it with a particular community.

Two major performances by the group were cancelled at a few hours' notice or at the very last minute during the same eight-month period, and the reasons for cancellation provide an important insight into the conditions under which theatre in Ghana operates. One performance at the Arts Centre was cancelled because a political function was given priority; the other, at the National Theatre, because there were so few people, fewer than ten, in the auditorium.

Obtaining audiences in the places near where people actually live is, however, never a problem so long as the entrance fee is reasonable and some music, songs and dances establish a suitable atmosphere. For evening performances in impoverished communities, simply the switching on of bright lights is all that is required to attract an audience.

An important aspect of theatre in the country can be seen during festivals and purification ceremonies, as well as in the rites associated with fishing, hunting, planting, fertility, the attainment of adulthood and funerals. There are elements of impersonation in all of these, the true theatrical base of Ghana. Certainly anyone who has attended a funeral at which episodes from the life of the deceased person are acted out will testify to the narrow dividing line that exists between dramatic representation and ordinary life in such ceremonies. In this sense, the national theatre community is large and inclusive and stretches across the length and breadth of the country.

With the Ghanaian calendar full of such festivals, one can find theatre somewhere at almost any time of the year. In them, theatrical elements abound: the heightened use of language, masquerades, symbolic actions, impersonation and group antiphonal singing. Underlying structures, however, are often concealed in such forms, and references tend to be allusive rather than explicit as they are in more mimetic theatre. Audiences are principally local, but usually include some of the scattered sons and daughters of that community who are encouraged to return for the celebrations. The occasion is often one to which visitors are also invited. Interpretations of the precise historical events being commemorated or the particular significance of specific elements in such proceedings may vary and much may be only vaguely understood, especially by those who have lost touch with the community. This is to be expected in societies in which the oral tradition was once strong.

Invaluable work on these Ghanaian festivals and events has been carried out and written up by J.H. Kwabena Nketia (b. 1924) who, while fully aware of the possibilities of change and innovation, has identified four broad festival categories. These include the festivals of the gods among which are Kpledzo, Chawe, Letsu and Okpei; festivals concerned with nature, such as Bakatue and Gonfifaa; festivals concerned with the solidarity of a local area represented by Adae and Odwira; and finally those devoted to the ancestors which include Danyibakaka, Avedegbe and Bugum.

There is, says Nketia, 'hardly any month in which a festival of some sort is not celebrated in some locality'. As one might expect, this tradition of festivals has been exploited and developed by politicians and ministries of culture, as well as by playwrights and choreographers.

Artistic Profile

The griotic storytelling tradition is still the root of much indigenous theatre. Storytellers begin by listening and earn special recognition if they are eloquent and fluent, if they marry wit with wisdom and originality with tradition. Some groups, or families, cultivate a tradition of storytelling – for example Efua Sutherland was drawn to the village of Atwia Ekumfi by the vigour of its storytelling tradition. Inevitably the advent of other forms of entertainment and instruction has challenged the position that storytelling once held, or has forced storytellers to come to terms with new forms of communication.

Singers and dancers, their shortcomings tolerated in youth, their particular accomplishments earning them praise as they grow up, also develop within a community in which participation is encouraged. In the early 1960s, when the decision was taken to start a National Dance Ensemble, able performers were recruited from villages and invited to Legon where they were instructed in the dances of parts of the country they were unfamiliar with.

Concert Parties, building on a tradition begun just after World War I by an elementary school teacher – Master Yalley – recruited actors from towns and villages, encouraging determined and talented performers to dance and act. Despite Yalley's background, classroom knowledge was not a very great asset, and more immediately valuable skills, such as comic timing and the ability to keep a deadpan expression, were learned on the job.

There were at one point more than forty such troupes making a living from touring their productions through the country. Even now, in a harsher economic climate and in competition with other forms of entertainment a number of such groups manage to survive. In 1960, there were some twenty-eight Concert Party companies and more than thirty in 1974. Numbers, however, declined by the 1990s.

The Concert Party form itself makes use of slapstick and satirical lyrics which comment on current issues. Bame describes a typical production in terms of a long musical introduction, a series of brief sketches, a choral song and a 'play'. The dramatic structure is loose by comparison with the conventions of the 'well-made play' and more akin to musical tradition. Opportunities are created for the singing of numerous songs in a variety of styles (traditional, hymns, high-life, soul, pop and so on), in telling a story in which sympathy is often evoked for the orphaned and downtrodden and in which trickster characters feature prominently. The vitality of the form, the volatility of the audiences and the precarious economic base on which companies operate

have been well described by John Collins in his numerous publications on the subject. The Concert Party 'play' is followed by a reprise of some of the most popular songs.

Always responsive to popular demand, the Concert Parties have a large popular following. Most audiences quite happily sit through a warm-up programme of songs that lasts for up to two and-a-half hours on uncomfortable wooden seats whose only saving grace is that they are usually in the open air. The dramatic part of the entertainment may range in subject matter from moralistic to domestic, from historical to political and is also punctuated with songs.

The early work in this tradition by Master Yalley was developed by later groups such as Ishmael 'Bob' Johnson, a founding member of the group Two Bobs and their Carolina Girl. This three-person company in their turn paved the way for the Axim Trio and later the Happy Trio. During the 1920s the tradition was carried on and made more accessible to a large popular audience by the Keta Trio, Jovial Jokers, Burma Jokers and Yankee Trio. Right through the 1960s, Concert Party groups continued to emerge, the names hinting at origins and aspirations: the Abuakwa Trio, Jungle Jokers, Kakaiku's Concert Party, Jaguar Jokers and Happy Brothers.

Titles from the Two Bobs' repertoire suggest the ambition and concerns – historical, political and moral – of the productions: *The Coronation of George VI* (a particularly popular play, mounted like all the others with just three performers), *The Bond of 1844, The*

The Jaguar Jokers' campaign bus.
Photo: Bokoor African Popular Music Archives.

Downfall of Adolph Hitler, Kwame Nkrumah Will Never Die, and *Love Is the Sweetest Thing*.

In 1962, when Nkrumah's 'African Socialism' was the dominant ideology, the Workers' Brigade Drama Group was formed to combine a Nkrumahist message with this populist theatrical tradition. The Brigade's repertoire included *Papa ye Asa, Obra ye ko* (*Life Is War*), *No Tears For Ananse*, and *The Faithless Wife*, an improvised drama based on Chaucer's 'Pardoner's Tale' that had become an established favourite by the late 1960s and was still drawing audiences in the 1990s.

While visitors with a background in conventional western theatre may find such performances difficult to relate to theatrically, they will find little or no difficulty in coming to terms with the European-style amateur, school and church drama performed in Ghana. Given the impact Europeans have made on the country over the last five hundred years, the strength of this tradition is not surprising. The missionaries who first proclaimed the Gospel in Africa also brought European theatre with them – or, at least, the tradition of doing Nativity plays and of dramatizing parables. On occasions, school teachers and tutors in teacher training institutions encouraged a similar approach to theatre. The examination system has also contributed to the form by suggesting that drama is primarily a matter of text, a branch of literature, rather than the more traditional African form of public performance.

A revealing insight into this approach from the 1930s is provided by material on 'Native Drama' that appeared in the British Drama League's publication *Drama* in 1932. Readers were informed then that 'the African native' can hardly distinguish fact from fiction when watching a play; that it is the instinct of the audience to participate in the play; that the natural method is for one or two players to perform to a rhythmic accompaniment by the audience; that rhythm is an essential part of their art; that the body of African folklore is small and entirely concerned with animals; and that a sense of comedy overflows everything.

Revd Kingsley Williams, then at the major secondary school in the Gold Coast, Prince of Wales College, Achimota (later Achimota School) contributed the following: 'So far as I know there is no native drama properly so called in the Gold Coast.' He listed only school productions of *Everyman, The Bishop's Candlesticks* (after Victor Hugo), a Nativity play in three scenes, and a play about Joseph. Subsequently correspondents to *Drama* drew attention to the fact that *Antigone* had been presented, at least partly in Greek, at St Nicholas's School, Cape Coast (now Adisadel). From this it is clear that the perspective from Achimota was partial and ill informed. Williams, for instance, did not know that Sekyi's *The Blinkards* had been done at Cape Coast in 1915 and made no mention of Concert Parties.

Later important work in school drama was carried out at Mfantsipim School in Cape Coast; during the 1950s by Caribbean poet Edward Kamau Brathwaite (b. 1930), who adapted *Antigone* as *Odale's Choice*; and by Joe de Graft (1924–78), who directed work by Nigerian dramatist James Ene Henshaw and subsequently wrote and produced his own *Sons and Daughters*.

The contemporary situation in schools and colleges continues to be characterized by diversity: productions can range from the tried and tested (*The Bishop's Candlesticks* remains a favourite) to presentation of work by local writers, Martin Owusu's *Sudden Return* and Asiedu Yirenkyi's *Kivuli*, for example. There are also explorations of the narrative theatre tradition which Sutherland encouraged and which she embodied in her text *The Marriage of Anansewa*. Beside these can be ranked bold attempts to come to terms with the combination of festival theatre and English language drama represented by Wole Soyinka's *Kongi's Harvest*, and a range of Theatre-in-Education experiments.

The important role played by dance in African society, and therefore in Ghana, has frequently been remarked upon. Because it exists at so many levels in the numerous cultural groups within Ghana's borders, and because it does not rely on language to communicate, dance has also been used to develop a sense of nationhood. The Ghana Dance Ensemble, under Niyi Yartey, has also moved from staging 'traditional dances' to presenting dance dramas using a range of expressive gestures and movements derived from the life of Ghana's bustling markets, from local dance forms and from his own experience as an international choreographer. Of the Ghanaian playwrights, Ben-Abdallah has been the most creative in integrating dance, dance drama and spoken drama.

Companies
Dramaturgy

The country's most influential playwright, Efua Sutherland, fostered decisive developments in the tradition of building drama from a narrative base. It must be noted as well that she also recognized the possibility of evolution in other directions.

Brought up in Cape Coast, educated at St Monica's Anglican School in Ashanti-Mampong and later at Homerton College, Cambridge, and at the University of London, Sutherland described herself as being on a journey of discovery into the culture and traditions of her people. From the establishment of the Experimental Theatre Group in the 1950s she encouraged those who gathered around her to perform plays based on the canon of *Ananse* stories, a cycle of tales built around the adventures of a spider. An early account describes a performance on the grounds of the Teacher Training College at Akropong in the course of which stories that might have been told in neighbouring compounds in a traditional manner – that is to say by a single storyteller with musical interludes (*mboguo*) provided by participating audience members – were given more theatrical treatments.

In the performance she described, the songs were sung by a rehearsed, imported chorus, and the characters introduced in the course of the story were played by different actors. Sutherland has argued that 're-created and contemporized [the *Ananse* folk tales] offer exciting food for dramatists' in Ghana. Plays based on such stories (*anansesem*) are, following Sutherland's use of the term, known as *anansegro*.

In *The Marriage of Anansewa* she produced, with the help of collaborators and with some inspiration from non-African theatrical traditions, an example of what *anansegro* might be. Significantly, although the published version is in English, the play was first performed in Akan – an indication of her commitment to African languages and a recognition of the need to communicate primarily with a mass audience.

An interest in *anansesem* can also be seen in works by Joe de Graft, Asiedu Yirenkyi and Martin Owusu such as *Ananse and the Gum Man, Anna Pranaa* and *A Bird Called* .... However, it is worth pointing out that other influences were also at work on these writers: de Graft was influenced by Pirandello; Yirenkyi by

Chekhov; and Owusu by Yeats. One might also note here that the popularity of these tales has spread far; in Jamaica the hero of the adapted Ananse stories is known as Aunt Nancy.

Another major Ghanaian playwright is Mohammed Ben-Abdallah. His early work, written after he had completed a diploma at Legon and while working with schools and with the Anokye Players attached to the Kumasi Cultural Centre, includes *Ananse and the Magic Drum* and *Ananse and the Rain God*. From those modest exercises, and partly while doing a doctorate in playwriting at the University of Texas in the United States, Ben-Abdallah moved on to much more complex manipulations of narrative traditions, seeking inspiration in legend, history, and contemporary politics. Significantly, he also retold Brecht's *The Good Woman of Setzuan*, transforming it in the process. His version, *The Land of a Million Magicians*, is clearly placed in Nima, an area of Accra in which groups from different parts of the country live side by side. The text was given a lavish production which drew on many of the theatrical resources available in the capital: the company included Abibigromma (there was then only the Legon group), Lord Bob Cole and his musicians, veterans of the Workers' Brigade Concert Party, dancing groups from the city and students from the School of Performing Arts. Such exploitation of resources and considerable expenditure was possible because the production in the Arts Centre (1991) was part of the celebrations marking a conference of leaders of countries that belonged to the Non-Aligned Movement.

In addition to advocating the creation of *anansegro*, Sutherland foresaw the possibility of creating *asafogro*, large-scale dramas along the lines of Greek tragedy based on the odes of the Asafo companies, or town regiments, which were familiar from her childhood in Cape Coast. The closest she appears to have come was in her adaptation of the Alcestis legend in her play *Edufa*.

Still another playwright of note is Ama Ata Aidoo (b. 1942), particularly important for her play *Anowa*. Though the play is based on a story, Aidoo allows the narrative element to be submerged in an examination of the pressures of family and commercial life. Against the backdrop of the slave trade, she shows the position of a childless woman with compassion.

The very idea of *anansegro* and *asafogro* indicate the concern to make use of the past. A recurring emblem in Ghanaian cultural discussions is provided by the Sankofa bird, an exhortation to artists to explore resources and performance patterns from the past. Such conventions have, so far, been most energetically pursued by Ben-Abdallah.

Directing and Acting

Within the country there is a tendency towards caricature in performance. Thus from primary school sketches on, one sees old women presented as crippled crones, Yoruba men as flamboyant and arrogant, and servants as scheming tricksters. Within the body of written texts there are calculated rejections of such stereotypes (see, for example, de Graft's *Through a Film Darkly*), but the tradition continues. It can even be detected in television and video where characterization relies heavily on exaggeration. Within the acting tradition of the Concert Parties it is significant that the white lips of the minstrel, derived from vaudeville and American films, are still sometimes used to identify clowns.

For the first fifty or so years of its existence, the Concert Party tradition also included female impersonators. These specialists developed a verisimilitude of appearance, gesture and movement that attracted admiration, and some actors achieved considerable renown for cross-dressing. In the other direction, girls' schools putting on plays with casts that include male and female roles often produced actresses who delighted audiences with their mannish swaggering and imitations of masculine movements.

Significantly, during 1994 three directors from outside Ghana were responsible for major productions in the National Theatre: Anton Phillips was brought in by the British Council and the American Steven Gerald worked within the context of a cultural link that has been established between Legon and the University of Texas. The première of a new play written and directed by Nigerian Femi Osofisan was given for those, many from the United States, attending an African Literature Association Conference. Such a dependence on imported talent has made the identification of a modern national style particularly difficult.

The Legon 7 production of *The Leader*.
Photo: James Gibbs.

Indeed the only Ghanaian theatre director who presented a play on the National Theatre stage during the first eight months of 1994 was William Addo. He directed Sackey Sowah's *Firestorm*, and there were those who felt that in coming to terms with the vast size of the main stage and auditorium, he was inevitably encouraging a declamatory style and relying on broad gestures. It may be possible to link this with the convention of caricature described previously, but it is also connected with the need to make an impact from an enormous stage. In other words, the style of a Ghanaian director was dictated by a space bequeathed to him by a Chinese architect.

Other recent attempts at finding a national directorial style include Sam Manu's production of James Baldwin's *Amen Corner* and Martin Owusu's production of *An Inspector Calls*. The only feature that might be said to have emerged, and this was mainly apparent in Owusu's work, was a tendency to underline somewhat insistently the dramatic high points of a scene. For those working in the National Theatre, this is clearly an attempt to communicate with a sparse and dispersed audience. In the case of *An Inspector Calls*, which was presented in the fairly intimate Drama Studio, the tendency may be linked with the kind of bold effects achieved in traditional storytelling.

Theatre for Young Audiences

This form of theatre is generally found in Ghana within the context of the country's many festivals. On some occasions, women and children – the uninitiated – are traditionally excluded, but on most occasions the whole community is able to take part and the participation of children in certain dramatic or symbolic dances is encouraged. Participation is essential in certain storytelling traditions in which actor-narrators direct certain narratives specifically at children. In such circumstances, children are expected to respond, within defined limits, and to interact with the narrator.

Missionaries used drama to teach and demonstrate and this didactic approach has been maintained by schools and evangelical groups. The position of drama within the church and within the educational system has already been touched on and the traditions, which included Nativity plays, dramatized parables, productions in Greek at St Nicholas and of *Everyman* at Achimota have been mentioned. But at Achimota the text-based foreign plays were consciously balanced by an educational policy that sought to retain links between pupils and their linguistic and cultural backgrounds.

Efua Sutherland's desire to develop a theatrical tradition from *anansesem* also produced a theatre that was accessible to children. But Sutherland went further by exploring children's songs and games, deriving from them the building blocks for scripted dramas. Her children's texts include *Vulture! Vulture!* and *Tahinta*, which she described as 'rhythm plays'.

They were published in 1968 with photographs showing children performing the plays and with a musical arrangement by Kwasi Baiden.

Sutherland's example was complemented by the influence of the British teacher-director Dorothea Alexandra who, under the auspices of the British Council, visited the country in 1968, ran workshops for teachers and encouraged them to help children create plays out of stories, both those familiar from home and those encountered in books. This work continues, although as is to be expected, it is now more formalized and often takes place within the context of Theatre-in-Education courses, and in response to current thinking about drama in the classroom.

Plays by children for children are also a feature of the Ghanaian education system from nursery schools onward. Even privately owned nursery schools clearly see the plays their children put on, sometimes with traditional dance and music, as part of a regular programme. Sometimes, perhaps in an attempt to woo ambitious parents, the plays are acted in English or French. Important occasions in the school calendar, or days of national celebration, provide other opportunities for the presentation of such theatrical entertainments.

The coordination of theatrical activities by children in school became the particular responsibility of Frances Sey, and she made use of experienced directors, including Paddy Animpong and Adelaide Amegatcher who worked with school groups, sometimes using plays they wrote themselves.

Examples of older groups working with or acting before young audiences are Legon Road Theatre, Anokye Players and Theatre for Extension Communication students from Legon. During the 1960s, Ben-Abdallah directed a group which presented extracts from secondary school set-texts; by the 1990s drama students were working with school drama societies, using drama as a way of raising awareness about social issues and to stimulate debate about problems.

Puppet and Mask Theatre

Although there are indigenous traditions of puppet theatre in parts of West Africa, there appears to be little, apart from the tradition of carving, on which puppeteers in Ghana have been able to build. The earliest references to puppet shows date from 1957 when mass education workers carried out a health campaign at the request of the Chamber of Mines and Ministry of Health. On that occasion, puppets were used as part of a programme that also included demonstrations, plays, lectures, films, drumming, music and an exhibition.

Support for the use of puppets for community development continued after Ghana became independent and in the Annual Report of the Department of Social Welfare and Community Development for 1961 it was noted that 'drama (and for that matter puppetry) is one of the most effective aids in the field in most situations'.

Writing on 'Theatre in Ghana', Peter Carpenter (1963) reported that puppetry in the country had been encouraged by the donation of a puppet caravan by the Elder Dempster shipping line and by the visit of the Bussells, a British husband and wife team. Three years later, in the *Ghana Cultural Review*, Ato Bedu-Addo reported that the Ghana Institute of Arts and Culture was 'aspiring to evolve a socialist theatre consonant to the aspirations of the liberated people of Ghana' and that as part of this broad drive a Puppetry Division, headed by E.A. Hanson, was ensuring that puppetry was increasingly gaining publicity. Bedu-Addo wrote: 'In all, 146 puppet shows were given by the Institute throughout the regions and Accra last year.' Since 1965, the programmes for festivals indicate that performances by puppeteers are frequently featured. The tradition is of hand-puppets, but the use of large marionettes has also been contemplated.

Within the corpus of written drama that has come into being in Ghana, it has already been remarked that Ben-Abdallah's work is remarkable for the range of theatrical resources exploited. At one point in *The Trial of Mallam Ilya*, he requires that actors enter with puppets. For example, an actor 'dressed as David Livingstone enters holding the strings of a puppet dressed as an African Christian preacher who hits the carved figure of a traditional African priest on the head with a Bible'. Other figures include Henry the Navigator, who manipulates a buccaneer and a naked African woman; and Queen Victoria, pulling the strings of Cecil Rhodes, who dances 'on the fat belly of a carved African chief labelled Chaka'. The stage directions reveal the playwright's awareness that the figures may not be instantly recognizable.

Design

Onto the indigenous tradition of processional masquerades – in which costumes are intended to be seen and assessed from all quarters of the assembled audience – has been grafted expectations from the European theatre. Some, in fact, *prefer* the picture-frame stage and European-style spoken drama. For many of these, a curtain is regarded as an essential ingredient and footlights are highly desirable. Realism is taken as the obvious objective for designers working in this way.

On the other hand, there are those who recognize that the symbolism and stylization present in the masquerades can also be essential ingredients of the plastic and performing arts and that such elements should be seen in Ghana's own theatrical forms. The *akuaba* fertility dolls, for example, with their enlarged and idealized heads, indicate this stylized tradition in carving, and the fluid movements which transform the action of harvesting into graceful gestures do the same in certain dances.

Here again, one turns to the work of Efua Sutherland for a highly stylized use of properties and for symbolic settings. Ben-Abdallah's work also has a design dimension; in *The Verdict of the Cobra*, for instance, there is not only a bare stage but also directed lighting, masks, highly stylized costumes and symbolic dances.

Constraints of budget and limited technical facilities have curbed the ambitions of most Ghanaian set and lighting designers. John Djisenu, based at Legon, and others have endeavoured to come to terms with the vast auditorium in the National Theatre without the resources to make a proper impact. At the same venue, lighting crews have struggled with unfamiliar Chinese equipment.

Ambitious set-design is often largely the work of directors and thus it is appropriate to talk about the relative success of George Andoh Wilson's multiple staging approach to *Kongi's Harvest* in 1970 or Ben-Abdallah's effective use of levels and symbolic scenery in *The Land of a Million Magicians*. The financial pressure under which groups work is the element which most often militates against large-scale set designs.

However, it should be noted that some designers have drawn effectively on indigenous resources. The large umbrellas that protect royal heads from the African sun make a distinctive impact in episodes with a court setting, and the use of *kente* and *adinkra* cloth in scenes where such materials are appropriate instantly impresses the eyes with a distinctive range of colours, patterns and symbols. For informed local audiences these materials are redolent with meaning, and they are used effectively by choreographers such as Opoku and Yartey.

The Concert Parties usually perform with such rudimentary equipment that design appears to have been eschewed: a curtained-off section of the performance area provides a dressing space where costumes – often elaborate, stylish and authentic – are changed. Illumination is provided by bare bulbs fixed to a pole, and microphones are arranged so as to impress the audience and dominate the movements of the actors. However, audiences relish special effects, such as 'discovery scenes' or coloured lights, and enterprising troupe leaders capitalize on this.

Theatre Space and Architecture

The National Theatre building in Accra is (as previously indicated) vast and somewhat alienating. Its main auditorium covers 11,896 square metres and seats 1,504 in plush armchairs that challenge any sense of intimacy. An open-air courtyard theatre at the side of the main building, with a seating capacity of 326, provides greater opportunities for establishing a relaxed and creative atmosphere. The stated goal is that the National Theatre 'replicate itself in the regions and ensure the availability of regional theatres, if so desired'. No copies have as yet been made, and it is unlikely that any ever will be.

Another regular venue in Accra used by companies is the Arts Centre, which, though somewhat dilapidated and shed-like, is favoured by some of the longest serving directors and writers. Entirely without pretension, it has a raised stage at one end. Since the seating is not fixed, it invites experimentation.

The British Council Hall, a modern building whose primary purpose is to serve as a venue for lectures, is regularly used by amateur groups particularly at Christmas when a pantomime is usually put on. The garden at the Goethe Institute has been laid out so that trees provide a natural background to a simple performance area, no more than a concrete circle, and this has been used by such groups as Audience Awareness. Churches and classrooms are also frequently put into service as theatres.

The campus at the University of Ghana, Legon, some 10 kilometres from Accra, was laid out on a grand scale with dining halls and quadrangles which deliberately recalled Oxbridge models. The architect's attempt to create a Greek amphitheatre at the top of Legon Hill offers, unfortunately, no more than a weak imitation of the real thing. Acoustics were not adequately considered and the sightlines are poor. A conventional picture frame stage is included in Commonwealth Hall.

The Fairfield Foundation, Fund for Tomorrow and Arts Council of Ghana contributed to the construction of a modest Drama Studio in

The set for Wole Soyinka's *Kongi's Harvest*, Drama Studio in Accra.
Photo: James Gibbs.

Accra. This was opened in 1961, and for many years was the major open-air venue in the capital. When, in 1989, the structure was demolished to make way for the National Theatre, a building was constructed at Legon, where it is now used by students of the School of Performing Arts, Abibigromma and various visiting amateur companies, including the Legon Players.

The structure is simple, conceived to resemble a courtyard, or perhaps the inside of a 'compound house', the outer walls make an octagon and enclose a central acting area, indicated only by an octagonal performing area that is raised an inch or two. On one side, a picture-frame stage stands flanked by ancillary buildings (which include a green room) and behind this there is a scenery workshop.

The Drama Studio was an urban expression of Efua Sutherland's idea of the kind of space required by a Ghanaian theatre based on narratives and on the domestic entertainments and rituals of an extended family. Her other experiment in architectural form is represented by the Kodzidan or House of Stories in Ekumfi Atwa, a village between Accra and Cape Coast. Inspired by the architecture of nearby clan houses, this is a covered building with opaque sheets in the centre of the roof which allow light to filter on to a sunken performance area

surrounded by tiers so broad they can accommodate tables and chairs. The tiers are broken on one side by what a visitor familiar with European theatre architecture would recognize as a cyclorama and a tier broad enough to be called a stage. The sidewalls of the building are so low that the audience can be cooled by the wind.

The Universities of Cape Coast and Kumasi have substantial halls, and there are structures that have clearly been built with the idea that they might be used for theatrical performances in secondary schools and teacher training colleges. In many cases the imagined requirement of a picture-frame stage, often pokey and lacking adequate access, has been met by an architect or contractor commissioned to design a hall for public use. Institutional budgets rarely stretch to provide adequate lighting equipment, indeed even those concerned with lighting the stage of the main auditorium of the National Theatre have found occasion to complain about the facilities there. At the expensive, privately owned International School in Accra, there is a well-lit stage and a set of electrically operated curtains.

For the Concert Parties groups the major requirement of a performing space is that only those who have paid should be able to see the performance. They have often used open-air cinemas, making use of the narrowest of stages, the most basic of sets and the simplest of lighting systems.

In another space, the Cultural Centre at Kumasi, there is an open-air amphitheatre where Saturday afternoon variety programmes bring together dance and theatre groups.

The creation of a National Commission on Culture, which extended the work pioneered in Kumasi, led to the creation – at least on paper

– of several regional cultural centres. In Navrongo, for example, there is a hall with raked auditorium and stage; in Cape Coast, on the other hand, where many notable and comparatively well-equipped schools flourish, the Centre's plans have yet to be transformed into bricks and mortar. Ambitious, uncompleted cultural centres can be found in other urban centres. Some are still open to the sky although building commenced in 1965.

Training

When Efua Sutherland started the Experimental Theatre Group, and later the Drama Studio Players, she built on Ghanaians' experience of storytelling and of informal dance schools. The Drama Studio Players, were, quite deliberately, stretched: drawing on the skills of experienced amateurs, an introduction to the various branches of the theatre was provided. The kind of training offered became a formal course of instruction in 1962 when the School of Music and Drama was opened at Legon.

Initially under the auspices of the Institute of African Studies and Ghanaian Institute of Art and Culture, the School was opened by Kwame Nkrumah, with the purpose, according to Kwabena Nketia in an article that appeared in the first issue of the *Ghana Cultural Review*, of giving approved courses and training to future artists. Those on the course would, he said, make use of the Drama Studio, the University Theatre in Town, where they would play to small, critical audiences. The intention was to combine an academic awareness of various traditions of the theatre with practical competence in as many areas of the theatre as possible. At that time, this was offered through an introductory, one-year certificate course that led to a two-year diploma course.

Inevitably, given the cultural and political situation, there were ideological, cultural, professional and linguistic tensions between members of staff, and with other elements and individuals in the university. In 1977, however, the School of Music and Drama became the School of Performing Arts.

For much of its history, Sutherland and de Graft were influential presences there. Opportunities occurred, or were created, for a select few of the students who had completed the diploma to proceed to post-graduate work

overseas. Thus Owusu went to Bristol and then to Brandeis University for a PhD; Yirenkyi did an MFA at Yale University; and, somewhat later, Mary Yirenkyi did a post-graduate degree at Leeds on drama and education. Those in the sister arts also completed higher degrees – Patience Kwakwa did an MA in the Institute of African Studies, and Adinku, who prepared 'A Model for the Development of Dance Education within the Ghanaian University System' in Surrey, was the first scholar at a UK university to obtain a PhD for a thesis on dance.

As a result of the variety of experience and specialization, the curriculum offered by the School of Performing Arts in the 1990s includes courses for drama students in music, dance and practical drama, in Theatre-in-Education, in theatre history, in the work of influential playwrights, critics and theorists from various continents, and in theatre communication. Students can select various options within a modular system, and the practical requirements of their courses ensure that there is a flow of one-act and full-length plays through the Drama Studio.

The selection of plays for production is revealing and shows the particular interests of the school. The 1990s have already seen productions of work by Ghanaians (including Aidoo, Acquaye, Yirenkyi, Owusu, Marshall, de Graft and Tamakloe) and by other Africans (such as Henshaw, Sofola, Rotimi, Lakoju, Ngugi and Soyinka).

In the early days of the school, there were employment opportunities for graduates in radio, film and television, and in teaching, the profession in which many of the students had trained before studying drama. The situation remains fundamentally unchanged, though the creation of a National Commission on Culture with regional centres has provided employment for some, while others have joined the forty or so on the payrolls of the professional drama groups. They and some of their classmates have also taken advantage of the opportunities offered by the interest in locally produced videos to act, write and direct in that medium.

Criticism, Scholarship and Publishing

As independence approached and just after it had been achieved there was an almost palpable sense that Ghana was carving a place in history and that what it achieved in matters theatrical and in other cultural fields should be debated, discussed and chronicled. *The Ghanaian, Okyeame* and *Ghana Cultural Review* provide coverage of this period since they carried articles about the issues confronting the National Theatre Movement.

After the overthrow of Nkrumah, the initiative for sustaining the debate moved to the university, and *The Legon Observer* regularly devoted space to reviewing productions and sometimes carried contributions on the language issue and the role of dance. When that platform for campus debate was rudely forced to close, there was no obvious successor.

Newspapers had occasional articles, but sometimes advertising material masqueraded as reviews and the tradition of informed criticism established by *The Legon Observer* was lost. Since 1989, *Urea* has emerged as a local publication that is committed to providing coverage of important cultural matters.

Scholarly articles on the Ghanaian theatre have regularly appeared in the *Research Review* published by the Institute of African Studies. Kofi Agovi, K.N. Bame, and John Kedjani have all produced work of interest, though it is noticeable that the range of investigation has rarely included examination of contemporary performance traditions other than those connected with the Concert Party.

Some theses by those active in the theatre have been presented for higher degrees, and these include John Collins and John Darkey's research on the Concert Party, Owusu's work on West African adaptations of classical dramas, and Mary Yirenkyi's analysis of Drama-in-Education.

The closing of the Cameroon-based *African Theatre Review* and the absence of a journal devoted specifically to African drama means that Ghanaian academics have often found it hard to place scholarly articles. Conference papers including a study by Asiedu Yirenkyi on Sekyi and Danquah, have been presented at conferences and important essays by Angmor and Sutherland have been published, but book-length studies are at a premium. Indeed readers are indebted to Bame for extended theatre analyses in book form.

Publishing in Ghana was initially in the hands of missionaries, and church-linked publishing houses were responsible for bringing Danquah and Fiawoo into print. During the 1960s, there were opportunities for Ghanaian playwrights to publish through international houses, and at that time Aidoo went to Longman and de Graft to Oxford. During the 1970s, when Heinemann was very active in publishing African writing, Patience Addo, George Awoonor-Williams, Derlene Clems and Owusu all appeared under its imprint. But in the 1980s, multinational interest in African publishing decreased and local imprints became important once more. A trickle of texts has recently appeared from smaller Ghanaian houses over the years: Dei-Anang from Waterville in 1963; Sutherland from the Ghana Publishing Corporation; and Bill Marshall from Sedco in 1992.

With paper in short supply, and pirates ready to take advantage of any title that makes it on to a syllabus, times have been lean for local publishers. Few have been willing to venture into the notoriously uncertain area of theatre. One that has boldly bucked this trend is Woeli, which currently includes five volumes by Ben-Abdallah, a total of nine plays, on its list.

Within those texts can be seen the range of thinking that has dominated the Ghanaian theatre movement. The Preface to Abdallah's first collection ends with a paragraph that is particularly meaningful and provides a convenient conclusion to this survey. Readers should now have some insight into why a teacher who turned into a political office-holder, who was educated at Wesley College, the School of Music and Drama and at universities in the United States should, in 1987, write:

> It is time for African playwrights to set their own standards, richly drawing from their own cultural heritage, our history and totality of the African experience to create the criteria for judging our own work. Our theatre must mirror to us what in our culture we must keep and improve upon and what we must reject and discard. At the same time, we must not be ashamed to take out of the examples of the western world what will help us in our bid for progress and development while at the same time we must learn not to repeat their mistakes.

Patience Rosina Addo, James Gibbs

Further Reading

Agovi, James K. 'The Ghana Dance Ensemble and the Contemporary Ghanaian Theatre'. *Legon Observer* 12, no. 9 (1980): 213–15.

Agovi, K.E. 'Towards an Authentic African Theatre'. *Ufahumu* 19, nos. 2 and 3 (1991): 67–79.

Agovi, Kofi. 'The Aesthetics of Creative Communication in African Performance Studies'. *Institute of African Studies Research Review* 4, no. 1 (1988): 1–9.

———. 'Is There an African Vision of Tragedy in Contemporary African Theatre?'. *Présence Africaine* 1st and 2nd quarters (1984): 133–4.

———. 'Joe de Graft'. In *The Dictionary of Literary Biography: Black and African Writers* no. 117, 134–40. Detroit, MI: Broccoli, Clark, Layman, 1992.

———. 'Of Actors, Performers and Audience in Traditional African Drama'. *Présence Africaine* 116, no. 4 (1980): 141–58.

———. 'The Origin of Literary Theatre in Colonial Ghana, 1920–1957'. *Institute of African Studies Research Review* 6, no. 1 (1990): 1–23.

———. 'The Philosophy of Communication in Traditional Ghanaian Society: The Literary and Dramatic Evidence'. *Institute of African Studies Research Review* 5, no. 2 (1989).

———. 'Sharing Creativity: Group Performance of Nzema Ayabomo Maiden Songs'. *The Literary Griot: International Journal of Black Oral and Literary Studies* 1, no. 2 (1989).

Angmor, Charles. 'Drama in Ghana'. In *Theatre in Africa*, eds Oyin Ogunba and Abiola Irele, 55–72. Ibadan, Nigeria: Ibadan University Press, 1978.

———. 'Drama in Ghana'. In *Ghanaian Literatures*, ed. Richard K. Priebe, 171–86. Westport, CT: Greenwood, 1988.

Antubam, Kofi. *Ghana's Heritage of Culture.* Leipzig: Koehler & Amelang, 1963. 221 pp.

Assimeng, J.M. *Traditional Life, Culture and Literature in Ghana.* New York: Conch, 1976.

Baker, Donald S. 'Shakespeare in Ghana'. *Shakespeare Survey* 16 (1963): 77–82.

Bame, Kwabena N. *Come to Laugh: A Study of African Traditional Theatre in Ghana.* Legon: Institute of African Studies, and New York: Lilian Barber, 1985. 102 pp.

———. 'Comic Play in Ghana'. *African Arts/Arts d'Afrique* 1, no. 4 (1968): 30–4, 101.

———. 'Popular Theatre in Ghana'. *Institute of African Studies Research Review* 3, no. 2 (1967): 34–8.

———. *Profiles in African Traditional Popular Culture: Consensus and Conflict.* New York: Clear Press, 1991.

———. 'Some Sociological Variables which Need Attention in Development Support Communication: Examples from a Ghanaian Family Planning Study'. *Greenhill Journal of Administration* 3–4 (1976–7): 76–84.

Carpenter, Peter. 'East and West: A Brief Review of Theatre in Ghana and Uganda Since 1960'. *Makerere Journal* 8 (1963): 35–9.

Collins, E.J. 'Comic Opera in Ghana'. in *Ghanaian Literatures*, ed. Richard K. Priebe, 61–72. Westport, CT: Greenwood, 1988.

Collins, John. *Highlife Time.* Accra: Anansesem, 1994.

———. 'Life on the Road – Modern African Minstrels: The Jaguar Jokers'. In *West African Popular Roots.* Philadelphia, PA: Temple University Press, 1992.

Kedjanyi, John. 'Masquerade Societies in Ghana'. *Institute of African Studies Research Review* 3, no. 2 (1967): 51–7.

———. 'The National Theatre in Ghana'. *East Africa Journal* 6, no. 7 (1969): 38–45.

———. 'Observations on Spectator–Performer Arrangements of Some Traditional Ghanaian Performances'. *Institute of African Studies Research Review* 2, no. 3 (1966): 61–6.

Kennedy, Scott. 'Language and Communication Problems in the Ghanaian Theatre'. *Okyeame* 4, no. 1 (December 1968): 103–9.

Lokko, Sophia D. 'Hunger-Hooting Festival in Ghana'. *The Drama Review: African Performance Issue* 25, no. 4 (winter 1981): 54–50.

———. 'Plays and Players: A Means of Transmission and Dissemination of Ghanaian Culture'. *Maske und Kothurn* 29 (1983): 261–71.

———. 'Theatre Space: A Historical Overview of the Theatre Movement in Ghana'. *Modern Drama* 23 (September 1980): 309–19.

Muhindi, K. 'L'Apport de Efua Theodorea Sutherland à la dramaturgie contemporaine' [Efua Theodora Sutherland's contribution to contemporary dramaturgy]. *Présence Africaine* 133–4 (1985): 75–85.

Nketia, J.H. Kwabena. *A Calendar of Ghana Festivals*. Legon: Institute of African Studies, 1964. 13 pp.

———. *Ghana – Music, Dance and Drama: A Review of the Performing Arts of Ghana*. Legon: Institute of African Studies, 1965. 50 pp.

———. 'National Theatre Movement and the African Image'. *The Pan African Review* 1, no. 2. (1964): 88–93.

Opoku, A.A. *Festivals in Ghana*. Accra: Ghana Publishing, 1970. 80 pp.

Ricard, Alain. 'Between the Oral and the Written: Theatre in Ghana and Nigeria'. Translated by Anthony Graham-White. *Educational Theatre Journal* 28 (May 1976): 229–38.

Theatre-Scribe [pseud.] 'Meet the Wooden Actors'. *The Ghanaian* 7, no. 10 (October 1964): 22–3.

Wyllie, R.W. 'Ritual and Social Change: A Ghanaian Example.' *American Anthropologist* 70 (1968): 21ff.

GOLD COAST

(see **GHANA**)

GUINEA

The first of the former French colonies in Africa to vote for independence when given the choice in 1958, Guinea (formerly called French Guinea) lies along a 280 kilometre stretch of the Atlantic coast of West Africa south of Sénégal and Guinea-Bissau and north of Sierra Leone and Liberia. It is bounded on the east by Côte d'Ivoire and Mali. A small country of some 7 million people, Guinea has a land area of 245,900 square kilometres (94,900 square miles). Its capital is the port city of Conakry.

More than two-thirds of the population are of the Fulani (Peul) and Malinke ethnic groups and another 20 per cent Sousou. The ancestors of modern Fulani moved into the region from northern Africa. Eight official languages are taught in schools including Fulani, Malinke, Sousou and French. A true synthesis of western Africa's geographic and cultural elements, Guinea possesses important mineral, agricultural, industrial and forestry resources.

Portuguese explorers first visited the region in the fourteenth century and were soon followed by French and British explorers and traders. The French gradually extended their control of the coast until they controlled the region from British Sierra Leone to Portuguese Guinea (now Guinea-Bissau). The colony of Guinea was established in 1891, and in 1895 it was joined to the newly created federation of French West Africa.

Samory Touré led a continuing battle against French control leading the Malinke people from 1882 until his capture by the French in 1898. At first governed like most French colonies as if it would become part of France, Guinea after World War II was given more opportunity to become self-governing. In 1958, when given a choice of becoming completely independent or retaining ties with France, the population voted for independence. Sékou Touré, a descendant of Samory, was elected the country's first president and remained in that position until 1984. Diplomatic relations with France were broken off in 1965 but restored in 1975. In 1984 the military took control of the country.

Rich in traditional dance and musically based performative events connected to celebrations such as births, circumcisions, weddings and burials, a European-style theatre was introduced into Guinea through missionaries and colonial government officials in the nineteenth century. Amateur groups emerged mostly in and around the French-language schools.

By the late 1930s, top Guinean students returning from teacher training at the prestigious William Ponty Normal School in Dakar brought to the country a deepened understanding of European theatrical form. One example was the play, *La Rencontre du Capitaine Péroz et de Samory* (*The Meeting Between Captain Péroz and Samory*, 1937). Several theatre groups of this same period were actually connected to the Boy Scout movement and in 1944 a scout group in Conakry staged an original play called *The Schoolmaster*. Though not an important piece in itself, it was typical of the work being done. Such pieces – when mixed in with song and dance – did much to popularize the European forms both within these community groups and within the school curriculum.

This said, such European-style plays actually exacerbated the division between the intellectuals of the country and the illiterate populace, between the urban population and those who lived in the rural parts of the country. It was probably the many visits of French music and dance groups in the early 1950s that inspired Fodéba Keita and Kanta Facely to bring together a group of young African and Antillean artists in a group known as Les Ballets Africains, staging both dramatic ballets and spectacular dance pieces, most based on traditional movements, rhythms and styles. The group began touring widely both in Africa and worldwide and subsequently achieved a major international reputation in the field. One of the major theatre-ballets is *L'Aube africaine* (*African Dawn*, 1965) about the shooting of African troops who had served for France in World War II by French troops in Thiaroye, Sénégal.

Other Guinean groups of the period were less spectacular and more connected to spoken drama. Among them were FRAG (the Guinean Brotherhood) and Justin Mangué's Fraternal Artistic Union (UFAJM) which as early as 1946 presented full-length plays, musical sketches and even dance pieces such as *The Girls Are Pretty in Bamako*.

Through the 1950s, community dramatic competitions evolved into regional and colony-wide competitions and interest in creating original plays began to grow. One of the strongest local groups, the Mamou Troupe from Conakry, won the national competition and then represented the Guinea region in the French West African competition. In 1956 in a new play competition, Guinean dramatist Sidi Mohamed Condé's *Le Sacrifice suprême* (*The Supreme Sacrifice*) was named one of the top five plays.

By the late 1950s, still other troupes emerged: L'Éetoile de Guinée (Star of Guinea), L'Étoile de la jeunesse (Youth Star), Kara Touré's L'Union des jeunes artistes de Sanfil (Young Artists' Union of Sanfil), La Jeunesse artistique (Artistic Youth), Le Djolé club (Djole Club), La Troupe artistique de Boké (Boke Art Troupe) of Cossa Bounama, and, more occasionally, the Habana Club and the Noung Club. The year 1956 also saw a special grant awarded to Les Ballets Africains to finance its first tour of Africa.

In the years immediately following independence Guinean theatre groups followed guidelines set down by the new government and the official state political party, the Parti Démocratique de Guinée (Guinean Democratic Party). The party urged cultural groups to defend the revolution from both internal and external enemies through the creation of a militant revolutionary theatre which would establish a cultural base for the Touré regime.

As well, the government helped to begin a Guinean School of Theatre at this time and supported expanded artistic competitions, seminars, debates and festivals. Local revolutionary committees were established for those under 25 and each had a cultural component. For all the activity, however, much was lost in terms of free expression. Even having the names of playwrights on scripts was discouraged in support of the notion of not collective but collectivist creation.

Yet certain plays of note did emerge from this period between about 1958 and 1984. Listed here is the name of the group, city or author pseudonym that was credited. Significant scripts included *Wagadou Bida* (Donka School, 1961); *Mory Wankon* (Kankan, 1963); *Et la nuit s'illumine* (*And the Night Is Lit*, Labé region, 1967); *Retour aux sources*

Abdoulaye Fanye Touré's drama *L'Ingrat* (*The Ungrateful One*).

(*Return to Source,* Conakry II, 1969); *Qui est victime de qui?* (*Who Is the Victim of Whom?*, Conakry I, *c.*1971); *Thiaroye* (Dabola region, 1973); *Le Train ne me laissera pas* (*I Won't Miss the Train,* Dabola, 1976); *Condeke* (Faranah, 1982); *Tchaka* (University Troupe, *c.*1983); *Le Waliou de Gomba* (*The Waliou of Gomba,* Kindia, *c.*1983); *Dina Salifon* (Boke, *c.*1984); and *Almamy Samory Touré* (Kankan, *c.*1984). Some of these scripts later played at theatre festivals in Algiers and Lagos.

Also established at this time was a second dance troupe – Ballet Djoliba – and a National Instrumental and Choral Ensemble. Like Les Ballets Africains, both troupes toured extensively.

The military coup of 1984 actually eased some of the political controls that had characterized the earlier period. With fewer artistic restrictions, groups were able to stage newer and slightly more critical works and, with less government support, theatre groups learned the challenges of a free enterprise system. Also established at this time was the country's first artistic association, l'Association guinéenne des hommes de théâtre (Guinean Association of Theatre People). The group's first president was Abdoulaye Fanye Touré.

Structure of the National Theatre Community

Most theatrical activity in Guinea is centred in and around Conakry where four state-supported 'national' companies operate on a regular basis: Les Ballets Africains, the National Music Ensemble (1961), National Ballet Djoliba (1961) and National Theatre Troupe (1989).

Each of these groups operates under contract with the Ministry of Culture which guarantees their costs and helps negotiate both national and international performances. Members of all these groups are considered professionals and they receive salaries, pensions and holiday pay. Revenues generated by the performances are channelled back into the public treasury where they are credited, for instance, against outlays for sets, costumes, equipment, salaries and travel.

In 1990 a cultural charter was adopted by the government defining various classifications of artistic groups and relations with government agencies. The particular status of Guinean artists is outlined clearly in this document.

In addition to these major professional groups, another five or so companies operate shorter seasons throughout the year in Conakry. Outside the capital, the amount of theatrical activity has continued to reduce since 1984.

In addition there are a number of semi-professional troupes whose work is seen regularly and several language-based amateur groups whose work is seen regularly on television. Also subsidized by the state, the television companies perform in the various official languages of the country. The state television provides them with recording and editing equipment and state-paid professional technicians. Each group does its own casting and chooses its own directors.

The National Concord Theatre Festival (FESCONA) was held for the first time in 1995 and provided a rare occasion for groups from the interior to introduce their work and productions to the public in Conakry.

Guinean groups are regular participants in the African Performing Arts Market (MASA) and have regular contact with both the Daniel Sorano Theatre in Dakar and Burkinabe Studio Theatre in Burkina Faso.

Artistic Profile

Companies

Music, dance and the oral tradition are intimately integrated in most Guinean performance events, making it difficult at times to recognize specific genres. This is seen most clearly in the theatre ballets of Les Ballets Africains which is as much of a theatre troupe as any other. Music too is very much a part of dramatic performances and it speaks clearly to those who know how to understand it.

As for those troupes which tend to emphasize spoken drama more, the National Theatre Troupe is the most heavily subsidized by the state. Focusing on plays by Guinean dramatists, it has represented Guinea at several international festivals including the African Festival of Francophone Theatre in Bouake (Côte d'Ivoire) and the International Festival of Theatre for Development in Ougadougou (Burkina Faso).

Run since its inception by Kalifa Condé and Sheik Mamadi Condé, the group's major directors include Marcellin M. Bangoura, whose major production was Ahmed Tidiane Cissé's *Au nom du peuple* (*In the Name of the People*, 1990); Siba Fasson, director of Yves Jamiaque's *Negro Spiritual*; Abdoulaye Fanye Touré's *Rigolade ou le procès au pays des sourds* (*It's a Piece of Cake or Trial in the Land of the Deaf*); and William Sassine's *Légende d'une vérité* (*Legend of a Truth*).

Other professional troupes include Pesse (founded in 1985), Lewru Djeere (1987), Nyl Palouwou (1990), Benso Sodia (1991) and Benda (1992). Each presents short seasons of productions in the capital, mostly of plays by Guinean writers. Pesse is run by Alkhaly Mohamed Keita and Abou Sylla; Lewru Djeere by Abdallah Diallo, Ammar Barry, Elhadj Nabika Sylla and Alpha Oumar Pathebarry; Nyl Palouwou by Togba Moriba and Laurent Kolie; Benso Sodia by Kalil Touré; and Benda by Joseph Tonguino.

Among the notable semi-professional troupes are Le Club artistique et culturel les Ambassadeurs de guinée (Guinean Ambassador's Artistic and Cultural Club, 1984), Afrique Style de Guinée (Africa Style of Guinea), Espoir de guinée (Hope of Guinea, 1986), Comédie guinéenne (Guinean Comedy, 1991) and Djibril Tamsir Niane Group (1991) founded by Tamsir Niane (b. 1932), author of the plays *Sikasso* and *Chaka*.

None of these groups is subsidized but they do charge admission or work under contract; all proceeds thus derived are shared among the company members. Costs are guaranteed by the company's management, usually the founder or founders of the group.

Other troupes exist specifically for the Islamic community. There is also a company called Kabako composed of physically disabled players. The company has produced several interesting productions including *La Fin du rouleau* (*The End of the Roll*) and *Avoir l'air d'autres* (*The Look of Others*).

Dramaturgy
Directing and Acting

Prior to independence, Guinea's dramaturgy was heavily composed of adaptations of French classics and more or less domestic comedies. In the period immediately prior to independence and in the years from 1958 to 1984 state involvement and cultural policy profoundly influenced dramaturgical style.

Dramatists – like all artists – were given a social responsibility in the revolutionary period: to inform, to mobilize and to educate. These cornerstones of public policy are still felt in the late 1990s in terms of dramatic structure and a style which is more akin to social realism than anything else. In virtually every play since 1958, historical and daily social issues can be seen as dominating themes.

To put this another way, fiction has little place within Guinean dramatic literature of this period except as a way to evoke social relations between individuals or groups. One of the few exceptions to this rule is Abdoulaye Fanye Touré's *Rigolade ou le procès au pays des sourds*. This is essentially an absurdist piece in which the essence is miscommunication.

As well, the notion of collective creation – whether or not a playwright actually worked as dramatist with the group – meant that many plays which might otherwise be credited to particular writers have been credited to groups or even to regions of the country. Nevertheless, a number of writers of note have emerged. Among them are Fanye Touré; William Sassine, author of *Légende d'une vérité*; Yves Jamiaque, author of *Negro Spiritual*; Ahmed Tidiane Cissé, author of *Au nom du peuple* and, of course, Sidi Mohamed Condé, author of *Le Sacrifice suprême*.

Ahmed Tidiane Cissé's *Au nom du peuple*, to give but one example of Guinean playwriting, is a three-act satire in which Cissé deals with the tricky problems of the administration, management and redistribution of goods across the country. Linked in is a plot to assassinate the president and another dealing with two brothers battling over which will inherit family land. Within his play Cissé takes

Abdoulaye Fanye Touré's absurdist drama *Rigolade*.

satirical shots at the former revolutionary tribunal with its clownish magistrates and ridiculous decisions, at blaspheming Muslim holy men and public figures who supposedly are acting in the name of the people.

Theatre for Young Audiences

The day after Guinea's independence in 1958, a comprehensive programme aimed at developing a rich and varied cultural inheritance was elaborated and quickly put into effect. The new situation and the cultural planning that went along with it affected all aspects of culture, including those dealing with young people.

One of the first elements of the new plan was the creation of a series of theatre festivals specifically for plays created by young people. Over the next years, nine such festivals were held involving elementary schools (choral playlets and poetry recitals) and secondary schools and universities (choral playlets, poetry recitals and scripted plays). High school students are expected to present plays of relevance to Guinea's social life or history while university groups are expected to deal with plays of significance nationally or across the African continent. Rehearsal time is given to the competing groups and awards are presented.

Also part of the planning, a theatre for young audiences – opened in 1973 – was built and a troupe from the National Theatre regularly plays there. This troupe has participated in the Pan-African Festival (FESTAC) in Lagos in 1977, in the twelfth International Festival for Youth and Students in Cuba in 1978 and in the Pan-African Festival held in Tripoli in 1983.

Other specific events are built around UNICEF or UNESCO-sponsored events such as the International Year of the Child and Africa's Month of the Child. Several groups now regularly perform plays for young audiences.

Puppet and Mask Theatre

Guinean masks hold a special place of honour within the country and though this is not puppet theatre in any European sense the form has real significance in terms of performance study and traditional culture. This can be seen especially during funerals when both men and women, to mark the occasion, don masks of various types.

These masks have a symbiotic relationship with the wearer allowing them to touch the power of not only the immediately deceased but all their ancestors. This force, released by the mask, is the material realization of ultimately sacred realities. In achieving this, they also assume important social roles: the protection of traditional values, the initiation of the wearer into the science and wisdom of the elders, the reaffirmation of eternal truths and the placing of myth in everyday life.

Design
Theatre Space and Architecture

A small number of spaces, mostly in Conakry, are used regularly for spoken drama events. While none of them is a playhouse in the European architectural sense, they are functional and do work for theatrical performances.

The largest of these is Le Palais du peuple (Palace of the People) which seats 2,000 and was built in 1966. Two other spaces used regularly are the National Museum theatre with 200 seats and the Franco-Guinean Alliance theatre which holds 100.

Similar small spaces exist in most of the thirty-three regions of the country and within each of the five administrative districts of the capital.

None is particularly well equipped but they are all functional.

Training
Criticism, Scholarship and Publishing

A Guinean School of Theatre, funded by the state, has existed almost since independence.

Research on theatre and study of its history is done almost exclusively at the University of Guinea, mostly at the graduate level.

Only a single publishing house exists within the country: La Société africaine des livres guinéennes (African Society of Guinean Books) run by Djibril Tamsir Niane, a professor at the university. Despite ongoing financial difficulties, it publishes a limited number of literary works but no scripts. The only play that has been published is Abdoulaye Fanye Touré's *Mask of the Empire* which appeared under the imprint Patrice Lumumba Press.

Abdoulaye Fanye Touré
Translated by Heather Lash

Further Reading

Cornévin, Robert. *Le Théâtre en Afrique noire et à Madagascar* [The theatre in Black Africa and Madagascar]. Paris: Le Livre africain, 1970. 334 pp.

Keita, Fodeba. *Le Théâtre de Fodéba Keita* [The theatre of Fodéba Keita]. Paris: P. Seghers, 1950.

Touré, J.M. 'Mobiliser, informer, éduquer; un instrument efficace: le théâtre' [To mobilize, to inform, to educate; an effective instrument: the theatre]. *Notre Librairie: La Littérature Guinéenne* 88–9 (July–September 1987).

GUINEA-BISSAU

(Overview)

Formerly known as Portuguese Guinea, Guinea-Bissau, a small country of 36,130 square kilometres (13,950 square miles), lies on Africa's Atlantic coast just south of Sénégal and north of Guinea. It had an estimated population in 1994 of just under 1.1 million people.

Some twenty different dialects and languages are spoken by the country's twenty-six different ethnic groups, four of which predominate – Balanta, Fulani (Peul), Mandyako and Malinke (Mandingo). Portuguese remains the official language although many people also speak Crioulo (a Portuguese-based Creole). Two-thirds of the population follow traditional animist religious beliefs with most others being Muslims.

The Portuguese were the first Europeans to visit the area and from the middle of the fifteenth century it became a centre for the Portuguese slave trade. This practice continued into the nineteenth century. In 1879, the Portuguese formally established the colony as Portuguese Guinea.

An independence movement led by Amílcar Cabral began in 1956 with the founding of the African Party for the Independence of Guinea and the Cape Verde Islands (PAIGC), the latter some 640 kilometres northwest of Guinea-Bissau and also ruled by Portugal. PAIGC eventually had to operate on an underground basis. Beginning a guerrilla war, PAIGC declared Guinea-Bissau independent in September 1973, just months after Amílcar Cabral was assassinated. Following the declaration, Luiz de Almeida Cabral, Amílcar Cabral's half-brother, was named president. In September 1974, Portugal recognized Guinea-Bissau's independence and a year later the independence

of Cape Verde. By 1976 majority ownership of Portuguese companies had been acquired by the government and universal education made possible. In 1993, however, literacy still stood at only 36 per cent.

As with most animist cultures, religion, a recognition and celebration of the forces of nature, and art are closely connected. Traditional practices include totemic mysticism which is expressed in a wide variety of rituals and taboos that include music and dance, shouts and pantomimes. Relying on form, colour, voice and gesture for their religious significance, such practices are proper to a world populated by spirits, sorcerers, furies, angels and demons, who govern the world and unleash the events that take place both on earth and in the afterlife.

Clearly such theatrical manifestations as storytelling, music and movement evolve from the attempt to capture the rhythm and movement of animals, people and gods, attempts which ultimately gave rise to sophisticated rituals and cults.

The occasions for representations are many. The oldest seem to be in connection to the harvest and in relation to ancestor cults. Others, probably nearly as old, are connected to fundamental events of human existence such as birth, marriage and death. In each situation, the theatrical action would take on a religious or secular guise through different emphases of gesture, word and rhythm.

Masks too became an important element within this belief system. The signification of a divine presence, the mask was the key instrument allowing the believer to dominate supernatural and malignant spirits in cere-monies which range from war dances to pantomimes of love, events which express human beings and show them in communi-cation with both spirits and people.

Masked events for the initiated include *fanado* (a celebration for the circumcised) and involve tales of tribal heroes. There are animal stories in which a *djidiu* (a traditionally trained narrator-actor) sings, dances and imitates various adventures, a more secular occasion which has the goal of providing entertainment for the community. The religious equivalent involves the community's official *griot* or praise singer who re-creates the drama and the history of the community while taking on himself all the roles (gods, humans, animals) and mixes all genres, blending laughter with tears.

Spectators in such events are participants and the performance is directed to the entire community. It is always free of charge and outdoors. Such traditional theatre both consoli-dates the community and transmits educational messages fundamental to its survival. But the didactic function does not minimize the aes-thetic role, which is essential, or the joy of such occasions which provide the community with promise, merrymaking, festivity and fun.

One such event among the Balanta people is *dança do boi* (ox dance) which tells a tale passed on from generation to generation. In it, two grazing bull oxen are approached by a cow; they begin to fight and eventually one of them wins the female. In Balanta celebrations connected to circumcision ceremonies, initiates are expected to narrate tales of their own youthful escapades imitating first one animal and then another. Those playing wolves might arrive from the woods while those playing crocodiles must imitate swimming.

Many dances of the Bolama/Bijagôs region are performed by women and contain scenic spectacle to the constant beat of strong drums. The dancers paint their faces, wear raffia skirts, necklaces, animal skins, feathers on their ankles and bells on their knees. Male dancers might also wear masks or coloured helmets. Thus costumed, the Bijagôs recall their history in such pieces as the cow or buffalo dance, the hippopotamus dance or fish dance, works in which one can see convulsive movements of body and feet, gesticulating arms, high jumps, and listen to claps, shouts and howls. To the unsophisticated observer, such movement might appear senseless; to the initiated it is precise knowledge that is being communicated.

Among the Mandyacos there are narrative performances which portray and praise the deeds of powerful chiefs. Even those who have converted to Islam – mostly Fulsas and Malinkes – have such forms of theatre.

One can also see among these events two opposite aesthetic tendencies – one recognized by its violent and rapid gestures and shrill, noisy music (drums, whistles, shouts); the other a harmonious slow movement with soft, gentle music and verse ballad narratives sung by choirs.

Balantas, for example, prefer significant movement and drums, the sound of horns, choruses shouting in frenzied pitches, sounds connected to recognizable events such as the theft of cows or, worse, theft of a community's women. In some cases, faces are covered with flour, powder or ash. All are part of the required ritual. There is also an annual carnival in Bissau which lasts several days each February and which includes such masks, costumes, music and dance.

As in many colonized countries of Africa, the arrival of European missionaries included the introduction of a literary drama usually used, however, more to further religious than literary interests. At the same time, attempts were made to devalue the traditional religious/artistic forms, the more extreme suggesting that there was, in fact, no indigenous Guinean art. Clearly this was a way of affirming the colonial culture and diminishing the local culture.

Throughout the colonial period, for example, the Portuguese did not make a single study of local theatrical forms and barely acknowledged the existence of African culture generally. So strong was the anti-African senti-ment and the destructive influence of this movement that later African scholars have themselves had trouble identifying and inter-preting some of those cultural expressions that remain.

In place of traditional forms, European forms began to emerge in Guinea-Bissau, first through Catholic missions. By the 1940s, regular amateur performances were being offered in the capital by a group under the direction of Henrique de Oliveira (also known as Oliveirinha). Later another group appeared under the direction of the Portuguese actor Antonio José Flamengo. In neither case was an attempt to create a popular theatre but rather a theatre for the educated colonials.

Some of the early scripts included social criticism within their satire, relating to such things as local corruption or even the lack of rice or insect repellent. Flamengo himself called this genre Revista Africana de Fantasia e Crítica (African Critical Fantasy Revues).

Flamengo's group also offered occasional 'artistic' evenings at the National Museum in Bissau. They included recitals of poetry and performances of piano music. Some even included choruses singing traditional songs and, on occasion, the performances of short plays such as Don Beltrano de Figueira and Don Ramon de Chapishuela by Julio Dantas. Some of these productions later toured the interior. When Flamengo died in 1959, however, the group disintegrated.

One form that grew during the 1950s was a theatre for children which did dramatizations of folk tales from both Europe and Guinea-Bissau, tales such as Sleeping Beauty, Cinderella, Festival of Sparrows, and The Cicada and the Ant. Some schools taught Portuguese folk dances such as the vira and the pauliteiro.

By the early 1960s a new group emerged in Bolana under the direction of Pori Costa, known by his stage name, Alanso. Entirely composed of Guineans, the group had little support but managed to perform several shows. Part of the early nationalist movement, the group was, however, regularly censored and harassed by Policia Internacional para a Defesa do Estado Fascista Português (PIDE; International Force for the Defence of Portuguese Fascism) and closed down as a result.

In an effort to stand up for local rights and cultural expression, a series of cultural conferences was organized at this time by the PAIGC. Included in the conferences were variety shows, poetry recitals, songs and pantomimes. Throughout the independence period, Theatre-for-Development performances were also encouraged, most involving satirical attacks against the Portuguese. As well, a number of plays were done to support the campaign for literacy.

After independence, a number of groups emerged. Perhaps the most important of these was Afrocid (Occidental Africa). A collective which operated between 1974 and 1976, Afrocid enabled many important Guinean theatre, film and television people of the 1980s and 1990s to obtain their initial experience. Among them were such artists as Rui Borges (Pantcho), who later moved to television, and Umbam N'Kesset, who later worked on stage in Dakar and eventually moved into film production in France.

From this group also came the play Miló (1976), about a husband who pays a high dowry price for his bride and then comes to feel he owns her. In the play, he works for PIDE as an informer; after independence he becomes a thief. The play focuses on his wife's growing awareness of her role as a citizen in the new society. Still another Afrocid play was Africa Liberdade (Free Africa) which dealt with the meaning of independence for both Africans and Portuguese.

Another play of note – it was created and staged by several former members of Afrocid including the actress Rosalina Gauffin – was Chassô. The title itself is a Balanta word meaning 'truth' and the play reveals how political prisoners were treated by PIDE. The play explores the role of women within Guinean society and the general subject of women's emancipation, a topic still controversial in the country in the 1990s.

Many members of the Chassô group returned to the stage shortly after in Se cussa Murri, Cassa cu Matal (Nothing Dies Without a Cause), directed by Carlos Vaz (b. 1954), one of the major Guinean men of the theatre. Born in Bissau, he studied acting at the Escola Superior de Teatro do Conservatório Nacional in Lisbon. After working in Lisbon and Madrid, he returned to Guinea-Bissau where he staged Se cussa Marri which dealt with Portuguese political repression and what actually happened in Guinean prisons.

Vaz quickly found himself the subject of political harassment, returned to Portugal and later moved to Cape Verde where he worked mostly in television. While in Portugal he published a book called Para um conhecimento do Teatro Africano (Toward Understanding African Theatre, 1978), one of the few important theatre works to be published by a Guinean.

Rosalina Gauffin remains on a par with Vaz in terms of commitment to the creation of a viable national theatre. Trained in the Soviet Union, she is both an actress and a writer as well as director of the country's only theatrical training school, the Instituto Nacional das Artes.

Other groups which have emerged through the years to make a contribution in the field include The Kin... 14 November, the Fire of the Revolution, Charma, the Flowers of Kobbournel and the Sons of Balana.

In 1976, to commemorate the twentieth anniversary of the creation of the Guinean independence party, a national theatre contest (Concurso Nacional de Teatro) was initiated through the efforts of José Carlos Schwartz, a pioneer in the composition of modern revolutionary music in Guinea-Bissau. The contest included prizes for the best scripted play and another for plays with dance and music. Schwartz's death the following year was a loss to the national performing arts and in his honour a national music school was founded, the José Carlos Schwartz School of Music.

One should mention here as well the creation of the Guinea-Bissau National Dance Troupe in 1975 under Jacqueline Ramous, a former dancer with Ballet Djoliba of Conakry in neighbouring Guinea. The company had some fifty members in the mid-1990s.

Though there are no purpose-built European-style theatres, the state does cover costs for students accepted into theatre school and social benefits for those involved in state-supported performing arts companies. Contacts with foreign performing arts festivals have enabled Guinean companies through the years to perform in Cuba (World Youth Festival, 1978), North Korea (Presidential Arts Celebrations, 1982) and Libya (Pan-African Performing Arts Festival, 1983).

Joaquin Rosa Pinto, Mamadu d'Jalo
Translated by Maria-Clara Versiani Galery
and Helen Heubi

Further Reading

Crowley, Daniel J. 'The Carnival of Guinea-Bissau'. *The Drama Review: A Journal of Performance Studies* 33, no. 2 (summer 1989): 74–86.

Vaz, Carlos. *Para um conhecimento do Teatro Africano* [Toward understanding African theatre]. Lisbon: Ulmeiro, 1978. 204 pp.

HAUTE-VOLTA

(see **BURKINA FASO**)

IVORY COAST

(see **CÔTE D'IVOIRE**)

KENYA

(Overview)

Known for more than two thousand years by merchants sailing from Arabia, Kenya is located on the Indian Ocean in eastern Africa between Tanzania to the south and Somalia and Ethiopia to the east and north. To the west the country is bordered by Sudan and Uganda, the latter with historical and cultural connections to Kenya. Covering an area of 582,700 square kilometres (225,000 square miles), the country is slightly larger than France. Kenya had a population estimated at 28.2 million in 1994. Swahili is the country's official language, with English used widely for administrative purposes.

Kikuyu, Luhya, Luo, Kalenjin and Kamba ethnic groups make up some 70 per cent of the country's population. From the seventh century on, Arabs settled parts of the coast and built trading centres at Mombasa and Malindi. In 1498, the Portuguese Vasco da Gama sailed around the Cape of Good Hope and landed at Malindi. The Portuguese later established their own trading posts which they held until 1740, when they were driven out by the Arabs. Throughout this period many East Africans were captured and sold into slavery.

By the middle of the nineteenth century other European explorers had discovered the potential riches of Kenya. In 1887, the Imperial British East Africa Company leased a ten-mile strip of land along the coast. In 1895, the British government took over the company's interests and built a railway (completed in 1903) from the coast to Lake Victoria. That same year the British made all of Kenya and Uganda into a protectorate known as the East Africa Protectorate and sought to stop the slave trade completely. Some years later, Kenya and Uganda became separate territories under British rule.

It was the construction of the railway linking Mombasa with the interior that opened up the country to European farmers, missionaries and commercial traders. The British government encouraged European immigrants to settle in Kenya's highlands and the arrival of the whites forced the local peoples, mostly Kikuyu, off their traditional homelands. At the same time, manufacturing developed in the country, particularly in Mombasa and the capital Nairobi. By the 1980s, Kenya was the most industrially developed nation in East Africa.

Kenya became an important base for the allies during World War II but the war effort itself helped to stimulate a sense of nationalism among many Kenyans. Despite an attempt at multiracialism in government, by 1952, a Kikuyu movement called Mau Mau, led by Jomo Kenyatta (c.1889–1978) tried to frighten whites out of the territory. Following a period of extended violence, Kenyatta was jailed by the British. In 1963, however, Kenya became an independent nation with Kenyatta as its first president. When Kenyatta died in 1978 he was succeeded by Vice-President Daniel Arap Moi (b. 1924) who was still president in 1996.

Dance and music have long played a part in Kenyan traditional cultures but modern formal theatre does not have deep historical roots in the country. It has its beginnings in the early part of the twentieth century when Kenya was a British colony. The creation of the railway line from Mombasa inland not only linked commerce, a new administration and new settlers in one network but also forged a new culture.

Kenyans watched with interest as amateur theatre groups sprung up in the settler communities and through the first half of the century educated Kenyans tried their own hands at the art, but always separated from the settler groups. The study of dramatic literature and the staging of plays, however, quickly became part of the school curriculum and drama competitions were soon a regular segment of the educational system, the major one being the annual Kenya Colleges Drama Festival. Not surprisingly, the criteria, the adjudicators and most of the scripts were foreign.

One of the few educators who tried to change this situation was Robert Beaumont. Encouraging the production of scripts which dealt with African issues and ultimately the production of plays by African writers, he helped to popularize as well as Kenyanize school theatre. As theatre gained prominence, the colleges began taking winning productions not only into other schools but also into community centres and even market-places.

By the 1990s, it was evident that the use of the local languages in festival productions was continuing to open up lines of communication between the schools and the community and involving other sectors of the population in both educational and theatrical endeavours. In terms of size and participation, the Kenyan Schools Festival became unrivalled in East Africa and great importance was placed on it by the Ministry of Education at not only the national level but also the local, district and provincial levels. At the same time, censorship continued to remain a problem, with government officials regularly questioning plays in terms of both their politics and their morality. In 1982, for example, two different school plays were actually banned by the state censor.

Theatre-for-Development evolved in Kenya just after World War II when the Nairobi African Dramatic Society took plays on specific social issues to local communities. In 1952, however, as winds of independence swirled around the country, the colonial government created a Cultural Centre in Nairobi which became home to an even more entrenched European theatre under the guise of being a Kenyan National Theatre. A breakthrough of sorts was achieved in 1955 when the Nairobi African Dramatic Society entered the National

Joe de Graft's 1976 production of *Muntu* for the All-Africa Conferences of Churches in Nairobi.

Drama Festival for the first time and won several awards. The festival was held that year at the National.

Developing at around this same time was the country's first important dramatist – Ngugi wa' Thiongo (b. 1938), also a novelist. Ngugi's play *The Black Hermit* (1962) is a clear statement of the issues facing young Kenyans caught up in the political struggles of the country. In it, the black hermit of the title, Remi, the first of his tribe to get a university education, has to decide whether to return to his people, whether to marry his brother's widow as tribal custom would require, whether to support the Africanist Party which replaced colonial oppression with another sort or whether to remain wandering in the city with his friend Jane. The play was written while Ngugi was studying at Makerere University in Uganda and was first produced by the Makerere College Students Dramatic Society at the Uganda National Theatre.

As Ngugi put it later in the introduction to the published version of the play:

> I thought then that tribalism was the biggest problem besetting the new East African countries. I, along with my fellow undergraduates, had much faith in the postcolonial governments. We thought they genuinely wanted to involve the masses in the work of reconstruction. After all, weren't the leaders themselves sons and daughters of peasants and workers? All the people had to do was to co-operate. All we had to do was to expose and root out the cancerous effects of tribalism, racialism and religious factions.

After independence, the Kenya National Theatre continued to be dominated by foreign plays and foreign administrators. By 1968, the Kenyan government had expressed a wish to have an African heading the National. The governing council of the Cultural Centre first named an African, Mark Mshila, as assistant director. In making the appointment, the council said that his duties would include working mainly outside the building encouraging work by less experienced groups.

Later that year, Seth Adagala was appointed director of the National Theatre. His mandate included the extending of theatrical activities beyond the confines of the building in Nairobi to the country as a whole. Adagala said that his hope was to arouse a theatrical consciousness among the Kenyan people by encouraging Kenyan writers to commit their talents to the theatre.

Among his first steps was the establishment of a National Theatre Drama School which would produce its first graduates in 1970 and which would supply the National Theatre with its own trained resident company. Offering seasons in Nairobi and also touring widely, the company did most of its shows in Kiswahili (Swahili) and/or English. All were done without charge for the general public with a small charge for schools and educational institutions. Producing comedies for the most part, the company's purpose was to win over the public to spoken drama and arouse interest in the form. Public reaction to these productions was generally positive.

By 1973–4, however, the Cultural Centre's governing council reported that 'little progress had been made in furthering African theatre appreciation among the public although some productions and plays by African playwrights had been staged during the two years'. Several people challenged the council report including Ngugi who, in an article called 'Handcuffs For a Play' (later published in his *Writers in Politics*, 1981) asked:

> Couldn't the reason be found in the fact that African plays were crammed into two or three nights and therefore gaining very little from the crucial word-of-mouth publicity given by the first three nights' audience? Couldn't it also be that the National Theatre has, over the years, created the image of a service station for irrelevant cultural shows?

Shortly thereafter Adagala resigned his position and was replaced by an English director, James Falkland. The justification? No African had the skills needed to take over the position. A major debate ensued over the role of the Kenya Cultural Centre with the majority of Kenyan Africans questioning the wisdom of having a white expatriate running of an institution charged with charting the cultural direction of the country.

Even the Writers' Union joined the fray, arguing that the appointment highlighted the problems facing Kenya's cultural development. 'The present National Theatre', said the writers, 'needs a director, but one who will conceive theatre in terms of local relevance.' Though the battle at the Cultural Centre was not won immediately, writers and students were encouraged more than ever before to explore their talents both in and out of the university, and theatre arts courses began to be taught within literature and education departments.

The year 1974 marked another landmark in Kenya's national theatrical development. It was in that year that the University Free Travelling Theatre was created under the direction of Ngugi wa' Thiongo and others. In 1976 Ngugi wrote *The Trial of Dedan Kimathi* with Micere Mugo which, with Francis Imbuga's play *Betrayal in the City*, were Kenya's entries in FESTAC '77. Both scripts were staged at the National Theatre. Later that year, Ngugi wa' Thiongo and Ngugi wa Mirii wrote a play in Kikuyu called *Ngahika Ndeenda* (published subsequently in English under the title *I Will Marry When I Want*), one of the first examples of a full-length play in Kenya to be written in the vernacular.

Staged at the Kamiriithu Community Education and Cultural Centre in Limuru, the play was an experiment in creating community theatre. All the actors helped shape the script, all were involved in the direction of the play and in building an open-air theatre. Utilizing song and dance, the play sought to explicate the villagers' material conditions and circumstances through an analysis of their significant history. The play, said Ngugi later, became 'part and parcel of their lives'.

The experiment, however, would come to an abrupt end when the government sought to suppress the play by withdrawing its licence for public performance. During the protests that followed, Ngugi was also detained by the Kenyan government without trial and Ngugi wa Mirii lost his university teaching position. In 1978, fearing for his life, Ngugi wa' Thiongo went into exile. Four years later, the Centre was denied a licence to perform Ngugi's play *Maitu Njugira* (*Mother, Sing for Me*) and in March 1982 the Centre was deregistered and the open-air theatre knocked down.

Through the 1980s, community theatre groups continued to emerge, however, some for short periods of time; others for extended periods. Significant among these in Nairobi have been the Capricorn Theatre Group, Mbalamwezi Players, Friends Theatre and Wanamtaa. In 1986, several community groups came together for a four-day festival.

In the 1990s, a more professional theatre movement began to be seen with such groups as Sarakasi Ltd (founded in 1990) and the Miujiza Players (1992) leading the way. In 1991 Sarakasi successfully toured a Kenyan play, Nderitu's *Wangu wa Maeri* in both English and Kikuyu. Clearly, the struggle for the development of a genuine Kenyan national

Oluoch Obura and Sibi Okumu in Janet Young's 1984 This Theatre production of *Woza Albert!* in Nairobi.

theatre had moved beyond the confines of the National Theatre or any other particular building. The idea of a Kenyan theatre that could express Kenyan values and Kenyan issues had finally appeared to take root.

Oluoch Obura

Further Reading

Björkman, Ingrid. '*Mother, Sing for Me*': *People's Theatre in Kenya*. London: Zed Books, 1989. 107 pp.

Brown, David M. 'The Form of Protest in Kenya: Drama or the Novel'. *Critical Arts* 1, no. 3 (1980): 47–58.

Fiebach, Joachim. 'On the Social Functions of Modern African Theatre and Brecht'. *Darlite* 4, no. 2 (1970).

Gachuka, E. and K. Akivaga, eds. *The Teaching of Literature in Kenya Secondary Schools*. Nairobi, 1979.

Gurr, Andrew and Angus Calder, eds. *Writers in East Africa*. Nairobi: East African Literature Bureau, 1974.

conflicts and skirmishes resulted between the original peoples and those newly arrived.

Another area of conflict was caused by the exclusion of the aborigines from government and decision-making processes. This continued until 1964 when the entire population was finally granted full political status. Despite this, the aboriginal majority culture was still suppressed and only western culture was recognized as official and acceptable.

Liberia is now composed of thirteen political subdivisions (counties), each one having an administrative headquarters or capital. The capital of the country as a whole is Monrovia.

As for Liberian theatre, as in many cultures it began with storytelling by the *gwayee-poyon* (a Krahn word for village storyteller). The tales of the *gwayee-poyon* were usually didactic, but comic tales were also included. Centred around animals and objects that related to everyday life and the immediate environment, each tale had a corresponding song and a special rhythm to go along with it. The tales would have stock characters such as the spider, the leopard or the king of the jungle.

Storytelling was also participatory in nature with the villagers responding to the rhythmic tales of the *gwayee-poyon*, tales which had no ends. The storyteller would go on far into the night and then resume the narrative the next evening. Working with the *gwayee-poyon* was the *gba-geahee* (drummer) who would create suitable rhythms for each song-story. When moved by the music, audience members would often stand up and dance.

Another traditional event was called *kwi*. In this, initiated society members (those who were circumcised) would hear one version, and everyone else another, less serious, version. In the *kwi* voices are used, voices believed to be of spirits which have been invoked from the great beyond. This *kwi* takes place only at night or in a space where no light or fire is allowed. The location must be so dark, in fact, that one cannot see one's own hand. If outdoors, performances must be away from the ground. Though the same kind of storytelling takes place as with the *gwayee-poyon*, the difference here is that the storyteller must have skills as a ventriloquist. Also, in the *kwi* no one is allowed to dance.

Another significant feature of traditional Liberian theatre, dance is done in all these forms of theatre, in symbolic imitation of events from daily life: death, birth, war, peace, harvest, hunting or fishing. An outward embodiment of some aspect of life for those performing, most dances are initiated by individuals and later refined within the secret societies where tutors would add to the steps. Traditional dances were usually performed at the 'breaking of bush' (when young initiates were expected to display their talents before an eager crowd gathered in the village circle). Specific dances might feature elephant, monkey, baboon or even leopard steps. Musical ballad is another traditional form which included storytelling, dance, music and speech.

Masks were used in many of these forms as a liaison between the living and the spirits of the dead. In this sense, the masks served a dual capacity: to give enjoyment as well as spiritual guidance to the people. Highly honoured, they have played a significant and meaningful role in the history of many African aboriginal cultures. Among the types of masks, some are used only in dance, others for comic effect, while still others are only for music or for war. Masks are believed, by virtue of their spirituality, to have supernatural powers which may not be questioned or challenged by the living. They are also used to perform many social functions, such as helping to resolve conflicts between families, clans and tribes. They also serve as a unifying and inspirational force during times of adversity.

Western-style theatre began with the coming of freed slaves in 1816 from the United States. Growing out of musical church concerts and school auditoriums, these were followed by Christian Nativity and Passion plays. Other forms evolved from debates, orations, monologues and recitations. Through the nineteenth century, scripted plays emerged in the cities but always in connection with traditional musical forms. Independence Day celebrations in Monrovia, for example, are still an opportunity for young people to sing, dance and see such entertainments. Street pageants (marching bands and decorated floats representing the various political subdivisions of the country) are also regularly seen.

Such performances increased in number in the 1940s and 1950s as did an interest in western lifestyles. Official functions, in fact, required western formal dress. By the late 1960s and early 1970s, however, the state's Integration and Unification Policy modified this behaviour to permit ethnic chiefs and elders to attend major functions in African traditional dress.

From the blending of both traditional and western culture have come two specifically Liberian comic folk forms: the Santa Claus and

Old Man Baker. The former is unlike the western gift-giving Santas at Christmas because the Liberian Santas dance and entertain to the accompaniment of music produced on the harksaw and drums, with a musical group as entourage during the Christmas, New Year and Independence Day periods. He also receives small tokens from those he entertains.

Old Man Baker, for his part, begs and amuses his audience. This figure usually has a protruding stomach, is dressed in rags and is accompanied by one or two persons. Both the Santa and Old Man Baker wear western masks.

In the early 1960s, the government began to develop a national policy on the preservation and promotion of traditional culture and established a Department of Information Services, including a cultural bureau. This, in turn, led to the creation of the Kendeja National Cultural Village in 1963. The function of the Village is to preserve the unique identities of Liberia's indigenous and settler ethnic groups.

By the 1970s, artists and various cultural groups had begun to be included in official Liberian political delegations. This gave real momentum to the promotion of culture in Liberia and many cultural organizations sprang up including the Blamadon Theatre Workshop, Dehkontee Artists Theatre, Womtee Dramatic Group, Tro-Tro Artists, Malawala Balawala and Kama Soko among others. With the opening of a national television station (ELTV), Liberians were able to view the works of their own artists on a regular basis and to learn about their own heritage.

The 1980s was a decade of both political turmoil and reconciliation. Most cultural performances during this time were concerned with mending political wounds, though political problems continued. By the end of the decade, arrests and executions, coup plots, the destruction and burning of homes of opposing ethnic and political groups and numerous accusations by the security forces of the day culminated in civil war. During this period, artists spearheaded campaigns aimed at reuniting Liberians by preaching a message of peace through culture.

Structure of the National Theatre Community

In each of the political subdivisions in Liberia, one can see traditional dance and musical groups which bear unique cultural imprints.

Most formal theatre activity is concentrated in urban areas – non-subsidized amateur groups, school cultural troupes or even individual ethnic troupes. These ethnic companies play during major national celebrations, holidays and activities. Occasionally such groups are asked by government officials to create performances for specific national events.

Given this background, it can be fairly said that no group operates on a commercial basis while the traditional groups perform only out of sheer love or social necessity.

The one group that the state does finance directly is Kendeja National Cultural Troupe based at Kendeja National Cultural Village. Earlier, support was also given to the Monrovia Players, a semi-professional group of Liberian and American nationals. Each of these theatres has about forty members including actors, dancers, musicians, painters, and scenic, makeup and property designers. For productions, rehearsals last up to three months.

With all this activity, unions have emerged, the central one being the Cultural Union of Liberia (comprising all genres of artists in the country). Others include the Liberia Painters' Association, New Breed Painters of Liberia and Liberia Musicians' Union. All are umbrella organizations which seek to promote arts and culture generally as well as to protect the individual interests of artists including rights and benefits. Ticket prices vary depending on the occasion and the group performing. Most are low by western standards.

Artistic Profile

Companies

There are five regularly producing theatre groups in Liberia, all in the Monrovia area and all working in forms involving music, dance and drama. These include Kendeja National

Cultural Troupe, the Cultural Ambassadors, Flomo Theatre Productions, Malawala Balawala and Dehkontee Artists Theatre.

The National Cultural Troupe, based at the Cultural Village, has won acclaim through the years for its spectacular mostly improvised music-dance performances. Composed of some of Liberia's best music and dance artists, the company blends traditional elements to create what is essentially an original series of pieces depicting ethnic events, customs and stories. Inspired by the success of Guinea's Ballets Africains, the group was founded in the early 1970s and has represented Liberia on many state occasions. One of its most popular pieces has been *The Village of So So Women* created by director-choreographer Boima N'gabla. The company is state subsidized and, though it performs regularly on indoor proscenium stages, its artists prefer to work outdoors.

The Cultural Ambassadors also perform dances and songs from the various ethnic groups, particularly those of the Mande (Kpelle, Lorma, Yai and Mandingo). Often included in official entourages, the company is noted for its elaborate traditional costumes and acrobatic dance steps and musical ballets.

Flomo Theatre Productions is headed by leading actor Peter Y. Ballah – known to all as Flomo (b. 1945) – who took his name from the comic role he played in *Gbengbar* (a local television series). Flomo Theatre Productions is a folk theatre; most of its plays and songs are improvised and spoken in simple English, which makes it easy for ordinary Liberians to understand. *Our People, One People* is one of its most popular shows. The group has received support from both individuals and institutions.

Dehkontee Artists Theatre blends traditional African and western theatre forms. The group was formed in 1977 at the University of Liberia out of a perceived need to promote Liberian arts and culture both at home and abroad. Composed of university and college students and professional traditional artists, it has a professional director and a resident playwright. All of the group's productions are scripted and these take a critical and analytical look at Liberian and African society. Various theatrical styles have been used. Among its important

The 1984 Dehkontee Artists Theatre production of Joe Gbaba's *The Resurrection* at the Monrovia City Hall Auditorium.

productions have been Joe Gbaba's (b. 1954) *Zon Ninneh Taryee*, a historical drama which deals with the life history of one of Liberia's traditional warriors; *The Resurrection* (1984), and *Chains of Apartheid*, another essentially realistic play by Gbaba. Dehkontee Artists Theatre attempts to create a national consciousness and a sense of national unity. Supported by various non-governmental organizations, it also receives sponsorship from the Gbaba Family Fund for the Promotion of Culture in Liberia, Liberian Jewish Heritage Society and Liberia Network for Peace and Development.

All these groups usually perform only during the dry season, when the weather is more conducive for public outings. All have been seriously affected in the 1990s by the civil war.

Dramaturgy
Directing and Acting

In Liberia there are two types of drama: indigenous genres (primarily oral) and written and spoken genres. In indigenous genres, appreciation is based on authenticity and probability. How well are the song and dance elements produced? How real are the songs? Do they relate to the story? Are the artists singing a funeral dirge when they should be singing a harvest or feast song? Is the lead vocalist speaking the indigenous language correctly? Is the drummer's introductory beat the usual one used to begin a harvest dance?

Indigenous art is very particular about such appropriateness. It must offer stories and songs in the exact language from which the materials originate. Usually, indigenous genres are lengthy and take place outdoors. They often last for four or five hours or more. Such settings provide ample room for acrobatic activities, and the improvised nature of the genres makes them appear different each time they are performed even though efforts are made to keep the central themes intact.

One of Liberia's most interesting productions used most of these elements plus elements of the spoken western drama – Kona Khasu's (b. 1942) *Homage to Africa*, which was performed at the 1977 World Black and African Festival of Arts and Culture in Lagos, Nigeria. This production begins with a storyteller entering, accompanied by music (a piercing female voice singing a song about the glory of Africa). To

the sound of a flute, very quiet and melodious, and drumming, the storyteller begins an invocation.

O Africa, we have come to pay homage to you, our motherland. We have come as your sons and daughters to honour you, to adore you, to worship you.

Khasu feels that images of Africa have been blurred both by Africans themselves and by others. He endeavours to put Africa's past, present and future in perspective. Using a free style of writing, he looks at society critically. His sentences are short and connected and he uses not dialogue but a storytelling approach.

Another professional playwright of note is poet and theatre director Joe Gbaba. His plays are socially critical of Africa as well as Liberia, and his diverse socio-political themes range from racial discrimination to political injustice and integration to cultural rebirth, healing and reconciliation. A pacifist, one of his key dramatic works is *Chains of Apartheid* (1977), written in support of the National Fund Drive for the Liberation of Southern Africa. Gbaba's plays are very direct and, within Liberia, controversial. Right from the opening scene, the subject matter – apartheid, and racial discrimination generally – is introduced. Gbaba criticizes not only white people but also Blacks who do not challenge racism. The latter he refers to as the Chains of Apartheid, the link that keeps the apartheid system intact.

In one scene, migrant labourers discuss how they can help undermine the system.

THAMBA: I think this whole issue of racial discrimination can be only solved by armed struggle and not dialogue.
SITHOLE: I think so myself. I think independent Africa should give us all the support necessary to wipe out this apartheid system.
YUKANI: There are some blacks who sell their birthrights for a few shillings and these are the blacks who are benefitting. Some African leaders also support apartheid. In these countries blacks are treating blacks no differently from the way we are being treated by whites.

The play ends with the renegades escaping to a nearby country to join the Liberation Front. *Chains of Apartheid* was staged at the University of North Carolina in the early 1980s.

Peter Y. Ballah (Flomo) is one of Liberia's rare theatre talents. Almost all of his works are improvised and are spoken in a local *patois*. Most of Ballah's plays are comic in nature.

Usually the comic nature of his drama out-weighs the stories – aiming for laughter rather than social points. His play *The Jealous Husband*, a typical example, revolves around a semi-literate man and his two wives.

In general, playwrights in Liberia direct their own work; this is standard for Khasu, Gbaba and Flomo.

Theatre for Young Audiences

The Kukatonon Children's Peace Theatre emerged on the Day of the African Child on 16 June 1992, out of a collaborative effort between Liberian UNICEF and Dehkontee Artists Theatre. The company was started to preach the messages of peace through drama, song and dance and has since travelled to various communities, schools and regions advocating national healing, reconciliation and reunification. The company emerged as a direct response to the civil war and to the fact that Liberian children and women were most often victimized. The goal was to give children an opportunity to tell their own stories, to explore their own traumatic experiences through song, dance and drama, effectively a psychocultural therapy for war trauma victims.

In order to create an ethnic and geopolitical balance in the company, the children were selected from the various ethnic groups in Liberia and educational materials were prepared by a core of Liberian artists including Boima N'gabla and Joe Gbaba. The company is an integral part of Dehkontee's season with the children also occasionally performing on the national radio as part of Dehkontee's radio series. Examples of some of the group's theatre work have been published in the *Kukatonon Training Manual of Conflict Resolution, Reconciliation and Peace* (1993). The word Kukatonon itself derives from the Kpelle language and means 'we are one'.

Puppet and Mask Theatre

Puppetry is unknown in Liberia and one rarely sees puppets of any type. What one does see, though, are mask performances, especially in traditional theatre. Hardly any feast or joyful occasion goes by without the participation of at least one mask or usually several of them. So powerful are some ethnic masks that they not only entertain but also execute judicial functions.

Liberian masks are ranked among the most beautiful in the world because of their natural and awesome appearances. Most have mysterious origins. While some are obviously human-made, others were discovered under water and in wild forests through dreams. For those not carved by a known craftsman, stories are told of their being discovered in dreams, during which people were ordered by the spirits of their forebears to find them. Usually specific instructions were also given as to how to manage the masks.

Some of the most powerful Liberian masks come from the Krahn, Gola, Dan, Yai Bundu, Bassa and Dei peoples. Due to their spiritual nature, masks do not usually appear in public unless some important ethnic, clan or family occasion occurs, such as the death of an elder, leader or warrior, the celebration of a successful harvest or during significant feasts where cows, sheep, goats and/or chickens are offered to gods to appease the spirits of their forebears or to intercede on their behalf.

Siah-you-wor-gle, for example, a powerful mask from the Krahn ethnic group in eastern Liberia, is noted for its judicial wisdom and is always called upon to settle inter-ethnic or extra-ethnic disputes. This mask is said to be thousands of years old and is passed down through *zoes* (teachers of or inheritors of the mask tradition). It is traditionally believed that a *zoe* does not die but lives on through the spiritual head of a family, clan or ethnic group. He possesses supernatural powers to heal, pardon and condemn and serves as a liaison between ancestral spirits and the living. As such, he may re-inherit the same mask and again become its *zoe*.

Gba-too is another fascinating mask from the Gola people in southwestern Liberia. *Gba-too* during its performance may grow taller or shorter in height (as tall as seven to eight feet or as short as three feet).

Still another Liberian mask of unique appearance is *gle-gban* or Gio devil. Unlike other masks which are carved of wood and are of normal human height, *gle-gban* performs on stilts as high as twelve feet and is usually made of cotton materials attached to a long head. Its special dance climaxes by hitting two stilts together and making a fast twist to the cheers of the audience. Because of its unusual height, *gle-gban* sits on rooftops when not being used.

A number of Liberian masks are literally hundreds of years old and have been preserved from one generation to the next by family members. In some unfortunate instances, some ancient masks were sold and carried across the Atlantic to western countries and other parts of the world where their spiritual significance and power are unknown.

All masks are accompanied by attendants who are usually friends or relatives of the *zoe* who ensure that the masks receive maximum physical and spiritual protection. It is traditionally believed that individuals dealing with masks must be very sure of their strength in African science or they run the risk of instant death. Because of this widely held belief and custom, masks are not 'tested' in any way, whether or not they are being used in performance.

Design

Traditional theatre requires traditional designs. Male performers generally wear colourful headgear made of raffia, a raffia skirt and have their faces marked with white chalk. They usually perform barefooted.

Female performers have their hair braided and decorated with cowries. They wear bangles made of brass, copper or silver, with bead necklaces spread around their breasts. Their bodies are decorated with white chalk and they too wear raffia skirts and perform barefooted. Because most performance occasions are held outdoors, there is no need for additional effects such as lights, set pieces or background scenery.

With respect to indoor theatre, design is usually limited to lighting. In this area, J. Lysander McCritty and Peter Lincoln work regularly for Dehkontee Artists Theatre.

Theatre Space and Architecture

Most theatrical performances in Liberia take place outdoors and those which occur indoors take place in halls and auditoriums which are not specifically designed for theatrical purposes. Any open-air space can be used for outdoor performances – the centre of the village or any square – anywhere artists can find sufficient space to express themselves. Generally outdoor audiences form themselves into circles with the artists performing in the centre. In village squares during festive occasions, elders and villagers might also seat themselves (or stand) on three sides of the performance space, leaving an outlet for performers to make entrances and exits.

Significant indoor spaces include Monrovia's Executive Pavilion, E.J. Roye Auditorium, Kendeja Cultural Village, Basao Cultural Village and the Relda Cinema. There are no technical facilities in any of these halls.

As for formal indoor theatrical spaces, most halls in which theatrical performances are held were constructed to host political gatherings. There are about two hundred such spaces in Liberia – thirteen of which are the city halls of the thirteen political subdivisions. Other spaces include cinemas, school and university auditoriums, fairgrounds, gymnasiums and church halls.

Training

There are no formal training institutions for theatre artists in Liberia except for the private village teaching lodges operated by and for the various 'secret societies'. Over the centuries, these schools – usually located in forest enclaves and called by outsiders 'bush schools' – have been the major source of perpetuating cultural history and practice. Mainly oral in nature, they teach traditional history, customs and practices as well as special crafts and skills such as music, dance, acting, directing, linguistics, weaving, hunting, architecture, medicine, fishing and daily life skills. Such schools are regularly found among the Sande, Poro, Gborh and Gee Negee societies.

The duration of training in bush schools differs from one ethnic group to another and from region to region. In some schools, a student may require seven to ten years in order to satisfactorily complete the work; in others, four to five years. Even after 'graduation' one may return for additional training in a specialized area of study or may choose to pursue a different craft altogether.

Fees are paid by parents in the form of food contributions and material support during the time of the training. Bush schools also receive the support of the ethnic group in which they are located.

Occasional training also takes place under the auspices of existing theatre groups such as Dehkontee Artists, Malawala Balawala, Flomo Theatre and the Cultural Ambassadors.

Among the professionals are zoe Ma Gbessie (a dancer and musician), Ndoma Golafalai (a dancer and musician), Flomo Togba, Deyougar Puu, Kpargbor Barclay (a traditional drummer and musician), Peter Ballah (actor and director) and Boimah N'gabla (a renowned choreographer based at the Kendeja Cultural Village). Kona Khasu, a professionally trained theatre director (MA, Boston University), also provided actor training with his Blamadon Theatre Workshop for a time. Joe Gbaba, another foreign-trained theatre expert (MFA, University of North Carolina), provides basic actor training for both adults and children who participate in the regular Dehkontee Theatre season and the Dehkontee Children's Peace Theatre performances.

Criticism, Scholarship and Publishing

The most important cultural research centre in Liberia is the Kendeja National Cultural Village established in 1963. The Village ensures the continuation of traditional art forms from the various ethnic groups of the country. It includes skilled artists in the areas of carving, weaving, dance, music, acting, directing, choreography, painting and drawing. Though most artists cannot read or write, they possess vast cultural knowledge about the history and culture of the country. These artists are the bedrock of traditional culture and they are noted for their authenticity.

Another centre is the Basao Cultural Village located in the Gola town of Basao, Bomi County. This centre is more local and is confined to the Gola and Vai as well as Dei cultures.

In specific cultural research, two names are significant: Tankabai Johnson (1908–82) and Bai T. Moore (c.1920–88), the father of Liberian culture. Moore for many years served as Deputy Minister for Culture at the Ministry of Information, Culture and Tourism. Moore and Tankabai Johnson are credited with the establishment of the Kendeja National Cultural Village and both conducted extensive research on cultural history.

Moore's research is in the safekeeping of his widow. His literary works include poems and novels and the ballet *The Village of So So Women*. The few Liberian novels, poems, short stories, histories and plays to be published were all done so outside Liberia at personal cost to the authors.

Criticism is hardly heard of in Liberian literary circles. Journalists rarely attend local theatrical performances and when they do, only occasionally do they write about them. Newspaper stories must be paid for by producers or they do not appear.

Joseph Tomoonh-Garlodeyh Gbaba

Further Reading

Best, Kenneth Y. *Cultural Policy in Liberia*. Paris: UNESCO, 1974. 59 pp.

Dempster, Roland T., Bai T. Moore and H. Carey Thomas. *Echoes from the Valley: Being Odes and Other Poems*. Robertsport, Liberia: Douglas Muir Press, 1947. 73 pp.

Dorsinville, Roger. 'Rediscovering Our Cultural Values'. In *Black People and their Culture*, 130–7. Washington, DC: Smithsonian Institute, 1976.

Gale, Steven H. 'Liberian Drama'. *Liberian Studies Journal 9*, no. 2 (1980–1): 69–74.

Henries, A. Doris Banks. *A Survey of Liberian Literature*. Tübingen, Germany: Horst Erdmann Verlag, 1970.

Johnson, S. and M. Jangaba. *The Warrior King Sao Boso: Liberian Writing*. Tübingen, Germany: Horst Erdmann Verlag, 1970.

Martin, Carlos. 'Blamadon: The Bud of Liberian Theatre'. *Liberia: Political, Economic and Social Monthly* 23–4 (1976): 28–32.

Moore, Bai T. *Categories of Liberian Indigenous Songs*. Chicago: African Studies Centre, Depaul University, 1970.

———. *Tribes of the Western Province and Dewoin People*. Monrovia: Department of Interior Folkway Series, 1955.

LIBYA

(Arab World volume)

MADAGASCAR

The fourth largest island in the world, Madagascar lies in the Indian Ocean 400 kilometres off Africa's east coast. Some 1,600 kilometres long and 580 kilometres wide, it has a land area of 587,000 square kilometres (226,700 square miles) and a population of 13.4 million (1994 estimate). In 1994, nearly 60 per cent of the population was 20 years of age or younger.

Though now known officially as the Republic of Madagascar, the island at independence in 1960 took the name Malagasy Republic and the people living in Madagascar still refer to themselves as Malagasy after the earliest inhabitants of the island, people who came from the Malay Archipelago and Austronesian areas. Others were Africans and Arabs who crossed the Mozambique Channel from the African mainland, Arabs and, since the sixteenth century, Europeans.

The first recorded European to sight Madagascar was Diego Dias, a Portuguese

explorer. He was followed by Dutch, English and French traders, the latter establishing a base on the southern coast. Most of the island was united under the Merina Kingdom by the end of the nineteenth century but in 1895, during the reign of Queen Ranavalona III, a French protectorate was established. The end of the Merina Kingdom came with the complete French takeover of the island in 1896.

Malagasy is the official language although French is spoken widely. More than half the population still follow traditional religious beliefs; 41 per cent are Christians and 7 per cent Muslim. A number of foreign cultural centres now exist in the capital of Antananarivo. Among them are centres from Lebanon, Indonesia, France, the United States, Russia and Germany. All are used for local theatrical activities and visiting performances.

Since independence, Madagascar's political history has been divided into three republics. The first, known as the Malagasy Republic, lasted from 1960 to 1972 and was led by Phillbert Tsiranana. He was overthrown in a popular uprising led by university students and intellectuals who objected to French interference in the country's economic, social and cultural life.

General Gabriel Ramanantsoa led the country during a transition period and in 1975 designated Colonel Richard Ratsimandrava to replace him. A week after his designation, however, Ratsimandrava was assassinated. In 1975 Didier Ratsiraka came to power and established the Second Republic as a socialist state, the République Démocratique de Madagascar. His presidency lasted sixteen years. In 1993, a Third Republic came into being under President Albert Zafy. During the 1990s, however, the country's per capita income has continued to decline to the point where it is now one of the lowest in Africa.

Like many countries in Africa, Malagasy culture can be divided into traditional oral culture and the more modern written one which emerged in the nineteenth century. The earliest form of Malagasy oral culture is found in the *hira gasy* (Malagasy Song) which emerged in the central highland of the island and, though typical of the people living in the capital area, can now be found throughout the country. A series of sung stories with established movements and gestures, *hira gasy* always has a moral. Originally done with the accompaniment of drums, flutes and the guitar-like *jejy*, early-nineteenth-century versions began to include violins, trumpets, clarinets and accordions. Now studied by scholars, the form and content have changed but its function has remained constant: to teach and to delight a popular audience. For most people, such oral performances were an important means of education whose intent was to bring communities together, to make people aware of their personal and social responsibilities.

The present style of *hira gasy* dates from the middle of the nineteenth century and includes acrobatics. Performed originally to entertain the court as well as to be seen on festival days by the community, the players always came from the lower classes. Costumes by the mid-nineteenth century began to be modelled on European military uniforms and fashionable women's clothing (long dresses, for example). Even the acrobats took on a military look.

All *hira gasy* performances contain five parts: a drum call to attract the audience followed by music and the entrance of the players; an oration mixed with chanted songs and proverbs whose goal is to introduce the company; the telling of a primary story; the telling of a second shorter story with dance and acrobatics; and a danced song of departure.

The development of a written literature changed the Malagasy way of living significantly and *hira gasy* along with it. During the Merina Kingdom, English missionaries first introduced the idea of western drama and used dramatic sketches to teach Bible stories in an effort to convert the indigenous population to Christianity. Under French colonization, French culture was imposed including operettas. Those soldiers who came to occupy the island in 1896, unable to find suitable local distractions, created their own Military Follies Theatre and performed at the estate of the former Prime Minister. During this same period, the Roman Catholic church in Madagascar banned *hira gasy*; the form, however, gained in popularity and it became a rallying point in the struggle for independence.

Under French administration, a Municipal Theatre of Anatananarivo was begun in 1897 and was inaugurated in 1899. It remained the only formal theatre on the island until its destruction in 1947. The first play performed there was *La Mascotte* (*The Mascot*) by Durus Chivot, done in French. A week later, a Malagasy adaptation of a French-style play was staged there by the Antananarivo Teatra. Entitled *Zéphine sy Armand* (*Zéphine and Armand*), it was written by Rajonah Taelatre and staged by Romain Andrianjafy.

Typical of scripts produced between 1897 and 1921, this play took a French story and reset it in Madagascar. A 1921 script by Naka Rabemanantsoa called *Iray Minitra* (*One Minute*) performed by Ny Tropy Anaiamanga (The Anaiamanga Group) while still French in form shows a Malagasy girl refusing to marry the man her parents had chosen for her.

From 1921, there is a very conscious turning away from western literature and an attempt to identify a specifically Malagasy form and subject matter, a period in which the island's lost identity is sought, a period called in Malagasy *Mitady ny very* (Search for Identity).

During the years of World War I, numerous performances took place at the Municipal Theatre, many as benefits for the war effort. After the war, popular music hall performances began to be seen more and more and interest in the legitimate theatre declined rapidly. As the

The 1995 Ra-Jean Marie's Company production of the *hira gasy* (*Malagasy Song*), directed by Ra-Jean Marie.

Malagasy independence movement gained strength culminating in violent revolt by 1947, local cultural events took precedence over foreign ones.

It was not until 1950 that new interest in western-style theatre returned, this time in the form of a spoken theatre dealing with Malagasy issues even though it was often written in French. Among the significant plays of this period are *Les Portes de la ville* (*Gates of the City*) and *Imaintsoanala*, both by Jean Joseph Rapearivelo (1901–37) and both with dance and music; *Les Boutriers de l'aurore* (*Boutriers of the Dawn*) and *Les Amants du Tritriva* (*The Lovers of Tritriva*), both by Jacques Rabe-mananjara (b. 1917), the latter having affinities with Shakespeare's *Romeo and Juliet*.

After independence, many new theatre groups were formed, some performing in French, some in Malagasy. Also returning to great popularity was *hira gasy* which, wherever it was played, attracted wide audiences including students and foreigners. Though still essentially a private entertainment, public performances are regularly given. When performed for a large audience, it is usually done in some open square with the audience standing around the artists in a circle. Audiences show their enthusiasm by shouting out praises, applauding and throwing money.

Structure of the National Theatre Community

Madagascar's professional theatre community is easily divided into traditional and modern companies. The forty or so traditional professional groups are known by their art form – *hira gasy*. Each village has its own group known by the name of the group leader and the village. For example, the *hira gasy* group called Ramilison Fenoarivo means that it is a company led by an actor-director called Ramilison from the village of Fenoarivo.

Directors of these traditional companies can be a man or a woman. The director is also the company's leading actor-orator. Each has twenty singers and dancers – ten men and ten women – plus two boy dancers, two percussionists, one or two players of the Malagasy violin, and two to six wind instrument players. The members of each group very often belong to the same immediate family.

For the most part, *hira gasy* groups perform on a commercial basis for individuals or community events, usually two companies comprising a performance. Because performances are generally staged in the open air, the players rehearse their shows during the seven-month rainy season when it is otherwise difficult to perform. Performances can last up to eight hours with each of the two competing groups performing twice for a minimum of two hours each time.

The modern dramatic and operetta groups perform a repertoire of spoken dramas – many with music and dance – primarily in the French and Malagasy languages. About twenty such groups exist in Madagascar, the oldest being the Ny Tropy Jeannette (Jeannette Company) created in 1929. Each group is composed of about twelve actors. Most are also singers and dancers. There is also usually a resident director and a costume designer.

The Malagasy-speaking groups jointly commit to about six different shows each season

with most running only one or two nights. Usually at least one is a new play. The French-speaking groups tend to stage only one major production each season in Anatananarivo but they often tour it as well.

Though all members of both the traditional and modern companies are paid, no one in Madagascar is able to survive on their theatrical earnings alone. Ticket prices are very low – generally about the equivalent of two packs of cigarettes – and rarely do audiences exceed 700 people. French-language performances are also sometimes sponsored by foreign cultural centres, embassies, or the French Cooperation Agency.

Three theatre associations exist in the country, one for each of the above groupings. For the *hira gasy* groups it is Fikambanan'ny Mpihira Gasy (Association of Malagasy Hira Gasy Players); for the Malagasy-speaking groups it is Fikambanan'ny Teatra Miteny Malagasy (Association of Malagasy-Speaking Theatres) founded in 1950; and for the French-speaking groups it is the Association des Théâtres Malagaches d'Expression Française (Association of Malagasy French-Speaking Theatres).

Artistic Profile

Companies

The many *hira gasy* companies can be found performing on public occasions throughout the country. Known as *Mphira Gasy* (players of *Hira Gasy*), these artists are hired by the state or by wealthy individuals for private events. During the winter, many *hira gasy* troupes appear at official exhumation and reburial festivities. In such ceremonies, the dead are removed from their tombs, given new shrouds, and joyously reinstalled by their descendants who honour their memories in the act.

Spoken theatre companies range from operetta groups to groups staging classical plays of the European repertoire to groups staging new plays by Malagasy playwrights. Production of plays by these groups tends to attract a mostly middle-class audience and students. The most popular venue for such shows is the Municipal Theatre of Isotry, the only western-style theatre now in the capital.

During the colonial period, one local writer working in the French language – Jacques Rabemananjara – wrote several plays in neo-classic style but using Malagasy themes. Another French language writer, Jean Joseph Rapearivelo, mixed text, song and dance in his works and in doing so created the only example of a Malagasy opera, *Imaintsoanala*.

As for major companies, the *hira gasy* troupes of Sahondraffnina Zanany and Ramilison Fenoarivo are two of the most famous. Both are, following the national tradition, hereditary companies led by outstanding actors who are themselves the descendants of leading actors who led the same company.

In the area of spoken theatre, two companies also stand out – Ny Tropy Georgette (Georgette Company) and Ny Tropy Jeanette (Jeannette Company). Among the oldest of Malagasy theatre groups, the Jeannette was founded by Charles Ravalison (1915–85) who was the first Malagasy theatre person to have studied abroad.

The 1995 Jeannette Company production of
Rodlish's *Ranomody*, directed and designed by
Rajonhson Andriambatosoa Ravaloson.
Photo: Marie Hélène Raheriniaina.

In 1962–3, he worked with France's Théâtre
National Populaire in Paris.

Also well known is the Ny Tarika Victor
Solo (Victor Solo Group), a company which
specializes in plays of strong social criticism
and strong national feelings. The Tarika
Rakotosolo Silver (Rakotosolo Silver Group),
in its turn, has made a specialty of mystery
plays.

A number of the newer groups – especially
some working in French – have turned to
collective creations. Among these are the Compagnie Johary (which has focused on Malagasy
customs) and the ATAF Miangaly (a group
sponsored by the Alliance-Française) whose
first major success was *En attendant le bus*
(*Waiting for the Bus*, 1996).

Two other groups of note include the Landy
Volafotsy, a company which specializes in

A 1996 ATAF Miangaly improvisation *Waiting for
the Bus*, directed by Christiane Ramanantsoa.

foreign plays translated into Malagasy as well
as original works and, at the University of
Tananarive, the Association Sportive et
Culturelle (University Sport and Cultural
Association) which both produces and offers
occasional training courses. Only one spoken
theatre company exists outside the capital, the
Atelier at the Alliance-Française in Antsirabe.

Dramaturgy
Directing and Acting

Hira gasy stories focus on everyday issues and
problems including conflicts between parents
and children, social prejudices and the need for
generosity. More modern versions have begun
to explore such contemporary issues as AIDS
and the environment. *Hira gasy* stories always
end with virtue rewarded and the guilty punished. Forgiveness is always requested for the
guilty.

French-language Malagasy musical theatre
takes its main influence from French operetta.
Songs are used to express strong emotion and
such plays also end with virtue triumphant. In
contrast, spoken French-language plays follow
a range of forms and thematic concerns. They
include historical pieces as well as plays that
are socially critical and politically provocative.
Among major writers in this genre have been
David Jaomanoro, Michèle Rakotoson, Henry
Andrianierenana, and Charlotte Rafenoman-
jato. Jaomanoro's best known play is *La
Retraite* (*Retirement*) a play about the life of
the lower class while Andrianierenana's best
play is *Elle* (*She*), a play dealing with the
environment.

As for performance styles, *hira gasy* is
essentially a sung art with the voices loud
and nasal. Because of this, microphones are
never used and the director's main role is to
ensure that the voices are clearly heard and the
artists clearly seen. Generally pieces are done
as solos, duets or trios. Women are always
seen as models of chastity and are never
allowed show their legs or to move
provocatively.

In western-style operetta as well, modesty is
the norm (especially for women) and songs are
generally subdued. Microphones are widely
used because of a lack of facilities with effective
acoustics. Only in the spoken drama are
women allowed to follow the emotions and
dramatic dictates of particular scenes playing
without restraint if required.

Theatre for Young Audiences
Puppet and Mask Theatre

Theatre for young audiences as such does not exist in Madagascar. Children, however, do sometimes attend *hira gasy* performances. Television, especially cartoons, has come to dominate the area of children's entertainment.

The only real exception to this is the occasional puppet theatre performance seen in the capital. One of the first Malagasy artists to work in this area was Paul Rakotovao who worked under the stage name of Paul Guignol in the 1940s and 1950s.

In the late 1960s and through the 1970s, puppet theatre took on a greater seriousness with several Russian puppet masters brought in to teach the art and to put on productions. Several of the shows used Malagasy tales and customs. It was from this work that the Ministry of Art and Culture established a state puppet group but the company performs only occasionally. For the most part, members of the group train teachers in the art working with children as young as 6 in schools. Trainers work both in and out of the capital and occasional puppet shows are now even seen on television.

Design
Theatre Space and Architecture

Because *hira gasy* is produced outdoors, setting is minimal with most emphasis focused on the colourful costumes worn by the barefooted performers. In Antananarivo performances take place weekly in venues ranging from parks to sports stadiums to natural amphitheatres on hillsides.

For operetta and spoken theatre, performances are generally limited to the Municipal Theatre of Isotry in Antananarivo. This theatre is a classical proscenium auditorium with 700 seats. Technical facilities are minimal.

Some companies also use the amphitheatre at the University of Antananarivo or halls in the various foreign cultural centres, which have slightly better technical facilities.

Training
Criticism, Scholarship and Publishing

Traditional theatre training in Madagascar tends to be done on a personal basis within the many *hira gasy* companies. Essentially this is training offered by masters to apprentices, with training often carried out from childhood on.

Since 1987, acting and singing classes have been offered on a subsidized basis by the Association of Malagasy French-Speaking Theatres. Several levels are offered and graduates are later placed with various groups.

Within the spoken theatres, classes are offered regularly by groups to their own members. Foreign cultural centres have regularly invited established foreign artists to give occasional classes to anyone interested.

There are no specialized journals or magazines for theatre nor are there any specialized collections. Newspapers rarely mention theatrical productions and never review them.

The standard book on Malagasy theatre is *Ny Teatra* (*The Theatre*), a study of Malagasy theatre from its earliest days until the modern period. It was written by Rajonhson Andriambatosoa Ravaloson, a director of spoken theatre.

Jeannine Rambeloson-Rapiera, Marie-Antoinette Rahantavololona, Marie Hélène Raheriniaina

Further Reading

Andrianjafy, Danielle Nivo. 'Le Théatre' [The theatre]. *Notre Librairie Madagascar: La Littérature d'Expression Française* 110 (July–September 1992). 7 pp.

Andriatsilaniarivo. 'Le Théâtre malgache' [The Malagasy theatre]. *La Revue de Madagascar* 26 (July 1946).

Artistic Department, Ministry of Art and Culture. *Fantaro ny teatra* [Know the theatre]. Antananarivo: Artistic Department, Ministry of Art and Culture, 1982.

———. 'The Hira Gasy' [Malagasy song]. *News of the Ministry of Art and Culture*. Antananarivo: Ministry of Art and Culture, 1984.

Ary, Michel Francis Robin. 'Le Théâtre à Madagascar' [Theatre in Madagascar]. *Bulletin of Madagascar* 72 (January 1953).

Bertrana, G. 'Une expérience théâtrale à Madagascar' [A theatrical experience in Madagascar]. *Education et Théâtre* 8 (1952).

Gerard, A. 'La Naissance du théâtre à Madagascar' [The birth of theatre in Madagascar]. *Université de Liège Bulletin d'Information* 8 (1967): 28–35.

Haring, Lee. 'Funeral Oratory: Living and Dead'. In *Verbal Arts in Madagascar: Performance in Historical Perspective*. Philadelphia, PA: University of Pennsylvania Press, 1992. 242 pp.

Puppet Group, Ministry of Art and Culture. 'Marionnettes'. *News of the Ministry of Art and Culture*. Antananarivo: Ministry of Art and Culture, 1984.

Ramiandrasoa, Jean Irénée. 'Le Théâtre malgache classique' [Malagasy classical theatre]. *Notre Librairie: Madagascar, La Littérature d'Expression Malgache* 109 (April–June 1992). 9 pp.

Ravaloson, Charles. *Ny Teatra Tany Am-pita Sy Eto Madagasikara* [Theatre from abroad and that of Madagascar]. Antananarivo, 1962–3.

Ravaloson, Rajonhson Andriambatosoa. *Ny Teatra sy ny fampandrosoana* [Theatre and development]. Antananarivo, 1986.

MALI

Situated in the heart of West Africa, the Republic of Mali is a landlocked nation of some 1,204,000 square kilometres (464,900 square miles). It is bordered to the east by Niger and Burkina Faso, to the west by Sénégal and Mauritania, to the north by Algeria and to the south by Côte d'Ivoire and Guinea.

Once the richest and most powerful of West African empires, Mali is a country of some 9.1 million people divided into two major categories each comprising several ethnic groups: the sedentary groups and the nomads. The sedentary ethnic groupings include the Mandingo group (Bambara and Malinke), the Sudanian grouping (Saracollé, Songhai and Dogon), and the Burkinabe grouping (Senoufo, Minianka and Bobo). The nomadic peoples comprise about 10 per cent of the population and include the Tuaregs and the Moors who live in the northern half of the country, and the Fulani (Peul) who live in the upper Niger Valley north of the capital, Bamako. Other important ethnic groupings include the Ouassoulounké, Khassonké, Toucouleur, Bozo, Wolof and Mossi.

Bambara (Bamana) is spoken by about 80 per cent of the population, although French is the official language of the country. About 90 per cent of the population is Muslim and less than 1 per cent Christian. Some 70 per cent of the country's land area is desert or semi-desert with 80 per cent of the labour force involved in agriculture and fishing.

Situated between the Saharan, Sahelian and Sudanian zones of the African continent, the Malian people created vast empires in the past: the Empire of Ghana from the seventh to the eleventh centuries; the Empire of Mali from the twelfth to the fifteenth centuries; and the Songhai Empire of the fifteenth century. Among the great kingdoms which are part of Malian history are the Fulani Kingdom of Macina, Bambara Kingdoms of Segou and Kaarta, and Senoufo Kingdom of Kenedougou.

Located at a major crossroads of Africa, the city of Timbuktu was once the most important stop on the caravan routes as well as a regional centre of learning and culture. In 1591, the city was captured by invaders from the north, and soon it declined in importance. Timbuktu's population is now small, and its once famous university is no longer in existence.

The French began to explore the region in the late nineteenth century and in 1893 they captured Timbuktu. Calling the territory the French Sudan, it became part of French West Africa. After World War II, France gave much of French West Africa some say in governing and by 1958 the French Sudan had achieved self-government. In 1959 it joined with neighbouring Sénégal to form the Federation of Mali but a year later the federation split in two. The Republic of Mali came into being in 1960 as a socialist state taking its name from the ancient Islamic Empire of Mali.

In 1968, the army overthrew the first president, Modibo Keita, and suspended the National Assembly. A new constitution was approved in 1974; President Moussa Traoré ruled from 1969 as a dictator. He was re-elected in 1979 and 1985 without opposition, through the only political party, the Democratic Union of the Malian People. This was dissolved in 1991 after a coup that deposed Traoré. A new constitution was approved in a popular referendum in 1992; this established Mali as a multi-party republic with a directly elected president. In 1992 the leader of the

Alliance for Democracy in Mali (ADEMA), Alpha Oumar Konaré, was elected president and a coalition government was formed.

From the earliest times, the Malian people used storytelling, music, dance and other performative events to convey their collective hopes and fears. Among these traditional forms have been the *kotéba*, the *gna*, the *kembe*, the *hore hollel* and the *do*; the latter is a masked initiation piece taking three months to perform. The *kotéba* – a giant snail dance – includes a chorus of female singers surrounded by five circles of musicians and dancers. There is also an active puppet theatre in the country. The creators of all these forms and their public were found among the rural masses who excelled in these forms and saw themselves reflected in them.

The modern history of the Malian theatre begins with the William Ponty Normal School in Sénégal. Founded in 1903 to train teachers, pharmacists and jurists for the colonial administration of French West Africa, this school, under the direction of Charles Béart, was in 1935 one of the most important laboratories of dramatic art in sub-Saharan Africa. Equivalents in other regions included the Tabora in Tanganyika (now Tanzania), the Alliance in Kenya, the Achimota School in Ghana and the Sierra Leone Grammar School in Freetown. Far from their native lands, the young students in training at Ponty devoted large periods of their leisure time to theatrical activities, collecting performance materials on their holiday trips home.

Well before the end of World War II, students from Bamako and other cities in modern-day Mali were staging plays at Ponty drawn from local tales and legends as well as creating new works dealing with colonial history. Among these collectively created plays were *Jégé's Ruse*, about the Mandingo Emperor Sundjiata Keita's conquest of the powerful sorcerer Sumanguru Sumaoro, King of Sosso; *Mali or Sundjiata*, an epic tale of Sundjiata's rise from infirmity in childhood to power; *Da Monzon*, dealing with the history of the Bambara Kingdom of Segou in the eighteenth century; *Bakarijan*, about a society based on violence; and *The Secret Meeting of the Almamy Samory* and *Tieba, Fama of Kenedougou*, among the first African works dealing with colonization.

Once back in their own country, many of the young Ponty-trained Sudanese became national leaders and many sought to give voice to the culture through theatrical endeavours. After World War II, a number of cultural centres were built in the major cities and it was again the Ponty graduates who organized evenings in them featuring not only theatrical performances but also lectures, readings and discussions. Writers emerged for and from these events working in many different genres. Among them are Sory Konaté, Mamadou Berthé, Dugokolo Konaré, Mamadou Ouattara, Sidiki Dembélé, Mamadou Sacko and Alphonse Dembélé.

Various amateur theatre groups also came into existence at this same time, many of them staging quite elaborate productions: Le Kotéba de Bamako, Les Tréteaux, L'Amicale, Arts et Métiers, Les Griots and Jeunesse Tam-Tam to name only a few. Their repertoires tended to favour militant and politically progressive themes, almost all involving song and dance. Warning against the dangers of denying one's African identity, and speaking against prejudice, the consequences of divide-and-conquer tactics by colonial rulers, and the conflict between the modern and the traditional, the best known titles of the period are *The Call of the Sorcerers*, *The Song of Mahdi*, *The Interview Between Samory and Captain Peroz*, *Sona's Marriage* and *Mukaila's Goat*.

Cultural competitions were also organized in French West Africa with each region's top groups gathering in Dakar for the finals. In 1958 a competition was held in Bamako. The following year, several of the leading groups in the French Sudan were again brought together, this time by the High Commissioner for Youth, with the specific intention of creating a Sudanese National Theatre.

With independence in 1960, all cultural organizations fell under the general supervision of the state, and the mission of the theatre was to interpret through fiction official political positions. In 1969 Le Groupe dramatique national (National Dramatic Group) was founded joining Les Ballets Maliens, the Malian Instrumental Ensemble, the National Orchestra, and in 1986 Troupe nationale de marionnettes (National Puppet Theatre).

The role of all these groups was to energize and reassert the value of the national cultural heritage. In 1962 an annual cultural week was established which would bring together the best performances of Malian arts groups. All the performances were well attended, filling public halls, youth centres, public squares and even stadiums. Called National Youth Week from 1962 to 1968, this community effort tried to shape both the political and historical visions toward socialism and Pan-African unity.

During this period, social and political messages were spoken, sung and danced in works such as *We Have Resisted the Invader* by Yaya Kané and *Tempest at Dawn* by Yaya Maiga and in such collective creations as *Whose Fault Is It?* and *Rural Exodus* (both done in the town of Segou), *The Mask Falls Off* (done in Mopti), and *The Verdict of the People* (done in Kayes).

After the army take-over of the government in 1968, the Cultural Weeks became biennial, ostensibly to allow more preparation time for the competitions. Yet censorship in both form and substance was reduced; this allowed writers to deal with all aspects of Malian social life. Among the plays of note seen during this period were *A Moral Affair* by Sada Sissoko, *Evil Is Vanquished* by Phorou Cissé, *Anfao* by Mamadou Bagna Maiga, *Who Benefits from the Rift?* by El Hadj Ladj, and *Nankama* by Pascal B. Coulibaly.

The creation of the National Institute of the Arts, a performing arts school, in 1964 infused the community with a large number of young, professionally trained artists, many of whom were interested in staging works by Malian writers. Among the national dramatists first staged during this time were Seydou Badian, Gaoussou Diawara, Moussa Konaté and Abdoulaye Diawara. A dramatization of the Senegalese novelist Aminata Sow Fall's *The Beggar's Strike* brought new audiences into the theatres.

During this same period, plays by internationally known dramatists were staged in Mali for the first time: Arthur Miller's *A View From the Bridge*; Bertolt Brecht's *Threepenny Opera* and his *Exception and the Rule*; Heinrich von Kleist's *Broken Jug*; Gogol's *The Government Inspector*; Gorki's *The Lower Depths*; plays by Molière, Racine, Corneille and Chekhov; as well as plays by African dramatists such as Wole Soyinka and Efua Sutherland.

Through the 1970s and 1980s, a number of private companies began to operate. On occasion banks or insurance companies would sponsor their performances. Since the early 1980s a number of Theatre-for-Development groups have begun to work as well, appearing for one or two productions and then disappearing. Among the issues being dealt with were AIDS, desertification, brush fires, deforestation, family planning, women's and children's health. At the same time, state companies continued to stage important national plays such as Alkaly Kaba's *The Tip Men*, and Massa Makan Diabaté's *Such a Fine Lesson in Patience* and *A Fasting Hyena*.

By the mid-1990s, a general economic malaise had set in across the country and the theatre was obviously being affected. Mali's artists were feeling it severely on a day-to-day basis.

Between 1945 and independence, Malian

Structure of the National Theatre Community

theatre was sustained by the artists themselves who gave time, talent and/or money to ensure that productions were staged. Wealthy patrons, however, were rare and both actors and playwrights were hard-pressed to earn any money from their efforts. Most artists had to work at other jobs to survive.

With independence, the state took over this responsibility and national performing arts companies came into existence with the most talented and committed individuals beginning truly professional careers. Salaries were guaranteed from this point along with social benefits for artists and administrators. On the other hand, this also meant that artists and administrators were subject to the political vicissitudes of the time. By the 1990s, Malian theatre had become a mix of both state and individual enterprise, with the state promoting theatrical activity generally on all levels from streets to neighbourhoods, from villages to regional and national communities.

The national companies all operate in Bamako, are subsidized by the state and therefore continue to serve as vehicles for state cultural policy. Les Ballets Maliens is the oldest of the groups dating from 1960. The National Dramatic Group began operations in 1969 and the National Puppet Theatre in 1986.

The National Dramatic Group has staged a wide range of plays including a number by national writers. These include plays by Séydou Badian, Alkaly Kaba, Amadou Hampaté Ba and Massa Makan Diabaté. The company has also staged a number of *kotéba* music and dance performances in Bambara. Its most successful productions in this genre include *Cétèmalo* (*The Artist's Destiny*), *Bugu ka moso* (*Bugu's Marriage*), *Muso jugu* (*The Shrew*), *Ce fali* (*The Vulgar Man*), *Morikè* (*The Charlatan*) and *Tègè magèlin* (*The Miser*).

Les Ballets Maliens has appeared on both national and international stages. Among its best known productions are *Biré*, a popular dance of the Khasso people; *Ciguélé* from Sikasso; *Bondialan* from Segou, and *Gomba* from Djitumu.

Of the private, legally incorporated companies, the most active are the Ba Bemba, Teriya and Nyogolon companies. Teriya specializes in theatre for young audiences.

A number of smaller groups perform for specific social groups. Danaya, for example, stages shows for railroad employees while La Troupe Enda Tiers-Monde (Enda Third World Company) is composed of abandoned children. Another group, the Kusun of Beledougou, performs traditional pieces during urban ceremonies.

Regional and national dramatic festivals take place regularly. The most important are the National Institute of the Arts biennial Cultural Weeks and the biennial storytelling festival La Grande parole de Bamako.

Artists are protected by state social practices. There is also a Malian Writers' Union.

Artistic Profile

Companies

It is rare for a theatre piece in Mali to be played without some kind of musical interlude. The *kotéba*, for example, includes several different varieties of music. At the root of many theatrical forms, however, is the *griot* – the storyteller and praise singer seen all across West Africa – who performs his art as a soloist, often taking on several different roles in the course of his performance.

Music and dance ensembles exist in various parts of the country. Among the major groups in and around Bamako are Sandia and Ambiance which perform operatic-type works with orchestral accompaniment. Their themes are based on traditional legends and stories from modern life. Among these are the Mandingo Epic, the Hymn to Kèmè Bourama, the Siege of Djokoloni, the Taara and the Djandjon.

Under the direction of Amadou Massamou Diallo, the National Instrumental Ensemble has moved in new directions with its work on comic opera. Its early efforts in this field were seen in the *Djarabi* (*The Unloved One*), a musical cycle.

As for dance, it is found everywhere in the country and is seen as a way to free the spirit since, as leading choreographer Kardiégué Laïco Traoré, head of the Kéléte Ensemble says, 'it helps people to discover through their bodies the essence, the soul of life and to enter into physical communication with freedom'.

The repertoire of Les Ballets Maliens and the National Folklore Company covers virtually all of Mali's cultural areas and reflects them through the aspirations and preoccupations of the various ethnic communities. Among the wide variety of programmes of Les Ballets Maliens are *The Serpent of Bida* from the Soninké people, a tale as well known in West Africa as the Iphigenia legend is known in the west about the dubious sacrifice of a young woman; *The Bondialan* of the Bambara of Segou; and *The Chagal* of the Tuaregs which teaches fidelity to one's community. Other major works by the group include the *Buffalo of Do*, *The Legend of Sundjiata*, *The Drama of Samagana* and *The Possessed*.

The National Folklore Company, on the other hand, finds its roots in rural communities whose daily life is reflected in the choreographic work of Mamadou Badian Kouyaté, founder of the company's Tam-Tam Youth group. As a form of meditation on the human condition, Mali's dance theatre finds its inspiration in both folk dance as well as in more abstract movement. These roots clearly include sacred dances such as the *gomba* and ritual dances such as *kanaga*, *céblengé* and *ciwarani*; profane dances such as *ciguélé*, *kofili* or *djitatlon*, and group dances such as *djondon*, *djanbara*, *sandja*, *tagué* and *domba*.

Other companies of note include Ba Bemba, La Troupe du district de Bamako, Nyogolon, La Troupe des Chemins de fer, La Troupe Djibi, La Troupe Dakan, La Troupe Badenya and La Troupe Koulé Diaka.

Among the key choreographers working with these groups are N'tji Diakité and Mamadou Badian.

Dramaturgy
Directing and Acting

Production of a play by the National Dramatic Group usually signifies that a writer has achieved a certain level of note. Four important dramatists whose plays have been produced by the National are Seydou Badian, author of *La Mort de Chaka* (*The Death of Chaka*, 1970) and *The Blood of the Masks*; Alkaly Kaba, author of *Nègres, qu'avez-vous fait?* (*Negroes, What Have You Done?*, 1974); Amadou Hampaté Ba, author of *Kaïdara* (1977); and Massa Makan Diabaté, author of *Une si belle leçon de patience* (*Such a Fine Lesson in Patience*, 1976) and *A Fasting Hyena* (1988), the latter staged by Ousmane Sow.

Other playwrights of note include Sada Sissoko, author of the socially critical *A Moral Dilemma*; Phorou Cissé, author of *Evil Is Vanquished*; Mamadou Bagna Maiga, author of *Anfao*; El Hadj Ladj, author of *Who Benefits From the Rift?*; Gaoussou Diawara, author of *Moriba Yassa* (*The Dawn of the Rams*), *La Parole donée* (*As Good As His Word*), a social satire, *Abubakari II* and *The Hour of Choice*; Moussa Konaté, author of *Le Cercle au féminin* (*The Feminine Circle*) and *L'Or du Diable* (*The Devil's Gold*); Abdoulaye Diawara, author of *Kadi and Safi No. 2* and *Dance of Death for Toumani*; Pascal B. Coulibaly, author of *Nankama*; Sory Konaté, author of *Le Grand Destin de Sundjiata* (*Sundjiata's Great Destiny*, 1973); and Samba Niaré.

All these writers challenge such things as the vanity of power and opportunism, and promote cultural rehabilitation.

Among the country's leading directors are Issa Falaba Traoré, Abdoulaye Ascofare and Victoria Diawara.

Theatre for Young Audiences

There are two Malian groups which regularly produce productions for children and young people – the Teriya Troupe and the young actors of the National Institute of the Arts. Teriya Troupe is composed of professional actors and the company has laid the foundation for continuing development in this field.

In 1995 Teriya Troupe presented an adaptation for young people in Bambara of Henrik Ibsen's classic, *A Doll's House*. Earlier productions of note have included *Janjo*, an epic by Massa Makan Diabaté, numerous sketches taken from folk stories such as *The Scatter-brained Girl* and *The Forced Marriage*, and an evening based on South African poetry called *Plural Cry*.

The company's most active dramatist is Gaoussou Diawara, author of *Madou and Queen Amina* and *How Young Simba Freed King Rain*. The first play features elements of the fantastic: trees that talk to the wind and the sun, and monkeys that converse with rabbits and ants. The hero is a hooky-playing pupil whose life is filled with trouble. The latter play includes space aliens, rockets, computers and sand dunes that open when the proper incantations are spoken. Many of Teriya's plays are adaptations of school texts or are based on experiences of children from their own lives.

Two festivals of note include the biennial Cultural Weeks and youth congress, and an International Festival of Folktales bringing storytellers to Bamako from all across Africa. This latter event, called Le Grande Parole de Bamako (Great Word of Bamako) attracts dozens of storytellers to the capital and entrances thousands of listeners.

The National Puppet Theatre has done work in the area of theatre for children and young people. One of its most popular productions has been *Banjugu the Trickster*, a script based on the nation's rich oral tradition. The company has invited various local groups to perform pieces for children using masks and puppets.

Puppet and Mask Theatre

Puppets and masks have origins in Mali going back more than a thousand years. As ancient as the Malian *kotéba*, work with puppets and masks is rooted in the oral tradition and involves a wide range of characters including both natural and supernatural animals.

Rod-puppets are the most common puppet form in Mali and the puppeteers themselves inherit their art from generation to generation, especially along the Niger River where several ethnic traditions have blended: Bambara with Sarakholé; Bozo with Somono; Fulani with Songhai. Puppets are also used in secular performance in both the Mégétan and the Bélédougo with those reserved for sacred performances found mostly in Baniko, the Bani Mono and the Djitoumou.

String-puppets and glove-puppets also exist and training programmes have been instituted to give puppeteers the skills they need to work in this area.

The puppets of Pélégana (in Segou) have represented Mali at various African and European festivals. Representing stock characters, they satirize the behaviour of jealous husbands and voluble wives and include such figures as evil genies and good fairies.

The puppet theatres of Lassa and of Sogonafing primarily use masks and draw their inspiration from folk tales and legends. They often include magicians, warriors and kings and are played mostly for children.

Puppet productions in general tend to be done after the harvest when people are best able to bear the cost of various entertainments involving these sumptuous figures, each crafted by gifted sculptors. Such shows involve reflections of everyday life – farming, fishing and even herding. At harvest time as well one tends to find a proliferation of popular festivities including rites of passage, weddings and the enthronement of chiefs.

Malian puppet performances include recognizable types from the various ethnic traditions such as *Faro*, a spirit of water and abundance; *Ci-wara*, a symbol of fertility; *Yayoroba*, the lady whom none can ignore; *Niéléni*, the typical village peasant woman; and *Bilissi*, a three-headed monster.

The state-subsidized Puppet Theatre for Children and Young People, based in Bamako, hosts the best productions each year from all regions of the country and also creates its own original performances. Involving music and dance, the most popular of the company's performances include *Bakaridian*, *Daba's Adventure*, *Badiougou the Trickster*, *The Cock and the Elephant*, *The Lion and the Hunter*, *The Schoolmaster*, and a three-episode epic, *Sundjiata, Lion of the Mandingo*.

Among major puppeteers are Djibril Diabaté, Adama Bagayoko, Yaya Coulibaly, Djénéba Sissoko, Awa Koné, Broulaye Diawara and Niakira Diarra.

Design
Theatre Space and Architecture

When Sudanese (Malian) students returned home from the William Ponty Normal School in Sénégal in the 1950s, they brought with them new ideas about stagecraft and particularly about stage design. Until that time, theatre in Mali – both traditional and modern – was conceived of as something that takes place in a natural setting – a town or village square under the stars with trees marking off the limits of the stage space. The sound of crickets and the light of the moon were all that was necessary in the area of sound effects and lighting.

But from the 1950s backdrops began to be introduced depicting savanna landscapes or other outdoor scenes. Moveable scenery soon followed representing the façades of particular locations such as public buildings or houses. Since those early days, theatrical architecture in the country's more established theatres has become more varied and more sophisticated reflecting a new movement toward evocative motifs, a symbolic suggestion of location and psychological states.

Nevertheless most settings remain simple and easily movable, clearly reflecting the continuing lack of suitable playhouses in the country. Indeed, only the French Cultural Centre, the Palace of Culture and Omni Sports Hall, all in Bamako, have stages of any size, the latter two conceived for large-scale musicals and too big for most local groups.

Among the major scenographers now working in Mali are Mamadou Badian Kouyaté at Les Ballets Maliens, Moussa Maiga at the Dramatic Group, Kardiégué Laïco Traoré at the National Puppet Theatre, Harounda Bary at the National Instrumental Ensemble and Modibo Sidibé, Bourama Diakité and Amadou

Bouaré – the latter three all graduates in plastic arts from the National Institute – at Teriya. Mamadou Rafi Diallo has also done some effective work, especially on Diawara's *The Dawn of the Rams*. Other designers of note are Claude Rollin and Lamine Sidibé.

Training

Training for the country's traditional theatre activities – including dance and music – is done through apprenticeships and study with traditional master artists. Actor-participants grow from imitators to interpreters. In reaching this point, the young learn dances, songs and mime techniques that will stimulate audiences and enable them to express themselves.

In addition to such techniques, these young people study folklore, learn proverbs and adages, customs and body language. Rooted in such work is the need to be both the person performing and one's self at the same time. As the Bambara say, to identify with a character too closely is to admit that one is without one's own ideas.

Techniques vary widely in such training for what the Bambara call the 'great spiral of existence', a term which designates performative activities of many sorts. Such community training schools strive to give participants an opportunity to share with his or her society, a means of letting the soul breathe in the same way that the body must breathe. Those who keep themselves isolated, it is said, are threatened with spiritual asphyxia and moral instability.

As for modern theatrical training, this is provided mostly by the National Institute of the Arts. The Institute, founded in 1933 as the House of Sudanese Artists and later called the Artisans' School, has long taught a range of skills from jewellery making and weaving to leatherwork and carpentry. When it became the National Institute of the Arts in 1963, the performing arts were added in along with visual arts and, later, socio-cultural promotion.

Formerly under the Ministry of Education, after 1963 it came under the aegis of the Ministry of Sports, Arts and Culture and had secondary school status. Its mandate has since been to train personnel in all areas of the arts, to train teachers of arts and music for the elementary and secondary schools, to promote modern art without rejecting traditional art and to research, collect and publish information on the traditional arts.

Included in the theatre section – a four-year programme of study – are courses in Black African theatre, history of art, aesthetics, scenography, directing, voice, corporal expression, sound, lighting and performance. In addition, students must also take courses in language, philosophy, ethics, civics and physical education. Participation in national and international arts events is mandatory. Plans are now underway to move the school into university level education as well.

Criticism, Scholarship and Publishing

There are two important publications in Mali which deal on a more or less regular basis with theatre issues and concerns: *Kalimu*, published by the Malian Writers' Union and *La Voix de l'Artiste* (*The Voice of the Artist*), a quarterly journal published by the National Institute of the Arts.

Occasional articles appear in the daily newspaper *L'Essor*, the weekly *Podium* and the monthly *Sundjiata*. A regular radio programme called *Arts et lettres d'Afrique* has also been valuable in helping artists remain aware of new developments. Reviews of new productions are done in newspapers, on radio and occasionally on television.

In recent years, research has been conducted at the National Institute of the Arts on stage design as well as on traditional and popular theatre topics. Theses have also been defended in all these areas. The sociology of performance has been studied at the Superior Normal School's letters and language departments, especially in the English, Russian and German departments. They have also done work on initiation rituals and the influence of oral sources on modern Malian theatre.

The only plays to be published have come from Les Editions–Imprimerie du Mali – Alkaly Kaba's *Negroes What Have You Done?* and Gaoussou Diawara's *The Hour of Choice*, while the Lino Printing Company has published Diawara's *As Good As His Word*. Jamana Publishing Company distributes published Malian dramatic works as well as essays dealing with Malian theatre that have been published abroad. Among these, the most important is Diawara's *Panorama critique du théâtre malien dans son évolution* (*Critical Overview of Malian Theatre in its Evolution*), published in Dakar by Sankoré.

Manuscripts of prize-winning plays from the various Cultural Weeks are kept on file at the Arts and Letters Division of the Ministry of Culture.

Gaoussou Diawara with Victoria Diawara
and Alou Koné
Translated by Sylvia Bâ

Further Reading

Arnoldi, M.J. *Bamana and Bozo Puppetry of the Ségou Region Youth Societies*. Lafayette, IN: University of Indiana Press, 1977.

———. 'Performance, Style and the Assertion of Identity in Malian Puppet Drama'. *Journal of Folklore Research* 25, nos. 1–2 (January–August 1988): 87–100.

———. 'Playing the Puppets: Innovation and Rivalry in Bamana Youth Theatre of Mali'. *The Drama Review* 32, no. 2 (summer 1988): 65–82.

———. 'Puppet Theatre in the Segu Region of Mali'. PhD dissertation, Indiana University, 1983. 450 pp.

Béart, Charles. 'Le Théâtre indigène et la culture africaine' [Indigenous theatre and African culture]. *Education Africaine* (1936).

Brink, James Thomas. 'The Conceptual Meaning of Theatre among the Beledugu Bamana: An Ethnographic Overview'. In *Discourse in Ethnomusicology II: A Tribute to Alan P. Merriam*, ed. Caroline Card, 67–82. Bloomington, IN: Archives of Traditional Music, Indiana University, 1981.

———. 'Organizing Satirical Comedy in Kote-Tlon: Drama as a Communication Strategy among the Bamana of Mali'. PhD dissertation, Indiana University, 1980. 242 pp.

Cornévin, Robert. *Le Théâtre en Afrique noire et à Madagascar*. Paris: Le livre africain, 1970. 334 pp.

Decock, Jean. 'Pre-théâtre et rituel: National Folk Troupe of Mali'. *African Arts/Arts d'Afrique* 1, no. 3 (1968): 31–7.

Diabaté, Massa Makan. *Première Anthologie de la musique malienne* [First anthology of Malian music]. Recording. Edition Barenreiter, 1983.

Diallo, Mamadou. *Essai sur la musique traditionelle au Mali* [An essay on traditional music in Mali]. Paris: ACCT, 1983.

Diawara, Gaoussou. *Panorama critique du théâtre malien dans son évolution* [Critical overview of Malian theatre in its evolution]. Dakar: Sankoré, 1981. 109 pp.

Hopkins, Nicholas S. 'Le Théâtre moderne au Mali' [Modern theatre in Mali]. *Présence Africaine* 25, no. 53 (March 1965): 162-93.

'Le Théâtre négro-africain' [Black African theatre]. Report of the 1970 Colloquium of Abidjan. *Présence Africaine* (1971). 249 pp.

Maiga, M. 'Le Kotéba'. *Notre Librairie: La Littérature malienne*, (July–October 1984): 75–6.

Messaillou. 'La Farce villageoise à la ville, le kotéba de Bamako' [The Village Farce in the City, the Koteba of Bamako]. *Présence Africaine* (November 1964), 55 pp.

MAURITANIA

(Arab World volume)

MAURITIUS

A small volcanic island nation in the Indian Ocean, Mauritius is located about 800 kilometres east of Madagascar off the south-eastern coast of Africa. It is some 2,000 kilometres from Durban, 1,800 kilometres from Mombassa and 4,700 kilometres from Bombay. Most Mauritians are descended from people who came to the island as slaves or workers; about two-thirds of them are of Indian ancestry.

Composed of one main island 61 kilometres (38 miles) long and 46 kilometres (29 miles) wide and several smaller islands, Mauritius has an overall land area of just 2,000 square kilometres (790 square miles). Mauritius was once the home of the dodo, a large flightless bird which became extinct by the eighteenth century.

The Portuguese sighted Mauritius in the sixteenth century but it was not settled until the Dutch took possession of it in 1598 and named it after Prince Maurice of Nassau (1567–1625). The Dutch abandoned the island in 1710. This marooned a large number of African slaves, mostly from Madagascar. The French claimed Mauritius in 1715. Changing its name to the Isle de France, they brought in additional slaves from Africa, built a port and planted sugar and other crops.

In 1810, the British captured the island from the Napoleonic navy and thousands of Indians were brought in to work the sugar plantations. When slavery was abolished in 1835, Mauritius had a population of 101,469. Of this number, 76,774 were black slaves, 18,019 were free Blacks and 8,135 were Europeans. In 1996, about 30 per cent of the population were Creoles, mainly descendants of Africans in an ongoing process of mixing with other ethnic groups. More than 60 per cent were Hindu and Muslim descendants of indentured labourers with the remainder of the total 1.2 million population made up of Sino-Mauritians and Euro-Mauritians. In 1968, Mauritius became independent. English is the island's official language but French and Mauritanian Creole are widely spoken. Hindi, Urdu, Hakka and Bhojpoori are languages preserved by the various ethnic groups.

A country of nearly full employment (the unemployment rate in the early 1990s was running at just over 2 per cent), Mauritius has enviable social services and a healthy balance of payments. Mauritius is the second largest exporter of knitwear in the world. The thousands of Mauritians who regularly leave the country – most to Australia, England and France – are well educated and multilingual. A relatively large number have distinguished themselves in cultural areas.

In general, English is used in Mauritius for business and technical studies while French is used socially or for writing. Most Mauritians communicate with one another in Creole although the island's seven newspapers are mostly published in French. Mauritius has also fostered solid links with various international groupings and organizations. It is, for example, a member of the British Commonwealth, of the Francophonie, of the Organization of African Unity, of the EEC/ACP Convention, and of the Preferential Trade Agreement of East and Southern Africa.

Given such a background, one would expect the arts and leisure in Mauritius to be flourishing. Unfortunately, this is not so. While words like consolidation, diversification and modernization are common to all, innovation, culture and creativity are notions that are apparently being left to some unspecified future development programme.

The island's theatre tradition dates back to the seventeenth century when plays from Paris were produced by enthusiastic amateurs living or stationed on Mauritius. A theatre was, in fact, built for production of these plays in a park at the heart of the capital, Port Louis. The park is still there but the theatre – La Comédie du Roy (King's Playhouse) – has disappeared.

By the time the British arrived, French language and culture were part of the island's traditions and the British accommodated it all, along with Roman Catholicism. The British were quite pragmatic – so long as the French settlers managed their sugar estates, paid their taxes and kept the peace, French culture was fine. A parliamentary system was established based on the British model, however, and a

British education and administrative system put into place. Mauritius's modern legal system too continues to reflect the compromise reached between the early French and English. Culturally, the French have managed to hold a stronger influence on the intellectual life, artistic expression in general and theatre life in particular.

By the twentieth century, theatre had become more of a social event than anything else with the Port Louis Theatre hosting three-month seasons of light opera featuring three or four productions by visiting troupes from France. Favourite composers included Franz Lehár, Giacomo Puccini, Jules Massenet, Charles Gounod and Gaetano Donizetti. Occasionally a piece by a lesser known composer such as Francis Lopez would be included. Talented Mauritian amateurs would often be used as part of the chorus. The productions – almost always sold out in advance – attracted virtually all the wealthy French Mauritians, most of them powerful landowners.

There was – and still is – a festive atmosphere for these music theatre seasons which usually took place from July to September. The visiting troupe always brought a sense of Paris style to the island and there was a festival atmosphere as wealthy islanders spared no effort to look glamorous as they left their homes by horse-drawn coaches for Port Louis. Most of the population, however, were simply curious onlookers.

To be sure, such activities were an important meeting point between the outside world and isolated Mauritians. The arrival of whatever *troupe lyrique* was performing was an event that many cherished to the point of actually going to the docks to welcome them. Artistic trends from Paris mattered and continue to matter. But it also mattered to show oneself as part of high society, to show oneself as cultured. The local expression 'ena dzimun kuma teat' ('people for the theatre') was clearly created to describe this social phenomenon.

By the end of the 1950s, more and more local people began to attend these performances and the interest in theatre grew. Even those who simply sat on the sidewalks and watched the social spectacle got interested. Most became familiar with the show songs which could be heard outside. Many would sing them later for both the audience as they left the theatre and for the artists themselves on their way back to their hotels.

Social gatherings at all levels would often end up including an exchange of extracts from the repertoires of the better known operettas. It was not unheard of for a young Creole man to be expected to be able to sing a piece from *The Merry Widow* or *The Mikado* to impress the parents of the girl he wished to marry.

In the 1990s, theatre attendance still remained a matter of education, privilege, and class and still revolves around imported culture. The *saison lyrique* was still the most likely theatrical event to find commercial sponsorship and to fill theatre seats.

On the English side, the Mauritius Dramatic Club staged its first production at the Plaza Theatre in Rose Hill in 1934, a British play called *The Last of Mrs Cheyney* by Frederick Lonsdale. The Club, composed mostly of British expatriates, civil servants, businesspeople, teachers and members of the Navy, remained in continuous operation through the 1970s and produced plays of a generally high quality. Among the dramatists it introduced to Mauritius were Sheridan, Wilde, Fry, Coward and Shaw. Few Mauritians, however, were cast in these shows whose audience was the economic and intellectual elite.

During this time a number of talented Mauritians left the country to advance their skills abroad – actors Max Moutia and Yves Forget among them, the former to France and the latter to Belgium. Both achieved respectable professional careers. After World War II, they returned to Mauritius and jointly took charge of theatre activities during the 1949 season on behalf of the Municipality of Port Louis and the Municipality of Beau Bassin-Rose Hill. Through their imagination and skills, a generation of younger artists was developed. Both these pioneers continued to perform and direct until their deaths.

Moutia, a classically trained singer-actor, also initiated a series of tours across the island through the 1950s while Forget trained younger actors and worked at the Plaza Theatre for many years.

One ongoing source of theatre activity has been schools and colleges. Most have good stages, some technical equipment and committed directors. During the 1960s productions of Molière and Jean Anouilh reached impressive standards at St Mary's College in Rose Hill.

It was a Frenchman married to a Mauritian, Denis Julien, who made the first serious attempt to create a multiracial, national troupe. In the late 1960s, Julien sought to establish such a company with a repertoire of French language plays to be both staged and televised. Julien's dream was never fully realized. Later, Daniel Labonne, an actor turned director who had worked closely with Julien (staging plays by Eugène Ionesco and René Obaldia), staged a number of his own productions. Far from a national theatre, however, Labonne used alternative venues such as restaurants, nightclubs and cafeterias.

Another serious attempt was found in the work of Serge Kimoun, an employee of the French Embassy. It was Kimoun who introduced popular Molière productions including in them lines in the Creole language. Later touring his productions, they introduced theatre to a wide audience across the island.

From 1966 to 1972, La Société des metteurs en scène (Society of Theatre Directors) attempted to bring together a group of artists working in French to stage major works from the French repertoire. Initiated by André Decotter, an occasional playwright, the group's members included such major directors as René Antelme, Michel Cervello, Roger Lecoultre and Yves Forget. The society staged four plays a season – classics, boulevard comedies, serious dramas and thrillers – mainly at the Plaza Theatre.

In the 1970s, a well-educated generation of young people emerged who tried to deal with the meaning of independence for the island. They questioned the direction of Mauritius society, and argued for the importance of the Creole language and against the elitist character of Mauritius's established theatrical culture. Research and innovation accompanied these concerns and accepted notions of theatre were severely challenged. The result was a new commitment to Creole as a language for cultural transmission, a new belief that artists on a stage did not have to speak French like a Parisian or English like a Cambridge professor, a belief that Mauritians needed to establish their own identity, and that issues of concern only to Mauritans did have a place on Mauritian stages.

Playwrights such as Dev Virahsawmy and directors such as Labonne responded with new enthusiasm. Virahsawmy began writing plays in Creole starting with *Li* while Labonne established his Atelier Theatre in an attempt to open the theatre to new audiences. Others followed and by the end of the decade the perception of theatre in Mauritius was both enriched and transformed.

Yet even in the 1990s theatre remained essentially an elitist art form in Mauritius and young people still thought of theatre as something connected to classroom texts. The taste of local audiences continued to be outward rather than inward looking and continued to be very conservative in style. Imitation of the successful styles of others appealed much more than originality. Nevertheless, government agencies were continuing to look at theatre as a way to reach out to all ethnic groups. Increased importance was being placed on the arts in general and a more active role for theatre in particular were views being supported by the Ministry of Arts, Culture and Leisure (whose minister was a poet, Tsang Man Kin), and even by the President of the Republic – Cassam Uteem – who was a versatile actor in his pre-political days.

Structure of the National Theatre Community

Government cultural policy since independence has focused on the fostering of a multicultural society with an emphasis on the learning of several languages and a recognition of the cultural heritage of all of Mauritius's ethnic groups. In practice this has tended to favour cultural forms and practices from India in particular and Asia in general. African culture has somehow lagged behind. As a result an African Cultural Centre was established in the 1980s but it has been poorly funded and not effective.

A Ministry of Culture was established in 1982 and shortly thereafter a National Arts Council began operation. The National Arts Council, however, never really got off the ground and in its short existence had no real impact on the arts.

For the most part, theatre is still essentially an amateur activity though there have been examples of productions making profits. The most professional of the operations and the one which does regularly earn a profit is the French light opera season in Port Louis. But in this instance, virtually all of the artists are from abroad and stay in Mauritius for only a few months.

Most local productions must be funded from box-office revenues or are modestly supported by local government, private firms, advertising agencies or the cultural services of foreign embassies.

Since the 1970s, theatre in Creole has joined theatre in French and English as a viable cultural outlet, becoming both respectable and popular.

Until that time, Creole was seen as a language for uneducated people and an affirmation of a lack of cultural sophistication. This was despite the fact that the language has always been the medium for popular storytelling and the only language used to express with humour and sadness the inner drama of the *sega*, a long popular dance theatre form. (See **Artistic Profile** section for more information on the *sega*.)

One attempt at establishing a viable commercial theatre in Creole was a production of Andrew Lloyd Webber and Tim Rice's musical *Joseph and His Amazing Technicolour Dreamcoat*. The show was adapted into the Creole language by Dev Virahsawmy. An exceptional success, the production attracted audiences from all ethnic groups on the island and packed the Port Louis Theatre for forty nights in 1981.

For the record it should be noted that there is a Board of Censorship on the island which officially regulates the propriety of public performances. Though stage productions are rarely affected, in 1975 a theatre practitioner did have to appear before the Board to justify his work.

The major festival seen in Mauritius is the annual Youth Drama Festival; other festivals have begun to be seen since the mid-1980s. Among them have been the Festival of Plays in Kreol organized by the Municipality of Port Louis, and an Alliance-Française Theatre Competition.

Artistic Profile

Despite the preponderance of western-style theatre in English, French and Creole, Mauritius also has a traditional theatre which can be seen in a number of celebrations, many fading in importance as the society's economic success has grown.

One such celebration is the Goon Festival celebrated by the Muslim community. For a period of ten days, the Festival commemorates the killing during war of the nephews of the Prophet Muhammad, Assen and Hussein. Involving self-inflicted punishment, the Festival begins with the sound of drums and is followed by barefooted men who begin to walk on sharpened machetes, striking themselves with sharp objects and swallowing bulbs. Spiritual guides ensure that no blood is spilled as celebrants move around the mobile shrine (the Goon).

Another South Indian tradition involves walking on fire, an act preceded by severe fasting and intense praying. The Holi Hindu Festival is a kind of joyful game that includes the throwing of a pink coloured liquid solution onto family and friends.

The Cavadee is a religious festival celebrated on the streets by Mauritian Tamils. In this colourful procession, men, women and children – their bodies pierced with pins of varying sizes – carry on their shoulders a wooden structure decorated with flowers. To the sound of trumpets, drums and cymbals and the incantations of a leader-priest, participants enter in a trance.

The Chinese Spring Festival each year is celebrated with performers moving beneath elongated dragon bodies made of satin, mirrors and fabric frills.

The national dance of Mauritius is the *sega*, perhaps the island's most theatrical and popular cultural expression. Now reduced to a commercial dance form, the *sega* was originally an all-night participatory theatrical event. Its participatory character is one of the few African elements still found along with the build-up of rhythms and chanting.

In the *sega*, first the performers and later the audience dance. Usually celebrated at nightfall, the event begins with two or three musicians performing a call on the *ravann*, a large circular tambourine. A storyteller then begins a dramatic

A scene from Le Théâtre de l'ACOI's (Cultural Alliance of the Indian Ocean) production of *The Barber of Seville*.
Photo: courtesy of Daniel Labonne.

tale in language full of riddles and poetry. Responses come from a largely female choir while the drums pick up momentum. The tale itself can be sad, ironic or comic and at its conclusion the choir breaks into loud singing and vibrant dancing usually executed in pairs with revolving partners. Sexually suggestive for some, the *sega* for younger generations is simply associated with party dancing and records.

Poetry is another form of expression favoured by the island's creative artists. Le Théâtre de l'ACOI (Cultural Alliance of the Indian Ocean) actually created a television show called Le Cabaret des Poètes as part of their own dramatic series. In 1975, the Atelier Theatre staged a dramatization of the poetry of Pierre Renaud in a show called *Pierre sur Pierre*. In 1981, a collection of short stories originally by the French writer LaFontaine but adapted to the Mauritian socio-political context in Creole was produced in a stage version. The production – *9 Fab Lafontenn* – was still touring in 1996. Another theatre production of note – *Mokko* – was created in 1994 based on *Petrusmok*, a 1951 piece by the poet and painter Malcolm De Chazal.

Companies

In December 1994, the Theatre of Port Louis reopened after being closed for renovations since 1989. For its ongoing season, a programme of productions was put together which gives a fair idea of the most active companies and individuals in the country at the time. Among those taking part was the Mauritius Drama League, founded in 1979 and headed by director Quisnarajoo Ramana; the innovative Favory Troupe of Henri Favory; Pro-Musica, founded in 1971 and directed by Philippe Ohsan, which specializes in light opera and classical music; the Arts Institute of Mauritius; Philippe Houbert who creates popular sound and light shows; Gerard Sullivan; and Les Amis du Théâtre.

In the 1950s, one of the most consistent producers was the Choral Society of Curepipe which staged such operas as *Samson and Delilah*, *Carmen*, *Aida* and *Faust* under conductor Joseph Leroy. During the 1960s and 1970s it was Théâtre Populaire with its *commedia*-style productions of European classics with a Creole touch. Another group of note in the early 1970s was La Société des Metteurs en Scène (Directors' Group).

Daniel Labonne's Atelier Theatre, founded in 1974, has through the years looked at core questions of actor training, audience education and the evolution of a new theatre form that could express the uniqueness of the Mauritian cultural experience. The results of his research were to be found in what he called his *exchange training method*. This method rests on the belief that each actor is a complete human being with his or her own set of human experiences. Theatre is created through the exchange of these sets of experiences even more so than from written plays or the mastery of vocal or physical theatrical techniques.

Labonne argued that theatre could happen anytime and anywhere, not just on a formal stage. He sought an authentic cultural experience, relevant to an audience and theatrically clear. In the group's work, psychological and physical barriers were explored. Scenography was innovative as were marketing approaches. Productions were taken to people's living rooms, to sugar factories, and performed under trees.

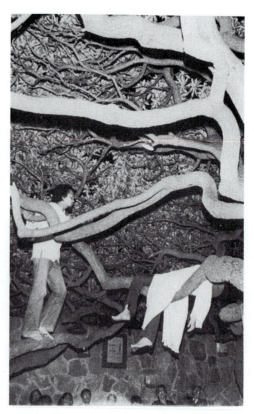

Theatre created and performed on a real tree on a beach in Mauritius.
Photo: courtesy of Theatre International.

The major theatrical performance evolving from this five-year experiment was *The Sega Story*, performed on the beach. Combining traditional and modern forms of theatrical expression, the production dealt with the notion of social and personal respectability, international recognition for the island and the question of appropriate theatrical expression for Mauritians.

Dramaturgy
Directing and Acting

There is only a handful of practising Mauritian playwrights and none who can live by their art. Probably the best known dramatist on the island is Dev Virahsawmy, an academic who writes plays in Creole. His first important play was *Li*, a play written in a Sartrean style; his most commercially successful was an adaptation into Creole of *Joseph and His Amazing Technicolour Dreamcoat*. In between these extremes, Virahsawmy, trained in linguistics, wrote a political adaptation of *Macbeth* in Creole, *Zeneral Makbet*.

Three other playwrights of note are Jean-Gérard Theodore, a poet and author of *L'Empereur des montagnes* (*Emperor of the Mountains*); Emmanuel Juste who wrote the first Mauritian television dramatic series,

Trames; and Daniel Labonne, author of the play *Sapsona* (1977). Labonne's work attempts to create a Mauritian mythology and sees the land through the eyes of dogs on the streets of Port Louis. The play was later revived and staged in Monaco in 1989.

Among those who have also written plays of note which have been staged since World War II are Malcom de Chazal, author of *Judas*; Arthur Martial, author of *Primauté* (*Primacy*); Robert Edward Hart, author of *L'Egide* (*The Shield*); Leoville L'Homme, author of *Le Dernier Tribut* (*The Last Tribute*); André Masson, author of *La Verrue* (*The Wart*); André Decotter, author of *La Terre des hommes* (*Men's Territory*); Yves Ravat, author of *L'Apôtre* (*The Apostle*); Azize Asgarally, author of *Home Again, The Hell Hot Bungalow,* and *The Chosen Ones*; and Marcel Cabon, author of *Malika et le Mendiant* (*Malika and the Beggar*).

Guy Lagesse, director of his own group in the 1970s, became known for his large-scale performances. His production of *Un homme parmi les autres* (*A Man Among Others*) was about the passion of Christ, had a cast of over 100 and was done at the Citadelle where it played to audiences of 3,000 for several weeks. The production had massive sponsorship from private business and large marketing support from the church.

Theatre for Young Audiences
Puppet and Mask Theatre

A Youth Drama Festival was begun in the 1950s to encourage the production of plays in English. Later a French section was added and in the 1990s sections for productions in the Indian and Chinese languages have been added.

The festival is open to any theatre club on the island wishing to stage a one-act play in competition. For the most part the plays are conservative in both style and content. Although it does tend to encourage the mimicking of Parisian French or Cambridge English accents, it is a good introduction to theatre for the participants. Awards are presented in each language grouping.

One of the few groups to participate regularly in both English and French is the Second

Tamil Scouts. Despite its name, the club, formed in the 1960s, was not a scout group nor was it restricted to Tamils. Through the years it has produced plays by Chekhov, Shakespeare and Labiche.

As for puppet theatre, the Marimootoo Company combines puppetry with traditional Creole-language stories for both children and adults. Storytelling is another form of popular theatrical expression pioneered by comedian Badoune Ducasse and later by Elie Topize, who later adapted his stage stories for television.

Theatre-for-Development has also utilized puppetry in its work, especially in its campaign for family planning.

Design
Theatre Space and Architecture

The Port Louis Theatre with its decorated ceiling, chandelier and proscenium stage was completed in 1822. Designed by the French architect Poujade and inaugurated by the then English Governor Robert Farquar, Port Louis Theatre is one of the oldest theatres in this part of the world. Refurbished in the 1990s thanks to a grant from the French government, the venue – which seats 400 – is generally under-utilized, at one point being rented out for weddings and prize-giving ceremonies. Even with amateur dramatic performances and occasional music concerts, the space is still used for only four months each year.

The same is true of the second largest and even more popular venue, the Plaza Theatre in the town of Rose Hill. Inaugurated in 1933 as a cinema and used as a cinema quite often through its history, the Plaza, like the Port Louis, has full-time employees including an administrator, a designer, a lighting engineer and stage managers. It was upgraded in the 1980s, has a revolving stage and seats 1,000. Many visiting companies make it a point to play at both Port Louis Theatre and at the Plaza during their stays on the island.

Other venues include Trafalgar Hall in the town of Vacoas, a venue built for social functions by the British Navy prior to independence; the Citadelle, formerly a fort overlooking the port in the capital and now an amphitheatre where productions can be seen by audiences of 3,000; the Mahatma Gandhi Institute, a cultural centre built in the 1970s with a 1,000-seat performance space and the venue where most visiting Indian companies specializing in dance and theatre play; and the French Centre Culturel Charles Baudelaire and the British Council Cultural Centre, both located in Rose Hill. Both these centres are used for small-scale productions and are managed and financed by the respective consulates. A Chinese Cultural Centre was built in the 1980s on the outskirts of Port Louis following an increase in economic ties between Mauritius and China. A number of Chinese music and dance groups have been seen there.

Serge Constantin and Gerard Barry are among the few experienced stage designers in Mauritius. Constantin trained in England and has been connected with the Plaza Theatre since 1965. Barry has been with the Port Louis Theatre since 1975.

Training

There is no formal theatre school in Mauritius. There has evolved a tradition of training workshops with leaders from India, Britain, France, the Reunion Islands, or from UNESCO. One such workshop led to the production of *Jesus Christ Superstar* with a Mauritian cast under the direction of a British expert, John Dryden.

Other significant workshops include one by the New Delhi director Mohan Maharishi in the 1970s which introduced quality Hindi theatre to Mauritius; an African Symposium Workshop in 1989 which looked at training methods across Africa and in other parts of the world; and continuing courses by Henri Favori, playwright and director, who runs a number of independent training workshops in Port Louis subsidized by the municipality.

Criticism, Scholarship and Publishing

There is a small Theatre Museum within the Plaza Theatre in Rose Hill but it includes almost exclusively material about performances at the Plaza Theatre itself. Beyond that, little is available.

To be a theatre critic in Mauritius is neither easy nor a specialty. The job is usually carried out by non-specialist journalists who talk more about spectator reactions than the work on stage. That said, Mauritian audiences can be quite difficult and vocal. One story tells of a visiting company that was mercilessly booed off the stage for having gone off-key in a particularly well-known piece of music.

Among the few knowledgeable writers on theatre has been Pierre Renaud whose theatre reviews in the 1960s and 1970s helped the island through a period of major cultural change. He was one of the island's few theatre critics who effectively engaged in a dialogue with creative artists and provided a guide for potential audiences.

Daniel Labonne

Further Reading

Decotter, A. André. *Le Plaza, un demi-siècle de vie théâtrale* [The Plaza Theatre: a half-century of theatre life]. Port Louis: Precigraph, 1983.

Gordon-Gentil, Alain. *Le Théâtre de Port Louis* [The Theatre of Port Louis]. Port Louis: Éditions Vizavi, 1994.

Morna, Colin Lowe. *Mauritius: Twenty-Five Years of Independence*. Port Louis: Institutional Investor, 1989.

MOROCCO

(Arab World volume)

MOZAMBIQUE

Located on the southeastern coast of Africa, Mozambique covers an area of approximately 785,000 square kilometres (303,100 square miles). It shares borders with South Africa and Swaziland to the south, Zimbabwe to the west, and Zambia, Malawi and Tanzania to the north. Because of the country's strategic location on the Indian Ocean, its ports have long been an important link to the sea for countries in central and southern Africa.

Arab (mainly in the north), Indian and Malay influences were already strong in Mozambique when the Portuguese explorer Vasco da Gama arrived there in 1498, the country's first contact with Europeans. By 1505 the Portuguese had established a profitable gold trade and gradually began to establish their influence further inland along the Zambezi River. From the seventeenth to the nineteenth centuries, the slave trade was the colony's primary source of income.

As part of Portugal's overseas empire, Mozambicans – in theory at least – had civil rights and job opportunities equal to the Portuguese. In fact, Mozambique was simply another African colony to them. After World War II, independence movements began all across Africa and Mozambique was no exception. By 1964, the Mozambique Liberation Front (FRELIMO) was formed, which led a guerrilla war that lasted for nearly a decade. The Portuguese government was finally overthrown in 1974 and the country became officially independent a year later with Samoira Machel, leader of FRELIMO, becoming its first president. Over the next few years most Portuguese nationals left the country. Civil war, however, continued into the 1990s, a major cause of the country's continuing economic problems. By 1989, for example, the country had amassed an external debt of US$4.7 billion.

Portuguese remains Mozambique's official language though a variety of indigenous languages are in common use. The capital and largest city is Maputo (formerly Laurenço Marques), a major port near the southern border. The second largest city is Sofala. Divided into ten provinces and a capital district, Mozambique in 1995 had a population of some 16 million people – almost all of them Bantu. More than 60 per cent of the country still followed traditional animist beliefs with the remaining 40 per cent divided between Christians and Muslims (the latter mainly in the north coastal region). The three major ethnic subgroupings include the Changana people in the south, the Senas in the central part of the country, and the Makway in the north.

Mozambique's wide variety of theatre styles – indigenous performance events and European-style spoken theatre – reflects the nation's history and cultural diversity. Traditional celebrations include song, dance, representation and pantomime.

Spoken theatre too – sometimes as a form of agitprop – can also be seen throughout the country and since the early part of the twentieth century, such theatre has been used to support the resistance to the Portuguese and to communicate messages of national cultural identity. Spoken drama eventually found its way into other events as well – religious celebrations, harvest celebrations, during prayers for rain and even during initiation rites. Within such pieces, mythological figures were often invoked to aid in the solution of various political, social and economic problems.

In the 1930s and 1940s theatre moved into urban locales where both Portuguese and well-educated Mozambicans lived. Most often such shows were sponsored by local clubs and social groups such as Associação dos Negros de Mozambique (Association of Negroes of Mozambique), Associação Africana (African Association) and the Lisbon Club. Most of the theatrical work sponsored by the first of these groups was done by NESAME, its secondary school wing under the direction of Samuel Dabula Ncumbula (1915–78). A teacher, playwright and director, his works were mostly satires about those who had become assimilated during the colonial period. His best known play in this style was *Marrumbo Freguês* (*Marrumbo Customer*) featuring the still well-known character of Mahantjase.

Other groups of note producing plays at this time were the Clube Feroviário (Railway Club), the Radio Club, and the Núcleo de Arte (Art Centre). The latter group is still in existence but now works almost exclusively in the visual arts.

By the 1960s, the two longest lived dramatic groups were Teatro dos Estudantes Universitários de Mozambique (TEUM; Mozambique University Students' Theatre) and Teatro de Amadores de Laurenço Marques (Amateur Theatre of Laurenço Marques). Both groups had a similar repertoire staging modern foreign plays by such authors as Samuel Beckett, Luis Sttau Monteiro and Branquinho da Fonseca. Clearly, Mozambican reality was not the essential reason for choosing the scripts.

Even the liberation armies had a theatre group – Grupo Cénico das Forças Populares (Popular Forces' Theatre Group) which regularly staged plays reflecting the movement's social preoccupations. The group's most active playwright was Teodato Hunguana (b. 1946).

Structure of the National Theatre Community

State subsidy for theatre is virtually unknown in Mozambique and it is equally unusual for private institutions to subsidize theatrical performances. On occasion, however, donations are received from non-governmental organizations and even from businesses interested in certain productions. Nevertheless it is rare for a production to show a profit and even rarer for performers to be able to take a real salary for their work. In this sense, then, theatre in Mozambique is almost exclusively done for the love of the art.

The only professional group is Mutumbela Gogo in Maputo, founded in 1986.

It should also be noted here that because of the high cost of importing foreign films, live theatre is unusually popular in the country and is seen not only in traditional theatre spaces but also in many under-utilized cinemas. Many companies also bring their shows to factories and schools.

Performances are generally seen only on weekends with ticket prices higher in Maputo

The 1992 Mutumbela Gogo production of *Amor, Vem*.
Photo: Georgios Theodossíadis/Zebra.

than in other cities, generally the equivalent of the price of two packets of cigarettes. Several groups usually share a theatre space during a season.

Most of the country's 150 or so groups also do some touring and the best participate in the many local theatre festivals that exist across the country.

Artistic Profile

Most productions make extensive use of song and dance, elements which clearly connect back to the audience's traditional roots. Such inclusions are important for artistic success even when dealing with adaptations of modern European authors.

In terms of theatrical dance, two forms are of particular importance: *nyau* from the province of Tete and *mapico* from the province of Cabo Delgado. In both, masks are used to satirize people and situations. Originally pure ritual, these forms are also seen today on public stages.

Other traditional theatrical forms to be seen are pantomime, storytelling and narration as well as the declamation of proverbs and poetry during festivals and traditional ceremonies. Modulation of voice is the artistic key. Usually

done for very large audiences, such performances are frequently used as vehicles for the transmission of social or political messages.

In the north, particularly on the islands of Ibo and Mozambique, the *borore* has also been part of the traditional theatrical arsenal. Essentially *borore* are songs of slander and exist in both written and oral forms. Historically these were performed at night on the doorstep of those to whom they were addressed.

Many groups outside the capital utilize local stories as a base for improvisation. Audience intervention is another feature of such performances.

More scripted literary forms – especially in the years immediately following independence – have tended to follow the principles of socialist-realism.

Companies

Amateur groups are most representative of theatre in the country and such groups can be found everywhere – secondary schools, cultural associations, churches, workers' unions, women's groups, youth organizations and community centres. There is much fluidity of personnel and vision within these groups. The oldest and strongest of these groups is Associação Cultural da Casa Velha. Performing mostly at Teatro Mapiko, the group has staged plays by many international dramatists including Eugene O'Neill (*The Emperor Jones*) and August Strindberg (*Miss Julie*). João Manuel Machado da Graça (b. 1946) has been its longtime director. Others who have staged productions with the group include the Portuguese-born Francisco Keil do Amaral (b. 1935) and Paula Ferreira (b. 1953).

The only stable professional group is Mutumbela Gogo. Begun in 1986, most of its plays have been staged by Manuela Soeiro (b. 1945) and the Swedish-born director Henning Mankell (b. 1948). Their productions have combined aspects of narration and traditional theatrical dance with elements of modern literary styles, scenography and even improvisation.

Popular with audiences, the company's repertoire under playwright Mia Couto (b. 1955) focuses on national dramatists but it has also done a number of successful collective

The 1989 Mutumbela Gogo production of *As Mãos dos Pretos* (*The Hands of the Blacks*).
Photo: Georgios Theodossíadis/Zebra.

creations. Scripts are often based on adaptations of local tales, folklore and poetry. Its productions have played at festivals in Portugal, Spain, Switzerland, France and Sweden as well as in South Africa, Tanzania and Mauritius. It works mostly at Teatro Avenida.

Another group of note in Maputo is the Companhia de Canto e Dance (The Song and Dance Company). Staging exclusively music and dance theatre, the company was founded in 1995 under the direction of David Abílio (b. 1949) who trained at the Berliner Ensemble. The group performs regularly at the Cine Teatro Africa. It has also played in South Africa and as far away as Cuba, the United States and Russia.

Dramaturgy
Directing and Acting

Moving away from the long tradition of local vaudevilles done mostly for colonial audiences, the country's most important dramatist in the post-World War II period has been Lindo Longhos (b. 1939). Focusing almost exclusively on the social and cultural reality of Mozambique, his best known play is *Os noivos ou Conferência Dramática sobre o Lobolo* (*The Engagement or Dramatic Discourse on the Purchasing of a Bride*) staged by Norberto Barroca in 1971. The play was later banned for its support of indigenous culture and the notion of Pan-Africanism. This was a fairly typical reaction during the censorship of the period. Another play of note by Lhongo was *As Trinta mulheres de Muzelene* (*The Thirty Wives of Muzelene*) which deals with traditional marriage and polygamy and the response to it by Europeans. João Fumene's *O Feitiço e a religião* (*Witchcraft and Religion*) deals with those who converted to Christianity while still holding on to traditional beliefs.

Several important national dramatists have been produced by the professional group, Mutumbela Gogo. Among them have been Mia Couto, Luis Bernardo Honwana (b. 1942), José Craveirinha (b. 1922) and Rui Nogar (1932–93).

Other dramatists of note include Afonso Ribeiro, author of the drama *Trés Setas Apontadas para o Futuro* (*Three Arrows Pointing to the Future*, 1959) and António Francisco, author of *Filhos da Noite* (*Children of the Night*).

Collective creation has been another popular form of dramaturgy since the 1960s with several groups using this production style.

The 1989 M'bêu production of *Para jovens* (*For Children*).
Photo: Georgios Theodossíadis/Zebra

Theatre for Young Audiences
Puppet and Mask Theatre

Theatre for young audiences in Mozambique is generally perceived to be theatre by young people. As such, it takes place mostly in schools and community centres. Utilizing improvisation usually around folk tales, two groups working regularly in these areas are Tejoco and M'bêu. Most shows also involve music. One popular play written especially for children is *Coisas que só acontecen na flor de lótus* (*Things That Only Happen in the Lotus Flower*) by Âlvaro Belo Marques.

Design
Theatre Space and Architecture

Much theatre in the country is performed outdoors – under a tree or even on a sports field – but there are a number of enclosed theatre buildings in large urban centres. Mostly built during the colonial period, they include cultural centres in Maputo, Sofala, Inhambane, Manica, Tete, Zambézia and Nampula.

Other major spaces in Maputo include the Teatro Avenida, Teatro Mapiko, Teatro João Vicente, Teatro Txova and Xita Duma. Many other cinemas are also used.

The only actual outdoor stage is in Maputo. It is used and operated by Casa Velha.

Designing for outdoor productions is difficult and therefore all but non-existent while designs for indoor spaces are generally put at the bottom of the theatrical list. It is rare, therefore, when one finds a production with more than a simple background.

Training
Criticism, Scholarship and Publishing

There are two national schools for the performing arts: one for music and the other for dance. Actors are expected to learn on the job, in school performances or from the occasional workshop offered by one of the local theatre groups.

A number of the country's theatre artists have studied abroad – mostly in Portugal, Sweden and France.

There are no specialized theatre libraries in Mozambique and criticism is limited to the occasional journalistic review published in a local newspaper. Most theatre history – as well as most performance skills – are therefore passed on orally. Various useful documents exist in the Historical Archives of Mozambique in the city of Maputo.

João Manuel Machado da Graça, João Manja,
Manuela Soeiro
Translated by Maria-Clara Versiani Galery

Further Reading

Ferreira, M. *Literaturas Africanas de expressão Portuguesa* [African literature in Portuguese]. Lisbon, 1977.

Fresu, Anna, and Mendes de Oliveira. 'Reflexão sobre teatro popular: origins do teatro em Mozambique e sua evolucão' [Reflections on popular theatre: the theatre in Mozambique from its origins to its evolutionary phase]. *Tempo* (7 October 1979): 55–7.

Gorodnov, Andrej. 'Mozambik – novaja žizn tradicii' [Mozambique – new life to the tradition]. *Teatr* 46, no. 9 (September 1983): 139–44.

Hamilton, R.G. *Literatura Africa, literature Necessária* [African literature, necessary literature]. 2 vols. Lisbon, 1981, 1984.

'Les Littératures africaines de langue portugaise' [African literature in Portuguese]. *Actes du Colloque International*, 28–30 November and 1 December 1984. Paris, 1985.

Mankell, Henning. 'Om att arbeta med teater i Mocambique' [On working with theatre in Mozambique]. *Entre* 16, no. 3 (1989): 10–29.

Salutin, Rick. 'Theatre, Language and Song in Mozambique'. *This Magazine* 13, no. 1 (1979): 26–30.

Vaz, Carlos. *Para um Conhecimento do Teatro Africano* [An introduction to African theatre]. Lisbon: Ulmeiro, 1978. 204 pp.

NAMIBIA

Lying on the southwest coast of Africa, Namibia, independent since 1990, has long evoked images of dry rivers and perennial drought. With a population of some 1.5 million (1992 estimate) in an area of 824,300 square kilometres (318,300 square miles), the country is overpopulated given its available groundwater resources. Divided geographically into three parallel strips – the Namib coastal desert, a central farmland belt and a semi-desert, the Kalahari – the country is filled with wild game, and the Etosha National Park is a sought-after tourist attraction.

Namibia's twelve ethnic groups are symbolized in the sunbeams of its national flag. These ethnic groups are Ovambo (50 per cent), white (German, Afrikaans and British), Nama, Damara, Herero, Kavango, Baster, Himba, Tswana, Khoikhoi, San and Khoisan. Half the population lives in the rural north some 700 kilometres from the capital of Windhoek (population 160,000).

Since 1990, English, though spoken as mother tongue by only a minority, has been the official language as well as the medium of instruction. At independence, some 60 per cent of the indigenous population was illiterate. With an economy made up predominantly of mining, fishing and tourism, the country relies heavily on South African imports. As in other parts of Africa, nineteenth-century trading and missionary work in the country culminated in colonial annexation. In 1878 the British government annexed the only deep-water port, Walvis Bay. In 1884 Germany declared the remainder of the territory a protectorate. German rule saw the familiar colonial scenario of land dispossession. The Nama, led by Hendrik Witbooi (his image is featured on the Namibian dollar notes) rose in rebellion as did the Herero. In the war of 1904–7, the German army reduced the Herero from some 90,000 to 16,000. Survivors fled through the desert, thousands dying of starvation.

During World War I, South Africa conquered German South West Africa and in 1919 Germany pronounced sovereignty in the Treaty of Versailles; in 1920 South West Africa was mandated by the League of Nations to be administered by South Africa until the indigenous population was ready for independence. In 1945 the South African government attempted to incorporate the frontier territory as a fifth province, increasingly applying its apartheid policies, while the indigenous population lobbied at the United Nations for independence. The South West African National Union (SWANU) and the South West African People's Organization (SWAPO) became the focus of the liberation struggle.

In the early 1960s, SWAPO, recognized and supported as the official liberation movement in exile, engaged in a bitter border war against South Africa. This battle was fought mainly in the north and in Angola. In 1989, SWAPO won a United Nations supervised election and established a government. The country became formally independent a year later.

Given this political and social history along with the scattered populations and a nomadic desert culture, it is no surprise that the development of an indigenous-style theatre was late in coming. Indeed, the historical constraints of various autocratic administrations worked almost directly against such ventures. Until the 1980s, therefore, Namibian theatre was mostly an imported commodity, which omitted the local people from the picture. Nevertheless, there was in the land an indigenous culture, manifested in a broad spectrum of collective expression – dance, song, sketches, storytelling and festivals.

In the 1960s and 1970s, with minor exceptions, Namibia seemed mostly a frontier society. As such, theatre activity in a European sense came from other places, usually South African and German productions done for audiences drawn from the white sector of the population. Even for this a population which itself was enacting the frontier myth, theatregoing was never a priority, though state funding kept ticket prices for such touring shows quite low.

Since the 1980s, a slow recognition of traditional performance has been seen – mostly centred on occasions such as weddings or initiation ceremonies and during which dramatic sketches were presented. In urban areas, these events even provided a sporadic underground commentary on those in power.

It was back in 1947, to coincide with a visit of the South African Prime Minister, that a South West African branch of the South African Arts Association was founded to provide, according to historian Olga Levinson, a 'unique opportunity for the three language groups of the white population to unite in a shared cultural interest'. Various South African administrators of the territory were honorary patrons. Membership in the Arts Association was nominally open to all races. Later, under the white administration, a South West African

Performing Arts Council was formed, largely as an extension of the apartheid regime's cultural agenda.

The Windhoek State Theatre, built in 1960 by the Arts Association, was upgraded and reopened in 1973. Despite a protest by the Arts Association, the theatre implemented a whites-only policy. In 1989, its name was changed to the National Theatre of Namibia, becoming a private company with a board of directors in a bid to retain control of cultural affairs through an arranged system of board rotations and approved membership. Since independence, the National Theatre has worked at reshaping its image and to honour its mission: to finance, utilize, present and promote the indigenous performing arts as much as possible.

Namibian-centred theatre – that is, work dealing with national issues – originated in the establishment of the Windhoek-based community organization, Bricks (founded in 1984), a non-professional group. Since 1986, the Drama Department of the University of Namibia has also produced a number of student workshop productions which tour to the outlying centres. The plays of both groups deal with Namibian historical themes from a contemporary political perspective.

Since independence there has been an attempt to merge the National Theatre with those more nationally focused official alternative streams. But in the mid-1990s, there remained a real gap between official and grassroots initiatives.

Structure of the National Theatre Community

After independence, a national effort was set in motion to encourage national cultural endeavours by all sectors of the population. Promoted by the Ministry of Education and Culture through the hiring of regional cultural officers and the organization of cultural workshops and seminars, efforts were made to organize cultural groups on both local and regional levels. Most such troupes have contact with the National Theatre of Namibia.

The National itself is contracted to and directly subsidized by the government to finance, utilize, present and promote indigenous culture as much as possible. Housed in the state-owned Windhoek Theatre – a 472-seat, well-equipped proscenium arch theatre – the National regularly produces its own productions

and hosts many international exchange programmes (ranging from Chinese acrobats, to Indian *kathak* dancers to the Red Army Choir). The Windhoek Theatre is also made available to local producers at subsidized rates.

For local productions, rehearsal periods range between six and eight weeks with a typical company drawn from amateur ranks in all categories – actors, directors and playwrights. Work continues to develop popular support for theatre but most people still tend to regard the National Theatre and theatregoing generally as something elitist and irrelevant.

When they occur, national tours are generally commissioned by non-governmental organizations for specific educational purposes such as AIDS awareness or literacy. A less formal venue, the Warehouse, in the capital, now offers playwrights and troupes low-cost production facilities.

Ticket prices range from about five Namibian dollars to about thirty – twice to twelve times the cost of a loaf of bread.

There are no Namibian theatre unions or national theatre awards.

Artistic Profile

As communities gain more confidence in articulating repressed cultural expression, the Namibian theatre has witnessed a steady shift away from predominantly western imports (mostly from its occupying neighbour, South Africa). Drama and dance groups tend to be informal associations of interested parties, gathering for specific productions occasioned by funding from foreign nongovernmental organizations or the National Theatre, or for some educational, socio-economic or political reason. These performances often centre on the atrocities of the apartheid regime and the popular resistance to it. More recently, dance-dramas have explored local legends and the lives of Namibian artists. These dramas take place all over the country, often at cultural festivals.

Rehearsals and play producing have also undergone a shift in approach away from European methodologies. Namibian theatre work is generally done through collective techniques – consensus and workshopping – so that productions generally reflect the input of participants on all levels. The 1991 production of Olga Levinson's *Forcible Love*, based on the life of the Namibian artist John Muafangejo, is an example of this approach at its best.

Increasingly, the Namibian Broadcasting Corporation (NBC) is also developing scripts and drama programmes for television and radio.

A typical season in Windhoek would include performances by the National Theatre or plays by local writers who gathered amateur actors into a temporary ensemble.

Companies

The National is Namibia's major professional troupe, and the company produces regular seasons of mostly international plays.

The Ministry of Education and Culture also employs a group of ten young musician-actors (known as Nanacut – National Namibian Cultural Troupe), whose function is to assist cultural groups in areas of indigenous cultural revival. Still in its initial phases of development in the mid-1990s, Nanacut works out of Windhoek. Afkawandahe is a group of committed amateur dancers and actors who explore the dynamics of adapting mainly indigenous dance forms from the north of the country for use in proscenium arch or thrust settings. The troupe has successfully restaged ritual circle pieces for wider audiences.

The northeastern Caprivi Cultural Troupe actively explores Caprivian culture and has built its own arts complex in Katimo Mulilo. Geographically at the crossroads between Angola, Zambia and Botswana, the troupe draws on many forms, including fire dances, mask rituals and indigenous dances.

Dramaturgy
Directing and Acting

Illiteracy and a strong oral tradition have not encouraged the emergence of written scripts. Rather, play production has largely involved collective creations. Nevertheless, a growing number of younger playwrights has begun to appear, almost all from the capital. Some have come from the University of Namibia, which has produced a new Namibian work annually. Others working with community groups have also contributed a number of scripts. Among those are the agitprop-kitchen sink plays of Frederick Philander (b. 1949): *The Beauty Contest*, *Papland* and the *King of the Dump*, which won a gold medal at the New York International Radio Competition in 1996; Dorian Haarhoff's (b. 1944) contemporary arrangements of Greek works (*Orange, Skeleton* and *Guerilla Goatherd*); the historical plays of Lazarus Jacobs (b. 1970) (*I've Been To the Mountain Top*, *Toivo*); the mime improvisations of the Bricks company (*Platforms 2000*, *Tables*) and the various attempts

Norman Job and Daphne de Klerk in Terence Zeeman's 1990 production of Brecht's *The Caucasian Chalk Circle* at the National Theatre.
Photo: Joe Roth.

at musical theatre: Haarhoff's *Alice In Welwitchialand* (1984); Bananna Shekupe's (b. 1959) *Circle Around the Moon*; and social commentary by Laurinda Olivier Sampson (b. 1955) (*A Woman's Dream*). Often, groups will simply perform a series of improvised scenes based on a loosely scripted plot and dialogue structure. Directing in such situations would involve facilitating rather than imposing and such a person would emerge as coordinator, organizer and energy giver more than they would as an interpreter.

Theatre for Young Audiences

In traditional settled communities such as the Ovambo, sketches and storytelling exist to entertain and teach children their culture. Western education has tended to disrupt such integrated approaches, replacing them with school concerts, Christmas pageants and children's ballet (mainly enactments of European texts). Until recently there has been little serious attention to drama as a form vital to the lives of children and their mode of expression.

Children's drama has recently been linked to environmental education. In 1992, the National Theatre revived *Alice In Welwitchialand* (the welwitchia is an ancient desert plant), originally produced by the Playmakers' Group in 1984. Haarhoff's *The Garbage Monster*, dealing with Namibia's fragile economy, was produced by the National in 1996.

Rural youth groups have continued to express drama mainly through dance forms. For example, Khoisan children have enacted ostrich dances at cultural festivals in the capital and in regional festivals.

In 1992, the Namibian government produced *A Commitment To Our Children* in response to the United Nations Convention on the Rights of the Child. Various articles of the convention referred to a child's right to education and cultural expression. This signifies a new departure from the traditional Namibian approach to children.

Puppet and Mask Theatre

Puppet theatre has not yet claimed a place in the dramatic canon but does exist in combination with other cultural forms. Puppetry, for example, is taught as part of Theatre-in-Education courses at the University of Namibia and in teacher training programmes. Shadow theatre has recently been introduced to Namibia.

In the capital and at rural centres, organizations such as the Namibian Children's Book Forum, founded in 1987, assisted by the National, have instituted book festivals which have incorporated puppetry. Puppet shows have also featured adaptations of traditional folk tales involving animals, humans and superhuman trickster figures. As with other forms of Namibian theatre, productions are usually on an *ad-hoc* basis with a temporary ensemble of amateurs gathered for the occasion.

Design

Productions at the National Theatre, the University of Namibia's Centre for Visual and Performing Arts and other venues vary considerably in their use of design. While no professional designers work full-time in the country, design elements range from constructivist cubes to expressionism to fully realistic sets built for thrust or proscenium productions.

Generally community theatres rely only on props and costume pieces to indicate situation and circumstances and neither the stage floor nor the cyclorama are treated as integrated design components. For most community theatre events, lighting entails a simple stage wash with occasional follow-spot accentuation. Sound design tends to be basic editing of found sound sources rather than production-specific composition.

Theatre Space and Architecture

The Windhoek Theatre is a proscenium arch space and is used by most groups. Other theatres exist in community halls across the country. Productions at the Windhoek Theatre have access to international standard lighting, sound equipment and workshop facilities. The octagonal Space Theatre at the University of Namibia is used for mainstream as well as more experimental work.

In rural areas, theatrical performances are adaptable and take place virtually anywhere – under trees, in the open, against the sides of trucks, on raised platforms in sports fields, in church halls, parking lots and in classrooms. Most outdoor performances choose a loose thrust or in-the-round orientation with a standing audience.

Training

Theatre arts and crafts training is offered as a major in a Bachelor's degree curriculum by the University of Namibia's Centre for Visual and Performing Arts. The department of drama offers modules in acting, directing, playwriting, crafts, history and criticism. The centre further offers a Theatre-in-Education diploma.

The Windhoek College for Education offers drama as a major in their teaching diploma and the College for the Arts (also in Windhoek) offers drama exposure to the licentiate level.

Tuition fees are subsidized by the state, although there are no theatre-specific scholarships available.

Drama graduates find work in television and radio, at the National Theatre, as teachers in schools across the country, in politics and in community theatre projects. Training and apprenticeships also occur regularly as on-the-job training and through regional workshops.

Criticism, Scholarship and Publishing

A number of journals and publications have encouraged theatre commentary. These include the University of Namibia's publication *Logos* and the Ministry of Education and Culture's *Kalabash*. Newspapers occasionally review theatre events. The National Archives (housed in Windhoek) are a valuable resource. *Ad-hoc* publications also appear from time to time. A large number of scholars are now undertaking continuing research in areas of indigenous Namibian culture.

Terence Zeeman, Dorian Haarhoff

Further Reading

Levinson, Olga. *Our First Thirty Years: The History of the South African Arts Association.* Windhoek, 1977.

O'Callaghan, Marion. *Namibia: The Effects of Apartheid on Culture and Education.* Paris: UNESCO, 1977. 169 pp.

NIGER

Situated between Black Africa and Arab-Berber Africa, Niger is a landlocked country of just over 8.6 million people. Bordering Bénin and Nigeria to the south, Algeria and Libya to the north, Burkina Faso and Mali to the west, and Chad to the east, Niger has an area of 1.19 million square kilometres (459,100 square miles), over twice the size of France.

For centuries a crossroads for black and white populations as well as for Muslims, Christians and animists, the land is primarily populated by Hausa, Djarma, Zarma-Songhai, Fulani (Peul), Tuareg and Kanuri people. Urbanization in Niger is minimal with over 90 per cent of the population living in rural areas. Even the present capital of Niamey was only a small village as late as 1901. Formerly a part of French West Africa, Niger became an independent nation in 1960.

The Niger River, from which the country takes its name, flows through the southwestern corner of the country and is not navigable above Niamey. Parts of the present republic are connected historically to several of West Africa's great empires. Among these were the Songhai (which flourished in the sixteenth century), and the Kingdom of Sokoto (founded early in the nineteenth century).

The first European to explore the area was a Scotsman, Mungo Park, in the late eighteenth century. Later came the Germans, most notably Heinrich Barth and his expeditions from 1851 to 1855. In 1890, France was given rights to the territory but the French occupation, which included massacres of segments of the local population, met considerable resistance. Among the Niger leaders remembered for their part in the resistance are Kaocen,

Tagama, Firhoun, Queen Sarraounia and Amadou Dan Bassa.

The French Colony of Niger was formally established in 1922 and following this military conquest, France put into place its own administrative and educational systems and made French the colony's official language. France continued to rule Niger until 1958 when, in a referendum, the colony voted for self-government. Full independence came on 3 August 1960 with Diori Hamani (1916–89) becoming its first president.

In 1974, a military *coup d'état*, led by Seyni Kountché, installed a dictatorship which continued until 1987 when Ali Seybou took over the leadership and inaugurated a period that he termed a period of *décrispation* (literally 'relief from tension') under the *Mouvement National pour la Société de Développement* (National Movement for Social Development), the country's only official political party at the time.

After a speech in La Cité de la Baule by French President François Mitterand in 1990, three students from the University of Niamey were killed during a demonstration. It was from this incident that a new, multi-party government was created and a national conference was called in 1991. A transitional government took over until new presidential elections could be held. In 1993 Mahamane Ousmane was elected the country's new president but in 1996 army colonel Ibrahim Mainassara Bare put the military in control once more.

Niger's political and social realities have allowed it a strong traditional continuity and a relative absence of European traditions. Its community life and the many exchanges between its diverse peoples have left the country with a rich artistic and cultural heritage.

Among the many traditional theatrical forms in Niger, the following are particularly noted: *gambara*, consisting of a musical debate between two actor-singers (usually *griots*, the traditional community praise singers); *dan kama*, where a solo performer addresses an audience, usually in a market, playing a range of character types including, for example, the fool or the glutton; *dabo*, a marionette theatre found in the regions of Maradi and Zinder, with wooden puppets used in sketches on such subjects as marriage and daily life; *tobey-tobey*, theatre for young people performed during the Muslim fasting period of *Ramadan*; and *wasan kara*, an event in the traditional harvest celebration, which in its modern form has been used to parody political leaders and colonial officials. Generally performed outdoors after some official function in the town, *wasan kara* is a re-creation of the event to which comic insights are added. In many instances, the people being satirized are also in attendance. Each of these forms of traditional theatre still exist especially in and around rural villages on market days.

The history of western-style theatre in Niger goes back to the 1930s when the country was officially part of what was called French West Africa. The male children of leading Niger families were chosen to attend the top teacher-training school in the region, the William Ponty Normal School in Dakar (now the capital of Sénégal). It was here that classical French plays were first encountered, especially the comedies of Molière. On returning home for holidays, students were encouraged to find themes for other plays that they could write and to perform the plays that they had seen at Ponty.

In 1940, a western-style community theatre was formed by students, *Amicale de Niamey* (Friends of Niamey), as was a similar group in Zinder. Though neither of these groups survived very long, they were the nucleus for ongoing western-style theatre during the period.

In the late 1950s and early 1960s, following the French model, a number of cultural centres were built in the major cities: Niamey, Zinder, Filingué, Tillabéri, Dosso and Tahoua. Though there was regular activity, the generally *ad-hoc* groups that performed in these spaces could not muster very large audiences mostly because the plays were in French (a language spoken by only a slender segment of the population and in a locally unknown style).

With independence, the state essentially took over control of culture and a number of significant events occurred. In 1964, an Artists' Week was held in Niamey and the following year a Youth Week was launched which was an annual event until 1973. During this event, virtually every performing group made its way to the capital. Pedagogical and ideological work was strongly encouraged.

But, the fact that most of the groups were performing in French (twenty-two out of twenty-seven plays were done in French between 1965 and 1973) meant that audiences still remained small and often attended out of simple curiosity. The situation was somewhat improved by the introduction of radio plays in the Hausa and Zarma languages in 1964 when ORTN (Office de Radiodiffusion et Télévision du Niger) the national radio and television corporation was founded.

With the dissolution of the First Republic, a new cultural policy was introduced. During this regime, village youth groups were organized as a support structure for cultural innovation and development. The annual Youth Week was replaced in 1976 by a National Youth Festival. Held first in Zinder, the festival moved to a different *département* each year. In 1984, the festival became biannual though its official function remained the same: to support national unity and to protect national cultural heritage by bringing together young people at cultural, artistic and sporting events.

Through the 1980s, the use of national languages increased at these events as well as on radio and television through a weekly two-hour 'popular' Sunday theatre. Seen widely, it made national stars of actors such as Yazi Dogo (b. 1943), Hima Adamou (b. 1936) and Oumarou Neino (b. 1945).

A National Sovereignty Conference in 1991 was the departure point for a new era of freedom and democracy and this led to an outburst of new theatrical activities. Among the groups that sprung up were Troupe Mourna at the University of Niamey (noted for its political satire) and Les Jeunes tréteaux du Niger (Strolling Players of Niger, formerly known as the Niger Youth Theatre), founded under the auspices of the Centre culturel franco-nigérien (Franco-Nigerian Cultural Centre). The company has toured regularly since 1993.

A number of private initiatives have also been seen during the 1990s, the best known being the Messagers du Sahel (Sahel Messengers). All of this activity speaks clearly to the growing vitality of theatrical art in Niger in the 1990s.

A production at the National Festival for Youth, Arts and Culture.

Structure of the National Theatre Community

Traditional theatre receives no particular government subsidies in Niger nor, as a rule, do other theatre performances. This has been so since the colonial period when spoken theatre was limited to school and academic circles. However, since 1960, the government has tried in various ways to support and promote educational and artistic development through a Ministry of Youth and Cultural Affairs.

Among the first manifestations of this support was the construction of a series of cultural centres as well as state-supported personnel to run them. In 1963, these centres were transformed into Youth and Culture Centres and in 1976 the Ministry of Youth reorganized itself to include a special department for Youth and Culture. Since 1976, all thirty-two townships (*arrondissements*) in the country and each of Niger's eight county seats (*départements*) have been equipped with infrastructures and personnel for programmes in theatre, education, cultural exchange and promulgation.

Each of the Youth and Culture Centres has its own open-air theatre which is used extensively during national holiday periods. The director of each centre acts not only as manager but also as artistic and stage director, creating informal groups for particular productions. Both men and women participate in the activities which attract people from a wide cross-section of the community including government workers and farmers.

Most of these informal companies are comprised of eight to twenty non-professional actors. In addition to their own productions, most of the established groups – Troupe de Yazi Dogo, Troupe de l'ORTN, Messagers du Sahel – create commissioned shows for national television, specific events and non-governmental organizations. In such instances, the groups receive a fixed price for the work plus a percentage of the box-office receipts. The latter are always modest since ticket prices must be kept low to attract audiences (rarely more than five French francs).

An annual Festival of Arts and Culture is the principal occasion for groups from across the country to meet but it is not the only one. For many years, Troupe de Yazi Dogo has hosted a Comedy Theatre Week (usually in February) at

The Centre Culturel Oumarou Ganda in Niamey.

the Centre Culturel Oumarou Ganda in Niamey. The benches at this open-air theatre are almost always filled.

Of the various troupes, Les Jeunes tréteaux du Niger is the most consistent in touring, taking their performances to over 50 different locations each year.

Messagers du Sahel has performed plays from its mainly French-language repertoire at Pan-African festivals such as one held in Burkina Faso during the Theatre Workshop for Development in 1992.

Artistic Profile

Companies
Dramaturgy
Directing and Acting

The most interesting and authentic of the traditional theatre forms – *gambara, dan kama, tobey-tobey* and *wasan kara* – were described in the opening, historical section. Elements of all of these can be seen in the western-style plays and dances that have emerged in Niger throughout the twentieth century.

During the colonial period, the new forms tended to be done almost exclusively in French and took their generally comic inspiration from the foibles and problems of daily life. The plays were about urbanization and rural exodus, the new elite, alcoholism, and the influence of foreign lifestyles.

Later, dramatists such as Boubou Hama (1906–82), André Salifou (b. 1942) and Joseph Keita (b. 1947) added depth and an historical perspective to social satire. This tradition was developed further in the work of Chaïbou Dan-Inna (b. 1952), author of *Une vie de cent carats* (*A Hundred Carat Life*), and Mahamane Coulibaly (b. 1962), author of *Le Devoir* (*Duty*). Dan-Inna's play is written in verse and was inspired by the traditional dramatic art of the

A production at the National Festival for Youth, Arts and Culture.

gambara as well as by Niger proverbs. Using Bertolt Brecht's alienation techniques, the play traces the life of the political leader Thomas Sankara, the head of state of neighbouring Burkina Faso who was assassinated in 1987. In *Le Devoir*, the dramatist focuses on the problems of taxation, questioning the morality of a state pillaged by corrupt politicians and dishonest businesspeople.

For the most part, however, plays in the national languages are created collectively and their structure tends to be similar to folk tales. Many depict public figures whose extreme actions lead them into danger while others contrast extremely good behaviour with extremely negative behaviour. Evil is always punished in an appropriate fashion in these plays.

The entertainment value of most productions lies in the audience's appreciation of verbal virtuosity together with the absurdity of the drama's situations.

There are five regularly producing troupes in the country. Messagers du Sahel generally works through collective creation and perform in French. Among its most successful productions have been *Rève déçu (Disappointed Dream)* and *Le Génie de Kamalo (The Spirit of Kamalo)*. Its productions tend to be realistic in style.

Les Jeune tréteaux du Niger has had success with adaptations of Molière plays such as *Georges Dandin* and *Le Médecin volant*. The group frequently collaborates with both African and French directors under the auspices of the Centre Culturel Franco-nigérien. The company uses more stage effects and lighting in its shows than do the other groups. An active touring group, Les Jeune tréteaux is run by Achirou Wagé Moussa, a director keenly interested in the physical – mime, gesture, even colour – more than in words.

Troupe de Yazi Dogo is one of the most popular groups in the country and the largest. Composed of more than thirty actors, many of them teachers, its collective creations are first improvised by the actors and later adapted into a text by the comic star Yazi Dogo. Another company that tours regularly, it tends to play at major Culture Centre venues. Because the actors work in the Hausa language, they have also found audiences in Nigeria.

Two other troupes of note are the ORTN troupe, which is connected to the national radio and television network, and Troupe Mourna (Joy), composed mostly of students from the University of Niamey; this troupe specializes in political satire.

A production at the National Festival for Youth, Arts and Culture.

Theatre for Young Audiences
Puppet and Mask Theatre

Children are included as part of the audience for most traditional performances, thus it is unusual when special shows are organized for them. However, many children are given opportunities to perform as part of shows done in the school curriculum.

As for puppets, the *dabo* tradition in the Zinder region utilizes wooden puppets to depict scenes from married life. Unfortunately, the tradition has virtually disappeared and can only rarely be found. Puppets in the European sense have been seen in Niger only on rare occasion, usually when a European company passes through Niamey.

Design
Theatre Space and Architecture

Performances, in traditional theatre in Niger, take place in the open air. Venues include markets and public squares and can be watched by anyone passing. Spoken theatre is available only to those who can pay an admission charge. This is usually not very high but it is not free as is traditional theatre.

Theatrical performances generally take place in Youth and Culture Centres, generally in an open-air theatre. In some centres, a

217

proscenium-style stage has been included. Two of the major open-air theatres in the country are the Centre Culturel Franco-nigérien and the Complexe culturel Oumarou Ganda, both situated in Niamey. These are not only used only for theatrical performances but are also available for conferences, political meetings and film showings.

Training
Criticism, Scholarship and Publishing

Certain aspects of theatre are studied at the National Institute of Youth and Sports in Niamey by those interested in becoming cultural animators and working with young people in the various Youth and Culture Centres across the country. There is, however, no specific school of dramatic arts, and usually actors and directors learn on the job.

Plays are rarely published. Nevertheless, the Imprimerie Nationale du Niger (National Press of Niger, now called the New Press of Niger) along with the Imprimerie de Issa Beri (Issa Beri Press) between them have published plays by André Salifou, Joseph Keita, Chaibou Dan-Inna and Harouna Mahamane Coulibaly. All were done in very limited editions.

The département de lettres modernes at the University of Niamey has regularly published papers on aspects of modern literature, including the occasional piece on theatre. Two magazines that present new points of view on literature and the arts are *Encres* and *Le Fleuve*.

Reports on new plays are found on radio and television as well as in the local newspapers *Le Sahel*, *Le Sahel-Dimanche* and *Le Démocrate*.

Chaibou Dan-Inna and Ousmane Tandina
Translated by Helen Heubi

Further Reading

Abdoulaye, Mamadou. 'Le Théâtre au Niger' [Theatre in Niger]. MA thesis, University of Abidjan, 1981.

Beik, Janet. *Hausa Theatre in Niger: A Contemporary Oral Art*. New York: Garland, 1987. 327 pp.

———. 'National Development as Theme in Current Hausa Drama in Niger'. *Research in African Literature* 15, no. 1 (spring 1984): 1–24.

Bovin, Mette. 'Ethnic Performances in Rural Niger: An Aspect of Ethnic Boundary Maintenance'. *Folk* 16–17 (1974–5): 459–4.

Dan-Inna, Chaibou. 'La Théâtralité en pays hausa' [Theatricality in Hausa country]. MA thesis, University of Abidjan, 1979.

Galadima, Dodo Idi. 'Le Théâtre moderne nigérien: naissance et évolution' [Modern theatre in Niger: birth and evolution]. Thesis; University of Niamey, 1987.

Harding, Frances. 'Continuity and Creativity in Tiv Theatre'. PhD dissertation, University of Exeter, 1988.

Illo, Bija. 'La Critique sociale dans l'oeuvre dramatique de Djibo Mayaki' [Social criticism in the dramatic works of Djibo Mayaki]. MA thesis, University of Niamey, 1994.

NIGERIA

The most populous country in Africa, the Federal Republic of Nigeria shares borders with Cameroon to the east, Bénin to the west, and Burkina Faso, Chad and Niger to the north. To the south is the Gulf of Guinea. Nigeria attained independence from Britain in 1960 and in 1994 had a population of some 100 million spread across the land's 923,800 square kilometres (356,700 square miles).

The history of Nigeria has been an oral one for thousands of years with tales passed down from generation to generation through legends, songs, myths and ethnic poems. The earliest known group in the region was the Nok, who lived in central Nigeria from about 700 to 200 BC.

One of West Africa's most powerful empires was the Yoruba state of Oyo, which ruled much of the land by the eighteenth century. With its religious and cultural centre in Ife, the Oyo Empire began to weaken by the nineteenth century because of the slave trade and fighting among Yoruba chiefs.

Bénin, in south-central Nigeria, was, like Ife, known for its visual art, especially its bronze figures. At one time it ruled the city of Lagos but by the eighteenth century its power was eroding. A Fulani-Hausa empire in northern Nigeria was founded in the early nineteenth century and its capital was Sokoto but by the end of the century it too had broken up into smaller states.

In Nigeria in the 1990s, the Hausa, Fulani (Peul), Yoruba and Ibo compose about 65 per cent of the national population.

The earliest recorded Europeans to reach the area were Portuguese explorers in 1472, who spoke of the wealth that they had seen in Bénin. In 1553, the British arrived and over the next decades several European nations vied for control of the slave trade that had developed. Gradually, the British gained control of the region and in 1861 they created the colony of Lagos, and in 1885 the Oil Rivers Protectorate. Bénin was conquered in 1897.

In 1914 the different parts of the region were brought together as the Colony and Protectorate of Nigeria. Ruled to a very great extent through local chiefs, the colony consisted of a large Muslim population in the north and an almost equally large Christian population in the south. Across the country, a British-style educational system was introduced.

After World War II, Nigerians took on more and more of a role in local government and by 1960 it became an independent federation and in 1963, a republic with the Ibo Nnamdi Azikiwe (1904–96) as president. With some 250 different ethnic groups in the country, however, numerous rivalries broke out, with hostility between the Hausa of the north and the Ibo of the east being particularly strong.

In 1966, a coup against the civilian government put a new military regime in power led by Johnson Aguiyi-Ironsi, an Ibo. A second coup, led by northern officers, overthrew Aguiyi-Ironsi and established a new military regime under Yakubu Gowon. A year later, Nigeria was divided into twelve states, three in the former Eastern Region.

In opposition to this new structure, the Eastern Region seceded from the federation and declared itself the Independent Republic of Biafra. For the next thirty months a civil war was fought which finally led to the return of Biafra to the federation. Elections were held in 1979 and the nation returned to civilian rule; a military government returned to power in 1983, a government which was still in power in 1996.

In 1995, the execution of Ogoni playwright and environmentalist Ken Saro-Wiwa (b. 1941) and eight other Ogoni human rights activists sparked international anger against General Sani Abacha's military regime. Saro-Wiwa had protested against the environmental devastation in Ogoniland caused by Nigerian and international oil companies. Oil accounts for 95 per cent of Nigeria's export earnings and 80 per cent of its public revenues.

Lagos, with a population of nearly 2 million, is Nigeria's largest city and the country's chief port. Ibadan is Nigeria's second largest city and parts of it have stayed as they were when founded by the Yoruba in the late eighteenth century. The most important city in northern Nigeria is Kano, a walled city whose market has been famous for five centuries. Sokoto is a Muslim religious centre in the north while Bénin and Port Harcourt are both located in southern Nigeria.

Nigeria's official language is now English, though other languages are widely spoken including Hausa (20.9 per cent), Yoruba (20.3 per cent), Ibo (16.6 per cent) and Fulani (8.6 per cent). In 1991 the capital was transferred from Lagos to Abuja.

With each ethnic group possessing a unique theatrical tradition, performative activities in Nigeria before 1945 were generally ritualistic in nature and associated with seasonal festivals. These included masked dances (some with short enactments), extended evenings of mainly dance, and dramatizations of historical stories.

The Yoruba theatre *alarinjo*, for example, evolved from and developed alongside the original Egungun masquerade from 1700. Much has been written of Ibo performative events – celebrative festivals that were both presentational and stylized in form. Functioning as a communion between the living and the dead, these festivals were intended to present models of ethical life. Much is also known of the Odo, Omabe, Mbom Ama and Ekpe festivals through the works of Ibo scholars.

Theatre among the Hausa has been traced to the sixteenth century when, as a result of military struggles and the establishment of an emirate system, there developed court theatres which included singers, drummers and actors. Apart from these, other theatrical groups organized themselves in guild systems. There are many theatre groups in Hausaland which still reflect these earlier traditions including Yan Gambara, Yan Kaura, Yan Ma'abba, Yan Zari, Yan Tauri, Yan Hoto and Yan Gardawa.

Among the minority ethnic groups are celebrative theatrical traditions that still serve as popular entertainment. Their requirements are simply an open space, time, and an audience. Of these groups, the Ibibio drama is the most sophisticated and developed, especially so since it is essentially a non-literate society. J.C. Messenger's studies indicate that the Ibibio Ekong drama was meticulously prepared with up to six years of daily rehearsal.

The Tiv people developed their own elaborate dance theatre as both historical documentation and dramatic enactment. These forms later developed into the *kwagh-hir* tradition, which uses puppets of varying sizes and descriptions as well as dance, music, masquerades and human actors. The Kanuri peoples also developed a puppet entertainment, *dabo dabo*.

Among the Idoma people, one of the performative forms is *ocha*, storytelling, for both community entertainment and education. Both adults and young people form the audience and also perform, the older people more than the young. *Ocha* is usually a night-time theatrical event, being a way of relaxing after a day spent on the farm.

Traditional theatre activities have received great support from arts councils, the mass media, theatre artists and scholars. As a result, such activities are becoming increasingly secular, more popular and certainly much better known, both nationally and internationally.

Nigeria's modern theatre tradition is largely a blending of such indigenous forms with western theatre traditions brought to the country by colonists, by foreign-educated Nigerians and by freed American slaves who had started to return to Nigeria in 1839.

During the last half of the nineteenth century and the first half of the twentieth, many small community theatre groups emerged playing to enthusiastic audiences mostly composed of the elite of Lagos society. Among the most popular of these were the Philharmonic Society, Rising Entertainment Society, Orplican Club, Lagos Glee Singers, Brazilian Dramatic Company and United Native Progressive Society.

It should be noted here that the content and format of most such performances were based on English music halls of the period, making no effort to integrate traditional performance modes. Rather, in imitation of English music halls, they concentrated on solos, duets, love songs, recitations, comic sketches and comic songs.

By 1945, the Church Missionary Society splintered into fourteen autonomous, separate national churches. Each reworked traditional Nigerian music and blended it into the worship services. Ultimately, developed into an autonomous form, these evangelical pieces included satires, musical dialogues and hymn tunes. Dramatizations were usually of biblical themes using traditional music and were utilized for the opening and closing sections.

It was in such a theatrical milieu that Hubert Ogunde (1916–90) found himself in the 1940s. Hired as organist and composer for the Aladura Church at Ebute Metta, Ogunde's African Music Research Party format emerged by 1946. Growing from this was the first modern professional theatre in Nigeria. A Yoruba, Ogunde influenced innumerable other artists, many of whom would also start their own groups – Kola Ogunmola (1925–73), Duro Ladipo (1931–78) and Moses Olaiya (b. 1946) among them. In total, these artists founded over a hundred of what became known as Travelling Yoruba Opera troupes.

Ogunde saw his work as essentially consciousness-raising. He attempted to use the new form to expose the ills of the British colonial administration. His more formal dramatic works – *Strike and Hunger* (1945), *The Tiger's Empire* (1946) and *Bread and Butter* (1950) – were all serious attacks on colonial government. In reaction, Ogunde's plays were banned in many parts of the federation, and Ogunde himself was imprisoned.

Following Ogunde was James Ene Henshaw (b. 1924) who also fought for the development of a truly African theatre. His best known plays include *A Man of Character* (1956), *This Is Our Chance* (1956), *Children of the Goddess* (1964), *The Jewels of the Shrine* (1965), *Medicine for Love* (1965) and *Dinner for Promotion* (1965), all written in English.

Also influential was the development of the populist Onitsha market plays in the 1940s, short, issue-oriented pieces of a generally didactic nature. The most prominent of the Onitsha playwrights were Ogali Agu Ogali (b. 1935) and Orlando Iguh (b. 1937).

Theatrical activities began to be centred at the University of Ibadan following its establishment in 1948. Two student dramatic societies – the University College Dramatic Society and the Arts Theatre Group – made extensive use of the University College Arts Theatre, staging a number of western plays including the Greeks, Shakespeare, Molière, and Bertolt Brecht.

Nigeria's more literary drama movement was born in 1960 in Ibadan. Its architects were members of the Mbari Club, a group which systematically gathered together the best local talents to forge a nationalist culture using theatre and other arts. It was from this movement that many of the country's leading writers and academics emerged: Wole Soyinka (b. 1934), John Pepper Clark (b. 1935), Segun Olusola (b. 1936), Dapo Adelugba (b. 1940), Kola Ogunmola and Joel Adedeji among others. Along with Gerald Moore, Ralph Opara, Geoffrey Axworthy, Martin Banham, Frank Speed and Peggy Harper, they infused a new spirit into the nationalist movement.

Other groups emerged in Ibadan as well. Especially important were the Players at Dawn and the 1960 Masks of Wole Soyinka, both English-language companies. The 1960 Masks' first production was Soyinka's own *A Dance of the Forests*. With this play, Nigerian theatre clearly had begun to use indigenous experiences – in this case Yoruba experiences – to comment on political developments and the future of the nation. Similar developments were taking place in the eastern part of the country at Enuga where John Ekwere transformed the Ogui Players into the Eastern Nigeria Theatre Group in 1961.

Outside of Ibadan, and particularly in towns like Lagos, Jos, Enugu and Kaduna, other amateur dramatic societies developed. But it was the experiments at Ibadan which contributed most significantly to giving the emergent Nigerian theatre a goal and respectability not only among its practitioners but also among audiences.

Viewing theatre as a medium for education, the University of Ibadan also initiated its populist Theatre on Wheels in 1961. The group took plays into student halls and beyond, adapting Molière's *Les Fourberies de Scapin* into *That Scoundrel Suberu* (translated into English by Yetunde Esan and Dapo Adelugba). Intended to bring theatre to the whole country, the group showed others what they could do with limited facilities.

By 1962, the department of music of the University of Nigeria at Nsukka was able to produce its own version of the immensely popular South African musical, *King Kong*.

The civil war of 1967–70 saw the breakup of this movement as both playwrights and critics became immersed in the conflict and ethnic rivalries sharpened. The euphoria of independence gave way to a new reality. Instead of a colonial oppressor, Nigeria saw one indigenous government after another essentially mismanaging the affairs of the nation.

In the 1970s a new genre of theatre known as Popular Theatre/People's Theatre emerged and began to be practised. The Popular Theatre practice in Nigeria derived inspiration from the radical pedagogies of scholars like Paulo Freire and Franz Fanon, and the socially committed theatre practices of Bertolt Brecht and Augusto Boal. This genre of theatre first began to be practised in Ahmadu Bello University, Zaria, in 1975. The beginning of this practice in Nigeria coincided with a period of radical/Marxist pedagogy which was interrogating the country's socio-political process. The practice, which has now been rechristened Theatre-for-Development, is a theatre of social and political commitment making use of indigenous performative forms in addition to western dialogue drama giving rise to a hybrid theatre created and performed communally.

While Ahmadu Bello University, Zaria, remains the earliest home and centre of this practice, it has spread to all Nigerian universities to become an integral part of theatre studies. It has also spread and gained respectability outside academia with the emergence of the Nigerian Popular Theatre Alliance (NPTA) since 1989. NPTA is a national non-governmental organization headquartered in Zaria. Its activities are coordinated by Oga Abah (b. 1953) who has also been one of the key persons in giving shape and direction to Theatre-for-Development as an academic practice.

Activists now seek to use drama for social change, a movement which has continued into the 1990s side by side with the creation of many new plays by a later generation of literary dramatists such as Ola Rotimi (b. 1938), Femi Osofisan (b. 1946), Bode Sowande (b. 1951) and Kole Omotoso (b. 1943).

The overall growth of theatre in Nigeria was given particular impetus by FESTAC '77, the World Festival of Black and African Arts and Culture hosted by Nigeria in 1977. After this festival, structures for the growth of theatre were actively promoted. A National Cultural Policy was eventually drafted, which recommended the establishment of Arts Councils at federal and state levels as well as committees of the arts at local government and district levels.

Structure of the National Theatre Community

There are three types of theatre to be seen in Nigeria in the 1990s – community-based traditional theatre, institutionally supported companies staging both modern and traditional performances, and private companies.

Of the institutional companies, the National Troupe, founded by Hubert Ogunde in 1986, was begun when the federal government asked Ogunde to assemble a company of talented artists from various State Arts Council groups with the view to establishing a national company. The Troupe began at the Iganmu Theatre in Lagos. Ogunde opened with a dance drama appropriately entitled *Destiny*. The success of this first *ad-hoc* 'national theatre' production led to the formal birth of the National Troupe in 1989 with Ogunde as its first artistic director. After his death in 1990, he was succeeded by Bayo Oduneye. Established to promote the various traditions of Nigerian performing arts, the National Troupe concentrated on producing Nigerian dances and plays, often taking them to international festivals in different parts of the world.

Apart from the National Troupe, each of the states of the federation has its own troupe under the auspices of its Arts Council. Arts Council troupes are mainly concerned with the preservation of traditional performing modes through research and presentation. The state troupes tend to be funded directly by the state Ministries of Information and Culture. They usually do not have specific budgets but receive grants for performances, running expenses and salaries. The troupes usually comprise twenty to fifty people, including performers, musicians, directors and administrative staff.

Six universities in the country also support their own theatre companies. These are Obafemi Awolowo University's Ife Performing Company, University of Ibadan's Performing Company, University of Lagos Centre for Cultural Studies, Ahmadu Bello University Centre for Nigerian Cultural Studies, University of Calabar Theatre Company and Cross-River State University Theatre Company. Most of these companies have resident playwrights, directors, designers and choreographers and many new works are conceived at these theatres.

A scene from the National Troupe's production of Ahmed Yenma's *The Silent Gods*.

Among the private companies of note are the Kakaun Sela, Orisun Theatre, Odu Themes, Parable Repertory Group from Zaria, Oyin Adejobi Theatre, Alawada Theatre Company, Ojo Ladipo Theatre, Jagua Theatre, Jimoh Aliu Theatre, Olofin Theatre, Lere Paimo Theatre, Funmilayo Ranko Theatre, Kola Ogunmola Theatre, Charles Sanyaolu Theatre, Star Sudan Repertory Company, Kuriya Mata Sabo of Kano, Maitama Sule Group of Kano, Karkuzu Company Jos, Dan Wanzam of Kano and Yantai of Kaduna.

Among the national theatre support organizations of note are the International Theatre Institute and the Society of Nigerian Theatre Artists. Both sponsor workshops, conferences and publish information.

Others include the National Association of Nigerian Theatre Arts Practitioners (NANTAP) which tries to protect the welfare of artists. However, this organization is restricted to trained performers or practitioners with university or some form of formal education. There is a parallel organization for performers or practitioners without formal education called the Association of Nigerian Theatre Arts Practitioners. Students of theatre and performing arts have a body called the National Universities Theatre Arts Students Association. Its activities are restricted to the universities. They hold an annual festival, the National Universities Theatre Arts Festival.

For now, the only performing arts award is given by the Society of Nigerian Theatre Artists. However, several performers have received individual honours for their performances.

Artistic Profile

Studies on the *alarinjo* theatre by Joel Adedeji, the *kwagh-hir* by Iyorwuese Hagher and the Hausa theatre by Ezekiel Kofoworola have shown that in the past, traditional artists (storytellers, dancers and oral poets among others) travelled from village to village performing their

John Pepper Clark, Soyinka's contemporary, is also a playwright, poet and director. Clark resigned his university chair to found a professional theatre group, the PEC Repertory Theatre in Lagos. In the early 1960s, Clark made his mark as both director and playwright with *Song of a Goat* (1964), *The Masquerade* (1964), *The Raft* (1964) and *Ozidi* (1966), all written in English.

Clark has also created literary drama out of traditional performance modes. *Ozidi* is probably his most successful play in this direction. Derived from a traditional Ijaw epic that is still told and enacted, the traditional story takes seven nights from beginning to end. Clark's ability to condense such vast material has earned him recognition as one of Africa's most Aristotelian dramatists.

Ola Rotimi's rise to fame came after the civil war and the collapse of the nationalist movement in drama that was pioneered by the Mbari Club. Rotimi established himself as a playwright and director during his sojourn at Obafemi Awolowo University (Ile-Ife) where he was the director of the Ori-Olokun Theatre. His major plays include *The Gods Are Not to Blame* (1968), *Kurunmi* (1971), *Ovonramwen*

Nogbasi (1974), *Our Husband Has Gone Mad Again* (1977), *To Stir the God of Iron* (1981), *If* (1983) and *Hopes of the Living Dead* (1988).

The Gods Are Not to Blame is based on Sophocles' *Oedipus Rex*. It shows Rotimi's ability to transpose legend into a rural Yoruba setting. His historical plays – *Kurunmi*, *Ovonramwen* and *The Gods Are Not to Blame* – have led him to be accused of falsifying history and of holding negative views and perceptions and even the paranoia of the post-colonial, indigenous ruling class.

As if to deny these allegations, Rotimi's later plays, such as *If* and *Hopes of the Living Dead*, were in the forefront of the 1980s radical theatre movement in Nigeria. Turning from Aristotle to Marxism, these two plays concern themselves with the plight of the common people who have become the protagonists of the later plays. Compared to Soyinka, Rotimi is obviously more accessible to Nigerian theatre audiences. His ability to find words, phrases and images that run close to the vernacular makes plays such as *If* and *Hopes of the Living Dead* clear demonstrations of class contradictions within the country. Preoccupied

Odukwe Sackeyfio's 1980 production of John Pepper Clark's *Ozidi* at Jos University.
Photo: Justice Onah.

with the need to raise the consciousness of ordinary people through collective action, he is unsurpassed in the country as a theatre director. He is particularly strong at staging plays with large casts and is noted for the rigour and thoroughness in his work with actors as well as for his attention to dramatic detail.

The leaders of the 1970s radical theatre movement were Femi Osofisan and Bode Sowande. Paradoxically, both were obviously influenced by Soyinka. As if to repudiate this fact, Osofisan often tried to stress his separation from Soyinka through the popular media. He sees himself as a much more revolutionary writer, even though his critics claim that his revolutionary zeal is elitist and seems to have adherents only in the academic world. His plays are in great demand among students as are Bode Sowande's *The Night Before* and *Farewell to Babylon*, both written in 1979.

Like many writers, Osofisan embraces a revolutionary zeal that calls for a social revolution in the political realm. His earlier plays, *Oduduwa Don't Go*, *Restless Run of Locusts*, *You Have Lost Your Fine Face* and *Behind the Ballot Box*, all from 1975, were not designed to sharpen social awareness or evoke change. By contrast, *The Chattering and the Song* (1976), *Once Upon Four Robbers* (1980), *No*

More the Wasted Breed* (1982) and *Morounto-dun* (1982) are unmistakably designed to evoke change in contrast to the tragic fatalism found in his earlier plays.

At the University of Ilorin, Zulu Sofola (1935–95), Nigeria's most popular female playwright, established her reputation with an adaptation of *Romeo and Juliet* called *Wedlock of the Gods* (1972). Using an Ibo traditional setting, the play remains very popular in schools as does her play *Wizard of Law* (1972).

Akanji Nasiru (b. 1946) is another product of Ibadan. His work was introduced by Michael Etherton, a British lecturer at Ahmadu Bello University in the late 1970s. In the 1980s, Nasiru was producing and writing plays at the University of Ilorin.

Ahmadu Bello University has produced two other playwrights of note: Segun Oyekunle, whose play *Katakata for Sufferhead* (1983) won many awards; and Iyorwuese Hagher whose plays include the much-produced *Anti-people* (1987), *Aishatu* (1987), *Swem Karagbe* (1987) and *Mulkin-Mata* (1991). At the University of Calabar, Chris Nwamuo (b. 1948) has charted a course for Theatre-in-Education in the country.

At the University of Jos, Sonny Oti (b. 1940), a musician, playwright and director,

Samson Amali's 1979 production of his drama *Orugbo Mloko* in Otukpo.

has written and directed many plays for the stage and television. One of Nigeria's finest actors as well, his most popular play is *Evangelist Jeremiah* (1983), a play obviously inspired by Soyinka's *Jero* plays. Oti also pioneered the use of recorded drama on tape, a form of popular theatre now popularized by the Masquerades of Owerri.

At the same university is Samson O.O. Amali (b. 1945), a playwright, poet and director whose plays have been published in bilingual editions, Idoma and English. Derived from the oral traditions of the Idoma people, among the ethnic minorities in the country, Amali's most popular play, *Orugbo Mloko* (1972), is derived from an ancient Idoma text. His other plays include *Ohe – The Witch* (1982), *Adela* (1983), *De Intafew* (1984) and *Nigerian Dreams and Realities* (1986).

Many theatre groups now perform in the pidgin language for urban workers, unemployed people and the rural populace. This fact has begun to influence Nigerian dramatists who are beginning to devise a pidgin orthography for their plays. These playwrights argue that since those who hear and speak pidgin are in greater number than those that hear and speak English, the language of Nigerian dramaturgy should be pidgin.

No overview of playwriting in Nigeria can be complete without some recognition of television drama which until the 1980s was flooded with foreign programming. By 1990, however, the Nigerian Television Authority had achieved over 80 per cent domestic programming. The first indigenous drama on television was Soyinka's play *My Father's Burden* (1961), a play which incisively criticized the Nigerian bourgeoisie.

Theatre for Young Audiences

Theatre for young audiences has existed in the traditional societies since ancient times. In the Bénin Kingdom period, for example, parents and other members of the extended family would gather the children together for an *ibota* session in the *ikun* – a dug-out space open to the sky. *Ibota* is essentially a storytelling performance meant mainly for children or young audiences. The storyteller could be the mother, father, grandfather, grandmother, uncle, or an aunt.

The stories could be told for simple entertainment or they could have a didactic function. The narrator would drive home the lesson dramatically, sometimes calling on one of the children to re-enact a portion. Like all theatrical forms in Africa, storytelling would be a mixture of various art forms including drama, narrative, poetry, mime, music and dance. Sometimes the narrator would use costumes and props to add colour to the performance. *Ibota*, in this sense, would be an effective and subtle instrument of education and socializing for the child.

Okpobhie, another storytelling form, is more complex than *ibota*. Done mostly for adults because of the time of staging – from about 10 p.m. till dawn – children usually are brought in for what are called the 'moonlight' plays (traditional theatrical games) before going to bed. This is not to say that some of the older ones do not remain for as long as the

performances last. They do and are usually kept awake by the musical accompaniment.

In *okpobhie*, audiences are also part of the performance, exchanging dialogue, gestures and facial and body expressions, a vital part of the whole. Interesting as this theatre is, tales of the past no longer seem adequate to satisfy recreational needs. As a result, many of the tales are being modernized.

Still another traditional theatre for young audiences is the *kwagh-hir* found in Gboko, Katsina Ala and Makurdi. This puppet theatre also originated in ancient storytelling. It re-emerged in the 1960s as a challenge to the oppression of the then Northern People's Congress, a political party which tried to reimpose a form of feudal government. The *kwagh-hir* stories of that time warned people against the government and suggested appropriate steps to take in overcoming oppression. This theatre effectively combines the educational function of storytelling performance with such changing socio-political circumstances.

Kwagh-hir is introduced by a narrator and ultimately also combines music, dance, song, dialogue and poetry. The narrator's many interpolated jokes and artistic versatility add to the overall festive mood. Audiences assist the musicians and act as a chorus for dances, mimes and interludes. Although the *kwagh-hir* was originally created for adults, children are always included as part of the audience.

Kwagh-hir puppets vary in size and style. Some are rod-puppets and string-puppets while others are closer to the mask tradition. The mask-puppets are mounted on top of large box-like structures. The puppet manipulators sit inside the *daghera* box and manipulate them from below. *Kwagh-hir* plays are episodic and a performance may last for five minutes or for a whole night. The best known plays are *Anum ior* (*Firing Squad*) featuring the execution of an armed robber; *Ortwer* (*Medical Doctor*) depicting the delivery of a baby through a Caesarean operation; and *Chankula*, an acrobatic show with drummers and dancers.

Masked figures for children also tend to have a didactic function. The *gaya nyum* (hippopotamus), for example, is meant to scare children into believing that they could be swallowed if they do not work hard. *Anyamagurugu*, another mask, is used to evoke fear in crying children to keep them silent.

As for western-style theatre for children, it has not gained much prominence in Nigeria despite occasional individual efforts, mostly by university institutions or private theatre companies. The National Council for Arts and Culture has a section for children though it does very little. What modest activity there is has come from the University of Ibadan, University of Jos, University of Calabar and Ahmadu Bello University. Most active are Ibadan, Jos and Ahmadu Bello Universities, which operate Theatre-in-Education, Drama-in-Education and education courses.

At Ibadan, the programme was started in 1963 when theatre historian Joel Adedeji began to do research in this field. The group that emerged was called the Saturday Theatre For Young People and it was run by a West Indian couple, Dexter Lyndersay and his wife. The theatre was later run by Nwafor Ejelima.

Until 1982, the group was a laboratory meant to serve the needs of undergraduate students at Ibadan. By 1982, graduate students studying theatre or those with a particular interest in theatre for young people were included in the group that assisted the directors.

Although the Saturday Theatre For Young People started in 1963, it did not make the desired impact, partly due to the fact that most of the plays done were foreign. From 1973, there was a re-orientation and an expansion of its scope with the result that more emphasis was placed on the needs of the Nigerian child.

Among the group's productions are many rooted in storytelling including *The Tortoise and the Lizard*, *The Quarrel Between the Barber and the Vulture*, *How Lizard Became a Red-Cap Chief*, *Why Cock Crows Before Dawn*, *Why the Tiger Has Spotted Skin* and *How Cat and Rat Became Enemies*. In 1978, the group became part of the Children's International Summer Village movement.

The University of Jos company – the Theatre Project for Young People – is an educational theatre group under the department of theatre arts. By combining original theatre productions, improvisation, playmaking, mime, dance and drama, the group motivates young audiences to examine pertinent social issues. Starting in 1979, fairytales were adapted: *Cinderella* as *Bemborella*, *Snow White* as *Ebony White*. The group also does regular tours to schools.

The Ahmadu Bello University Children's Theatre programme runs production workshops with primary and post-primary institutions around Zaria. In addition, dramatized indigenous folk tales with contents changed to reflect contemporary reality are toured round the local schools every year.

The aims of the group are to help children develop the ability to use words effectively and creatively in ordinary conversation, simultaneously allowing them to express and affirm perceptions of reality and the world around them; to help children have control over intellectual and linguistic powers; and to establish a workshop for undergraduate students offering courses in children's theatre, Drama-in-Education, Theatre-in-Education and theatre for young audiences.

Another touring group is the Educational Theatre run by Gure Emoisiri. A small company, it covers the country twice each year. The performances are mainly modernized folk tales in which children are participants. Funded privately, the group operates on box-office proceeds and the occasional corporate gift.

Writing for children has become a specialized occupation which few address themselves to, particularly writers of adult plays. Notable among those who do work in this area is Irene Salami who has written about twenty plays for children. Salami writes as a 'former child' and her plays reveal a sense of universal mystery. In the early 1990s, nine of her plays were approved for the Junior Secondary School Certificate Examination and several have been anthologized for junior secondary schools in the country.

Other children's volumes include *Let's Play Together* by Boniface Nzeako and Tess

Onwueme (the latter a successful adult playwright) and *Udoo's Journey* by Tar Ahura.

Televised children's programming has also helped promote children's theatre. Mostly modelled on the US programme *Sesame Street*, its emphasis is nevertheless on local cultural content and educating the Nigerian child. The television station in Jos is leading in this work.

Puppet and Mask Theatre

In almost all Nigerian communities, there exists not a puppet theatre in the western sense but rather a masked theatre which has not detached itself from the moorings of ritual. There are as well some distinct puppetry traditions whose primary aims are entertainment and education. The mask tradition is considered as a most serious form, one which inhabits the thin line dividing the living world and the supernatural one.

In Yoruba tradition, masked performance can be seen in both *egungun* and in *gelede* dancers. A more elaborate, secular development of this tradition is seen in the *alarinjo* theatre, which evolved from and developed alongside *egungun* performers. Like the Tiv *kwagh-hir* puppets discussed earlier, the Yoruba used masked puppets in the *Alarinjo* tradition to criticize antisocial behaviour. More significantly, they have also used it for social cohesion by presenting other ethnic groups in a derisive and satiric way.

The Tapa and Idahomi masks recall the Nupe and Dahomeyan ethnic groups that border Yoruba areas. Several other smaller figures, especially those of totemic significance such as birds, snakes, lizards and other animals, are sometimes mounted on top of other masks or simply attached to performing platforms held on the heads of manipulators.

Like the *kwagh-hir*, the Kalabari *ikaki*, and the *Ekong* masks of the Annang Ibibio are also well rehearsed and performances are elaborate affairs. The *ekong* theatre, like the *kwagh-hir*, reflects contemporary realities. The rehearsals for *ekong* plays go on for several days. Performances are staged as collaborative efforts of many artists – carvers, stage designers, musicians and singers.

The plays of the *ekong* satirically exploit family, social and political conflicts and attack people within the society whose behaviour is considered contrary to the general well-being.

In the state of Borno there exists another puppet form called *dogo dogo*. A remnant of a more broadly based puppetry tradition called *dabo dabo* in Hausa, the *dogo dogo* seems to have gone completely underground as a result of suppression by Muslims who were averse to making images and especially images that moved. The *dogo dogo* puppets are rag dolls manipulated with hands and fingers. A performance involves manipulation through a slit made in the neck of a flowing gown under which the manipulator crouches. Musicians play drums between scenes and the puppeteers modify their voices by half-swallowing two pieces of ostrich eggshell bound together with thread.

Design
Theatre Space and Architecture

Traditional performative events in Africa are meant to be viewed by a general public in an open space where spectators can observe and, as is sometimes required, participate. This venue is normally the village or town 'square', where people gather around the performers, most often in a circle. From this tradition, it could be expected that the most appropriate, and therefore prevalent, architectural form in Nigerian theatre would be the arena stage or theatre-in-the-round. This is not so, however. A very powerful non-African influence was first introduced by the so-called 'Sierra Leonean emigrants' – mainly liberated slaves, or their descendants, primarily Yoruba, between about 1839 and 1866. When their first 'public concert' was offered in Lagos, the newly acquired European (especially English and Portuguese) cultural set-up of these emigrants clearly clashed with the traditional open space in many ways.

Architecturally, this resulted in the predominance of the face-to-face configuration of performers and audiences to be found in European-style proscenium theatres. The country's first modern stages therefore were wooden platforms in churches, easily dismantled so the rooms could be restored. For lighting, candles, kerosene, gas and palm oil were used. Public halls were soon demanded in response to objections to the use of churches for such secular entertainment.

Renovations of an old customs warehouse in Lagos began in 1887 but this first public hall, eventually called Glover Memorial Hall, after John Hawley Glover, a popular colonial governor, took twelve years to complete and was not officially opened until 1899.

A new Glover Hall was built after the first had burned down in 1919. It is still used but mostly as a cinema and is not an effective theatre space. Other halls, such as Ilupesi Hall and Tom Jones Hall, appeared later in Lagos.

Lagos now boasts several theatres of different styles, the most prominent being the National Arts Theatre, a cultural complex of Bulgarian design. In addition, there is J.K. Randle Hall, a small European-style theatre of about 200 seats; three theatres at the University of Lagos; and some spaces identified and enhanced by a team led by theatre technologist Sunbo Marinho as performance venues specifically for FESTAC in 1977. These include Tafawa Balewa Square, a vast tiered structure, and the National Stadium Sports Hall.

One of the National Theatre's two 500-seat cinemas is also in almost constant use as a theatre. The National Theatre's Main Hall can seat some 6,000 in one of its configurations. This can be changed in eighteen minutes by rotating the stage on the vertical plane to reveal a wide bank of tiered seats that emerge from under the stage to join several balcony seats at the back of the stage in facing the other seats in the hall. Some of the seats are tiered from the floor to just under the balcony rail and these can also be rolled into a recess under the balcony. An alternative configuration, though primarily provided for sports, has been praised by a prominent Nigerian theatre academic as flexible enough to accommodate more traditional performer–spectator relationships or even modern experiments based on the traditional forms. Film projection equipment and a screen, as well as an impressive sound system and controls, complete the Main Hall's facilities.

On the National Museum grounds at Onikan, Lagos Island, is the Museum Kitchen, which is a theatre-restaurant combination. Dining patrons are seated in a circle around the performers.

A range of flexible theatre architecture can be found on the various university campuses. The University of Ibadan's Arts Theatre is an

The National Theatre in Lagos, Nigeria.

———. 'Form and Function of Satire in Yoruba drama'. *Odu* 4, no. 1 (July 1967): 61–72.

———. 'The Nigerian Theatre in English and its Audience'. In *Das Theater und sein Publikum.* [The theatre and its audience], 238–57. Vienna: Österreichische Akademie der Wissenschaften, 1977.

———. 'The Place of Drama in Yoruba Religious Observances'. *Odu* 3, no. 1 (July 1966): 88–94.

———. 'Theatre Forms: The Nigerian Dilemma'. *Nigeria Magazine* 128–9 (1979).

Agu, Ogonna. 'Dance Theatre, Ritual and the Ibo Drama'. *Nigeria Magazine* 55, no. 2 (1987): 78–84.

Ahura, Tar. 'Popular Theatre and Social Education in Benue State of Nigeria'. *Nigeria Magazine* 53, no. 2 (April–June 1985): 57–65.

Alagoa, E.J. 'Delta Masquerades'. *Nigeria Magazine* 93 (1967): 145–55.

Alston, Johnny Baxter. *Yoruba Drama in English: Clarification for Productions.* Iowa City: University of Iowa, 1985. 226 pp.

———. *Yoruba Drama in English: Interpretation and Production.* Lewiston, NY: Edwin Mellen, 1989. 192 pp.

Amankulor, James Ndukaku. 'The Concept and Practice of the Traditional African Festival Theatre'. PhD dissertation, UCLA, 1977. 526 pp.

———. '*Odo*: The Mass Return of the Masked Dead Among the Nsukka-Ibo'. *The Drama Review* 26, no. 4 (winter 1982): 46–58.

Anpe, Thomas Uwetpak. 'An Investigation of John Pepper Clark's Drama as an Organic Interaction of Traditional African Drama with Western Theatre'. PhD dissertation, Madison: University of Wisconsin, 1985. 367 pp.

Art and Culture in Nigeria and the Diaspora. Studies in Third World Societies Series. Williamsburg, PA: William and Mary College, 1991.

Asagba, Austin. 'Roots of African Drama: Critical Approaches and Elements of Continuity'. *New Literature Review* 14 (1985): 47–57.

Asomba, Domba. 'The Role of Theatre in a Developing Society: The Nigerian Example'. *Nigeria Magazine* 54, no 3. (1986): 71–81.

Badejo, Dierdre Lorraine Gómez. 'Yoruba Theater: A Case Study in Continuity and Change'. PhD dissertation, UCLA, 1970. 218 pp.

Banham, Martin. 'The Beginnings of a Nigerian Literature in English'. *Review of English Literature* 3, no. 2 (1962): 88–99.

———. 'African Literature II: Nigerian Dramatists in English and the Traditional Nigerian Theatre'. *Journal of Commonwealth Literature* 3 (1967): 97–102.

———. 'Ola Rotimi: Humanity Is My Tribesman'. *Modern Drama* 33, no. 1 (March 1990): 67–81.

Begho, Felix O. 'The Dance in Contemporary Nigerian Theatre: A Critical Appraisal'. *Nigerian Journal of the Humanities* 2 (1978): 18–33.

Clark, Ebun. 'The Rise of Contemporary Professional Theatre in Nigeria, 1946–1972: Second Part'. *Nigeria Magazine* 115–16 (1975): 9–24.

———. *Hubert Ogunde: The Making of Nigerian Theatre.* London: Oxford University Press, 1979.

Clark, John Pepper. 'Aspects of Nigerian Drama'. *Nigeria Magazine* 89 (June 1966): 118–26.

Cole, Herbert M. and Chike C. Aniokor. *Ibo Arts: Community and Cosmos.* Los Angeles: Museum of Cultural History, 1984. 256 pp.

Corbett, Delbert Franklin. 'Theatrical Elements of Traditional Nigerian Drama'. PhD dissertation, University of Oregon, 1980. 288 pp.

Degen, John A. 'Cultural Identity and the Cross-Cultural Assimilation: The Case of Nigerian Drama in English'. *South African Theatre Journal* 1, no. 2 (1987): 52–62.

Enekwe, Osmond Onuora. 'Ibo Masks: The Oneness of Ritual and Theatre'. PhD dissertation, Columbia University, 1982. 268 pp.

Epskamp, Kees P. 'Training Popular Theatre Trainers: A Case Study of Nigeria'. *Maske und Kothurn* 29 (1983): 261–71.

Etherton, Michael. *The Development of African Drama.* New York: Hutchinson African Library, 1982.

Euba, Femi. 'Soyinka's Satiric Development and Maturity'. *Black American Literature Forum* 22, no. 3 (fall 1988): 615–28.

Ezeokoli, V.C. 'African Theatre: A Nigerian Prototype'. PhD dissertation, Yale University, 1967.

Feuser, Willfried F. 'Wole Soyinka: The Problem of Authenticity'. *Black American Literature Forum* 22, no. 3 (fall 1988): 555–75.

Folarin, Agbo. 'Modern Scenography in Western Nigeria'. *Nigeria Magazine* 53, no. 2 (April–June 1985): 14–24.

Gidley, C.G.B. 'Yankamanci: The Craft of the Hausa Comedians'. *African Language Studies* 8 (1967): 52–81.

Gotrick, Kacke. *Apidan Theatre and Modern Drama: A Study in a Traditional Yoruba Theatre and its Influence on Modern Drama by Yoruba Playwrights.* New York: Humanities Press, 1984. 271 pp.

Hagher, Iyorwuese Harry. 'The *Kwagh-hir*: An Analysis of a Contemporary Indigenous Puppet Theatre and Its Social and Cultural Significance in Tivland in the 1960s and 1970s'. PhD dissertation, Ahmadu Bello University, 1980.

Harding, F. 'Continuity and Creativity in Tiv Theatre'. PhD dissertation, Exeter University, 1988.

Harper, Peggy. 'Dance and Drama in the North'. *Nigeria Magazine* 94 (September 1967): 219–25.

Jeyifo, Abiodun. *The Yoruba Popular Travelling Theatre of Nigeria*. Lagos: Ministry of Social Development, Youth, Sports and Culture, 1984. 213 pp.

Jones, Eldred Durosimi. *The Writings of Wole Soyinka*. London: Heinemann, 1973.

Kidd, Ross. 'Popular Drama Workshops in Northern Nigeria: From Outside-In to Inside-Out'. *Theatre International* 6, no. 2 (1982): 25–44.

Kofoworola, E.O. and Yusef Lateef. 'Hausa Performing Arts and Music'. *Nigeria Magazine* (1988).

Lakoju, J.B. 'A Critical Evaluation of the Nature and Function of Theatre-in-Education in Britain and a Proposed Model for Nigeria'. PhD dissertation, University of Cardiff, 1985.

Laurence, Margaret. *Long Drums and Cannons: Nigerian Dramatists and Novelists*. New York: Frederick A. Praeger, 1969.

Lindfors, Bernth, ed. 'Interview with Eight Nigerian writers'. *Nigerian Theatre Journal* 1, no. 1 (1983).

———. 'Nigerian Drama in American Libraries'. *Afro-Asian Theatre Bulletin* 3, no. 2 (February 1968): 22–7.

———. 'A Preliminary Checklist of Nigerian Drama in English'. *Afro-Asian Theatre Bulletin* 2, no. 2 (February 1967): 16–21.

MacRow, D.W. 'Folk Opera'. *Nigeria Magazine* (1954): 329–45.

Maduakor, Obiajuru. 'Soyinka as Literary Critic'. *Research in African Literature* 17, no. 1 (spring 1986): 1–38.

Moore, Gerald. *Wole Soyinka*. London: Evans, 1971.

Nwoko, Demas. 'Search for a New African Theatre'. *Présence Africaine* 75 (1970): 49–75.

Nzewi, Meki. *The Drama Scene in Nigeria*. Enugu: Fourth Dimension, 1985. 240 pp.

Obafemi, Olu. 'Revolutionary Aesthetics in Recent Nigerian Theatre'. *African Literature Today* 12 (1982): 118–36.

Obiechina, Q. *An African Popular Theatre: A Study of Onitsa Market Pamphlets*. Cambridge: Cambridge University Press, 1973.

Obuh, Sulvanus Onwukaike Stanley. 'The Theatrical Use of Masks in Southern Ibo Areas of Nigeria'. PhD dissertation, New York University, 1984. 294 pp.

Oduneye, B. 'Theatre in Ibadan'. *Cultural Events in Africa* 21 (August 1966): 1–11.

Ogonna, Nnabuenyi. *Mmonwu: A Dramatic Tradition of the Ibo*. Lagos: Lagos University Press, 1984. 226 pp.

Ogunba, Oyin. 'Theatre in Nigeria'. *Présence Africaine* 30 (1966): 65–88.

Ogunbiyi, Yemi, ed. *Drama and Theatre in Nigeria: A Critical Sourcebook*. Lagos: Nigeria Magazine Publishing, 1981. 522 pp.

'Our Authors and Performing Artists'. *Nigeria Magazine* 88 (March 1966): 57–64 (part one); 89 (June 1966): 133–40 (part two).

Richards, Sandra L. 'Nigerian Independence Onstage: Responses from "Second Generation" playwrights'. *Theatre Journal* 39, no. 2 (May 1987): 215–27.

Riggs, Rose, and Richard Festenstein. 'Puppets in Zaria'. *Animations* 6, no. 4 (1983): 12–13.

Rotimi, Ola. 'The Drama in African Ritual Display'. *Nigeria Magazine* 99 (1968): 329–30.

Sekoni, R. 'Metaphor as a Basis of Form in Soyinka's Drama'. *Research in African Literature* 14, no. 1 (spring 1983): 45–57.

Soyinka, Wole. *Myth, Literature and the African World*. Cambridge: Cambridge University Press, 1976.

Stratton, Florence. 'Wole Soyinka: A Writer's Social Vision'. *Black American Literature Forum* 22, no. 3 (fall 1988): 531–53.

Urpokodu, Iremkokiokha Peter. *Socio-Political Theatre in Nigeria Since Independence*. San Francisco, CA: Mellen Research University Press, 1992. 300 pp.

'Wole Soyinka'. *Black Orpheus* 15 (August 1964): 46–51.

'Wole Soyinka and the Nigerian drama'. *Tri-Quarterly* 5 (spring 1966): 129–35.

Wren, Robert M. *J.P. Clark*. Boston, MA: Twayne, 1984. 181 pp.

The Tutsi *ntore* war dance.
Photo: Michel Huet.

body and gesture. A ballet troupe, its best known works include Rugamba's *La Bataille de la frontière* (*Border War*), *La Nativité* (*The Nativity*), *L'Ami véritable* (*The True Friend*), *La Passion* (*The Passion*), *Bwiza la belle* (*Bwiza the Beautiful*) and *Igitego* (*The Challenge*).

Both these dance troupes are interested in a synthesis of the traditional and modern styles of African performing arts as well as a synthesis of African and western styles.

A new generation of university-trained directors began to emerge in the 1980s. Among them were Landoald Ndasingwa, Joseph Nsengimana and Damien Rwegera. By 1985 Nsengimana and Rwegera had instituted a national theatre training programme at the National University leading to the institution of an expanded Concours National d'interprétation théâtrale (National Theatre Performance Competition) under the auspices of the Ministry of Higher Education and Scientific Research.

The Concours of 1985 included performances by thirty-five groups from across the country – eighteen in Kinyarwanda and seventeen in French. Of these, the strongest through the late 1980s and into the early 1990s were Iryamuje – Soleil du vallon (Iryamuje – Sun of the Vale) from the University campus of Ruhengeri; Cercle St Paul from the Nyaki-banda Seminary; La Troupe de l'Ecole Sociale de Rambura (Troupe of the Rambura Social School); La Troupe Rafiki from the Kigali Rafiki Club; Irebero from Kigali; and Indamutsa, a company sponsored by the Rwandan Information Office in Kigali. The occasional independent group also emerges from time to time.

The Iryamuje company is headed by Joseph Nsengimana and, appropriate to its university setting, takes as its motto 'entertainment through education'. A company committed to socio-political research through theatre, it has experimented with a range of ideas from André Antoine to Bertolt Brecht, from Jerzy Grotowski to Augusto Boal, and has also done work in Theatre-for-Development. Its major productions have included Marcel Aimé's *La Tête des autres* (*The Head of Others*), Cocteau's *Les Parents terribles* (*Terrible Parents*), Ivoirian playwright Bernard Dadié's *Mhoi-Seul* (*Me Alone*) and Joseph Nsengimana's *Sinalinze ko zica*.

The Indamutsa troupe, directed by Joséphine Mukarushema, specializes in radio drama and only occasionally works away from this field. Its repertoire is exclusively Rwandan and the company generally adapts plays which have won awards during the annual competitions.

Among the dramatists who have specialized in radio drama are Innocent Bahinyuza, François-Xavier Byuma, Mathias André Sebanani, Eliphas Abaganizi, Jean-Baptiste Nkuriyingoma and Silas Mbonimana.

The seminary-based Cercle St Paul is one of the oldest groups in the country and the first to stage western-style plays in Kinyarwanda in the 1950s. From its work came the talented playwright Emmanuel Gasana.

The Rafiki Club was a creation of the Dominican fathers and offered many cultural activities, among them theatre. Under the direction of François-Xavier Byumas who wrote many of the group's plays, the Rafiki Club focuses its work – almost exclusively Rwandan – around social issues. Its best known productions are *Mpariye abaseka* (*Too Bad for the Scoffers*) and *Ijamabo ryiza* (*The Comforting Word*). The club also publishes inexpensive editions of Rwandan plays.

Several companies of note existed in the 1970s but had stopped producing by the 1980s. Among them were Damien Rwegera's Compagnie du délire (Frenzy Group). Funded by the Franco-Rwandan Cultural Exchange Centre, the group staged two productions which remain in the national theatrical memory – Rwegera's adaptation of Jacques Roumain's novel *Gouverneurs de la Rosée* (*Masters of the Dew*) and a production of Wole Soyinka's *Dance of the Forest*.

Another company that is now gone was the Indangamuco Troupe of the Institut National Pédagogique, an institution which merged with the National University in 1981. The company's importance rests with the production of the Rwandan play *Natacye bitwaye* (*Never Mind*) by Evariste Nsabimana.

A third troupe that has now disappeared is the privately operated Landoald Ndasingwa Company, headed by Ndasingwa himself. This group's major productions include Marcel Pagnol's *Topaze* and *La Famille africaine* (*The African Family*).

Other than in Kigali, the capital, there are regular theatre activities in Butare and Gisenyi. Kigali has the country's best-equipped theatre – le Centre d'Echanges Culturels Franco-Rwandais (Franco-Rwandan Cultural Exchange Centre); Butare has the largest theatre in Rwanda, located on the campus of the university; and Gisenyi has the modern SODEVI auditorium.

The development of theatre was interrupted in 1994 by the civil war, which stopped theatre activity in the country almost entirely.

Joseph Nsengimana, Jean-Baptiste
Nkuriyingoma
Translated by Linda Toriel

Further Reading

Houdeau, Serge. *Panorama de la littérature rwandaise: bilan, bibliographie, choix de textes en français* [An overview of Rwandan literature: assessment, bibliography and selected French texts]. Butare, 1979. 209 pp.

Jadot, J.M. *Les Écrivains du Congo belge et du Ruanda-Urundi: une histoire, un bilan, des problèmes* [Writers of the Belgian Congo and Ruanda-Urundi: a history, an assessment and some issues]. Brussels: ARSC, 1959. 167 pp.

Kabasha, Théobald. 'Aspects historiques, dramaturgiques et thématiques du théâtre rwandais' [Historical, dramaturgical and thematic aspects of Rwandan theatre]. MA thesis, Université Nationale du Rwanda, Butare, 1981. 156 pp.

Munyarugerero, François-Xavier. 'La littérature rwandaise: bilan, problèmes et perspectives' [Rwandan literature: assessment, issues and perspectives]. MA thesis, Université Nationale du Rwanda, Ruhengeri, 1982. 244 pp.

Rugamba, Cyprian, Damien Rwegera and Médard Mwumvaneza. *Théâtre et enseignement* [Theatre and education]. Kigali.

SÉNÉGAL

Situated on the westernmost point of Africa, Sénégal covers an area of 197,200 square kilometres (76,100 square miles). Bounded to the north by Mauritania, to the east by Mali and to the south by Guinea and Guinea-Bissau, Sénégal surrounds the small nation of Gambia which occupies the lower valley of the Gambia River. Major ethnic groups in the country include the Wolof (36 per cent), Fulani (Peul; 19 per cent), Serer (9 per cent), Diola (9 per cent) and Toucouleur (9 per cent). French is the country's official language but most people speak Wolof. Over 90 per cent of the people are Muslim.

The Wolof, Serer and Toucouleur ethnic groups were the earliest known peoples to inhabit the region and they established flourishing kingdoms. Europeans reached Sénégal as early as the fifteenth century and by the end of the seventeenth the French had built several fortified trading posts in the area. During the Napoleonic Wars (1803–15) the British took over the settlements, which were returned to France in 1815.

In 1895, the colony of French West Africa was created, a federation of the eight French territories in the region. Saint Louis, a port city in the north of the country, was made the capital. In 1902, Dakar was named the new capital of French West Africa though Saint Louis remained the capital of Sénégal. In 1957, Dakar became the national capital. In June 1960, Sénégal and the former French Sudan (now Mali) established a federation. Called the Mali Federation, the new state was dissolved in August 1960 when profound differences could no longer be settled. Sénégal then established its total independence, with poet, philosopher and politician Léopold Sédar Senghor as its first president and he continued in the position through successive elections until his voluntary retirement in 1981.

Prior to colonial occupation, Sénégal had its own varied forms of dramatic expression and popular spectacles performed before large rural audiences. Among these were *kassak* (initiation songs), *baks* (gymnastic songs), *taasu* (praise or critical songs), and *ndeup*, a therapeutic ritual involving animal sacrifice and a musical and dance performance. More specifically, *kassak* aims to educate candidates for circumcision during the initiation period as well as to entertain the public in the case of urban forms; *baks* is a poetic entertainment done for the public at wrestling matches; *taasu* are praise songs, done primarily to entertain the public; and *ndeup* is connected to freeing the possessed from evil spirits.

Such traditional art forms combine elements of spoken theatre with spectacle and utilitarianism with entertainment almost without differentiation. Requiring a direct relationship between the oral production by the creators and the spectators who receive it, such performative events are by their very nature theatrical.

Two other modern types of theatre have emerged in the country since the colonial presence: a generally improvised theatre in the various national languages dealing with daily issues in a quite direct form of performance, and a European-style literary theatre – mostly in French – dealing with a wide range of topics from social history to contemporary issues. Works in the improvised theatre are rather like *commedia dell'arte* pieces with the actors improvising from an outline conceived by an author who is more often than not the director as well.

The more literary theatre is the direct result of colonization and especially two of its institutions: the church and the school. The earliest examples date back to the end of the nineteenth century when church-supported schools staged religious playlets in Saint Louis with their black and mixed-race students.

But it was not until the 1930s and the opening of the École normale supérieure William Ponty (William Ponty Normal School) on Gorée Island (off Dakar) that such dramatic works began to be systematically produced and that they began to move away from religious subject matter. The most prestigious and important teacher training school in all of the French West Africa colony, it became the key place to send a male child for his education and it attracted top students in many fields from throughout the region. The fact that the school, under the direction of Charles Béart, had a keen interest in the pedagogical value of theatre meant that the Ponty School – and the many Pontins who graduated from it – were destined to bring the idea of theatre to all of French-speaking Africa.

The Ponty School was at its most influential between the two world wars and it is no coincidence that spoken theatre in French emerges at this time in Sénégal, Côte d'Ivoire, French Sudan (Mali), Upper Volta (Burkina Faso), Dahomey (Bénin) and other areas of French influence.

From an aesthetic point of view, such use of the French language within this formal theatre was also the beginning of the break with indigenous Senegalese theatrical modes. First performed in the front of the Chamber of Commerce Meeting Hall in Dakar, this new European theatre attracted a curious public. Eventually settings suitable for an Italian-type stage were introduced. It also became obvious that the actors in such a theatre would need a different type of training from traditional theatrical modes, that a system of formal rehearsals would have to be introduced and that scripts reflecting Senegalese issues would have to be created. The Ponty influence continued strong until after World War II.

By 1953, French cultural policy – as carried out by Bernard Cornut-Gentil, the French High Commissioner in French West Africa – was moving toward decentralization of the arts and cultural centres were created in almost all the large cities in the territory. As well, a Concours théâtral inter-africain (Inter-African Theatrical Competition) was instituted bringing together top performances for a wide public, and a publication, Trait d'union (Hyphen) was created to stimulate the art and to publish the best of the new plays that began to emerge. The finals of the competition were held at the Palace Theatre in Dakar in 1955, 1956 and 1957.

The Palace Theatre (the restaurant in Dakar's Palace Hotel) was itself the first non-institutional European-style theatre created in Sénégal. Later transformed into a more formal theatre with funds from the French High Commissioner primarily so that French troupes on tour would have a suitable space in which to perform, it seated about 400 and had as its director a young Senegalese, Maurice Sonar Senghor (b. 1927), whom the High Commissioner had met in Paris in 1953. No regularly producing troupes were in operation at that time.

Senghor, with the assistance of French actor Roland Bertin, created a troupe at the Palace Theatre as well as a theatre school. Classes were conducted each evening from 6 to 8.30 p.m. and rehearsals began at 9 p.m. Funding came from the High Commissioner's office. A playreading committee advised on scripts for production. Composed of several members of Dakar's intellectual elite, the committee included Assane Seck (b. 1919), Amadou Makhtar Mbow (b. 1921), Lamine Diakhaté (b. 1927) and others.

The first production at the Palace was Sarzan (the Wolof pronunciation of the word sergeant) by Diakhaté, an adaptation of a folk tale by Birago Diop, which opened in April 1955. In short order, Senghor began to make plans for the company – led by Alé Samba Diouf, Bassirou Diakhaté, Oulimata Fall and Ousmane Madamel Cissé – to become a professional troupe. Another success was with Abdou Anta Kâ's (b. 1931) play La Chant de Madi (The Song of Mahdi). As well, the Palace welcomed foreign troupes both from France and from other countries. Among these was the distinguished Guinean dance troupe of Fodéba Keita.

A number of local Dakar groups performed occasionally at the Palace in the Wolof language including the Brothers of Africa troupe directed by Ahmet Ndiaye, Mansour Gueye's Rakadiou and the troupe of Emile Cissé and the Yéou Troupe, the forerunner of such contemporary troupes as Diamonoy Tey and Daaray Kocc.

Unfortunately, the next High Commissioner was less interested in theatre and the direct subsidy to the Palace Theatre was discontinued. From this situation grew L'Union des artistes et des techniciens du spectacle (Union of Artists and Technicians of the Performing Arts) in 1958. Its first president was Patrice Diouf; its second, Lamine Diakhaté.

With the creation of the Mali Federation in 1959, the Minister of National Education commissioned Maurice Sonar Senghor to organize a celebratory artistic programme. The resulting music and dance troupe was called Troupe du Mali. When the federation dissolved in 1960, the troupe's name was changed to l'Ensemble de Ballet du Sénégal (Ballet Ensemble of Sénégal). Two years later the Palace Theatre building was demolished as part of the proposed creation of a cinema and theatre complex. The project, however, was never realized.

Prior to 1960 Senegalese theatre was essentially organized, oriented and controlled by the colonial administration and this was reflected in the on-stage products. Most works were in a French style and dealt with Sénégal as a colonized country. This ideology was also evident in the published plays of the period from the early creation of the Ponty School to the end of the Palace Theatre.

One can look for proof of this in the plays of Amadou Cissé Dia (b. 1915) and Abdou Anta Kâ. Scripts such as Dia's *La Mort du Damel* (*The Death of the Damel*) and *Les Derniers Jours de Lat Dior* (*The Last Days of Lat Dior*, 1947) and Kâ's *La Fille des dieux* (*Daughter of the Gods*, 1955) lack any significant criticism of the colonial system and the perspective of their historical figures is much more passive than that of plays produced after independence.

In fact, Senegalese theatre takes on a whole new energy and point of view after independence. In the major cities, a politically committed, militant theatre was founded whose subject matter was predominantly historical. Indeed, African history as a whole was to be reinterpreted by everyone during these years.

New plays by writers such as Cheik Aliou N'dao (b. 1933), Thierno Bâ (b. 1926) and Mamadou Seyni Mbengue (b. 1925) re-created historical figures in much more aggressive ways in the plays such as N'dao's *L'Exile d'Albouri* (*The Exile of Albouri*, 1967), Bâ's *Lat Dior ou le chemin de l'honneur* (*Lat Dior or The Path of Honour*, 1971), and Mbengue's *Le Procès de Lat Dior* (*The Trial of Lat Dior*, 1971). The differences are less clear in the area of dramatic technique in these two periods.

Through the late 1960s and well into the 1980s, a number of other companies emerged, including the Daniel Sorano National Theatre with its beautiful western-style building, the only state theatre in Sénégal. Founded in 1965, the Sorano National Theatre's prestige quickly spread across the country and abroad. By 1995, it had staged more than fifty productions and had represented Sénégal and won prizes in Algiers (1969), Lagos (1977), Lyon (1979) and Carthage (1987 and 1995).

By the early 1990s, however, the Sorano Theatre's energy, like that of many of the dozens of companies that had come into existence during this period, had begun to wane. The National Theatre's budget had also been cut between the late 1970s and 1992 from 200 million African francs annually to 12 million, an extraordinary drop. As a result, the company was reduced from thirty to fifteen actors and few new faces were added.

In 1980, the National Conservatory's actor training programme was closed down; it would not reopen for six years. It was 1990, in fact, before a new class of trained actors would graduate.

In 1994, the Sorano National Theatre seemed economically marginalized and artistically in a kind of purgatory awaiting some reform that would allow the company to again improve working conditions and return to the top rank of African dramatic companies.

By 1991, the National Theatre turned to the production of popular plays in an effort to reach a wider public and generate more income at the box office. A number of comedies in Wolof were produced, the most successful being *Poot-mi*, a social commentary whose music and dance sequences underscored the satire. The show also had impressive sets, sound and lighting effects. A commercial success, *Poot-mi* was followed by a historical drama in 1992, *Nder en flamme* (*Nder in Flames*) by Alioune Badara Beye (b. 1945) staged by Seyba Lamine Traoré (b. 1949). An impressive and spectacular historical epic, the production again attracted a wide audience including a number of government leaders. This was followed by another historical drama, *La Dame de Kabrousse* (*The Lady of Kabrousse*) by Marouba Fall and directed by Abdoulaye Diop Dany (b. 1948), director of the National Drama Troupe, one of the troupes of the National Theatre. Opening in 1993, the production was, however, not the success that had been hoped. It was followed by another popular comedy in Wolof, *Khar Yalla* by Boubacar Guiro (b. 1946), an actor and production manager at the Sorano National Theatre.

In 1995, a play by the late Congolese dramatist Sony Labou Tansi, *Le Coup de vieux* (*Sudden Aging*) attracted new attention to the company. Representing Sénégal at the 1995 Carthage Theatre Festival, the Sorano production was awarded First Prize.

Structure of the National Theatre Community
Artistic Profile

Companies

During the first two decades of independence, culture was a major concern for the government and particularly for President Léopold Sédar Senghor, who supported the arts in almost every way possible. Ultimately, the government opted for the creation of a single, subsidized national theatre company with dramatic, musical and dance sections as opposed to widespread support for a range of producing companies. Hence, the Daniel Sorano National Theatre – home of Ensemble de Ballet du Sénégal, Ensemble Lyrique Traditionnel (Traditional Music Ensemble) and Troupe Nationale d'Art dramatique (National Drama Troupe) – received the bulk of state funding and, when that funding was severely reduced during the late 1980s, the companies paid a heavy price. All of these national groups have regular seasons in Dakar and often perform abroad.

The building was named in honour of Sorano, who was born in Toulouse, southwest France, in 1920 into a family of Franco-Senegalese origin. Growing up in Dakar, he later studied acting at the Conservatoire in Toulouse and become a member of the Grenier de Toulouse company. In 1952 he joined Théâtre National Populaire in Paris where he worked with Jean Vilar and Gérard Philippe until 1961. He died in 1962.

Through the 1980s and 1990s, many other small, privately supported companies were created and continued to manage a precarious existence, struggling to be self-sufficient and earning the bulk of their income at the box office. Most, however, have had short lives. Of these short-lived groups, the most artistically interesting were Tréteaux Sénégalais (created in 1969) and Nouveau Toucan (created in 1976). Among the private groups which have survived are the Jamonoy Tey and Daaray Kocc companies. Both perform in Wolof. Also popular is Les Ballets Africains, founded by Mansour Gueye.

There are a large number of semi-professional and amateur groups in existence across the country. Of note is Awa Sene Sarr's (b. 1953) Pettaaw bi troupe; Gueustou troupe of Mame Birame Diouf; Faro of Oumar N'dao (b. 1957); Zenith Art International founded by Pape Faye; Meteo Theatre of Marouba Fall; Atelier de Recherche et de Pratique Théâtrales of the Cheik Anta Diop University in Dakar, directed by Ousmane Diakhaté (b. 1949) in collaboration with actors Jacqueline (b. 1927) and Lucien (b. 1923) Lemoine.

Among groups involving young people, Cercle de la jeunesse de Louga (Louga Youth Circle) is one of the most consistently interesting and is regularly seen at the annual youth festival.

Sénégal's most prestigious national cultural award is the Grand Prix du Président de la République pour les Arts (Presidential Grand Prize for the Arts). In 1993 actor Coly Mbaye (b. 1943) of the Daniel Sorano National Theatre won the award, while in 1995 it went to the National Theatre's Jean-Pierre Leurs (b. 1941), a director.

Dramaturgy
Directing and Acting

Several of Sénégal's important modern playwrights have focused on historical themes in their works, among them Amadou Cissé Dia and Cheik Aliou N'dao. Dia is the country's first important modern playwright and his plays include *La Mort du Damel and Les Derniers Jours de Lat Dior*.

Ndao's plays – especially *L'Exil d'Albouri*, one of five to have been produced – show him a more attentive witness and partisan of the development of Africa from the colonial period to modern self-rule. He shows better control of

Coly Mbaye and Serigne Ndiaye Gonzales in the Daniel Sorano National Theatre's 1967 production of *L'Os de Mor Lam*.

his material than Dia and his writing is more confident. *L'Exil d'Albouri* was awarded first prize at the Pan-African Festival in Algiers in 1969. Among his other works of note are *La Décision* (*The Decision*, 1967), *La Case de l'homme* (*The Initiate's Hut*, 1973), and *Le Fils de l'Almamy* (Almamy's Son, 1973). N'dao writes in both French and Wolof and has regularly utilized music and dance in some of his plays.

Other writers such as Thierno Bâ and Mamadou Seyni Mbengue have also demonstrated significant skills and creativity in dealing with historical themes, both in terms of character and dramatic movement. Bâ is the author of three plays, the most important of which is *Lat Dior ou le chemin de l'honneur*. He has also been successful in integrating music and song into his historical plays (*Bilbassy*, 1980). Mbengue has written one play, *Le Procès de Lat Dior*.

Among playwrights of note writing in the 1980s and 1990s have been Abdou Anta Kâ, author of several plays including the stage adaptation of Jacques Roumain's novel, *Masters of the Dew*; Ibrahima Sall (b. 1949), author of *Le Choix de Madior* (*Madior's Choice*, 1981) and *La République* (*The Republic*, 1987); Mamadou Traoré Diop (b. 1944), author of *La Patrie ou la mort* (*The Native Land or Death*, 1986); Mbaye Gana Kébé (b. 1936), a committed poet and dramatist; Bilal Fall (b. 1943), author of *L'Intrus* (*The Intruder*); and Boubacar Boris Diop (b. 1946), whose re-creation of the massacre of Thiaroye in *Thiaroye terre rouge* (*Thiaroye Red With Blood*, 1981) is a powerful evocation of a bloody period of history.

One should mention the work of Alioune Badara Beye, author of *Nder en flamme* and *Dialawali terre de feu* (*Dialawali, Land of Fire*); and Marouba Fall, who also writes in both French and Wolof, author of *La Dame de Kabrousse* and especially *Chaka roi visionnaire* (*Chaka, Visionary King*). These two writers are among the most prolific and produced of the country's younger generation of dramatists.

In total, there are about thirty produced playwrights in Sénégal.

Two directors are noteworthy in the development of theatre in Sénégal over the modern period – Maurice Sonar Senghor and Raymond Hermantier, the latter a Frenchman who spent many years in Sénégal as Artistic Adviser to the Daniel Sorano National Theatre. Between them, they staged virtually all the productions at the National Theatre through the 1970s.

During the 1980s and into the 1990s, the most interesting directorial work has come from four talented creators – Boubacar Guiro, Abdoulaye Diop Dany, Mamadou Seyba Traoré and Jean-Pierre Leurs. Their names have been connected with the most important productions since the late 1970s.

The best known Senegalese actor has been without doubt Douta Seck (1919–93), creator of the title role in Aimé Césaire's *La Tragédie du Roi Christophe* and of the role of Bienaimé in Abdou Anta Kâ's play, *Général Manuel Hô*. After leaving Sénégal for a successful career in Paris where he was a long-time member of Jean-Marie Serreau's Toucan company, Seck returned to Sénégal in 1973 as a member of the Daniel Sorano National Theatre. After his death, the National Conservatory of Dramatic Arts, Dance and Music became the Douta Seck National Conservatory of Dramatic Arts, Dance and Music.

Seck's equivalent among actresses is Jacqueline Lemoine, who began acting in her native Haïti before joining Serreau's company in Paris. She joined the National Theatre in Dakar in 1966 and later became a Senegalese citizen. She continued to act well into her 70s.

Another actor of particular note is Doura Mané (1939–76) who was part of the Sorano National Theatre from 1965 to 1972. Born in Guinea, he played the title role in a 1968 Africanized production of *Macbeth* and Albouri in *L'Exile d'Albouri*. One must also mention here the career contributions of such other stars as Awa Sène, Farba Seck, Omar Seck, Assi Dieng Bâ, Joséphine Zambo, Isseu Niang and Fatim Diagne.

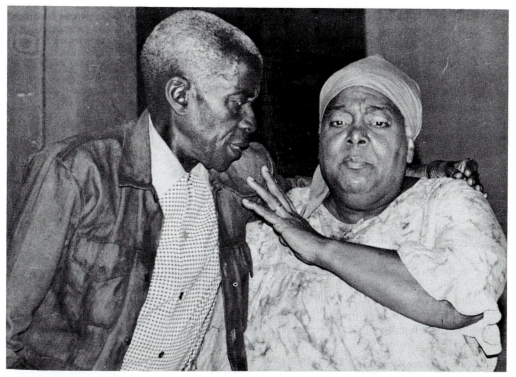

Douta Seck and Jacqueline Lemoine in Abdou Anta Kâ's 1979 Daniel Sorano National Theatre production of *Général Manuel Hô*.

Doura Mané as Macbeth in the 1967 Daniel Sorano National Theatre production of *Macbeth*.

Theatre for Young Audiences
Puppet and Mask Theatre

Children are regularly included as part of audiences for traditional theatre events. As a result, the western concept of a separate theatre for young audiences has had little impact in Sénégal.

Among the few groups to try their hands in this field is the Roy Baax Troupe, an independent company that eventually received some state support and has injected real dynamism in this area.

Theatre companies made up of young people have become more of a focus, particularly school groups. There is now an annual Festival of Young Creators which brings together such groups in all the arts.

One of the recent experiments in spoken theatre for children was done by the National Theatre actress, Assi Dieng Bâ, who participated in a French training programme for children's theatre in 1993. On her return she staged *Qui dort dine* (*He Who Sleeps Dines*), one of the first full plays done specifically for young audiences in the country.

There is an annual Inter-School Theatre Festival, organized by the Franco-Senegalese Alliance of Dakar, which has been valuable in encouraging young actors and directors.

Design
Theatre Space and Architecture

Assi Dieng in Aminata Sow Fall's *Batu Cassé* at the Daniel Sorano National Theatre, 1984.

The use of stage settings in both traditional and western-style theatre performances has been quite minimal. In the traditional theatre, settings are not required at all. Performances usually take place in the open air with audiences standing or sitting around the performers in a circle. From this position audience members – essential participants in the event – are able to comment directly on the performance and interrelate with the performers through gestures and words. A growing interest in linking traditional theatrical events with western style productions has led some directors to re-establish precisely this relationship and to move away from face-to-face performance styles and Italian-style theatrical spaces.

Even in the production of western plays, little has been done in the area of set design for economic reasons. There is simply no money for most groups to include significant design elements.

The major theatrical venue in the country is the Daniel Sorano National Theatre, a large space seating 1,128. Inaugurated in 1965, its main entrance hall (900 square metres) is often used for exhibits. It is equipped with modern lighting and sound systems.

Training
Criticism, Scholarship and Publishing

The Douta Seck National Conservatory of Dramatic Arts, Dance and Music was founded as a general training school for all areas of the visual and performing arts. In 1960 it began an autonomous dramatic arts division.

In general, theatre has received virtually no research support in the country and there is little in the way of theatre criticism being published either in journals or the daily press. University-based research has tended to focus on traditional theatre forms in their relation to modern theatre forms.

Senegalese plays were first published by the Frenchman Pierre Jean Oswald, who created an

African theatre list at Honfleur in Paris. He began his series in 1967 with N'dao's two plays, *L'Exil d'Albouri* and *La Décision*. The Concours théâtral inter-africain, organized by the Office de Radiodiffusion et de Télévision Françaises (ORTF), has enabled a number of Senegalese plays to be both produced and broadcast. Among them are *Le Procès de Lat Dior* by Mamadou Seyni Mbengue, and *L'Afrique a parlé* by Mbaye Gana Kébé. All of these plays have also been published by ORTF. In recent years, Nouvelles Èditions Africaines in Dakar, Editions Khoudia of the African Centre for Cultural Exchange in Dakar, and l'Harmattan in Paris have all published useful editions of the works of Senegalese authors.

Ousmane Diakhaté, Madior Diouf
Translated by Jennifer Hutchison

Further Reading

Acogny, Germaine. *Danse africaine* [African dance]. Frankfurt am Main: Verlag Fricke, 1988.

Bâ, Bocar. 'Point de vue sur le théâtre africain' [A stock-taking of African theatre]. *Trait d'union* 12 (March–May 1995).

Béart, Charles. 'Le théâtre indigène et la culture africaine' [Indigenous theatre and African culture]. In *L'Education africaine*. Sénégal, 1937.

Diakhaté, Lamine. 'Poésie et théâtre en Afrique noire' [Poetry and theatre in Black Africa]. *Ethiopiques* 2, nos. 2–3 (1984).

——. 'Un Théâtre africain d'expression française' [An African theatre in French]. *Paris-Dakar* (5 March 1965).

Diahkaté, Ousmane. 'Antonin Artaud et Wole Soyinka: l'imaginaire ancien aux sources de la théâtralité' [Antonin Artaud and Wole Soyinka: the imagination of antiquity at the sources of theatricality]. *Annales de la Faculté des Lettres et Sciences Humaines de l'Université de Dakar* 24 (1994).

——. 'Bertolt Brecht et l'Afrique noire' [Bertolt Brecht and Black Africa]. *Brecht Then and Now* 20 (1995).

——. Culture traditionelle et influences européennes dans le théâtre négro-africain moderne' [Traditional culture and European influences in modern Black African theatre]. MA thesis, Université Paul Valéry, Montpellier, 1984.

——. 'De l'espace théâtral' [On dramatic space]. *Annales de la Faculté des Lettres et Sciences Humaines de l'Université de Dakar* 19 (1989).

——. 'Figures et fantasmes de la violence dans le théâtre africain francophone' [Figures and fantasies of violence in francophone African theatre]. *La Deriva delle francofonie* (vol. 1): *l'Afrique Sub-Saharienne*. Naples: Instituto Universitario Orientale, University of Bologna (November–December 1990).

——. Préface à *Nder en flamme* [Preface to *Nder in Flames*] by Alioune Badara Beye. Dakar: Nouvelles Éditions Africaines, 1990.

——. 'Regard africain sur l'esthétique occidentale de l'interprétation: l'exemple de Diderot-Brecht' [An African reading of the western aesthetics of acting: the examples of Diderot

and Brecht]. *Annales de la Faculté des Lettres et Sciences Humaines de l'Université de Dakar* 17 (1982).

——. 'Le Théâtre sénégalais, saisons 1992–1993, 1993–1994' [Senegalese theatre for the 1992–1993 and 1993–1994 seasons]. In *Le Monde du Théâtre* [The world of theatre]. Tunis: International Theatre Institute, 1995.

——. 'Théories du jeu de l'acteur en Europe au XXe siècle: une lecture africaine' [Theories of acting in twentieth century Europe: an African reading]. PhD Dissertation, Université de Dakar, 1993.

Diop, Alioune Oumy. 'Réflexions sur le théâtre africain pré-colonial et contemporain' [Thoughts on pre-colonial and contemporary African theatre]. In *Quel théâtre pour le développement en Afrique?* [Which theatre for development in Africa?]. Institut Cultural Africain, 1985.

——. *Le Théâtre traditionnel au Sénégal* [Traditional theatre in Sénégal]. Dakar: NEA, 1990.

Diouf, Madior. 'Un Baobab au milieu de la brousse: le théâtre de langue française' [Baobab in the middle of the bush: French-language theatre]. *Notre Librairie* 81 (October–December 1985).

——. 'Le Théâtre francophone d'Afrique noire depuis 1960' [Francophone theatre in Black Africa since 1960]. *Revista de la Universidad Complotense 'El Teatro Actual'* 27, no. 114 (October–December 1978).

Fall, Marouba. 'Le Théâtre sénégalais face aux exigences du public' [Senegalese theatre and the demands of the public]. *Ethiopiques* 2, nos. 2–3 (1984).

Harris, Jessica. 'French-speaking Theatre in Senegal'. PhD dissertation, New York University, 1983. 194 pp.

——. 'Toward a New Senegalese Theatre'. *The Drama Review: African Performance Issue* 25, no. 4 (winter 1981): 13–18.

Hermantier, Raymond. 'Art dramatique et animation culturelle au Sénégal' [Dramatic art and cultural animation in Sénégal]. In *Notes, Actes du Colloque sur le théâtre négro-africain* [Notes, Colloquium on Black African theatre]. Paris: Présence Africaine, 1970.

Kâ, Abdou Anta. 'Passé et présent du théâtre africain' [The past and present of African theatre]. *Trait d'union* (November–December 1956).

Kesteloot, Lilyan. 'Les thèmes principaux du théâtre africain moderne' [The main themes of modern African theatre]. In *Notes, Actes du*

Colloque sur le théâtre négro-africain, Paris: Présence Africaine, 1970.

Kum'a Ndumbe, Alexandre III. 'Le Théâtre sénégalaise' [The Senegalese theatre]. *Cameroun Littéraire* 2 (1983): 44–52.

Lemoine, Lucien. *Douta Seck ou la tragédie du roi Christophe.* [Douta Seck or The tragedy of King Christophe]. Paris: Présence Africaine, 1993.

N'dao, Cheik Aliou. 'Le théâtre historique'. *Notre Librairie* 81 (October–December 1985).

Répertoire culturel: le Sénégal, inventaire des activités, ressources et infrastructures culturelles des pays membres de l'Agence de Coopération culturelle et technique (l'ACCT) [Cultural repertory: Sénégal, inventory of the activities, resources and cultural infrastructures of the member countries of the Agency for Cultural and Technical Cooperation]. Paris: Gamma Pair, 1982.

Scherer, Jacques. *Le Théâtre en Afrique noire francophone* [Theatre in Black francophone Africa]. Paris: Presses Universitaires de France, 1992.

Senghor, Léopold Sédar. 'Le Groupe *Yewu* de Ousmane Cissé et les frères du théâtre de Samb: meilleures troupes pour 1969' [Ousmane Cissé's *Yewu* Group and Samb's Frères du théâtre: best troupes of 1969]. *Mali Magazine* 2 (August 1969).

———. 'Poésie et théâtre' [Poetry and theatre]. *Ethiopiques* (nouvelle série) 2, nos. 2–3 (1984).

Senghor, Léopold Sédar and Hossman. 'Situation du théâtre Sénégalais' [The position of Senegalese theatre]. *Afrique* (1965).

Senghor, Maurice Sonar. 'Les Tendances actuelles dans le théâtre africain' [Contemporary trends in African theatre]. *Présence Africaine* 75 (1970).

———. 'Le Théâtre africain au Festival Culturel Pan-Africain d'Algerie' [African theatre at the Pan-African Cultural Festival of Algeria]. *Présence Africaine* 72 (1970).

Traoré, Bakary. Preface à *L'Exil d'Albouri* et *La Décision* [Preface to The Exile of Albouri and The Decision] by Cheik Aliou N'dao. Paris: Honfleur, 1967.

———. *Le Théâtre négro-africain et ses fonctions sociales* [Black African theatre and its social functions]. Paris: Présence Africaine, 1958.

Vievra, Paulin Soumanou. 'Où en sont le cinéma et le théâtre?' [What is the present state of cinema and theatre?]. *Présence Africaine* 13 (April–May 1957).

SEYCHELLES

The Republic of Seychelles, the world's smallest independent nation, consists of a group of 115 islands with a total land area of 450 square kilometres (about 170 square miles). Located just south of the Equator in the western Indian Ocean, the islands are scattered over a land area of 1.03 million square kilometres (400,000 square miles) about 1,600 kilometres (1,000 miles) east of the African mainland.

More than 85 per cent of the population of 73,000 live on the main island of Mahé (142 square kilometres; 55 square miles) with most of the remaining 15 per cent living on Praslin and La Digue. Most of the country's cultural activities are to be found on Mahé in the capital city of Victoria.

Largely uninhabited until the middle of the eighteenth century, when England and France began to vie for power in the Indian Ocean, Seychelles was settled by the French in 1770 and by the African slaves they brought with them (mostly of Bantu origin). In 1756, France laid legal claim to the islands, naming them after the Vicomte Moreau de Séchelles, Minister of Finance in the court of Louis XV.

In 1794, the British captured the islands, which in 1814 were ceded to Britain by the Treaty of Paris. Ruled by Britain as a dependency of Mauritius until 1903 when the Seychelles became a British Crown Colony, the Seychelles Order of 1967 granted the islands a governing council under a governor appointed by Britain. On 29 June 1976, Seychelles became an independent republic. A *coup d'état* brought a government led by F.A. René to power in 1977. Important economic and social changes ensued in the following years which also saw the encouragement and active support of the theatre among other cultural forms. A

new constitution was promulgated in 1993 and multi-party elections in the same year returned both President René and his party to government.

Despite the lengthy British role in Seychelles' history, French influence has remained strong and both French and English are widely spoken. French was, in fact, the language of school instruction until the 1940s. English and French are both official languages while the French-based Creole, also an official language, is the mother tongue of the majority of the population. Some 14.4 per cent of the country's exports and 12.8 per cent of its imports are with France, while 55 per cent of the islands' exports and 13.3 per cent of imports are with the UK. Other major trading partners are Yemen, South Africa, Singapore and Pakistan. Tourism remains the primary source of foreign exchange.

Because of the absence of reliable records, no one knows for sure about the origin of theatre on the islands. One can catch a glimpse, however, in a diary entry by A.N. Gordon, Governor of Mauritius in the 1870s, when he wrote 'In the evening, the Negroes on the estate had an elephant dance. It was a curious sight. It was an opera rather than a dance for the whole hunt was sung and acted as well as danced'. A year later, he wrote 'I told you last year about their dance in imitation of an elephant hunt. We had that again and then a war dance which was equally curious'.

Another hint is found in the writings of the French musicologist Bernard Koechlin, who wrote about *sokwe*, traditional masked dancing. Along with *sokwe*, he described a kind of *commedia dell'arte*. He wrote 'The king and his officers enter. ... The doctor gives life with his stethoscope. ... After an introductory dialogue the king falls down paralyzed ... the doctor steps in ... the actors improvise a comic dialogue'.

Koechlin has also produced two recordings of traditional music in 1976 and 1977, while Gordon wrote in the 1870s.

If, on the outer islands, the actors still performed these *commedia*-like shows until quite recently, it was usually confined to a particular segment of the community – those most deprived of cultural activities. Generally these were private performances done with music.

Mauritian-born scholar and playwright Guy Lionnet has also written of this proto-theatre in Seychelles consisting of half-danced and half-sung scenes. Lionnet adds that these pieces are also done for healing or resurrection with typical characters being the sick or the dead, the healer and his helpers. He has spoken of a type of one-person improvised theatre, half-spoken and half-mimed and staged during celebrations such as weddings. The folk-rooted and melodramatic wedding dance sequences are generally known as *moutya*.

It was the primary schools which introduced European-style forms and themes. The taste for spoken theatre spread to private homes and adult actors became involved. Eventually, religious groups performed spoken plays. On the island of La Digue, for example, the Sisters of Savoyard staged productions from 1862 on. Even the exiled King Prempeh of the Ashanti (modern-day Ghana) staged melodramas and dances to which no less a personage than the British governor was invited.

From the 1940s on, plays with Seychellois themes began to be seen and in the 1950s community theatre clubs emerged. One of the pioneers was Dolfin César (b. 1928), who staged productions all across Mahé and Praslin both outdoors and in the community centres. Some of her plays were socially rooted. *Carolin*

and Carola, for instance, dealt with a woman who had been abandoned in the forest because of her infidelity.

After 1977, plays depicting the Seychellois efforts toward independence became popular. Among the best of these historical pieces is *Lalit en Pep* (*Struggle of a People*) by Marie-Thérèse Choppy, a woman who later became Director-General of Culture; and *Kastor*, a musical play about a runaway slave by Patrick Victor. *Kastor* has since been played more than seventy times.

Another popular Creole play from the period is *Bolot Feray* by Geva René, which recalled traditional wedding customs. It was first produced during the independence celebrations of 1976.

In 1990, Radio-Television Seychelles produced another historical play – partly in French and party in Creole – *Les Exilés de 1801*. The play recalled the exile in Seychelles in 1801 of seventy Jacobins from France who had been accused of trying to assassinate Napoleon on Christmas Eve 1800. The play was adapted from a text by Guy Lionnet.

By the 1990s, the Seychelles had seen local adaptations of many of Europe's best known classical dramatists, most often Shakespeare and Molière. Of the more modern dramatists, the most successful in Seychelles have been France's Jean Anouilh and Albert Camus.

In the first years after independence, censorship existed but was often rationalized as protecting decency or fighting for 'decent language'; by the 1990s, however, virtually anything could be seen on a stage, even sexual themes, up until then considered taboo. Through such work, theatre was quickly moving from being only for educated people to being an art for everyone, and theatre artists were gaining new respect for their ability to expand the limits of accepted social norms.

Structure of the National Theatre Community

There is no national theatre structure *per se* in Seychelles. Only one of the country's four regularly producing groups is subsidized by the state – the National Theatre in Victoria. The others are sponsored privately. Because of the small population base, it is rare for a group to stage more than one play a season. Even then

it is usually in conjunction with some public occasion such as the popular Creole Festival held annually in October.

Virtually all the island's artists are therefore amateurs in the truest sense of the word. As a result rehearsals tend to take place over many months because of other commitments by those involved. The only exception is at the National Theatre where the company members can best be described as semi-professionals.

With the minimum wage in Seychelles just under US$100 per week, it was rare that a production was able to charge more than US$10 for a ticket, a price that was still considered high in 1996.

Shows done in Creole reach wide audiences and successful Creole plays are now seen by thousands of people. Theatre has now become an art for the masses in Seychelles rather than an art for only an educated elite or for those who are literate in English or French.

Seychelles has no theatrical unions nor are there any specifically theatrical festivals.

Artistic Profile

Dance and music are integrated in traditional folk forms and can still be seen on occasion. More and more, however, spoken theatre has come to dominate. Most popular are socially based comedies done in Creole. There are occasional performances of original ballets staged by students of the Seychelles School of Dance in Mahé.

Companies

The major theatre groups in Seychelles include the National Theatre Troupe of the Ministry of Education and Culture, Victoria Theatre, Veyez, and Théâtre de la Jeunesse. Christian Servina (b. 1963) works most closely as a director with Veyez, while John Etienne (b. 1965) directs at the Victoria Theatre, and Angelin Marie at Théâtre de la Jeunesse.

Of these, the National Theatre is the largest; it plays in Mahé and tours to other islands. The company receives subsidy directly from the state while other troupes work with private sponsorship.

The Mahé Players is composed mostly of foreign expatriates living in Seychelles.

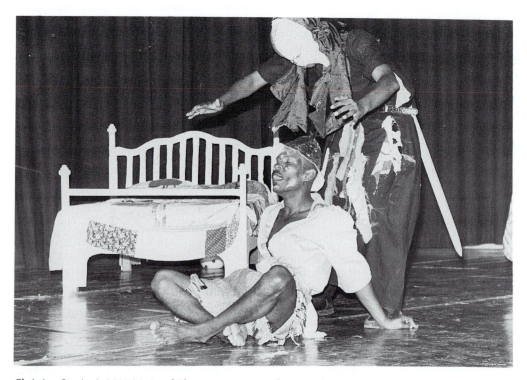

Christian Servina's 1995 National Theatre Troupe production of *Sen Disparet* at the Creole Festival.
Photo: Seychelles Nation.

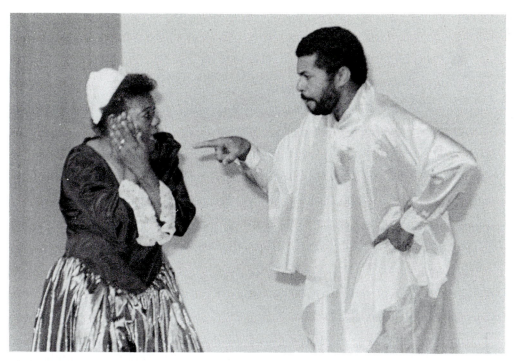

John Etienne's 1992 Ministry of Education Theatre production of *Le Malade Imaginaire*.
Photo: Seychelles Nation.

Christian Servina's 1995 Veyez production of his *Goula i la*.
Photo: Seychelles Nation.

It is rare that more than one play a season is staged by any of these groups.

Dramaturgy

Spoken drama in the European sense is still in its infancy in Seychelles. There are perhaps a half dozen or so writers who have offered plays of some note to the country.

Perhaps the most important of these writers is Christian Servina, a social satirist who has dealt with political, social and sexual issues in plays such as *Lo stenn* (*The Bus Station*) and *Solisyon fatal* (*Fatal Solution*).

Other writers of note include Angelin Marie, author of *Lanver bouke*; Marie-Cécile Médor, author of *Vaz a fler larm*; Marie-Thérèse Choppy and Patrick Victor.

Directing and Acting

The country's best known and important director is the Russian-trained John Etienne. A graduate of the state theatre school in Moscow (GITIS), Etienne's work is rooted in the Stanislavski system as interpreted by Michael Chekhov. He has said that his goal is to find 'the internal roots of each character's actions' as well as to stage plays that affirm the realities of Seychelles. Etienne and other local directors have regularly tried to incorporate folk elements within their work.

Theatre for Young Audiences
Puppet and Mask Theatre

There are no companies in Seychelles which specifically focus on theatre for young audiences. That said, most of the country's theatre groups try to include some children's work. This has ranged from local adaptations of *Cinderella* and *Snow White* to plays such as Christian Servina's *Goula i la* which attracted large audiences of young people because of its many animal folk figures.

The Ministry of Education and Culture has consistently encouraged theatrical activities in schools and students regularly perform at the national inter-schools competition during the Kreol Festival.

Discussion has taken place over many years about the use of dramatic literature in schools and even, on occasion, about the possibility of establishing theatre courses. In the mid-1990s, however, no such courses existed.

Puppet theatre is often used in school programmes involving storytelling. Puppet shows are also seen regularly on local television in French and English although not yet in Creole. Despite the appearance from time to time of *sokwe*, the masked dances mentioned earlier, the mask tradition is not as significant in Seychelles as it has been in other African societies.

Design
Theatre Space and Architecture

Design is, for the most part, still an unknown and unpractised profession in Seychelles. In general, directors are responsible for design elements although from time to time others are brought into the work. John Etienne, for example, has involved the Russian-born and Russian-trained designer Marina Malvina, who is now resident in Seychelles, while the National Theatre has on occasion utilized artists from the School of Art and Design at the Seychelles Polytechnic.

There are three theatre buildings which are regularly used for public performances – the National Theatre of the Ministry of Education and Culture (162 seats), Polytechnic Theatre (624 seats) and Maison du Peuple (also with 624 seats). All are multi-use spaces which are generally set up in a proscenium format.

Occasional outdoor performances, usually involving the folk forms such as *sokwe* and *moutya*, are generally staged around a fire under moonlight.

Training
Criticism, Scholarship and Publishing

Since there is no national theatre school or extended training programme in theatre, anyone interested in advanced training must go abroad. This has been the example of the country's two major theatre professionals – Christian Servina, who received training in the UK and Denmark, and John Etienne, who studied at GITIS in Moscow. Both now offer their own training courses.

Since 1977, organizations such as UNESCO and Théâtre International de la Langue Française (TIL; International French Language Theatre) have offered occasional workshops in cultural animation.

During 1982, Fabio Paccioni made a study of the Seychelles' performing arts for UNESCO. That document was published in Paris in 1983 and is entitled simply *Animation théâtrale*. Other than this single study and a few small references to Seychelles in journals or magazines, little has been written about cultural life on the islands.

Theatre performances are nevertheless regularly written about and reviewed in Seychelles' newspapers, magazines and journals. Among these are the daily government paper, *The Nation*, *The Weekend Nation* and weeklies such as *Regar, The Independent, People* and the fortnightly *L'Echo des Iles*. The national radio and television network, SBC, also provide occasional theatrical coverage.

Jean-Claude Pascal Mahoune
with *Christian Servina and John Etienne*

Further Reading

Gordon, A.N. *Mauritius: Records of Private and Public Life*. Edinburgh: R. and R. Clark, 1894. 231 pp.

Koechlin, Bernard. *Les Seychelles et l'océan indien* [Seychelles and the Indian Ocean]. Paris: L'Harmattan, 1985.

Lionnet, Guy. *Regard sur la culture seychelloise* [A look at Seychelles culture]. Lagazet: Ministry of Information, Culture and Sports. 8 pp.

Paccioni, Fabio. *Animation théâtrale* [Theatrical animation]. Paris: UNESCO, 1983. 13 pp.

Skerrett, A. and D. Skerrett. *Spectrum Guide to Seychelles*. Nairobi: Camerapix, 1991. 65 pp.

SIERRA LEONE

One of the smallest countries in Africa, Sierra Leone has a total area of about 72,300 square kilometres (27,900 square miles). It is bordered on the north by Guinea, on the east by Liberia and on the west by the Atlantic Ocean. Its population was estimated at about 4.7 million in 1995.

For administrative purposes the country is divided into three provinces and the Western Area, which includes the capital, Freetown. Up to 1992, Sierra Leone was a republic with a single party government. Since then the country has been ruled by a military government and the constitution suspended, though timetables for the return to civilian rule have been announced.

There are fourteen ethnic groups in Sierra Leone, each with its own distinctive language. The largest are the Mende and the Temne, each comprising about 30 per cent of the population. Smaller groupings include Limba, Loko, Kono, Kuranko, Mandingo, Vai, Krim, Susu and Foulah. Creoles – descendants of liberated slaves – inhabit the Western Area and form about 1 per cent of the total population. However, they have wielded significant cultural and political influence and their language, Krio, is regarded as the country's *lingua franca*. English is the official language, although its use is restricted to a literate minority numbering only 21 per cent. Major religions include Islam, Christianity and traditional animism. There is great religious tolerance in Sierra Leone, with all segments of the population participating in religious festivals such as Christmas and the Eve of Ramadan.

The first western people to visit the land which is now called Sierra Leone were the Portuguese, who landed in 1453 and called the country they saw Sierra Leoa, or Lion Mountains. It is certain that from this time onward slaves were taken from Sierra Leone, as from other parts of West Africa, to the West Indies, South America and North America. Sierra Leone's modern history dates from 1787, when a group of Blacks comprising liberated slaves from North America, ex-soldiers (Maroons) from the West Indies, and the so-called Black Poor from England, were settled by the British on land bought from the indigenous peoples and called Freetown. Freetown thus became a haven for liberated slaves; after a difficult start, the colony grew, the numbers of the settlers being augmented not only by more freed slaves from North America but also by those liberated by the British before their ships actually reached North America. It was the descendants of these liberated slaves who became the Creoles and it was their language which became Krio. Along with Creoles came not only the English language, Christianity and western education, but also Islam and certain Yoruba-oriented customs associated with the former slaves from Nigeria.

For the next one hundred and fifty years or so the Creoles were to be a very important force not only in Sierra Leone, but also in the whole of West Africa for, as pioneers in education, they were in charge of the Civil Service, formed professional cadres, and were extensively used by the British in other parts of British West Africa. From the colony, the British gradually extended their influence over the rest of the country despite resistance from the north, where the great Temne monarch Bai Bureh led the Hut Tax Rebellion. Declared a British Protectorate in 1896, Sierra Leone from that time on was regarded and administered as a British colony with the British governor wielding the major power. In 1951, the first steps toward a representative democratic government were taken with the appointment of Sierra Leoneans as Chief Minister, Cabinet Ministers, and popularly elected Members of Parliament. Gaining its independence from Britain in 1961, Sierra Leone was declared a republic in 1971 with a one-party constitution.

The development of theatre in Sierra Leone follows more or less the same pattern as the development of the country's literature and can be described as the quest for a Sierra Leonean identity. As in most African countries, theatre from the pre-colonial era – traditional theatre as it is otherwise known – was not an end in itself but rather a means to an end. Part of the rituals of various cults and groups, part of the religious activities of the people in general, part of the ceremonies of secret societies such as the Poro and Bundu peoples, performative events included masquerades and boasted rich dramatic components which even in the 1990s a powerful source of inspiration for dramatists. Similarly, the rich, age-old tradition of storytelling demonstrates a clear penchant for dramatic narrative. Storytellers often enhance the quality of their tales through a skilful use of facial expression, voice, dialogue, gesture and questions to the audience as well as incorporating mime, drumming and singing.

European-style spoken drama, however, started in the colonial era with the introduction of Christianity and western education. Part of a general attempt to inculcate religious knowledge and stimulate Christian consciousness, the dramatization of biblical stories and passages by organizations within the church was a regular feature of colonial life. The fact is that such performances can still be seen in the country in productions of plays such as *Everyman*, *The Bishop's Candlesticks* and T.S. Eliot's *Murder in the Cathedral*.

A more secular drama, started and developed in the schools, also had a religious or missionary orientation. These productions, generally under the direction of English teachers and principals and usually of European authorship, were a staple ingredient of the annual speech day and prize-giving ceremony. Though some might regard these activities with condescension, it is certain that they afforded people, particularly the young, valuable dramatic training and led to the establishment of theatre groups outside school and church. Such groups

became regular features of Freetown life during the 1940s and 1950s.

The development of theatre was given a significant boost with the formation of the British Council Dramatic Society in 1948, spearheaded by Sierra Leonean Nada Smart, who had been sent to England in 1946 for a British Council drama course. For the next twenty years the Dramatic Society was to set the pace for Sierra Leone's theatrical development and be a pattern for other theatre groups. That it was called the British Council Dramatic Society meant that it was run largely under the auspices of the British Council. This made it a major outpost of British culture in the African colonies. Most of its members were British; the few Sierra Leonean members belonged to the educated elite – teachers, lecturers, top civil servants and professionals who felt at home in English culture. The plays produced at the British Council were, of course, also British. Its first two productions in 1948 set the tone that would be followed for decades to come – J.B. Priestley's *Laburnum Grove* and Noël Coward's *Blithe Spirit*. For the next fourteen years, in fact, the society would concentrate on such British fare with the plays of Priestley and Coward regularly joined by those of Somerset Maugham, Wilde, Sheridan, Goldsmith and Shakespeare.

In the 1950s, the example of this Dramatic Society led to the formation of similar groups such as the Brunswick Cultural Circle in 1952 (and continued functioning until 1980), the Cascader Circle and the Drama Circle. Meanwhile, at the university, Fourah Bay College Dramatic Society was formed. All of these, like the British Council Dramatic Society, staged almost exclusively British plays such as Shakespeare's *The Merchant of Venice*, Wilde's *The Importance of Being Earnest*, Eliot's *The Family Reunion* and Emlyn Williams's *A Murder Has Been Arranged*. The reason for such choices is to be found in the nature of both the groups and the audiences. Considered essentially an upper-class interest, theatre activity for the actors and audience alike was a means of demonstrating their preference for British culture. Going to the theatre became a means of proving one's membership in the elite. Such was the lack of cultural self-confidence among Sierra Leonean members of the group that the idea of staging a play by an African or of writing plays themselves did not occur until much later.

In 1957, however, a significant change was heralded by the first Sierra Leone Festival of the

Arts. The festival encouraged Sierra Leonean scripts and opened the way for the production of a number of them including plays by John Akar (b. 1927), author of *Valley Without Echo* (1954) and *Cry Tamba* (1961). The attainment of independence in 1961 provided a further boost. The drama competition that was organized as part of the independence celebrations produced Sierra Leone's first major dramatist, Raymond Sarif Easmon (b. 1913), whose prize-winning play, *Dear Parent and Ogre* (1961), was the first African play produced by the British Council Drama Society.

The plays of Sarif Easmon clearly herald a dawning of cultural self-confidence among Sierra Leoneans. But the break with the past was to be gradual rather than sudden. A medical doctor, Easmon was himself a member of the educational and social elite to whom the conservative and western-oriented British Council Dramatic Society (BCDS) catered, and his plays, though set in Sierra Leone, still exuded a British tone. Although dealing with genuinely African topics and themes such as the gap between the generations, the clash between old and new, ethnicity, and the rise of a meritocracy and corruption in government, the lifestyle and values of his leading characters, who are themselves very much members of the elite, are much more British than African. They demonstrate a penchant for champagne, luxurious cars, western cities (New York, London and Paris), the music of Wagner, and the poetry of Lord Byron. Their language and homes are almost completely western, and at the end of the plays it is undoubtedly the values of this kind of aristocracy that Easmon is endorsing. Structurally, too, the plays make little or no use of elements that have now become part and parcel of African plays such as drumming, singing and dancing, or any other aspects of the rich native African theatrical traditions.

Significant also was the establishment of the National Theatre League in 1964, bringing together most of the amateur societies. This was taken several stages further toward professionalism during the mid- and late-1960s largely due to changes in the social, political and cultural climate of the country. With independence and the achievement of majority rule, the new elite came largely from the provinces and were much less committed to a western lifestyle.

The feeling grew that more emphasis should be placed on indigenous culture; that an atmosphere in which British plays were staged for a British-oriented audience was alien if not undesirable; that the continued staging of British plays (even those of Shakespeare) was anachronistic; that the BCDS in particular was too stiff, too conservative, too British-oriented; that the BCDS membership was too restricted to a small number of elite who were connected with the British Council; that the theatre audience itself was too restricted by class and education and that ordinary members of the public were being denied the enjoyment of theatre; that ordinary people who were interested in acting were inhibited from doing so by the social atmosphere pervading the established drama societies; and that theatre should be for the people and that one need not be highly educated or even literate to enjoy it.

Three forces gave impetus to this trend. The first was dramatist Yulisa Amadu Maddy (b. 1936), who changed his name from Pat Maddy to reflect his African consciousness. Maddy was almost the exact antithesis of Sarif Easmon. Where Easmon was a member of the educational and social elite, Maddy unashamedly paraded the fact that he was a man of the people. Without a university degree, he had attended drama school in England, produced African plays for Danish radio, and trained the Zambian National Dance Troupe for Expo '70. He was, therefore, a professional actor and a man of the theatre with professional awareness of the possibilities of the stage. Where Easmon's leading characters were taken from the elite, Maddy selected his from school drop-outs, street-corner boys, thugs, prostitutes, criminals, even murderers. Where the language of Easmon's characters was western and 'elegant', Maddy's was earthy. Where the western atmosphere of Easmon's plays and the lifestyle of his characters was clear, Maddy's characters were genuinely African, as was the atmosphere of his plays in general.

He was also the first Sierra Leonean to incorporate singing, dancing and other elements of the African tradition into his plays which include *Obasai* (*Over Yonder*, 1976), *Yon-kon* (*Clever Thief*, 1968), *Alla Gbah* (*The Big Man*) and *Gbana-Bendu* (*Tough Guy*). All of these titles were taken from languages such as Krio.

The second determining factor in the future of Sierra Leonean drama was the translation into Krio by Thomas Decker of Shakespeare's *Julius Caesar* in 1965. This was performed to great acclaim by the newly formed National

Theatre League. Decker saw that there was still a place for the plays of Shakespeare but, to conform with the temper of the times, they needed to be made accessible to a wider audience.

A third factor was the performance of two plays in Krio by Juliana John (b. 1938) – *Nar Mami Born Am* (1968) and *E Day E Nor Do* (1969). Following Decker's success, these plays showed the possibilities of the use of Krio and other indigenous languages in the theatre and paved the way for the evolution of a vernacular drama as a means of opening up the theatre.

The result was a tremendous upsurge in dramatic activity during the late 1960s and 1970s, a major development in Sierra Leone's modern cultural history. Within a few years, many new groups sprang up, most of them committed to performing plays in the vernacular, although plays in English were not ruled out. New groups emerged and include Tabule Experimental Theatre, founded by Raymond Dele Charley (1948–94) and Adeyemi Meheux in 1968; Gbakanda Tiata, founded by Yulisa Amadu Maddy in 1968; Songhai Theatre, founded by Clifford Garber and John Kolosa Kargbo (1954–94) in 1973, and also known as the Shegureh Players; and Balangi Dramatic Group, formed in 1974.

The differences between these groups and the British Council Dramatic Society, which soon became defunct, could not be more marked. Their very names suggest the members' wish to make a clean break with the past and to affirm indigenous or traditional culture. *Tabule*, for example, is the name of a traditional drum, and *shegureh* and *balangi* are also traditional musical instruments. Whereas the members of the BCDS were more or less of the social elite, the new dramatic groups drew their membership from all walks of life, but especially from very ordinary people and from the young. While members of the BCDS were highly educated (many were graduates of overseas universities), the dramatists and members of the new groups were in most cases high school graduates, and in some cases drop-outs; only a very few had university degrees or teacher's diplomas. Where the older Sierra Leonean writers and actors came from the Western Area and were largely Creoles, the playwrights and actors of the new generation, though still based in the Western Area, came from various ethnic groups – Mende, Temne, Creole, Limba – as well as from various parts of the country. Where the plays of someone like Easmon reflected the values of a Creole-Susu aristocracy, the works of the new generation reflected traditional customs, cultures, and values. It has been these groups which have carried Sierra Leonean theatre into the 1990s.

Structure of the National Theatre Community

At best, theatre activity in Sierra Leone can be regarded as semi-professional. No playwright or actor can make his or her living entirely from theatre. The fact that individuals are not full-time professionals, however, and that all of the groups started out with amateur status does not imply that they are not interested in financial rewards. Though it cannot be described as lucrative, the theatre in Sierra Leone can bring fairly high returns on an investment. Since the 1970s, theatre has become enormously popular, and a play that captures the attention of audiences can make a considerable profit. The government, recognizing such profits, has even begun to levy an entertainment tax. But, even after the payment of this tax, most groups are able to make enough for the playwright and actors to be paid a decent honorarium, though not a salary.

One of the reasons for the recent enormous popularity of theatre is the relative dearth of other forms of entertainment. The government's economic stringency in the late 1980s and through the 1990s has adversely affected most aspects of life including cinemas, nightclubs, radio and television (which have been badly hurt by power cuts), the shortage of foreign exchange (which made it difficult to import first-rate films), and even the shortage of beer and soft drinks, which affected pubs. House parties, too, were reduced because of the soaring cost of living. In this situation, theatre and football ministered to a vital need as virtually the only means of entertainment open to most people. Indeed, some entrepreneurs, having discovered the profits that could be made in the theatre, have conceived ingenious means of financing productions. The

English, *The Great Betrayal* (1980) by Bakarr. Bakarr is also an accomplished painter who designs the sets for all of his productions.

Songhai Theatre, which came into existence in 1973 under the name Shegureh Players, has been associated with two playwrights, Clifford Garber and John Kolosa Kargbo. The plays produced by this group include the Krio plays *Rayday Rahoon* and *Ibosio* by Garber, and *Poyo Togn Wahala* (1979) by Kargbo, and the English-language play, *Choice of the Gods*, by Kargbo. Of these, *Poyo Togn Wahala* was probably the most effective. A biting socio-political satire, it raised the curtain on the political and social corruption that characterized the country after independence.

Fourah Bay College English Department Dramatic Society came into being in 1976 with the aim of performing plays that students normally study. Its productions, mostly in the Mary Kingsley Auditorium, included the Nigerian playwright Ola Rotimi's *The Gods Are Not to Blame* and *Our Husband Has Gone Mad Again*; Wole Soyinka's *Jero* plays; Nikolai Gogol's *The Government Inspector*; Eldred Jones's *Crowther's People* (1977); and *Ojukororo* (*Ojukokoro*) (1985), based on Ben Jonson's *Volpone*. Staging two productions a year, the group ceased operating in 1986 when drama studies were incorporated into the English Department.

Julius Spencer, an original member of Tabule Experimental Theatre, is the only Sierra Leonean director-playwright to have been trained at the PhD level. A professor in the English Faculty at Fourah Bay College with special responsibility for directing the department's theatre programme, he also established his own group, Freetong Players. Trained in all aspects of stagecraft, Spencer brought a professional touch to the theatre that has often been missed in the country. He took the first real steps towards establishing a professional company by incorporating his group.

Another group of interest is The Professionals, which has been in existence since 1990. Strictly speaking, this is not a theatre group since it never stages plays. Its medium is mainly radio, and it can best be regarded as the Sierra Leonean equivalent of a radio sitcom or of BBC productions like *Hancock's Half Hour* or *Here's Archie*. For an hour or so at a time, the company entertains radio audiences with light-hearted, satirical sketches of various groups or institutions. Stock characters and stereotypes are used particularly in representations of members of various ethnic groups. The material is generally improvised and The Professionals' show is enormously popular. It often takes shows on the road and plays in hotels or even at parties in homes. It makes skilful use of aspects of traditional verbal art such as proverbs and songs.

Dramaturgy
Directing and Acting

Since 1970, more than a hundred plays have been written by Sierra Leoneans and most of these have been performed, though for reasons discussed below only a few of them, including Dele Charley's *Petikot Khona*, which was written in Krio, have been published.

In plays such as *Big Berin* by Yulisa Amadu Maddy, and *Poyo Togn Wahala* by John Kolosa Kargbo, social and political ills that have characterized life in the country since the 1970s have been exposed. Enormously popular, *Big Berin*, for instance, was produced twice and was later taken on a tour of the provinces.

During the 1980s, however, social commentary disappeared because of the heavy hand of censorship. As a result, some playwrights have turned to harmless topics such as marriage, love and the relationship between old and young. Love and marriage are still the most common themes; dramatists no longer seem willing to write on anything controversial.

Playwriting outside Freetown is virtually non-existent due, in part, to the problem of orthography. Many of the nation's languages simply have not yet been rendered in written form. Even in languages like Mende that do have an orthography, little writing has been done. This problem affects Krio as well, which until very recently was not really a written language, which presented writers with formidable problems. Of great value in this area was the publication by the English Department at Fourah Bay College of a Krio/English dictionary which helped to standardize the orthography and give respectability to Krio as a language in which one could write. Attempts are now being made to standardize the orthography of other Sierra Leonean languages.

Patrick Muana, a member of the English Faculty at Njala University College, wrote a play called *Ndaawa* (1992) about a Mende warrior of the same name. Although written in English, the play included a number of bold experimentations with form and language. Set up as a traditional storytelling session with actors in the audience from where they interject Mende jibes, it was performed countrywide by the Njala University College African Studies Society. Other plays written in local languages have been designed to spearhead campaigns by various organizations about issues such as vaccinating children.

The role played by the audience during dramatic performances in Freetown is worth commenting on. It differs markedly from that of both the western audience and the British-oriented audience of the colonial and pre-independence periods, and it reflects the change that has occurred in the concept of theatre. The audience members in a Freetown theatre are not passive; they are active participants and constantly react to what is happening on the stage. Plays in the vernacular have clearly brought a greater diversity of people into the theatre and have changed the dramaturgy. Audience members actually offer advice to actors, shout warnings, extend words of sympathy, or hiss their disgust. Some audiences have been known to throw things at particularly repulsive characters. The audience regularly joins in when familiar songs are sung, especially those that have been popularized by the particular play, and they are quick to learn new songs. They are never slow to complete a well-known proverb or riddle as soon as the first few words are mentioned.

The playwrights and actors themselves often invite the participation of the audience by directing questions at them and even, at times, asking them to join in the songs. During scenes involving traditional dancing, drumming, and singing, particularly those with masked dancers, members of the audience have gone up to the stage and, in the traditional way, pressed money on the foreheads of dancers and actors who have impressed them. Some players may even encourage this kind of audience involvement by putting a plate for this purpose on the stage.

Unfortunately, audience reaction has not always led to happy results. The Freetown playgoing public does not like short plays even though they may get bored if the play is extraordinarily long. An audience at one performance of Tabule's *Petikot Kohna* made no bones about showing their displeasure when the play lasted for only an hour and twenty minutes. In response, some playwrights have been forced to lengthen their plays by including scenes which are irrelevant, thus badly affecting the unity of the drama and the pace of the production.

Freetown audiences also like plays that make them laugh, so playwrights therefore seem to go out of their way to satisfy this need by including as many farcical scenes as possible and creating the kind of stock characters that are always calculated to amuse – the decrepit old man, for example, or the semi-literate servant.

Dele Charley has some twenty-five plays in both English and Krio to his credit. Born in Freetown, he attended the Milton Margai Teachers' College where he earned his teacher's certificate in 1973, specializing in physical education. He was also a teacher of English and drama and in that capacity played a leading role in generating dramatic awareness among school children. His contribution in the field was recognized by various embassies which sponsored him for training courses and visits overseas. A highly competent and versatile writer and director, he was a graduate of the Master's Programme in Drama at Leeds University. His early death in 1994 was a tremendous loss to Sierra Leonean theatre.

Through the late 1960s and early 1970s, adaptations of European classics were part of the drive to create an indigenous theatre in the country. These works were later included in the high school syllabuses and began to be taught in schools and colleges alike. In addition to Tabule's *Wan Poun Flesh* and *Makuba*, Bai Bureh Theatre mounted an adaptation of Sheridan's *The Rivals*, while the English Department Dramatic Society at Fourah Bay College staged a successful production of *Ojukororo* (*Ojukokoro*) (1985), a Krio translation by its director Eustace Palmer (b. 1939) of Jonson's *Volpone*, which, with its focus on materialism and corruption, reflected a very topical mood.

Akmid Bakarr has written over a dozen plays, more than half of which are in Krio and all of which he has directed himself. Commercially successful, his most captivating play is *The Great Betrayal*, about betrayal, sacrifice, treachery, greed, and patriotism, which makes full use of African cultural traditions.

Until his death in 1994, John Kolosa Kargbo was the most exciting and possibly the most promising of Sierra Leone's playwrights. Educated at the Prince of Wales School in Freetown, he worked as a journalist and then as Assistant Information Officer in the Government Information Service. His difficulties with the government over *Poyo*

Student members of the cast of Eustace Palmer's 1977 Fourah Bay College English Department Dramatic Society production of Eldred Jones's documentary play *Crowther's People*.

Togn Wahala forced him to leave government service. He moved to Nigeria to study theatre arts and communications at the University of Ibadan. He was the author of ten plays in Krio and English. These included, in addition to *Poyo Togn Wahala* and *Choice of the Gods*, the Krio plays *Aminata*, *Otogu*, *Ekundayo* and *Tabita Broke Ose* and the spectacular and highly impressive *Let Me Die Alone* (1979). The last five were written for the African Heritage Workshop, the group that Kargbo made particularly his own. *Otogu* is noteworthy for the ingenuity of some of its stage effects while *Tabita Broke Ose* was a successful comedy about love and infidelity in the style that the Sierra Leone audience has come to demand.

It is probably *Let Me Die Alone* that assured Kargbo's reputation. A meticulously researched and well-constructed script, the play is about a legendary Sierra Leonean traditional ruler, Madame Yoko. It is also about relationships between the colonial powers and the traditional ruler, about political intrigue, rivalry and the lust for power, about sacrifice, treachery and loyalty; but above all, it is about the tensions that exist in a woman who wishes to be on a par with men and to prove that she can be a capable ruler and yet wishes at the same time to fulfil her instincts for motherhood. *Let Me Die Alone* is a tragedy that marked its author as a dramatist of great promise. Kargbo's early death was, to an even greater extent than Dele Charley's, a tremendous blow to the development of dramatic literature in the country.

Theatre for Young Audiences
Puppet and Mask Theatre

There is no puppet theatre in Sierra Leone, nor is there a theatre exclusively for young audiences. Masks, however, play a very important role in the cultural life of the people.

Usually associated with secret societies, both male and female (i.e. the Hunting society, the Ojeh society and the Bundu society), the masks usually appear whenever the relevant society is observing an occasion which calls for a performance. These occasions might range from the initiation of new members to the death of a member. Performances are usually private – that is, restricted to members of the secret society – or they may be held openly in fields or courtyards or take the form of processions through the streets.

Masks of all kinds used to appear regularly during festivities such as Christmas and Easter, but this is no longer the case. Until the 1990s, two particular masks – Paddle and Firestone – would regularly pass through the streets of Freetown on certain public holidays, followed by enormous crowds. The practice was discontinued because authorities felt that such processions posed a threat to public order.

It should be noted that young boys still create their own small puppet masks, and these are still paraded in the streets at Christmas. A regular and apparently undying feature of Good Friday observances in Freetown is the creation by young boys of a puppet Judas figure which is usually propped against a wall or post and then severely beaten.

Design
Theatre Space and Architecture

There is only one professional designer – Sallu Deen of the Wara Dramatic Company – although Randy Wright, formerly of Tabule Experimental Theatre and now of Afromerica Collective, studied scenography, stage design and children's theatre in France in 1981.

Elaborate sets, such as those called for in some western plays, are rare. When one is used, it is usually constructed on one-half of a long stage and remains there for the rest of the play while less elaborate scenes are acted on the other half. This method was used by Goombay Theatre for *Love Wahala* and by Wara Dramatic Company in *Tradition*. During a performance of Dele Charley's *The Blood of a Stranger*, one of whose scenes requires a cave, a wooden platform with exits at both ends was used. The part of the cave facing the audience was painted to resemble stones. In Kailondo Theatre's production of Alieu Sannoh's (b. 1960) *Tink You Do Me* (1983), an actual classroom was constructed on the stage.

The lack of sophisticated lighting systems in theatres has presented playwrights with problems but also with splendid opportunities. For instance, when Akmid Bakarr's *The Great Betrayal* was produced in the British Council Theatre (which has the most modern lighting system in the country), a scene in which the gods are revealed sitting in council was swathed in an awesome reddish glow to emphasize their majesty; when the same play was performed at Fourah Bay College's Mary Kingsley Auditorium (which lacks a sophisticated lighting system), candles were used, throwing the gods and the forest into semi-darkness, thus emphasizing the sense of mystery and foreboding. Great inventiveness is also shown in the production of sound effects: the amplified thudding of feet on the stage can represent thunder; the repeated blinking of lights can represent lightning; and fire when commanded by the gods or when caused by an accident can be simulated by spraying kerosene from someone's mouth against a lighted match. In the 1975 production of *Seal for the Deal*, directed by Raymond De Souza George, a can of insecticide sprayed over the flames of potted candles was used to indicate the descent of the gods.

Strictly speaking, there is no real theatre building in Sierra Leone. The only building that approximates a theatre is the auditorium of the Institute of African Studies at Fourah Bay College, one of the constituent colleges of the University of Sierra Leone. Although built as an auditorium and largely used for university lectures and public meetings, it is a thrust stage with the audience on three sides. It also includes a balcony above a trapped stage, both of which have been put to use by imaginative directors.

The British Council Hall, with traditional proscenium stage and curtain, was the main theatrical venue until the end of the 1960s. Since then it has been enlarged, but the structure of the stage has been retained. The hall also has a modern lighting system. Much in demand for meetings, film showings, and other activities, none the less, it is associated with an old-fashioned attitude towards drama. Until the mid-1980s some groups preferred to use the Town Hall, which has no such associations, but the stage and lighting system there are inadequate.

The construction of the new City Hall in 1970 gave a great boost to dramatic activity because of its 2,000-seat auditorium. Still, the auditorium was constructed with political rallies rather than cultural events in mind. Later allowed to fall into disrepair, its facilities were not operative in the 1990s. During the 1970s and 1980s, it was the main venue for drama performances in Freetown. In the early 1990s, however, the civic authorities took the view that the staging of plays in the City Hall was harming its reputation and destroying the physical facilities. As a result, dramatic performances were banned.

Groups such as Tabule have successfully staged outdoor productions on tennis courts and in the forecourts of hotels. The English Department at Fourah Bay College and the Institute of African Studies have also staged shows outdoors.

Training
Criticism, Scholarship and Publishing

There are very few professionally trained actors, playwrights, designers or technical people in Sierra Leone. Of the playwright-director-actors, only five – Eric Hassan Deen of Nomoli Theatre; Raymond De Souza George, formerly of Tabule and later of Afromerica Collective; Alusine Kebbay of Ronko Theatre; Frederick Borbor James; and Julius Spencer of Freetong Players – hold university degrees. (Spencer holds a PhD from Ibadan University in Nigeria while George and the late Dele Charley had Master's degrees in drama from the University of Leeds.)

No school of drama exists in Sierra Leone. The English Department at Fourah Bay College, conscious of this need, brought in a consultant in 1983 under the auspices of UNESCO to study the situation and investigate the possibility of the establishment of a Department of Drama at the College. The report recommended the establishment of such a department, stressing that it was long overdue and that in addition to offering courses to students working towards a university degree, it could offer extension courses to members of theatre groups who would like to broaden their expertise. The report still awaits implementation.

During this period, the university's Institute of African Studies introduced a two-year diploma course in Cultural Studies, a major component of which is theatre. The English Department also has added a practical drama component to its literature courses. The department has run theatre workshops over the years involving not only its own students, but also members of the groups in Freetown. In 1968, 1970, 1972 and 1976, it invited Martin Banham, the director of the Leeds University Workshop Theatre, and his technical director, Trevor Faulkner, to Freetown under the auspices of the British Council. The workshops in 1970, 1972 and 1976 led to spectacular productions of the Nigerian Ola Rotimi's *The Gods Are Not to Blame*; *Mosquito* (a documentary written by members of the workshop); and Shakespeare's *The Taming of the Shrew*. These workshops provided valuable training, and the one in 1968 in particular was a tremendous boost to new drama groups.

The groups themselves frequently organize workshops and seminars either individually or collectively. Embassies, especially those of Britain, the United States and France – have also helped by giving bursaries to actors and playwrights to attend courses in their countries.

There is very little theatre criticism in Sierra Leone. The general view seems to be that the Sierra Leone press, which is very weak, has not served the theatre well. Reviews of plays appear infrequently and when they do they are usually uninformed. There are also few critical articles or books on theatre written by Sierra Leoneans, although there have been general articles by critics such as Eustace Palmer and Jack Moore on the plays of Easmon and Maddy, and chapters of books by Banham and Ogunda have been devoted to Easmon's plays. Predictably, these scholars have focused on plays as literary works rather than as plays for the stage. Students of the English Departments at Fourah Bay College and Njala University

College have begun to write theses based on original research as part of the requirements for their Bachelor's and Master's degrees, and Spencer wrote his doctoral dissertation on theatre in Sierra Leone.

The fact that few of the new wave of Sierra Leonean plays have been published is a reflection of the almost total absence of publishing houses in the country. Obviously plays written in Krio are not likely to have a very wide readership. Umea University Press in Sweden has published Dele Charley's *Petikot Khona* and Decker's Krio translation of *Julius Caesar*.

Eustace Palmer
with *Raymond De Souza George*

Further Reading

Akar, John. 'The Arts in Sierra Leone'. *African Forum* 1, no. 2 (fall 1965): 87–91.

Dele Charley, Raymond. 'A Theatre for My Country'. MA thesis, London Drama Board, 1981.

Graham-White, Anthony. 'African Drama: A Renaissance?'. *Ba Shiru* 5, no. 1 (1973): 78–83.

Harding, Hannah. 'The Development of Sierra Leonean Drama'. BA thesis, Fourah Bay College, 1978.

Palmer, Eustace. 'The Development of Sierra Leonean Writing'. In *A Celebration of Black and African Writing*, eds Bruce King and K. Ogungbesan, 245–57. Oxford: Oxford University Press/Ahmadu Bello University Press, 1975.

——. 'The Plays of Sarif Easmon'. *Journal of the New African Literature and the Arts* 8 (1973): 242–64.

Porter, Abioseh Michael. 'Krio Literature: The Most Popular Literature of Sierra Leone'. In *Signs and Signals: Popular Culture in Africa*. ed. Raol Granquist. Stockholm: Umea University Press, 1990.

Rowe, Sylvester E. 'Sierra Leone's Newly Born Theatre'. *African Arts* 9, no. 1 (October 1975): 56–9.

Sheriff, Mohamed. 'Recent Trends in Sierra Leone Drama'. BA thesis, Fourah Bay College, 1984.

Spencer, Julius. 'A Historical Background to the Contemporary Theatre in Sierra Leone'. *International Journal of Sierra Leone Studies,* no. 1 (1988): 26–35.

Warritay, Batilloi I. 'Cultural Misdirection and the Sierra Leone Theatre'. *Afriscope* 5, no. 8 (1975): 50–3.

SOMALIA

(Arab World volume)

SOUTH AFRICA

The Republic of South Africa lies at the southern tip of the African continent and is bordered to the north by Namibia, Botswana, Malawi, Zimbabwe, Swaziland and Mozambique. Completely surrounding the tiny Kingdom of Lesotho, the country is 1.22 million square kilometres (471,400 square miles) in size and extends from the Atlantic Ocean on the west coast to the Indian Ocean on the east.

Formerly divided into four provinces (Cape of Good Hope, Orange Free State, Transvaal, and Natal) and a number of ethnically based 'homelands', the country was redivided into nine provinces in 1993 (Western Cape, Northern Cape, Eastern Cape, Free State, Kwazulu/Natal, Gauteng, Northern Province, Northwest and Mpumalanga). The capital cities are Cape Town (legislative) and Pretoria (administrative).

The centre of some of the earliest human development, dating back over 3 million years, the region was settled by various African peoples over the course of many centuries. While exact information is scanty and often debatable since no written history has been handed down, numerous theories have been proposed over the past century.

The general belief seems to be that the early hunter-gatherer communities (the San, or 'Bushmen' as they were previously known) have lived in the region for approximately eight thousand years, meeting up with the early herders and farmers (the Khoi, previously known as 'Hottentots') about two thousand years ago, as the latter moved down from present-day Botswana. These related communities, usually referred to as the Khoisan, shared a number of linguistic and cultural traditions, and eventually settled in what is now known as the Western and Eastern Cape regions, where they were to meet up with the Bantu from the north and European settlers in about the fifteenth century.

The present-day Bantu peoples (broadly grouped linguistically into the Nguni, Tsonga,

Sotho and Shona groups) have their origins in the first centuries of the Christian era, when iron-working communities who farmed with crops and cattle and presumably shared a common base language, moved into the area south of the Limpopo. For the next thousand years the majority seem to have been confined to the savannah bushveld of what was later known as the northern and eastern Transvaal. One group, Nguni, gradually moved further south along the coast, into what became Zululand, Natal and Transkei. In the rich grazing lands they turned to tending cattle, and milk became a central feature of their diet and cattle a symbolic feature of the culture.

In the central part of the country, other groups, sharing the Sotho language, began to evolve their own culture, while the Shona, who had settled along the northern coast, spilled down as well. Because of the topography, they too took to cattle farming and the raising of crops. Thus, gradually, the period between AD 1100 and 1400 saw the more permanent establishment of the numerous chiefdoms and larger empires among the various groups with which the Khoisan and the European settlers were to make contact over the next three centuries, a period in which they eventually evolved into the broader groupings known today. Scholars tend to classify them broadly as the Nguni groups (Zulu, Xhosa, Swazi, Ndebele) and the Sotho groups (North Sotho, South Sotho, Tswana), the Venda and the Tsonga.

This period also saw the gradual evolution and formulation of distinctive ethnic and cultural customs, traditions and beliefs which were to find expression in the dance, song and narration that make up early southern African performance.

European connections to the region date to the Portuguese discovery of the sea route around the Cape of Storms (later the Cape of Good Hope) in the fifteenth century. This led to the first Dutch settlement in 1652 and a century and-a-half later the British annexation of the Cape (1814) and Natal (1843). The subsequent colonial expansion into the interior by farmers, missionaries, civil servants and troops extended British control over the outreaches of Cape Province and Natal, while rebellious Dutch farmers who trekked inland to escape the British influence founded the independent republics of the Transvaal and Orange Free State. In a century punctuated by military clashes between European settlers and indigenous African farmers, the latter gradually had to retreat to border areas to retain their autonomy, or else had to adapt to the encroaching capitalist life by becoming paid workers, often on their own ancestral lands.

The discovery of diamonds in Hopetown (1867) and gold on the Witwatersrand (1886) accelerated the process. The interior was quickly overrun by speculators, diggers, business people and – inevitably – politicians and imperialists from across the globe. Rapid urbanization, mechanization and more aggressive exploitation of labour followed, as did a myriad of secondary industries and organizations. The evolving capitalist society also brought touring theatre companies and entertainers from Britain and other parts of Europe in its wake, a factor of crucial importance for the way South African theatre and its theatrical system were to evolve over the twentieth century.

The Anglo-Boer War of 1899–1902 was an international *cause célèbre* in which the world rallied to support the 'gallant little republics' of Transvaal and Orange Free State in their struggle against the might of Britain. The war was also to become an important theme in South African literature. In 1910 the country was granted home rule as the Union of South Africa, with a Westminster-style democratic parliament. In 1961 it became the Republic of South Africa and seceded from the British Commonwealth – to which it returned only in 1995.

The parliament it created was predominantly for Europeans (that is to say whites) in much of the country with the so-called 'Coloureds' (people of mixed blood) and some Blacks being accepted in regions such as Cape Province. Thus individuals of African and Asian descent were treated as second-class citizens. As the new century dawned, a growing sense of injustice over this system began to emerge. This resulted in a clear drive towards resistance especially among the non-European population. Symptomatic of this was the founding, in 1912, of the South African Native National Congress (later to become the African National Congress or ANC), which was to go on to become one of the most prominent voices of opposition, in conjunction with a number of similar organizations founded during the course of the century.

Meanwhile Afrikaner cultural nationalism, a fully fledged drive to political, social and economic empowerment, stimulated the fight for autonomy for Afrikaners (speakers of

Afrikaans – the locally developed version of Dutch). This culminated in the 1948 victory by the National Party which would rule the country for the next forty-two years and which would devise and implement the notorious laws and policies which became known as 'apartheid' ('separateness'). Apartheid thinking was to dominate all aspects of life, including South Africa's arts and culture, for decades.

The initial resistance to racism and discrimination tended to be predominantly peaceful, but between 1960 and 1976 a series of bloody confrontations between the protesters and the police (e.g. at Cato Manor, Sharpeville, Langa and Soweto) changed everything irrevocably. Affected by the post-war winds of change blowing over the rest of Africa, the struggle for liberation – backed up by international boycotts and pressure – became militant, while white resistance to change generally hardened into ever-increasing political and social oppression. Between 1960 and 1990 this struggle was to inform every social, cultural and economic act, and give direction to the arts and artists of the country.

In 1990 the situation changed radically when President F.W. de Klerk (b. 1936) committed the National Party to negotiations by unbanning all political parties and eventually releasing all political detainees. This paved the way for discussions between all parties, the formation of an interim Government of National Unity and, in 1994, the first democratic elections and the inauguration of Nelson Mandela (b. 1918), a black lawyer and ANC leader who had been jailed by the government from 1963 to 1990, as the new republic's first State President.

Approaching the year 2000, South Africa was perhaps the most highly industrialized country in Africa as well as one of the most productive agricultural centres on the continent. Sociologically it remains a mixture of underdevelopment (particularly in rural areas) and highly developed urbanization, with the major cities constantly growing, western-style metropoles characterized by high-rise buildings, high-density living and technological sophistication. The removal of the apartheid laws restricting free movement has led to an unchecked increase in the urbanization process causing a major housing crisis in urban centres and the development of vast squatter communities – reputedly some 7 million people – on the outskirts of most cities.

This said, one legacy of the colonial and apartheid eras was that every city and virtually every major town also boasted well equipped cultural amenities: theatres, galleries, museums, libraries. In addition, South Africa had twenty-one major universities – a number with international reputations – eight influential scientific research councils, fifteen technikons and 123 technical colleges. In general, the education, health and social welfare systems were based on British models and worked well within the limits set for them. On the other hand, for most of the century such amenities were provided for and built in areas reserved exclusively for the white population, with only a fraction of state funds being allocated for the black population. The effect was catastrophic in most cases; rectifying these imbalances was a major priority of the Mandela government.

In 1995, South Africa's population numbered over 40 million, speaking eleven languages (Afrikaans, English, Ndebele, Xhosa, Zulu, Swati, Sesotho, Leboa, Setswana, Tshvenda and Xitsonga). In the 1910 Union constitution, English and Dutch (from 1925, Afrikaans) were declared the official languages of the country, with all other languages seen only as regional languages, but the post-1990 interim constitution recognized all eleven as official, though English still tends to serve as the *lingua franca*. This posed unique problems for public broadcasting (South African Broadcasting Corporation – SABC) and other such institutions.

This cultural mix has also impacted heavily on the range of cultural expression in the country, particularly since 1970. In this period, as the restrictions of apartheid were slowly lifted, African – rather than European – art forms began to receive both academic and artistic recognition, and African artists gained confidence and exposure. As a result, crossover forms and styles became more and more prominent, and multicultural and multilingual expression became the norm rather than the exception, leading to the creation of uniquely South African approaches and styles. Dance, music, oral poetry and storytelling have, of course, existed as prominent cultural and social activities on the continent for almost six thousand years. It was the coming of European colonization which introduced the notion of spoken theatre (as a formal and distinctly separate system) to the region. Over time, two performance systems developed: on the one hand there were the indigenous forms which were initially largely found within tribal contexts, particularly in non-urban areas, but later developed in a variety of more urbanized forms and styles. While they were a fundamental part of African cultural life and taken seriously by the African population itself, such forms were considered by the whites as only curiosities for tourists. They were not made part of the colonial theatrical system and were manifestly ignored by scholars and historians (anthropologists and ethnologists being the exceptions) until midway through the twentieth century.

On the other hand, the European-style theatre that the Dutch, French, German and particularly the British introduced between 1790 and 1880 provided the basis for most of the theatre system found in South Africa today. This was seen in both amateur dramatics and through regular visits of touring companies from London and Australia, 'playing the Empire'. It affected all aspects of the formal theatre system including the physical form of theatre spaces, the organizational system and the fundamental principles behind theatre as a representational art.

By about 1880 this imported theatre was becoming 'naturalized' and was beginning to adapt itself to local circumstances. This occurred under the influence of such contradictory impulses as British imperialism, Afrikaner nationalism and African nationalism, as well as the socio-political and economic events of the time: the Anglo-Boer War, establishment of the Union of South Africa in 1910, World War I, the enormous growth of the country as a commercial force and the devastating effect of the Great Depression in the 1930s.

Local authors, including the farceurs Stephen Black (c.1880–1931), Melt Brink (1842–1925) and C.J. Langenhoven (1873–1932) as well as the more seriously minded Louis Leipoldt (1880–1947) and H.I.E. Dhlomo (1903–56), now began to write and produce original South African texts, initially for the expanding amateur theatre movement, then for the emerging professional theatre system, led by producers such as Leonard Rayne (1869–1925), Hendrik Hanekom (1896–1952) and Andre Huguenet (1906–61). Shrewd investors, including the powerful African Consolidated Theatres of I.W. Schlesinger (1871–1949) and Harry Stodel (1869–1951), seized the opportunity and constructed a network of impressive theatres throughout the country.

Thus by the mid-1930s there were numerous professional companies operating in the cities, while more than thirty touring companies were servicing the rural towns, travelling by road and rail. The network of amateur groups was strong and prominent, leading to the formation of the Federation of Amateur Theatrical Societies of South Africa (FATSSA – 1934–60), under the directorship of P.P.B. Breytenbach (1904–84). Another important factor was a widespread publishing industry and an influential press which supported the arts. At the same time, black performance forms were evolving in their own way in the urban ghettos under such diverse influences as African traditional dance and music, the evolution of urban jazz and contemporary dance competitions, and the advent of radio and film.

A devastating drought, the Great Depression and World War II meant the virtual end of professional theatre. The rise of radio and film caused many of the major theatres to be turned into bioscopes (movie houses) and even the touring companies found themselves without audiences. So for almost fifteen years theatre largely became the province of the amateur or semi-professional again, with only the more powerful societies (e.g. the various repertory societies, Shakespeare circles and Gilbert and Sullivan societies in the major cities, as well as a number of large and dominant Afrikaans societies) providing occasional job opportunities for professional directors and actors.

This semi-amateur basis was – and would long remain – standard practice in the black community, deprived as it was of facilities and unable to develop its own performance traditions professionally because of the Eurocentric attitudes of the artistic and critical community.

This situation continued through the war years, further complicated by the fact that the war effort kept many talented artists in Europe and North Africa. In South Africa, the theatre was largely kept going by a number of highly qualified and experienced women, including Marda Vanne, Gwen ffrancon-Davies, Margaret Inglis, Leontine Sagan, Muriel Alexander, Anna Neethling-Pohl (1906–94) and Hermien Dommisse. A positive aspect of the war effort was the founding of the Union Defence Force (UDF) Entertainment Unit, set up by Major Myles Bourke to entertain the troops in the African and European campaigns with vaudeville-type shows. After the war, the entertainment industry could thus draw on a much larger pool of professionally experienced men and women of the theatre when setting up the new professional theatre which was to dominate the industry for the next twenty years.

After the war professional theatre in English resurrected itself quite rapidly. Directors such as Brian Brook (b. 1911), Taubie Kuschlick, and others mounted superb productions of the West End and Broadway hits of the season, while others (Leon Gluckman and Leonard Schach (b. 1918) did the more risky work of Tennessee Williams, John Osborne and the like, and even the occasional local play.

Formal classical theatre and Afrikaans theatre were slower in getting going again, but a superb Afrikaans *Hamlet* in 1947 brought a major breakthrough. After years of pressure from cultural organizations, the government relented and established the first state-supported theatre organization in the British Commonwealth: the National Theatre Organiz-ation (NTO – 1948–62). Directed by P.P.B. Breytenbach, NTO was a bilingual (Afrikaans and English) organization, centred in Pretoria, and intended to provide professional theatre for South African citizens, to provide work for local performers and to provide an outlet for local writing. In the course of its existence, this organization would undertake many tours through the country and perform over a hun-dred plays, classical as well as some by a wide range of local authors. By the late 1950s NTO had employed and trained a vast number of the performers, technicians and authors who were to go on and create the much more dynamic theatre of the 1960s and 1970s.

However this 'national' theatre was not national in any real sense: it was intended to serve the interest of whites only. In later years attempts were made to cater for and involve black needs in the planning, but this was largely tokenism and generally ignored the genuine needs and desires of the black commu-nities. As a result the townships surrounding the cities gradually strengthened and expanded their own cultural style and industry. Ironi-cally, a significant influence was once more the UDF Entertainment Unit. A number of the best township jazz artists had worked for the unit and on their return to their townships some of them formed a variety company which was to pioneer black entertainment in the cities. Tour-ing with an enormously popular variety show called *Zonk*, playing for white and black audiences, they paved the way for a whole range of such shows over many years. Embed-ded in a broader artistic explosion than occurred in Sophiatown during the 1950s, a renaissance led by the artists, writers, journal-ists, singers and musicians of the time, these performances paved the way for one of the most significant theatrical events of the period: an enormously popular indigenous musical about the rise and fall of a heavyweight boxer entitled *King Kong*. Put on in 1959, the pro-duction was a collaborative effort of black artists and white entrepreneurship which gave the local story and local performance styles a legitimacy they had previously lacked in the world of fashionable show business.

By popularizing a vital and distinctively black urban style of performance, these pro-ductions spurred a new industry in the 1960s and 1970s: the so-called 'township musical', perhaps best represented by the work of the extremely successful Gibson Kente. These writers adopted the musical comedy style and the melodramatic content of the *King Kong* format for purely commercial purposes.

By the mid-1950s, however, a growing wave of resistance had developed among writers and artists both in Afrikaans and English. This led to the first real break with the received tradi-tion of the British colonial theatre heritage and the beginnings of what was to become a long-term rift between the artist and the state. Much of this work shared a basic set of ideas: that theatre has to be politically relevant, that it has a right to be oppositional, that it should have its own voice.

This all started off rather slowly as a whole world of non-institutionalized and serious theatre began to evolve, revolving around such diverse organizations and individuals as Leon-ard Schach and the Cockpit Players, Athol Fugard (b. 1932) and the Serpent Players, and the Union of Southern African Artists and Natal Theatre Council in Durban. This period saw the appearance, for example, of a large number of so-called 'try-for-white' plays, including Athol Fugard's *Bloodknot*, Lewis Sowden's (1905–74) *Kimberley Train*, Basil Warner's *Try for White* and Bartho Smit's (b. 1934) *Die Verminktes* (*The Maimed*).

As it settled into power, the government gradually imposed segregation at all levels of social, political and cultural life. The 1960 clampdown on political organizations and resistance movements made segregation a political issue, but the promulgation of a series of Acts intended to separate the races, culmi-nating in the Group Areas and Separate Amenities Act (1965), directly affected the performing arts by effectively banning the presence of racially mixed casts on stage and racially mixed audiences in the theatre. Conversely, national and international pressure brought to bear on the government and the artists working in the country also impacted on the theatre.

At Athol Fugard's behest, an international playwrights' boycott was put in place by 1963, followed in 1966 by British Equity's ban on performers working in South Africa. Actions like these effectively set in motion the gradual isolation of artists and academics in the country. Ironically the initial effect of this was far more positive than negative, for it forced local writers and performers to make theatre by using and developing their own resources. In this way it enabled a playwriting tradition in English to establish itself firmly alongside the Afrikaans tradition.

The beginning of the 1960s also saw a troubled NTO make way for a larger, more ostentatious governmental scheme. In 1962 four regionally based Performing Arts Councils (PACs) were formed: Natal Performing Arts Council (NAPAC), Performing Arts Council of the Transvaal (PACT), Performing Arts Council of the Orange Free State (PACOFS) and Cape Performing Arts Board (CAPAB). Lavishly funded, they were responsible for theatre, music, opera and ballet in the four provinces. Over the next thirty years the councils were to do much to improve the quality of theatre for they offered fixed employment, expansive budgets and well-equipped theatres. As permanent companies of trained performers, they could mount a wide variety of fine productions ranging from the classical repertoire to the modern.

Unfortunately the PACs, like the NTO, were for whites only and focused exclusively on Eurocentric forms of theatre. However, they did offer writers in Afrikaans and English an opportunity for developing a quite formidable canon of new dramatic writing, and not all of it supportive of the regime. Indeed, some of the first essays into resistance theatre boldly occurred within the PACs' own workshop-theatres, notably PACT's Arena in Johannesburg, CAPAB's Theatre Laboratory in Cape Town and PACOFS's Presidensie Teater in Bloemfontein. Prominent writers whose works premièred with the PACs during this period include Chris Barnard (b. 1939), André P. Brink (b. 1935), Guy Butler (b. 1918), P.G. du Plessis (b. 1934), Pieter Fourie, Adam Small (b. 1936) and H.W.D. Manson (1926–69). However, the PACs did little for the other performance traditions until the beginning of the 1980s, when the government was forced to allow them to open up to all races and thus considerably broadened the scope of their activities.

All these trends came together at the beginning of the 1970s with the development of the so-called 'alternative' theatre movement. As the initial excitement of the PACs wore off and disillusion slowly set in, many came to believe that the real liberating influence could come only from groups outside the governmental sphere. The whole concept of improvisational and experimental performances as ways of raising the political consciousness of the performers and public attracted those opposing the status quo. As a result, a growing number of politically inclined independent theatrical producers surfaced in this period, and began to push the limits of the indigenous theatre beyond its European roots. Along with the groups mentioned earlier, these included Robert (Mshengu) Kavanagh's Theatre Workshop '71 (founded 1971), the Music, Dance, Arts and Literature Institute (MDALI – 1972), The People's Experimental Theatre (1973) and Junction Avenue Theatre (1976). However, two groups in particular are inextricably linked with the major thrust forward experienced in the 1970s. When Brian Astbury and Yvonne Bryceland (d. 1995) linked up with Athol Fugard and founded the Space Theatre in Cape Town in 1972, the tentative movement towards a serious and locally grown theatre of opposition became a virtual revolution. And when Mannie Manim and Barney Simon (1934–85) followed suit in Johannesburg and founded The Company in 1974 and the Market Theatre in 1976, a new pattern was firmly set. By focusing on a multifaceted agenda of oppositional theatre, by promoting local work, by allowing experimentation and training for disadvantaged people, these groups not only actively helped to broaden the scope and alter the form of South African theatre, but also gave it a distinctive character and status. By the 1980s the Market had become South Africa's unofficial 'national' theatre.

Such was the situation until the late 1980s when the collapse of apartheid and the new political realities in the country altered much of this, particularly since many of the plays from this earlier period had lost much of their impact. During the 1990s, the role and funding of the arts became a point of heated debate. Structurally, however, South African theatre

The 1972 PACT production of P.G. du Plessis's drama *Siener in die Suburbs* (*Seer in the Suburbs*), directed by François Swart for the Performing Arts Council of the Transvaal.
Photo: Bob Martin.

remained much as before, though the straitened economy and altered attitudes towards the importance of the arts impacted heavily on the industry. Essentially the same four basic traditions (spoken Eurocentric drama, western-style indigenous theatre, crossover workshop theatre and traditional indigenous performance forms) continue to develop in the country, mostly along parallel lines. However, there are clear signs that increasing cross-fertilization may be taking place, that the individual forms are less clearly linked to specific companies and groups and that the country in the 1990s was in the midst of a search for new structures, forms and styles to suit the rainbow nation of a newly emerging South Africa.

Structure of the National Theatre Community

The colonial legacy in South Africa left a very well-developed infrastructure for formal theatre ranging from subsidized state and civic theatre companies to commerical and experimental groups with their own range of venues.

State-funded buildings such as the Pretoria State Theatre, Nico Theatre Complex in Cape Town, Sand du Plessis Theatre in Bloemfontein and Natal Playhouse in Durban are primarily used by the state-funded Performing Arts Councils for their own productions, or productions co-sponsored by them. Buildings in smaller urban centres are also managed by PACs (e.g. Windybrow Complex in Johannesburg, the Opera House in Port Elizabeth and the Oppenheimer Theatre in Welkom).

There are as well a variety of civic theatre complexes, mostly in cities without state theatres. Johannesburg Civic Theatre is by far the largest and most prestigious of these and has its own production company. Other civic theatre venues, such as those in Bellville, Roodepoort, Witbank, Bloemfontein and Kimberley, are provided by the cities and hired out by local and touring companies, amateur groups and even schools.

Some cities even have independently endowed theatre complexes. The Baxter Theatre (1977) in Cape Town, for example, was built with money donated by the Baxter family and other donors, on ground provided by the University of Cape Town. A superb design by Jack Barnett, the multipurpose complex houses a concert hall, a main theatre, a studio theatre and many other facilities. Run as a commercial venture, it had for a period of time its own company, but is also let to visiting companies and boasts having never had one dark night. Over the years it has presented a wide spectrum of work, from militant protest theatre to new indigenous plays and European classics to drawing-room comedy and popular musicals.

There are more than a hundred purely commercial performance venues across the country. The most prominent name in this area is that of the entrepreneur Pieter Toerien, whose modest but comfortable proscenium-style theatres include the extremely successful Richard Haines, Leonard Rayne and Alhambra Theatres in Johannesburg, and the Theatre on the Bay in Cape Town. Other well-known and successful commercial theatres are the African Cultural Centre in Johannesburg, Dock Road Theatre in Cape Town, Orient Theatre in Durban, Intimate Theatre in Johannesburg and Winston Churchill Theatre in Pietermaritzburg.

The best known summer theatre and one of the most magical to attend (complete with picnic basket and chilled bottle of Cape wine) is the open-air Maynardville Theatre in Cape Town. The annual Shakespeare production at Maynardville was the brain-child of Cecilia Sonnenberg and René Ahrenson, aided by the British director and actor Leslie French. Opened in 1956, it has presented an annual Shakespeare production to packed houses for more than forty years. Other such venues include Mannville in Port Elizabeth, the Pieter Scholtz Open Air Theatre in Durban and the Oude Libertas Amphitheatre in Stellenbosch.

The intimate revue and cabaret venue became exceedingly popular in the 1980s and early 1990s. Often combined with a restaurant and/or bar, these transient, generally urban venues number in the several hundreds offering the individual artist a space in which to perform at a time when state funding for larger theatre and media projects was being drastically curtailed and full-time employment scarce.

Tickets for virtually all performances in South Africa may now be bought from the ubiquitous Computicket outlets (created by Percy Tucker), a nation-wide computer network, which allows one to reserve tickets for any show, anywhere in the country.

Producers tend to consider South African theatre tickets cheap, since they hardly cover production costs, but the truth is they are expensive for the country's mass of potential consumers. The average play at a state or commercial theatre would cost about 25 rand (whereas in comparison, cinema tickets are 15 rand and a loaf of ordinary white bread 2.50).

As a result shoestring and/or alternative theatre groups make use of cheaper 'found' spaces. This is especially true in the so-called 'townships' and the shanty towns around the cities. Marketing is by occasional poster and word of mouth, while the performances are difficult to access for outsiders. Usually one has to work through local cultural associations or cooperatives to get invited and to find (or be escorted to) the particular venue.

More traditional African indigenous performance forms are mostly found in rural areas, in spaces allocated for this. Again, access is through community organizations rather than commercial channels.

The country hosts a number of annual cultural festivals, the largest and most notable being the Standard Bank National Arts Festival (more popularly known as the Grahamstown Festival). Held every July (during the South African winter) this heavily sponsored festival has a full-time office in the Monument Theatre. The formal side of the conference encompasses a main festival of invited artists, performers and performances, a jazz festival, a film festival, a student drama festival and a schools drama festival. The informal side of the festival, which groups and individuals join on application, takes the form of an enormous and constantly expanding fringe of theatre, music and other activities, including a sprawling flea market, countless buskers, and numerous food stalls. Many academic and other societies and associations combine their annual conferences with this event. Main festival events are booked out months in advance. Involving as it does representatives from almost all spheres of the performing arts, at all levels, this festival is a vast showcase of South African theatre.

Other festivals of note are the Potpourri Festival of new plays in Pretoria and Johannesburg, the Johannesburg Arts Alive Festival in September, Durban Arts Festival and Kleinkaroo Kunstefees (Little Karoo Arts Festival) in Oudtshoorn over Easter. In 1996 the latter combined with the annual Kampustoneel (Campus Theatre) festival (started in 1981), an extremely successful exercise in promoting playwriting. Over the years a large number of new Afrikaans plays have been tried out by student companies from the various university drama departments. A number of the major Afrikaans playwrights originally made their début there.

Theatre awards in the country are usually sponsored by large commercial companies and the majority are regional in nature. For example, there are the Dalro Awards in Gauteng and the Fleur du Cap Awards in the Western Cape recognizing excellence in performance, directing, design and the like. The Vita Awards are the only ones awarded on a regional basis as well as on a national basis. Besides awards for best text of the year in all the above, there are a number of specific awards for dramatists as well. The best known is the large Amstel Playwright of the Year Award, a playwriting competition. Dramatists also qualify for the numerous literary awards, among which are the Hertzog Prize (for writing in Afrikaans, awarded in turn for prose, poetry and drama), and the CNA (Central News Agency) Prize.

The theatre industry is organized by and around a number of organizations and agencies. While there are a large number of casting agencies in the country and some very comprehensive casting directories (e.g. The Limelight and Contacts), there are virtually no literary agents; authors negotiate their own contracts with publishers and companies, while prominent local authors make use of agents in England and the United States. Performing rights for all plays produced in the country may be obtained from the Dramatic, Artistic and Literary Rights Organization (DALRO) in Johannesburg, a private organization founded in 1968 to represent virtually all South African authors and a large number of international agencies. Another useful institution is the National Drama Library in Bloemfontein (founded in 1933), which supplies its members (mainly schools, universities and amateur theatre groups) with complete performance sets of plays and publishes regular catalogues of its holdings.

There are a number of theatre and performing arts related organizations and trade unions, some of the more important being the South African Institute of Theatre Technicians, Arts and Entertainment Peace Committee, Consultative Committee (work permits for the entertainment industry), Film and Allied Workers Organization (FAWO), Performing Arts Workers Equity (PAWE) and the South African Theatre Producers Forum.

Artistic Profile

There are, broadly speaking, four types of theatre in the country – a European tradition, a European-styled indigenous tradition, traditional indigenous performance forms and what can be called a crossover workshop tradition. In each there are a variety of combinations of music, dance and spoken drama. The first three are relatively autonomous, but the last one is perhaps the most pervasive and difficult to pinpoint.

European-style spoken drama is still very central to South African theatre and the formal distinctions between the various genres are retained. There are formal musicals (from popular musical comedy to full-scale opera), dance (ballet and contemporary), and the classical and contemporary works of everyone from Shakespeare and Molière to Tom Stoppard and Heiner Müller. The state-funded theatres and fully commercial companies tend to do this kind of work. Classical opera and ballet companies are run by the four subsidized Performing Arts Councils, being too expensive for any single commercial company to afford and maintain.

Within the European-style indigenous theatre the categories remain musicals, dance, opera, and formal drama. The few local operas written are usually presented by the Performing Arts Councils, but the plays and dances (particularly contemporary forms) are produced by commercial companies as well. The plays produced in this category make up the bulk of the canon of South African drama. At the same time an explosion took place in contemporary dance and particularly dance drama from the mid-1980s, with a number of new companies and choreographers coming to the fore. Among them are the Gauteng-based PACT Dance Company, Free Flight Dance Company and Soweto Dance Theatre (1994); Cape Town's Jazzart Dance Company (1975) and Gary Gordon's First Physical Company in Grahamstown (1994). The works tend to be uncompromising, focused on social and other issues, and drawing on a wide range of traditions, often also on indigenous African styles and forms.

The term 'traditional indigenous performance' is a rather contentious notion, but the best available to refer to the range of African performance forms and styles in the country. Given the heterogeneity of the population it is impossible even to mention them all, but good examples are found in the indigenous dances, music and praise poetry which featured so prominently in the internationally televised inauguration ceremony for President Nelson Mandela. However, (South) African jazz, African gospel music, funeral services, Hindu dances, Afrikaner, Xhosa, Zulu and Sotho storytelling, are all notable examples of performance events which contain a sizeable theatrical component in their execution. Indeed they have recently become the focal point of research and writings by both local and international scholars, presenting as they do tantalizing glimpses of the region's vibrant oral culture.

However, the real growth-points of South African theatre have been those works which seem to pull the above three traditions together in one performance, often incorporating a sizeable music, song and/or dance element. Referred to inter alia as 'alternative theatre', 'hybrid theatre', 'syncretic theatre' and

'crossover theatre', this kind of performance text had its genesis in the 'township musicals' of the 1950s and 1960s and the experimental workshops of the 1970s and early 1980s. This improvisational approach relies heavily on performance and makes use of an eclectic mixture of performance traditions and acting styles to tell a story or address a problem. Even more conventional productions make use of it today: from the semi-professional and amateur township plays to the more formal works of the PACs and the Market Theatre. With all its weaknesses (such plays are often aurally and visually stimulating, but thematically unstructured and textually unfocused), the process has produced some of the most vibrant theatrical experiences from the 1970s through the 1990s. Among them are such memorable works as *Women of Crossroads* (Theatre Workshop '71, produced 1975), *Woza Albert!* (Simon, Kani and Mtwa, 1981), *District Six – The Musical* (Kramer and Pietersen, 1987), *U'Phu Van Der Merwe* (Market Theatre, 1987), *Sophiatown* (Junction Avenue Theatre, 1986), *Sarafina* (Mbongeni Ngema, 1987) and *Marabi* (Junction Avenue Theatre Company, 1982, revived 1995). The annual festivals, such as the Grahamstown National Arts Festival, are excellent places to view such works.

One of the major spin-offs of this kind of work has been the evolution of community-based theatre into what is broadly referred to as 'theatre-for-development'. Encompassing everything from people's theatre and workers' theatre to industrial theatre and live advertising, the central notion is that of social intervention through techniques of dramatization. An extremely important consciousness-raising weapon during the cultural and political struggles of 1970–90, the needs of the new South African democracy have made special demands on these companies. The new government's Reconstruction and Development Programme gives priority support to projects such as health programmes (including AIDS education), voter education programmes, and job training programmes. The process, however, is causing a gap between this kind of functional dramaturgy and the more aesthetic playmaking processes of the formal theatre.

Companies

Theatre companies range from full-time professional companies to part-time amateur

Friedman also became hugely popular with the country-wide Puppets Against AIDS tours he undertook with his assistant Nyanga Tshabalala in 1989 and 1994.

The Johannesburg and Pretoria areas have been growth points for marionettes. For example, the Johannesburg Civic Theatre not only formed the first permanent professional marionette group but also presented the first national marionette workshop in 1977 in association with the Department of National Education. The quality of the work done by Little Marionette Company, a semi-professional group from Pretoria under the leadership of Hansie Visagie, led to this group representing South Africa in 1983 at marionette festivals in Austria.

The state-subsidized Performing Arts Councils unfortunately never really accepted puppetry as an art form and therefore did not create permanent puppet companies, but rather tended to contract private groups to visit schools as part of their theatre for youth work. As a result professional puppetry never really developed in the country.

However, one company has really done much to reverse this trend and rekindle a wide interest in the puppet theatre as a versatile theatrical form and the puppet as an invaluable aid to theatre in general. Handspring Puppet Company is South Africa's most prominent professional puppet troupe at present. A fully professional company with Adrian Kohler and Basil Jones as permanent members, its activities include formal performances for both children and adults, involvement in health-care and development work, lecturing at tertiary institutions and even mounting exhibitions (the most extensive of which was 'Unmasking the Puppet' at UNISA during 1987). Productions for children have included *Mbira for Passela* and other plays based on African folktales, and original animal stories such as *Gertie's Feathers*, which also toured Namibia and Botswana.

One of Handspring's most significant contributions has been in the field of puppet theatre for adults. In a country which still associates puppets mostly with children – in spite of pioneering work with puppet cabarets by players such as Toby van Eyck (b. 1942) – they managed to break away and create a niche for themselves. In 1985 Esther van Ryswyk directed them in a puppet play based on David Lytton's indigenous political radio drama, *Episodes of an Easter Rising*. The main

character is a wounded and unjustly treated black man, portrayed as a Christ-like figure. In the open performance area lighting effects were used not only to focus attention on the marionettes, but also at times to illuminate the manipulators.

In 1988 van Ryswyk used the Handspring Puppet Company for her own production of *A Midsummer Night's Dream*, combining puppets and actors. The visual impact and African character of Kohler's puppets (representing the fairy denizens of the dreamworld) were astounding. Operated on long rods, they were not the conventional idea of fairies, but almost nightmarish apparitions in the form of huge fish, skeletal flying creatures, goblin-like beings, and in the cases of Oberon and Titania, 4-metre-high statues with movable arms and heads. The actors spoke some of their lines from inside the puppets, and then – as the characters assumed more human qualities – they stepped out of the puppets to become human sized performers. In the Pyramus and Thisbe play-within-a-play, crude rag-doll puppets were used to charge the broadly comic interlude.

In a bold new collaboration with artist and film-maker William Kentridge as director, designer and animator, and using Louis Seboko, Busi Zokufa and Tale Motsepa as the three principal actors, the company did a puppet and film adaptation of Büchner's *Woyzeck* in 1992. Entitled *Woyzeck on the Highveld*, the play commented on modern South Africa through a multilayered structure using rear-projected animation of filmed charcoal drawings and ink-drawn shadow puppets. In front of the screen, roughly carved wooden rod-puppets were manipulated by four puppeteers and an actor. On the animated backdrop, Woyzeck's explosive inner world not only conveyed a sense of his South African environment, but also gave the audience an interpretation of his visions. The distance between the inner world as projected on the screen and the action on stage form the thin line between Woyzeck's twisted dream and reality.

In 1995 Handspring the experimentation further with its production of *Faustus in Africa*. With Kentridge directing, the play once again integrated film animation, actors and puppets. The script combined sections of *Part One* and fragments of *Part Two* from Bulgakov's *The Master and Margarita* and new material by the South African poet Iesega Rampotokeng, so that the idealism of Goethe's

The 1992 Handspring Puppet Company production of *Woyzeck on the Highveld,* directed and designed by William Kentridge.
Photo: Ruphin Coudyzer.

Faust is tested against the more earthy materialism of colonial Africa.

By integrating art forms such as dance, music, animated film, live actors and object animation into a new *Gesamtkunstwerk,* the productions of the Handspring Puppet Company reflect and reinforce the belief that puppetry can be a powerful tool in the evolution of the new crossover theatre in the country.

On an organizational basis, South Africa long retained its links with the international community through affiliate membership in the Union Internationale de la Marionette (UNIMA; International Puppeteers' Union). In 1977, under the leadership of Lily Hertzberg in Cape Town and Alida van Deventer (b. 1962) in Johannesburg, South Africa became a full member of this international body.

Marie Kruger

Theatre Space and Architecture

Most theatre in South Africa takes place in formal spaces, usually theatre complexes reserved for the performing arts, or multi-functional public halls in the case of the more informal, semi-professional and amateur theatre. Such spaces vary greatly in their adaptability, but proscenium theatre remains a favourite configuration, with the thrust stage and theatre-in-the-round found in more experimental venues. This tendency is reinforced by theatre architecture in the country as well as by the theatre training, trends at the various festivals and spaces of the sponsored cultural facilities (e.g. Barlow Arts Trust Centre in Durban and Market Theatre Precinct in Johannesburg).

There are in total five large-scale, multipurpose European style and superbly equipped theatre complexes in the country. Each city has at least one fully equipped major theatre, larger centres have more. The state theatres typically contain large proscenium-style drama and opera theatres, often a concert hall, one or more smaller, more experimental spaces, rehearsal rooms, workshops and design studios and administrative offices. The majority of the civic theatre complexes are well-equipped proscenium style theatres, seating upwards of 300 people. Thus the Oppenheimer Theatre in Welkom, Sasol Theatre in Sasolburg and Secunda Theatre in the Northern province were built by local governmental structures in conjunction with large local businesses, and are used in the same way as civic theatres.

Similarly, the Monument Theatre in Grahamstown was built as a multipurpose theatre and conference venue by the 1820 Settler's Foundation to commemorate the contribution of the British settlers. With its fine climate, the country has a number of open-air theatres, mainly used for summer festivals (November to February).

There are more than fifteen university, college and technikon theatres (the majority are professionally equipped, multipurpose teaching facilities) and numerous amateur theatres, including some quite impressive structures (e.g. the Playhouse in Somerset West, Ford Little Theatre in Port Elizabeth, Breughel Theatre in Stellenbosch and Joseph Stone Auditorium in Athlone, Cape Town). Then there are the innumerable school halls, civic halls and informal theatre venues, which are utilized as theatre spaces in nearly every town in the country.

The traditional use of a flexible and open public space is still very evident in performances in rural areas, though that too is being adapted to other venues as these performance forms are brought to festivals and urban theatres as formal performance pieces. However, the ideas of the village 'common' as a performance space, or the campfire as scene for storytelling, are also filtering back into mainstream theatrical form, affecting the structure and style of contemporary writing and performance as new forms and styles evolve.

Training

Theatre training occurs both informally and formally. Informal training occurs primarily through direct involvement in the semi-professional and amateur theatre organizations that proliferate in the country, particularly in historically disadvantaged communities. Numerous performers have made their way into the professional theatre and media through this kind of apprenticeship, particularly as the discriminatory measures of the apartheid regime began to crumble toward the end of the 1970s and theatres became more fully integrated. For most non-white performers that

was the only way, since formal theatre training had been largely reserved for white students only until the late 1970s. By the mid-1990s formal training was widely accessible to everyone.

Formal training takes place in three ways. The oldest form (beyond pure apprenticeship) is the private drama and elocution class. There are still hundreds of such teachers and private schools, working independently or through primary and high schools and most of them are affiliated to the South Africa Guild of Speech Teachers (founded 1945). The students usually take an international certification exam. In the late 1980s a number of more theatre-oriented schools opened, either as private schools and training cooperatives or affiliated with professional theatre companies. Notable examples are the Funda Centre in Soweto, the Federated Union of Black Artists, Afrika Cultural Centre and Market Theatre Laboratory in Johannesburg; the Community Arts Project and Jazzart in Cape Town.

There are high school drama classes, offered by a limited number of schools in the various provinces as a formal part of the curriculum. The five-year course in drama (theory and practice) falls under the auspices of the various provincial education departments and students write a departmental examination. The graduates tend to go directly into the industry, or continue their studies at a tertiary institution.

Eleven tertiary institutions offer full diploma and degree courses in drama and theatre. They tend to follow the North American model, combining theoretical study with practical training in their own theatre complexes. While they have different emphases in terms of teaching, there is a move to coordinate and evolve a core syllabus, in order to facilitate interchange of students between institutions.

University and technikon fees are partially subsidized and there are extensive bursary and loan schemes in most cases. Jobs come in various ways. For instance, annual auditions are held on every campus by the state-funded Performing Arts Councils and some other private theatre, film and television companies, while talent scouts from the various organizations attend the many student festivals during the year. Open auditions are advertised by many companies and most students are also encouraged to obtain an agent as soon as possible.

The only non-university institution offering a complete course in theatre is the Pretoria Technikon founded in 1974 and offering largely practical courses in theatre technology, design, acting, film, dance, opera and musical theatre. Students obtain Technical Diplomas in the field. A number of other technikons do offer courses in selected aspects of theatre and the performing arts.

The universities all provide a basic Bachelor of Arts degree in drama, some also have a four-year Bachelor of Drama degree, and they all offer post-graduate options (usually Honours, MA and PhD). By and large they train students in the fundamentals of stage acting and the theory and history of theatre, though each university also has a few areas of specialization, which distinguish it from the rest.

The University of Cape Town (UCT) School of Speech and Drama is the oldest such institution in the country, starting speech classes in 1919 and becoming a fully fledged department in 1942, with Rosalie van der Gucht as first professor. Besides degree courses, UCT also has a specialized Performer's Diploma. This department concentrates on undergraduate training and has long had the reputation of being the best acting school in the country. Its teaching staff has included some of the country's foremost directors, including Robert Mohr and Mavis Taylor. Other specializations include Drama-in-Education and Theatre-for-Development.

The Department of Speech and Drama at the University of Natal, Durban, was founded by Elizabeth Sneddon in 1949 and started out with an emphasis on speech communication. Its strengths have now expanded to theatre design and children's theatre. There is also a department on the Pietermaritzburg campus of the same university, with the same profile, but with a focus on Drama-in-Education and community theatre.

The University of Stellenbosch near Cape Town had been teaching voice and oratory since 1910, but was formally constituted in 1953 with the appointment of Belgian actor/director Fred Engelen as the first professor. Originally an Afrikaans medium institution, it now trains performers, directors and theatre technicians in Afrikaans and English. Other areas of specialization include cabaret, children's theatre, puppetry and film and media studies. The department plays a prominent role in contemporary theatre research and houses a Centre for Theatre and Performance Studies.

The School of Dramatic Art at the University of the Witwatersrand in Johannesburg (founded 1975 with David Horner as first head) offers a host of specializations including movement, design and community theatre. The department also has a comprehensive and influential course in film and television production, while it has for many years featured a strong interest in research, a point reflected in a substantial post-graduate enrolment and staff members' involvement with various academic journals and publications. Its Performing Arts Centre, managed by Mannie Manim, has become an important venue in the country.

The Drama Department of the University of Pretoria was founded in 1965 with philosopher-sociologist Geoff Cronje as its first professor. For many years it was the most prominent research university in the country, employing three major theorists and historians as staff members (the most prominent being F.C.L. Bosman (1898–1981)). The subsequent appointment of experienced performers as staff members (notably Anna Neethling-Pohl) caused the emphasis to shift considerably, the department gaining renown for its acting and directing courses. Its children's theatre and puppetry courses are also of importance.

The University of the Orange Free State's Drama Department in Bloemfontein (founded in 1965 by Belgian actor Jo Gevers) offers playwriting and children's theatre among its specializations, while the Drama Department at Rhodes University (founded in the 1960s by Roy Sergeant) focuses on movement and physical theatre, and has a growing post-graduate component as well as a professional performing company devoted to these two aspects.

The two remaining university drama departments have long had a specific ethnic focus and in a sense retain these, having turned them into points of specific growth. The University of Durban-Westville was founded to cater for the Asian (mostly Indian) community in the country, and the drama department (begun by David Horner in 1975) has gradually focused its attention – in training and, perhaps more importantly, in research and publication – on the vastly underrated tradition of what they term Indic theatre in the country.

The University of Zululand was founded as a state university to take in Zulu students; its drama department, started by Johan Bernard (b. 1945) in the 1970s, has turned this narrow focus to its advantage, by exploring training in and research on aspects of indigenous theatre not accessible to other departments. The department has achieved wide recognition for its research programmes, particularly in the fields of Drama-in-Education and Theatre-for-Development.

Criticism, Scholarship and Publishing

A few early actor-managers, journalists, dilettantes and travellers have left descriptions of the theatrical, cultural and social life among the colonial settlers from the seventeenth to the nineteenth centuries, while a few of these and other travellers, missionaries and anthropologists have provided scanty but invaluable descriptions and interpretations of what they saw as the 'pagan practices' among the 'African natives' during the same period.

However, in South Africa the whole concept of academic theatre research in the western sense really dates from two disparate sources. First, there was the formidable and painstaking historical detective work by F.C.L. Bosman. His doctoral dissertation was entitled 'Drama en Toneel in Suid-Afrika' (Drama and Theatre in South Africa) and was published in 1928. Based on his meticulous reading of all the newspapers, brochures, posters and programmes in the state archives and the state libraries of the country, it describes the history of colonial theatre in the country from 1652 to 1855. A monumental work, the book is the starting point for any researcher in the field. Bosman continued his study of theatre in the

country to the end of his life, publishing a second volume (1855–1916) in 1980. A number of his students, or researchers influenced by his work, continued the task of writing the history of theatre and dramatic literature in the country, focusing particularly on the contribution of Afrikaans and English playwrights and players. An extremely valuable English summary of Bosman's main findings was produced by Jill Fletcher in 1994.

While the work produced by these researchers was of immense value for understanding the colonial contribution to theatre and performance, their recognition of the African contribution was scant, as was their contribution to theory. H.I.E. (Herbert) Dhlomo, playwright, journalist, teacher and cultural activist, was a catalyst in this respect. Dhlomo not only was involved in promoting drama and amateur theatre among the black population, but also wrote and published an extraordinary series of articles in the 1940s in which he explored the nature and purpose of drama in (Southern) Africa. These articles were rediscovered and published in the journal *English Studies in*

Africa in the 1970s, as part of the renaissance in theatre studies in South Africa.

Much of the research remained focused on generalized literary histories and overviews until the mid-1970s, with the notion of performance studies receiving scant attention and local writing in English or the African languages not being considered an important field of study. But then, led by Stephen Gray (b. 1941), a number of younger researchers began to publish articles and research papers focused on theatre and performance in the country, particularly of contemporary and non-western forms. This revival culminated in the establishment of four major journals, a commitment to the publication of local plays by a number of dynamic new publishers, the formation of a national Association of Drama Departments, a sharp increase in post-graduate enrolment in theatre and performance studies at certain universities and the founding of a formal Documentation Centre for the Performing Arts (1971–8) at the Human Sciences Research Council under the directorship of P.P.B. Breytenbach and Rinie Stead (b. 1914). Housing more than 300,000 documents, this expanded further to become the Centre for South African Theatre Research (1979–88), under the directorship of Temple Hauptfleisch (b. 1945).

The years 1984–5 were particularly important, because five book-length publications and one unpublished thesis appeared, which in a sense radically changed the direction and focus of research in the country by focusing on a range of neglected yet exciting areas. Thus Peter Larlham (b. 1945) introduced the study of indigenous performance forms, while David Coplan, Robert Kavanagh and Ian Steadman (b. 1951) did the same for black urban performance. Kavanagh, in particular, introduced a strong cultural-materialist approach which was to influence such studies for much of the 1980s.

Another kind of shift came with Hauptfleisch and Steadman's 1984 volume of South African plays which, for the first time since Bosman's pioneering work, sought to incorporate a more representative range of local playwriting into the history of South African theatre. Controversial though some of its introduction was, it influenced the direction of research by pointing to the shift taking place from a segmented, linguistically and ethnically defined set of theatre subsystems to a more encompassing South African system. This notion was to become a central feature of evolving theories of post-apartheid theatre.

Following on this initial burst of activity, other individual researchers joined those mentioned above in making significant contributions (through research reports, theses, articles, lectures and books) to broaden the scope of research to encompass fields beyond the narrow confines of written literature or formal theatre. Particularly prominent were Lynn Dalrymple, Martin Orkin, Ari Sitas and Keyan Tomaselli.

There are now numerous public and private archives and libraries in the country with sizeable holdings in South African theatre. Of these, four specialize in particular aspects of the performing arts: the South African Centre for Information on the Arts in Pretoria, which had taken over the vast holdings of the now defunct Centre for South African Theatre Research in Pretoria and combined them with their own considerable holdings on South African film; National English Literary Museum in Grahamstown; Nasionale Afrikaanse Literêre Museum en Navorsingssentrum in Bloemfontein, and Mayebuye Centre at the University of the Western Cape.

As far as research centres go, there is one focused purely on theatre: the Centre for Theatre and Performance Studies at the University of Stellenbosch (founded 1994) is a clearinghouse, information centre and an active research centre engaged in a number of research programmes on the theory, history and function of theatre in South Africa.

There are a number of other centres which touch on aspects of theatre and performance. These include the Centre for Cultural and Media Studies at the University of Natal in Durban, Institute for the Study of English in Africa at Rhodes University, and Centre for the Study of African Language and Literature at the University of Durban, Westville.

Most of the South African academic literary journals (there are more than a dozen) take articles on drama, but three journals specialize largely in the academic study of theatre and performance. The *SAADYT Journal* (founded 1979) focuses on drama and theatre for youth and is published by the South African Association for Drama and Youth Theatre. *Shakespeare in South Africa* (founded 1988) is edited by Laurence Wright for the society and is published by the Institute for the Study of English in Africa. *The South African Theatre Journal* (founded 1987) is edited by Temple Hauptfleisch and Ian Steadman and published by the Centre for Theatre and Performance

Studies at the University of Stellenbosch. *Critical Arts* (founded in the 1980s), edited by Keyan Tomaselli and published by the University of Natal, focuses more widely on media and cultural issues, but has a particular interest in performance studies as well.

The publishing industry in South Africa is varied and well established; despite the small market for published plays, many publishers have plays and critical works on theatre on their lists. Besides numerous international publishers which have offices in the country (e.g. Oxford University Press, Routledge, Methuen, McGraw-Hill), the major publishing houses are Tafelberg, Van Schaik, Human en Rousseau, Juta, Kagiso (formerly HAUM Publishers), Ravan Press, Ad Donker, David Philip, Jonathan Ball and Witwatersrand University Press.

Temple Hauptfleisch

Further Reading

Astbury, Brian. *The Space*. Cape Town: Moira and Azriel Fine, 1979.

Blecher, Hilary. 'Goal Oriented Theatre in the Winterveld'. *Critical Arts,* 1 no. 3 (1980): 23–39.

Bosman, F. Christiaan Ludolph. *Drama en Toneel in Suid-Afrika, Deel I: 1652–1855* [Drama and theatre in South Africa. Volume 1:, 1652–1855]. Amsterdam/Pretoria: J.H. de Bussy, 1928. Volume II: 1855–1916. Pretoria: J.L. van Schaik, 1980.

——. *The Dutch and English Theatre in South Africa, 1800 till Today, and the Afrikaans Drama*. Pretoria: J.H. de Bussy, 1951.

Brink, André P. *Aspekte van die Nuwe Drama* [Aspects of the new drama]. Pretoria: Academica, 1986.

Brown, Duncan, and Bruno van Dyk, eds. *Exchanges: South African Writing in Transition*. Pietermaritzburg: University of Natal Press, 1991. 125 pp.

Chapman, Michael, Colin Gardner and Es'kia Mphahlele, eds. *Perspectives on South African English Literature*. Johannesburg: Ad Donker, 1992.

Coplan, David B. *In Township Tonight! South Africa's Black City Music and Theatre*. Johannesburg: Ravan, 1985.

Daymond, M.J., J.U. Jacobs and M. Lenta, eds. *Momentum: On Recent South African Writing*. Pietermaritzburg: University of Natal Press, 1984.

Dhlomo, H.I.E. *Collected Works*. Nick Visser and Tim Couzens, eds. Johannesburg: Ravan, 1985.

Du Toit, P.J. *Amateurtoneel in Suid-Afrika* [Amateur theatre in South Africa]. Pretoria: Academica, 1988.

Fletcher, Jill. *The Story of the African Theatre 1780–1930*. Cape Town: Vlaeberg, 1994.

Friedman, Gary. 'Puppets Against Apartheid: From a Series of Letters, Papers and Press Cuttings'. *Animations* 9, no. 3 (February–March 1986): 48–9.

Fuchs, Anne. *Playing the Market: The Market Theatre, Johannesburg, 1976–1986*. Contemporary Theatre Series. London: Harwood, 1990. 183 pp.

Fugard, Athol. 'Scenes from a Censored Life'. *American Theatre* 7, no. 8 (November 1990): 30–5.

Glasser, Mona. *King Kong: A Venture in the Theatre*. Cape Town: Norman Howell, 1960.

Gray, Stephen, ed. *Athol Fugard,* Cape Town: Maskew Miller, 1980.

——. 'Desegregating the Theatre'. *Index on Censorship* 14, no. 4 (1985): 11–14, 17.

——. *Southern African Literature: An Introduction*. London: David Philip, 1979.

——. 'Women in South African Theatre'. *South African Theatre Journal* 4, no. 1 (1990): 75–87.

Greyvenstein, Walter. 'The History and Development of Children's Theatre in English in South Africa'. DLitt and PhD dissertation, Rand Afrikaans University, 1988.

Gunner, Liz, ed. *Politics and Performance: Theatre, Poetry and Song in South Africa*. Johannesburg: Witwatersrand University Press, 1994.

Hammond-Tooke, David. *The Roots of Black South Africa*. Johannesburg: Johnathan Ball, 1993.

Hauptfleisch, Temple, ed. *The Breytie Book: A Collection of Articles on South African Theatre*. Johannesburg: Limelight, 1985.

——. 'From the Savoy to Soweto: The Shifting Paradigm in South African Theatre'. *South African Theatre Journal* 2, no. 1 (1988): 35–63.

Hauptfleisch, Temple and Ian Steadmen, eds. *South African Theatre: Four Plays and an Introduction*. Pretoria: HAUM Educational, 1984. 250 pp.

Hauptfleisch, Temple, H.C. Gruenewals, P. Kohler and J.L. Marais, eds. *Research on South African Literature and Race Relations*. Pretoria: Human Sciences Research Council, 1986. 80 pp.

Hauptfleisch, Temple, Wilma Viljoen and Câeleste Van Greunen. *Athol Fugard: A Source Guide*. Johannesburg: Ad Donker, 1980. 126 pp.

Kannemeyer, J.C. *Geskiedenis van die Afrikaanse*

Literatuur I [The history of Afrikaans literature I]. Pretoria: Academica, 1978.

———. *Geskiedenis van die Afrikaanse Literatuur II* [The history of Afrikaans literature II]. Pretoria: Academica, 1983.

Kavanagh, Robert Mshengu, ed. *South African People's Plays*. London: Heinemann, 1981.

———. *Theatre and Cultural Struggle in South Africa*. London: Zed Books, 1985. 237 pp.

Kruger, M.S. 'Poppespel: 'n Ondersoek na die historiese ont wikkeling, die spelbeginsels, karakter en gebruiksmoontlikhede van die toneelpop' [Puppetry: a study of the historical development, the acting principles, character and uses of the puppet]. MA thesis, University of Stellenbosch, 1987.

Larlham, Peter. *Black Theatre, Dance, and Ritual in South Africa*. Ann Arbor, MI: UMI Research Press, 1985.

Luther, C.M. *South African Theatre: Aspects of the Collaborative*. Leeds: University of Leeds, 1987.

Ndlovu, Duma, ed. *Woza Afrika! An Anthology of South African Plays*. New York: George Braziller, 1986.

Orkin, Martin. *Drama and the South African State*. Johannesburg: Witwatersrand University Press, 1991.

———. *Shakespeare against Apartheid*. Johannesburg: Ad Donker, 1987.

Read, John. *Athol Fugard: A Bibliography*. Grahamstown: NELM, 1991.

Sachs, Albie. 'Preparing Ourselves for Freedom: Culture and the ANC Constitutional Guidelines'. *The Drama Review* 35, no. 1 (spring 1991): 187–93.

Scheub, Harald. *The Xhosa 'Ntsomi'*. Oxford: Clarendon, 1975.

Schwartz, Pat. *The Best of Company: The Story of Johannesburg's Market Theatre*. Johannesburg: Ad Donker, 1988. 280 pp.

Schwenke, Astrid. 'Poppeteater in Suid-Afrika: 'n oorsig' [Puppet theatre in South Africa: a survey]. *Lantern* 34, no. 3.

Steadman, Ian P. 'Drama and Social Consciousness: Themes in Black Theatre on the Witwatersrand Until 1985'. PhD dissertation, University of the Witwatersrand, 1985.

Storrar, Patricia. *Beginners Please: A History of Children's Theatre in South Africa*. Johannesburg, 1988.

Taylor, Norah. *Towards a History of the South African Guild of Speech and Drama Teachers*. Johannesburg: Norah Taylor/The Guild, 1989. 84 pp.

Theatre Quarterly 7 (winter 1977–8). Special issue on South African theatre.

Urpokodu, Peter I. 'Plays, Possession and Rock-and-roll: Political Theatre in South Africa'. *The Drama Review* 36, no. 4 (1992): 28–53.

Vandenbroucke, Russel. *Truths the Hand can Touch: The Theatre of Athol Fugard*. Johannesburg: Ad Donker, 1986.

Von Kotze, Astrid. *Organise and Act: The Natal Workers Theatre Movement 1983–1987*. Durban: Culture and Working Life, 1988. 127 pp.

Walder, Dennis. *Athol Fugard*. London: Macmillan, 1984.

White, Landeg and Tim Couzens. *Literature and Society in South Africa*. Cape Town: Maskew Miller Longman, 1984.

SOUTHERN RHODESIA

(see **ZIMBABWE**)

SUDAN

(Arab World volume)

TANGANYIKA

(see **TANZANIA**)

TANZANIA

Situated on the eastern African coast, the modern state of Tanzania grew out of a union in 1964 between Tanganyika and the islands of Zanzibar off its coast. Bordered by the Indian Ocean to the east, Kenya and the highest mountain in Africa, Kilimanjaro, to the northeast, and the states of Uganda, Rwanda, and Burundi to the north and northwest, Zaïre and Zambia to the west, and Malawi and Mozambique to the south, Tanzania boasts the three biggest lakes in Africa – Lake Victoria, Lake Tanganyika and Lake Nyasa in the northwest, west and southwest respectively. Tanzania's 939,800 square kilometres (362,900 square miles) is home to 120 different ethnic groups, each with distinct linguistic and cultural characteristics as well as several groups of Asian origin. Most of the country's exports go through Dar es Salaam on the east coast, the largest of the ports as well as the business and commercial capital. In 1994 Tanzania had an estimated population of 27.9 million, 35 per cent of whom were Muslim, 45 per cent Christian with another 20 per cent following traditional, mostly animist beliefs.

Archaeological findings have placed some of the earliest ancestors of humankind in the Ngorongoro area in northern Tanzania, now the centre of one of Africa's largest wildlife preserves, the Serengeti National Park. Contact with the outside world started early. In the seventeenth century BC the area was colonized by people from Arabia. By the tenth century AD trade and commerce were thriving between the east African coast, Zanzibar (then known as Azania) and the Orient.

European interest in east Africa began when Vasco da Gama rounded the Cape of Good Hope in 1497. The Portuguese used the coastal towns to service their ships on the way to India. By the beginning of the eighteenth century the Portuguese had been almost entirely forced out by the Omani Arabs.

In general, the hinterland at this time was still organized in communal or semi-feudal societies while the coast and the islands were organized into a city-state with a mixture of indigenous people and those from the Middle East. From 1804 until 1963, Zanzibar was ruled by the dynasty founded by Sultan Sayyid Said (1791–1856). Under the Sultan, trade was expanded and in 1840 the capital was moved to Zanzibar.

It was the Germans, however, who managed to colonize the hinterland and create a German East Africa Company which also administered Tanzania until 1891. German colonization lasted from 1885 to 1918. Resistance to German rule manifested itself in various struggles including the Maji Maji Resistance of 1905–7 and Chief Mkwawa's battles against the colonialists. After World War I, the then Tanganyika was made a mandate of the League of Nations to be administered by the British and in 1946 a trust territory of the United Nations under British administration. In 1961, Tanganyika became the first British East Africa territory to win independence. The islands of Zanzibar, however, continued to be ruled by Arab clans until 1963 when a bloody revolt brought an end to their rule and paved the way for the union with Tanganyika in 1964.

One of the major results of the eclectic interaction between various ethnic groups as well as with those from the outside has been the development of the Kiswahili (Swahili) language which is the national language but also spoken in neighbouring countries such as Kenya, Uganda, Zaïre, parts of Mozambique and Malawi. English is also widely spoken.

The post-colonial history of Tanzania can be said to have had three phases so far – pre-socialist, socialist, and post-socialist. The pre-socialist period covers the years from 1961 to 1966. With independence and the resultant political and economic problems, concerted efforts were made to address the colonial legacies of illiteracy, poverty and ill health. These efforts culminated in the revolutionary Arusha Declaration in 1967 which sought to move the country towards a socialist economy and political system and away from the inherited capitalist system. By the mid-1970s, however, it became clear that socialism would not become a reality as centralized planning, nationalization of the major forms of production and reorganization of societies in the nation's villages and communities were floundering. From the early 1980s, liberalization was slowly allowed to creep in and

became policy by the late 1980s. Even though socialism has not been officially declared dead, new policies and government actions indicate the country is already living in a post-Arusha era. The country's modern history moved into a new chapter with the adoption of a multi-party democratic system in 1994, replacing the one-party state that had operated since 1965.

The history of Tanzanian theatre can itself be traced through three major eras: the pre-colonial, the colonial and the socialist or *ujamaa* era.

The pre-colonial period for the mainland covers the years up to 1885. Theatre was then traditional and ethnic-based, reflecting a wide variety of forms including dance, storytelling, heroic recitations, and ritual events. Except for the heroic recitations, generally limited to feudal and warring societies, most groups had forms from all these genres. Every ethnic group, for example, had a minimum of three dances. As such, these forms ran into the hundreds.

Pre-colonial theatre was function based. Theatre was done to educate, criticize, mobilize, appease, regulate behaviour and generally monitor the welfare of the community. Theatre was also done within specific contexts such as education, mobilization, worship or celebration. Dances, for example, were an integral part of traditional educational systems like initiation rites. These included *mkole* of the Wazaramo people in the coastal region, *digubi* of the Wakaguru in Morogoro, and *ikumbi* of the Wagogo in Dodoma. Dances were also part of worship like *livangala* of the Wahehe in Iringa. Wedding dances included *mbeta* of the Waluguru in Morogoro and *selo* of the Wazigua in Tanga. The *abasimba* dance of the Wajita from Ukerewe is an example of a hunting dance while the *bugobogobo* of the Wasukuma is a farming dance. Dances were also an integral part of healing rituals as was the case of *mbayaya* of the Wahehe and *madogori* of the coastal area. Details of many of these forms have been documented elsewhere; some still remain to be recorded.

Heroic recitations were often pre- or post-war displays of heroism meant to motivate valour and pride. The *ebyebugo* of the Wahaya of Bukoba, *ambasimba* of the Wajita of Ukerewe and *ibivugo* of the Wahangaza of Ngara are some examples of this very specific form of art. Their aesthetic needs to be understood within the context of the social functions from which they emerge. The pre-colonial period also shows Arabic influence in such dances as the *chama*, *chakacha* or *lelemama* practised in the coastal area.

The colonial era saw the introduction of western theatre forms – specifically English drama – which was introduced into schools around 1920. Although western drama was primarily done as entertainment for expatriate teachers and students, it was also a colonial tool for inculcating western cultural values among the colony's subjects. Dramatic literature was part of the teaching of both the English language and English literature. Proper accent, diction and pronunciation became a point of focus in later school productions.

Between the 1920s and the 1950s school productions were dominantly European with Shakespeare and Bernard Shaw as the leading playwrights. *Julius Caesar*, *The Merchant of Venice*, *Henry VIII*, *Macbeth* and *Romeo and Juliet* were some of the more popular Shakespearian plays. Other favourites included Shaw's *Pygmalion*, Gow's *The Sheriff*, Milne's *The Ugly Duckling* and Gilbert and Sullivan's *The Gondoliers*.

Western drama generally was promoted through the patronage of the British Arts Council, which sponsored an annual Schools Drama Competition beginning in 1957. The competition was later known as the Youth Drama Festival. Although the British Council withdrew its support in 1963 after independence, the festival continued up to 1973 and was a significant catalyst in the emergence of early Tanzanian playwrights, including Ebrahim Hussein, George Uhinga and Faraji Katalambula. Hussein's *Alikiona* (1970) and Uhinga's *Martin Kayamba* (1968) were the products of this movement. Since these original entries were emerging in the early and mid-1960s, a time of strong nationalist sentiments, it is not surprising that all the entries were in Kiswahili. Kiswahili translations of Shakespeare also emerged, including *Julius Kaisari* (*Julius Caesar*, 1968) and *Mabepari wa Venice* (*The Merchant of Venice*, 1969) by the then President of Tanzania, Mwalimu Julius K. Nyerere (b. *c*.1922). Others included *Makbeth* (1968). Since then all plays written by Tanzanians have been in Kiswahili, the national language and the language of the theatre in general.

During the same period, western drama was supported in the European and expatriate communities through the formation of Drama Associations. The Dar es Salaam Players, commonly known as Dar es Salaam Little Theatre, was established in 1947, and Arusha Little Theatre in 1953. The main objective of these theatres was to provide entertainment for the European community in Tanzania. In general, they have ignored the local theatre community and remained unconnected and generally unknown to the local population.

Western-style theatre was introduced to Tanzania in the late nineteenth century by church missionaries. As part of their evangelical efforts, missionaries introduced morality plays and pageants that became part of the mass, especially at Easter and Christmas. *Imekwisha*, an Easter pageant, and *Safari ya Msafiri* (*Travellers' Adventures*), a morality play, were widely performed by the Anglican church communities and schools. Mvumi Middle School in Dodoma, for example, staged annual performances of *Imekwisha* in the 1950s and 1960s. Recognizing the importance and effectiveness of communicating through indigenous mediums, the church also used Tanzanian stories for evangelical purposes, adapting and retelling them during church services. Paul White's collection *Jungle Doctors' Fables* (1950) and Daudi Muhando's *Hadithi za Kiafrika zimekuwa za kikristo* (*African Tales Tamed Christian*, 1943) are examples.

Despite these attempts, traditional theatre continued to be practised despite the fact that it was incompatible with colonial strategies to deculturalize and thus control the population. As a result, a deliberate war began to be waged against the indigenous theatre forms by colonial forces, particularly the school system and the church. Tanzanians who entered the colonial education system or converted to Christianity were discouraged and often forbidden to participate in indigenous dances, rituals, heroic recitations and other performances on the argument that they were 'pagan' and 'uncivilized' activities. At no time were these indigenous performances recognized as legitimate cultural expressions. The Tanzanians, therefore, like many Africans, came to associate the term 'theatre' only with the type of dramatic performances found in Europe.

In 1948, colonial cultural policy underwent a change. Apprehensive because of the unrest and demands for independence that were emerging in its colonies – particularly in Asia, the colonial office hatched a plan to brighten the lives of colonial subjects and thus gain acceptance of the colonial system. Believing that the native was a natural performer, music, dances, traditional festivals and national celebrations were encouraged. Agricultural shows and exhibitions were organized with dance performances as highlights. Because the colonial government did not want financial investment in African artistic forms, however, the policy emphasized the use of existing groups. Nevertheless, new indigenous theatre groups emerged. In Dar es Salaam, for example, there were fifty-eight cultural troupes by 1954, most organized along ethnic lines. The more outstanding ones were the dance unions of the Wakami, Wakwere, Wazigua, Wapogoro, Wanyasa and Wamatengo peoples. In other urban centres, as well as in Christian Mission Centres, still more indigenous dance performances were organized.

As a result, European Christian missionaries and school teachers, who previously played the role of overseer to ensure that children and Christian converts stayed away from indigenous theatre performances, now patronized these indigenous dance performances. Specific evenings were set aside for school children in boarding schools to stage dance performances. Troupes were invited to perform at colonial events including Empire Day, the Queen's Birthday or during visits of colonial officials.

Care was taken, however, that the dances were 'acceptable' to the British. Dances were therefore modified or new dances, without such characteristics as gyrations or courting scenes, were encouraged. The *mpendoo* of the Wagogo in Mvumi Dodoma and the *beeni* of Wakaguru in Berega Kilosa emerged from this movement. Interestingly, neither *mpendoo* nor *beeni* spread beyond the mission centres in Mvumi and Berega and both died out after independence. Another dance, however, also called *beni*, which emerged under the same circumstances, survived and spread, and several adaptations of it exist today, such as *mapenenga* and *mganda*.

While colonialism, in spite of its efforts, did not kill traditional cultural practice, its policies and attitudes did not enhance them either. It took the gaining of independence for a new cultural chapter to be ushered in. It was in 1962 that a Ministry of National Culture was inaugurated with the mandate of supporting traditional cultural practices. President Julius Nyerere's slogan – 'Culture is the soul of a nation' – became national cultural policy. In theatre, new plays written by nationals or from other parts of Africa began appearing. A National dance troupe as well as two workers' drama groups were formed. It was not, however, until after 1967 that the efforts begun at independence picked up momentum. In that year, the Arusha Declaration came into effect. This was to provide Tanzania with a blueprint for socialism. Much of the history and practice of theatre in present-day Tanzania was framed by this policy and the subsequent reactions to it.

Responding to Nyerere's call of 'go and propagate *ujamaa*' (socialism), theatre practitioners wrote and composed plays in support of the tenets of the declaration. Theatre was encouraged in the primary and secondary schools while autonomous cultural troupes performed dance, music, dramatic skits and plays in institutions of higher learning, in factories and in various branches of the armed forces. Courses in theatre arts, which had begun in 1965 at the University of Dar es Salaam, became translated into a full department in 1967 and were further strengthened. In 1972 and 1974, courses in music and fine art were added to reflect the interrelated arts characteristic of African cultural practice. Two other institutions were created to cater for theatre training – the College of Arts (in 1976) and Butimba College of National Education's Programme in Theatre Arts (in 1982). All these institutions aimed at producing artists, cultural facilitators and teachers.

The period between 1967 and 1995 saw further developments in the use of local forms of theatre, including narrative performances, dance-musical-dramas and much experimentation. *Ngonjera*, a dramatic-verse-dialogue drama, developed into a form which was closely interlinked with the *ujamaa* era. The form became an important mouthpiece for *ujamaa* policies and aspirations.

Focus was also put on research which investigated traditional African forms and this fed into the practice of theatre. Such works as Hussein's *Kinjeketile* (1970) and *Mashetani* (1971), Penina Muhando's *Pambo* (1975) and *Lina Ubani* (1984), Paukwa Theatre's *Ayubu* (1982), Amandina Lihamba's *Hawala ya Fedha* (1980), and Emanuel Mbogo's *Giza Limeingia* (1980) were written and/or produced during this period. Some of these were also translated into English, Japanese and German. It was also during this time that Theatre-for-Development was institutionalized.

To popularize theatre activities further, the government organized various cultural programmes beginning in 1980. These included

Amandina Lihamba's 1982 Paukwa Theatre production of *Ayubu*.

competitions at the village, district, regional, zonal and national levels between 1980 and 1984. This programme has received minimal attention in recent years, however.

The politicization of the theatre as a result of the Arusha Declaration and *ujamaa* policies was in evidence not only in those plays which supported them but also in those after the mid-1970s that questioned its practices and failures.

The inauguration of a multi-party era in 1994 actually intensified the use of political issues in theatre. Finally, the period also witnessed developments in the commercialization of theatre and fierce competition among such popular groups as the Mandela Theatre, Muungano Cultural Troupe and Tanzania One. They have moved from being purely non-profit performance groups to business enterprises which travel through the country providing entertainment.

Structure of the National Theatre Community

With the majority of the people living in rural areas and continuing to practise indigenous forms, traditional theatre is still a major force in Tanzania. Narrative performances such as storytelling, and heroic recitations, dance-musical dramas as well as ritual theatre continue to be part of the daily activities of the majority of the people. Besides these, however, there are formally and informally constituted theatre groups in both rural and urban areas, for example Bagamoyo Players in Bagamoyo, Paukwa Theatre Group in Dar es Salaam and

Kajiwe Theatre Group in Mbeya. There are also groups sponsored by such institutions as religious communities, educational and industrial institutions.

Since the early 1980s, there has been a growing number of commercial or semi-commercial groups which are mostly urban based but travel throughout the country performing, most often, variety shows which include dramatic sketches, plays, music and dance pieces. There were over one hundred such groups in the country in 1995 according to the National Arts Council.

Some of the most popular groups include the Muungano Cultural Troupe, Tanzania One Theatre, Parapanda Arts, The Lighters and the Mandela Theatre, all based in Dar es Salaam.

There are several festivals and annual competitions which bring together many of the groups. The Bagamoyo Festival held each year in September, Bujora Dance Festival in Mwanza, the dance contest festivals in the southern highlands, the National Cultural Competitions held every year in different parts of the country, the primary and secondary schools zonal and national competitions as well as an annual Children's Festival held at the University of Dar es Salaam every September are some of the more public events.

The growing commercialization of theatre activities in the country has been for the most part the result of the inability of the government to provide material and financial support to groups. There were great expectations after the Arusha Declaration that the government's intentions to support cultural activities would give the theatre sufficient subsidy to avoid commercialization. However, the proclamation did not translate itself into concrete support. Liberalization policies pursued from the early 1980s made theatre a commodity for sale like any other.

The National Arts Council of Tanzania (established in 1984) is the umbrella arts organization under which all cultural organizations operate. Since its establishment, the Council has mobilized artists in the various disciplines to organize themselves into associations but has met with only limited success. Its Department of Theatre Arts, however, has managed to mobilize performers in campaigns against AIDS as well as to work closely with the Department of Theatre Arts of the University of Dar es Salaam in the use of Theatre-for-Development.

Artistic Profile

The contemporary theatre scene is a combination of genres and styles emerging from the indigenous, colonial and *ujamaa* heritage. The indigenous theatre forms are now dominating after having received deliberate nurturing during the *ujamaa* era.

Dance is the most popular theatrical form in both rural and urban areas. Most theatre groups – commercial, amateur, school or community – have dances in their repertoires. Storytelling and *ngonjera* are also common forms whereas ritual theatre and heroic recitations are restricted almost exclusively to the rural communities. It is of interest to note that urban commercial theatre companies also base their performances on indigenous theatre forms, especially dance. Their shows are normally a kind of variety evening where dance, *vichekesho* (comic skits), *ngonjera* and music (*taarab*, orchestral, choir) may all be featured. Single-genre performances, such as play productions are rare and tend to be found only in amateur, school or college theatre groups.

Major artistic styles can be divided into indigenous genres, western-influenced dramatic genres, and Theatre-for-Development. Indigenous genres include dance, storytelling, heroic recitation, *ngonjera*, ritual theatre and *vichekesho*.

Dance Since dance is tied to social function, the more than five hundred dances found in Tanzania are performed in the context of social events such as weddings, initiations, burials, worship, healing processes, courting, work, war or celebrations. The content, form and performance techniques are, therefore, determined by the function within which the dance exists.

A proper interpretation of the content requires an understanding of each dance's social function. For example, wedding dance songs deal with roles and responsibilities pertaining to married life. Work dances set standards for accepted levels of work performance, ridiculing the lazy and praising hard work. Initiation into adulthood dances are basically lessons about adult life.

Most dances call for broad community participation because they are part of public functions or ceremonies. The dance form in terms of movement, music and formations is such that it accommodates and encourages wide community participation and is not restricted to performances by specialized artists. People participate in particular wedding dances because they are relatives of the bride or groom, or initiation rites because they are fulfilling their adult duty to instruct young people in the village. Whether they are good artists or not is of secondary importance.

Anyone can therefore perform without having to undergo rigorous artistic training. As such, most Tanzanian dances have a simple basic movement which is repeated over and over again. A person can join in at any time and can easily fall into step with the movement. Similarly, the dance music often includes short songs with repeated phrases as chorus. The *msunyunho* and *nindo* of the Wagogo from Dodoma region and the *hiari ya moyo* of the Wanyamwezi are some exceptions where the songs can be quite long. Indeed, a dance performance never stops for a new song to be taught.

Because of the simplicity of the song forms, the artist introduces a song and the performer/participants catch the tune and words as they continue dancing. The widest section of those attending the social function can therefore participate in a dance and thus ensure the fulfilment of the dance's particular social function.

In some cases, participation is limited. For example, in an initiation rite into adulthood dance, participation is restricted to people who are already initiated. Similarly, healing dances are restricted to members of healers' associations or to relatives of the sick.

Participation in a dance represents the fulfilment of duty in executing a particular function. For example, the relatives of a bride and groom dance because such participation will determine the success of the marriage. Similarly the better the initiation dance is performed the more effective the instructions contained therein. The relatives of the initiates therefore participate in the dance to ensure that their child is properly trained. This accounts for the active participation of the audience which may watch and cheer but in most cases feels obliged to step into the dance as performers.

Improvisation is another common characteristic of dance especially in the creation of the dance songs. Songs are often handed down from one performer to another. Some dance songs, like those of initiations, healing rites or work dances could be handed down for several generations. New songs are, however, often composed during performances and performed in addition to those in the standard repertoire. Such impromptu compositions are also often done as collective creations. One artist may start the first few phrases and others will come

A 1991 dance musical drama production at the University of Dar es Salaam.

in with additional phrases while everybody else joins in a chorus, thus making the final product a true group composition.

Dance song composition is therefore also not restricted to defined artists. Any performer who wants to introduce a new song or improve an old one can be accommodated. In many cases, people use this opportunity to express through song their feelings on issues that touch their welfare. Dance song creations are in this sense revelations of a person's inner feelings. For example, the mother of the bride may in a wedding dance express her sense of loss now that her daughter is leaving to set up her own home. The improvisational nature of these pieces can be extended even to the dance movement where variations from the basic motif can be improvised by anyone present.

The more ritualistic dances – such as healing or initiation dances – have less improvisational character. Instead, songs are handed down from earlier generations and new ones emerge only very selectively. Clearly, the content of such dances represents society's accepted doctrines, values and attitudes. The content is considered a sacred heritage and tampering could disrupt the society's way of life. As such the content remains fairly fixed and is repeated with little or no improvisation.

Storytelling Like dance, storytelling is a very popular form present among all ethnic groups. Its main function is educational. Used to teach children the morals and values of the society, the stories are often told by grandparents, often the grandmother, who teaches the children the virtues of good behaviour, love, cooperation, sharing, endurance, hard work, obedience, loyalty, honesty and bravery. All are enforced through stories in which the lack of such virtues lands the concerned characters in trouble.

Storytellers exploit the intimate relationship with their audience to capture the audience's imagination. Using suspense, urgency or pauses, the storyteller often makes this narrative art as effective as a staged drama. At the end, the culprit is always apprehended and punished. The moral becomes clear with the message that it does not pay to do evil or to be bad mannered.

Like dance, storytelling is characterized by collective creativity, improvisation, and audience participation. Although one storyteller is normally the main performer, those present can at any time also become the storyteller. In fact, there is deliberate encouragement for the audience to perform also. One storytelling session therefore may have several storytellers. Stories also often include songs which are structured in such a way that the storyteller need sing only the main phrase and the audience will sing the chorus.

In many Tanzanian communities, storytelling is structured so that the audience has to utter a certain response. For example, there are set ways of starting a narration where the audience has to respond before the story can even begin. Among the coastal people, for example, stories begin this way:

STORYTELLER: Paukwa (Once upon a time…)
AUDIENCE: Pakawa (There was…)
STORYTELLER: Hadithi Hadithi (A Story… A Story…)
AUDIENCE: Hadithi njoo (Tell the story.)

During the narration the audience also utters responses meant to assure the storyteller that the audience is with her. Responses vary from one ethnic group to another but include such words as *eee* or *mmmh* (many groups), *Naam Twaib* (coastal Swahili) or *Dii* (Wakaguru). The audience will also interact by adding other viewpoints during the performance. The storyteller will usually incorporate these commentaries and viewpoints into the narration, thus creating a unique sense of collective creativity.

Heroic recitation This is a theatrical form whose basic function is to glorify heroism, deeds performed in war, hunting or some other dangerous encounter. Recitations would be performed before the soldiers go to war in order to motivate them into heroic combat and after the war to allow the soldiers to display their heroism. Heroic recitations would also be done at the court to pledge loyalty to the king.

In a typical recitation, the performer recites at a very quick pace. Holding a shield and spear, he jumps and dances about, jabbing his spear backwards and forwards as if to strike an enemy. He re-enacts his heroic deeds in combat. Reciters stand in line and recite in turns. Sometimes two reciters compete, weighing their acts of bravery against one another. In feudal structures, like the traditional Bahaya, the recitation is directed at the king. Each reciter ends his performance by presenting himself to the king for recognition. If the king endorses his heroism, blessings or a gift are presented to the reciter but if the reciter cannot prove his heroism he is jeered and presented with cowdung. The audience responds by cheering in a chorus of *Eeee* or *Yeeee*. The better the reciter presents his heroism, the more enthusiastic the response from the audience.

Sometimes heroic recitations are accompanied by intervals of drumming. Among the Bahaya, for example, the drum starts off and marks the end of the reciter's performance. The recitations are normally original poetic compositions of the reciters covering their own heroic deeds as well as those of their ancestors. The poems contain boastful phrases and epithets to portray the reciter as a formidable force. The reciter often likens himself to lightning and portrays actions that he says can be done only by people as fierce as himself.

Apart from the Bahaya, heroic recitations are found also among the Wakurya, the Wazanaki of the Musoma region, the Wahangaza of Ngara and the Wajita of Ukerewe Island.

Ngonjera This is a poetic contest between two antagonistic characters with each trying to prove superiority in virtue. Each side can have one or several characters who may add dramatic sketches, costumes and props to the poem. *Ngonjera* poems are usually long and to win, the losing side must concede defeat or claim enlightenment and cross to the other side. *Ngonjera* can deal with any theme. The more traditional forms involved qualities of people or families. For example, the family of a bride could claim superiority over the groom's family in work performance, bravery or hospitality. The more contemporary *ngonjera* are, however, highly political. *Ngonjera's* heyday was during the *ujamaa* era when they were deliberately used as propaganda tools for socialist ideology. The contest was normally between the evils of capitalism and the virtues of socialism. Exploitation, corruption, disregard for human values and materialism were pitted against socialist egalitarian values.

The traditional *ngonjera* also shares the characteristics of improvisation, audience participation and collective creativity. The contemporary *ngonjera* is, however, differently structured in that there is now often a script. As such, improvisation, audience participation and impromptu creativity are limited.

Ritual theatre This genre includes theatre forms tied to particular rituals. Utilizing dance, mime, recitations, narration or any combination of these, the rituals may include worship, healing, initiation, burial or the installation of leaders. These forms are part of structured ritual processes from which they cannot be separated without affecting the essence of the ritual.

Examples are *digubi*, an initiation dance of the Wakaguru of Morogoro region; *selo*, a healing dance of the Wagogo of Dodoma region; *ing'oma*, a burial dance of the Wanyakyusa of Mbeya region; and the *lindende* of the Wapogoro of Morogoro.

Ritual theatre is more restrictive than other indigenous forms in terms of timing, those who participate, the role of the audience and the performing space itself. A rain-making ritual may be conducted only once in five years because it is the time people need to appeal to the gods for rain. Performers in a burial dance may be restricted to their connections to the deceased. A worship dance may have the village shrine as the only acceptable performing space.

The content of ritual theatre is often sacred and handed down without modification from one generation to another. There is no individual claim to the authorship of the content. Instead it is considered societal property which the individual has no right to change. Indeed, tampering with such content is believed to be calling upon the wrath of the ancestors on the community.

Ritual performance is also the least common of all the genres. To see such a performance one requires sufficient knowledge of the community as well as knowledge of when the ritual occurs. A burial dance, for example, is performed only when certain people die and the performance is not necessarily open to all.

Influenced by European dramatic forms, the improvisational nature of *vichekesho* is suitable for quick commentary on topical themes. Urban commercial theatre troupes as well as secondary and primary school groups engage primarily in *vichekesho*. Aimed at making people laugh, *vichekesho* of the colonial era laughed at the African's inability to cope with European civilization while those of the *ujamaa* era ridiculed capitalism. *Vichekesho* now ridicules social evils. Domestic characters such as the irresponsible husband, the unfaithful wife, the stepmother or in-law relations are common topics. Like other genres, however, *vichekesho* can also play educational roles and plots are designed to drive home some moral at the end.

Most *vichekesho* are not documented. Theatre groups similarly improvise them or use plots from old pieces to come up with new ones. There is also no individual claim to authorship with *vichekesho* since they are truly collective creations. In this, they are close to *commedia dell'arte*.

Western-influenced dramatic genres European influences can be seen in genres where an actual script forms the basic structure. Developing from the colonial period – particularly the theatre of Shakespeare, the form has led to the development of plays written or improvised by Tanzanian subject matter; these plays are written in Kiswahili.

Productions are centred around universities, colleges, schools and urban areas. Groups usually operate on an amateur basis. Adapting to the traditional social function of theatre, plays have leaned towards the didactic. They are often highly political with common themes that discuss social problems such as corruption, mismanagement of the economy, bad leadership, injustice or exploitation of the poor.

Traditional Tanzanian forms have also greatly influenced such scripted plays. Through a deliberate effort, spearheaded by the Theatre Department of the University of Dar es Salaam, plays often mix spoken drama with dance, storytelling or recitations.

Improvised plays in this style often start with an idea. All members of the group contribute towards the making of a final performance.

Paukwa Theatre group is a leading exponent of this process. Its productions of *Ayubu* (1980), *Mafuta* (1986), *Chuano* (1980) and *Mitumba Ndui* (1989) were all in this style.

It should be noted that even when a production is based on a script, improvisation is not ruled out and playwrights learn to tolerate such changes.

Theatre-for-Development Involving the wider community in the theatre creation process, Theatre-for-Development seeks to identify problems and analyse them with a view to finding solutions. The performance is not an end in itself but rather a catalyst for community discussion on appropriate action to take.

Theatre-for-Development in Tanzania, also sometimes referred to as Popular Theatre or Community Theatre, emphasizes the active participation of the community at all stages. The community identifies the problems and discusses them. The people create the theatre performance and become the performers. Animateurs, from both within and outside the community, guide the process; they are basically catalysts who steer the process towards awareness, creation and deeper analysis.

Post-performance discussion at a Theatre-for-Development production in Bagamoyo in 1983.

The process also emphasizes the use of theatre forms indigenous to the community. Indigenous dances, recitations, storytelling, *ngonjera* and skits tend to characterize Theatre-for-Development performances.

Companies

Just after independence, the Tanzanian government established a National Dance Company (1963) and a National Drama Company (1974). Both were dismantled in 1981. Established with the money thus saved was the Bagamoyo College of Arts. This policy saw logic in training many artists and sending them to promote theatre all over the country instead of having just one company in each field purporting to represent the Tanzanian theatre.

There are as a result a number of commercial or semi-commercial groups that try to subsist on theatre. These groups operate as registered companies and spend most of their time on theatre. The best of these include the Mandela Theatre group, Muungano Theatre, Tanzania One Theatre, National Service, Kajiwe Drama Group (Mbeya), The Lighters, Magereza, Nyumba ya Sanaa, Bandari (Tanga), Kilombero Sugar Company (Morogoro) and CDA (Dodoma). Unless otherwise noted, these groups are located in Dar es Salaam.

Many amateur theatre groups are based in educational institutions such as the University of Dar es Salaam and Bagamoyo College of Arts; some can be found in secondary schools and colleges. Such theatre groups include Paukwa (University of Dar es Salaam), Bagamoyo Players (Bagamoyo), Dar es Salaam University Players, BAWA (Bagamoyo), MAPA (Dar es Salaam) and Parapanda (Dar es Salaam). Members of these groups engage in theatre as a part-time activity and do not make much or any income from it.

In addition, many temporary groups emerge to perform on specific occasions. The artists are well known and recognized in the community and the best are sought after and rewarded with gifts during or after the performances. These artists see their participation as part of their responsibility to the community especially since such performances are tied to social functions. Such groups do not have names but are identified by the name of the dance or the theatre performance they specialize in.

Dramaturgy
Directing and Acting

Without exception, the major playwrights use Kiswahili as their language of expression. Few of their works have been translated into other languages. Besides the published plays there are numerous unpublished ones which have been produced and received national acclaim.

Leading writers include Penina Muhando, Ebrahim Hussein, Emanuel Mbogo, Amandina Lihamba and Ibrahim Ngozi. Most of the writers began in a realistic style. This is evidenced in the early works of Penina Muhando, such as *Hatia* (*Guilt*, 1974), *Talaka si Mke Wangu* (*I Divorce You*, 1976) and *Heshima Yangu* (*My Honour*, 1974), and Hussein's *Wataki Ukuta* (*Time Is a Wall*, 1970) and *Alikiona* (*She Was Punished*, 1970).

From the mid-1960s, writers tended to move to a style which used more African forms and cultural expression such as storytelling, heroic recitations, ritual, dance and music. Hussein's *Mashetani* (*Devils*, 1971) started this trend, which was picked up later in *Jogoo Kijijini* (*A Cock in the Village*, 1976) and *Ngao ya Jadi* (*The Ancestral Shield*, 1976), Muhando's *Pambo* (*Ornament*, 1975), *Nguzo Mama* (*Mother Pillar*, 1982) and *Lina Ubani* (*There Is an Antidote for Rot*, 1984).

The works of the Paukwa Theatre Group – *Ayubu* (*Job*, 1982) and *Chuano* (*The Contest*, 1980) – and Lihamba's *Mkutano wa Pili wa Ndege* (*The Second Conference of the Birds*, 1992) are also centred in this area.

The move towards the use of African traditional performance forms was both a political and aesthetic move. On the one hand, the move was a revolt against the dominance of western theatre forms and, on the other, it was a deliberate move to exploit the dynamism and complexity of traditional African performance modes. However, conventional western dramatic styles are still being used. Mbogo's *Tone la Mwisho* (1981), Ngozi's *Machozi ya Mwanamke* (*A Woman's Tears*, 1977) and *Ushuhuda wa Mifupa* (*The Bones' Witness*, 1992) are examples of realism in Tanzanian theatre. This, however, is being overshadowed by dance musical narrative dramas, both written and otherwise.

Politics is a major factor in the content of the works and their themes. Issues of liberation and its struggles in the economic and political arenas (*Kinjeketile, Mkwava wa Uhehe Tone la Mwisho*), the relationship between state and civil society (*Ayubu*) and relationships of individuals and groups within specific social and political systems (*Mashetani, Machozi ya Mwanamke*) are continuing preoccupations.

The Arusha Declaration also inspired works which have over the years supported its tenets. *Chuano* criticized the manifestations of its implementation while *Ayubu, Lina Ubani, Kijiji Chetu (Our Village)* and *Giza Limeingia (The Dawn of Darkness)* celebrated its successes. The corruption and exploitation of the masses by the ruling elite as well as the resulting disillusionment and helplessness continue to be major thematic concerns. This preoccupation with political issues has resulted in characterizations based on types rather than psychologically developed ones in plays that are often episodic and close to Brechtian aesthetics.

Both the Department of Theatre Arts of the University of Dar es Salaam and the Bagamoyo College of Arts have experimented by merging African and western performance motifs to create productions which are mixtures of the two. Such plays as *Nyani na Mkia Wake (The Monkey and its Tail), Baba Yetu (Our Father)* by the department and *The Challenge and the Gap* by Bagamoyo are good examples of this effort.

Because improvisation has become one of the dominant ways of creating theatre productions, responsibility for directing often takes a collective or semi-collective form. Ghonche Materego (*The Challenge and the Gap, Tunda*), Amandina Lihamba *Ayubu, Harakati za Ukombozi, Chuano Mitumba-Ndui, The Burdens, The Island, Mafuta, The Beggars' Strike*), Eberhard Chambulikazi (*Lina Ubani*) and Juma Bakari in Bagamoyo are leading directors whose directing methodology is similar. Theirs is a mixture of what in the west are called Brechtian and Stanislavskian styles but another element is African style utilizing dance, music, storytelling and heroic recitations.

Amandina Lihamba's 1986 Paukwa Theatre production of *Mafuta*.

Theatre for Young Audiences
Puppet and Mask Theatre

In the traditional theatre, theatre for the young is basically storytelling, dance and children's theatre games. Most ethnic groups also have dances for the young. Examples include *mtunya* of the Wakaguru of Morogoro, *mangaka* of the Wamakonde, *kajanja* of the Wabondei, *endongo* of the Wakerewe. These dances are sanctioned opportunities for boys and girls to interact and even court each other. The young also get the opportunity to display their physical qualities, to be praised for their heroism or for upholding societal values.

Children's games take a large variety of forms. Some of the games, though, are very theatrical, often combining song and dramatization, song and dance, or poetry and dance. Examples include *tumemwona simba yule* in the coastal area, *dobodobo* in the Morogoro region, *engulube* in Shinyanga, *kimgongo binuka* in Iringa, *saka mke wangu* in the coastal area, and *mbangano* in Zanzibar.

Theatre in Tanzania is a family affair. Everybody, young and old, participates in theatre both as performer and especially as audience. Dances, for example, are performed by both adults and children. Only initiation dances are restricted to adults as well as some religious rituals or secret society performances. Other forms, however, are all open to children.

The western-style contemporary theatre for and by young audiences is almost totally school based. During the *ujamaa* era, schools took a very active part in the socialist movement. Primary and secondary schools became centres for political mass mobilization. School buildings were meeting-places for political rallies as well as development-related campaigns. All schools had theatre groups which performed dances, *ngonjera* or *vichekesho*, as part of the mass mobilization strategies. Campaigns for literacy, health, establishing villages, agriculture, forestation, sanitation and so on also used school theatre groups.

Unfortunately, the children were used as tools to communicate campaign messages not designed by them. The *ngonjera* poems or dance songs were composed by the teachers or extension workers with content for adult consumption and often on issues beyond children's comprehension. Principles of child care, nutrition, health care, good governance, modern agriculture and adult literacy were some of themes of these performances.

The need to redirect theatre to school children resulted in various actions in the 1990s. The most significant step has been the creation of the Children's Theatre Project conducted by the University of Dar es Salaam's Department of Art, Music and Theatre in collaboration with the National Arts Council. The project trains primary school teachers in the skills of running children's theatre groups. Trained teachers then establish children's theatre groups in their schools.

Workshops are conducted in schools with children's groups as part of the training. Every September, the school groups participate in a Children's Theatre Festival. Started in 1990, by 1995 sixty-four teachers were trained and forty-seven groups established in primary schools. The project has also produced twenty research reports on Tanzanian indigenous theatre for children.

The September Festivals, held at the University of Dar es Salaam, also feature

The 1991 Children's Theatre Festival at the University of Dar es Salaam.

children's films, children's workshops in dance, storytelling, *ngonjera*, drama, music and painting. Some 4,000 children attend the festival daily.

As for puppetry, it has not become a significant form in the country. There is, however, the Katamaji group in Dar es Salaam which has been trying to popularize the art through the use of hand puppets.

Masks, however, do play an important part in certain indigenous theatre practices. The Makonde of the southern part of Tanzania, for example, have popular and ritual theatre performances where masks are commonly used.

Design

For most of the groups, design for productions is a collective effort where discussions lead to consensus in terms of costuming, props, performance space and set. This pattern is a continuation of the indigenous theatre design process which is effected collectively under the leadership of individuals or teams specifically designated to do so.

Even in spoken theatre performances, the director or the director together with the performers are responsible for designs. Simplicity is the guiding principle. Constructed sets or complicated heavy props are rare. Most productions are designed to travel and so a backdrop with movable props are all that is needed.

While this is a matter of practicality, it is also prompted by an aesthetic conception of non-realistic effects. The backdrops, for example, are covered with designs which are more symbolic and metaphorical than realistic.

The holding of theatre events during the daytime has meant that lighting design is also minimal. Bagamoyo College of Arts, however, has a lighting designer and equipment which are not only used for their shows but also rented out to interested groups. The theatre there is also fully equipped with lighting equipment.

The use of face and body design is another feature from indigenous performance. Specific patterns on the face and body are used to give identity to events, characters and their relationships. Designs are drawn from history, myth and even contemporary life.

Theatre Space and Architecture

Village squares, courtyards, backyards and street corners are still popular spaces for performances. Spaces are organized to suit the demands of the performance in which the audience surrounds the performers in the round or on three sides. This arrangement best lends itself to participation by the audience, which is a major factor within African theatre conventions.

There are three other types of spaces which are used for inside performances. First, there are theatres which have been left from the colonial era. The Little Theatres in Dar es Salaam and Arusha have been operating since 1947 and 1953 respectively. Built with proscenium stages, they continue to be used by groups interested in producing western plays for the expatriate communities in the respective cities. Rarely are they available for indigenous performances.

In this category are several school auditoriums built in the colonial era which also have proscenium stages. Auditoriums at Azania and Zanaki Secondary School and Msimbazi Centre in Dar es Salaam, and Kilakala in Morogoro are examples of these. Unlike the Little Theatres, these auditoriums are used by both school and indigenous theatre groups utilizing a variety of styles.

A second type of space is the multipurpose hall. These can be found everywhere in the country and include such institutional spaces as Nkrumah Hall at the University of Dar es Salaam, Vijana and Urafiki Social Halls, Nyumba ya Sanaa (all in Dar es Salaam) and the many halls at industrial, government and parastatal (semi-government-owned) organizations. From the late 1970s, there have been clubs which have spaces for performances and these have become popular with commercial or semi-commercial troupes.

The only space constructed specifically for theatre after independence is at the Bagamoyo College of Arts. With assistance from the

Swedish International Development Agency, the theatre was opened in 1990. It takes its inspiration from African architectural design and has an open-air auditorium (like a Greek amphitheatre), a thatched roof which covers a proscenium stage, and space for workshops. Situated about 40 kilometres from Dar es Salaam, the theatre complements the historical sites which Bagamoyo is famous for but its use is limited to the groups in Bagamoyo and the College.

Ritual performances use specifically arranged sites and include enclosed spaces in the bush or temporary arenas inside or outside village boundaries. Rites of passage ceremonies and performances utilize such spaces. An inherited space convention is the use of the whole community as performance area. This includes houses, squares, fields and roads. Festivals and contest events in which one village hosts the events and several other villages are invited to participate demand the use of such space. The contests held in Njombe and Songea in the southern part of Tanzania each year after the harvest are good examples.

Training

There are three theatre training institutions in Tanzania. The Department of Art, Music and Theatre of the University of Dar es Salaam offers degree training at both the undergraduate and post-graduate levels. The department was established in 1967. The undergraduate programme lasts three years and offers both theoretical and practical training. Courses include Theory and History of Theatrical Forms, Dramaturgy, Traditional African Theatre, Criticism, Playwriting, and Introduction to the Arts of the Theatre. Applied courses include acting, directing, choreography, stagecraft, design, writing for theatre, television and radio as well as production for theatre for children and young people.

Students also engage in research in various aspects of theatre with an emphasis on indigenous theatre. MA theses and PhD dissertations have been produced covering a wide spectrum of Tanzanian theatre.

Students are challenged to explore indigenous theatre practice and to create original productions combining indigenous and contemporary techniques.

Significant theatre writings and plays have emerged out of the department's efforts to develop an authentic African theatre. These include *The Contest* (Rugyendo, 1977); *Jogoo Kijijini, Ngao ya Jadi* (Hussein, 1976); *Pambo* (Muhando, 1975); *Lina Ubani* (Mhando, 1984); *Ayubu* (Paukwa, 1982); *Mafuta* (Paukwa, 1986); *Harakati za Ukombozi* (Lihamba *et al.*, 1982); *Nembo* (Lihamba, unpublished, 1995); *Matanga* (Muhando, unpublished, 1993); and *Dude Dude* (Muhando, unpublished, 1994).

The department has also led the Theatre-for-Development movement in the country. It has done workshops in many rural communities including Malya, Mwanza, the Bagamoyo Coast region, Mkambalani, Morogoro, Msoga, Bagamoyo, Namionga, Mtwara, Mbeya, Rukwa and Tanga.

The Bagamoyo College of Arts, located on the seafront of historic Bagamoyo in the coastal region, trains at the certificate level. A three-year course is offered to secondary school graduates. Established in 1981, the college's objective is to train cultural personnel for cultural promotion activities in the regions and districts. The college also offers short-term courses for foreigners. The curriculum is heavily practical covering dance, drama, music and fine art. Indigenous forms are also emphasized.

The Butimba College of Art in Mwanza specializes in the training of art teachers for primary and secondary schools. A teacher training certificate in art is given at the end of a two-year programme. Theatre, music and fine art are taught at Butimba. Educational theatre is accentuated with practical work in schools. Emphasis on indigenous Tanzanian theatre is seen at Butimba College as well. Examples of such works are *Azenga and Azota* (1981), and *Mapambano na Muungano* (1984) in which storytelling and dance take a central role.

Most of those interested in indigenous theatre practice, however, learn from master artists and develop their artistic talents through participation in actual performances. Artists of the contemporary urban theatre groups also train on the job.

Criticism, Scholarship and Publishing

There are no specific publishing houses for theatre works in the country. For the most part, works on theatre have been published by such local companies as Tanzanian Publishing House and Dar es Salaam University Press as well as foreign companies such as Heinemann and Oxford University Press.

Critical essays by academicians and researchers can be found in journals such as *Kiswahili, Research in African Literatures, The Drama Review* and others. The defunct *Darlite, Mulika, Umma, Zinduko* and *Kioo cha Lugha* carried critical essays and articles on theatre up to the 1970s.

Since theatre criticism has not yet become a profession, reviews on specific productions, artists and theatre groups are generally done by journalists and have appeared in *The Daily News, Mfanyakazi, Uhuru* and, since 1993, in such independent papers as *Dimba, Heko* and *The Express*.

Much research has been done on the aesthetics of African traditional theatre. Among the major studies have been Penina Muhando's 'African Traditional Theatre as a Pedagogical Institution' (PhD dissertation, University of Dar es Salaam, 1984), Robert Leshoai's 'Drama as a Means of Education in Africa' (PhD dissertation, University of Dar es Salaam, 1978), and Godwin Kaduma's 'A Theatrical Description of Five Tanzanian Dances' (MA thesis, University of Dar es Salaam, 1972). Criticism on theatre since the advent of colonialism can be found in such works as Ebrahim Hussein's 'The Development of Theatre in East Africa' (PhD dissertation, Humbolt, 1974) and Amandina Lihamba's 'Politics and Theatre in Tanzania after the Arusha Declaration, 1967–1984' (PhD dissertation, Leeds, 1985). In these works, dramaturgical analysis and the socio-political context of the theatre are given critical evaluation.

In the area of popular theatre and development, an important study is Penina Muhando Mlama's *Culture and Development: The Popular Theatre Approach in Africa* (1991). The process and practice of Theatre-for-Development are both described and criticized. Besides this seminal work, reports and unpublished works on popular Theatre-for-Development are housed at the University of Dar es Salaam, the National Arts Council and Bagamoyo College of Arts.

Penina Muhando Mlama, Amandina Lihamba

Further Reading

Balisidya, N. *Fasihi ya Kiswahili: Wakati Ukuta* [Time is like a wall]. Dar es Salaam: Mulika, 1970.

Carlson, Ebbe. 'Teater i Bagamoya' [Theatre at Bagamoya]. *ProScen* 14, no. 4 (1990): 5–12.

Etherton, Michael. *The Development of African Drama*. London: Hutchinson, 1982.

Fiebach, Joachim. 'On the Social Function of Modern African Literature and Brecht'. *Darlite* 4, no. 2 (1970).

Hussein, Ebrahim. 'The Beginning of Imported Theatre in Tanzanian Urban Centres'. *Wissenschaftliche Zeitschrift der Humboldt Universität zu Berlin* 23 (1974): 405–10.

Kazooba, B. 'The Art of Heroic Recitations at a Bahaya King's Court'. University of Dar es Salaam, 1977. Unpublished.

Leshoai, Bob. 'Tanzania Socialist Theatre'. *New Theatre Magazine* 12, no. 2 (1972).

Lihamba, Amandina. 'Politics and Theatre in Tanzania after the Arusha Declaration, 1967–1984'. PhD dissertation, University of Leeds, 1985.

——. 'Theatre and Political Struggle in East Africa'. In *Between State and Civil Society in Africa: Perspectives on Development*, ed. Eghosa Osaghae. Dakar: Codesria, 1994. 281 pp.

Makoye, Herbert. 'Modification and Use of Traditional Dances in Tanzania Plays'. Unpublished, 1993.

Masanja, John. 'Production Technique and Contemporary Dance Troupes in Tanzania'. University of Dar es Salaam, 1984. Unpublished.

Mbaga, N. 'Ngonjera'. MA thesis, University of Dar es Salaam, 1980.

Mbughuni, L.A. *The Cultural Policy of the United Republic of Tanzania*. Paris: UNESCO, 1974.

——. 'Old and New Drama from East Africa: A Review of the Works of Four Contemporary Dramatists, Rebecca Njau, Ebrahim Hussein, Penina Muhando and Ngugi'. *African Literature Today* 8 (1976).

Mbwana, Ali. 'The Contribution of Modern Dance Troupes Towards the Development of Traditional African Theatre'. Unpublished, University of Dar es Salaam, 1984.

Mlama, Penina Muhando. *Culture and Development: The Popular Theatre Approach in Africa*. Uppsala: Nordiska Afrikainstitutet [Scandinavian Institute of African Studies], 1991. 219 pp.

Mlama, P.O. 'African Theatre: The Case of Tanzania'. University of Dar es Salaam, 1981. Unpublished.

———. 'Digubi: A Tanzanian Indigenous Theatre Form'. *The Drama Review* 25, no. 4 (1981): 3–12.

———. 'Music in Tanzanian Traditional Theatre'. MA thesis, University of Dar es Salaam, 1973.

———. 'Reinforcing Existing Indigenous Communication Skills: The Use of Dance in Tanzania'. In *Women in Grassroots Communication: Furthering Social Change*. Pilar Riaño, ed. Thousand Oaks, CA: Sage, 1994. 315 pp.

Mlama, P. and A. Lihamba. 'Women in Communication: Popular Theatre as an Alternative Medium'. *Women and the Mass Media in Africa*/Femmes et média en Afrique. Dakar: AAWORD/AFARD, 1992. 216 pp.

Mollel, Jesse. 'The Drama of Penina Muhando'. MA thesis, University of Alberta, 1979.

Ranger, T.O. *Dance and Society in Eastern Africa, 1890–1970: The Beni Ngoma*. London: Heinemann, 1975.

Rugyendo, M. 'Towards a Truly African Theatre'. *Umma* 1, no. 2 (1974).

TOGO

(Overview)

Located on a strip of land 145 kilometres across (90 miles) and less than 600 kilometres long (360 miles) between Bénin and Ghana on the Gulf of Guinea in West Africa, Togo has a total land area of just 56,600 square kilometres (21,900 square miles). Formerly administered by France, Togo became an independent nation in 1960.

The Ewe people, the largest of Togo's more than thirty ethnic groups, are a branch of the Adja-Tado peoples, who themselves migrated from the Niger valley in the twelfth century. Portuguese sailors visited the coast in the fifteenth and sixteenth centuries. Eventually, ships began to carry slaves from the coastal villages to the Americas. French trading posts were established in the seventeenth and eighteenth centuries. Germans began to arrive in the mid-nineteenth century and in 1885, with European colonial powers carving up Africa at the conference table, Germany established Togoland as a protectorate. Most of the Togolese ethnic groups were thus divided among three colonial administrations – the Germans (in German Togoland), the French (in Dahomey, now Bénin) and the British (in the Gold Coast, now part of Ghana).

During World War I, the British and French took Togoland from Germany and in 1922 it became a mandate of the League of Nations and later a trust territory of the United Nations, the western part of the area under British control and the eastern part under the French. In 1956, British Togoland voted to become part of the independent Gold Coast and in 1957 Ghana came into being, composed of the Gold Coast and British Togoland. In 1960, French Togoland became the independent country of Togo.

With a population of 4.25 million (1994 estimate), Togo's official language is French but other languages are widely spoken including Ewe and Mina in the south, Kotokoli, Kabyè and Moba in the north. About 70 per cent of the population follow traditional animist religious beliefs; some 20 per cent are Christian and about 10 per cent Muslim. Lomé, located on the Gulf of Guinea, is the capital and chief port. Rail lines go from Lomé along the coast and some distance into the interior.

With a one-party presidential system in transition to a multi-party democratic system, the country is divided into twenty-three circumscriptions and is dependent on subsistence agriculture and phosphate mining. Some 70 per cent of Togo's exports and imports go to and from the European Union. The national literacy rate is approximately 43 per cent.

The performing arts have long been a part of traditional Togolese life. Dance and music are clearly to be found in virtually every aspect of ritual and public events. It was European missionaries as well as French teachers who introduced western-style theatrical forms into the country as part of their 'civilizing mission' and as part of teaching the colonial language. From these experiences emerged amateur groups, mostly in and around schools.

By the beginning of the twentieth century, established companies began visiting French Togoland from the Gold Coast and by the 1920s many Gold Coast Concert Party troupes were touring to Lomé. Part vaudeville variety show, part storytelling and part improvised sketches on topical issues, the Concert Party groups were enormously popular and the style was soon copied. The leading company in the mid-1990s is the Kokovito Concert Band, whose founder is both an actor and the owner of the necessary musical equipment. With many groups having to rent musical equipment at exorbitant prices, this group is able to survive in a way that others are not.

Shows take place in dance clubs and community centres for the most part, with ticket prices extremely low. Despite the public fame of many modern Concert Party artists, they still live on the fringes of society. Because of their social status, women rarely work with these groups (in Ghana, it should be noted, both men and women perform). The Togolese version, therefore, puts greater emphasis on cross-dressing as a comic technique.

Among the major individual stars have been Ayi d'Almeida of Happy Star, Kokovito, Boboe, Azeko Kovivina and Zorro among others. All are known for their most popular roles: the silly old man, the servant boy, the prostitute, the country bumpkin or the sour-tempered woman.

By the mid-1940s, as a result of more widespread educational programmes and urbanization, more modern theatre forms began to flourish including spoken drama in French and other local languages. The French theatre was mainly limited to school groups until the 1970s. Mostly written by teachers for their classes, there is barely a trace today of these early unpublished, largely handwritten scripts.

For the most part, these plays took French classics as their models and it became essential for students to learn to speak French as it was spoken in France. The goal was clearly to demonstrate to students the superiority of French culture and civilization and to show the 'barbaric' nature of Black African culture. Public performances in the vernacular were discouraged by many schools. The same attitude existed within the Christian churches whose leaders worked closely with the school system.

After independence, a number of Togolese dramatists emerged, able not only to use the modern dramatic forms but also to include within them elements of Togo's rich traditional performing arts. This crossover has opened the way for new growth of theatrical art. Written, for the most part, by students and intellectuals, the subject matter of these scripted plays in the vernacular has tended to deal with Togolese

issues, especially the cultural conflicts arising from the vast changes taking place in the 1960s and 1970s in Africa.

Among notable plays to appear during this period were Célestin Abalo's *Kalia ou les malheurs d'un héritier* (*Kalia or the Misfortunes of an Heir*, 1964); Henri Ajavon's *Datchi, l'esclave marronne* (*Datchi, the Runaway Slave*, 1965); Modeste d'Almeida and Gilbert Lacle's *Kétéyouli, l'étudiant noir* (*Ketéyouli, the Black Student*, 1966); Joseph Amegboh's (b. 1937) *Fo-Yovo ou sang mêlé* (*Fo-Yovo or Half-Caste*, 1965); Senouvo Agbota Zinsou's (b. 1946) *On joue la comédie* (*Let's Play the Play*, 1972); Julien Guenou's *Agokoli, cruauté ou devoir* (*Agokoli, Cruelty or Necessity*, 1976); Koffi Gomez's (b. 1941) *Gagio ou l'argent cette peste* (*Gagio or That Plague Called Money*, 1993); and Gnavo Akodegla's *Une fille à l'école* (*A Girl at School*, 1981). Such plays by Togolese and other African writers proved popular and began to take precedence over the production of plays by French dramatists.

Moorehouse Amavi Tuli Apedo-Amah, creator of the Togolese Cantata.
Photo: Ayayi Togoata Apedo-Amah.

One of the more unusual forms of theatre to be found in Togo is the religious cantata. Sung in the Ewe language, the form was originally used for evangelical purposes in the Gold Coast but found wider audiences. The cantata made its début in Togo in 1943 in Amavi Tuli Apedo-Amah's (b. 1911) play *Le Mariage d'Isaac et de Rébecca* (*The Marriage of Isaac and Rebecca*), based on the Old Testament story. The Togolese form – music and rather formal movement – was inspired by cantatas done by the Gold Coast's Evangelical Church of Kéta and later seen in Lomé. Though only a small number of cantatas have ever been produced, its rarity and unusual form make it unique. Among the few other cantatas of note have been Apedo-Amah's *Ruth and Naomi* (1945) and Aboki Essien's (b. 1917) *Fia Salomon* (*King Salomon*, 1959).

Subsequent cantatas slowly veered from religion and dropped many of the emphatic gestures used in early productions. Other writers found the blend of music and movement of great interest and the form secularized through the years to the point where folk instruments and dances are included along with non-religious stories. A cantata production of *Ali Baba and the Forty Thieves*, for example, was regularly performed between 1947 and 1954. In Togo, any play using dance and movement can be referred to as a cantata.

Another form which seems to exist almost exclusively in Togo is the rarely performed *albéra*. Seen solely in Togo's Muslim communities, the word itself is Hindu in origin and comes from the name of a famous Hindu film star who was adored by working-class film *aficionados*. *Albéra* plots are simple and straightforward, usually intertwining a power struggle and a love story. Full of kings and princes and the women they love, these plays closely resemble Indian sentimental and melodramatic films. All *albéras* are punctuated by song and dance and are done with percussion and flute accompaniment.

The *albéra* is usually played in either the Haoussa or Kotokoli languages and always outdoors. The songs, dances and costumes of these sentimental comedies are clearly oriental in inspiration. Aimed at showing audiences the mysteries and unpredictable nature of the human heart, the form, though performed only in the Muslim community, is not religious but secular.

Besides these traditional and literary theatres, what can be called a media theatre has also

Azeko Kovivina, Concert Party comedian.
Photo: Ayayi Togoata Apedo-Amah.

emerged in the country; that is to say, plays and other performances on radio and television. Even the Concert Party is now seen regularly on television, a medium which did not appear until 1974 in Togo. Audiences seem to see the Concert Party's broad comedy and didactic folk tales as reinforcement of the pervasive animist philosophy.

On radio as well theatre has become popular, mostly through the French-sponsored Concours théâtral inter-africain (Inter-African Theatre Competition) which has allowed a relatively large number of Togolese plays to be heard both at home and abroad. Since the 1960s, this competition has presented outstanding plays by Togolese and other African playwrights, many of which have become famous without ever having been staged or published in their home countries.

Performances of literary plays on television are to some extent a logical extension of the French radio competition. Many include dance and music and such productions are immensely popular. Probably the most important of Togo's television directors is Kofi Hantz (b. 1946), who has produced more than twenty plays for the medium, among them Senouvo Agbota Zinsou's well-known *La Tortue qui chante* (*The Singing Tortoise*, 1986).

In general all the theatre groups in the country are amateur in the truest sense of the word. Artists perform for the love of the art and though some occasionally earn money, very few are able to survive on this income. Almost all youth organizations and almost all schools have some sort of French-language drama group and several of the country's community centres have their own groups as well.

Only two troupes stand apart from the rest: Troupe Nationale (National Troupe) is composed of a dramatic company, a dance company and a music company, while Association des Amis Artistes is known to all as 'Les Trois A' (Association of Artistic Friends). Both companies are professionally structured and operate on a more or less professional basis. Troupe Nationale also receives a state subsidy which is used almost exclusively for production costs rather than salaries. The company is connected to the Ministry of Culture and was founded and run by playwright and director Senouvo Agbota Zinsou from 1978 until 1992.

Zinsou, born in Lomé, attended the University of Bénin in Togo and later the Institut d'Études Théâtrales at the University of Paris. After returning from France, he founded the Troupe Nationale. Zinsou is also a prize-winning short story writer whose fiction and plays have been published in France by Hatier and in English translation by Ubu Repertory in New York.

Zinsou's plays include *On joue la comédie*, which includes elements of the Concert Party form. The play won first prize in the radio Concours and Zinsou himself directed it for the 1977 Festival of Black Arts and Culture in Lagos. Other plays include *Le Club* (*The Club*, 1983), *La Tortue qui chante*, which integrates aspects borrowed from both the Concert Party and popular folk tales; *La Femme du blanchisseur* (*The Laundryman's Wife*), and *Yévi au pays des monstres* (*Yevi in the Land of the Monsters*, 1987). Koffi Hantz's television production of *La Tortue qui chante* won first prize for francophone television films in Montréal in 1987.

Another dramatist of note is Josué Kossi Efoui (b. 1962), author of *Le Carrefour* (*The Crossroads*, 1988). An actor as well as playwright, Efoui's play also won first prize in the Concours in 1989 and the play was published in 1990 in the French journal *Théâtre Sud* and in an English translation by Ubu Repertory in New York in 1991. In 1990 the play was performed at the French Cultural Centre in Lomé. Efoui is also a short story writer.

There are three theatre scholars of note with expertise in Togolese theatre forms – Ayayi Togoata Apedo-Amah (b. 1952) and Noble Akam from Lomé and the French scholar Alain Ricard. All have done studies of both the Concert Party and the cantata traditions. Other scholars of note are Huenumadji Afan in the area of theatre reception, and Tohonou Gbeasor, who has done studies on the works of Zinsou.

Two publishing houses in Togo have included plays on their lists – Les Nouvelles Éditions Africaines and Les Éditions Haho, the latter publishing several of Zinsou's plays. The state publishing house L'Editogo has also published plays but always at the author's expense.

Specialized journals are *Annales* (*Annals*) published occasionally by the University of Bénin in Lomé, and *Propos scientifiques* (*Scientific Commentaries*), founded in 1984. The latter appears twice a year and includes regular theatre reviews.

Ayayi Togoata Apedo-Amah
Translated by Jennifer Hutchison

Further Reading

Akam, Noble. 'Le Concert party togolais' [The Togolese Concert Party]. PhD dissertation, Université de Bordeaux, 1985.

Apedo-Amah, Ayayi Togoata. 'Le Concert-party: une pédagogie pour les opprimés' [The Concert Party: instruction for the oppressed]. *Peuples noirs, peuples africains* 8, no. 44 (1985): 61–72.

——. 'Peinture sociale et théâtre populaire en Afrique noire' [Social portrayal and the popular theatre in Black Africa]. PhD dissertation, Université de la Sorbonne-Nouvelle, Paris III, 1982.

Messa, Abotsi Fo. 'Les promesses togolaises' [The Togolese promises]. *Bingo* (November 1978): 65–7.

Reisner, Gena. 'Three Ceremonies in Togo'. *The Drama Review: African Performance Issue* 25, no. 4 (winter 1981): 51–8.

Ricard, Alain. 'Concours et concert: théâtre scolaire et théâtre populaire au Togo' [Contest and concert: scholarly theatre and popular theatre in Togo]. *Revue d'Histoire du Théâtre* 1 (January–March 1975): 44–86.

——. 'Concert Party as Genre: The Happy Stars of Lome'. *Research in African Literatures* 5 (fall 1974): 165–79.

————. *L'Invention du théâtre: le théâtre et les comediens en Afrique noire* [The invention of the theatre: the theatre and actors in Black Africa]. Lausanne: L'Age d'Homme, 1986. 134 pp.

————. 'Reflexions sur le théâtre à Lome: la dramaturgie du concert-party' [Reflections on the theatre in Lome: Concert Party dramaturgy]. *Recherche, Pedagogie et Culture* 57 (1982): 63–70.

————. 'Texte moyen et texte vulgaire: essai sur l'écrivain public Félix Couchoro et les comédiens ambulants du Happy Star Concert' [Established text and popular text: an essay on public writer Felix Couchoro and the Travelling Artists of the Happy Star Concert Party]. PhD dissertation, Université de Bordeaux III, 1981.

Zinsou, Senouvo Agbota. 'La Naissance du théâtre togolais modern' [The birth of modern Togolese theatre]. *Culture Française* 31–2 (1982–3): 49–57.

TUNISIA

(Arab World volume)

UGANDA

Lying across the equator, landlocked Uganda is roughly the size of the United Kingdom, about 236,000 square kilometres (91,100 square miles). Bounded by Sudan to the north, Kenya to the east, Tanzania and Rwanda to the south and Zaïre to the west, Uganda has a multi-ethnic population of some 19.1 million (1994 estimate). Kampala is the national capital and the largest city in the country. Though English is the country's official language, Luganda is the most widely spoken language, with Swahili also spoken by many. About two-thirds of the population follow Christianity (almost evenly divided between Roman Catholicism and Protestantism) while 16 per cent follow Islam. The country is presently divided into 39 districts.

With over fifty different ethnic groups and languages, communication has long been one of the country's major problems. For centuries, Bantu, Nilotic and Hamitic peoples arrived in present-day Uganda. In the south and west several hereditary kingdoms emerged, the strongest during the seventeenth and eighteenth centuries being the Bunyoro. Buganda was the chief kingdom during the nineteenth and early twentieth centuries.

Arab traders from Zanzibar (now part of Tanzania) began to visit Buganda in the mid-nineteenth century, establishing an active slave trade while introducing Islam amidst traditional, generally animist, worship. Later came the British who introduced Protestantism from 1877 on and the Italians who introduced Roman Catholicism in 1879.

Arab power was severely reduced after 1890 following agreements among the European powers. Control of the country was given to the Imperial British East Africa Company which ruled through the Buganda chiefs. In 1894, the British government annexed Buganda and two years later a loose protectorate was extended over most of the rest of the country and the name Uganda was adopted.

The Kingdom of Bunyoro, a historical enemy of Buganda, was declared a British Protectorate in 1896 and in 1899 its ruler was exiled.

By 1921, a colonial legislative council was put in place but no Africans became members of it until 1945. Such indirect rule by the British long favoured Buganda, which created political turmoil after independence was achieved in 1962. A succession of dictators emerged under the Nilotic leader Milton Obote (b. 1924) who became president in 1966. Obote was ousted in a military coup by Idi Amin (b. 1925) in 1971 and took refuge in neighbouring Tanzania. When Amin took control of the government, thousands fled the country or were killed, among them most of the country's once-prosperous Asian community. At about the same time, Arab immigration to the country increased. In 1978, Amin's forces seized land in Tanzania. The next year, Tanzanian troops and Ugandan rebels invaded Uganda and overthrew him.

These dictatorships effectively ruined the country both politically and economically, cost Uganda significant human resources and saw the widespread repression of the country's leading artists. The national decline was finally halted by the National Resistance Movement's victory in 1986 led by Yoweri Kaguta Museveni (b. 1945), who later became president. Museveni introduced a grassroots democracy, a constitution-making process and economic development policies. He also welcomed back many of the Asians who had been ousted by Amin. Since 1986, the arts have enjoyed a period of unprecedented growth and freedom.

Before colonialism, communal performances of traditional rituals along with ceremonies comprising song, music, dance, mime, recitation and narration regularly took place outdoors, generally in the round, for religious and social purposes. The kings of Buganda, Bunyoro and the other major kingdoms of Toro and Ankole also held occasional indoor performances by court musicians and dancers.

The British introduced spoken drama, choral music and Scottish country dances in schools and colleges. Performed in indoor halls with raised stages, these school and missionary performances led to the emergence of a number

Sam Mugalasi as Claudius and Margaret Macpherson as Gertrude in David Rubadiri's 1975 Theatre Lovers production of *Hamlet*, designed by Leonard Ondur.
Photo: P.R. Francomb.

Robert Serumaga, playwright.
Photo: courtesy of Charles Buyondo and Charles Tumwesigye.

of British and Asian amateur groups across the country. Also to be seen were numerous music hall shows in the British variety tradition. The first of the indigenous amateur theatre groups was the African Artists' Association, founded in 1954 by Wycliffe Kiyingi-Kagwe.

In the years prior to independence, a new interest developed in the arts and a government-supported Ugandan National Theatre opened in Kampala in 1959. Audiences, however, remained primarily British and Asian though playwrights were being trained through the Makerere College English Department's Inter-hall Competition for Original Short Plays, a competition run continuously from 1947 to 1967. In 1962 Ngugi wa'Thiongo's *The Black Hermit* was premièred by the university, the first major play by this major Kenyan dramatist.

In 1963, the African Artist's Association produced Kiyingi's *Gwosussa Emwani* (*The Ignored Guest Becomes the Saviour*), the first full-length play staged in the Luganda language, and in 1968 an opera, *Nyakake* (*Nyakato's Marriage*) by Mbabi Katana (b. 1922), a work that integrated traditional African performing arts with western forms. Both were done at the National Theatre. In 1970, Byron Kawadwa (d. 1977) and Wassanyi Serukenya's (d. 1977) *Makula ga Kulabako* (*A Gift for Kulabako*) was staged.

Makerere Travelling Theatre was founded in 1965 at Makerere College (later Makerere University) and brought English language theatre performances across the country and as far as Kenya and Tanzania. In 1971, a Department of Music, Dance and Drama was established offering a range of courses in the performing arts. In that same year, a new play by Byron Kawadwa, *Oluyimba lwa Wankoko* (*Song of the Cock*) was premièred at the National.

It was the impact of foreign values on Ugandan society which most occupied national dramatists of this post-independence period. Plays of political criticism began to be seen during the Obote years with Kiyingi's radio serial, *Wokulira* (*By the Time You Grow Up*) being very popular in 1965. It was to mark the beginning of direct political reprisals, however; that same year, the serial was banned and everyone who had participated in the production arrested.

Charles Tumwesigye in the 1976 Abafumi Company production of *Ekikekenke*.
Photo: courtesy of Charles Buyondo and Charles Tumwesigye.

Amin's 1972 economic policies put all local theatre in Ugandan hands and foreigners fled the country. The most important company at this time was Robert Serumaga's (1939–82) Abafumi Company (1972–6). The only truly professional group operating in Uganda, Serumaga experimented with indigenous forms; he explored the use of mime, song, movement and ritual in creating a company that dealt with human issues from an African perspective. Among his most important plays and productions of this period were *Renga Moi* (1972) and *Amayirikiti* (1974), a play without dialogue. As an indication of *Renga Moi*'s importance, Abafumi played it in twenty-six countries during that company's existence.

By 1975, Amin had closed all cinemas and even football matches had been banned. Audiences did patronize, however, the theatre. The National, for example, was staging a series of escapist farces and musicals in the Luganda language. Other theatre spaces were created in bars, cinemas and nightclubs but the quality of both the plays and the performances was less than impressive. In 1977, Byron Kawadwa was murdered under Amin's direct orders.

Since 1986, a new generation of writers, directors and actors has emerged more willing than ever to speak freely about social issues such as corruption, childhood neglect and nepotism. Among writers of note are Fagil Mandy (b. 1948), author of *Bush Trap* (1989) and Alex Mukulu (b. 1954), author of *Wounds of Africa* (1990) and *Thirty Years of Bananas* (1991).

A Theatre-for-Development movement also began in 1986 at Makerere University's Department of Music, Dance and Drama. The movement was aimed at sensitizing communities to issues of empowerment and community health.

Structure of the National Theatre Community

Theatrical activities in Uganda generally operate on an amateur basis with dozens of companies in operation at any given moment across the country, most in and around Kampala. While there is a Ministry of Culture, none of the companies receives any type of subsidy. Though there is a National Theatre building, there is no National Theatre company and local groups utilize the National Theatre space on a first-come, first-served basis. Box-office income is shared between the National and the renting group.

Performances take place almost exclusively on weekends because actors and other company members are generally unavailable because of their work during the week. Audiences come mainly from the business community or the political elite or, if a script is on a school reading list, students. With artists having other jobs, rehearsals must take place at night, usually over an extended time period. Some rehearsals have been known to go on all night.

Audiences are generally largest for plays in the Luganda language which have music and dance included. Plays in English find virtually no audiences, a far cry from the pre-1972 period when productions were almost totally done in English or other foreign languages and were written only by non-Ugandan dramatists.

Ticket prices of necessity are kept very low, often less than the cost of a loaf of bread and rarely more than the cost of five loaves.

A number of festivals take place at various times each year; among them are the Uganda Dance Festival and National Schools Music Festival (both July/August), National Schools Drama Festival (May/June) and Makerere University Culture Festival (December).

The National Theatre makes a series of annual performance awards as does the Riverside Theatre and *Munakatemba*, the Luganda language national theatre newsletter.

There are also a number of theatre service organizations now operating. The most important are the Theatre Guild of Uganda which offers workshops and does general promotional activities for the theatre community; the Uganda Theatrical Groups Association, which, though it is not legally a trade union, acts as one and also arbitrates inter-group disputes; the Uganda Performing Rights Society which is a not-for-profit group dealing with rights and intellectual property issues; the Uganda Traditional Dancers Association; and the Uganda Centre of the International Theatre Institute which brings together various organizations to celebrate such events as International Music Day and World Theatre Day. A Uganda Arts Council is in the process of being established.

Artistic Profile

Companies

Ugandan theatre tends to be a mixture of music, dance and drama along with ritual, mime and folk elements. Each of the country's many ethnic groups has its own performative events utilizing variations on these basic elements. Dance and music are central with dialogue – spoken or sung – rather lower on the scale of significance. Dance-based performances can be found everywhere as social celebrations, as concerts or even included as part of western-style plays.

A number of experiments have also been tried in creating multi-ethnic productions which cut across Uganda's complicated language barriers. Perhaps the most successful example of this was the 1987 play, *Mother Uganda and her Children* by Rose Mbowa (b. 1943). Theatre-for-Development performances have dealt with a range of issues from children's health to AIDS.

One of the few efforts at establishing a permanent troupe was the creation of the Uganda National Theatre, which had for a short time both a drama group and a dance group, the latter called the Heartbeat of Africa. Both groups were founded in 1967 but were closed during the Amin regime. The National Theatre is itself now just a theatre building which until 1994 received a small amount of state subsidy to help promote the performing arts nation-wide.

Among the many semi-professional groups of note are Bakayimbira Dramactors under the direction of Andrew Kibuuka, Black Pearls under the direction of Omugave Ndugwa, Theatrikos under Christopher Mukiibi, Ngaali Ensemble, N'dere Troupe, the Diamond Ensemble, and Impact International under Alex Mukulu. All of these groups operate in Kampala in the Luganda language.

Among the groups producing in English in Kampala are the Miando Theatre Company,

Rose Mbowa's 1987 Ngaali Ensemble production of *Mother Uganda and Her Children*, designed by students of the School of Fine Art, Makarere University.
Photo: Andrew Wiard.

325

Teamline, and Ngoma Players. Outside the capital, groups of note include Kigezi Kinimba Company and Rugo Players in Kabale, Ntuha Drama Performers in Kabarole, and Linda Performers in Mbale.

Most of these groups are centred around the energy and talents of a single person, sometimes an actor-director, sometimes a playwright-director. Many of their plays are developed collectively and are connected to issues of importance to their regular audiences. As such they are perhaps closer to Theatre-for-Development than to fully scripted plays.

Dramaturgy
Directing and Acting

The country's first western-style dramatists in the 1960s worked in a tradition of accepted social values and rich performance traditions. Their plays reflected these elements along with the vast changes that occurred during the twentieth century with colonialism. Two early playwrights of note working in this style are Wycliffe Kiyingi-Kagwe and Elvania Zirimu

Namukwaya. Kiyingi's *Pio Mberenge Kamulali* (1954) and Namukwaya's *Keeping Up With the Mukasas* (1961) were both realistic plays with significant social criticism dealing with the loss of indigenous values through the introduction of Christianity and western materialism.

Other writers reflected Kiganda and Luo myths, for example, Kironde's *Kintu* (1960) and Tom Omara's *The Exodus* (1965). Following *Kintu* came an unusual recording from the Luganda Language Society called *Kabbo Ka Muwala* (*The Girl's Basket*), a spoken documentation of Kiganda marriage customs.

Other dramatists of note include Christopher Mukiibi (b. 1933), a social satirist, and Andrew Kibuuka (b. 1962) and Alex Mukulu, both political satirists. Among dramatists who write in English are Cliff Lubwa p'Chong, Fagil Mandy and Charles Mulekwa (b. 1965); p'Chong wrote *Song of Prisoner* in 1988, an adaptation of a well-known novel. Mandy is best known for *Endless Night* (1981), a play about the rigged elections of 1980, and Mulekwa for *The Woman In Me* (1992).

Byron Kawadwa used the folklore of Kiganda palace life and the political reality of

Alex Mukulu's 1990 Concern International production of his *Wounds of Africa*, designed by Fabian Mpagi, at the Seattle Pacific University Theatre Stage, Washington.

abolished kingdoms to attack Ugandan political exploitation in *Oluyimba Lwa Wankoko* (1971). The political points were taken further in Namukwaya's *When the Hunchback Made Rain* (1974) and Nuwa Sentongo's *The Invisible Bond* (1975). The latter play was a clear attack on Amin distanced through a tale of how gods exploited their believers. Shared signs clearly linked the audience to the political messages.

To mask political meanings during the Amin period, Ugandan dramatists turned more and more to symbolism and absurdist dramaturgical approaches. Among plays which followed this direction were several Serumaga works: *A Play* (1967), *Majjangwa* (1971), *Renga Moi* (1972) and his wordless play *Amayirikiti* (1974), the latter about Amin's numerous murders. Others included John Ruganda's *The Burdens* (1972) and *The Floods* (1979), and Mandy's *Endless Night* (1981).

Austin Bukenya's more Aristotelian play *The Bride* (1972) used African ritual and symbolism to depict a destructive culture gradually giving way to a new albino culture, a call for bloodless revolution and integration in place of violence.

Since the mid-1980s, social dramas and moralistic farces have dominated the national stages. Among the social dramas of note during this time have been Lubwa p'Chong's *The Minister's Wife* (1983), Rose Mbowa's *Mine By Right* (1985), Steven Rwangyezi's *Time Bomb* (1993) on women's rights; Mulekwa's *The Eleventh Commandment* (1994); and two plays on AIDS: *The Riddle* (1991) and *The Hydra* (1992) by Harriet Masembe, Peter Lwanga, Sarah Birungi and Kiyimba Musisi.

Popular farces that have had successful runs during this period include Christopher Mukiibi's *Omuzadde n'Omwana* (1982), a play about the generation gap; Ebonita's *The Inspector* (1991), about corruption; Charles Senkubuge's *Omunaala* (*The Tower*, 1990), on national language; and Patrick Mangeni's *The Prince* (1995), a play about power. A number of popular musicals with a political edge have also been done during this period, the most famous being *Thirty Years of Bananas* (1993).

Since many playwrights are also their own directors, it may be useful to say a few words here about some of the significant directorial styles being used. Fagil Mandy tends toward

The Abafumi Company's 1974 production of *Renga Moi* by Robert Serumaga. Robert Serumaga, right.
Photo: courtesy of Charles Buyondo and Charles Tumwesigye.

The Abafumi Company's 1974 production of *Renga Moi* by Robert Serumaga.
Photo: courtesy of Charles Buyondo and Charles Tumwesigye.

expressionism and symbolism in his directorial work while Christopher Mukiibi is a refined realist. Abby Mukiibi and Joseph Omugave Ndugwa both include dance and music in their work. The politically-oriented productions of Alex Mukulu in the mid-1970s were deeply influenced by the absurdist production style of Byron Kawadwa and the theatrical commitment of Robert Serumaga. Kawadwa blended realism and symbolism in his works. Other directors of note include Matovu Joy Alosysus (b. 1962), Kennedy Sekisambu (b. 1965),

Andrew Benon Kibuuka (b. 1962), Charles Senkubuge (b. 1962) and Steven Rwangyezi (b. 1955). Jessica Kaahwa directs mostly African plays in English from her position as a teacher of directing at Makerere University.

One foreign director who has made a significant contribution to Ugandan theatre is Damien Grimes from Britain. A talented choreographer, his modern dance productions at Namasagali College have influenced many local groups.

Theatre for Young Audiences
Puppet and Mask Theatre

There are no theatre groups working specifically for children. If a script is available and found interesting, it can be done by any group interested. One of the few dramatists writing regularly in this area is Fagil Mandy

whose plays include *Drunken Mary Anne* (1985), *Bush Trap* (1988) and *Flowers* (1989). Mandy usually directs his own productions and tries to use children as actors. In his work, the children are the champions of common sense and often undermine the assumptions of the adults involved. It was Mandy who championed the annual schools festivals begun in the 1970s.

Other writers working in the theatre for young audiences field include Kaaya Kagimu (b. 1964), author of *The Present*, and Eria Kizza Lwanga whose work grows out of local legends and has been done by primary schools.

Puppet theatre has been used almost exclusively as an effective tool in community education, especially Theatre-for-Development.

Introduced to Uganda as a medium for community health education by the German Agency for Technical Cooperation (GTZ) in western Uganda in 1992, it was picked up and further developed by the Makerere University Institute of Adult and Continuing Education. Puppets are made of bamboo and foam with the puppeteers themselves chosen from school children between the ages of 7 and 15. Each performance ends with an open discussion of the issues raised.

Design
Theatre Space and Architecture

There is a thin line in Uganda between scenography and stage decoration. With most productions operating on minimal budgets, design is usually seen as something of a luxury. In this sense, design is improvised more often than not. Training is just beginning in this field at Makerere University. Among the only artists working in this area are Fagil Mandy, who favours symbolist and abstract designs, Fabian Mpagi and the London-trained Augustine Bazaale.

The National Theatre, Pride Theatre and Riverside Theatre are the primary spaces used by companies in Kampala. All three have modern and operational stage and lighting equipment. Most other spaces are less well equipped. The National has a proscenium arch stage; virtually all other indoor stages are simply raised platforms.

Makerere University's multipurpose Main Hall is used almost exclusively for university performances. It too has a proscenium arch and is quite well equipped. The Victoria Terrace View Theatre, one of the few spaces actually built as a formal theatre, lacks both front-of-house and backstage facilities and is difficult to use for most performances. As a result, it has been used regularly for non-theatrical activities.

There is one outdoor amphitheatre in Uganda located at the Kitante Primary School in Kampala. It has a capacity of 600. Plans are underway for the construction of two additional public amphitheatres which would be used during festivals. Theatre spaces outside of Kampala tend to be located in hotels, resorts, lodges and schools.

Traditional theatre events always take place outdoors and the borderline between performer and audience, and between public space and audience space is quite fluid. Because every spectator is a potential performer, the circle which surrounds the performer's space is likely to become part of the performance in just minutes. The only exception to this is with ritual and ceremonial events where more specific rules must be followed. Such events include storytelling by bonfire and ritual enactments which often use village courtyards or public squares.

Training
Criticism, Scholarship and Publishing

Makerere University's Department of Music, Dance and Drama offers both applied and scholarly training in all areas of the performing arts on both the undergraduate and graduate levels. Theses and dissertations are kept in the university library.

Uganda Museum is a national museum stocking a large collection of artefacts pertaining to the performing arts including an impressive collection of musical instruments and traditional costumes.

Uganda Cultural Centre opened in 1959 and boasts a year-round cultural village within the complex. In addition to regular performances, it has a large collection of documented photos and publishes an occasional newsletter, *Munakatemba*.

Newspaper or magazine coverage of theatre and the performing arts is rare in the country.

Rose Mbowa with Andreas H. Schott,
Augustine Bazaale and Mercy Mirembe

Further Reading

Breitinger, Eckhard. 'Popular Urban Culture in Uganda'. *New Theatre Quarterly* 8 (1992).

———. 'Theatre and Political Mobilisation: Case Studies from Uganda'. In *Southern African Writing: Voyages and Explorations*, ed. Geoffrey V. Davis. Amsterdam and Atlanta, GA: Rodopi, 1994. 226 pp.

Carpenter, Peter. 'East and West: A Brief Review of Theatre in Ghana and Uganda Since 1960'. *Makerere Journal* 8 (1963): 35–9.

Cook, David. 'Theatre Goes to the People: A Report'. *Transition* 25, no. 2 (1966): 23–33.

Frank, Marion. *AIDS – Education Through Theatre: Case Studies from Uganda*. Bayreuth African Studies Series 35. University of Bayreuth. 205 pp.

Horn, Andrew. 'Uganda's Theatres: The Exiled and the Dead'. *Index on Censorship* 8, no. 5 (September–October 1979): 12–15.

———. 'Uhuru to Amin: The Golden Decade of Theatre in Uganda'. In *Essays in African Literature*, ed. H.H. Anniah Gowda, 22–49. Mysore, India: Centre for Commonwealth Literature and Research, 1978.

Mbowa, Rose. 'Artists under Siege: Theatre and the Dictatorial Regimes in Uganda'. In *Theatre and Performance in Africa*, ed. Eckhard Breitinger, 123–35. Bayreuth: African Studies Series 31, 1994.

———. 'Cultural Dualism in Ugandan Theatre since Colonialism'. In *Contemporary Drama in English: Centres and Margins*, vol. 2, ed. Bernhard Reitz, 163–73. Trier: Wissenschaft Verlag, 1994.

Mbowa, Rose and Eckhard Breitinger, eds. *Uganda: The Cultural Scenery*. Bayreuth African Studies Series 33. University of Bayreuth, 230 pp.

Middleton, J. 'The Dance among the Lugbara of Uganda'. In *Society and the Dance*, ed. P. Spencer, 165–82. Cambridge: Cambridge University Press. 165–82.

Sentongo, Nuwa. 'The Role of Theatre in Adult Education in Uganda'. *Makerere Adult Education Journal* 1, no. 1 (1977): 24–32.

UPPER VOLTA

(see **BURKINA FASO**)

ZAÏRE

A mostly Bantu nation in central Equatorial Africa, Zaïre is sub-Saharan Africa's largest nation with a land area of 2.35 million square kilometres (905,100 square miles), about one-quarter the size of the United States. With a small coastline along the south Atlantic Ocean, it is bordered by Congo and the Central African Republic to the west and north, by Sudan, Uganda, Rwanda, Burundi, Tanzania and Zambia to the north, east and southeast, and Angola to the south. Its population in 1994 was estimated at 42.6 million.

Zaïre includes more than 200 ethnic groups, each with its own language. Pygmies were the earliest people to live in the region but by about AD 800 were pushed into the northern areas by various Bantu peoples who came from what is now Cameroon. Several important states emerged between the thirteenth and nineteenth centuries, the most powerful being the Kongo nation, which dominated the area by the fifteenth century. It was the leaders of

Kongo who encountered the first recorded European to reach the area, the Portuguese explorer Diego Cão who explored the estuary of the Congo River in 1482. In 1487, the Kongo king, Nzinga a Nkuwu, allowed some younger members of his court to be taken to Lisbon where they were baptized and taught Portuguese. In 1491, Nzinga became a Catholic and took the name João I. The Portuguese made treaties with the Kongolese Kingdom and established an active trading base there; slaving was one of the major sources of commerce with upwards of 150,000 people being shipped from the area annually by the nineteenth century. By 1665, with the flow of trade shifting to Luanda, the kingdom declined severely and by the end of the eighteenth century Kongo had virtually disappeared as a kingdom. During the last part of the seventeenth century, non-Bantu groups had moved into the region as well.

Two other traditional groupings of note which grew up in the region during this period include the Bakuba Kingdom, known for its visual arts and extended oral chronicles, and the Luba Empire, which between the fifteenth and eighteenth centuries covered most of Katanga Province (now Shaba).

Between the sixteenth and eighteenth centuries, European explorers, miners, business people and missionaries moved into the area, all seeking to capitalize on Zaïre's enormous natural resources – copper, cobalt, manganese, gold, lead, zinc, tin, diamonds and later uranium. The land ultimately produced rich crops of coffee, palm oil, cotton and rubber.

Even after European and Arab slavery was outlawed in the nineteenth century, explorers continued to pass through the region, the most famous being the Welshman Henry M. Stanley (1841–1904) who in 1876–7 became the first European to journey the entire length of the Congo River. King Léopold II of Belgium (1835–1909) hired Stanley to set up a series of protectorates and a development company between 1878 and 1884 in association with local chiefs, the company to be called the International Association of the Congo with Léopold II as its chief stockholder. At the 1884–5 Berlin Conference on Africa, Léopold II was recognized as the head of what was now called the Congo Free State, still a more or less private economic entity rather than a political one.

Léopold leased and sold pieces of the area to private industry, the largest being the copper-mining company Union Minière du Haut-Katanga. This company developed the southern province of Katanga and it became one of the richest of all the colonial investments in Africa. Many of the companies exploiting the area, however, were less than humane toward the indigenous population and colonial cruelty in the area was among the harshest anywhere on the continent. International criticism led Belgium to take over the Congo Free State in 1908 as a political rather than as a personal entity to be called the Belgian Congo.

Local government was all but unknown under Belgian rule through the first half of the twentieth century and the indigenous population of the Belgian Congo lacked many civil rights. In the late 1950s, however, as winds of independence spread across most of colonial Africa, the Congolese began their first significant moves toward independence. Belgian political reforms came in 1959, too late to avoid riots in the capital.

Belgium moved quickly to recognize local demands for independence assuming that such speed would force the new nation to continue to depend on foreign expertise. In 1960, the Belgian Congo became the independent nation of Congo with Patrice Lumumba (1925–61) as Prime Minister and Joseph Kasavubu as President. Shortly after independence, though, the Congolese army mutinied and Europeans fled the country. Katanga Province soon announced that it was seceding and the United Nations was asked to send troops to help reunite the country.

In 1961 Lumumba was murdered and the same year a new government was formed. In 1963 Katanga was brought under central government control. Civil strife continued for four more years, however. The country's name was changed during this period to Congo (Léopoldville) and then Congo (Kinshasa) to distinguish it from the Congo Republic that had Brazzaville as its capital. In 1972, the country's name was officially changed to Zaïre, a name based on the original Kongo word for 'river'.

In 1973, the government nationalized some 2,000 foreign companies and turned them over to Zaïreans, mainly members of the political elite. By the 1980s, mismanagement and political corruption turned Zaïre into one of the largest debtor nations in all of Africa. The International Monetary Fund helped Zaïre reschedule its national debt in 1985 and the economy was liberalized.

Under the presidency of Sese Seko Mobutu (b. 1930), who came to power in a military coup in 1965 and was still president in 1996, numerous constitutional changes occurred and the economic situation remained difficult. As a result, Zaïrean artists found themselves able to work only under difficult conditions.

Zaïre's official language remains French which is used for government, administrative and legal purposes. More widely spoken is Lingala (being promoted as the national language), Swahili, Kikongo and Tshiluba. About 75 per cent of the country in the mid-1990s were Roman Catholic or Protestant with most of the rest following traditional animist religions.

To comprehend Zaïre's modern theatre it is necessary to understand something of these various indigenous communities and their history of traditional performative events. As in many African countries, cultural manifestations – both profane and sacred – existed long before contact with the European world. Public performances for the entire community were used to commemorate historical events, important burials, rites of passage, enthronements and the cycles of the seasons. All were called festivals and all were occasions for enormous spectacle, much of it participatory and much of it involving dance, music and re-enactment.

Early European traders and missionaries no doubt took some pleasure in viewing these events but by the nineteenth century and the formal colonization of the country, such performances were deemed to be primitive, heathen and lacking in cultural sophistication. At best, they were considered as folkloric displays and relegated – until well after 1945 – to the realm of anthropological rather than cultural study. Missionaries urged the abolition of all such performances apparently fearing that they might popularize spirits who would divert the population from their now Christianized lives. But rather than eliminate them entirely they finally allowed them to be contained under the rubric of indigenous folk events.

A commission was even established in 1935 (by 1938 it included the colonial Governor Maquet) to defend traditional folklore and to help protect the Belgian Congo's indigenous arts. A huge festival was organized in the capital in 1938; in 1949, the Colonial Fair in Brussels was used to show just exactly how exotic and museum-worthy Congolese dancers, musicians and artists could be.

From the mid-1920s, missionaries had been introducing into these traditional communities a more western style of dramatic structure (dialogue, characterization and an Aristotelian mimetic sense). More medieval in tone than modern and usually built around Christian themes, these modern mystery plays – many of them quite spectacular – mark the emergence of western-style drama in the country. Many of these religious performances took place over several days, used hundreds of actors, elaborate designs and ingenious stage machinery. Such events became a regular feature of theatrical life in the Belgian Congo. In 1934 came another major production, *Allo Congo*, which led one Belgian cultural leader to say that 'from these mysteries will be born a true indigenous theatre'. There were, of course, indigenous models to follow including the three-day Mongo performance festival called the Liandja (much closer in style to the medieval mysteries than the modern Christian efforts) but most

missionaries refused to believe that such events could be put into the service of Christianity.

During the colonial period, the indigenous people lived a double life, supporting both traditional and modern events. On the one side was their own living theatre represented by festivals and manifestations of Congo traditions; on the other, presentations organized by the Belgians which needed to be supported for political and social reasons.

These elements began to come together in the early 1950s with a series of dance and music performances representing both Congolese and European traditions done in a British music hall style. Presented mainly in Léopoldville (now Kinshasa) and Elisabethville (now Lubumbashi), the movement was labelled *spectacles popularisés* (people's performances). Included were music, dance, pieces of European ballet, circus and spoken drama. These performances were later toured through the provinces with Albert Mongita often hosting the shows coming out of Elisabethville and Adolphe Kisimba the ones from Léopoldville.

One such group was the popular Circus of Jonghe composed of thirty Europeans and seventy Congolese musicians, clowns, actors and dancers. This group tried to capture the authentic spirit of indigenous performance styles in their many tours between 1952 and 1960. Though attracting large audiences and clearly part of the people's performances movement, it was, however, completely unauthentic.

In 1956, the National Theatre of Brussels helped to launch a new Municipal Theatre in Léopoldville (Théâtre de la Ville, now called Théâtre du 30 Juin) with two productions, an adaptation of John Patrick's *Lotus and Bulldozer* and *The Witch Hunt*, an adaptation of Arthur Miller's *The Crucible*. That same year, J. Marc Landrier organized a popular Indigenous Folk Festival. Another indigenous festival highlighted the opening of another new theatre building, Théâtre de Verdure in Kolowezi.

The Universal Exposition in Brussels of 1958 saw a large-scale production involving Congolese artists, a show called *Yetu: notre allégresse à nous* (*Yetu: Our Very Own Joy*), a hodgepodge of traditional songs, dance and music brought together from the four corners of the country. Out of this curious performance, however, a number of talented artists were discovered and the following year a national Congolese dance company was created, Le Corps National de Ballet Congolais, under the direction of Diatako and Mulenda.

Congolese dance and theatre groups working in a more or less western style had been appearing across the country since the 1940s – Jeunes Comédiens de la Zone Kenya, created in 1948 in Elisabethville; Jeunes Comédiens de Katanga; Jeunes Comédiens de Matadi; and the company of Master Taureau in 1957 – but none had the prestige of the new Ballets Congolais.

The honour of calling itself Zaïre's first modern theatre company goes to the Ligue Folklorique du Congo, founded in 1955 by Mongita. Known to all as LIFOCO or, as Mongita later called it, LIFOTHAC (Ligue du Folklore et du Théâtre Congolaise/Folk and Theatre League of the Congo), this attempt to blend folkloric elements and theatre was more effective than most.

During this period an active religious-based theatre emerged from the many missionary seminaries. In the seminary of Bulongo, for example, Father R.P. Bontink (Father Bongolo as he was known), later an eminent historian at the University of Kinshasa, created a series of Christian moral comedies and historic dramas using a troupe of seminarians who toured through remote villages. Their repertoire was based on myths, legends, epics and local customs and they used the traditional circle actor–audience relationship for their shows in the Lingala language.

Other seminaries followed their lead including the seminary of Kabwe in the province of Kasai. Other respected authors in this religious style were Monsignor Six (author of *Le Pardon des offenses/Pardoning Sins*) and Joseph Malula. The influence of this theatre could even be seen within the large-scale performances of the Circus of Jonghe. *Les Belles Heures de Marie* (*The Happy Times of Mary*) was shown between a juggling number and a lion-tamer. Such pieces were also shown at school events, awards ceremonies, anniversaries and jubilees.

A Christian cultural circle was eventually established for these groups led by P. Mbaya and Albert Mongita (1916–85) and performances increased in number. Among the major productions was an adaptation of *Everyman* called *Bisa Batu* (*Mister Everybody*). Even plays by Molière were done.

As far back as 1945, the first issue of the monthly review *La Voix du Congolais* (*The Voice of the Congolese*), published under the auspices of the government information agency, hinted in a paternalistic way at the political and cultural restlessness in the country even then. Three years later, another government-supported magazine began to appear called *Elite Noire* (*The Black Elite*) which aimed at reaching the black community with information on living well from a colonial standpoint.

La Voix du Congolais encouraged study groups, conferences, libraries, leisure activities and dramatic groups. Interestingly, theatre was absent from the literary competitions sponsored by the publication in 1946 and again in 1948. Included in 1950, plays had to be at least fifteen pages and could contain no more than five principal characters. They had to deal with the life and customs of the country.

In 1952, winning scripts in Kiswahili, Ciluba and Lingala were published: Dominique Membounzhout's Kiswahili play *Mangaiko Zuhula*; Gilbert Mbayi's *Cilembele Watshimuenapale* and Zébédée Nkongolo's *Katshinguka Kuma Nsanga*, both in Ciluba; and Pascal Madudu's *Edongolo Bana* in Lingala. Also published in other issues of *La Voix du Congolais* were plays by Mongita, Pascal Kapela and Christophe Tshimanga. Mongita's plays were of a high literary level though neither revolutionary nor critical.

In April 1956, Patrice Lumumba wrote in this journal about 'the idea of evolution of the Congolese within the norm of western civilization'. Such a norm was seen in other plays by Mongita such as his *Mongenge*, awarded the publication's first prize that year. Mongita's later play *Mgombe* was published in a paperback edition the next year.

Numerous bilateral organizations came into existence at this time involving Belgium and the Belgian Congo – the Association of Artists, Writers and Journalists, the Belgian–Congo Cultural Association and Les Amis de l'art indigène (Friends of Indigenous Art). It was within the framework of this latter group that Mongita's LIFOCO was created in 1955.

Although these associations tried to encourage cultural exchanges, these tended to be one way. Among the Belgian groups seen between 1947 and 1960 were Théâtre Royal du Parc, Théâtre National Flamand, Théâtre du Rideau de Bruxelles, Les Coureurs de Bois (a puppet troupe), Théâtre National de Bruxelles, Théâtre des Galeries de Bruxelles, Théâtre de Poche and Théâtre Royale du Gymnase de Liège. Among the French authors whose works were seen were Jean Anouilh, Sacha Guitry, Jean Giraudoux, Armand Salacrou, Jean Cocteau and Paul Claudel.

Albert Mongita's 1972 production of *Ambeya* at the National Theatre of Zaïre.
Photo: courtesy of CRASA.

Because of this one-way traffic, it can be said that the attempt to develop a modern theatre in the Belgian Congo was effectively smothered. Nevertheless, attempts continued to be made.

One approach was to establish groups more exclusively for Europeans in the Belgian Congo (the Rideau Congolais, for example, which was reserved for Walloons and operated out of Léopoldville). There were also many Alumni Dramatic Associations founded at Congolese schools. The former attempts had virtually no impact whatsoever on Congolese theatre while the latter gave black actors and directors an occasional opportunity for cultural expression. Important groups in Léopoldville included the Alumni Association of the Brothers of Christian Schools (ASSANEF), founded in 1928, and the Alumni Association of the Fathers of Scheuts (ADAPES) founded in the early 1930s. In Elisabethville it was the Alumni Association of Students of the Athénée in Katanga (founded in 1957).

Most of these groups included Blacks and were supported by members of the appropriate Belgian religious order. ASSANEF had as its director in the 1950s the Congolese writer-actor-director Justin Disasi. ASSANEF also published a review, *Signum Fidei* (begun in 1929) and organized soirées in which music and theatre were performed. The ASSANEF model began to be copied by religious groups across the country; in 1954 a 100-seat theatre was built for it which became a key stopping point for many foreign theatre groups. ADAPES included among its prestigious members Patrice Lumumba (its vice-president in 1952) and Albert Mongita. The Katanga group was in a way the meeting-point for theatre of the colonial Belgian Congo and theatre of modern Zaïre. Its theatre group was called Theatre East Africa or THESTAF, and its most noteworthy production was *Papa Bon Dieu* (*Papa God*) by Luthois Sapin. The piece was ultimately judged to be impious by church officials and the director, a member of the clergy, was sent back to Belgium. Nevertheless, a small flag of rebellion had been raised and THESTAF became an early leader in the independent theatre movement from 1960 on.

With only a few notable exceptions the focus of this quickly growing movement was not on the play but rather on creating a theatrical outlet for indigenous voices and artists. Most of the shows by these groups were in French but more and more the language was shifting to Lingala.

There were at least five local theatre groups operating in the capital from the mid-1950s – two in the standard western style, Mongita's LIFOCO and Disasi's Kokodioko; two working street theatres, Libike Lya Bangala and the Amis de Kongoyongo Theatre Association; and Alhadeff, funded by foreign business people. There were also three Katanga groups – Jocoke (Young Actors of Kenya), Jocokat (Young Actors of Katanga) and the aforementioned THESTAF.

All these groups participated in the Challenge Perpetuel d'Art Dramatique (Permanent Theatre Challenge), a festival organized by the Governor of Katanga in 1957. In the first competition, twelve companies participated.

Among the dramatists whose work was presented at the festival were L.S. Bondekwe, author of *Athanase ou Le Professeur de Lunière*; Joseph Kiwele, author of *Chura Na Nyoka* (*The Frog and the Snake*); G. Kitenge, author of *Ujanja Wa Ntumba*; Hippolyte Kbamba, author of *Nkongolo*; and A. Ngongo, author of several pieces – *Le Citadin, Mbutamuntu, Les Deux Médecins* and *Les Frictions*.

The Association for Bakongolais-Kwangolais was created in 1953 for the unification, conservation, perfection and expansion of the Kikongo language. Part of its mandate was to create a Kikongo dictionary. Theatre was to be used in pursuing this mandate and the association organized special soirées for theatrical and folk performances. Patrice Lumumba was again actively involved in this ethno-cultural association.

By 1958, a number of independence newspapers began to appear which gave the organizations and their related theatrical activities extraordinary attention. Among these papers were *Notre Congo, Indépendance, Emancipation, La Voix du Peuple, Congo, Liberté, Solidarité Africaine* and *La Nation Congolaise*. From 1959, these associations more and more openly were evolving into political parties. In fact, life itself became more theatrical and theatrical events *per se* no longer made any sense on their own.

Lumumba, called by Aimé Césaire the Socrates of Black Africa, began making a series of impassioned speeches whose revolutionary power was captured by Jean-Paul Sartre in the introduction to his 'La Pensée de Patrice Lumumba' in the journal *Présence Africaine* in 1963. Political meetings and public assemblies took on spectacular theatrical dimensions at this time. The 1960 National Theatre Festival was, in fact, a revolutionary festival of independence and it went far to place theatre at the core of both the society and its people. Following independence in 1960, a new consciousness could be seen among the country's theatre people. Among the new troupes to emerge was the Theatre Union of Africa troupe, which represented the country in the first Festival of Negro Arts held in Dakar in 1966 with Seydou Badian's Malian play *La Mort de Chaka* (*The Death of Chaka*); the Théâtre de Douze and Lokole Theatre.

In 1967 the government funded the new Théâtre National Congolais (National Theatre of the Congo) with grants from the Department of Culture, Arts and Tourism. Through the 1970s, collective creation emerged as the most active form in the country with work in this area occurring under the auspices of the National Institute of the Arts, a wing of the Centre d'Études et de Diffusion des Arts (CEDAR; Centre for the Study and Propagation of the Arts). A national arts research centre created in 1977, the company sought a new theatrical language.

Among other collective companies during this period were Théâtre Populaire Mwangazo with its production of *Bolozi*; Mwondo Theatre of Lubumbashi with productions such as *Buhamba* and *Tafisula* based on indigenous rituals; and the company of actor-director Bukasa Oshosho in Shaba and later in Ngandu Tshibutu.

It was from these groups that the Theatre-for-Development movement emerged, stimulating an awareness in environmental and health issues. Mwambayi Kalengayi (b. 1942), as one example, organized Theatre-for-Development workshops and festivals in towns such as Boma, Idiofa and Yassa. This work, involving the various communities, was almost exclusively carried out in the local languages.

One of the few who actually wrote scripted plays on these themes was Katshimbika Katende, who worked in Shaba. His best play on this subject is *À la croisée des chemins* (*At the Crossroads*).

Konzi wa Tudu's 1985 production of *Muzang* at the National Theatre of Zaïre.
Photo: courtesy of CRASA.

A number of multidisciplinary experiments were also seen during this period in works by director Konzi wa Tudu (b. 1946) in the capital and productions such as *Muzang*, an adaptation of a classical poem by Mwamb'a Musas done in 1975 by the National Ballet troupe.

During this same period director-actor-teacher Bokomba Katik Diong returned from theatre studies in Belgium and began a series of monthly ateliers in which theatre people could come to discuss their work and compare experiences. These ateliers were extremely useful in bringing out new ideas which were then tried by many groups.

Into the 1980s several groups turned to scripted plays, mostly comedies with social themes. For example, Mutombo Buitshi (b. 1950) and his company Théâtre de Malaika worked mostly in the local languages; the group toured widely. Another was Compagnie Lokombe, directed by Tshisungu Kalimbo and Paul Mbunga. The group did popular satires, many growing out of workshops. Among them were *Lisapo, Lokasa* and *Muam's*.

The Théâtre des Intrigants (Theatre of the Intriguing), directed by Katanga Mupey, adapted a number of foreign plays into the reality of Zaïrean life while the AS company of Mobien Mikanza and Théâtre Icone of Mabanza and Kabesa based their work on the French classical repertoire.

During the late 1980s, theatre reached even further into the country. In Kisangani it was Gazelles de la Thiopo headed by Jules Mishia; in Kasayi Ben Tshibangu staged a number of innovative solo performances such as the social satire *L'Honorable Sentinelle* (*The Honourable Sentinel*); in Kasongolunda, Mitendo wrote the revue that was seen in productions such as *Mgongo-Dioko;* and in Mayombe it was Mavungu Yongo and his Bana Boma Cosmos company attacking social ills in such pieces as *Aujourd'hui j'accuse* (*Today I Accuse*).

Into the 1990s, other international influences had become evident. Wembo Ossako (b. 1946), a director and writer, was experimenting with Boal's Theatre of the Oppressed style, most often in schools with his *Amour et Préjugés* (*Love and Prejudice*) programmes.

Structure of the National Theatre Community

In Zaïre, there are more than a hundred theatre troupes, only a handful of them operating on a professional basis. The capital Kinshasa is the centre of most of these activities and boasts two professional groups including the National Theatre. Other companies exist in Lubumbashi (with one professional troupe), Bandundu, Kasai, Lower Zaïre, Upper Zaïre, Kivu and the Equatorial region. Only three of these groups receive state or municipal support.

The majority of other theatre companies survive on box-office income or on donations from sponsoring schools, companies, churches or other community groups. Numerous national, regional and municipal theatre associations now exist to provide advice and information to their various members. The major grouping is Fédération Nationale du Théâtre.

In 1963 a national theatrical union was established, Union Théâtrale d'Afrique. There is as well the Mobutu Fund which was introduced by the President of Zaïre to cover exceptional social services for artists including medical and death benefits.

There are a number of national branches of international theatre organizations in the country including the Union of African Performing Artists (UAPA); International Theatre Institute; International Association of Amateur Theatre; and the International Society of Libraries and Museums of the Performing Arts.

Artistic Profile

Companies
Dramaturgy
Directing and Acting

Traditional performative activities abound across the country, most involving dance and music and taking place at celebrations and during rituals. Many of these forms are now being seen in experiments involving spoken drama.

Spoken drama itself is used in the many collective creations that dominate community theatre activities in Zaïre and is seen as well in the scripted productions staged by theatre clubs and on a more *ad-hoc* basis among writers – both black and white – who work independently.

Experiments are also seen from time to time in western-style dance and musical theatre.

Among the early modern dramatists of note is playwright and director Albert Mongita, one of the leaders of the national theatre movement in the decades after World War II. A graduate of the St Joseph Institute and later a teacher, Mongita moved into educational religious theatre and then found work as a radio editor where he produced sketches, translated traditional songs and produced music performances by various ethnic groups. In the early 1950s, he joined ADAPES and later became its theatrical animator. With André Schoy, he organized several national popular theatre festivals and tours of foreign theatre groups to Léopoldville. Among his original pieces is *Soko Stanley* (*Thanks to Stanley*, 1954).

In 1955, he staged his first production with LIFOCO, the theatre group of Les Amis de l'art indigène. The group's goal was to combine education with entertainment and it received a substantial subsidy from the Léopoldville government to do its work. Its early productions were in French, even when trying to show the life and customs of the non-French communities. Shows were presented on stages in streets, in hospitals, military camps, work sites, in schools and in association with other cultural groups. Mongita's plays and productions are filled with keen observation of the details of both the comic and tragic elements of everyday life.

Another major group is Justin Disasi's Kokodioko company which performed almost exclusively in the Lingala language. A graduate of the École des Frères, he later became the school's theatre director and subsequently vice-president of the Belgian–Congo Cultural Committee. A director-writer and entrepreneur, he, like Mongita, was involved in the organization of various festivals.

Disasi's work is spoken of in terms of its humour and its cunningly moral viewpoints. Among his earliest successes was *Bolingo Mpe*

Mokuya (*Love and the Occult*). In May–June 1957, *Presence Congolaise* published his piece *Tala se na Miso* in French. Another success was *Arrivée Tardive*. In general, the repertoire of Kokodioko is rather similar to Mongita's LIFOCO group. Both tried to show everyday life in a morally uplifting way utilizing numerous folk elements.

Other authors of note from the 1950s were Hippolyte Kbamba, author of *Nkongolo*, and A. Ngongo, author of *Le Citadin, Mbutamuntu, Les Deux Médecins* and *Les Frictions*. Buabua Wa Kayembe has written several pieces dealing with class and race prejudice. His play *Les Flammes de Soweto* (*Flames of Soweto*) is one of the most performed works in Zaïre's university theatres.

One playwright standing apart from others has been the religious writer, Father Nghenzi Lonta (b. 1932). Even after independence, he wrote a large number of plays which explored questions relating to ethnicity and religion. Many of his protagonists were women in such plays as *La Fille du forgeron* (*Blacksmith's Daughter*), *Njinji, une fille de Ngola sauvera le peuple Ngola* (*Njinji, the Daughter of Ngola Will Save the People of Ngola*) and *La Tentation de soeur Hélène* (*The Temptation of Sister Hélène*).

Among the companies receiving state or municipal support in the 1990s were the National Theatre and the Théâtre Expérimental Maisha (the latter funded by the Department of Higher Learning, University and Scientific Research) at the Institut National des Arts and, in Shaba, the Mwondo Theatre (a regional branch of the National).

The National produces plays on a regular basis with a full-time company and a large number of supporting artists. Its productions tend to have a national focus and are often political. This said, some of its major successes have been with Molière, especially *Le Bourgeois Gentilhomme* which made a star of the actor Kalend Yav (1942–78), known to many as Mundele Ndombe. During three different periods the company was under the direction of Norbert Mobyiem Kikanza (1944–94), later the director of the company Arts et Spectacles.

Maisha Theatre tends to present new plays and styles of theatre that are new to Zaïre. The Mwondo group does theatre of popular ritual.

Theatre for Young Audiences
Puppet and Mask Theatre

Masks have long been part of traditional rituals and have been seen for hundreds of years in performative events. An art of the people, many of the masks speak to one another during such events, being both worn and operated by the creators.

European-style puppet theatre has been seen in Zaïre only since 1980, when workshops began to be offered at the National Institute of the Arts. Through these workshops, participants were led to establish the country's first formal puppet theatre. Those involved in the work include Tshingombe Kalombo, Tshiamala, Velo, Kazadi Musungayi, Kulumbi, Makitu and Mavesse. All of these puppeteers are members of the national centre of UNIMA, the International Puppeteers' Union.

Playwright and director Norbert Mobyiem Kikanza is one of the only people in the country to have experimented with Chinese shadow-puppets, bringing into them social criticism in such pieces as *Le Procès à Makala* (*The Trial in Makala*) and *Biso*.

In 1979, a theatre company and school for children – Théâtre de 2000 Acteurs – opened in Bandalungwa (Kinshasa). Founded by Mwambayi Kalengayi, the school's basic pedagogy is based on Stanislavski's writings. Later run by actress Mpia Agzebi, it is composed of children aged 6 to 12. The group has toured to various parts of the country. Following this model, a number of children's troupes have also been established in schools.

In 1986, an annual festival was created by Katanga Mupey, a festival now called the Journée de Zaïroise de Théâtre pour l'Enfance et la Jeunesse (Youth and Children's Theatre Day). During the festival, children not only perform but also participate in conferences and workshops.

Design
Theatre Space and Architecture

African traditional theatre generally takes place outdoors within a circular space defined by the actors and audience/participants. Such space was based on ritualistic demands. Symbolically, the performance area represented cosmic space and time.

The notion of enclosed playhouses emerged in the first half of the twentieth century with the advent of colonial Little Theatres in major cities. There are several in the capital and others can be found across the country. Some theatre spaces are found in community halls, missionary buildings and foreign cultural centres.

Among the major independent spaces have been Théâtre du Cultrana in the centre of Kinshasa, destroyed to make way for a football stadium; Théâtre du Zoo near the old park of Bock, Théâtre du Centenaire (Centennial Theatre) in Lubumashi; and Théâtre de Verdure, an open-air space in Kinshasa; a campus theatre at the University of Kinshasa.

The best equipped spaces in the country are the private Little Theatres.

Training
Criticism, Scholarship and Publishing

The first professional training school in the arts was created in 1967 – Conservatoire Nationale de Musique et d'Art Dramatique (National Conservatory of Music and Dramatic Art). In 1971, the Conservatoire merged with the National University of Zaïre and in 1972 it became the National Institute for the Arts.

The National Institute is a technical school dealing with all elements of the performing arts. It provides instruction in music, dance, theatre, design and cultural animation. It offers a three-year programme, one general year and two specialized years. A unique institution nationally, the institute had graduated more than 350 people by 1995, some of whom have been subsequently hired by the institute as teachers, researchers and administrators.

There are as well two preparatory National Institutes working at the secondary school level, one in Kinshasa and the other in Bandundu. Additional secondary level schools are planned for other parts of the country. At all these schools, more and more efforts are being made in the performance areas to refocus programmes toward African-based techniques and traditions.

Many have led in the public discussion about theatre in Zaïre, its social role, responsibility and form. Bokomba Katik Diong conducted a series of influential monthly discussion groups and ateliers in the 1970s; Ndundu Kivwila (b. 1944), a director of the National Institute of the Arts organized many conferences, seminars and broadcasts in the 1980s on subjects of importance to the theatre community. Kivwila is also a former director of the Théâtre des Masques Terribles (Theatre of the Terror Masks), a group later run by Nkanga and Mobinzo Damien.

Yoka Lye Mudaba (b. 1947) is another professor at the National Institute, a playwright (author of the play *Tshira*) and a deputy general of the National Theatre. He has written widely on the theatre of Zaïre.

Much national theatrical research has been done at CEDAR (Centre d'Études et de Diffusion des Arts). CEDAR's main publication is *Maisha* (*Life*). Among research projects of note which have received funding from the centre are Mwambayi Kalengayi's study of 'Symbolism in the Dance of Royal Kuba' (1978); research into puppet theatre by Tshsungu Kalomba; a project on ethno-musicology in central Africa; a project on 'Ritual Masks' by Bukasa Oshosho; and a children's theatre study by Bangala Duam. Funding for these came via special grants from the Ministry of Higher Education and Scientific Research.

One major project put together by CEDAR scholars themselves was the development of an African theatre bibliography (1992).

A number of publishers have issued theatre titles including Éditions Lokole, the Zaïre University Press, Éditions des Filles de St Paul,

Éditions Bobiso, Editions CEDI, Éditions Zazeta, Éditions Suka and Éditions Catarsis.

One organization is dedicated to the collection and conservation of objects related to African performing arts – (Centre de Recherche d'Arts de Spectacle Africain (CRASA)).

Most of the major theatre festivals are covered in newspapers and magazines such as the dailies *Elima* and *Salongo*, *The Zaïre Weekly* and the bimonthly *Objective*; and in the more scholarly journals such as *Kin-Media* and *Ngongodioko*. Several television and radio programmes also focus on the arts including *Avant Scene, Culture and the Arts* and *Une Heure au Théâtre*.

Mwambayi Kalengayi
Translated by K. Scott Malcolm

(*Author's Note: This article could not have been written without the extensive research done in the 1970s and 1980s by Professor Henry Lebailly, most notably his book* La Fête révolutionnaire, le théâtre au Zaïre avant 1960 *(1983). He is, in a very real sense, the co-author of this article, which is a modest addition to his groundbreaking work in this field. – MK*).

Further Reading

Actes du colloque sur le théâtre africain, Abidjan, 15–29 avril 1970' [Proceedings from the Conference on African Theatre, Abidjan, 15–29 April 1970]. *Présence Africaine* (1977).

Biebuyck, Daniel P. *The Arts of Zaïre*. Berkeley: University of California Press, 1986.

Bokonga Ekanga Botombele. *Cultural Policy in the Republic of Zaïre: A Study*. Paris: UNESCO, 1976. 119 pp.

Collard, J. 'Vers un théâtre congolais' [Towards a Congolese theatre]. *La Jeune Afrique* 27 (1958).

Cornévin, R. *Histoire du Congo, des origines préhistorique à la République Démocratique du Congo* [History of Congo, from prehistoric origins to a democratic republic]. 3rd edn. Paris: Berger Levrault, 1970.

Crine Navar, B. 'L'Avant-tradition zaïroise' [Before the Zaïrean tradition]. *Revue zaïroise des sciences de l'homme* 3 (1974).

De Rop. *Théâtre Nkundo*. Léopoldville: Édition de L'Université, 1959.

Duvignaud, J. *Sociologie du théâtre, essai sur les ombres collectives* [Sociology of theatre, an essay on Collective Shadows]. PUF, 1965.

Edibiri, Unionmwan. 'Le Théâtre zaïrois à la recherche de son authenticité' [Zaïrian theatre in search of itself]. *L'Afrique littéraire et artistique* 40 (1976): 70–6.

Hulstaert, G. 'Théâtre Nkundo'. *Aeguatoria* 16 (1953).

Jadot, J.C. 'Contribution à l'histoire littéraire du Congo-Belge' [Contribution to the literary history of the Belgian Congo]. *Revue Coloniale Belge* 147 (November 1951): 842–4.

——. *Les Écrivains africains du Congo-Belge et du Rwanda-Urundi* [African writers of Belgian Congo and Rwanda-Urundi], vol. 17. Brussels: Royal Academy of Colonial Sciences, 1959.

——. 'L'Entrée de nos pupilles négro-Africaines dans la littérature de langue Française' [The entry of Black African pupils into French language literature]. *Revue Colonial Belge* 81 (February 1949): 109–10.

——. 'Les Lettres et les arts en Belgique coloniale et au Congo Belge en 1954' [The arts and letters in colonial Belgium and the Belgian Congo in 1954]. *Zaïre* 12, no. 1 (January 1955): 67–7.

——. 'Les Lettres et les arts en Belgique coloniale et au Congo-Belge en 1957' [The arts and letters in colonial Belgium and the Belgian Congo in 1957]. *Zaïre* 12, no. 2 (1958).

——. 'Le Théâtre des marionnettes au Congo-Belge' [Puppet theatre of the Belgian Congo]. *Bulletin des séances de l'Institute Royal Colonial Belge* 21, no. 3 (1950): 559–70.

Kadima-Nzuji, Mukala. 'La Littérature du Zaïre: un parcours critique … le théâtre' [A critique of the theatre of Zaïre]. *Zaïre-Afrique* 153 (1981): 161–9.

Kikufi, Mikanda, Kilesa Ndona, and Tayaya Lumbombo. *Théâtre populaire de Bandundu* [The popular theatre of Bandundu]. Bandundu: CEEBA, 1980. 149 pp.

Lapissade, G. *L'Arpenteur*. Paris: EPI, 1971.

Latere, Ama Buli. 'Le Devin, Le feticheur et le sorcier dans le théâtre zaïrois de langue française' [Divination, fetishism and sorcery in the Zaïrean theatre]. *Zaïre-Afrique* 15, no. 98 (October 1975): 467–83.

Lebailly, Henry. *Catharsis, viol-violence* [Catharsis, rape-violence]. Lubumbashi: PIC, 1979.

——. *La Fête révolutionnaire, le théâtre au Zaïre avant 1960* [The Revolutionary Festival Theatre in Zaïre before 1960]. Lubumbashi: Éditions Catharsis, 1983.

Le Théâtre zaïrois, dossier du premier festival [Theatre of Zaïre: record of the first festival]. Kisantu, 1977.

'Le Théâtre zaïrois' [The theatre of Zaïre]. *Poètes et Conteurs noire*.

Malatuma du Ma-ngo. 'L'Action théâtrale au Zaïre hier et aujourd'hui' [Theatrical activity in Zaïre yesterday and today]. *Ethiopiques* 24 (October 1980): 48–56.

Mawene, Buying. 'Le Théâtre zaïrois' [The theatre of Zaïre]. PhD dissertation, University of Caen, 1978.

Mikanza, Mobiem M.K. 'Les Nouvelles perspectives des arts scéniques africaines: le cas du Zaïre' [New perspectives on African scenic art: the case of Zaïre]. *Zaïre-Afrique* 22, no. 168 (1982): 487–93.

Mudaba, Yoka Ly. 'La critique coloniale et la naissance du théâtre au Zaïre' [Colonial criticism and the birth of the theatre in Zaïre]. *L'Afrique littéraire et artistique* 37 (1975): 83–91.

Mukala, Kadima Nzuji. *Bibliographie littéraire de la République du Zaïre, 1931–1972*. Lubumbashi: Centre d'étude des littératures romanes d'inspiration africaine, Université nationale du Zaïre, 1973. 60 pp.

Mwambayi, Kalengayi. 'L'Arbre à Palabres chez les Bambagani: symbolism et espace scénique' [The Tree of Speech at the Bambagani: symbolism and scenic space]. PhD dissertation, National Institute of the Arts, Kinshasa, 1976.

———. *Initiation au théâtre Africain, technique du mouvement et de regroupement dans la création collective, guide pédagogique du maître* [Introduction to African Theatre, Regrouping Techniques of Collective Creations, Pedadogical Guide of the Master]. Legon: Institute of African Studies, University of Ghana, 1981.

Ngandu, K. 'La Littérature au Zaïre avant 1960' [The literature of Zaïre before 1960]. *Zaïre-Afrique* 58 (October 1972): 493–4.

Ngandu Nkashama, Pius. 'La Théâtre et la dramaturgie du masque au Zaïre' [The theatre and dramaturgy of masques in Zaïre]. *Culture Française* 31–2 (1982–3): 58–76.

———. 'La Théâtre zaïrois: vers une dramaturgie fonctionnelle' [Zaïrean theatre: towards a functional dramaturgy]. *Notre Librairie* 63, no. 1 (1982): 63–74.

Nguisi, N. 'Naissance et évolution des "spectacles populaires" à l'époque colonial à Kinshasa' [Birth and evolution of popular spectacles during the colonial period in Kinshasa]. PhD dissertation, National Institute of the Arts, Kinshasa, 1984.

Povey, John. 'The Mwondo Theatre of Zaïre. *Yale/Theatre* 8, no. 1 (1976): 49–54.

Sang 'Amin, Kapalanga Gazungil. *Les Spectacles d'animation politique en République de Zaïre* [Political rallies as performance in Zaïre]. Louvain-la-Neuve: Cahiers Théâtre Louvain, 1989. 262 pp.

Sartre, Jean-Paul. 'La Pensée politique de P. Lumumba' [The political thought of P. Lumumba]. *Présence Africaine* (1963).

Schicho, Ndala M. *Le Groupe Mafwankolo* [The Mafwankolo Group]. Vienna, 1981.

Traore, B. 'Le Théâtre négro-Africain et ses fonctions sociales' [Black African theatre and its social functions]. *Présence Africaine* (1958).

Ugeuc, E. 'Congo, mon beau théâtre' [Congo, my beautiful theatre]. *Théâtre de Belgique* 9 (1956).

———. 'Le Théâtre congolais cherche sa voie' [The theatre of the Congo in search of its path]. *Revue nationale* 253 (September 1954): 277–8.

Van Den Bosche, J. 'Mongita, peintre, speaker et auteur de théâtre' [Mongita, painter, speaker and author of theatre]. *Brousse* 8 (1956): 13–14.

Yoka, L.M. 'Les Problémes du théâtre au Zaïre' [Problems of the theatre of Zaïre]. *Dombi* 3–5 (August–September 1972): 3–5.

———. 'Le théâtre africain d'expression française, mémoire de licence' [African theatre in French]. Licentiate thesis.

———. *Le Rôle du théâtre au Zaïre, conférence au Goethe Institut, Kinshasa, 4 Juillet 1972* [The role of the theatre in Zaïre, conference at the Goethe Institute, Kinshasa, 4 July 1972]. Kinshasa: Goethe Institute, 1972.

ZAMBIA

Located in south-central Africa, Zambia is a landlocked country surrounded by Tanzania to the north, Malawi to the east, Mozambique to the southeast, Namibia, Zimbabwe and Botswana to the south, Angola to the west and Zaïre to the northwest. Formerly known as Northern Rhodesia, the country is 752,600 square kilometres (290,600 square miles), about three times the size of the United Kingdom. The population was estimated at 9.1 million people in 1993. Areas of highest population concentration are the copper-mining towns in the northeast, the capital city of Lusaka, and the nine provincial administrative centres.

Ethnically the country is divided into seventy-three different Bantu groups that speak the same number of languages. Six of these languages (Bemba, Tonga, Nyanja, Lozi, Lunda and Kaonde) are used for education at primary school level and broadcast on radio. English is the official language for national administration as well as secondary school and university level education.

David Livingstone, a Scottish missionary, was among the first Europeans to reach the area. His explorations of the region began in 1851 and lasted until 1873. In 1888, Cecil Rhodes (1853–1902) signed agreements with local leaders granting him mineral rights to the copper-rich land. Three years later, Lewanika, King of the Lozi people, placed the country under British protection to escape the slave trade which had extended into the region.

In 1899, the British South African Company (run by Rhodes and already administering Southern Rhodesia) took over the administration of most of what is now Zambia and in 1911 renamed it Northern Rhodesia. It came under direct British administration in 1924. In 1953, Northern and Southern Rhodesia (now Zimbabwe) along with Nyasaland (now Malawi) joined to form the Federation of Rhodesia and Nyasaland. The African majority in the territories opposed the federation, however, because it was dominated by whites. The federation dissolved in 1963. A year later – 24 October 1964 – Northern Rhodesia became the independent Republic of Zambia with Kenneth Kaunda (b. 1924) as its president.

Economically the country is dependent on copper mining, which contributes some 90 per cent of export earnings and 60 per cent of the national budget. Zambia's primary trading partners are the European Union, Japan, South Africa, and the United States.

Historically, the development of mining as an industry in the country led to the creation of copper mining towns such as Kitwe, Luanshya, Chingola, Ndola and Kalulushi in the Copperbelt Province and Kabwe (lead and zinc) in the Central Province. These towns attracted workers from across the country and from different ethnic groups.

Each also brought to the new areas their own traditional art forms and styles. Such performances and practices, however, were denigrated by the Europeans and officially discouraged. Without support, traditional forms survived only in the rural communities. In the cities, traditions involving music, dance and drama blended with the newly observed European dramatic forms to create what can be described as 'new traditional' forms.

One example of such fusion is *mbeni*. Created by African soldiers during World War II and full of militaristic miming, this form is nevertheless rooted in both national and local

A Ngoni in full costume with shield and knobkerrie in a team of *ngoma* dancers.
Photo: Zambia Information Services.

choreographic and musical aesthetics. Similar roots can be found in *kalela*, a dance form performed by both the Bisa and Ushi tribes of Luapula Province. Easily the most popular of the 'new traditional' forms, early on it regularly attracted audiences of up to thirty thousand people.

By the 1950s, regular weekend performances of the 'new traditional' forms began to be held in many of the mining towns. Through the Department of Community Development, these weekends were eventually organized into local and regional competitions.

It was in 1966 that the newly independent and very nationalist government of Zambia created the Zambian National Dance Company by recruiting performers from many of the different ethnic groups. Originally created simply to represent Zambia's traditional art forms at the first World Festival of Negro Arts in Sénégal that year, the group proved so popular that it remained together. Now supported by government grants, the National Dance Troupe tours widely and performs regularly at important national functions including the opening of parliament, convocation ceremonies and ceremonies involving foreign dignitaries.

Western-style spoken drama came to the country as part of the British religious and education system during the colonial period. By 1945, dramatic literature was regularly included in English courses in the schools. In the late 1940s, recreational clubs were formed in many towns and cities and some began to include dramatic performances as part of their regular activities.

In 1950, a number of British and South African drama and opera companies toured the country performing European plays at church and school fêtes. This tour gave impetus to the creation of formal theatre clubs particularly among the Europeans living in the country. In 1951, the Northern Rhodesian Dramatic Association was formed from six clubs that had previously been doing performances on an *ad-hoc* basis. Two years later, the clubs – Kitwe, Lusaka, Chingola, Broken Hill (now Kabwe), Luanshya and Livingstone – organized Zambia's first National Drama Festival with only western plays in English allowed to compete. The festival became a national event.

Between 1954 and 1958, many dramatic clubs built their own theatres or converted existing buildings into theatres with the

The Zambian National Dance Company at Kabwata Cultural Village, 1989.

assistance of federal grants, municipal councils and even the mining companies themselves. The first to be completed was Rados in Luanshya (a proscenium-style theatre) built in 1954.

In 1958, British theatre expert Adrian Stanley was hired by the federal government to tour the country for six months and train theatre artists. That same year, the Waddington Theatre Club (the country's only multiracial club) was created in Lusaka under the leadership of the Revd John Houghton (b. 1916). Admitted in 1960 only reluctantly to full membership in the National Drama Association, Waddington produced such fare as Audrey Obey's *Noah* (1960) and Lorraine Hansberry's American drama *A Raisin in the Sun* (1963). In 1966, Waddington ceased operation and, interestingly, many of its members – among the country's best educated Africans – took up important posts in the new national government.

In 1958, the Southern Rhodesia Drama Association joined with the Northern Rhodesia Drama Association to form the Federal Drama League. For the next five years, the new League organized the National Drama Competitions.

Between 1958 and 1960, the Northern Rhodesia Youth Council organized an annual Youth Drama and Choir Festival for high school students, trade school students and youth clubs. Following the same rules as earlier western plays in English, the festival terminated in the wake of the national independence movement as another vestige of colonialism.

In 1963, the Kitwe Drama and Cultural Society was formed. Another alternative for Africans who could not be admitted to the all-white Kitwe Little Theatre, the group began to crumble when some of its leaders were convinced that they should affiliate with the Northern Rhodesia Drama Association.

Later that same year, the Zambia Arts Trust was formed. Running parallel to the Theatre Association (formerly the Northern Rhodesia Drama Association), the Trust catered exclusively to Africans and organized its own festivals, encouraging production of plays in Zambian languages as well as music competitions and art exhibitions. Eventually, the Trust created its own paid company and began touring the country with productions such as *Iyi Eyali Imikalile* (*This Is the Way We Lived*) by Gideon Lumpa, *The Long Arm of the Law* by Kabwe Kasoma (b. 1933), and *Three Faces of Man* by Johannes Mutombela, the pen-name of John Houghton, founder of the multiracial

Waddington Theatre Club. The Trust also organized a major dramatic pageant to mark the country's independence. It disbanded in 1969 when some of its key leaders, including Lumpa, were absorbed into the leadership of the newly created Department of Cultural Services.

In 1966, the University of Zambia was founded and three years later, a University Drama Society was created there. The society first tried to work within the Theatre Association of Zambia but differing philosophies emerged. Composed of students and faculty, the group eventually emerged as the Chikwakwa Theatre, travelling widely, performing plays, doing workshops in many different parts of the country and staging both collective creations and individually authored plays by writers such as Stephen Chifunyise (b. 1947), Grant Lumbwe and Kabwe Kasoma.

A number of independent theatre groups were also formed. In 1966, Sierra Leonean playwright Pat Maddy (later known as Yulisa Amadu Maddy) was recruited by Zambian businessman and publisher Titus Mukupo (b. 1929) to create a professional troupe to be called the Zambia Dance Company. The group produced mainly Mukupo's own works although they did one production of a play by Nigerian Wole Soyinka (*The Road*). The company lasted four years (1966–70), and then became the Zambian National Dance Company.

In 1970, Bazamai Theatre was founded by Masautso Phiri (b. 1945) and Stephen Moyo (b. 1944). The group travelled for the most part, producing in its first season Nigerian writer Chinua Achebe's *Things Fall Apart* and Phiri's *Nightfall*.

The Zambia National Theatre Arts Association (ZANTAA) was formed in 1974 to support the growing number of independent theatre troupes as well as the many school drama groups. As with the Theatre Association of Zambia, one of its functions was to organize an annual drama festival. Instead of using external adjudicators, however (usually from Great Britain), ZANTAA opted to have Zambians in these positions and stressed the production of local plays.

By the 1980s, competition between the nationalistic ZANTAA (with a membership of some 300 groups) and the much older Theatre Association of Zambia was strong and ongoing. In the early years, for example, groups could enter plays in both annual festivals. In 1983, however, ZANTAA forced the issue and from that point on groups had to choose between them. In June 1986, with government support, a merger was effected and a new National Theatre Arts Association of Zambia created.

In the late 1980s and into the early 1990s, Zambia also witnessed the emergence of a Theatre-for-Development movement. Using local languages to address local social issues, the movement included traditional forms that had been marginalized through the years. The new focus – education through theatre – brought artists into many communities across the country. Leading Theatre-for-Development groups now include Kanyama Theatre, Africa 2000, Mwananga Theatre, Fwebena Africa, Modern Images, and Tiyende Pamodzi. So important has this form become that at the annual Zambian National Theatre Festival, Theatre-for-Development productions now have their own special category. In 1991, a separate organization – Zambia Popular Theatre Alliance – was formed with a current membership of over 400. Those in the alliance work with both non-governmental agencies and governmental ministries in promoting their educational messages. In 1994, a National Arts Council was created by the government.

A three-drum ensemble from the Zambian National Dance Company.
Photo: Zambia Information Services.

Structure of the National Theatre Community

In Zambia in the mid-1990s, there were over fifty regularly operating theatre companies and an even larger number of school and college theatre groups but no actors, directors, designers or playwrights who earned their living entirely from theatre. Most theatre artists have other jobs or, if talented and lucky, wind up working in radio, television and film to supplement their theatre incomes. Most of the regularly producing groups are based in Lusaka and the Copperbelt.

Performances generally take place on weekends. Using indoor proscenium stages with from 100 to 500 seats, tickets cost the equivalent of four packets of local cigarettes to attend. Rehearsals generally take place over an eight-week period with the average evening rehearsal lasting two hours.

Government subsidy of theatre activities is limited to support for the National Arts Council of Zambia which acts as an umbrella group for all theatre activities. In total, grants from the Ministry of Culture amount to less than 1 per cent of the government's overall budget. Individual artists are not eligible for grants and even companies rarely get support for more than a portion of their costs.

The National Theatre Festival is held each year in April under the sponsorship of the Zambia National Theatre Arts Association. Sixteen companies from across the country are selected to perform, with special prizes awarded in various categories.

Traditional performances involving dance and music generally take place on days of special ceremonial events in the community and are generally open to the public. Since 1966, public performances based on traditional forms have been done by the Zambian National Dance Company and can be seen regularly in Lusaka. There are no unions. The National Arts Council is the country's central clearing house for cultural information and activities.

Artistic Profile

Ritual theatre, specifically initiation ceremonies, though primarily educational in nature, also emphasize artistry. An initiate in *mukanda* or *makishi* ceremonies, as well as the *gule wa mukulu* ceremony, not only learns about adult life but also is initiated into learning how to dance and how to drum. These skills reflect themselves clearly during the National Theatre Festival when different groups compete.

The festival now recognizes traditional performing arts as an important part of the national culture and *makishi* (a masquerade), *gule wa mukulu* (a masked dance), and traditional forms such as *beena chisungu*, *kalela* and *umutomboko fwemba* are common entries. Each reflects the personal experiences of the young people who have undergone traditional education. Urban youth, without the same experience, often imitate traditional art forms but are equally influenced by modern movies. Workshops are often organized to show the distinctiveness and changing patterns of the traditional art forms.

A number of crossover forms have also emerged blending traditional African with western forms. Two productions, *Kalicheli* and *Mawe*, written and directed by Kwaleyela Ikafa, used such a combination of drama, dance and music as part of the creation of a significant dramatic spectacle. The choreography was close to traditional art forms – a combination of foot-tapping and hip-dancing and the dance as a whole was close to the South African *ipi tombi*.

Edwin Manda (b. 1944), former Deputy Director of Cultural Services, used traditional art forms to produce full-length dance dramas. The different traditional dances were pieced together to tell a complete story rather than being left as static elements. Manda's style has been adopted by other writer/directors such as Stephen Chifunyise and Masautso Phiri. Chifunyise used mime dance in his play *The Slave Caravan*, a historical re-enactment of the Arab slave trade in the region that portrayed the capture of slaves, and their transport to Mombasa on the east African coast. Such adaptation of dance to drama had unprecedented influence on school productions in the 1970s, especially in Lusaka.

Companies

The Tikwiza Theatre Club (founded in 1975) was created by people who had been associated with the University of Zambia Drama Club and Chikwakwa. The group consisted of lawyers, teachers, accountants and a few students. In 1976, Tikwiza came into the limelight when it produced the play *Soweto* by Masautso Phiri which was later taken to FESTAC '77 in Nigeria. It made a strong impression on many people including the President of Zambia, who personally requested the group to travel to other parts of the world and show the suffering of black South Africans. The company subsequently toured Botswana, Cuba and Kenya, and became a *de facto* national theatre company. Its works have often been political. In 1982, the group produced *The Cell* by Dickson Mwansa (b. 1947), a satirical play about prison conditions which upset government officials and cost the group some of its support and good will.

Bakanda Theatre (founded in 1978) was created by a mixed group of students and workers. Bakanda received support from Kitwe City Council in the form of a club facility. Bakanda has produced plays from both east and west Africa, including *Bana Bendu* by Maddy and *The Trial of Dedan Kimathi* by Kenya's Ngugi wa'Thiong'o and Mugo Micere, and such Zambian plays as *Do You Love Me Master?* by David Wallace (b. 1937), and David Watt's (b. 1938) play *Freedom to Be Wrong*. In 1979, they produced Mwansa's *The Cell* which later won awards as Best Original Play and Best Production. Subsequently chosen to represent Zambia at the International Amateur Theatre Festival being held in Canada, the production was unable to find funding and the play was not seen abroad. The situation led Mwansa to say that the play was being silenced for political reasons.

The Zambia National Service Club (founded in 1980) is supported by the Zambian army and mainly stages plays that were successful on television, many by Graig Lungu (1961–92).

The less professional but still important Little Theatres (Mufulira Arts Council, Chingola Little Theatre, Nkana Arts Society, Roan Antelope Dramatic Society, Lusaka Playhouse and Lowenthal Theatre) are the most active groups in the country. Dating back to the 1950s and supported by a racially mixed, middle-class audience, their productions are of a consistently high quality. The Lusaka Playhouse, for example, attracted national attention in 1989 when the president of Zambia attended its production of Mwansa's *The Family Question*. One is likely to see African as well as European plays at Lusaka Playhouse. Roan Antelope Dramatic Society is the country's second most active Little Theatre group, followed by Nkana Arts Society.

Bwananyina (Humanism) Theatre, founded in 1980, is a breakaway group from the Bakanda Theatre. Performing in the various Zambian languages, the group's play *Samaala*, which depicted an irresponsible miner who neglected his family and took to heavy drinking, was among its first important productions.

Chikwakwa Theatre, founded in 1970 at the University of Zambia, became both a movement and a philosophy of theatre with wide-ranging influence on national theatre development. Several non-Zambians were involved in its creation including the British scholar Michael Etherton (acknowledged as the real founder), Andrew Horn, John Reed, Fay Chung, Alison Love and Ezekiel Mphalele. In 1970, Chikwakwa became a travelling theatre. During

holidays, on an annual basis, students and staff travelled up country performing plays originally written in English but translated into the languages of the provinces to which they travelled. Performing in schools and community halls, they have also held training workshops and festivals giving many young people an opportunity to acquire writing and production skills.

The group's first tour in 1970 was made to the Eastern Province and performances consisted of English-language literary translations into Nyanja of works by Mphalele, Fwanyanga Mulikita (b. 1928) and Ireland's Lady Gregory. Throughout the 1970s, Chikwakwa travelled to all parts of Zambia and was instrumental in the creation of the Zambia National Theatre Arts Association. The company also produces the *Chikwakwa Review*, a theatre journal written in English. The work of Chikwakwa has been formally incorporated into the work of the Centre for the Arts at the University of Zambia.

Kanyama Theatre, founded in 1980, has been the most consistent theatre company

The Chikwakwa Theatre stage during a student production of Andreya Masiye's *Lands of Kazembe*.
Photo: University of Zambia Information Desk.

working in the area of Theatre-for-Development. Another is the Mwananga Theatre, based in Luangwa, a typically rural and remote part of the country. Mwananga is part of a non-governmental organization that spearheads community development through focus on the environment. Active in the area of wildlife conservation, Mwananga made a film on this subject, *The Problem*, in 1988.

Umondo Wesu Theatre is a semi-professional company supported by the Bank of Zambia and based in Ndola; the company also produces television shows. Another commercially supported group is the Zambia National Commercial Bank Theatre which is mainly involved in the production of television shows. In a country where historically theatre has not received funding from the business sector, the setting up of a business-supported theatre company ushered in an era not known before.

Dramaturgy
Directing and Acting

Until the 1960s the repertoire of Zambian spoken theatre consisted of mainly western plays. The works of Shakespeare, Brecht and Molière were commonly played in English or adapted for the Zambian stage. Mostly these plays catered to the interests of the British settler community. What was noticed after independence was a lack of plays that reflected the culture of Zambian society. Thus the number of national playwrights is rather small and their histories quite recent.

Andreya Masiye (b. 1922) began his career as a broadcaster soon after World War II. While working for the Broadcasting Corporation he wrote a play, *Kazembe and the Portuguese*. Based on the history of Portuguese journeys of exploration by de Leerda from the eastern coast of Africa into Zambia, the play as broadcast attracted attention because of its subject as well as its racially mixed cast. Produced at a time when racial mixing was virtually taboo, the play was performed on stage at the University of Zambia in 1974. Masiye, however, did not continue writing drama but turned instead to novels and short stories.

Gideon Lumpa wrote *Iyi Eyali Imikalike* (*This Is the Way We Lived*) and *Kalufyanya* for the Zambia Arts Trust. These works toured the country and reflected the change in life between the old and new African ways of living, as well as issues of urbanization and colonization. Lumpa later trained as an actor in Israel. When he returned, he became director of the Zambian National Dance Company.

Kabwe Kasoma also wrote for the Zambia Arts Trust in the mid-1960s. His major works include *The Long Arm of the Law*, *Black Mamba Lobengula* and *Fools Marry*. His plays focus on Zambian history and social life.

Another 1960s writer of note is Fwanyanga Mulikita who wrote *Shaka the Zulu*, a dramatization of the life of an historical African warrior. The work attracted attention for its realistic portrait of its central character, quite famous in Zambia, to whom some ethnic groups trace their ancestry. Like Masiye, though, Mulikita also did not continue writing for the stage but diverted his creative attention to written folklore.

The period from 1970 to 1995 saw the coming of age of a number of writers whose concern was with the conflicts that arose as the country was grappling with issues of development and modernization. Plays tended to focus more on the contemporary and less on the historical. Most writers of this era were products of the new University of Zambia and were associated with the University's Drama Group or the University of Zambia Writers' Association.

Stephen Chifunyise began writing in 1973 as part of the University Drama Society. His major works include *The Blood*, *I Resign*, and *The District Governor Comes to the Village*. Also important is Chifunyise's influence on Zambian theatre through his leadership role in the Zambia National Theatre Arts Association and the Department of Cultural Services. He was able to communicate effectively with many groups, wrote for them and helped them to deal with written scripts rather than simply improvisation.

Darius Lungu is the first Zambian playwright to focus on the problems of the betrayal of the promise of independence. Dealing with issues of unemployment among urban youth, his best works include *The Graduate and the Mishanga Sellers* and *The Man in the Street*.

Dickson Mwansa began his career with *The Cell* (1979), followed by *What's in the Title? Father Kalo and the Virus* and *The Family Question*. Both *The Cell* and *The Family Question* won Best Play Awards. Mwansa's works are primarily satirical and look at social contradictions in a country in transition. Mwansa has also provided leadership to the

Zambia National Theatre Arts Association and the International Theatre Institute, and has tried to relate adult education and theatre in his work as an adult educator at the University of Zambia.

Masautso Phiri wrote and directed *Soweto* (1976), *Soweto Remembered* and *Soweto Flowers Will Grow*, a trilogy that focused on the political upheavals in South Africa, the country to which Zambia is connected for its seaports. His works are realistic portraits of the problems associated with apartheid and have been performed in other parts of Africa as well as in Cuba.

The plays of Graig Lungu, one of Zambia's most talented writers, have been successfully adapted for both stage and television. His appeal is to a wide audience and his works deal with conflicts within families, child abuse, child neglect, and peace. Known also for a weekly television programme where he produces mainly improvised works, Lungu's written works have achieved great critical acclaim, especially *Farewell to Babylon*, *Imbangala* and *School Leaver's Note Book*.

Other significant writers whose works have been staged include Kwaleyela Ikafa (b. 1956), Moses Kwali (b. 1951), Julius Chongo (1944–94), Killian Mulaisho and Nora Mumba (b. 1955). Three British writers with intimate knowledge of Zambia whose works have been written and performed on Zambian stages are David Kerr, David Wallace and Stewart Crehan.

Theatre for Young Audiences

Modern western drama for young audiences has been introduced to young people through schools as both literature and as part of co-curricular activities. The actor Wesley Kaonga began his career as a student. Later he studied in the United States (at the California Institute of the Arts), and returned home to become a leading performer and a model for others.

Such theatre has attracted large numbers of participants; it is intense, highly competitive and has grown to incorporate poetry and choirs. Some of these works have even filtered into national television and have been seen by large audiences.

The American International School in Lusaka provides training in drama and music to young people. A school privately run from 1984 to 1988 by Jessie Martin provided training in drama and dance but closed due to lack of financial support.

Puppet and Mask Theatre

The use of puppets as a form of theatre is not widespread since puppetry has been associated with witchcraft in a number of ethnic groups.

In the 1980s, European-style puppetry began to grow as an urban art form used by solo performers in the streets. Such solo puppeteers can regularly be seen at bus stops and market-squares in Lusaka. Performers carry single figures that are manipulated with strings attached to a wooden frame. Most solo puppeteers have become social satirists and audiences have become quite attracted to these shows. Most ask for a token contribution before beginning their performance. Some have fixed fees and after a short performance will not begin again until another contribution is made. Puppeteers operating in this way are always men and, in most cases, have no other source of income. Puppetry has also been incorporated into many 'popular' theatre projects. It is one of the forms taught in training workshops on Theatre-for-Development.

Masks, however, are widely used in many ritual performances, particularly in *makishi* and *gule wa mukulu*. In the *makishi* masquerade, the dancers wear masks to represent ancestral spirits who are to guide initiates on their way into adulthood. Initiates are also taught how to make the masks themselves. The mask thus made is given the name of one of the maker's ancestors and for the rest of his or her life the maker will dance only with that mask on. Clearly, such masks are not interchangeable.

In *gule wa mukulu*, dancers wear masks that represent animals or a combination of both human and animal qualities. These are both abstract and naturalistic. In the colonial period, masks were created that parodied the behaviour of the Europeans for the amusement of local audiences. In the 1990s, masks were still used to parody the behaviour of the greedy and the mean.

Mariya, a Nyan female mask character, caricaturing colonial missionaries at Chadiza Boma, 1993.
Photo: Mapopa Mtonga.

Design
Theatre Space and Architecture

Theatres in Zambia have been built in two basic styles – the traditional proscenium arch and open-air structures. Most of the proscenium theatres are located in Kitwe, Mufulira, Luanshya, Ndola, Chingola and Lusaka and seat between 200 and 300 people. The best known of these are the Rados Theatre (built in 1954) and the Lusaka Playhouse (built in 1951). Most are equipped with modern technical devices and follow traditional European styling.

The outdoor theatres, in contrast, have been built for traditional performances. Most were created by the Department of Cultural Services in order to provide room for traditional performers for whom the structures of modern theatres were not suitable. Such theatres can be found in Livingstone, Lusaka and Ndola. Most are thrust stages and are of pole and thatch construction. The thatch has to be changed about every two years and obviously can be used only in clear weather. The seating pattern is similar to the ancient Greek amphitheatres. Most open theatres have seats built out of mud and concentrically arranged with seating capacities of 200–300 people while others do not have any seats and performances are watched while standing and involve audience participation. Admission fees are usually charged and the performances attract both local audiences and tourists. Outside the open-air theatres are special booths where craftspeople and artists work and sell their products.

Training

There is no national theatre school or licensing system for theatre artists in Zambia. Much of the theatre training that exists is provided through training workshops organized by the National Theatre Arts Association of Zambia, by resources drawn within the country and sometimes brought from outside by organizations such as the British Council and the American Cultural Centre. Training workshops are short, lasting only one or two weeks and focusing on specific aspects of theatre.

During national festivals, workshops are organized for playwrights, actors, directors, traditional dancers and administrators. Usually, the workshops alternate with competitions. A training school for young actors exists in Lusaka and the American International School has a Theatre Department where music and drama are taught. Each theatre group also offers some form of training.

The Centre for the Arts at the University of Zambia offered for a time more training in drama, music and fine arts leading to degrees, diplomas and certificates. It was closed in 1994, however, due to a lack of financial support and the staff transferred to the Department of Literature and Languages.

For traditional art forms, training is offered for those who have passed through traditional education and have shown skills as dancers and drummers. Performance is part of the pedagogy of traditional education and is taught during a period of intensive and confined training that coincides with initiation into adulthood. Generally this takes place at age 13 for girls and 15 for boys. Master drummer Mapopa Mtonga, a product of the *nyau* traditional school of drumming, offers training in traditional dances and drumming at the Centre for the Arts at the University of Zambia. The *nyau* school is found among the Ngonis of the eastern part of Zambia. Others are the *makishi* school in Northwestern Province, and the *nachisungu* school of Northern Province.

Western music training is provided by the Everlyn Home College of Further Education. It trains teachers who later are attached to theatre and choir clubs in schools.

Criticism, Scholarship and Publishing

Theatre criticism is done by journalists or correspondents attached to the country's two major daily newspapers – the *Daily Mail* and the *Times of Zambia*. The *Daily Mail* usually covers happenings in theatre and reviews major productions. The *Times of Zambia*, in its Sunday edition, covers one major production each week.

The *Mining Mirror*, a fortnightly published by the mining industry, provides a more detailed and thorough coverage of theatre although its coverage is generally confined to productions in the mining towns.

The *Chikwakwa Review* at the University of Zambia offers theatre criticism as well. Another more scholarly publication is the *Ngoma Journal*, produced by the University of Zambia's Department of Literature and Languages.

Research in the field is done as part of scholarship in literature and languages by university scholars. The Institute of African Studies at the University of Zambia has a cultural unit that focuses on oral literature and

theatre, while the School of Humanities and Social Sciences, Centre for the Arts and Centre for Continuing Education have staffs with academic and professional interests in theatre.

Two key publishing houses for theatre are the Kenneth Kaunda Foundation and Multimedia Zambia. The National Theatre Arts Association of Zambia also publishes occasional works.

Dickson Mwansa

Further Reading

Balcomb, J. 'The Beginning of a New Beginning for Zambia'. *Le Théâtre dans le Monde* (1965).

Batsford, R. 'Zambians Steal the Show at TAZ Festival'. *Stage* (September 1973).

Brelsford, W.V. 'African Dances of Northern Rhodesia'. In *The Occasional Papers of the Rhodes-Livingstone Museum*, University of Lusaka/University of Manchester, 1974.

Chakulanda, P. 'Towards a Zambian National Theatre'. *Chikwakwa Review* (1974–5).

Chifunyise, Stephen. 'An Analysis of the Development of Theatre in Zambia'. MA thesis, University of California, Los Angeles, 1977. 222 pp.

———. 'Problems of Transposing Traditional Narratives, Myths and Legends into Contemporary Performing Arts'. *Bulletin of the Zambian Language Group* 3, no. 2 (1978): 37–42.

Chifunyise, Stephen, David Kerr and F. Dall. *Theatre for Development: The Chalimbana Workshop, 1979.* Lusaka: Zambian Centre of the International Theatre Institute, 1980. 65 pp.

Chirwa, A. and F. Chung. 'Children's Theatre Production'. *Chikwakwa Review* (1971).

Crehan, Stewart. 'Fathers and Sons: Politics and Myth in Recent Zambian Drama.' *New Theatre Quarterly* 3, no. 9 (1987): 29–43.

Dall, F. 'Theatre for Development: An Approach Tool for Extension Communication and Non-Formal Education in Zambia'. *Education Broadcasting International* 13, no. 4 (1980): 183–7.

Epskamp, Kees P. 'Historical Outline of the Development of Zambian National Theatre'. *Canadian Journal of African Studies* 21, no. 2 (1987): 157–74.

Etherton, Michael. 'The Development of a Radio Programme Series in Zambia'. *University of Zambia Institute for Social Research Bulletin* (1968).

Idoye, Emeka Patrick. 'Ideology and the Theatre: The Case of Zambia'. *Journal of Black Studies* 19, no. 1 (September 1988): 70–8.

———. 'Popular Theatre and Politics in Zambia: A Case Study of the University of Zambia (Chikwakwa) Theatre'. PhD dissertation, Florida State University, 1981. 296 pp.

Kamlongera, Christopher F. 'Problems in the Growth of a Popular Art Form: The Relationship Between Drama and Society in Malawi and Zambia'. PhD dissertation, University of Leeds, 1984.

Kasoma, K. 'Participatory Communication and Development'. *Journal of Adult Education* (1983).

Kerr, David. 'Didactic Theatre in Africa'. *Harvard Educational Review* (1980).

Kerr, David and Stephen Chifunyise. 'Popular Theatre in Zambia: Chikwakwa Reassessed'. *Theatre International* 11–12 (1984): 54–80.

McCaffrey, Oona. 'The Nyau Dance'. *The Drama Review* 25, no. 4 (winter 1981): 39–42.

Maxwell, Kevin B. *Bemba Myth and Ritual: The Impact of Literacy on an Oral Culture.* New York: P. Lang, 1983. 197 pp.

Mensah, Atta Annan. *Music and Dance in Zambia.* Lusaka: Zambia Information Services, 1971. 22 pp.

Mitchell, J. Clyde. *The Kalela Dance: Aspects of Social Relationships among Urban Africans in Northern Rhodesia.* Manchester: University of Manchester Press, 1956.

Msimuko, A.K. 'The Theatre of Awareness: Its Use in Health in Africa'. *Zango* 10.

Mtonga, Mapopa. 'The Drama of *Gule wa Mkulu*'. MA thesis, Legon University, 1980.

Mwansa, Dickson. 'Theatre as a Tool for Communication'. *Journal of University Adult Education Programme* 24, nos. 1–3 (1985): 85–95.

———. 'Theatre Situation in Africa'. *Young Cinema and Theatre* 1, nos 3–5 (1985).

Mwondela, Willie R. *Mukanda and Makishi in Northwestern Zambia.* Lusaka: National Educational Council of Zambia, 1972. 58 pp.

Pownall, D. 'European and African Influences in Zambian Theatre'. *Theatre Quarterly* 10 (1973).

Richards, Audrey I. *Chisungu: A Girl's Initiation Ceremony Among the Bemba.* London/New York: Tavistock, 1982. 224 pp.

———. 'Theatrical Situation in Zambia'. *World Theatre* 15, no. 1 (1966): 56–57.

Turner, Edith. 'Phillip Kabwita, Ghost Doctor: The Ndembu in 1985'. *The Drama Review* 303, no. 4 (winter 1986): 12–35.

ZANZIBAR

(see **TANZANIA**)

ZIMBABWE

Located in south central Africa and surrounded by Zambia to the north, Malawi to the northeast, South Africa to the south and Botswana to the southwest, Zimbabwe is a landlocked country of 390,300 square kilometres (150,700 square miles), with a population of 10.9 million, 95 per cent of whom are Shona and Ndebele people of Bantu extraction. Shona constitute 70 per cent of the population and are made up of Karanga, Zezuru, Manyika, Ndau and Korekore ethnic groups.

Bantu arrived in the region as early as the fifth century AD displacing Pygmies and Khoisan. It was the Bantu who between the ninth and thirteenth centuries built the extraordinary stone fort and temple complex which they called Zimbabwe and after which the modern nation is named.

In the late 1880s, the British empire-builder Cecil Rhodes persuaded the Ndebele king, Lobengula, to grant mining rights to him. Soon after, Rhodes's British South African Company was granted a charter by Britain to rule the area, which was to be called Southern Rhodesia. Over the next few years, the settlers instituted laws and land tenure systems that dispossessed the indigenous peoples and used forced labour to create wealth for the settler community with the natives moved to reserves.

A major anti-settler challenge by the Ndebele in 1896 – the Chumurenga Uprising – was brutally suppressed by Rhodes and the white community. A number of Shona spirit mediums who had led the uprising were executed and the colony was more than ever in Rhodes's hands.

Southern Rhodesia became a self-governing colony in 1923 after its white population – the only ones allowed to vote – decided against joining the Union of South Africa. But soon after 1945, the indigenous people, especially those who had fought in World War II, returned home determined to fight against the racism and colonialism that had dispossessed them.

In 1953, the government joined with Northern Rhodesia and Nyasaland to create the Federation of Rhodesia and Nyasaland but the federation collapsed in 1963 because of pressure from Black Africans who refused to accept ongoing political control by whites. In 1964 Rhodesia dropped the word 'southern' from its name and demanded sovereignty but Britain refused insisting that Black Africans be given a larger role in governing. The white government unilaterally declared Rhodesia independent in 1965.

Only South Africa recognized Rhodesia's announced independence and over the next years black nationalist political parties adopted armed struggle as the only way to wrest the country from its colonial and racist occupation. This led to a twenty-year war of liberation that was fought both within the country and from Mozambique and Zambia. Led by the Zimbabwe African People's Union (ZAPU) under Joshua Nkomo (b. 1917), and the Zimbabwe African National Union (ZANU) of Robert Mugabe (b. 1924), the guerrillas received active support from the Soviet Union, China and North Korea. A brutal and violent struggle, it also resulted in the deaths of hundreds of thousands of peasants, black nationalists and white settlers, ending in 1979 with a peace agreement that formulated the constitution of Zimbabwe and guaranteed the rights of white landowners for a period of ten years. Formal independence was achieved in 1980.

Mugabe's ZANU party emerged as the overwhelming winner of the first general election, an election which ushered in a Marxist government of national unity that also shared ministerial posts with Nkomo's ZAPU and members of Ian Smith's (b. 1919) white Rhodesian Front Party. When ZAPU was later accused of plotting to overthrow the government, a five-year civil war began that was ended in 1987 by a Unity Accord that forged the two nationalist parties into the single Zimbabwe African National Union Patriotic Front.

An Economic Structural Adjustment Programme in the early 1990s initiated open-market reforms leading Zimbabwe to abandon its socialist policies in favour of market-driven capitalist ones, especially in Zimbabwe's two largest cities, Harare (the capital, formerly Salisbury) and Bulawayo.

It is against this political background that the country's rich theatrical heritage may be understood. When the white settler community first arrived in large numbers, Zimbabwe had its own African performing arts traditions which were an integral part of the life of the people. Among the Shona, for example, after harvest each year, pre-adolescent children would meet in the moonlight to perform *mahumbwe*, which dramatized and explained to them various aspects of adult life. Performances would last most of the evening. As adolescents, the children would no longer be expected to participate in *mahumbwe* but would be expected to put their knowledge of adult life into practice. Urbanization, the impact of modern education and Christianity have slowly eroded the meaning of this particular children's traditional drama and the form has all but disappeared from most Shona communities. In rural communities, it has become merely a child's game.

At funerals, other performative events take place among Shona ethnic groups. For example, in-laws (usually the younger sisters of a widow and/or the wives of a dead man's sons and nephews) would dress up in the dead man's clothing and perform scenes highlighting aspects of the dead man's life. These enactments, performed before the burial, were important for the community and were part of every all-night funeral wake. Generally including music, dance and mime, these quite joyous events were, however, discouraged by the Christian church, which called them evil. The form, though, still survives as an important aspect of the funeral rites of the Shona.

Storytelling performances were also popular among all indigenous groups. This form of theatre, where the storyteller plays various characters, offered opportunities for the audience to take active roles in the songs, dance and music that were always part of these stories. Such performances still survive and have begun to be utilized in various ways in modern theatrical performances.

Similarly, performances of praise poetry and ritual chants, especially totemic and royal praise dramatized by solo performers who portrayed a multitude of characters, have also remained vibrant, dynamic and adaptable and can be seen in modern theatre forms, especially those presented in indigenous languages.

Probably the most misunderstood and dominant form is the traditional dance, which is in fact traditional dance-drama. In Shona there are dances such as *chinyambera*, a dance performed by returning hunters to dramatize their adventures and to show the skins of the animals they killed. Other traditional dance-dramas were performed at communal rain-making ceremonies, marriage and inheritance rituals, fertility rituals and initiation ceremonies, as well as the installation of chiefs at harvest ceremonies.

These traditional forms, passed from generation to generation, and now performed out of context as entertainment, mean that the integrity and the socio-dramatic aspects of these pieces have been undermined. Nevertheless, they are still alive and helping to create new and innovative theatre forms.

During the colonial period, such traditional theatre forms were declared barbaric by the church, and banned by the Witchcraft Suppression Act. Those who performed them were condemned by the church for witchcraft. After independence, this Act was among the first to be revoked.

Given such a background, one can say only that white colonial historians such as George Maxwell Jackson were clearly wrong in saying that the first theatrical entertainment in the country took place only after the British flag was hoisted in Fort Salisbury in 1890 – a production of *Regiment Sergeant* by William Fleming King, 'a knockabout farce' with a 17-year-old soldier playing the sole female part. This type of closed-minded colonial history has been responsible for the continuing ignorance about the many indigenous theatrical traditions. It is true that from the early 1890s until the 1920s the dominant theatre seen by officials and settlers in the colony was that of visiting companies from Britain and South Africa, but theatrical activities did also exist among the indigenous population.

A number of colonial theatre clubs emerged whose operation, constitution, production philosophy and techniques – for example, the REPS Theatre, founded in 1931 as Salisbury Repertory Players – were moulded on British theatre practice and that of the general run of touring companies travelling throughout southern Africa.

Competitive drama festivals and the annual events of the Rhodesian Institute of Allied Arts, formed in 1947 (the Eisteddford Society), and the many national theatre festivals run by the Association of Rhodesian Theatrical Societies (established in 1958) became the backbone and *raison d'être* of the colonial theatre movement.

An examination of the plays produced by these theatre groups between 1931 and 1980 also shows the dominance of plays that had been successful in South Africa, London's West End or on Broadway. Plays by Shakespeare, Arthur Miller, Edward Albee, Samuel Beckett, Harold Pinter, Agatha Christie, Eugène Ionesco, Oscar Wilde, William Butler Yeats, Gilbert and Sullivan, George Bernard Shaw, John Osborne, John Arden, Molière and Ibsen were the staples of both visiting companies and this Little Theatre movement.

By 1945, European and US theatre was dominant in Rhodesia's schools and theatre clubs. During the 1950s and 1960s many new Little Theatres were built in segregated town council halls and sports club facilities in Harare, Bulawayo, Kadoma, Mutare, Gweru, Masvingo and Kwekwe.

Except for REPS – where full-time directors were employed, among them Adrian Stanley and John Cobb – most clubs were part-time operations. In later years, full-time technical crews were added along with building management personnel. By the 1970s, the quality of productions seen at the Little Theatre festivals was comparable to most professional theatres. With the annual festivals adjudicated by theatre artists from Britain and South Africa, it was clear that the goal was mostly to maintain ties with the mother country.

Among the best of the Little Theatre directors were Stanley, Cobb, Noel McDonald, A. Morgan Davies, Tony and Margaret Weare, Susan Hains, John Keeling, Joyce Belton and Ken Buchanan. A few playwrights were involved as well but none of any note – George Yiend, Ken Marshall, Frank Clements, John Watson and Myer Bloom among them. It was not that their plays were irrelevant or poor but rather that there was an obvious preference for London or New York than for plays that would discuss local issues or even question the notion of colonialism.

For example, Yiend's 1973 play, *Someone in the House*, had been successfully performed by the University of Rhodesia Players and had attracted critical attention. Yet the play was not deemed to be acceptable to the Little Theatres despite having been declared by adjudicators as Play of the Year. Foreign adjudicators were also influencing the theatre clubs to seek out plays that compared favourably to the repertoires of the provincial theatres in Britain, or elsewhere in Europe. This was to be done in an obvious attempt to prove that high standards were possible even in the rough conditions of an African colony.

Theatre was also encouraged in the schools through both the teaching of English literature and the Association of Rhodesian Theatrical Societies' National High Schools Drama Festival. Because most of the school festival adjudicators were themselves working in the Little Theatre movement, the rules and regulations of the theatre festivals were used to determine what was acceptable and consequently what would be performed, even in black schools.

Indigenous theatre forms were, of course, totally discouraged. When local authorities such as the Salisbury City Council's Native Affairs Department actively began to utilize theatre in the black townships, it was again European plays which were presented, especially Shakespeare. Translated into indigenous languages, these plays were ultimately performed by black groups.

There was a total silence, however, in the colonial press on black theatre activities (even when they were imitations of western theatre). This was consistent with the racist policies of the government which continued to repress traditional arts and culture. There were indeed many significant theatre activities that could have been reported. Organizations had come into being such as the church-based Ecumenical Arts Workshop which was founded in the early 1960s to promote the development of writing and the production of music and drama among black people. A group that later played a significant role in producing writers for the black majority theatre movement.

The College Drama Association and its annual competitions also actively promoted black theatre. Some of Zimbabwe's most notable directors and playwrights – Tobby Moyana, T.K. Tsodzo and Ben Sibenke – were products of this association. Equally important were groups such as the Rhodesian Association of Youth Clubs, which organized annual competitive drama festivals for black youth; Neshamwari Festival (formed in the 1960s); Mashonaland African Drama Arts and Cultural Association (formed in the 1970s); and Manyikaland Drama Association and Matebeleland Drama Association, which all promoted solidarity among black theatre groups using the drama festival format.

One of the most dominant features of the urban black theatre movement in colonial Rhodesia was the work of church youth organizations such as the Mabvuku Catholic Youth Club, formed in the 1960s. The club produced several plays in English and Shona and toured to many black townships. A similar club which also had success in promoting theatre among black people under very oppressive conditions was the Senka Christian Youth Club in Gweru, formed in the 1970s.

Because mission schools all over the colony encouraged the production of Christian Nativity and Passion plays, the first play to be performed in Shona in the colony was *Mutambo Wapanyika*, an adaptation of a Spanish morality play by Calderón. One of the most popular theatrical performances in the black mission schools was Dumi Maraire's *Mazuva Ekupedzisira* (*The Last Days*), a cantata about the Passion of Christ written in the late 1960s. It was through the Ecumenical Arts Workshops and the drama clubs in mission schools that morality plays such as *Everyman* and many different versions of the Christian Nativity story became dominant in black schools.

At the height of the country's nationalist struggle for liberation in the 1970s, the nationalist liberation armies used all-night festivals called *pungwe* (theatre, songs, dances, drama, tales and poetry recitals) in camps and villages to articulate the reasons and character of the nationalist struggle. One example was the bush drama group led by Fay Chung. A lecturer in drama at the University of Zambia in the early 1970s, Chung's group was formed in 1973 in Mozambique. Over a period of several years, the group put together a powerful series of performances for the camps.

In 1974 John Haigh, a white liberal, established the Sundown Theatre Company, a major multiracial group. Its 1979 productions of *Othello* gave John Indi the kind of public attention that had never been given to black actors in colonial Rhodesia. In the early 1980s Sundown featured many black actors including Walter Mparutsa and Dominic Kananenti. The company achieved international acclaim with its productions of plays such as *Kongi's Harvest* by the Nigerian Wole Soyinka and plays by the South African playwright Athol Fugard such as *Blood Knot, Master Harold and the Boys, Boesman and Lena* and *The Island*. The staging of such obviously political theatre at a time of black and white reconciliation in independent Zimbabwe was a bold move and one which could never have happened by itself in colonial Rhodesia.

When Haigh left for Australia in the mid-1980s, Sundown's leading black actors joined with white playwright-director Andrew Whaley in establishing a new group, Zimbabwe Arts Productions, which continued with the idea of multiracial theatre with productions of Athol Fugard, John Kani and Winston Ntshona's *Sizwe Bansi Is Dead*, and Whaley's own *Platform 5*, the latter a critical look at the quality of life of indigenous people in independent Zimbabwe.

Another experiment in multiracial theatre in the early 1980s was the joint effort of Ben Sibenke, a prominent black actor and playwright, and Carl Dorn, a white liberal businessman who was also a playwright and director, to establish the People's Theatre Company. In 1982 the company produced Sibenke's *My Uncle Grey Bonzo*, a comedy set within a traditional Shona community. The play was named Best Production in the formerly all-white National Theatre Festival, an award which drew attention to the work of multiracial and black theatre groups.

The People's Theatre Company went on to pioneer 'black theatre' through its nationally acclaimed productions of Sibenke's *Dr Madzuma and the Vipers* (1983) and *Chidembo Chanhuwa* (*The Polecat Stank*, 1993), Dorn's *Home Holds the Heart* (1987) and Stephen J. Chifunyise's *Shocks and Surprises* (1988). Each of these plays examined the cultural disorientation felt by black youth after years of foreign-oriented education and cultural imperialism.

Independence in 1980 ushered in a political Theatre-for-Development movement committed to changing the formerly all-white theatre environment into a much more genuinely African theatre, one more consistent with the new ideology of non-racial cultural development and the formation of a Zimbabwean cultural identity. The newly established black, multiracial and non-racial theatre groups soon found that the well-established whites-only theatre clubs and Little Theatre facilities, however, were still not accessible to black groups. These theatres were declared private cultural institutions and the personal property of the white community.

The style and subject matter being presented by the indigenous theatre groups were considered by many white theatre groups as too political for their audiences. The argument was that white audiences were interested neither in indigenous theatre forms nor in plays about Africa, especially those that showed black Africans asserting political and economic independence. White theatre clubs claimed the right to a separate cultural development as part of the guarantee of their now minority rights.

The 1993 People's Theatre Company production of Ben Sibenke's *The Polecat Stank*.
Photo: Zimbabwe Ministry of Information.

The Boterekwa Dance Theatre Company's *Dinhe* dance drama.
Photo: Zimbabwe Ministry of Information.

often priced beyond the reach of most although some are subsidized and are taken on tours of schools and colleges.

Zimbabwe's dance theatre community – comprising the mostly white National Ballet, the black Zimbabwe National Dance Company and another eighteen or so smaller groups – is a growing sector of the theatre community. The establishment of a Zimbabwe Dance Council has spurred activity in this area. Income comes mainly from tours and commercial performances in collaboration with popular bands.

Except for the national groups, which do receive corporate and donor funding, most dance companies receive no outside support. Many members make their livings by teaching traditional dance in primary and secondary schools.

Artistic Profile

Companies
Dramaturgy
Directing and Acting

At the height of the armed struggle for national independence in the early 1970s, national liberation movements used theatre to present the history of the colonial occupation of the country. This style used traditional African performing arts and included much audience participation. Such theatre featured a dynamic mix of music, dance, song, poetic recital, epic and praise chants, storytelling, and dialogue drama.

After independence, many Zimbabwean theatre artists began to try to find a way to use these same forms to help the country reassert its cultural identity. Artists and groups in urban centres were in the forefront of this movement, the result of which was the emergence of a highly political, collectively based Theatre-for-Development movement. These groups effectively created an agitprop theatre adaptable for performances in streets, market-places, playgrounds, community halls, churches and stadiums. It is this style which has remained strong in the decades since independence.

Among major productions in this style have been Amakhosi Theatre Productions' *Workshop Negative* (1985); University of Zimbabwe's Faculty of Arts production of *Mavambo* (*First Steps*, 1985); Zambuko/Izibuko Theatre's *Katshaa!* (1985) and *Samora Continua* (1988); Zimbabwe Theatre Workers' *Vashandi Neupfumi* (*Workers and Wealth*, 1987); Zvido Theatre Productions' *Chirwirangwe Ona Mawere* (*Beware Fighting Patriots*, 1987); Iluba Elimnyama Experimental Theatre's *Blood Brothers* (1987); and Tsungubvi Drama Club's *Aluta Continua* (1987).

Issues on women and development, and the place of traditional customs, have been used in productions of such plays as *Stitsha* (1990) by Amakhosi Theatre Productions and *Who Is To Blame?* (1991) by Glen Norah Women's Theatre Company. Batsiranayi Theatre Productions' *Disease in the House* (1993) explored the social and economic implications of AIDS; and Zambuko Izibuko's *Simuka Zimbabwe* (*Arise Zimbabwe*, 1994) dealt with the negative effects of the Economic Structural Adjustment Programme.

Dance has been used effectively since Zimbabwe National Dance Company's production of *Mbuya Nehanda* (*The Spirit of Liberation*, 1981), choreographed by Peggy Harper. Other dance-based works were undertaken by the University of Zimbabwe's Faculty of Arts with Rugyendo's *The Contest* (1986); Batanai Dance Company, which has produced dance-dramas written by Stephen J. Chifunyise, such as *Tatenda (Thank You)* (1983), *Jekesa* (1994), and *Tsotso* (1994), which dealt with the handicapped, environmental degradation and corruption.

An experiment of note was Clayton Ndlovu's *Madhunamutuna* (1994), which used music, masquerade, dance and ritual to present a traditional story. Using students of the ethnomusicology programme at Zimbabwe College of Music and members of the Batanai Dance Company, the production utilized a mixture of indigenous visual and performing arts to revive the tradition of storytelling in dance-drama.

Since 1987 a number of community theatre companies have used dance-drama and puppets to deal with such subjects as AIDS and family-planning awareness, while other companies such as Black Umfolosi, Tumbuka Dance Company and Sunduza Dance Company have used dance to portray general aspects of Zimbabwean culture.

Prior to colonization, music, like storytelling, was used as a part of traditional moral

Stella Chiweshe in the National Dance Company's *The Spirit of Liberation*.
Photo: Zimbabwe Ministry of Information.

education as well as in religious, marriage, burial and inheritance rites. During the colonial era the church exploited this musical heritage to produce religious musicals. In the early 1970s, Dumi Maraire even created a modern Shona Passion play, *Mazuva Ekupedzisira*.

By 1978, the whites-only Salisbury Repertory Theatre sought to show its support for indigenous culture during the war of liberation by producing Arthur Chipunza's *Svikiro* (*My Spirit Sings*), which dealt with the role of spirit mediums in the Shona culture. The musical was performed in English.

After independence Basil Chidyamatamba wrote and directed *Sounds of Zimbabwe* (1982) which several critics considered a 'breakthrough in African music theatre'. Portraying the traditional life of the rural indigenous people through music, it was successfully performed for both indigenous and non-indigenous audiences.

In 1985, the People's Theatre Company performed in English *Home Holds the Heart* again using traditional music. Later came even more ambitious musicals such as Savannah Theatre Arts Production's *Moneyland* (1992), which dealt with problems caused by unemployment and unequal distribution of wealth in Africa. Oliver Mtukudzi, one of Zimbabwe's leading popular musicians, wrote, directed and acted in *Was My Child* (1994), which explored the lives of street children in Zimbabwe and featured a number of popular local musicians.

At the big theatre clubs, foreign musicals dominate. In the 1990s, operettas have been performed while small theatres have concentrated on small-cast comedies and farces.

The 1990s have seen an increase in the number of scripted plays in English dealing with contemporary issues of a socio-political and economic nature. Most are small-cast productions mainly presented for an urban, multiracial audience. Many are by foreign writers. In the early 1990s this type of theatre was exemplified by Sundown Theatre, which specialized in plays by Fugard; Meridian Players, which performed Whaley's political plays; and by People's Theatre Company and Zimbabwe Arts Productions. In the 1990s, Rooftop Productions and Mhekiya also did several of Chifunyise's short topical plays – *Two Angry Young Men* (1994), *The Candidate* (1994), *Inmates* (1995) and *Strange Bedfellows* (1995).

Writers such as Aaron Chiundura Moyo, Agnes Taruvinga and King Dube have dealt

The chorus in Basil Chidyamatamba's *Sounds of Zimbabwe*, directed by the author.
Photo: Zimbabwe Ministry of Information.

with contemporary socio-political, economic and religious issues through television theatre which is dominated by dialogue drama in indigenous languages.

Rooftop, Meridian, Mhekuya, Savannah, Sunduza, Black Umfolosi, Tumbuka Dance Company and Batanai Dance Company are among the growing number of independent companies whose approach is often commercial and tour-oriented. Most of their plays use music, dance and dialogue, usually in English. These companies are mainly based in Harare and Bulawayo, and have demonstrated the fact that it is possible to survive doing theatre full-time using indigenous forms while dealing with issues of national and universal concern.

Five important companies dominate the 1990s including Amakhosi, Zambuko/Izibuko, Rooftop, Glen Norah Women's Theatre and the Young Warriors. Amakhosi was formed in 1982 by Cont Mhlanga after he attended a drama workshop with the National Theatre Organization. *Book of Lies* (1982) and *Diamond Warriors* (1982) were Amakhosi Theatre's first efforts. Written in English, these plays were action-packed and included impressive karate sequences. *Book of Lies* deals with the theft of African heritage by European colonizers. *Diamond Warriors* is a metaphor for the colonialization of Africa.

Amakhosi's third play, *Ngizozula Lawe* (*I Will Elope With You*), is a tragic story of two lovers. Written in 1984, the play was performed in Ndebele and was Amakhosi's first hit in their home area of Makokoba. Amakhosi's fame spread nationally in 1985 when *Nansi Lendoda* (*Here Is the Man*) won five trophies at the National Theatre Organization's festival.

The focus of Amakhosi began to shift away from action theatre in 1986 in its controversial *Workshop Negative*. The play caused a stir in government circles because of its hard-hitting comments on corruption and hypocrisy. *Children On Fire* (1987) maintained a critical eye on corruption in Zimbabwe by looking at drug pushing. In this play, a mother manages to unearth the illegal drug-related activities of a city councillor.

Cry Sillio (1988) looked at workers and trade unions. The following year, *Citizen Mind* depicted the conflict between indigenous and imported cultures. Women played major roles in the group's *Stitsha* (1990), the story of a woman who wants to become a theatre producer but is thwarted by authoritarian male relatives. Women's issues were also highlighted

in *Jazzman: The Story of My Life* (1990), a show commissioned by the International Labour Organization for a project called 'Improved Livelihood for Disabled Women'.

Another controversial play was *Dabulap*, which traced the lives of street vendors who decide to *dabulap*, or cross illegally into South Africa. Amakhosi Theatre's 1994 production of *Hoyaya* dealt with the spread of AIDS. All of Amakhosi's plays feature dance, songs and often original music. Several have toured nationally and internationally.

Amakhosi has also organized several annual arts festivals. During March and April each year, its INXUSA festival attracts performing arts groups from around the country, while in September, its Youth Festival brings together children in youth centres and children's theatre groups.

The name Zambuko/Izibuko means 'river crossing' in both Shona and Ndebele. A socialist-oriented political theatre consisting of workers, intellectuals and unemployed youth, it was founded at the University of Zimbabwe by Robert Mshengu McLaren in 1985 to respond to South African apartheid. The group eventually came to see itself as a frontline political company, committed to raising public consciousness and mobilizing support in the struggle for peace and social justice.

Zambuko/Izibuko has produced four full-length plays: *Katshaa!* (*The Sound of the AK*, 1986), *Samora Continua* (1987), *Mandela: The Spirit of No Surrender* (1990) and *Simuka Zimbabwe* (*Arise Zimbabwe*, 1994). In addition it has produced two shorter plays: *Socialism or Death* and *Chris Hani: Revolutionary Fighter* (1993). It has also performed numerous *ngonjeras* (short pieces for special occasions) as a contribution to a wide variety of political and other programmes, and a video on co-ops entitled *Chickenfeed*.

Katshaa! was a militant fusion of poetry, mime, freedom songs and dance designed to inform Zimbabweans about the political situation in South Africa and to win their solidarity and support. *Samora Continua* was a response to the death of Samora Machel, President of Mozambique. Many people in Zimbabwe believed that his death was plotted by the apartheid regime in South Africa. The play was similar in format to *Katshaa!*, with the addition of slides depicting aspects of Mozambican history.

Mandela: The Spirit of No Surrender (1988) was a large-scale collaboration originating in a *ngonjera* (short sketch) performed on the occasion of Nelson Mandela's seventieth birthday. It was further developed with cultural cadres of the African National Congress in Mazimbu, Tanzania, and then taken up by Zambuko/Izibuko, which presented it with the help of another theatre group, Chevhu Ndechevhu, from the Mount Hampden Training Institute.

Socialism or Death was a dramatization of a speech by Fidel Castro in which he supported socialism at a time when the Soviet Union and eastern Europe were abandoning it; it also honoured those Cubans who died on overseas missions, particularly in Africa. *Chris Hani: Revolutionary Fighter* was a dramatic tribute created shortly after Hani's murder. Zambuko/Izibuko's 1994 play, *Simuka Zimbabwe*, was about the effects of International Monetary Fund economic policies as they have been applied in Africa. All Zambuko/Izibuko's plays are developed collectively. Its shows have been performed all over Zimbabwe as well as in Zambia, Botswana and South Africa.

Young Warriors Theatre Company is a Bulawayo-based group that was established in 1985 by Norman Takawira. In 1987 the group became a full-time theatre company. Involved in community and popular theatre, Young Warriors collectively creates plays in Shona, Ndebele and English. In its production of *What Is Socialism?* (1989), Young Warriors critically evaluated the development of Zimbabwe under socialism and what the people's expectation of socialism was, while in *My Struggle* (1990) the group portrayed the plight of former combatants in independent Zimbabwe and their failure to realize their dreams. In *They Are Ours* (1993) the group dealt with the sensitive issue of caring for AIDS patients. In 1994 the group produced *Under the Death*, which dealt with sex education and its absence in many schools in Zimbabwe. Young Warriors has presented its work both in Zimbabwe and in Zambia, Namibia and the United Kingdom.

Established in 1990, Glen Norah Women's Theatre is a full-time group whose main objective is to use its collectively created works to raise awareness among women in urban and rural communities on social problems and how they can be solved. The group's first major production, *Who Is To Blame?* (1991), highlighted the problems that young girls face as a result of extended families. In *Ngozi* (1992), the group explored the negative effects of the traditional Shona custom in which under-age women are given away in marriage to men whose relatives had been killed by the woman's relatives in order to appease the spirit of the dead.

Glen Norah's *Mai Tapiwa* (*Mother of Tapiwa*, 1993) dealt with the causes, symptoms and effects of depression on women in urban areas and suggested ideas for a community approach to solving the problem. *My Piece of Land* (1994) dealt with how the shortage of land affects the welfare and status of women while *Temporary Market* (1992), written by Stephen Chifunyise, examined the effects of environmental degradation and the role of women in the promotion of environmental awareness.

In most of these groups there are influential playwrights whose ideas dominate content, structure and style as well as the philosophy of the group. For example, in Zambuko/Izibuko Robert McLaren has been the dominant writer; in Glen Norah Women's Theatre, Tisa Chifunyise; in the Young Warriors Theatre, Norman Takawira; in Batsiranai Theatre, Simba Pemenha; and in Siyakha Theatre, Elisha Ndumiyana.

Among published playwrights who use the techniques of collectively created plays as well are Cont Mhlanga and Stephen Chifunyise, Mhlanaga for Amakhosi Theatre Productions and Chifunyise, especially for his television plays.

Leading directors working in the field include Andrew Whaley, Dave Guzha, Daphne Jackson, Cont Mhlanga and Ben Sibenke.

In the theatre clubs, which produce mainly European plays, well-known directors include Adrian Stanley, Susan Hains, Dawn Parkinson, Vicki Hastings and Gloria Prentice.

Theatre for Young Audiences
Puppet and Mask Theatre

Until quite recently, traditional children's theatre thrived in rural parts of Zimbabwe. *Mahumbwe* – a theatre by children taking place in the open air during moonlight periods after harvest with children themselves depicting aspects of adult life – features music and dance and serves as a cultural training exercise. Major changes, however, in rural culture and the impact of modern education drastically reduced the appearance of this unique form.

Even storytelling, where adults were the dominant actors and young people listened, has declined in general popularity. Most to blame in this area are changes in social patterns brought about by urbanization, radio and television.

In 1989, writers Robert McLaren and Stephen Chifunyise created the Children's Performing Arts Workshop (CHIPAWO) to demonstrate techniques of theatre training for young people and to experiment with young people collectively creating their own plays. Involving children from 5 to 18 years of age, CHIPAWO later established an annual festival.

Other theatre companies such as Amakhosi Theatre Productions and Young Warriors followed suit by establishing children's theatre groups with the same philosophy – theatre for children by children. In 1992 CHIPAWO participated in the World Children's Festival organized by ASSITEJ in Nairobi. Later a national centre for ASSITEJ – the Zimbabwe Association for Theatre for Children and Young People – was formed. The association includes both adult groups producing for young audiences and groups involving children. The association has also recently begun organizing workshops for writers and the publishing of plays for children.

Theatre for young audiences is one of the few areas of Zimbabwe theatrical life to receive financial support from government. By providing facilities within their premises, schools and colleges have also been supporters of this type of theatre.

Zimbabwe has no tradition of puppet theatre except for isolated cases of 'wooden figures

A children's dance drama project.
Photo: Zimbabwe Ministry of Information.

on a string' used by young people in the Shona culture. Muppets, although quite popular among street theatre groups, are generally inapplicable in the overall Zimbabwean theatre reality.

Design
Theatre Space and Architecture

Zimbabwe's little theatres and playhouses were largely built during the colonial era in urban centres for European-style theatre. Inaccessible to the majority of indigenous theatre groups and indigenous audiences, they are owned by and used almost exclusively for the white and expatriate community.

Most indigenous theatre groups as a result perform in open-air theatres, schools and college halls which have few technical facilities such as lights. Except for the University of Zimbabwe and the cultural centres of foreign embassies, spaces designed for theatre are not seen very often by these groups. The result is that most Zimbabwean productions are compact, portable and very adaptable to different environments. Costumes are colourful, very original and visual but normally are taken from personal wardrobes. In the theatre clubs, on the other hand, elaborate designs and complex lighting, sets and specially designed costumes dominate. Construction of many of the modern little theatres began in the early 1950s. Built for whites only with funds from government and the business sector, these theatres – about fifteen proscenium spaces in all – are exclusively used for theatre productions.

Most other groups perform in spaces that were not specifically built for theatre such as community halls, cinemas and pubs. These facilities are normally of poor acoustical quality and are not technically equipped. Most groups create theatre-in-the-round and thrust configurations in the centre of these spaces.

In Harare, there are three additional halls mainly used for commercial musicals and pantomimes. These are the Harare Conference Centre, whose main auditorium has a seating capacity of 5,000; the 7-Arts Theatre (2,500 seats) and the Girls' High School Hall (500 seats). Bulawayo's City Hall is another 2,500-seat facility. Most of the little theatres and playhouses in Harare, Bulawayo, Mutare, Kwekwe and Masvingo have seating capacities that range from 100 to 300; the Gweru theatre is somewhat larger.

Theatre spaces at the three universities in Harare, Bulawayo and Mutare and at the fifteen teachers' training and technical colleges across the country generally seat in excess of 300. Most of these are multipurpose halls, again with no specifically designed stage facilities or lights.

Training

Since 1945, theatre training has been mainly by apprenticeship. Special workshops were occasionally organized by the then Southern Rhodesia Theatre Organization and in the 1960s festival adjudicators – usually from Britain – ran acting and technical production workshops. It was during these workshops that exceptionally good talent was identified and sponsored for advanced training in South Africa or Britain.

Black theatre artists were generally excluded from these workshops and limited to practical training in school and church-based efforts.

More serious training was occasionally obtained by indigenous theatre artists at youth cultural centres in pre-independence Rhodesia. These were run by community service departments or church youth programmes. From these latter theatre training programmes came many of the indigenous theatre artists of the 1970s such as Domini Kanaventi, Ben Sibenke, Walter Mparutsa, Simon Shumba, Safirio Madzikatire and Susan Chenjerai.

In 1982, the then Ministry of Education and Culture, through the foundation of Education Through Production, employed two Kenyans,

Ngugi wa'Mirii and Kimani Gecau, to help in the development of community theatre. This led to a series of workshops within Chindunduma School. The following year Zimbabwe hosted a UNESCO-funded ITI and IATA Workshop on Theatre-for-Development which featured theatre artists from twenty-two African countries and a number of local amateur theatre artists. Other Theatre-for-Development workshops followed. From 1987, both the National Theatre Organization and ZACT initiated different types of short-term and specialist theatre skills training at both the regional and national levels.

Recently established organizations such as the Children's Performing Arts Workshop, Amakhosi Performing Arts Workshop and the Zimbabwe Association for Theatre for Children and Young People have established more regular theatre skills training programmes for children and young people using permanent training centres with full-time resource people or festivals for shorter workshops.

At the University of Zimbabwe, a lecturer was appointed in 1984 by the Faculty of Arts as a first step towards establishing a full drama programme that would be in keeping with the process of democratization, *Zimbabweanization*, Africanization and socialist transformation. The department's first production was a dramatization of Wilson Katiyo's novel, *A Son of the Soil*, called here *Mavambo*. The play was performed in all three major Zimbabwean languages – Shona, Ndebele and English – and the staging rejected the proscenium arch in favour of a more fluid form of staging more appropriate to Africa. A policy statement made by the production team became a guideline for theatre work thereafter. This statement said that the university would base its work 'in the lives, experiences, thoughts and culture of the Zimbabwean people and their brothers and sisters in other parts of Africa and the progressive world', and that it would be part of 'the liberation struggle, the struggle for majority rule, the struggle against racism, colonialism and imperialism, and the struggle for a socialist Zimbabwe'.

Drama courses were subsequently introduced into the curriculums of the English and African languages departments as well. With most producing performances and other forms of practical work, an integrated strategy was developed. By 1985 the university was encouraging the use of Zimbabwean materials in literature and Zimbabwean plays in performance. In 1987, theatre from other parts of the world was reintroduced and plays by Brecht, Shakespeare and Russian dramatists were performed.

As a result of the popularity of such practical drama courses, a second year of drama was introduced in which students worked with various outside communities. A wide variety of projects resulted including work in army barracks, prisons, with the police, women's cooperatives, consumer groups, musicians and in schools.

The university also set out to study Zimbabwean theatre and launched a University Playscripts Series, which published two titles, *Mavambo* and *Katshaa!*, both by the Zambuko/Izibuko Group.

In 1993 a full Department of Theatre Arts was established and in 1995 a four-year honours programme was introduced. The department established as its major long-term goals the development of a theatre arts programme up to Master's level, service courses in other departments and faculties, and diploma and certificate courses in different aspects of theatre arts for teachers, cultural and media workers, actors, playwrights and directors. The department organizes with the Ministry of Education and Culture an annual Theatre-in-Education workshop to popularize its methods among teachers and theatre groups.

Criticism, Scholarship and Publishing

Mambo Press, a Catholic publishing house, has been the major publisher of theatre in Zimbabwe since 1968, when the company published Paul Chidyausiku's *Ndakambokuyambira (I Warned You)*. Mambo has published plays and criticism/history in English, Shona and Ndebele. College Press, Zimbabwe Publishing House, Longman and Baobab Books, and the University of Zimbabwe Press have published plays mainly for the school market. Only the University of Zimbabwe Press has paid attention to the collectively created political theatre.

Theatre research is still in its infancy in Zimbabwe. Among the few who have published on the general subject of Zimbabwean theatre are Stephen Chifunyise, Robert McLaren, M. Ranga Zinyemba and George Maxwell Jackson. Newspaper reviews are almost exclusively about theatre in English.

Stephen J. Chifunyise

Further Reading

Anthrope, Raymond, and John Blacking. 'Field Work Co-operation in the Study of Nsenga Music and Ritual'. *Africa* 32, no. 1 (1962).

Bourdillon, Michael. *Where Are the Ancestors? Changing Culture in Zimbabwe*. Harare: University of Zimbabwe Publishers, 1993.

Chifunyise, Stephen. *Medicine for Love and Other Plays*. Gweru: Mambo Press, 1984. 113 pp.

Dube, Caleb. 'Amakhosi Theatre Ako-Bulawayo'. *The Drama Review* 36, no. 2 (1992): 44–7.

Gelfand, Michael. 'A Description of the Ceremony of Kurova Guva'. *Zambezia* 2 (December 1971).

Globerman, Evie. 'Backstage on the Frontline'. *Journal of Southern African Studies* 16, no. 2 (1990).

Kaarsholm, Preben. 'Mental Colonisation or Catharsis? Theatre, Democracy and Cultural Struggle from Rhodesia to Zimbabwe'. *Journal of Southern African Studies* 16, no. 2 (1990).

Kavanagh, Robert. 'Theatre for Development in Zimbabwe: An Urban Project'. *Journal of Southern African Studies* 16, no. 2 (1990).

Kidd, Ross. *From People's Theatre for Revolution to Popular Theatre for Reconstruction: Diary of a Zimbabwean Workshop*. The Hague: Centre for the Study of Education in Developing Countries, 1984. 89 pp.

——. 'Theatre for Development: Diary of a Zimbabwe Workshop'. *New Theatre Quarterly* 1, no. 11 (May 1985): 179–204.

McLaren, Robert. 'Theatre on the Frontline: The Political Theatre of Zambuko/Izibuko'. *The Drama Review* 36, no. 1 (1992).

McLaren, Robert and Stephen J. Chifunyise. *Zimbabwe Theatre Report, University of Zimbabwe*. Harare: University of Zimbabwe Press, 1989.

Thompson, G. Caton. *The Zimbabwe Culture: African Pre-History*. London: Frank Press, 1971.

Welsh-Asante, Kariamu. *Zimbabwean Dance: An Aesthetic Analysis of the Jerusarema and Muchongoyo Dances*. New York.

Wortham, C.J. 'The State of the Theatre in Rhodesia'. *Zambezia* 1, no. 1 (January 1969): 47–53.

Zakes, M.D.A. 'Maratholi Travelling Theatre: Towards an Alternative Perspective of Development'. *Journal of Southern African Studies* 16, no. 2 (1990).

Zinyemba, Ranga M. *Zimbabwean Drama: A Study of Shona and English Plays*. Gweru: Mambo Press, 1986. 112 pp.

FURTHER READING

The following selected bibliography was prepared by the WECT staff, principally Mayte Gómez, in association with the Theater Research Data Center at Brooklyn College, publishers of the *International Bibliography of* *Theatre*. Essential books that deal with particular countries included in this volume can generally be found at the end of the respective National Articles. The books included here tend to be of a more general nature.

Reference Works/Dictionaries Encyclopedias/Bibliographies

Banham, Martin, Errol Hill and George Woodyard, eds. *The Cambridge Guide to African and Caribbean Theatre*. Cambridge: Cambridge University Press, 1994.

Biebuyck, Daniel. 'Drama: African Religious Drama'. In *The Encyclopedia of Religion*, ed. Mircea Eliade, vol. 4, 462–5. New York: Macmillan, 1987.

'Drama in Africa'. *African Literature Today 8* (1976). Special issue.

The Drama Review. 32, no. 2 (summer 1988). Special issue on African theatre.

East, N.B. *African Theatre: A Checklist of Critical Materials*. New York: Africana, 1970. 47 pp.

Graham-White, Anthony. 'A Bibliography of African Drama'. *Afro-Asian Theatre Bulletin* 3, no. 1 (1967): 10–22; 5, no. 2 (1970): 5–9.

Gray, John. *Black Theatre and Performance: A Pan-African Bibliography*. Westport, CT: Greenwood, 1990. 414 pp.

Jahn, Janheinz, and Claus Peter Dressler. *Bibliography of Creative African Writing*. Nendeln, Liechtenstein: Kraus-Thomson, 1973. 446 pp.

Kom, Ambroise, ed. *Dictionnaire des oeuvres litteraires negro-africaines de langue française des origines a 1978* [A dictionary of Black African literary works in French from the beginnings to 1978]. Paris: Agence de Coopération Culturelle et Technique, 1983. 671 pp.

Magnier, Bernard. *Dramaturgies africaines d'aujourd'hui: inventaire d'un imaginaire (dans les pays de l'Afrique noire d'expression française).* [Present-day African theatre: inventory of the imaginary person in French Black Africa]. In *Congés International de Teatre a Catalunya 1985. Actes. Vol. II. Seccions 1,2 i 3.* Eds Jordi Coca and Laura Conesa, 225–39. Barcelona: Institut del Teatro, 1986.

Salien, François O. *Panorama du théâtre africain d'expression française: historique, analyse, critique, perspectives* [A panorama of francophone African theatre: history, analysis, criticism, perspectives]. Bandundu: CEEBA, 1983. 218 pp.

Scherer, Colette, ed. *Catalogue des pièces de théâtre africain en langue française* [Catalogue of African plays in French]. Paris: Presses de la Sorbonne Nouvelle, 1996.

Shemanski, Frances. *A Guide to World Fairs and Festivals*. Westport, CT: Greenwood, 1985. 309 pp.

Theatre Research International. 7 (autumn 1982). Special issue on African theatre.

———. 9, no. 3 (1984). Special issue on black francophone theatre.

Trapido, Joel, Edward A. Langhans, and James R. Brandon, eds. *An International Dictionary of Theatre Language.* Westport, CT: Greenwood, 1985. 1,032 pp.

Warren, Lee. *The Theater of Africa: An Introduction.* Englewood Cliffs, NJ: Prentice Hall, 1975. 112 pp.

Wurtz, Jean Pierre, and Valérie Thfoin. *Guide de théâtre en Afrique et dans l'Ocean Indien* [Guide to theatre in Africa and the Indian Ocean]. Paris: Afrique en Créations, 1996. 337 pp.

Zimmer, Wolfgang. *Catalogue des pièces de théâtre africain en le langue française* [Catalogue of francophone African plays]. Paris: New Sorbonne University, Institute for Theatrical Studies, 1995. 129 pp.

Theatre History

Adandre, Alexandre. 'Le Théâtre africain d'expression française' [African theatre in French]. *L'Eveil du Bénin* (August 1952).

Awoonor, Kofi. 'The Modern Drama of Africa'. In *The Breast of the Earth: A Survey of the History, Culture, and Literature of Africa South of the Sahara.* New York: Doubleday, 1975.

Barrow, Brian, and Yvonne Williams Short. *Theatre Alive: The Baxter Story 1977–1987.* Cape Town: Baxter Theatre at University of Cape Town, 1988. 132 pp.

Béart, Charles. 'Les Origines du théâtre dans le monde: position actuelle du théâtre africain' [The origins of theatre in the world: the present state of African theatre]. *Bulletin de l'Académie des Sciences d'Outre-mer* 12 (2 April 1962): 143–63.

Bekale, Meyong. 'Quelques théâtre négro-africaines: le *mvet* – l'opera – le théâtre de masques – le théâtre de marionnettes' [Black African theatre: the *mvet*, the opera, the masks, puppets]. PhD dissertation, University of Paris VIII, 1978.

Condé, M. 'Naissance du théâtre en Afrique de l'ouest' [The birth of theatre in West Africa]. *Notre Librairie* 41 (April–June 1978).

Cornevin, Robert. *Le Théâtre en Afrique noire et à Madagascar* [The theatre in Black Africa and Madagascar]. Paris: Le Livre africain, 1970. 334 pp.

———. *Le Théâtre en Afrique de l'ouest* [Theatre in West Africa.] Paris: Société d'Histoire du Théâtre.

Dailly, Christophe. 'L'Histoire comme source d'inspiration' [History as a source of inspiration]. In *Actes du colloque sur le théâtre négro-africain: Université d'Abidjan, 1970.* Paris: Présence Africaine, 1971.

Dathorne, O.R. 'African Drama in French and English'. In *The Black Mind: A History of African Literature.* Minneapolis: University of Minnesota Press, 1974.

Denga (June 1977). Special issue on theatre in Malawi.

Diakhaté, Ousmane. 'Culture traditionnelles et influences européennes dans le théâtre négro-africaine modern' [Traditional culture and European influences in modern Black African theatre]. MA thesis, University of Montpellier III, 1984.

Duvignaud, J. 'Sociologie du théâtre' [The sociology of theatre]. *Cahiers International de Sociologie* 23 (1955).

Edebiri, Unionmwan. 'The Development of the Theatre in French-Speaking West Africa'. *Theatre Research International* 9, no. 3 (fall 1984): 168–80.

Etherton, Michael. *The Development of African Drama.* London: Hutchinson, 1982. 368 pp.

———. 'Trends in African Theatre'. *African Literature Today* 10 (1979): 57–85.

Fiebach, Joachim. *Die Toten als die Macht der Lebenden: Zur Theorie und Geschichte von Theater in Afrika* [The dead life power: on theory and history of theatre in Africa]. Berlin: Henschelverlag, 1986. 447 pp.

Gibbs, James. 'Experience of Censorship and Theatre in Malawi'. *Literary Half-Yearly* 26, no. 2 (1985): 65–73.

———. 'Of Kamuzu and Chameleons: Experiences of Censorship in Malawi'. *Literary Half-Yearly* 23, no. 2 (July 1982): 69–83.

Goyemide, Etienne. 'Le Théâtre centrafricain' [The theatre of the Central African Republic]. *Culture Française* 3–4, no. 1 (1982–83): 83–90.

Graham-White, Anthony. *The Drama of Black Africa.* New York: Samuel French, 1974. 220 pp.

Hoover, Deborah A. 'Developing a Cultural Policy in the Gambia: Problems and Progress'. *Journal of Arts Management, Law and Society* 18, no. 3 (fall 1988): 31–9.

Horn, Andrew. 'African Theatre: Docility and Dissent'. *Index on Censorship* 9, no. 3 (1980): 9–15.

Hourantier, Marie-José. *Du rituel au théâtre-rituel: contribution à une esthétique théâtrale négro-africaine* [From ritual to ritual-theatre: contribution to the Black-African theatre aesthetics]. Paris: L'Harmattan, 1984. 284 pp.

———. *Du rituel au théâtre-rituel: esquisse ethnosociologique d'une esthétique théâtrale négro-africaine* [From ritual to ritual-theatre: ethno-sociological approach to Black-African theatre aesthetics]. Paris: Université de Paris III, 1983. Vol. 1: 439 pp. Vol. 2: 785 pp.

Irwin, Paul. *Liptako Speaks: History from Oral Tradition in Africa*. Princeton, NJ: Princeton University Press, 1981.

Jeyifo, Biodun. *The Truthful Lie: Essays in a Sociology of African Drama*. London: New Beacon, 1985. 122 pp.

Johnson, A.C. 'Language and Society in West African Literature: A Stylistic Investigation into the Linguistic Resources of West African Drama in English'. PhD dissertation, University of Ibadan, Nigeria, 1982. 420 pp.

Jones-Quartey, K.A.B. 'The Problems of Language in the Development of the African theatre'. *Okyeame* 4, no. 1 (December 1968): 95–102.

Kalu, Ogbu. *African Cultural Development*. Engu: Fourth Dimension, 1980.

Kamlongera, Christopher F. 'Art and Development in Africa'. *Africana Marburgensia* 16, no. 2 (1983): 14–32.

———. 'Development of Contemporary Theatre in Malawi'. MA thesis, University of Leeds, 1977.

———. 'An Example of Syncretic Drama from Malawi: Malipenga'. *Research in African Literatures* 17, no. 2 (summer 1986): 197–210.

———. 'Theatre and Censorship in Africa: A Preliminary Study'. *Africana Marburgensia* 20, no. 2 (1987): 18–37.

Kennedy, J. Scott. *In Search of African Theatre*. New York: Scribners, 1973. 306 pp.

Kerr, David. 'An Experiment in Popular Theatre in Malawi: The University Travelling Theatre to Mbalachanda'. *Society of Malawi Journal* 35, no. 1 (1982): 34–51.

Kotchy, Barthélémy. 'Les Sources du théâtre négro-africaine' [The sources of Black African theatre]. *Revue de littérature et d'esthetique négro-africaines* 2 (1979): 91–103.

Laude, Jean. 'A l'origine du drame' [The origins of drama]. *Théâtre Populaire* 6 (1954).

Leloup, Jacqueline. 'De la specificité de l'histoire du théâtre négro-africain' [On the specificity of Black African theatre]. *Annales de la Faculté des Lettres et Sciences Humaines, Yaoundé* 2 (1983): 47–65.

L'vov, Nikolai Ivanovich. *Sovremennyi Teatr Tropicheskoi Afriki* [Contemporary theatre of tropical Africa]. Moscow: Nauka, 1977. 247 pp.

Lyakhovskaya, Nina D. 'French-Language Comedy in Tropical Africa as a Form of Mass Literature'. *Research in African Literature* 18, no. 4 (winter 1987): 458–71.

Mahood, M.M. 'Le Théâtre dans les jeunes états africains' [Theatre in the new African states]. *Présence Africaine* 32, no. 60 (1966): 23–39.

Malanda, Ange S. 'Mythe et histoire dans le théâtre africain d'expression française' [Myth and history in francophone African theatre]. *Mois en Afrique* 22, no. 247–8 (1986): 116–26.

Midiohouan, Guy Ossito. 'Le Théâtre négro-africain d'expression française depuis 1960' [Black African theatre in French since 1960]. *Peuples noirs, peuples africains* 31 (January–February 1983): 54–78.

Morisseau-Leroy, Felix. 'Le Théâtre dans la révolution africaine' [Theatre in the African revolution]. *Présence Africaine* 24, no. 52 (October 1964): 63–70.

Ndiaye, P.G. 'La Création dramatique, spectaculaire et musicale en Afrique' [Dramatic, spectacular and musical creation in Africa]. In *Patrimonie et création contemporaine en Afrique et dans le Monde Arabe*, ed. Mohamed Aziza. Dakar-Abidjan: Les Nouvelles Éditions Africaines, 1977.

Ngandu Nkashama, Pius. *Le Littérature africaine écrite en langue française: la poesie, le roman, le théâtre* [French African literature: poetry, the novel, theatre]. Issy-les-Moulineaux: Les Classiques Africaines, 1979.

Nidzgorski, Denis. *Arts du spectacle africain: contributions du Gabon* [African theatre arts: the contributions of Gabon]. Bandundu: CEEBA, 1980. 373 pp.

Ogunba, Oyin. *The Movement of Transition*. Ibadan: Ibadan University Press, 1975.

Ogunba, Oyin and A. Irele, eds. *Theatre in Africa*. Ibadan: Ibadan University Press, 1978. 224 pp.

Okagbue, O.A. *Aspects of African and Caribbean Theatre: A Comparative Study*. Leeds: University of Leeds, 1990.

Okpaku, Joseph, ed. *The Arts and Civilization of Black and African Peoples*. 10 vols. Lagos: Centre for Black and African Arts and Civilization, 1986.

Owomoyela, Oyekan. 'Drama'. In *African Literature: An Introduction*. Waltham, MA: Crossroads, 1979.

————. 'Give Me Drama, Or…: The Argument on the Existence of Drama in Traditional Africa'. *African Studies Review* 28, no. 4 (December 1985): 28–45.

Paricsy, Pal. 'The History of West African Theatre'. In *Studies on Modern Black African Literature*, 51–69. Budapest: Centre for Afro-Asian Research of the Hungarian Academy of Sciences, 1971.

Peterson, Bhekizizwe. 'Apartheid and the Political Imagination in Black South African Theatre'. *Journal of Southern African Studies* 16, no. 2 (1990).

Plastow, J.E. *The Development of Theatre in Relation to the States and Societies of Ethiopia, Tanzania and Zimbabwe*. Manchester: University of Manchester, 1991.

Ribas, Tomaz. 'O Tchilôi ou as tragédias de São Tomé et Príncipe'. *Espiral* 6–7 (1965): 70–7.

Ricard, Alain. 'Francophonie et théâtre en Afrique de l'ouest: situation et perspectives' [*Francophonie* and theatre in West Africa: present situation and future perspectives]. *Études littéraires* 7, no. 3 (December 1974).

————. *L'Invention du théâtre: le théâtre et les comediens en Afrique noir* [The invention of theatre: the theatre and comedians of Black Africa]. Lausanne: Age d'Homme, 1986. 134 pp.

————. *Théâtre et nationalisme* [Theatre and nationalism] Paris: Présence Africaine, 1972.

Ries, Fernando. *Doro Floga o Povo Brinca: Folklore de São Tomé e Príncipe*. Camara Municipal, 1969.

Ringel, Pierre. *Molière en Afrique noire; ou, le journal de 4 comediens* [Molière in Black Africa; or the journal of 4 comedians]. Paris: Presse du Livre Française, 1951.

Scherer, Jacques. 'Le Théâtre en Afrique noire francophone' [The theatre in francophone Black Africa]. In *Le Théâtre moderne II: depuis la deuxieme guerre mondial* [Modern theatre II: since World War II], ed. Jean Jacquot. Paris: Éditions du Centre de la Recherche Scientifique, 1967.

————. *Le Théâtre en Afrique francophone* [Theatre in francophone Africa]. Paris: Presses Universitaires de France, 1992.

Schipper-De-Leeuw, Mineke. *Theatre and Society in Africa*. Translated by Ampie Coetzee. Athens: Ohio University Press, 1982. 170 pp.

————. 'Traditional Themes and Techniques in African theatre and "Francophonie"'. *Theatre Research International* 9, no. 3 (autumn 1984): 215–32.

Schumacher, Claude, and Derek Fogg, eds. *Small Is Beautiful: Small Countries Theatre Conference, Glasgow 1990*. Glasgow: Theatre Studies, 1991.

Shore, Herbert L. 'African Theatre and Drama'. *African Studies Bulletin* 5, no. 2 (May 1962): 49–53.

————. 'Drums, Dances…and then Some: An Introduction to Modern African Drama'. *Texas Quarterly* 7, no. 2 (summer 1964): 225–31.

Silbert, Rachel. *Southern African Drama in English: 1900–1964*. Johannesburg: University of Witwatersrand, 1965.

Soyinka, Wole. 'Theatre in African Traditional Culture: Survival Patterns'. In *African History and Culture*, ed. Richard Olaniyan, 237–49. Ikeja: Longman, 1982.

Theatre and Society in Africa. Braamfontein: Ravan, 1982. 170 pp.

Turchin, N.M., ed. *Puti Razvitiia Teatral 'Nogo Iskusstva Afriki Sbornik Nauchnykh Trudov* [The paths of development of the theatrical art of Africa: a collection of scientific studies]. Moscow: GITIS, 1981.

Université d'Abidjan. *Actes du colloque sur le théâtre négro-africain 1970*. Paris: Présence Africaine, 1971.

University of Malawi, Department of English. *Theatre in Malawi 1970–1976*. Zomba: University of Malawi, 1977. 105 pp.

Urpokodu, Peter I. 'Theatre as Socio-political Power in Africa: Some Contemporary Experiments'. *Theatre Annual* 45 (1991): 39–64.

Valbert, Christian. 'Le *Tchilôi* de São Tomé. Un Exemplo de Subversion Culturelle' [The *Tchilôi* of São Tomé. An example of cultural subversion]. In *Les Littératures africaines de langue portugaise* [African literatures in Portuguese]. Paris: Calouste Gulbenkian Foundation, 1985. 437 pp.

Vaz, Carlos. *Para um Conhecimento do Teatro Africano* [Towards an understanding of African theatre]. Lisbon: Ulmeiro, 1978. 204 pp.

Warner, Gary. 'The Use of Historical Sources in Francophone African Theatre'. *Theatre Research International* 9, no. 3 (fall 1984): 180–94.

Waters, Harold A. 'Black French Theatre of the Eighties'. *Theatre Research International* 9, no. 3 (fall 1984): 195–215.

————. *Black Theatre in French: A Guide*. Sherbrooke, Canada: Éditions Naaman, 1978. 91 pp.

Webb, Jugh. *Drama, Society and Politics: African Impact*. Murdoch, Australia: African Studies Seminar, Murdoch University, 1980. 23 pp.

Criticism and Aesthetics

Agovi, K. 'Is There an African Vision of Tragedy in Contemporary African Theatre?' *Présence Africaine* 39, nos. 133–4 (1985): 55–74.

Ahura, Tar. 'The Playwright, the Play and the Revolutionary African Aesthetics'. *Ufahamu* 14, no. 3 (1985): 93–103.

Alphonse, T. *Vérité première du second visage africain* [Truth first from Africa's second face]. Paris: G.P. Maisonneuve et Larose, 1975. 135 pp.

Alston, J.B. *Yoruba Drama in English: Clarifications for Productions*. Iowa City: University of Iowa, 1985. 226 pp.

——. *Yoruba Drama in English: Interpretation and Production*. Lewiston, NY: Edwin Mellen, 1989. 192 pp.

Annan, Adaku Tawia. 'Revolution as Theater: Revolutionary Aesthetics in the Works of Selected Black Playwrights'. PhD dissertation, University of Wisconsin, Madison, 1987. 221 pp.

Anpe, Thomas Uwetpak. *An Investigation of John Pepper Clark's Drama as an Organic Interaction of Traditional African Drama with Western Theatre*. Madison: University of Wisconsin, 1985. 367 pp.

Asgill, Edmondson. 'African Adaptations of Greek Tragedies'. *Fourah Bay Studies in Language and Literature* 1 (1980): 67–92.

Ashaolu, Albert Olu. 'The Classical Temper in Modern African Drama'. In *Comparative Approaches to Modern African Literature*, ed. S.O. Asein, 77–93. Ibadan: University of Ibadan, 1982.

Baldo, Suleiman. 'Dramaturgie du théâtre négro-africain d'expression française (1930–1976)' [The dramaturgy of French Black African theatre (1930–1976)]. PhD dissertation, University of Dijon, 1978.

Banham, Martin with Clive Wake. *African Theatre Today*. London: Pitman, 1976. 103 pp.

Banks, Thomas. 'African Drama'. In *Critical Survey of Drama: English Language Series*, ed. Frank N. McGill, vol. 6, 2, 416–23. Englewood Cliffs, NJ: Salem, 1985.

Barber, Kevin, Joachim Fiebach, and Alain Ricard. *Drama and Theatre in Africa*. Bayreuth: Eckhard Breitinger & Reinhard Sander, 1986. 87 pp.

Blair, Dorothy S. 'Dramatic Literature'. In *African Literature in French: A History of Creative Writing in French and Equatorial Africa*, 84–142. Cambridge: Cambridge University Press, 1976.

Breitinger, Eckhard, ed. *Theatre and Performance in Africa: Intercultural Perspectives*. Bayreuth African Studies Series 31. Bayreuth, Germany: University of Bayreuth, 1994. 220 pp.

Brink, André. *Aspekte van die Nuwe Drama* [Apects of the new drama]. Pretoria: Academica, 1986. 268 pp.

Chesaina, Ciarunji. 'Women in African Drama: Representation and Role'. PhD dissertation, University of Leeds, 1988.

Chraibi, Driss. 'Théâtre noir' [Black theatre]. *O.R.T.F. Cahiers Littéraires* 4 (1965).

Cornévin, Robert. 'Littérature et théâtre en Afrique noire' [Literature and theatre in Black Africa]. In *Folklore in Africa Today*, ed. Szilard Biernaczky, 531–50. Budapest: Lorand Eotvos University, 1984, vol. 2.

——. 'Le Théâtre de langue française en Afrique noire' [Theatre in French in Black Africa]. *Culture Française* 3–4, no. 1 (1982–3): 18–32.

Dagry, Lucie. *Images et mythes de la femme dans le théâtre de Dadié* [Images and myths of woman in the theatre of Dadié]. Paris: Université de Paris III, 1984. 87 pp.

de Graft, J.C. 'Dramatic Questions'. In *Writers in East Africa*, eds Andrew Gurr and Angus Calder, 33–67. Nairobi: East African Literature Bureau, 1974.

Deldime, Roger. *Foi de théâtre* [Faith in theatre]. Morlan Welz: Lansman, 1993. 127 pp.

Diakhaté, Lamine. 'Au théâtre africain d'expression française' [French expression in African theatre]. *Paris–Dakar* (5 March 1955).

Duerden, Dennis. *African Art and Literature: The Invisible Present*. London: Heinemann, 1977.

Ezenwa-Ohaeto. 'The Nature of Tragedy in Modern African Drama'. *Literary Half-Yearly* 23, no. 2 (July 1982): 3–17.

Fiebach, Joachim. 'On the Social Function of Modern African Theatre and Brecht'. *Darlite* 4, no. 2 (1970): 5–19.

Gerard, Albert. 'Tragédies africaines' [African tragedies]. *La Revue Nouvelle* 41 (1965): 184–94.

Goisbeault, Nicole. 'Nationalisme et pouvoir dans le théâtre négro-africain contemporain'. [Nationalism and power in contemporary black African theatre]. PhD dissertation, University of Paris IV, 1982. 470 pp.

Graham-White, Anthony. 'West African Drama: Folk, Popular, and Literary'. PhD dissertation, Stanford University, 1969. 434 pp.

Hagher, Iyorwuese. 'The Aesthetic Problem in the Criticism of African Drama'. *Ufahamu* 10, nos. 1–2 (fall–winter 1980–1): 156–65.

Jones, Eldred Durisimi, ed. *Drama in Africa: A Review*. African Literature Today Series, no. 8. London: Heinemann, 1976.

Kennard, Peter. 'Recent African Drama'. *Bulletin of the Association for African Literature in English* 2 (March 1965): 11–19.

Kesteloot, Lilyan. *Les Écrivains noirs de langue française: naissance d'une littérature* [Black writers in French: the birth of a literature]. 2nd edn. Brussels: Université Libre de Bruxelles, 1965.

McElroy, Hilda-Njoki. 'Traditional Wit and Humor in Pan-Afrikan Drama'. PhD dissertation, Northwestern University, 1973. 212 pp.

Malan, Charles, ed. *Spel en Spiëel: Besprekings van die Moderne Afrikaanse drama en Teater* [Play and mirror: discussions of the modern Afrikaanse drama and theatre]. Johannesburg and Cape Town: Perskor-Uitgewery, 1984. 177 pp.

Mbele, Majola, ed. *Viewpoints: Essays on Literature and Drama*. Nairobi: Kenya Literature Bureau, 1980.

Mbughuni, L.A. 'The Development of English Drama in East Africa: A Study of the Emergence of New Trends of Modern Theatre and Drama'. In *The Writing of East and Central Africa*, ed. G.D. Killam, 247–63. London: Heinemann, 1984.

Meyong, B. 'Un dialogue de sourds: le théâtre négro-africain n'a de leçons à recevoir de personne' [A dialogue of the deaf: African theatre needs lessons from no one]. *Afrique-Asie* no. 177 (1978).

Midiohouan, Guy Ossito. 'Le Nouveau théâtre négro-africain' [The new Negro African theatre]. In *L'Ideologie dans la littérature négro-africaine* [Ideology in Negro-African literature], 155–76. Paris: L'Harmattan, 1986.

Mutia, Babila Joseph. 'Patterns of Alienation and Identity in African Fiction and Drama'. PhD dissertation, Dalhousie University, 1987.

'Negro Theatre at the Theatre of Nations'. *World Theatre* 9, no. 4 (winter 1960): 344–51.

Ngandu Nkashama, Pius. 'Le Théâtre vers une dramaturgie fonctionnelle' [Towards a functional dramaturgy in theatre]. *Notre Librairie* 63 (January–March 1982).

Orkin, Martin. *Drama and the South African State*. Johannesburg/Manchester and New York: Witwatersrand UP/Mancester UP, 1991. 263 pp.

Polycarpe, Oyi-Ndzie. *Le Chef dans le théâtre négro-africain d'expression française* [The chief in French Black-African theatre]. Paris:

Université de Paris III, 1985. Vol. 1: 348 pp. Vol. 2: 866 pp.

Ricard, Alain. 'Theater Research: Questions about Methodology'. *Research in African Literatures* 16, no. 1 (spring 1985): 38–52.

Roscoe, Adrian H. 'A Footnote on Drama'. In *Uhuru's Fire: African Literature East to South*. Cambridge: Cambridge University Press, 1977.

Sandoval, Enrique. *The Metaphoric Style in Politically Censored Theatre*. Montréal: Concordia University, 1986.

Sidibe, Valy. *La Critique de pouvoir politique dans le théâtre de Bernard Dadié (1966–1980)*. [Criticism of political power in Bernard Dadié's theatre (1966–1980)]. Paris: Université de Paris III, 1984. 323 pp.

Smit, Barto, and Charles Malan, eds. *Barto Smit*. Johannesburg: Perskor, 1984. 122 pp.

Smith, Rowland. *Exile and Tradition: Studies in African and Caribbean Literature*. New York: Africana, 1976.

Sofola, Zulu. 'The Theater in the Search for African Authenticity'. In *African Theology en Route*, eds Kofi Appiah-Kubi and Sergio Torres, 126–36. Maryknoll, NY: Orbis, 1979.

Soyinka, Wole. 'Modern Negro-African Theatre'. In *Colloquium: Function and Significance of African Negro Art in the Life of the People and for the People*, 495–504. Paris: Présence Africaine, 1968.

———. *Myth, Literature and the African World*. Cambridge: Cambridge University Press, 1976.

Taiwo, Oladele. *An Introduction to West African Literature*. London: Thomas Nelson, 1967.

Thomsen, Christian W. *Menschenfresser in der Kunst un Literature, in fernen, Ländern, Mythen, Märchen und Satiren, in Dramen, Liedern, Epen und Romamen* [Man-eaters in art and literature in distant countries: myths, tales and satires in drama, song, epic and the novel]. Vienna: Christian Brandstätter, 1983. 223 pp.

Traoré, Bakary. *The Black African Theatre and Its Social Functions*. Translated and with a preface by Dapo Adelugba. Ibadan: Ibadan University Press, 1972. (Originally published in French as *Le Théâtre négro-africain et ses fonctions sociales*, 1958.) 130 pp.

———. 'Meaning and Function of the Traditional Negro–African Theatre'. In *Colloquium: Function and Significance of African Negro Art in the Life of the People and for the People*, 481–93. Paris: Présence Africaine, 1968.

Uka, Kalu. 'Drama and Conscientization'. In *African Cultural Development: Readings in African Humanities*, ed. Ogbu U. Kalu,

185–204. Enugu, Nigeria: Fourth Dimension, 1978.

Vanni Menichi, Carlo, ed. *Le Maschere dell'-uomo. Segni plastici de oriente ad occidente* [The masks of man: plastic signs from east to west]. Pistola: Tellini, 1986. 80 pp.

'West African Drama in English'. *Comparative Drama* 1, no. 2 (summer 1967): 110–21.

Theatre Arts

Adedeji, Cecelia Folosade. 'African Stage Design: Problems of Collecting, Cataloguing and Conserving Documents'. *Performing Arts Resources* 8 (1983): 6–9.

Anthologies/Playwrights' Studies

Black, Stephen, and Stephen Grey, eds. *Three Plays.* Publications of the Centre for South African Theatre Research, no. 8. Johannesburg: Ad Donker, 1984. 260 pp.

Burness, Donald. *Fire: Six Writers from Angola, Mozambique and Cape Verde.* Washington, DC: Three Continents Press, 1977.

Gibbs, James. *Critical Perspectives on Wole Soyinka.* Washington, DC: Three Continents Press, 1980.

———. 'Nine Malawian Plays: An Introduction to an Introduction'. *African Theatre Review* 1, no. 1 (1985): 18–31.

Henderson, Gwyneth, ed. *African Theatre: Eight Prize-Winning Plays for Radio.* Nairobi: Heinemann, 1973. 150 pp.

Jones, Eldred Durisimi. *The Writings of Wole Soyinka.* London: Heinemann, 1976.

Kalejaiye, Oladipo. *The Father of Secrets, a Play, and the Defiance of Imitation, an Essay on African Drama.* Palo Alto, CA: Zikawuna, 1978. 31 pp.

Kesteloot, Lilyan. *Anthologie négro-africaine: panorama critique des prosateurs, poètes, et dramaturges noirs de XXe siècle* [Negro-African anthology: a critical panorama of Black prose writers, poets and playwrights of the twentieth century]. Revised edn. Brussels: Marabout, 1987. 480 pp.

Kotchy, Barthélémy. *La Critique sociale dans l'oeuvre théâtre de Bernard Dadié* [Social criticism in Bernard Dadié's work]. Paris: L'Harmattan, 1984. 253 pp.

Long, Kathryn Louise. *The Past and Future with Apartheid: The Function of Temporal Elements in Eight Plays by Athol Fugard.* Ann Arbor: University of Michigan, 1985. 231 pp.

Moore, Gerald. *Seven African Writers.* London: Hutchinson, 1980.

———. *Wole Soyinka.* London: Evans, 1971.

Owasu, Martin. *Drama of the Gods: A Study of Seven African Plays.* Roxbury/Nyangwe: Omenana, 1983. 134 pp.

Robaux, A. 'L'Art dramatique indigène en A.O.F' [Indigenous dramatic art in French West Africa]. *Europe nouvelle* 22 (January 1938).

Vandenbroucke, Russel. *Truths the Hand Can Touch: The Theatre of Athol Fugard.* Johannesburg: Ad Donker, 1986. 306 pp.

Walder, Dennis. *Athol Fugard.* London: Macmillan, 1984. 142 pp.

Wren, Robert M. *J.P. Clark.* Boston, MA: Twayne, 1984. 181 pp.

Theatre-for-Development

Abah, O.S. *Popular Theatre as a Strategy for Education and Development: The Example of Some African Countries.* Leeds: University of Leeds, 1987.

Breitinger, Eckhard, ed. *Theatre for Development.* Bayreuth African Studies Series 36. Bayreuth, Germany: University of Bayreuth. 80 pp.

Byram, Martin. 'Training for Theatre for Development: An Example from Swaziland'. *Theaterwork* 3, no. 5 (July–August): 53–9.

Colletta, Nat J. 'Folk Media, Popular Theatre and Conflicting Strategies for Social Change in the Third World'. In *Tradition for Change: Indigenous Sociocultural Forms as a Basis for Non-Formal Education and Development,* ed. Ross Kidd and Nat J. Colletta. German Federation for International Council for Adult Education, 1980.

Delafosse, Maurice. 'Contribution à l'étude du théâtre chez les Noirs' [Contribution to the study of Black people's theatre]. In *Annales et mémoires du Comité d'études historiques et scientifiques de l'A.O.F.*, 1916.

Edebiri, Unionmwan. 'Drama as Popular Culture in Africa'. *Ufahamu* 12, no. 2 (1983): 139–49.

———. 'L'utilisation du Pidgin française dans le théâtre africain francophone modern' [The use of Pidgin French in modern francophone African theatre]. *Peuples noirs, peuples africains* 7, no. 40 (1984): 97–114.

Eyoh, Hansel Ndumbe. *Hammocks to Bridges: An Experience in Popular Theatre*. Yaoundé: BET, 1986.

———. *Hammocks to Bridges: Report of the Workshop on Theatre for Integrated Rural Development, Kumba, Cameroon, 1–16 December, 1984*. Yaoundé: BET, 1986. 219 pp.

Institute Culturel Africain. *Quel théâtre pour le développement en Afrique?* [Which theatre for development in Africa?] Dakar: Nouvelles Éditions Africaines, 1985. 149 pp.

Kamlongera, Christopher F. 'The Growth of Popular Theater in East and Central Africa'. *New Literature Review* 13 (1984): 17–28.

———. 'Problems in the Growth of a Popular Art Form: The Relationship between Drama and Society in Malawi and Zambia. PhD dissertation. University of Leeds, 1984.

———. *Theatre for Development in Africa with Case Studies from Malawi and Zambia*. Bonn: DSE, 1989.

———. 'Theatre for Development: The Case of Malawi'. *Theatre Research International* 7, no. 3 (autumn 1982): 207–22.

Kerr, David. 'Didactic Theatre in Africa'. *Harvard Educational Review* 51, no. 1 (February 1981): 145–55.

———. 'Theatre and Social Issues in Malawi: Performers, Audiences, Aesthetics'. *New Theatre Quarterly* 4, no. 14 (May 1988): 173–80.

Kidd, Ross. *The Popular Performing Arts: Non-Formal Education and Social Change in the Third World*. The Hague: CESO, 1982.

Mda, Zakes, ed. *Marotholi Travelling Theatre: The Theatre for Development Project of the National University of Lesotho*. Lesotho: Mazenod Institute, 1986. 45 pp.

———. *When People Play People: Development of Communication Through Theatre*. London: Zed Books, 1993.

Mlama, Penina Muhando. *Culture and Development: The Popular Theatre Approach in Africa*. Uppsala: Nordiska Afrikainstitutet, 1991.

Steadman, Ian. *Drama and Social Consciousness: Themes to Black Theatre on the Witwatersrand Until 1984*. Johannesburg: University of Witwatersrand, 1985.

———. *Popular Culture and Performance in South Africa*. Durban: Contemporary Cultural Studies Unit, 1986. 76 pp.

Puppet and Mask Theatre

Adams, Monni. 'Current Directions in the Study of Masking in Africa'. *Africana Journal* 14, nos. 2–3 (1987): 89–114.

Bernolles, Jacques. *Permanence de la parure et du masque africains* [Permanent ornamentation and African mask]. Paris: G.-P. Maisonneuve et Larose, 1966. 632 pp.

Chesnais, Jacques. 'African Puppets'. *World Theatre* 14, no. 5 (September–October 1965): 448–51.

Cole, Herbert M., ed. *I Am Not Myself: The Art of African Masquerade*. Los Angeles: Museum of Cultural History, University of California, Los Angeles, 1985. 112 pp.

Dagan, E.A. *Emotions in Motion: Theatrical Puppets and Masks from Black Africa*. Montréal, PQ: Galerie Amrad African Arts, 1990. 309 pp.

Darkowska-Nidzgorska, Olenka. *Théâtre populaire de marionnettes en Afrique sud-Saharienne* [Popular puppet theatre in sub-Saharan Africa]. Bandundu, Zaïre: Centre d'études ethnologiques, 1980. 259 pp.

Froschan, Frank. *The Puppetry Tradition of Sub-Saharan Africa: Descriptions and Definitions*. Austin: University of Texas, 1980.

Gründ-Khaznader, Françoise. 'Masked Dances and Ritual in Tanzania, Mozambique and Zambia'. *The Drama Review: African Performance Issue* 25 no. 4 (Winter 1981): 25–38.

Harding, F. *Continuity and Creativity in Tiv Theatre*. Exeter: Exeter University, 1988.

Obuh, Sulvanus Onwukaike Stanley. *The Theatrical Use of Masks in Igbo Areas of Nigeria*. New York: New York University, 1984. 294 pp.

Traditional Theatre

Adedeji, 'Yinka. 'Drama: Art or Way of Life'. *Third World First* 2, no. 1 (1980): 30–8.

Agovi, James Kofi. 'Of Actors, Performers and Audience in Traditional African Drama'. *Présence Africaine* 116 (1980): 141–58.

Agovi, K.E. 'Towards an Authentic African Theatre'. *Ufahamu* 19, nos. 2–3 (1991): 67–79.

Amankulor, James N. 'The Condition of Ritual in Theatre: An Intercultural Perspective'. *Performing Arts Journal* 33–4 (1989): 45–58.

———. 'The Traditional Black African Theater: Problems of Critical Evaluation'. *Ufahamu* 6, no. 2 (1976): 27–46.

Balikuddembe, Joseph Mukasa. 'Traditional Elements in Contemporary African Drama'. PhD dissertation, University of California, Santa Barbara, 1981.

Bame, Kwame N. 'Drama and Theatre in Traditional African Society'. *The Conch* 6, nos. 1–2 (1974): 80–98.

Béart, Charles. *Recherche des éléments d'une sociologie des peuples africains à partir de leurs jeux* [Research on elements of a sociology of African peoples in their games]. Paris: Présence Africaine, 1960.

Drewal, Margaret Thompson. 'Ritual Performance in Africa Today'. *The Drama Review* 32, no. 2 (summer 1988): 25–30.

Enekw, Osmond Onuora. *Igbo Masks: The Oneness of Ritual and Theatre*. New York: Columbia University, 1982. 268 pp.

Essien, Arit Essien. *A Study of Efik Folk Drama: Two Plays by E.A. Edyang*. Urbana Champaign: University of Illinois, 1985. 188 pp.

Finnegan, Ruth. *Oral Literature in Africa*. Oxford: Oxford University Press, 1970. 558 pp.

Friedrich, Rainer. 'Drama and Ritual'. *Themes in Drama* 5 (1983): 159–223.

Hussein, Ebrahim. 'Traditional African Theatre'. In *The East African Experience*, ed. Ulla Schild, 35–53. Berlin: Reimer, 1980.

Kerr, David. 'Unmasking the Spirits – Theatre in Malawi'. *The Drama Review* 31, no. 2 (summer 1987): 115–25.

Kirby, E.T. 'Indigenous African Theatre'. *The Drama Review* 18, no. 4 (December 1974): 22–35.

Lindfors, Bernth, ed. *Forms of Folklore in Africa: Narrative, Poetic, Gnomic, Dramatic*. Austin: University of Texas Press, 1977. 281 pp.

Liyong, Taban Lo. *Popular Culture of East Africa: Oral Literature*. Nairobi: Longman, 1972. 157 pp.

Okpewho, Isidore. *The Epic in Africa: Towards a Poetics of the Oral Performance*. New York: Columbia University Press, 1979. 240 pp.

Person, Yves. 'L'Aventure de Porèkèré et le Drame de Waima'. *Cahiers Et. Africa* 5 (1965): 248–316.

Schipper-De-Leeuw, Mineke. 'Origin and Forms of Drama in the African Context'. In *The East African Experience*, ed. Ulla Schild, 55–64. Berlin: Reimer, 1980.

Scheub, Harold. *The African Storyteller: Stories from African Oral Traditions*. Kendall/Hunt, 1990.

Music and Dance Theatre

'African and African-American Dance, Music and Theatre'. *Journal of Black Studies* 15 (June 1985): 355–479.

Honore, Jasmine. *Towards a Transcription System for Xhosa Umtshotsho Dances*. Stellenbosch: Department of Physical Education, University of Stellenbosch, 1986.

Huet, Michel. *The Dance, Art and Ritual of Africa*. Intro. by Jean Laude. Text by Jean-Louis Paudrat. New York: Pantheons, 1978.

Katsenellenbogen, Edith. 'Die dokumentasie en ontleding van sosio-etniese danse en musiek van bepaalde volksgroepe in Suider Afrika, in antropologiese verband' [The documentation and analysis of socio-ethnic dance and music of specific cultural groups in southern Africa, in an anthropological context]. PhD dissertation, University of Stellenbosch, 1986.

Keita, Fodéba. 'La Danse africaine et la scène' [African dance and the stage] *Présence Africaine*, 14–15 (1957).

———. 'La Danse africaine et la scène' [African dance and the stage]. *World Theatre* 7, no. 3 (1958): 164–78.

Kennedy, J. Scott. 'The Use of Music in African Theatre'. *African Urban Notes* (winter 1970).

Kotchy, Barthélémy. 'Place et rôle de la musique dans le théâtre négro-africain modern' [The place and role of music in the modern Negro-African theatre]. *Annales de l'Université d'Abidjan*, Serie D: Lettres, vol. 4 (December 1971): 143–51.

Lalham, Peter. *Black Theatre, Dance and Ritual in South Africa*. Ann Arbor, MI: UMI Research Press, 1985. 172 pp.

Mensah, Atta Annan. *Music and Dance in Zambia*. Lusaka: Zambia Information Services, 1971.

INTERNATIONAL
REFERENCE

SELECTED BIBLIOGRAPHY

The following is a list of significant theatre books that have been published since the early 1950s. For a complete listing of world theatre publications, see volume 6 of this encyclopedia, *World Theatre Bibliography/Cumulative Index*. This section was prepared with the collabor- ation of the Belgian scholar René Hainaux and the Centre de Recherches et de Formation Théâtrales en Wallonie with the assistance of collaborators from Europe, North and South America, Africa, the Arab World and Asia.

Reference Works/Dictionaries/ Encyclopedias/Bibliographies

Attisani, Antonio. *Enciclopedia del teatro del' 900.* [Theatre encyclopedia of the twentieth century]. Milan: Feltrinelli, 1980. 598 pp.

Bailey, Claudia Jean. *A Guide to Reference and Bibliography for Theatre Research.* 2nd ed. Columbus, OH: Ohio State University Libraries, 1983.

Banham, Martin, ed. *The Cambridge Guide to World Theatre.* Cambridge: Cambridge University Press, 1988. 1,104 pp.

Brauneck, Manfred, and Gérard Schneilin, eds. *Theaterlexikon: Begriffe und Epoche. Bühnen und Ensembles* [Theatre lexicon: terms and periods. Stages and ensembles]. Hamburg: Rowohlt, 1986. 1,120 pp.

Cao, Yu, and Wang, Zuo Ling, eds. *China's Great Encyclopedia of World Theatre and Drama.* Beijing/Shanghai: China's Great Encyclopedia Press, 1989. 583 pp.

Cohen, Selma Jeanne, ed. *International Encyclopedia of Dance.* Oxford: Oxford University Press, 1996.

Corvin, Michel. *Dictionnaire encyclopédique du théâtre* [Encyclopedic dictionary of theatre]. Paris: Borduas, 1991.

Couty, Daniel, and Alan Rey, eds. *Le Théâtre* [Theatre]. Paris: Borduas, 1980.

D'Amico, Silvio, ed. *Enciclopedia dello spettacolo* [Encyclopedia of the performing arts]. 11 vols. Rome: Le Maschere, 1954–66.

Dahlhaus, Carl. *Pipers Enzyklopädia des Musiktheaters* [Piper's encyclopedia of music theatre]. 5 vols. Munich: Piper, 1986– .

Esslin, Martin, ed. *The Encyclopedia of World Theater.* New York: Scribner, 1977.

Fielding, Eric, gen. ed. *Theatre Words: An International Vocabulary in Nine Languages.* Prague: Publication and Information Exchange Commission of OISTAT, 1993.

Gassner, John, and Edward Quinn, eds. *The Readers' Encyclopedia of World Drama.* New York: Thomas Y. Crowell, 1969. 1,030 pp.

Giteau, Cécile. *Dictionnaire des arts du spectacle: Théâtre-Cinéma-Cirque-Danse-Radio-Marionettes-Télévision-Documentologie* [Dictionary of the performing arts: Theatre-Film-Circus-Dance-Radio-Puppetry-Television-Documentation]. Paris: Dunod, 1970. 430 pp. In French, English and German.

Gregor, Josef, and Margret Dietrich. *Der*

Schauspielführer: der Inhalt der wichtigsten Theaterstücke aus aller Welt [The play guide: Synopses of the most important plays from the whole world]. 15 vols. Stuttgart: Anton Hierseman, 1953–93.

Hainaux, René, ed. *Stage Design Throughout the World*. 4 vols. London: Harrap; New York: Theatre Arts Books, 1956–75.

Hartnoll, Phyllis, and Peter Found, eds. *The Concise Oxford Companion to the Theatre*. 2nd ed. New York: Oxford University Press, 1992. 586 pp.

———. *The Oxford Companion to the Theatre*. 4th edn. London: Oxford University Press, 1983. 934 pp.

Hawkins-Dady, Mark, ed. *International Dictionary of Theatre*. Vol. 2: *Playwrights*. Detroit/London/Washington, DC: Gale Research International/St James Press, 1994. 1,218 pp.

Hochman, Stanley, ed. *McGraw-Hill Encyclopedia of World Drama*. 2nd edn. 5 vols. New York: McGraw-Hill, 1984.

Hoffmann, Christel, ed. *Kinder- und Jugendtheater der Welt* [Children's and youth theatre of the world]. 2nd edn. Berlin: Henschelverlag, 1984. 276 pp.

Kienzle, Siegfried. *Schauspielführer der Gegenwart: Interpretation zum Schauspiel ab 1945* [A guide to contemporary plays: An interpretation of plays since 1945]. Stuttgart: Alfred Kröner Verlag, 1978. 659 pp.

Koegler, Horst, ed. *The Concise Oxford Dictionary of Ballet*. Oxford: Oxford University Press, 1987. 458 pp.

Kullman, Colby H, and William C. Young. *Theatre Companies of the World*. 2 vols. New York/London: Greenwood Press, 1986.

Leleu-Rouvray, Geneviève, and Gladys Langevin, eds. *International Bibliography on Puppetry: English Books 1945–1990*. Paris: Institut International de la Marionnette/Associations Marionnette et Thérapie, 1993. 281 pp.

Matlaw, Myron. *Modern World Drama: An Encyclopedia*. London: Secker & Warburg, 1972. 960 pp.

Mikotowicz, Thomas J., ed. *Theatrical Designers: An International Biographical Dictionary*. Westport, CT: Greenwood Press, 1992. 365 pp.

Mokulski, S.S., and P.A. Markov, eds. *Teatralnaia Entsiklopedia* [Theatre encyclopedia]. 6 vols. Moscow: Sovietskaia Entsiklopedia 1961–7.

Ortolani, Benito, ed. *International Bibliography of Theatre*. 7 vols. New York: Theatre Research Data Center, 1985–93.

Pavis, Patrice. *Dictionnaire du théâtre: termes et concepts de l'analyse théâtrale* [Dictionary of the theatre: Terms and concepts of theatrical analysis]. 2nd edn. Paris: Editions Sociales, 1987. 477 pp.

Philpott, A.R. *Dictionary of Puppetry*. London: MacDonald, 1969. 291 pp.

Queant, G., ed. *Encyclopédie du théâtre contemporain* [Encyclopedia of contemporary theatre]. Paris: Olivier Perrin, 1959. 211 pp.

Rischbieter, Henning. *Theater-Lexikon* [Theatre lexicon]. Revised edn. Zurich-Schwäbisch Hall: Orell Füssli, 1983. 484 pp.

Sadie, Stanley, ed. *The New Grove Dictionary of Opera*. 4 vols. London: Macmillan, 1992.

Schindler, Otto G. *Theaterliteratur. Ein bibliographischer Behelf für das Studium der Theaterwissenschaft* [Theatre literature. A bibliographic guide for theatre studies]. 3 vols. Vienna: Institut für Theaterwissenschaft, 1973.

Shigetoshi, Kawatake, ed. *Engeki Hyakka Daijiten* [Encyclopedia of world theatre]. 6 vols. Tokyo: Heibonsha, 1960–2.

Swortzell, Lowell, ed. *International Guide to Children's Theatre and Educational Theatre. A Historical and Geographical Source Book*. Westport, CT: Greenwood Press, 1990. 360 pp.

Trapido, Joel, ed. *An International Dictionary of Theatre Language*. Westport, CT: Greenwood Press, 1985. 1,032 pp.

Veinstein, André, and Alfred Golding, eds. *Performing Arts Libraries and Museums of the World/ Bibliothèques et musées des arts du spectacle dans le monde*. 4th edn. Paris: Centre National de la Recherche Scientifique, 1992. 773 pp.

Wilcox, R. Turner. *The Dictionary of Costume*. New York: Scribner, 1969. 406 pp.

Theatre History

Anderson, Jack. *Ballet and Modern Dance: A Concise History*. 2nd edn. Princeton, NJ: Princeton Book Company, 1992. 287 pp.

Arnott, Peter. *The Theatre in its Time*. Boston, MA: Little, Brown, 1981. 566 pp.

Aslan, Odette. *L'Art du théâtre* [The art of theatre]. Verviers: Marabout, 1963. 672 pp.

Award, Louis. *Al masrah al âlami* [World theatre]. Egypt, 1964.

Brockett, Oscar G. *History of the Theatre*. 6th edn. Boston, MA: Allyn & Bacon, 1990. 680 pp.

Calendoli, Giovanni. *Storia universale della danza* [General history of dance]. Milan: Mondadori, 1985. 288 pp.

Dumur, Guy, ed. *Histoire des spectacles* [History of the performing arts]. Encyclopédie de la Pléiade Collection. Paris: Gallimard, 1965. 2,010 pp.

Jurkowski, Henryk. *Dzieje teatru lalek: Od wielkiej reformy do współczesnoŝi* [History of the puppet theatre: From theatre's reform to today]. Warsaw, 1984.

———. *Ecrivains et marionnettes: quatre siècles de littérature dramatique* [Writers and puppets: four centuries of dramatic literature]. Charleville-Mézières: Institut National de la Marionnette, 1991.

Kuritz, Paul. *The Making of Theatre History*. Englewood Cliffs, NJ: Prentice-Hall, 1988. 468 pp.

Kybalova, Ludmila, Olga Herbenova, and Milena Lamarova. *The Pictorial Encyclopedia of Fashion*. New York: Crown, 1968. 604 pp.

Londré, Felicia Hardison. *The History of World Theater*. 2 vols. New York: Continuum, 1991.

Molinari, Cesare. *Teatro*. [Theatre]. Milan: Mondadori, 1972.

———. *Theatre Through the Ages*. New York: McGraw-Hill, 1975. 324 pp.

Mordden, Ethan. *The Fireside Companion to the Theatre*. New York: Simon & Schuster, 1988. 313 pp.

Nagler, A.M. *A Sourcebook in Theatrical History*. New York: Dover, 1952. 611 pp.

Nicoll, Allardyce. *The Development of the Theatre: A Study of Theatrical Art from the Beginnings to the Present Day*. 5th edn. London: George G. Harrap, 1966. 318 pp.

Niculescu, Margareta. *Teatrul de păpuşi in lume* [Puppet theatre in the world]. Berlin: Henschelverlag; Bucharest: Meridiane, 1966. 230 pp.

Nutku, Ŏzdemir. *Dünya Tiyatrosu Tarihi* [A history of world theatre]. 2 vols. Ankara: Ankara Universitesi dil ve Tarih Coğrafya Fakültesi Yaylonlan, 1973.

Ottai, Antonella, ed. *Teatro oriente/occidente* [Oriental/occidental theatre]. Biblioteca Teatrale no. 47. Rome: Bulzoni, 1986. 565 pp.

Pandolfi, Vito. *Storia universale del teatro drammatico* [World history of dramatic art]. 2 vols. Turin: Unione Typografico-Editrice, 1964. 1,626 pp.

Pronko, Leonard C. *Theater East and West: Perspectives Toward a Total Theater*. Berkeley, CA: University of California Press, 1967. 280 pp.

Roose-Evans, James. *Experimental Theatre: From Stanislavksi to Peter Brook*. 2nd edn. London: Routledge, 1989. 224 pp.

Sallé, Bernard. *Histoire du théâtre* [History of the theatre]. Paris: Librairie Théâtrale, 1990. 320 pp.

Zamora Guerrero, Juan. *Historia del teatro contemporáneo* [History of contemporary theatre]. 4 vols. Barcelona: Juan Flores, 1961–2.

Criticism and Aesthetics

Appia, Adolphe. *Oeuvres complétes* [Complete works]. 3 vols. Ed. Marie L. Bablet-Hahn. Lausanne: L'Age d'Homme, 1983–8.

Artaud, Antonin. *Oeuvres complétes* [Complete works]. 25 vols. Paris: Gallimard, 1961–90.

Barba, Eugenio. *Beyond the Floating Islands*. New York: PAJ Publications, 1986. 282 pp.

———. *The Floating Islands*. Holstebro, Denmark: Thomsens Bogtrykkeri, 1979. 224 pp.

———, and Nicola Savarese. *The Secret Art of the Performer. A Dictionary of Theatre Anthropology*. Edited and compiled by Richard Gough. London: Routledge, 1991. 272 pp.

Bawtree, Michael. *The New Singing Theatre*. Bristol UK: Bristol Classical Press; New York: Oxford University Press, 1991. 232 pp.

Beckerman, Bernard. *Dynamics of Drama*. New York: Drama Book Specialists, 1979. 272 pp.

Bentley, Eric. *The Dramatic Event*. Boston, MA: Beaucou Press, 1956. 278 pp.

———. *The Life of the Drama*. New York: Atheneum, 1964. 371 pp.

———. *The Playwright as Thinker*. New York: Reynal & Hitchcock, 1946. 382 pp.

Bharucha, Rustom. *Theatre and the World: Performance and the Politics of Culture*. London/New York: Routledge, 1993. 254 pp.

Birringer, Johannes. *Theatre, History and Post-Modernism*. Bloomington, IN: Indiana University Press, 1991. 240 pp.

Boal, Augusto. *Theatre of the Oppressed*. New York: Theatre Communications Group, 1985. 197 pp.

Brecht, Bertolt. *Kleines Organon für das Theater* [A little organum for the theatre]. Frankfurt: Suhrkamp Verlag, 1958.

———. *Schriften zum Theater* [Writings on the

theatre]. 7 vols. Ed. Werner Hecht. Berlin: Aufbau Verlag, 1963–4.

Brook, Peter. *The Empty Space*. London: MacGibbon & Kee, 1969. 141 pp.

Brustein, Robert. *The Theatre of Revolt*. Boston, MA: Little, Brown, 1964. 435 pp.

Carlson, Marvin. *Theories of the Theatre: A Historical and Critical Survey, from the Greeks to the Present*. Ithaca, NY/London: Cornell University Press, 1984. 530 pp.

Clark, Barrett H. *European Theories of the Drama*. New York: Crown, 1965. 628 pp.

Craig, Edward Gordon. *On the Art of Theatre*. London: Heinemann, 1911, 1968. 295 pp.

———. *Towards a New Theatre*. London: J.M. Dent, 1913.

Dort, Bernard. *Théâtre en jeu* [Drama in performance]. Paris: Seuil, 1979. 334 pp.

———. *Théâtre réel* [Real theatre]. Paris: Seuil, 1971. 300 pp.

Epskamp, Kees P. *Theatre in Search for Social Change: The Relative Significance of Different Theatrical Approaches*. The Hague: Centre for the Study of Education in Developing Countries, 1989.

Esslin, Martin. *The Field of Drama*. London: Methuen, 1987. 190 pp.

———. *The Theatre of the Absurd*. Garden City, NY: Doubleday, 1961. 364 pp.

Frye, Northrop. *Anatomy of Criticism*. Princeton, NJ: Princeton University Press, 1957. 383 pp.

Goodman, Lizbeth. *Contemporary Feminist Theatres*. London: Routledge, 1992. 272 pp.

Grotowski, Jerzy. *Towards a Poor Theatre*. New York: Simon & Schuster, 1968. 262 pp.

Innes, Christopher. *Avant-Garde Theatre, 1892–1992*. London/New York: Routledge, 1993. 262 pp.

Ionesco, Eugène. *Notes et contrenotes* [Notes and counternotes]. Paris: Gallimard, 1962. 248 pp.

Kidd, Ross. *The Performing Arts, Non-Formal Education and Social Change in the Third World: A Bibliography and Review Essay*. The Hague: Centre for the Study of Education in Developing Countries, 1981.

Kott, Jan. *Shakespeare Our Contemporary*. Garden City, NY: Doubleday, 1964. 241 pp.

Mackintosh, Iain. *Architecture, Actor and Audience*. London/New York: Routledge, 1993. 184 pp.

Mitchell, Arnold. *The Professional Performing Arts: Attendance Patterns, Preferences and Motives*. 2 vols. Madison, WI: Association of College, University and Community Arts Administrators, 1984.

Pavis, Patrice. *Theatre at the Crossroads of Culture*. London: Routledge, 1991. 256 pp.

River, Julie, and Germaine Dellis. *L'Enfant et le théâtre* [The child and the theatre]. Brussels: Labor, 1992. 155 pp.

Schechner, Richard. *Between Theatre and Anthropology*. Philadelphia, PA: University of Pennsylvania Press, 1985. 342 pp.

———. *Environmental Theatre*. New York: Hawthorne, 1973. 339 pp.

———. *Performance Theory*. London: Routledge, 1988. 320 pp.

Schutzman, Mady, and Jan Cohen-Cruz, eds. *Playing Boal: Theatre, Therapy, Activism*. London/New York: Routledge, 1994. 246 pp.

Seltzer, Daniel. *The Modern Theatre: Readings and Documents*. Boston, MA: Little, Brown, 1967. 495 pp.

Stanislavski, Konstantin. *The Collected Works of Konstantin Stanislavski*. Ed. Sharon Marie Carnicke. 10 vols. London: Routledge, 1993– .

———. *Sobraniye Sochinenii* [Collected works]. 7 vols. Moscow: Iskusstvo, 1954–60.

Strehler, Giorgio. *Per un teatro umano: pensieri scritti parlati e attuali* [Towards a humanized theatre: contemporary written thoughts and discussions]. Milan: Feltrinelli, 1974. 363 pp.

Turner, Victor. *From Ritual to Theatre: The Human Seriousness of Play*. New York: PAJ Publications, 1982. 127 pp.

Ubersfeld, Anne. *L'École du spectateur* [The school for theatregoers]. Paris: Éditions Sociales, 1981. 352 pp.

———. *Lire le théâtre* [Reading performance]. Paris: Editions Sociales, 1977. 280 pp.

Wandor, Michelene. *Carry On, Understudies: Theatre and Sexual Politics*. London: Routledge, 1986. 224 pp.

Theatre Arts

Bablet, Denis. *Les Révolutions scéniques du XXième siècle* [Scenic revolutions of the twentieth century]. Paris: Société Internationale d'art XXième siècle, 1975. 388 pp.

Barton, Lucy. *Historic Costume for the Stage*. London: A. & C. Black, 1961. 609 pp.

Bellman, Williard F. *Scenography and Stage Technology*. New York: Thomas Crowell, 1977. 639 pp.

Braun, Edward. *The Director and the Stage: From*

Naturalism to Grotowski. London: Methuen, 1982. 218 pp.

Cole, Toby, and Helen K. Chinoy. *Actors on Acting: The Theories, Techniques and Practices of the Great Actors of all Times as Told in Their Own Words.* New York: Crown, 1970. 715 pp.

Duerr, Edwin, ed. *The Length and Depth of Acting.* New York: Holt-Rinehart & Winston, 1962. 590 pp.

Gaulme, Jacques. *Architectures scénographiques et décors de théâtre* [Scenographic architecture and theatre design]. Paris: E. Magnard, 1985. 144 pp.

Gillibert, Jean. *L'Acteur en création* [The actor in creation]. Toulouse: Presses Universitaires du Mirail, 1993. 206 pp.

Gorelik, Mordecai. *New Theatres for Old.* New York: Dutton, 1962. 553 pp.

Grebanier, Bernard. *Playwriting.* New York: Thomas Y. Crowell, 1961. 386 pp.

Izenour, George C. *Theater Design.* New York: McGraw-Hill, 1977. 631 pp.

Jones, David Richard. *Great Directors at Work: Stanislavsky, Brecht, Kazan, Brook.* Berkeley, CA: University of California Press, 1986. 290 pp.

Machlin, Evangeline. *Speech for the Stage.* New York/London: Routledge/Theatre Arts Books, 1992. 254 pp.

Malkin, Michael R. *Traditional and Folk Puppets of the World.* New York: A.S. Barnes, 1977. 194 pp.

Mello, Bruno. *Trattato di scenotecnica* [A treatise on scene design]. Novara: G.G. Gorlich, Istituto Geografico de Agostini, 1979.

Niccoli, A. *Lo spazio scenico: storia dell'arte teatrale* [Scenic space: a history of theatre art]. Rome: Bulzoni, 1971.

Pilbrow, Richard. *Stage Lighting.* New York: Drama Book Specialists, 1979. 176 pp.

Saint-Denis, Michel. *Theatre: The Rediscovery of Style.* London: Heinemann, 1960. 110 pp.

———. *Training for the Theatre.* New York: Theatre Arts Books, 1982. 242 pp.

Spolin, Viola. *Improvisation for the Theatre: A Handbook of Teaching and Directing Techniques.* Evanston, IL: Northwestern University Press, 1963. 397 pp.

Tidworth, Simon. *Theatres: An Architectural and Cultural History.* New York: Praeger, 1973. 224 pp.

Watson, Lee. *Lighting Design Handbook.* New York: McGraw-Hill, 1990. 458 pp.

WRITERS
AND NATIONAL
EDITORIAL COMMITTEES

ANGOLA

Writer: Domingos Van-Dunem (Ambassador, Permanent Delegation of Angola to UNESCO, Paris)
Readers: Samuel Aco (Instituto Nacional du Patrimoine Culturel, Luanda), Manzambi Vivu Fernando (Museu Nacional de Antropologia, Luanda)

BÉNIN

Writers: Guy Ossito Midiohouan (Professor of Literature, Université du Bénin, Cotonou), Akambi Akala
National Editorial Committee: Bienvenu Koudjo (Professor, Université du Bénin, Cotonou), Guy Ossito Midiohouan, Tinjile Daniel (Actor), Hovetin Lazare (Actor), Akambi Akala (Actor), Hado Philippe (Journalist)
Readers: Romain-Philippe Assogba (Musée d'Ethnographie, Porto Novo), Alexis Adandé, Codjovi Joseph Adandé, Coffi Guillaume Adjaho (Conseiller Technique à la Culture, Cotonou), Léonard Ahonon (Musée Historique d'Abomey, Abomey), Dénise Sossouhounto (Ministère de la Culture et des Communications, Cotonou)

BURKINA FASO

Writer: Jean-Pierre Guingané (Professor of Theatre, Université d'Ouagadougou, Ouagadougou)
National Editorial Committee: Jean-Pierre Guingané, Jacob Sou (Actor; Director; Secretary-General, Union des Ensembles Dramatiques de Ouagadougou), Boukary

Nako, Christophe Sandwidi, Seni Bokolov, Simon Pierre Nikiema, Idrissa Zio, Prosper Kampaoré (Director of Cultural Promotion, Ministère de l'information et de la culture, Ouagadougou)
Readers: Oumarou Nao, Steven H. Gale (Endowed Chair in the Humanities, Kentucky State University), Ato Quayson (Pembroke College, University of Cambridge), Oga Steve Abah (Associate Professor, Department of Theatre and Drama, Ahmadum Bello University, Zaria; Director, Nigerian Popular Theatre Alliance), Jean-Baptiste Kiethèga

BURUNDI

Writer: Marie-Louise Sibazuri (Playwright; Director; President, La Société d'Acteurs et Auteurs Dramaturges; Vice-President, L'Association des Ecrivains du Burundi)
Readers: Juvénal Ngorwanubusa (Dean, Faculty of Letters and Human Sciences, University of Burundi, Bujumbura), Henri Boyi (Professor, Faculty of Letters and Humanities, University of Burundi), Marie-Louise Baricako (Chairperson, Department of English, University of Burundi), André Schils (Les Palmiers Troupe, Bujumbura)

CAMEROON

Writers: Hansel Ndumbe Eyoh (Director of Academic Affairs, University of Buea, Buea), Asheri Kilo, Bole Butake, Gilbert Doho, Oyi-Ndzie Polycarpe
Readers: Ato Quayson (Pembroke College, University of Cambridge), Sylvia Bâ (Professor, Faculté des lettres et sciences

humaines, Université Cheikh Anta Diop, Dakar), Bernard Ayuk (Ministry of Information and Culture, National Museum, Yaoundé), Raymond N. Asombang (Centre for Anthropological Studies and Research, Yaoundé)

CHAD

Writer: Garang Ko-Tourou
Readers: Dangde Laobele (Dean, Faculté des lettres et sciences humaines, Université du Chad, Ndjamena), Sylvia Bâ (Professor, Faculté des lettres et sciences humaines, Université Cheikh Anta Diop, Dakar)

CONGO

Writer: the late Sony Labou Tansi (Novelist; Playwright)
National Editorial Committee: Sony Labou Tansi, Donga La, Matando Kubu Turé, Sony S. Bemba, M. Leontine Isibinda, Ifunde Dao, Biahouila, Nicolas Bissi, Mza Lamu, Paul Kibangu, Sylvain Bemba (Playwright)
Readers: Sylvia Bâ (Professor, Faculté des lettres et sciences humaines, Université Cheikh Anta Diop, Dakar), Rémy Mongo-Etsion

CÔTE D'IVOIRE

Writers: Barthélémy Kotchy (Dean, Faculté des lettres, arts et sciences humaines, Université National de Côte d'Ivoire, Abidjan), Valy Sidibé (Professor, Faculté des lettres, Université National de Côte d'Ivoire, Abidjan), Aboubakar C. Touré (Professor, Faculté des lettres, Université National de Côte d'Ivoire, Abidjan)
Translator: Helen Heubi
Readers: Victor Diabete (Institut d'Histoire, d'Art et d'Archéologie Africaine, Université d'Abidjan), Jacqueline Alewsse (Centre Culturel Americaine, Abidjan), Oga Steve Abah (Associate Professor, Department of Theatre and Drama, Ahmadum Bello University, Zaria; Director, Nigerian Popular Theatre Alliance), Tiohona Moussa Diarrassouba (Institut d'Histoire, d'Art et d'Archéologie Africaine, Abidjan), Sery Bailly (Professor, Département d'Anglais, Université d'Abidjan)

ETHIOPIA

Writers: Tamirat Gebeyehu (Doctoral candidate, Graduate Centre for Drama, University of Toronto), Aida Edemariam (Master of Arts, Department of English, University of Toronto), Debebe Eshetu (Former Director, National Theatre of Ethiopia and the Hager Fikir Theatre; Actor; Playwright; former President, Union of African Performing Artists)
National Editorial Committee: Ayalneh Mulatu (Playwright; Director; former government Cultural Coordinator; Founder and Director, Candle Theatre Company), Debebe Eshetu, Fikre Tolossa (Playwright), Nebiyou Tekalign (Playwright; Director; Artistic Director, Ras Theatre, Addis Ababa), Tesfaye Simma (Actor; Director), Ahmed Zekarias (Institute of Ethiopian Studies Museum, Addis Ababa University, Addis Ababa)

GHANA

Writers: Patience Rosina Addo (Graduate, University of Ghana; Writer), James Gibbs (former Lecturer, Department of English, University of Ghana; Writer)
Readers: Kwame Arhin (Institute of African Studies, University of Ghana), Francis Duah (Ghana National Museum, Accra)

GUINEA

Writer: Abdoulaye Fanye Touré (Director, Association guinéenne des hommes de théâtre, Conakry)
National Editorial Committee: Bailo Taliwel Diollo (Director-General of Culture), the late Sidi Mohamed Condé (former Director of Arts and Letters), Mohamed Salif Keita (Director, Division of Literature, Direction-General of Culture) Celestin Camara, W. Doukoure, A. Jeansky Soumah, M.M. Bangoura, J. Tonguino
Readers: Sylvia Bâ (Professor, Faculté des lettres et sciences humaines, Université Cheikh Anta Diop, Dakar), Abdourman Bigné Camara (Direction Nationale de la Culture, Conakry)

GUINEA-BISSAU

Writers: Joaquin Rosa Pinto (Director, Département d'information du S.E.G.P.), Mamadu d'Jalo

National Editorial Committee: Rosalina Gauffin (Director, L'I.N.A.R.T., Secrétariat d'état à la culture et aux sports, Bissau), Louisa Borges (Director of Culture, Government of Guinea-Bissau), Joaquin Rosa Pinto, Fernando Pina (Choreographer, Ballet National), Florentino Flora Gomes (Film Producer)
Readers: Sylvia Bâ (Professor, Faculté des lettres et sciences humaines, Université Cheikh Anta Diop, Dakar) Carlos Lopes (Instituto Nacional de Estudos e Pesquista, Bissau)

KENYA

Writer: Oluoch Obura (Dean, Faculty of Arts, Maseno University College, Maseno)
Readers: Corinne A. Kratz (Institute of African Studies, Emory University, Atlanta), Oga Steve Abah (Associate Professor, Department of Theatre of Drama, Ahmadu Bello University, Zaria; Director, Nigerian Popular Theatre Alliance), Steven H. Gale (Endowed Chair in the Humanities, Kentucky State University), Ato Quayson (Pembroke College, University of Cambridge, Cambridge), Peter Amuka (Professor, Department of Literature, Moi University, Eldoret)

LIBERIA

Writer: Joseph Tomoonh-Garlodeyh Gbaba (Founder and Director, Dekhontee Artists Theatre, Monrovia; Playwright; Director; Actor; Theatre Manager)
Readers: G. Henry Andrews (Former Minister of Information, Culture and Tourism of Liberia), Hawa Goll-Kotchi (Secretary-General, Liberian National Commission for UNESCO, Ministry of Education, Monrovia), Charles Wingrove Dwamina (Vice President, Administration, University of Liberia, Monrovia)

MADAGASCAR

Writers: Jeannine Rambeloson-Rapiera (Professor, Faculté des lettres et sciences humaines, Université d'Antananarivo, Antananarivo), Marie-Antoinette Rahantavololona (Professor, Faculté des lettres et sciences humaines, Université d'Antananarivo), Marie Hélène Raheriniaina

National Editorial Committee: Jean Victor Rajosoa (Professor, Université de Madagascar; Secretary-General, Centre Malgache de l'IIT, Antananarivo), Henri Randrianierenana (Actor; Producer; Director), José Edouard Randriamanampisoa (Professor, Université de Madagascar), Jean-Marie Rakotoarisoa Andrianiain (Archivist)
Readers: Violette Ramanankasina (Professor and Chairperson, Département des études anglais, Faculté des lettres et sciences humaines, Université d'Antananarivo, Antananarivo), Nivo Danielle Andrianjafy (Professor of French, Faculté des lettres et sciences humaines, Université d'Antananarivo), Christine Ramanantsoa (Director, Atelier Théâtre de l'Alliance Française), Haja Ravaloson (Director, Ny Tropy Georgette), Rajonhson Andriambatosoa Ravaloson (Director, Ny Tropy Jeannette), Jean Aime Rakotoarisoa (University Museum, Université d'Atananarivo)

MALI

Writer: Gaoussou Diawara (Higher Teachers' Training School, Bamako) with Victoria Diawara and Alou Koné
National Editorial Committee: Alfomaye Sonfo (Professor, Higher Teachers' Training School), Moussa Maiga (Director, Groupe dramatique du Théâtre National), Ismaïla Samba Traoré, Abdoulaye Ascofare, Gaoussou Diawara, Oumar Kanouté (Professor, Higher Teachers' Training School)
Readers: Sylvia Bâ (Professor, Faculté des lettres et sciences humaines, Université Cheikh Anta Diop, Dakar), Klena Sanogo (Institut des sciences humaines, Bamako)

MAURITIUS

Writer: Daniel Labonne (Actor; Director; Playwright; Drama Teacher; former Advisor to the Minister of Education and Culture; Director and Founder, Theatre Atelier)
National Editorial Committee: Daniel Labonne, Guy Dupuch, Paul Hosenie, Serge Constantin

MOZAMBIQUE

Writers: João Machado da Graça; João Manja; Manuela Soeiro (Grupo Mutumbela Gogo, Maputo)

Readers: Renato Matusse (Coordinator, Culture, Information and Sports, Southern African Development Community, Maputo) Manuel Araujo, Alda Costa (Director, Departamento de Museus, Ministério da Cultura, Maputo), Gilberto Cossa (Museu Nacional de Arte, Maputo)

NAMIBIA

Writers: Terence Zeeman (former Senior Lecturer, Department of Drama, University of Namibia; former Director, National Theatre of Namibia, Windhoek); Dorian Haarhoff (Professor and Chairperson, Department of English, University of Namibia, Windhoek)
Readers: Oga Steve Abah (Associate Professor, Department of Theatre and Drama, Ahmadu Bello University, Zaria; Director, Nigerian Popular Theatre Alliance), Steven H. Gale (Endowed Chair in the Humanities, Kentucky State University)

NIGER

Writers: Chaïbou Dan-Inna (Professor, Faculté des lettres et sciences humaines, Université de Niamey, Niamey), Ousmane Tandina (Professor, Faculté des lettres et sciences humaines, Université de Niamey)
National Editorial Committee: Chaïbou Dan-Inna, Ousmane Tandina, Lailaba Hamidou (Professor, Faculté des lettres et sciences humaines, Université de Niamey), Dioulde Laya (Celtho, Niamey), Djibo Mayaki (O.R.T.N., Niamey), Issaka Soumaila (A.N.P.A., Niamey), Abdou Louché (I.N.D.R.A.P., Niamey), Saadou Galadima (M.E.N./E.S.R., Niamey), Imoussa Ousseini (M.C.C., Niamey), Imne Marcel (I.N.D.R.A.P., Niamey)
Readers: Steven H. Gale (Endowed Chair in the Humanities, Kentucky State University), Antoinette Titus-Tidjani, Sylvia Bâ (Professor, Faculté des lettres et sciences humaines, Université Cheikh Anta Diop, Dakar)

NIGERIA

Writers: Iyorwuese Hagher (Minister of State for the Federal Ministry of Power and Steel, Lagos; Playwright; former Professor, Faculty of Arts, University of Jos) with Saint Gbilekaa,

Ziky Kofoworola, Irene Salami (Playwright), K.W. Dexter Lyndersay
Readers: Oga Steve Abah (Associate Professor, Department of Theatre and Drama, Ahmadu Bello University, Zaria; Director, Nigerian Popular Theatre Alliance), Zaccheus Sunday Ali (former Director, Centre for Black and African Arts and Civilization, National Theatre, Lagos), Sylvia Bâ (Professor, Faculté des lettres et sciences humaines, Université Cheikh Anta Diop, Dakar), Sule Bello (National Council for Arts and Culture, Iganmu, National Theatre, Surulere, Lagos), Nuradeen Abubakar (Centre for Nigerian Cultural Studies, Ahmadu Bello University, Zaria), Bayo Adebowale (African Heritage Research Library, Oshum State), C.O. Adepegba (Institute of African Studies, University of Ibadan), Babatunde Agbaje-Williams (Institute of African Studies, University of Ibadan), Kokie Agboutaen-Eghafona (Department of Sociology and Anthropology, Université du Bénin)

RWANDA

Writers: Joseph Nsengimana (Professor, Université Nationale du Rwanda, Ruhengeri), Jean-Baptiste Nkuriyingoma (Journalist)
Readers: Sylvia Bâ (Professor, Faculté des lettres et sciences humaines, Université Cheikh Anta Diop, Dakar), Steven H. Gale (Endowed Chair in the Humanities, Kentucky State University), Oga Steve Abah (Associate Professor, Department of Theatre and Drama, Ahmadu Bello University, Zariai Director, Nigerian Popular Theatre Alliance)

SÉNÉGAL

Writers: Ousmane Diakhaté (Professor, Faculté des lettres, Université Cheikh Anta Diop, Dakar), Madior Diouf (Critic; Faculté des lettres, Université de Dakar)
National Editorial Committee: Moustapha Mbaye (Professor, Conservatoire), Madior Diouf, Lucien Lemoine (Professor, CESTI), Jacqueline Lemoine (Actress), Alioune B. Beye (Playwright), Ousmane Diakhaté, Abdoulaye Diop Dany (Director, Troupe Nationale d'art dramatique), Jean Pierre Leurs (Director of Production, Théâtre Daniel), Saïba Lamine Traoré (Secretary-General, Théâtre National

Daniel; Director), Alioune Fall (Fédération National du Théâtre Populaire)
Readers: Oga Steve Abah (Associate Professor, Department of Theatre and Drama, Ahmadu Bello University, Zaria; Director, Nigerian Popular Theatre Alliance), Steven H. Gale (Endowed Chair in the Humanities, Kentucky State University)

SEYCHELLES

Writers: Jean-Claude Pascal Mahoune (Senior Archivist, National Archives, Victoria, Mahé) with John Etienne (Director; Playwright), Christian Servina (Director; Playwright)
Readers: Marie-Thérèse Choppy (Director-General, Culture Division, Ministry of Education and Culture, Government of the Seychelles, Victoria, Mahe), Bernard Sham Laye (Ministerial Advisor)

SIERRA LEONE

Writer: Eustace Palmer (Professor, Department of English, Speech and Journalism, Georgia College, Milledgeville, Georgia; former Chairperson, Department of English, Fourah Bay College, Freetown) with Raymond De Souza George (Research Fellow, Institute of African Studies, Fourah Bay College)
Readers: Arthur Abraham (Institute of African Studies, Fourah Bay College), Steven H. Gale (Endowed Chair in the Humanities, Kentucky State University), Patrick Muana (Department of Language and Linguistics, University of Sheffield), Abioseh Porter (Associate Professor, Department of Humanities and Communications, Drexel University), Julius Spencer (Lecturer, Department of English, Njala University College, University of Sierra Leone, Freetown)

SOUTH AFRICA

Writers: Temple Hauptfleisch (Director, Centre for Theatre and Performance Studies; Chairperson, Department of Drama, University of Stellenbosch; Editor, *The Companion to South African Theatre*; Co-Editor, *South African Theatre Journal*) with Marie Kruger (Lecturer, Department of Drama, University of Stellenbosch)
Readers: Edwin Hees (Senior Lecturer,

Department of English, University of Stellenbosch; Assistant Editor, *The Companion to South African Theatre*), Yvette Hutchison (Research Assistant, Centre for Theatre and Performance Studies; Assistant Editor, *The Companion to South African Theatre*; Assistant Editor, *South African Theatre Journal*), Ato Quayson (Pembroke College, University of Cambridge), Neville Dubow (Michaelis School of Fine Art, University of Cape Town), Keith Bain (Department of Drama, University of Stellenbosch)

TANZANIA

Writers: Penina Muhando Mlama (Professor of Theatre Arts and Chief Academic Officer, University of Dar es Salaam), Amandina Lihamba (Associate Professor of Theatre Arts and Head, Department of Art, Music and Theatre, University of Dar es Salaam)
Readers: Elias Jengo (Professor, Department of Art, Music and Theatre, University of Dar es Salaam), Fachili Mshana (Professor, Department of Art, Music and Theatre, University of Dar es Salaam)

TOGO

Writer: Ayayi Togoata Apedo-Amah (Theatre Critic; Professor, Faculté des lettres, Université du Bénin, Lomé)
National Editorial Committee: Ayayi Togoata Apedo-Amah, Huenumadji Afan (Université du Bénin), Gbeasor Tohonou (Université du Bénin), Agbek S. Amegbleame
Readers: Adimado Aduayom (Professor, Department of History, Université du Bénin), Ato Quayson (Pembroke College, University of Cambridge, Cambridge), Steven H. Gale (Endowed Chair in the Humanities, Kentucky State University), Oga Steve Abah (Associate Professor, Department of Theatre and Drama, Ahmadu Bello University, Zaria)

UGANDA

Writers: Rose Mbowa (Professor, Department of Music, Dance and Drama, Makerere University, Kampala) with Andreas H. Schott, Augustine Bazaale, Mercy Mirembe
Readers: George Seremba (Actor; Playwright), Steven H. Gale (Endowed Chair in the

Humanities, Kentucky State University), Oga Steve Abah (Associate Professor, Department of Theatre and Drama, Ahmadu Bello University, Zaria), Ephrim R. Kamuhangire (Department of Antiquities and Museums, Kampala)

ZAÏRE

Writer: Mwambayi Kalengayi (Professor, Department of Dramatic Arts, University of Zaïre; National Institute of the Arts, Kinshasa; CRASA, Kimbanseke)
National Editorial Committee: Mazingi Pepo (Director, Théâtre National Zaïrois; President, Fédération National de Théâtre), Mwambayi Kalengayi
Readers: Steven H. Gale (Endowed Chair in the Humanities, Kentucky State University), Oga Steve Abah (Associate Professor, Department of Theatre and Drama, Ahmadu Bello University, Zaria; Director, Nigerian Popular Theatre Alliance), Ato Quayson (Pembroke College, University of Cambridge), Guy de Plaen (Musée National de Lubumbashi)

ZAMBIA

Writer: Dickson Mwansa (Professor, Department of Adult Education, Centre for Continuing Education, University of Zambia, Lusaka)
National Editorial Committee: Dickson Mwansa, Kabwe Kasoma (National

Chairperson, Zambia National Writers' Association; Senior Lecturer, Centre for the Arts, University of Zambia, Lusaka), Billy Nkunika (Programme Officer, UNICEF, Lusakai; Director, Centre for Continuing Education, University of Zambia, Lusaka; former Chairperson, ITI Zambia Centre), Moses Kwali (Poet; Playwright; former Chairperson, Zambia National Writers' Association), Wina Kanyembo (Department of Cultural Services, Republic of Zambia, Lusaka)
Readers: Grazyna Zaucha (Curator, Choma Museum, Choma), Mapopa Mtonga (Chairperson, Department of Drama, Centre for the Arts, University of Zambia, Lusaka), Godfrey Setti

ZIMBABWE

Writer: Stephen J. Chifunyise (Ministry of Sport, Recreation and Culture, Government of Zimbabwe, Harare; former Chairperson, Department of Language and Literature, University of Zambia, Lusaka; former Lecturer, Department of Drama, University of Zimbabwe, Harare)
Readers: Catherine Mondragon (Zimbabwean National and Student, Department of Cultural Studies, York University, Toronto), Robert McLaren (Professor, Department of Theatre, University of Zimbabwe, Harare; Chairperson, Zimbabwe Association of Theatre for Children and Young People, Harare)

INDEX